D0464733

NATIONAL UNIVERSITY
LIBRARY   SAN DIEGO

THE ORGANIZATIONAL FRONTIERS SERIES

The Organizational Frontiers Series is sponsored by the Society for Industrial and Organizational Psychology (SIOP). Launched in 1983 to make scientific contributions to the field, the series has attempted to publish books that are on the cutting edge of theory, research, and theory-driven practice in industrial/organizational psychology and related organizational science disciplines.

Our overall objective is to inform and to stimulate research for SIOP members (students, practitioners, and researchers) and people in related disciplines, including the other subdisciplines of psychology, organizational behavior, human resource management, and labor and industrial relations. The volumes in the Organizational Frontiers Series have the following goals:

1. Focus on research and theory in organizational science, and the implications for practice
2. Inform readers of significant advances in theory and research in psychology and related disciplines that are relevant to our research and practice
3. Challenge the research and practice community to develop and adapt new ideas and to conduct research on these developments
4. Promote the use of scientific knowledge in the solution of public policy issues and increased organizational effectiveness

The volumes originated in the hope that they would facilitate continuous learning and a continuing research curiosity about organizational phenomena on the part of both scientists and practitioners.

Previous Frontiers Series volumes, all published by Jossey-Bass, include:

Emotions in the Workplace

Emotions in the Workplace

Understanding the Structure and Role of Emotions in Organizational Behavior

Robert G. Lord

Richard J. Klimoski

Ruth Kanfer

Editors

Foreword by Neal Schmitt

 JOSSEY-BASS
A Wiley Company
www.josseybass.com

Published by

JOSSEY-BASS
A Wiley Company
989 Market Street
San Francisco, CA 94103-1741

www.josseybass.com

Copyright © 2002 by John Wiley & Sons, Inc.

Jossey-Bass is a registered trademark of Jossey-Bass Inc., a Wiley company.

No part of this publication may be reproduced, stored in a retrieval system, or transmitted
in any form or by any means, electronic, mechanical, photocopying, recording, scanning,
or otherwise, except as permitted under Sections 107 or 108 of the 1976 United States
Copyright Act, without either the prior written permission of the Publisher or authoriza-
tion through payment of the appropriate per-copy fee to the Copyright Clearance Center,
222 Rosewood Drive, Danvers, MA 01923, (978) 750-8400, fax (978) 750-4744. Requests to
the Publisher for permission should be addressed to the Permissions Department,
John Wiley & Sons, Inc., 605 Third Avenue, New York, NY 10158-0012, (212) 850-6011,
fax (212) 850-6008, e-mail: permreq@wiley.com.

Jossey-Bass books and products are available through most bookstores. To contact
Jossey-Bass directly, call (888) 378-2537, fax to (800) 605-2665, or visit our website
at www.josseybass.com.

Substantial discounts on bulk quantities of Jossey-Bass books are available to
corporations, professional associations, and other organizations. For details and
discount information, contact the special sales department at Jossey-Bass.

We at Jossey-Bass strive to use the most environmentally sensitive paper stocks available to
us. Our publications are printed on acid-free recycled stock whenever possible, and our
paper always meets or exceeds minimum GPO and EPA requirements.

Library of Congress Cataloging-in-Publication Data

Emotions in the workplace : understanding the structure and role
   of emotions in organizational behavior / Robert G. Lord, Richard
J. Klimoski, Ruth Kanfer, editors.—1st ed.
       p.   cm.—(The Jossey-Bass business & management series)
   (The organizational frontiers series)
   Includes bibliographical references and index.
   ISBN 0-7879-5736-4 (alk. paper)
     1. Organizational behavior. 2. Emotions. I. Lord, Robert G.
(Robert George), 1946– II. Klimoski, Richard J. III. Kanfer,
Ruth. IV. Series. V. Series: The organizational frontiers series
HD58.7 .E439 2002
158.7—dc21

2001007830

FIRST EDITION
HB Printing   10 9 8 7 6 5 4 3 2 1

The Jossey-Bass
Business & Management Series

The Organizational Frontiers Series

SERIES EDITOR

Neal Schmitt
Michigan State University

EDITORIAL BOARD

Angelo S. DeNisi
Texas A & M

Robert L. Dipboye
Rice University

Katherine J. Klein
University of Maryland

Richard J. Klimoski
George Mason University

Cheri Ostroff
Teachers College-Columbia University

Robert D. Pritchard
Texas A & M

Contents

Foreword

This is the sixteenth book in a series initiated by the Society for Industrial and Organizational Psychology (SIOP) in 1983 and published by Jossey-Bass. Originally published as the Frontiers Series, the SIOP Executive Committee voted in 2000 to change the name of the series to Organizational Frontiers Series in order to sharpen the identity and visibility of the series. The purpose of this series is to promote the scientific status of the field. The first editor of the series was Ray Katzell, and he was followed by Irwin Goldstein and Sheldon Zedeck.

The topics of the volumes and the volume editors are chosen by the editorial board. The series editor and the editorial board then work with the volume editor in planning the volume and occasionally suggesting and selecting chapter authors and content. During the writing, the series editor often works with the editor and the publisher.

The success of the series is evident in the high number of sales (now over forty thousand). Volumes have also received excellent reviews, and individual chapters as well as volumes have been cited frequently. A recent symposium at the SIOP annual meeting examined the impact of the series on research and theory in industrial/organizational (I/O) psychology. Although such influence is difficult to track and volumes have varied in intent and perceived centrality to the discipline the conclusion of most participants was that the volumes have exerted a significant impact on research and theory in the field and are regarded as being representative of the best the field has to offer.

This volume, edited by Robert Lord, Richard Klimoski, and Ruth Kanfer, represents a significant and successful effort to compile in one volume psychological theory about the role of emotions in human behavior in the workplace. The chapter authors include individuals who have done basic work on the nature and measurement of emotion and authors who have investigated the applied and theoretical implications of this research in a work setting. Bringing the best of psychological science to bear on work-related problems and to the attention of organizational researchers has been the major goal of the Organizational Frontiers series, and I believe this combination of authors' knowledge and expertise has helped achieve that goal in this volume.

The book is organized in four parts. The objective in Part One is to develop the theoretical and methodological bases necessary to understand how emotions affect work. Discussions of the valence and intensity of emotions as they affect the relationship between emotion and behavior; evolutionary, cognitive, and physiological approaches to emotion as each relates to the understanding of important outcomes in organizations; and a stimulus-organism-emotional response (S-O-R) framework that provides for an examination of individual differences in emotional sensitivity and response output processes provide an exceptional wealth of knowledge and researchable hypotheses regarding emotion.

In Part Two, the chapters consider emotional regulation, that is, how individuals learn and exhibit norms and rules for feeling and displaying emotions. An information-processing approach is used to examine these issues at the intraindividual level; a process similar to the S-O-R model is used to examine input and output processes and automatic and controlled processes in the regulation of emotion at the individual and dyadic level; and at the organizational level, the various processes that regulate affect in groups and organizations are examined. The group and organizational processes involved in affect are seen as determinants of some of the cognitive and motivational processes that take place at the individual level.

In Part Three, the authors consider several basic applied problems in which emotion often plays a central role in understanding human behavior. Common to these chapters is the notion that affective events produce emotional shocks to individuals, so one must understand events as well as individuals to achieve a more complete understanding of behavior. Another recurrent theme in these chapters is the notion that emotions involve social processes. The chapters in this part explore these themes while exploring knowledge about workplace violence and aggression, customer service, work-family interactions, organizational entry, and other topics.

In Part Four, two of this book's editors discuss the research issues that should be addressed if we are to improve our understanding of the relationship between emotions and work behavior. They also develop conceptual frameworks for integrating prior material.

Our target audiences for this book include graduate students in I/O psychology and organizational behavior, as well as doctoral-level researchers and practitioners who want to gain knowledge on the most up-to-date data and theory regarding emotions and workplace behavior. I believe that this book will make recent literature on emotions and behavior accessible to professionals who do not often read the basic literature in this area and in that way will meet the primary goal of the Organizational Frontiers series.

I also believe that this book will stimulate and promote more intelligent reading of the basic research literature on emotions and stimulate a greater understanding of the role of emotions in the workplace, as well as promote investigation of a wide array of interesting and important questions. The chapter authors deserve our gratitude for pursuing the goal of clearly communicating the nature, application, and implications of the theory and research described in this book.

Acknowledgments

Production of a volume such is the result of the hard work and cooperative effort of many individuals. The chapter authors and the editorial board played important roles in this endeavor. Because all royalties from the series volumes are used to help support SIOP financially, none of them received any remuneration. They deserve our appreciation for furthering our understanding of organizational science.

We express our sincere gratitude to Cedric Crocker, Julianna Gustafson, and the entire staff at Jossey-Bass. Over many years and several volumes, they have provided support during the planning, development, and production of the series.

January 2002

NEAL SCHMITT
Michigan State University
Series Editor, 1998–2003

Preface

When we developed the idea for this book almost three years ago, we had three major objectives. First, we realized that the theoretical basis for understanding emotions and emotional regulation had developed in many areas that may not be familiar to organizational researchers or practitioners. Our goal was to make this scientific literature more accessible. Consequently, Part One of this book brings together a variety of theoretical perspectives for understanding emotional behavior and the regulation of emotions. Second, we recognized that emotional regulation in organizations is a multilevel phenomenon and that although emotions could be investigated by research that focused on only one level, practical use of such research required the integration of individual-, dyadic-, group-, and organizational-level phenomena. Our second goal, then, was to have authors cover these various levels of analysis; this material is in Part Two of the book. Third, we recognized that organizational research is increasingly focusing on emotions after many years of neglect. Consequently, we wanted to bring together much of the applied research in one convenient volume. Part Three therefore addresses this objective, covering many applied topics such as aggression at work, emotional labor, courageous behavior, employee recruitment and socialization practices, cross-cultural effects, and the work-family interface.

We viewed Part Four as a forum for integrating prior material, identifying needed research, and developing models or frameworks that could aid future research and practice. As the book developed, we were delighted with the contributions of the chapter authors and pleased with the progress in understanding emotions and their regulation at work that was being made in both this book and other recent organizational literature. We sent the first three parts of the book to the publisher on September 10, 2001, believing we had largely accomplished our main objectives.

As we watched the terrorist attacks of September 11, 2001, the courageous responses by many workers involved in directly responding to these tragedies, and the subsequent responses of individuals, nations, and worldwide organizations, we realized that emotions are one of the most crucial elements of these responses. Often, people put emotions aside so they could do what had to be done at the time. At other times, emotions overwhelmed cognitive and behavioral attempts at regulation, providing a direct medium to express profound reactions and elicit support from others. In other instances, emotions were used instrumentally by leaders such as President Bush in his efforts to rally and unite a nation. And, sadly, at other times, emotions provoked stereotyping and aggression directed at religious or ethnic groups.

These world events and observations created two clear realizations. One was that in addressing emotions and emotional regulation, we were indeed focusing on a fundamental aspect of human experience that influences cognition, motivation, and behavior. The second was that our coverage of this topic was incomplete. We did not directly address the topic of fear and how it is managed in the context of work task, in family situations, or by solitary individuals. Our multilevel perspective stops with the organization, yet national and international environments are increasingly important. Societal and organizational norms for emotions also seem to have changed, with the open expression of strong emotions being tolerated and sometimes encouraged, while much of the current literature still emphasizes controlling emotions.

Given other constraints, it was not possible to revise the book to address such issues fully. Furthermore, although we do touch on some of the issues associated with the terrorist attacks and their effects on work behavior in the final part of the book, our focus in the last two chapters is more on integrating the material covered in prior chapters and developing needed theoretical frameworks. This focus reflects our fundamental belief in the value of trying to integrate science and practice. We hope that ideas that emerge from this activity, such the heuristic meta-framework developed in the final chapter, can be used to integrate the applied topics covered in the book, as well as many of the topics such as fear that we did not have the foresight to include. We invite readers and future researchers concerned with emotions to use the theories and research covered to understand both the issues that are explicitly addressed and the many additional concerns created by recent world events.

Acknowledgments

This book would not have been possible without contributions from many people. Foremost, we thank the chapter authors. We were fortunate to persuade researchers with a wide range of interests in emotions to contribute to this book, and they responded with grace, enthusiasm, and hard work. We are delighted with their contributions.

A number of other people also made important contributions to the book. We thank Jason Lord and Steve Shamp for creating a Web site that allowed authors to see the overall framework for the book as it was developing. The contributions of Jennifer Harvey in conducting initial research on many areas of emotions at work were also invaluable. Rosalie Hall read and commented on several sections of the book. Neal Schmitt, the Society for Industrial and Organizational Psychology Frontiers Series editor, and Julianna Gustafson, our editor at Jossey-Bass, have provided consistent support and encouragement. Finally, we thank our families—Nicole, Jason and Rosalie; Gretchen; and Phillip and Sarah—for their patience and support throughout this project.

January 2002

Robert G. Lord
Akron, Ohio

Richard J. Klimoski
Fairfax, Virginia

Ruth Kanfer
Atlanta, Georgia

The Contributors

Robert G. Lord is a professor of psychology at the University of Akron, Ohio. He received his Ph.D. in organizational psychology from Carnegie-Mellon University. He is a Fellow of the American Psychological Association, the American Psychological Society, and the Society of Industrial and Organizational Psychology. He currently serves on the editorial boards of *Organizational Behavior and Human Decision Processes, Leadership Quarterly,* and *Journal of Applied Social Psychology.* He coauthored *Leadership and Information Processing: Linking Perceptions and Performance* (1991) with Karen J. Maher. His research focuses on emotional regulation, motivation, self-regulation, social cognition, leadership processes, and information processing.

Richard J. Klimoski is professor of psychology, director of the Center for Behavioral and Cognitive Studies, and director of the A-E Area Program in Psychology in the Department of Psychology, and associate dean, College of Arts and Sciences, at George Mason University in Fairfax, Virginia. His teaching and research interests revolve around the areas of organizational control systems in the form of performance appraisal and performance feedback programs and team performance. His research has appeared in the *Journal of Applied Psychology, Personnel Psychology, Academy of Management Journal, Journal of Management, Administrative Science Quarterly,* and *Journal of Conflict Resolution.* He is coauthor with Neal Schmitt of *Research Methods in Human Resource Management* (1991) and coeditor with Stephen Zaccaro of *The Nature of Organizational Leadership* (2001). He is on the editorial review board of *Human Resource Management Review* and *Organizational Research Methods.*

Ruth Kanfer is a professor of psychology in the School of Psychology at Georgia Institute of Technology, Atlanta. She received her Ph.D. from Arizona State University. She is a Fellow of the American

Psychological Association, American Psychological Society, and the Society of Industrial and Organizational Psychology. She served as chair of the Organizational Behavior Division of the Academy of Management in 1999–2000 and has served on the editorial boards of several journals. She is the recipient of the American Psychological Association's Distinguished Scientific Award for an Early Career Contribution and the Academy of Management's Outstanding Publication in Organizational Behavior Award. Her research focuses on applications of motivation, self-regulation, and emotion. Her current research interests include the development of whole-person assessment strategies for use in personnel decision making and the role of self-regulation and emotion processes as they affect job search and work role transitions.

Richard D. Arvey is a professor of human resources and industrial relations at the University of Minnesota. He received his Ph.D. from the University of Minnesota. His research interests include staffing and selection, training evaluation, job satisfaction, and organizational behavior. He is the author of *Fairness in Selecting Employees* (1988) and has published widely in many of the academic journals associated with human resource management.

Blake E. Ashforth is a professor of management in the College of Business at Arizona State University. He received his Ph.D. in organizational behavior from the University of Toronto. His research interests include workplace identity and identification, socialization and newcomer work adjustment, emotions in organizational life, the dysfunctions of organizational structures and processes, and the links among individual-, group-, and organization-level phenomena. His most recent work has focused on role transitions, dirty work, and workplace spirituality. He recently wrote *Role Transitions in Organizational Life: An Identity-Based Perspective* (2001).

Analea L. Brauburger is a graduate student in industrial and organizational psychology at the Pennsylvania State University. She received her B.S. degree in psychology from Arizona State University. Her primary research interests are exploring interpersonal mistreatment and incivility in the workplace and expanding the criterion domain of job performance. Her other research interests include determining culture and climate effects on individual well-being and performance, as well as understanding perceptions of discrimination and unfair treatment in university settings.

Ed Diener is Alumni Professor of Psychology at the University of Illinois. He received his Ph.D. from the University of Washington in Seattle. He is past president of the International Society of Quality of Life Studies and president of the Society of Personality and Social Psychology (and Division 8 of the American Psychological Association). He is the editor of the *Journal of Personality and Social Psychology* and *Journal of Happiness Studies*. He recently won the Distinguished Researcher Award from the International Society of Quality of Life Studies and a Distinguished Alumni Award from California State University at Fresno.

P. Christopher Earley is the Randall L. Tobias Chair of Global Leadership at the Kelley School of Business, Indiana University. He received his Ph.D. in industrial and organizational psychology from the University of Illinois, Urbana-Champaign. His research interests include cross-cultural and international aspects of organizational behavior. Recent publications include *Face, Harmony, and Social Structure: An Analysis of Behavior in Organizations* (1997) and, with Miriam Erez, *The Transplanted Executive: Managing in Different Cultures* (1997). In addition, he is the editor of *Group and Organization Management*.

Clare Anne Francis is an assistant professor in the Management Department, Kelley School of Business, Indiana University, Bloomington. Her research interests focus on the linkages between face, affect, and related behaviors in a cross-cultural context. (Face refers to the internal and external presentation of oneself defined within a social system.) Behaviors of interest include organizational citizenship behavior and performance.

Jennifer M. George is the Mary Gibbs Jones Professor of Management and professor of psychology in the Jesse H. Jones Graduate School of Management at Rice University. She received her Ph.D. in management and organizational behavior from the Stern Graduate School of Business Administration at New York University. Her research interests include affect, mood, and emotion in the workplace; creativity; personality influences; groups and teams; prosocial behavior and customer service; values and work-life linkages; and stress and well-being. She is a Fellow in the American Psychological Association, the Society for Industrial and Organizational Psychology, and the American Psychological Society and a member of the Society for Organizational Behavior. She is on the Editorial Board of the SIOP Organizational Frontiers Series and an incoming associate editor of the *Journal of Applied Psychology*.

Theresa M. Glomb is an assistant professor in the Department of Human Resources and Industrial Relations at the University of Minnesota. She received her Ph.D. in industrial/organizational psychology from the University of Illinois. She has conducted research and published in the areas of anger and aggressive behaviors in organizations, emotional expression in organizations, sexual harassment, and job attitudes and behaviors. She has published in the *Journal of Applied Psychology, Organizational Behavior and Human Decision Processes,* and the *Journal of Occupational Health Psychology.*

Alicia A. Grandey is an assistant professor in industrial/organizational psychology at Pennsylvania State University-University Park. She earned her Ph.D. at Colorado State University. Her two research streams are concerned with the expression and regulation of emotions in service interactions and the barriers to family-supportive policy effectiveness. Her work has been published in *Academy of Management Journal, Journal of Vocational Behavior, Journal of Organizational Behavior, Journal of Occupational Health Psychology,* and several edited books on emotion. Her work on the topic of emotional labor has been heard on national radio and discussed in *Ms.* Magazine and national and international newspaper columns.

Jennifer L. Harvey is an associate in the personnel research group at Caliber Associates and has developed selection assessments for various organizations. She received her Ph.D. in industrial/organizational psychology from the University of Akron. Her research interests have focused on motivation, leadership, and emotional regulation. She has coauthored work on leadership and social influence in *Blackwell's Handbook of Social Psychology* (2001) and work on leadership prototype generation in *Leadership Quarterly*. She is a member of the Society for Industrial and Organizational Psychology.

Tracy M. Kantrowitz is a doctoral student in industrial/organizational psychology at the Georgia Institute of Technology, Atlanta. Her research interests include personality and motivational influences on job search behavior and employment outcomes, cognitive and noncognitive predictors of training and job performance, and investigation of motivational traits and skills.

Randy J. Larsen is the Stuckenberg Professor of Human Values and Moral Development in the Psychology Department at Washington University in St. Louis. He received his Ph.D. in personality psychology from the University of Illinois at Champaign-Urbana. His research is broadly in the area of emotion and personality, for which he has received a number of awards, including a Distinguished Scientific Achievement Award for Early Career Contribution from the American Psychological Association and a Research Scientist Development Award from the National Institute of Mental Health. He coauthored *Personality Psychology: Domains of Knowledge about Human Nature* (2002) with David Buss and is widely published.

Richard E. Lucas is an assistant professor in the Department of Psychology at Michigan State University. He received his Ph.D. in personality psychology from the University of Illinois at Urbana-Champaign. His research interests lie in the areas of personality and subjective well-being, and he has published a number of papers investigating these topics. Most recently, he has focused on examining the affective underpinnings of the extroversion personality dimension.

Shelley M. MacDermid is professor and director of the Center for Families at Purdue University and a faculty member in the department of Child Development and Family Studies. She also codirects the Military Family Research Institute at Purdue. She earned a Ph.D. in human development and family studies and an M.B.A. from the Pennsylvania State University. Her research focuses on relationships between job conditions and family life, particularly in smaller workplaces. Her work has been published in scientific journals, including the *Journal of Marriage and the Family* and the *Academy of Management Journal.* Her research has won awards from the Groves Conference and Gamma Sigma Delta.

S. Douglas Pugh, assistant professor of management at the University of North Carolina at Charlotte, received his Ph.D. degree in organizational behavior from Tulane University. His primary research focuses on emotion processes in organizations, particularly as they relate to customer service and employee-customer interactions. Other research interests include organizational citizenship behavior, layoffs, and race and diversity issues in organizations. His research has appeared in the *Academy of Management Journal, Academy of Management Executive,* and *Organizational Behavior and Human Decision Processes.*

Anat Rafaeli is an associate professor of organizational behavior at the Faculty of Industrial Engineering and Management at the Technion, Israel's institute of technology. She received her Ph.D. from Ohio State University. She is interested in emotional and symbolic self-presentation in organizations, especially as they occur in service interactions. She has spent three years as a visiting scholar at the University of Michigan, where she developed work on symbols and organizational interactions.

Alan M. Saks is associate professor of human resources in the School of Administrative Studies at York University. He received his Ph.D. in organizational behavior from the University of Toronto. He is the author of *Research, Measurement, and Evaluation of Human Resources* (2000), coauthor with Gary Johns of *Organizational Behavior: Understanding and Managing Life at Work* (2001), and coauthor with Monica Belcourt and Philip Wright of *Managing Performance Through Training and Development* (2000).

Brenda L. Seery is an assistant professor of human development and family studies at Penn State Worthington Scranton. She received her Ph.D. in human development and family studies from the Pennsylvania State University. Her research has focused on women's emotion work in families and the life experiences of low-income women living in rural areas.

Piers D. G. Steel, a doctoral student in industrial and organizational psychology at the University of Minnesota, received his B.A. from University of Toronto in psychology and philosophy. His research interests include the refinement of meta-analysis, personality at higher levels of analysis, and the motivational problem of procrastination.

Howard M. Weiss is professor of psychological sciences at Purdue University and codirector of the Military Family Research Institute, which is funded by the Department of Defense and dedicated to conducting research on the relationships between quality of life and job satisfaction, retention, and work performance. He received his Ph.D. in industrial/organizational psychology from New York University. His research interests focus on emotions in the workplace and on job attitudes. His most recent published work is related to his theoretical framework, affective events theory.

Monica C. Worline is a doctoral candidate in organizational psychology at the University of Michigan, where she is completing a dissertation on courage and social life. She is an interdisciplinary scholar who uses psychology, literature, art, poetry, drama, and philosophy to understand organizational life better. Prior to pursuing graduate study, she had a career in Silicon Valley. She received her B.A. from Stanford University.

Amy Wrzesniewski is an assistant professor of management and organizational behavior at New York University. She received her Ph.D. in organizational psychology from the University of Michigan. Her research interests focus on how people make meaning of their work in challenging contexts and the experience of work as a job, career, or calling. She is currently studying how employees shape their interactions and relationships with others in the workplace to change both their work identity and the meaning of the job.

PART 1

Conceptual Foundations and Measurement

Chapters One through Three develop the theoretical and methodological basis for understanding how emotions can affect work behavior. Although emotions influence every aspect of human life, their impact on work behavior has only recently received much attention. Consequently, the conceptual basis for understanding emotional processes must be borrowed from a number of other areas of psychology: evolutionary, cognitive, social, and neuropsychology. Methodological approaches show similar variability, although there is still a predominance of questionnaire-based research.

Chapter One, by Lord and Kanfer, focuses on the relationship of emotions to organizational behavior, explaining that the strength and specificity of this relationship vary with both the valence and intensity of emotions. Building on Scherer's (1994) argument that emotions mediate between environmental stimuli and behavior, the authors maintain that this emotional interface decouples stimuli and responses, providing flexibility in adjusting to environmental differences. They also note that emotions influence other important intra- and interindividual processes that are prevalent in organizations. Emotions modulate many internal processes such as information processing activities, which can be broadened or narrowed and accelerated or slowed by emotion-related neurochemical changes. Emotions also influence and are influenced by motivational processes. For example, individual differences in the regulation of emotions such as anger and fatigue play a central role in the effective pursuit of goals that involve sustained attentional effort, whereas the effect of motivation on emotions occurs through appraisals of affective events in terms of their relation to one's welfare or current goals. Emotions, particularly as expressed by facial, postural, and vocal variation, also provide a rapid, ubiquitous, and generally automatic guide to social interactions. Rules for displaying and reading emotions reflect both the human evolutionary heritage and the effects of formal and informal socialization processes that may be culturally or organizationally based. Through such processes, emotions provide the underlying structure for many cognitive and social processes in organizations. Thus, as Lord and Kanfer explain, emotions influence organizational behavior through many different routes.

In Chapter Two, Howard Weiss stresses that organizational researchers have adopted a very narrow perspective on affect and emotions. This chapter serves as a primer that seeks to broaden the perspective of applied researchers. It reviews evolutionary, cognitive, and physiological approaches to emotions, arguing that all approaches are needed to understand important outcomes in organizations. Weiss explains that evolutionary psychologists view the mind as being highly modular, comprising numerous systems dedicated to specific tasks (for example, mating, prey avoidance, resource acquisition) that had a critical impact on hominid evolution. Emotions can be viewed as "superordinate programs" that coordinate many subprograms pertaining to issues like facial expression, attention, and memory in the service of adaptational problems. Although evolution may have engineered the human system for problems found in a hunter-gatherer environment, behavior in modern organizations co-opts these systems and procedures to address contemporary issues. Thus, societal and organizational cultures as well as individual learning overlay and to some extent modify this emotion-based command structure.

Many applied issues such as aggression in the workplace or difficulties in emotional regulation can be understood in terms of using a highly modular mind that was optimized to an ancient environment to pursue modern objectives in a contemporary setting. For example, evolution may have engineered many emotions to facilitate fast-paced, physical responses, whereas modern organizations emphasize slower-paced, cognitive activity. The difficulty in using a system engineered by evolution for modern purposes can also be seen in more abstract issues, such as the interplay between emotions and cognitive processes. Weiss notes that one cognitive tradition sees interpretive or appraisal processes as being central in generating emotions, a view that gives causal priority to conscious cognitive systems in structuring and regulating more ancient emotional systems. A contrasting tradition emphasizes the effects of affective experience on a variety of cognitive processes, with factors such as positive versus negative moods affecting the comprehensiveness and internal versus external orientation of cognitive processes. The validity of both views can be appreciated by recognizing that cognitive and emotional processes are reciprocally related through many structures and processes and that conscious cognitive processes, which include emotional appraisal, are only part of the conceptual structure of emotions.

Weiss notes that research stemming from a physiological tradition provides an additional perspective on emotions. This research, aided by newer neuroimaging techniques, shows that emotions involve complex functional networks in many brain regions, a view consistent with conceptualizing emotions as being higher-level, co-ordinating systems and with the perspective that only part of the structure of emotions may be consciously experienced. Weiss also discusses an important recent development: the capacity to understand individual difference variables (positive versus negative affectivity, extroversion, neuroticism) in terms of the reactivity of certain brain networks to positive or negative stimuli. Emotional reactivity, in turn, is closely associated with motivational systems related to approach or avoidance (Gray, 1990; Higgins, 1998), and it has been argued that emotional, or "hot," systems have a greater role in generating behavior than "cold" cognitive systems (Metcalf & Mischel, 1998).

In Chapter Three, Larsen, Diener, and Lucas draw on the evolutionary, cognitive, and physiological traditions to examine individual differences in characteristic emotions and emotional regulation skills. They conceptualize emotions as arising from a multiattribute process involving experience, expression, behavior, cognition, and physiology, with the different attributes unfolding at different rates. Larsen, Diener, and Lucas advocate a stimulus-organism-emotional response (S-O-R) framework that distinguishes between an individual's sensitivity to stimuli (S-O) and his or her amount of response output (O-R). The value of this framework is that sensitivity and response output processes may be affected by different individual capacities, different aspects of organizations, or different cultures, as suggested by Earley and Francis (Chapter Eleven, this volume). Larsen, Diener, and Lucas use this framework to understand the relation among many personality measures and discuss their potential relevance to organizational behaviors. For example, they discuss Gray's (1990) distinction between behavioral approach and behavior inhibition systems (BAS versus BIS) in terms of S-O processes and analyze emotional regulation in terms of O-R processes.

Larsen, Diener, and Lucas also carefully review a number of techniques for measuring emotions. These techniques vary in terms of content and type of measurement technology. Single- and multi-item self-report inventories are often used to measure felt emotions, and expressed emotions are often measured using carefully developed coding systems and highly trained observers to rate facial or vocal expressions. Emotion-sensitive tasks and physiological measures are also reviewed. Larsen, Diener, and Lucas blend discussion of the practical problems in using such measures in organizations with more theoretical issues such as the meaning of constructs like reliability when there is both substantial variability in an individual's emotions over time and significant differences among individuals in average level of emotions. They also discuss the trend among emotion researchers of increasingly relying on dimensional representations of emotions rather than emphasizing basic or primary emotions such as happiness, anger, and sadness. However, it is not yet clear whether understanding emotions and emotion-related behavior in organizations is better served by dimensional representations or analysis in terms of primary emotions such as anger and fear.

References

Gray, J. A. (1990). Brain systems that mediate both emotion and cognition. *Motivation and Emotion, 4,* 269–288.

Higgins, E. T. (1998). Promotion and prevention: Regulatory focus as a motivational principle. In M. P. Zanna (Ed.), *Advances in experimental social psychology.* Orlando, FL: Academic Press.

Metcalfe, J., & Mischel, W. (1999). A hot/cool-system analysis of delay of gratification: Dynamics of willpower. *Psychological Review, 106,* 3–19.

Scherer, K. R. (1994). Emotion serves to decouple stimulus and response. In P. Ekman & R. J. Davidson (Eds.), *The nature of emotion: Fundamental questions* (pp. 127–130). New York: Oxford University Press.

CHAPTER 1

Emotions and Organizational Behavior

Robert G. Lord
Ruth Kanfer

During the past two decades, substantial advances have been made in understanding the structure and role of affect and emotions in human behavior. Industrial/organizational (I/O) psychologists and other applied researchers have recognized the relevance of such advances for understanding workplace behavior, producing a number of recent articles, special issues (Deiner, 1999; Fisher & Ashkanasy, 2000; Larsen 2000; Rosenberg & Fredrickson, 1998; Weiss, 2001), and books (Ashkanasy, Hartel, & Zerbe, 2000; Lewis & Haviland-Jones, 2000) on emotions and emotions at work. Building on this progress, a growing number of organizational researchers have begun to integrate these advances into theory and research pertaining to employee cognition, affect, and behavior. In some areas of I/O psychology, such as job satisfaction, new perspectives on affect have begun to reshape the domain (Fisher, 2000; Judge & Hulin, 1993; Weiss & Cropazano, 1996). In other areas, basic research on affect and emotions has been used as a foundation for new perspectives on established topics, such as leadership (Fitness, 2000; Glomb & Hulin, 1997; Lewis, 2000) or group processes (George, 1990). This research is also relevant to such timely issues as employee violence and employee reactions to organizational justice (Cropanzano, Weiss, Suckow, & Grandey, 2000). Concerns with emotions have spawned new areas of research, such as emotional labor in the workplace and its costs and benefits (Grandey, 2000; Grandey and Brauburger, Chapter Eight, this volume).

Many researchers interested in this topic (and, we suspect, most applied readers of this literature) may not have been exposed to a comprehensive coverage of the scientific literature on emotional regulation. Along with others (Rosenberg & Fredrickson, 1998; Weiss, this volume), we believe there are many advantages to taking a broad perspective when trying to understand emotions, and such a perspective brings the need to cross specialization boundaries within psychology or organizational behavior. The purpose of this volume is twofold: to provide applied psychologists (1) a concise and state-of-the-art scholarly introduction to new developments in this area of inquiry and (2) an overview of how basic theory and research in affect and emotions can influence the science and practice of I/O psychology.

It is important to define emotions carefully and distinguish emotions from moods. Izard (1993) notes that defining emotions is a complex issue, but he stresses that the experiential component of emotions—the experience of pain, anger, and joy—is central and manifests itself as an action tendency, a biasing of perceptions, or a feeling state. He maintains that emotional experiences are activated by neural, sensorimotor, motivational, and cognitive systems, but he also notes that neural systems can activate emotions without cognitive mediation. Emotions are generally of short duration and are associated with a specific stimulus; mood, in contrast, is more enduring, more diffuse, and less related to specific stimuli (Frijda, 1993). Emotions also have a stronger linkage with specific behaviors than moods do. *Affect* is a more general term and can refer to either mood or emotions.

We should also stress at the outset that our focus is on emotions and emotional regulation in normal, healthy individuals. Clinical applications and pathological aspects of emotional regulation are beyond the scope of this book. Readers interested in such issues might consult excellent works by Keltner and Kring (1998) on psychopathology and the social aspects of emotions or work by Globus and Arpaia (1994), which explains emotion-based disorders from a neural network perspective.

Among the many reasons to be interested in human emotions in the workplace, foremost is that as applied scientists, one of our aspirations is to increase human welfare. Rather than being objective, welfare is subjectively defined by people in terms of their affective reactions to organizational events. Consequently, if we can find ways to alter organizational practices, social processes, or task designs in ways that increase positive emotions and reduce negative emotions, the welfare of organizational members is directly increased.

Emotions are also central components of human reactions to many types of stimuli. Hence, they can directly cue specific behaviors, as well as indirectly influence behavior by their effect on physiological, cognitive, or social processes. For these reasons, attempts to change behaviors in organizations to more effective patterns may require that emotions also be changed, as is often the case with organizational interventions.

Emotions and Organizational Behavior

Emotions can influence organizational behavior in a number of ways, as we discuss in the following sections. Some of the ways are direct, such as the triggering of behavior by emotions, whereas other ways are indirect, such as emotions influencing behavior through mediating mechanisms like motivation or cognition.

Emotions as an Environment-Behavior Interface

Scherer (1994) provides a compelling reason for concern with emotions. He maintains that emotions are an interface that mediates between environmental input and behavioral output. This interface has strong ties to motivational-implementation systems and helps ensure that the central needs of an organism (or social system) are met. In lower-level organisms, such needs are generally met by hard-wired responses, producing a rigid link between specific releaser stimuli and behavioral responses. In human beings, the emotional interface decouples stimuli and responses, allowing for much greater flexibility in adjusting to environmental differences. Scherer argues that flexibility accrues from the combination of two processes. First, while emotions prepare and energize appropriate action tendencies, responses are not immediately released, providing a latency period in which additional information can be processed and alternative responses considered. Second, this latency period is shorter for stronger emotions. Thus, in critical situations, which produce strong emotional responses, pre-programmed responses can be reliably executed, but in less critical situations, continuous evaluation and more thoughtful choice of behavior can occur. Importantly, this continuous evaluation often takes into account the reactions of others.

Scherer's perspective helps us understand why the basis for emotions and related responses can change with emotional intensity. Figure 1.1 shows this relation graphically, emphasizing that as the latency between the triggering stimulus and responses increases, there is wider participation of cognitive and social processes in emotional responses, and consequently, the range of potential affective and behavioral reactions increases. As Scherer notes, intense emotions produce behavior reliably and rapidly; less intense emotions result in more variable, delayed behavior. This functional principle is important for understanding how cognitive and social-organizational processes influence emotions and behavior. Cognitive processes, which are the focus of Chapter Four, are often effective in modulating emotional responses, but when individuals are under cognitive load, attempts at emotional regulation are often ineffective (Wegner, 1994). The modulation of emotions and behavioral responses by social and organizational processes is also important, but it may be overlooked because social communications regarding emotions are often implicit. This topic is briefly addressed in this section as well as in separate chapters by Pugh and George (respectively, Chapters Five and Six).

The modulation of emotional responses to potentially threatening situations by social processes is an important issue for I/O psychologists to understand. This social component of emotions is often automatic and unrecognized, and as a result, it may cause difficulty in many organizational processes. Emotional responses can be intensified by reactions such as panic in others, or they can be reduced by the reassuring calm responses of others, particularly formal leaders. Modulation of emotional reactions by social cues would need to operate reliably and quickly to complement the emotional interface that Scherer discusses; hence, it is likely to be produced by relatively automatic reactions to the nonverbal signals of others. Such reactions tend to be learned through socialization

Figure 1.1. Increased Behavioral Variability as Greater Latency Between Stimulus and Response Permits More Cognitive Processing.

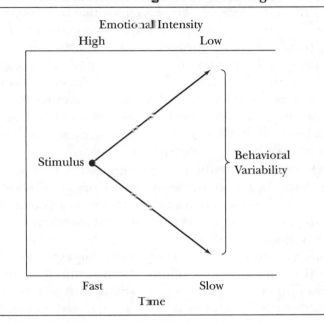

to a particular culture, although some have argued that there are universal aspects to facial expressions of emotions (Keltner & Ekman, 2000). Because such responses are relatively automatic, they are rarely part of formal organizational training processes. Instead, a worker's implicit understanding of how to use social cues to modulate emotions is likely to predominate, and that understanding may have been learned in different situations where emotional expression was more common (such as family or social situations) than in typical work situations.

Emotion-Behavior Linkages

Most theories of emotions recognize the linkage between specific emotions and specific types of behaviors (Fredrickson, 1998; Levenson, 1994). Indeed, this linkage is so reliable that Russell and Barrett (1999) propose that there are prototypical emotional events that follow specific emotions (*core affects,* in their terms), and Lazarus (1999) develops a complementary view maintaining that proto-typical events lead to specific emotions. For example, in the Russell and Barrett (1999) theory, emotions like fear, anger, love, or pity may each trigger a unique prototypical sequence of events involving core affect, appropriate overt behavior with respect to the emotional stimuli, attention toward and appraisal of the emotional stimuli, emotional experience, and neurochemical changes. The emotion-behavior linkage also depends on whether emotions are positive or negative (Fossum & Barrett, 2000), with positive emotions being associated with slower and more variable responses than negative emotions (Fredrickson, 1998).

Negative emotions often have strong associations with specific types of behavior, and strong negative emotions are likely to produce such behaviors with minimal guidance from concomitant cognitive processing because responses occur too fast for much processing to occur. For this reason, regulating the experience of strong negative emotions is an important aspect of behavioral regulation. Lord and Harvey (Chapter Four, this volume) address this issue from an information processing perspective, building on an emotional regulation framework that Gross (1998) suggested. Grandey (2000; Grandey and Brauburger, Chapter Eight, this volume) addresses this issue in the context of emotional labor, but it may be equally relevant to many other applied issues, such as workplace aggression. The important point for application is that many work behaviors may have strong and consistent linkages to negative emotions. In such cases, attempts to change behavioral patterns without first changing associated emotions are likely to be unsuccessful.

Positive emotions have garnered less attention than negative emotions, for several reasons: they are less differentiated, they are not associated with specific problems needing solutions, and they are not associated with specific action tendencies thought to be necessary for survival (Fredrickson, 1998). Nevertheless, positive emotions may have critical functions that are necessary for the survival of species or the effective functioning of organizations, although intense positive affect may have psychic costs as well (Diener, Colvin, Pavot, & Allman, 1991). Fredrickson (1998) has developed a "broaden-and-build" perspective on the value of positive emotions. She maintains that positive emotions are important in that they broaden attention and create situations where cognitive, physical, and social resources can be built. For example, she maintains that joy promotes play, which helps to build physical, social, and intellectual skills. Similarly, contentment broadens the self and worldview and creates the urge to integrate; love triggers other positive emotions and solidifies individual and social resources.

Generalizing from Fredrickson's perspective, positive emotions should promote a number of important organizational processes, such as skill building, creativity, effective social relations, organizational commitment, collective orientations, and prosocial behaviors. Fredrickson also notes that positive emotions serve as an antidote to the harmful physiological and cognitive effects of negative emotions. Consistent with such arguments, recent organization research has again raised the issue of whether happier workers are more productive. Wright and Staw (1999) suggest that they might be, but only when happiness is defined in enduring dispositional rather than more variable state terms. Dispositional positive affect may be required to build individual and social resources.

Emotions and Motivation

Emotions play an integral role in motivation. Individual differences in emotional tendencies interact with organizational events and social interactions to yield emotional reactions that importantly shape an individual's goals and the persistence of effort in the face of obstacles. The influence of emotional reactions to organizational events, such as downsizing, may seriously weaken personal commitment to organizationally desired goals and, in turn, job performance.

Emotional processes are also implicated in the accomplishment of complex and longer-term goals. Individual differences in the regulation of different emotions, such as anger and boredom, play a central role in the effective pursuit of goals that involve sustained attentional effort. In organizational contexts, such individual differences may be particularly important in the prediction of training outcomes and performance in jobs that involve substantial autonomous functioning.

Motivational processes also play an important role in the elicitation and expression of emotions. Theories of cognitive appraisal, for example, posit the critical importance of appraisals of personal significance for the elicitation of emotional responses. As such, the emotional significance of an event depends on the extent to which the event is appraised as relevant to the individual's goal concerns.

Implications of the interplay of motivation and emotion for organizations are discussed in several chapters in this book. For example, Kanfer and Kantrowitz (Chapter Thirteen) address motivation-emotion relations in the context of maturation and skill training. Worline, Wrzesniewski, and Rafaeli (Chapter Nine) and MacDermid, Seery, and Weiss (Chapter Twelve) discuss the role of emotions from the perspective of an individual's motives in achievement and balancing work-family demands, respectively.

Emotions and Social Processes

An important characteristic of emotion-evoking stimuli and emotional reactions is that they are often very fast, frequently producing initial effects before conscious, symbolic-level processing can occur. This aspect may have had critical survival value when fast reactions were needed to avoid threats, but it also has an important social consequence. That is, it allows emotions to serve as a rapid, and ubiquitous guide to social interactions. As Levenson (1994) noted, facial expressions, voice tone, and posture communicate how we feel to others and can draw us to or repel us from others. This argument has been developed into a social-functional approach to emotions, which posits that emotions coordinate interactions related to formation and maintenance of social relationships (Keltner & Kring, 1998). Three assumptions underlie this theory: (1) expression of emotions signals socially relevant information, (2) evoked responses in others are associated with benefits, and (3) emotions serve as incentives for other people's actions. For example, Keltner and Kring note that the experience and expression of embarrassment evoke forgiveness in others and produce reconciliation after social transgressions.

Because emotions are communicated and perceived rapidly, such processes often occur outside awareness, but they can still have an impact on important social processes, such as trust in others, perceptions of honesty, interpersonal attraction, and group commitment. The capacity to read and display emotions can be learned explicitly (emotional labor is a good example), but normally such learning may be largely implicit, reflecting regularities in family, ethnic, organizational, or national cultures. To the extent that rules for displaying and reading emotions are hard-wired, they reflect a repository for the influences of evolution, as Levenson (1994) notes. However, to the extent that they are learned, they provide a means of transmitting a culturally based structure for social interactions or organizational processes (see Ashforth and Saks, Chapter Ten, this volume). To be effective, applied efforts at understanding or changing social interactions at work need to be attuned to this continuous, often implicit emotional structure.

Emotions and Information Processing

Emotions are both bodily states and mental states, and they are also part of a larger information processing system (Clore, 1994; Isen, 2000). Considerable research shows that styles of information processing are influenced by both moods and emotions. Strong emotions can short-circuit cognitive processing, which can often be too cumbersome, too excessive, and too inconclusive for action (Levenson, 1994). Moods, in contrast, often have more subtle effects on information processing. For example, positive moods have been associated with tendencies toward heuristic processing (but see Isen, 2000), and negative moods are associated with more careful, systematic processing. Positive mood elicits the use of stereotypes, scripts, and categorical social information processing, whereas negative mood increases the use of individuating information (Gohm & Clore, 2000). Positive mood also elicits more exploration and enjoyment of new ideas and can enhance creativity (Isen, 2000).

Such general relations between mood and the extent of conscious processing are common (Isen & Baron, 1991; Gohm & Clore, 2000); however, others have made the argument that we need to describe specific processes to understand the relationship of cognitions and emotions (LeDoux, 1994; LeDoux & Phelps, 2000). That is, it is more useful to examine how specific emotions (fear, anger, pleasure) and specific types of cognitive processes (object perceptions, memory) interact than to make general arguments regarding the nature of cognitive-emotional interactions. One good starting point for developing greater specificity would be the circumplex model of Russell and Barrett (1999), which links core

affect (basic emotional categories) to prototypical emotional episodes and specific cognitive and behavioral processes.

To understand the interaction of emotions and cognitions, it
also helps to think of the mind as a "wet computer"—that is, a
spongelike mass of neurons in a constantly changing and locally
differentiated chemical medium. In such computational hardware,
information processing properties change as different chemicals
are supplied to or depleted from physically distinct subsystems.
Thus, processing networks can be broadened or narrowed and
made more or less sensitive by neurochemical changes associated
with hormones involved in emotional reactions (Globus & Arpaia,
1994). For example, fear releases stress-related hormones (glucocorticoids and epinephrine). When glucocorticoids reach the brain,
they inhibit the hippocampal-dependent (conscious or declarative)
memory but enhance the amygdala-dependent (emotional) memory. Consequently, intense stress impairs the ability to form conscious
memories but enhances the capacity for emotional memories.
Such chemical modulation by emotions shows why the "wet computer" metaphor is more useful for seeing emotion-cognitive interactions than using the typical modern computer as a model of
the human mind.

Evolution and Emotions

Much of the literature on emotions has strong ties to evolutionary
psychology; thus, understanding emotions helps us grasp the way
that evolution has shaped and continues to limit human behavior.
Cosmides and Tooby (2000) stress that cognitive, behavioral, and
emotional systems were all haphazardly but exquisitely designed
by adding specific components that dealt effectively with long-en-
during, ancestral adaptive problems. Yet in modern humans, many
of these components are co-opted and interact to produce emotions and behavior. The interaction of emotional and cognitive systems is a good example of how specific components can interact.

The interaction of cognitive, behavioral, and emotional systems
often underlies many other human phenomena, and adopting an
evolutionary perspective helps to bring such interactions into
focus. For example, one argument that evolutionary psychologists
and emotional researchers often make is that strong negative emo-

tions arise from the type of events that had important survival value for earlier humans. Emotions can then serve as a trigger for the type of behaviors that would have had adaptive value to ancient humans. However, this does not mean that the same emotions or emotion-related behaviors are instrumental in contemporary life or modern organizations. Hence, cultural, social and intraindividual processes are needed to regulate negative emotions and associated behavior. Appropriate socialization of emotional regulation and emotional displays may therefore be necessary for the effective functioning of organizations (Ashforth and Saks, Chapter Ten, this volume). Consistent with this argument, Mastenbroek (2000) views such socialization procedures as an important development that predates industrial organizations.

Another important point related to an evolutionary perspective is to recognize that the ability to work as a group and manage social processes was pivotal in human evolution. Consequently, emotions have a fundamental linkage with social capacities, providing a nonverbal means to communicate emotions through facial expressions, body posture, and voice tone. This heritage is ubiquitous in contemporary human interaction, and it provides an underlying structure for many social processes. When we overlook such processes in investigating organizational phenomena, we miss an important component of the processes we are studying. For example, studies of social processes such as charismatic or transformational leadership have often focused on abstract properties such as a leader's vision, while ignoring the effects of a leader's nonverbal behavior. Yet recent work shows that nonverbal behavior explains much more variance in perceptions of charismatic leadership than does visionary content (Awamleh & Gardner, 1999), which is not surprising when we think in terms of the nonverbal, emotional structure for social interactions shaped by evolutionary processes.

Objectives and Plan of This Book

Clearly, there are many theoretical and practical reasons for being interested in emotions at work. In this book, we seek a middle ground between the scientific literature on this topic and the desire of many practice-oriented individuals to apply thinking and findings on emotions in real-world situations. Thus, in Parts One and Two, we develop the scientific and methodological framework needed to address the applied issues covered in Part Three.

This book is divided into four parts that address the major themes: foundations, regulatory processes, applications to work situations, and issues and future directions. Part One consists of the first three chapters that, in addition to this introductory chapter, cover the historical and conceptual foundations in the emotions literature (Chapter Two) as well as methodological techniques and concerns (Chapter Three).

Processes related to emotional regulation and level of analysis concerns are examined in Chapters Four through Six in Part Two. Chapter Four maintains that information processing is guided by an emotional architecture that complements the neural network and symbolic architectures that underlie most popular information processing models. Chapters Five and Six illustrate that emotions unfold differently as the complexity of the social context increases. Chapter Five examines effects associated with individual differences, as well as constraints from dyadic interaction partners, and Chapter Six examines group and organizational constraints on emotions and emotion-related behaviors. In combination, these three chapters provide a basis for understanding how cognitive, personality, and social processes affect emotional regulation and expression and how these processes, in turn, affect organizational behavior.

Part Three turns to more specific applied issues, such as aggression and workplace violence, recruitment and selection, customer service, cross-cultural differences, performance in challenging situations, and work-family conflict. That emotions are central to such a wide range of applied topics illustrates the need for scholars and practitioners interested in organizational behavior to understand emotions at work better.

The past several years have been characterized by a renewed scholarly and practical interest in emotion. Although the chapters in this book show that much progress has been made, they also identify many unresolved issues and areas needing research. The two chapters in Part Four thus describe and catalogue such issues and propose future research agendas for understanding emotions and organizational behavior. Both chapters also provide integrative frameworks to guide future research and practice.

References

Ashkanasy, N. M., Hartel, C.E.J., & Zerbe, W. J. (Eds.). (2000). *Emotions in the workplace: Research, theory, and practice*. Westport, CT: Quorum Books.

Awamleh, R., & Gardner, W. L. (1999). Perceptions of leader charisma and effectiveness: The effects of vision content, delivery, and organizational performance. *Leadership Quarterly, 10*, 345–373.

Clore, G. L. (1994). Why emotions require cognition. In P. Ekman & R. J. Davidson (Eds.). *The nature of emotion: Fundamental questions* (pp. 181–191). New York: Oxford University Press.

Cosmides, L., & Tooby J. (2000). Evolutionary psychology and the emotions. In M. Lewis & J. M. Haviland-Jones (Eds.), *Handbook of emotions* (pp. 91–115). New York: Guilford Press.

Cropanzano, R., Weiss, H. M., Suckow, K. J., & Grandey, A. A. (2000). Doing justice to workplace emotion. In N. M. Ashkanasy, C.E.J. Hartel, & W. J. Zerbe (Eds.), *Emotions in the workplace: Research, theory, and practice*. Westport, CT: Quorum Books.

Diener, E. (1999). Introduction to the special section on the structure of emotion. *Journal of Personality and Social Psychology, 76*, 803–804.

Diener, E., Colvin, C. R., Pavot, W. G., & Allman, A. (1991). The psychic costs of intense positive affect. *Journal of Personality and Social Psychology, 61*, 492–503.

Fisher, C. (2000). Mood and emotions while working: Missing pieces of job satisfaction? *Journal of Organizational Behavior, 21*, 185–202.

Fisher, C. D., & Ashkanasy, N. M. (2000). Emotions in organizations. *Journal of Organizational Behavior, 21*, 121–234.

Fitness, J. (2000). Anger in the workplace: An emotion script approach to anger episodes between workers and their superiors, co-workers and subordinates. *Journal of Organizational Behavior, 21*, 147–162.

Fossum, T. A., & Barrett, L. F. (2000). Distinguishing evaluation from description in the personality-emotion relationship. *Personality and Social Psychology Bulletin, 26*, 669–679.

Fredrickson, B. L. (1998). What good are positive emotions? *Review of General Psychology, 2*, 173–186.

Frijda, N. H. (1993). Moods, emotion episodes, and emotions. In M. Lewis & I. M. Haviland (Eds.), *Handbook of emotions* (pp. 381–403). New York: Guilford Press.

George, J. M. (1990). Personality, affect, and behavior in groups. *Journal of Applied Psychology, 75*, 107–116.

Globus, G. G., & Arpaia, J. P. (1994). Psychiatry and the new dynamics. *Biological Psychiatry, 35*, 352–364.

Glomb, T. M., & Hulin, C. L. (1997). Anger and gender effects in observed supervisor-subordinate dyadic interactions. *Organizational Behavior and Human Decision Processes, 72,* 281–307.

Gohm, C. L., & Clore, G. L. (2000). Individual differences in emotional experience: Mapping available scales to processes. *Personality and Social Psychology Bulletin, 26,* 679–698.

Grandey, A. A. (2000). Emotion regulation in the workplace: A new way to conceptualize emotional labor. *Journal of Occupational Health Psychology, 5,* 95–110.

Gross, J. J. (1998). The emerging field of emotional regulation: An integrative review. *Review of General Psychology, 2,* 271–299.

Isen, A. M. (2000). Positive affect and decision making. In M. Lewis and J. M. Haviland-Jones (Eds.), *Handbook of emotions* (2nd ed., pp. 417–435). New York: Guilford Press.

Isen, A. M., & Baron, R. A. (1991). Positive affect as a factor in organizational behavior. In B. M. Staw & L. L. Cummings (Eds.), *Research in organizational behavior* (Vol. 13, pp. 1–53). Greenwich, CT: JAI Press.

Izard, C. E. (1993). Four systems for emotion activation: Cognitive and noncognitive processes. *Psychological Review, 100,* 68–90.

Judge, T. A., & Hulin, C. L. (1993). Satisfaction as a reflection of disposition: A multiple source causal analysis. *Organizational Behavior and Human Decision Processes, 56,* 388–421.

Keltner, D., & Ekman, P. (2000). Facial expression of emotions. In M. Lewis & J. M. Haviland-Jones (Eds.), *Handbook of emotions* (2nd ed., pp. 236–249). New York: Guilford Press.

Keltner, D., & Kring, A. M. (1998). Emotion, social function, and psychopathology. *Review of General Psychology, 2,* 320–342.

Larsen, R. J. (2000). Emotion and personality: Introduction to the special section. *Personality and Social Psychology Bulletin, 26,* 651–655.

Lazarus, R. S. (1999). *Stress and emotion: A new synthesis.* New York: Springer.

LeDoux, J. E. (1994). Cognitive-emotional interactions in the brain. In P. Ekman & R. J. Davidson (Eds.), *The nature of emotion: Fundamental questions* (pp. 216–223). New York: Oxford University Press.

LeDoux, J. E., & Phelps, E. A. (2000). Neural networks in the brain. In M. Lewis & J. M. Haviland-Jones (Eds.), *Handbook of emotions* (pp. 157–172). New York: Guilford Press.

Levenson, R. W. (1994). Human emotions: A functional view. In P. Ekman & R. J. Davidson (Eds.), *The nature of emotion: Fundamental questions* (pp. 123–126). New York: Oxford University Press.

Lewis, K. M. (2000). When leaders display emotion: how followers respond to negative emotional expression of male and female leaders. *Journal of Organizational Behavior, 21,* 221–234.

Lewis, M., & Haviland-Jones, J. M. (Eds.). (2000). *Handbook of emotions* (2nd ed.). New York: Guilford Press.

Mastenbroek, W. (2000). Organizational behavior as emotion management. In N. M. Ashkanasy, C.E.J. Hartel, & W. J. Zerbe (Eds.), *Emotions in the workplace: Research, theory, and practice* (pp. 19–35). Westport, CT: Quorum Books.

Rosenberg, E. L., & Fredrickson, B. L. (1998). Overview to special issue: Understanding emotions means crossing boundaries within psychology. *Review of General Psychology, 2,* 243–246.

Russell, J. A., & Barrett, L. F. (1999). Core affect, prototypical emotional episodes, and other things called *Emotion*: Dissecting the elephant. *Journal of Personality and Social Psychology, 76,* 805–819.

Scherer, K. R. (1994). Emotion serves to decouple stimulus and response. In P. Ekman & R. J. Davidson (Eds.), *The nature of emotion: Fundamental questions* (pp. 127–130). New York: Oxford University Press.

Wegner, D. M. (1994). Ironic processes of mental control. *Psychological Review, 101,* 34–52.

Weiss, H. M. (Ed.). (2001). Affect at work: Collaborations of basic and organizational research [Special issue]. *Organizational Behavior and Human Decision Processes, 88.*

Weiss, H. M., & Cropanzano, R. J. (1996). Affective events theory: A theoretical discussion of the structure, causes, and consequences of affective experience at work. In B. M. Staw & L. L. Cummings (Eds.), *Research in organizational behavior* (Vol. 18, pp. 1–74). Greenwich, CT: JAI Press.

Wright, T. A., & Staw, B. M. (1999). Affect and favorable work outcomes: Two longitudinal tests of the happy-productive worker thesis. *Journal of Organizational Behavior, 20,* 1–23.

CHAPTER 2

Conceptual and Empirical Foundations for the Study of Affect at Work

Howard M. Weiss

A comparative examination of the basic literature on affect and the literature on affect in organizations indicates that organizational researchers have focused on only a few of the interesting topics of affect. It also indicates that too often, organizational researchers have only a cursory understanding of affect processes. The objective of this chapter is to help improve this situation by familiarizing readers with the basic literature on emotions and moods. Because that literature is too enormous to be covered in detail, the chapter is presented as a primer; it looks at the broad topics of basic research on affect, the key questions and findings in the topic areas, and sources for more detailed information. The breadth of this research will become apparent as the chapter unfolds. The focus on basic affect processes will not, however, make apparent the narrowness of research on affect in organizations, and so it is appropriate to comment on this first before we begin.

It is fair to say that the late 1980s and the 1990s saw a rebirth of interest in true affective experiences—that is, moods and emotions—in the workplace (Weiss & Brief, 2001). I use the term *rebirth* deliberately. The very early studies of affect in organizations had discussions of "emotional maladjustment" (Fisher & Hanna,

---

Thanks to Dan Beal, Joe Forgas, and Bob Meisel for their comments and suggestions.

1931), collected data with daily mood diaries and accompanied these with physiological measurements (Hersey, 1932), and examined individual differences in affective dispositions (Kornhauser & Sharpe, 1932). At the end of the 1930s, affect had become job satisfaction, and questionnaires had become the method of choice. True affective experiences disappeared from the research scene for five decades, resurrected only in the past ten years or so.

Armed with these basic historical facts, some might argue that the "job satisfaction as affect" perspective was overly narrow and that we can take encouragement from the broader array of affective studies over the past decade. I think this argument would paint an overly optimistic picture. Job satisfaction, as we will see, was never properly the study of affective experiences at work, and the recent research, although admittedly more truly affective in character, is overly narrow in problems and approaches.

Any thorough examination of the state of research on affect in organizations (see, for example, Brief & Weiss, 2002) will note the preponderance of research on moods, the almost exclusive reliance of positive and negative affectivity to describe the structure of moods, both in state and trait terms, and the lack of conceptual clarity in understanding the differences between affective states and attitudinal judgments. Few studies on the causes and consequences of discrete emotions will be discovered. Little research tying organizational conditions to the appraisal processes that drive affective states will be seen. Only rarely will the information provided by current physiological research on emotions be encountered in discussions about appropriate conceptualizations of affective dispositions. The proliferation of field verifications of basic findings about mood-outcome relations (for example, that mood predicts absenteeism, helping, and creativity) will be observed simultaneously with the lack of attention to the performance implications of basic emotion regulation processes.

I am hopeful that by exposing readers to some of the areas of basic emotion research, I might encourage research that goes beyond the narrow confines of mood, positive and negative affectivity, and similar other topics. Because I cannot hope to familiarize readers with the full range of information available, my objective is simply to point motivated readers to areas of further inquiry. In addition, I have not made any decisions about what to present and what to exclude based on any preconceived ideas about relevance to organizational research.

Key Terms and Taxonomic Structure

It is useful to begin with a definitional section, so that readers will understand which constructs are being discussed. Many constructs inhabit the same conceptual space of relevance to us. These constructs are often the product of different research traditions, and this can and has created confusion. Some of the constructs that inhabit this space are mood, emotion, affect, attitude, well-being, stress, and temperament. There are few discussions that focus on defining all simultaneously, but there are very useful discussions that try to distinguish among pairs. For example, the distinction between mood and emotions and temperaments is thoughtfully discussed in a number of chapters in Ekman and Davidson's book *The Nature of Emotion* (1994). Good presentations of the differences between moods and discrete emotions can also be found in Morris (1989) and Frijda (2000). Lazarus (1991, 1993; Lazarus & Folkman, 1999) discusses the differences between the constructs of stress and emotion. Diener, Suh, Lucas, and Smith (1999) review the enormous literature on subjective well-being and in doing so discuss the affective and nonaffective components of the construct. I have discussed the differences between affective states and attitudes, particularly job satisfaction (Weiss, in press; Weiss & Cropanzano, 1996).

Let me try to present a framework that organizes most of these constructs and thereby allows us to understand the focus of this chapter. Readers may wish to refer to Figure 2.1 while reading this section. There is a conceptual space called affect. Metaphorically, in the taxonomy of psychological variables, it would be a family of concepts. Within this family are the various genera of affect—such constructs as moods, emotions, and stress. It is at this genus level that I will try to make the necessary distinctions. However, let us not forget that genera themselves are composed of various species: the genus "emotion" contains anger and guilt and pride, for example, and the genus "mood" may be composed of positive and negative affect or perhaps pleasantness and activation. We shall see. Above the family of affect is the order of evaluative constructs. Affect is one family in that order; attitude is another.

Figure 2.1. Construct Taxonomy.

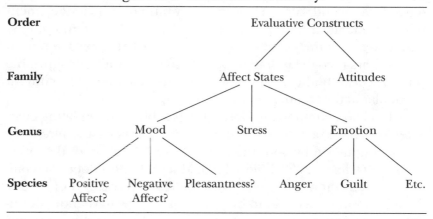

I use this taxonomic model instead of a prototype model because I do not want readers to think that the structure necessarily reflects the way ordinary people think about the constructs. I use the taxonomic model instead of a hierarchical factor-analytic model because I do not want readers to think that the structure has within it some inherent mathematical relationships. Instead, I want readers to think in terms of some common and unique features of these scientific constructs, which I will describe shortly. In addition, as in biology, the taxonomic model allows for revision of structure as the importance of new features becomes apparent or new variables are developed.

Let me first define the key genera (constructs) that comprise the affect family. These are moods, emotions, and stress. We will start with emotion. Emotion, everyone knows, has been a very difficult construct to define. Part of the problem is that an emotion is not really one thing but a constellation of physiological, subjective, and behavioral responses that cohere as a unified construct. This multicomponent nature of emotion is quite understandable when one recognizes that emotions serve adaptive functions and therefore recruit multiple systems in the service of dealing with adaptive problems. Frijda (1993) provides a nice summary of the general consensus among emotion researchers as to the components of an emotion. First, there is the experiential component of affect, that is, the subjective appreciation of the emotional state.

Part, but not all, of this experience is valence. Emotions are valenced states, and valence is a necessary but not sufficient element of emotion. Second, this subjective experiential element is always connected to some person, object, or event. Third, most emotion researchers recognize that emotional states include recognizable physiological, bodily changes. Finally, discrete emotions contain particular action tendencies.

Mood and emotion are closely related, but differentiating characteristics have been described. Frequently, moods and emotions are distinguished by both the intensity and duration of the affective state (Larsen, 2000; Frijda, 1993; Morris, 1989). Moods, as compared to emotions, are thought to be less intense and of longer duration. Emotions tend to be punctuated; they have more definable beginnings and endings. These differences in duration and intensity are not as useful as they may first appear to be. Moods can vary greatly in duration, as can emotion episodes. The brevity of mood states is well understood by anyone trying to manipulate mood in the laboratory. Similarly, some diffuse affective states best described as moods can be rather intense, and some discrete emotions can be rather mild. Although duration and intensity may generally be different for moods and emotions, these do not appear to be at the core of the difference between the constructs.

More central to the difference is what can best be called diffuseness. Many researchers have noted that while emotions always seem to be affect in relation to a particular object or event (I am angry with my colleague; I feel guilty about having lied to my friend), moods lack such an object or defining event. They exist more as background affective states. This does not mean that they are not caused by something particular or that we are not aware of the state. Rather, it means that the cause is not part of the experience itself. The diffuseness of the mood, its disconnection from particular objects or circumstances, is often central to its broad cognitive and behavioral effects (Fiedler, 2001).

Russell and Barrett (1999) provide a new structure to affect that distinguishes between core affect and prototypical emotional episodes. Prototypical emotional episodes are emotional experiences as most people understand them, with referent objects and events, affective experience, behavior tendencies, discrete time frames, and so forth. Interestingly, they suggest that prototypical emotional episodes are infrequent occurrences. Core affect is the accessible, subjective, affective feeling. It is present in prototypical emotion episodes, but such episodes are not necessary for the experience of core affect. Core affect can be free floating, exists at some level (including a neutral level) all the time, and need not be associated with an object. In some ways, core affect is like mood. More precisely, it seems to be the subjective experiential component that is mood when it is not part of a prototypical emotion episode.

For some, the concept of stress is subsumed under the concept of emotion (Lazarus, 1993), but here we will try to identify differentiating features. I use the term *stress* to describe an immediate psychological and physiological state. I recognize that some people prefer to reserve the term *stress* to refer to the causal agent and then use *strain* to refer to the state I am describing. However, the terminology is not well worked out, and I think most readers will understand my use of the term *stress*. Although stress and emotion share many features, inherent in the concept of stress is the experience of demand or challenge. Stress research began with the study of responses to physical demands, and the stress concept itself is borrowed from analysis of the effect of physical demands on man-made structures (Lazarus, 1993). The key qualitative element of stress appears to be the demand or challenge placed on the individual in a taxing situation. Of course, different types of stress have been proposed, including eustress and distress to differentiate positive and negative stress situations (Selye, 1974) and harm, threat, and challenge (Lazarus, 1993). Lazarus believes that the concept of stress can be subsumed under the concept of emotion. Eventually, this may turn out to be a more productive way of understanding these constructs. However, for now, we will maintain a separation and reiterate that the focus of this chapter is on moods and emotions.

Looking at the common features of the family helps us decide which genera belong and which do not. Three common features predominate. First, all members of the affect family are states; that is, they describe transient psychological experiences. Second, there is a common subjective component. This is the feeling component, the experience of the affect that is sensed by the individual, the knowledge that we are in some affective state and can distinguish it from not being in such a state. Third, all of these states—emotions, moods, and stress—appear to have a physiological element.

Although there is debate over how much and in what ways the particulars of this physiological component vary across the affect states, there is a clear consensus that these states are accompanied by activation and deactivation of various bodily systems (Larsen, 2000). A fourth common feature can also be identified: these states—moods, emotions, and stress—all have an evaluative component as well: people prefer some of the states to others.

Using this taxonomy helps us to eliminate certain variables from the family and thereby clarify differences among variables often treated as equivalent. First among these is attitude and, by extension, job satisfaction. I have argued elsewhere that attitude is not affective in the same way that moods and emotions are (Weiss, in press; Weiss & Cropanzano, 1996), and now, by way of clarifying that position, I argue that attitude does not belong in the family of affective states, although it does belong in the order of evaluative constructs in which affect is also a member. Attitude, as defined by many social-psychological researchers (Eagly & Chaiken, 1993; Petty, Wegener, & Fabrigar, 1997), is an evaluation or evaluative tendency with reference to an object. As such, it has none of the defining features of the affect family. It is not a state, it does not have the same subjective experiential character, and it has none of the typical physiological correlates. The fact that it shares an evaluative component is not enough to put it in the same family of constructs as other affect genera, in the same way that having a backbone is not enough to make an alligator a hominid. Instead, it might be better to define a separate family of constructs within the order of evaluative constructs and label that family "attitudes." Subcategories (genera, species) might include, for example, self-esteem (evaluation of self) and non-self object evaluation (job satisfaction, attitude toward the president). Our purpose here is not to describe the different types of attitudes but rather to try to show why attitude does not fall within the family of affect constructs. As we continue our discussion of affect, the exclusion of research on satisfaction will seem only natural.

The Structure of Moods and Emotions

Everyday language suggests to us that the subjective experiences of emotions and moods are rich with variety. When my wife says to me, "You're in quite a mood," she can be calling attention to any one of a number of states (not all of which are obvious to me). Averill (1975) developed a list of 558 emotion-related words. Shaver, Schwartz, Kirson, and O'Conner (1987), working from Averill's list and others and focusing only on nouns and eliminating obvious redundancies, created a list of 213 emotion names. Yet, as in most other areas of psychology, researchers have concluded that the search for underlying simplicities, that is, organizing structures, dimensions, typologies, and so forth, will better serve the cause of theory development than will a strictly experiential analysis. This search has taken two directions. In one direction, researchers have sought the basic emotions that serve as the building blocks of discrete emotional experience In the other direction, researchers, and primarily mood researchers, have sought the underlying dimensions that best capture the structure of relationships among affect terms. We start our discussion with the search for basic emotions.

Basic Emotions

An important tradition in the study of emotion structure takes the form of a search for "basic" emotions. These basic emotions comprise a small set of central or fundamental emotions from which the full range of emotion experience derives. Researchers who argue for the existence of these basic emotions generally do not deny the validity of the wide variety of human emotional experiences that go beyond the set of basic emotions. However, they propose a universal set of core emotions and, with varying degrees of clarity, processes by which the diversity of emotions we experience grows out of these basic emotions.

Interestingly, most of the important recent work on the topic have not focused on determining which emotions can be considered basic. Rather, it has focused on the legitimacy of the concept of basic emotions. Ekman and Davidson have a section in their book, *The Nature of Emotion: Fundamental Questions* (1994), that contains short essays with arguments for and against the usefulness and validity of proposing basic emotions. Ortony and Turner (1990) presented a thorough critique of the concept, and Ekman (1992) and Izard (1992) had rejoinders.

Not surprisingly, the advocates of the basic emotion position generally come from an evolutionary psychology tradition of emotion research, and the critics generally come from a cognitive appraisal tradition. Psychoevolutionary-focused emotion researchers view individual emotions as programmed adaptations to specific problems shaped over the course of human and animal evolutionary history (see, for example, Izard, 1994; Plutchik, 1994; Cosmides & Tooby, 2000). The various emotions evolve to deal with particular adaptive problems, and basic emotions themselves are therefore discrete and limited.

On what basis would we be willing to call an emotion "basic"? Again, the answer comes from the evolutionary development and the adaptive significance of emotions. For example, Izard (1992) proposes three criteria: basic emotions have innate and unique neural substrates, unique and universal facial expressions (the adaptive significance of facial expressions of emotions will be discussed later), and unique feeling states. Ekman (1994a) presents more criteria, including the presence in primates and automatic appraisal, but also includes distinct physiology.

Universality and distinct physiology appear to be important and agreed-on criteria for a basic emotion driven by natural selection. Consequently, both have been active areas of research. Postulating that a basic emotion has unique physiological or neural substrates does not mean the uniqueness is to be found in any one physiological system (like unique autonomic nervous system activity for each emotion, for example) or that a neural structure need be found for each emotion. Natural selection is often a process of jerry-rigging existing structures for new purposes, and the underlying physiological uniqueness for a particular emotion is likely to be found in the pattern of responses among various existing systems.

The critique of the basic emotion position by Ortony and Turner (1990) is interesting and thoughtful. So too are the responses by Ekman (1992) and Izard (1992). I will not go into the details except to point out the validity of the criticism that agreement among researchers as to which emotions are basic does not exist. Ortony and Turner present a table illustrating the wide diversity among the various lists of basic emotions and also show that some emotions in these lists are not really emotions at all. Ekman (1992) responds that researchers do agree that six emotions meet most criteria (happiness, surprise, fear, sadness, anger, and disgust), but in a later work (Ekman, 1994a) he lists seventeen candidates.

The argument for a basic set of emotions driven by natural selection is compelling. However, because the problems for which these emotions evolved cannot be identified a priori, the research strategy often seems to be to find a universal emotion and deduce a problem it is meant to solve. Thus, the logic of an adaptational underpinning to emotional experience may be sound but also practically limited. Furthermore, it is still possible that a more involved cognitively driven superstructure of emotions can be built from the basic evolutionary-driven foundation, and one cannot easily make a case for where the best explanatory system will be found.

An alternative approach to identifying basic emotions can be found in the work of Shaver et al. (1987), who examined the mental representation of emotion concepts using prototype theory (Rosch, 1973). Prototype theory argues that mental representations of normal objects or concepts are organized in hierarchical category systems In any system, three levels of the hierarchy are considered to be important for mental representation: superordinate, basic, and subordinate levels. For example, furniture (a superordinate category) is composed of basic categories like chairs, tables, and cabinets, which are in turn broken down into subordinate categories (sofas, settees, and recliners—all types of chairs). More important for our discussion, the basic categories have certain properties that suggest that they are the most fundamental level of representation. Among these are shorter latencies for recognition, more precise visual imagery, and earlier learning during language acquisition (Shaver et al., 1987).

Shaver et al. (1987) applied prototype theory to examine the structure of meaning in emotion words. They did this by applying hierarchical cluster analysis to judgments of similarity among the emotion terms and found six "basic" categories of emotion words—love, joy, anger, sadness, fear, and surprise—although they argued that surprise should not be considered an emotion. They also found that these basic emotion categories were further subdivided into twenty-five subordinate-level categories, with these subcategories distinguishable primarily in terms of the intensity of the basic emotion or the antecedents or context for the expression of the emotion. Two superordinate categories were identified comprising positive and negative emotions. Shaver et al. (1987) also identified the prototypical episodic structure of each basic emotion.

The approach of Shaver et al. (1987), being based on the structure of emotional language, has the same limitations of other lexical approaches to conceptual structures. That is, it describes whether certain emotion words and categories are basic but does not bear directly on the question of whether the emotions themselves are in some way basic (Ortony & Turner, 1990). Nonetheless, their approach is an interesting bridge between evolutionary- and cognitive-based emotion researchers.

Dimensional Structures

An alternative approach to summarization has sought to determine the underlying dimensional structure that best captures the relationships among affect states and terms. This area presents perhaps more heated exchanges among scholars expressing divergent viewpoints than any other area of emotion research. Papers, responses, and counterresponses dot the landscape. Among the more important pieces are Russell's and Carroll's "On the Bipolarity of Positive and Negative Affect" (1999a) and the response to it by Watson and Tellegen (1999) and the response to the response by Russell and Carroll (1999b); the special issue of the *Journal of Personality and Social Psychology* edited by Diener (1999) with articles by Russell and Barrett (1999), Watson, Wiese, Vaidya, and Tellegen (1999), Cacioppo, Gardner, and Berntson (1999), and Green, Salovey, and Truax (1999); and the special issue of *Psychological Science* in 1999 with articles by Tellegen, Watson, and Clark (1999a), the response by Green, Salovey, and Truax (1999), and the Tellegen, Watson, and Clark (1999b) counter-response. Russell must have been out of the office when *Psychological Science* called.

At any moment, people describe their affective states using terms like *happy,* or *fearful,* or *sad,* or *stressed.* They use these terms when they are aware of the cause, when the affect has an object as in discrete emotions, and when the cause is not part of the experience itself, as in moods. Is there an underlying structure to these affect states, and can the structure be identified? Of what value would the structure be, and if it had value, what would be the best way to measure it? These are the questions that have occupied those working in this area.

Simple introspection appears to point to one dimension of the underlying structure. Our states, whatever their discrete qualities, seem to fall along a bipolar dimension ranging from positive to negative. This bipolar dimension is referred to by such terms as *valence, hedonic tone,* and *pleasantness.* Further introspection might also discover that our states, whether positive or negative, are sometimes aroused, as in elation and anger, and sometimes quiescent, as in serenity and sadness. Consequently, an arousal or activation dimension would be a useful complement to the valence dimension.

However, as is often the case, things are not always as they seem. In the 1960s Bradburn (1969) applied factor-analytic techniques to self-reports of affect states and found that positive affective states and negative affective states appeared to fall out as two separate dimensions. Such research led to the idea that the underlying structure of affect is best described by dimensions of positive and negative affectivity. This proposition, most notably advocated by Watson, Tellegen, Clark, and their associates, has spawned an enormous amount of research, both in favor of and against the proposition, as well as the development of those ubiquitous scales to measure activated positive affect (PA) and activated negative affect (NA)—the Positive Affect Negative Affect Schedule (PANAS). The articles I have noted present one side or the other of the debate over whether affect is better understood with bipolar pleasantness and activation or positive affectivity and negative affectivity. Readers who are interested in doing mood research in organizations should read each of these articles in order to make an informed decision about structure and therefore measurement. The following is my take on some of the issues.

A general consensus appears to be that a circle can geometrically represent the similarity structure of affect terms (although see Tellegen et al., 1999a, 1999b). This circle, shown in Figure 2.2, is called the affect circumplex, and in this structure, affect terms are arranged along the circumference of a circle with similarity of meaning between two terms represented by how far apart the terms are along the circle's edge. In such a structure, the location of any term can be determined using two dimensions at right angles to each other, and the meaning of those dimensions will be generated by the particular affect terms that fall at the dimension's poles. Two such dimensions are pleasantness and activation; two others are positive and negative affectivity. The important thing to remember is that any set of two right-angled dimensions will do an equally good job of positioning the affect terms. The choice from among dimension pairs cannot be made in terms of usefulness for describing the similarity of affect terms. All right-angled dimensions are equally capable.

Figure 2.2. Affect Circumplex.

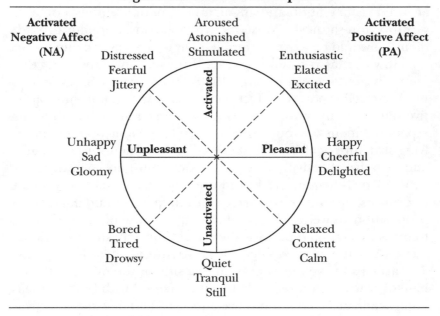

This point is well understood by all researchers in this area, regardless of their side in the debate. It has important measurement and conceptual implications. Russell and Carroll (1999a) provide a nice summary of many of these conceptual and measurement issues. For example, the relative independence of NA and PA (these scales generally show low to moderate negative correlations) cannot be taken as evidence against the validity of a bipolar valence scale because items in the PANAS are sampled only from the high activation ends of the PA and NA dimensions. Thus, the items included do not represent the opposite poles of any dimension structure and should therefore not be expected to be either perfectly negatively correlated or independent, and they are neither. Green, Goldman, and Salovey (1993) make this same argument in their discussion of how measurement error masks the bipolarity of momentary affect.

Consequently, the choice of appropriate dimensional structure must be made based on external criteria. Watson et al. (1999) acknowledge this point when they argue for the PA-NA structure based on its compatibility with physiological approach and avoidance systems and by their observation that affect words seem to pile up at the poles of activated positive and negative states. Russell and Carroll (1999) dispute this latter point, and regarding the former, as we will see, organization at the physiological level need not be isomorphic with organization at the psychological level.

External criteria can also be used to support the valence-activation structure. Behavioral responses are clearly bipolar in terms of approach and avoidance, even recognizing the potential for vacillation, and overall evaluative structure based on bipolar valence appears to be a ubiquitous component of attitude and meaning. In our own research on affective influences on attitudes (Weiss, Nicholas, & Daus. 1999), we showed that the pleasantness but not the activation dimension of momentary mood states at work predicted job satisfaction. This suggests the utility of keeping these dimensions separate.

Overall, research seems to indicate that when appropriate measures are created and latent variables examined, pleasantness and activation appear to be most useful for describing momentary affect (Russell & Carroll, 1999a). However, momentary affective experience is a blend of these two dimensions, or any other two dimensions, and the affective experience itself is more than the dimensional reduction. People do not experience dimensions; they experience states. At any moment, people feel a particular way (for example, sad or angry). How much meaning and predictive utility is lost by reducing discrete states to dimensions is an important research question. Anger and fear are near each other on any dimensional configuration and yet have very different subjective meaning and behavioral implications.

Three Traditions in the Study of Emotions

Now that we have discussed the definition and structure of moods and emotions, we are ready to get to the core of the research on the topic. I have organized the discussion along the lines of three traditions in the study of emotions—the evolutionary tradition, the cognitive tradition, and the physiological tradition—because these categories appear to capture the way the literature is organized. General textbooks on emotions roughly organize the material in these ways (see, for example, Plutchik, 1994). Judging by references within articles, researchers within these traditions seem to talk to each other more than they talk to researchers across traditions. Most important, the three traditions focus on internally coherent sets of problems. This organization should not imply that these traditions are completely independent. Important bridgework is being conducted. Nonetheless, the categories provide a useful heuristic for summarizing the issues and pointing to important papers. Left out is the clinical tradition, including the psychodynamic tradition, mostly for reasons of space and interest.

The Evolutionary Tradition

The past decade has seen the emergence of evolutionary psychology as a major theoretical approach to the study of human behavior and cognition. The frameworks of natural section, sexual selection, and inclusive fitness have been applied to, among other things, the study of language, altruism, cooperation, family violence, sexual attraction, and jealousy. Buss's recent textbook (1998) provides a reasonable introduction to the topic, although it is weighted toward social processes at the expense of evolutionary examinations of cognitive processes. Cartwright (2000) has a more balanced treatment. Both are worth reading. The *Handbook of Evolutionary Psychology* (1998) and Barkow, Cosmides, and Tooby's *The Adapted Mind* (1992) provide good collections of essays on various topics. Tooby and Cosmides (1992) is a tour de force that every psychologist should read.

This recent explosion of interest in evolution-based explanations of behavior for broad classes of behaviors contrasts with a long tradition of evolution-based thinking about emotions. Darwin's *The Expression of the Emotions in Man and Animals* (1872), a classic, provided the blueprint for a continuing study of emotions and emotional expression, both theoretical and methodological. More recent ideas on evolution and emotion are represented by Plutchik (1980, 1984, 1994), Izard (1993), and Cosmides and Tooby (2000). Darwin was greatly interested in the expression of emotion, and much of the recent evolution-inspired work on emotions does indeed focus on emotional expression, particularly facial expression. Embedded in that research are also assumptions about the nature of emotions, apart from their expression, and still other research examines emotions from the point of view of evolution with less focus on expression.

The Basic Evolutionary Argument

Izard (1992) well expresses the basic idea of all psychoevolutionary theories of emotion: "Emotions are specific neuropsychological phenomena, shaped by natural selection, that organize and motivate physiological, cognitive and action patterns that facilitate adaptive responses to the vast array of demands and opportunities in the environment" (p. 561). Cacioppo et al. (2000) express the same idea, perhaps more lyrically: "We may sing in choirs and bridle our rages behind placid countenances, but we patrol the world under the auspices of an affect system sculpted over millennia of evolutionary forces" (p. 173). The key is that emotions are "programs" that have arisen through the course of human evolutionary history to help organisms solve problems of adaptation and survival.

Evolutionary psychology generally views human behavior and cognition as modular in structure. That is, what has evolved are domain-specific adaptations, each developed to deal with a specific type of problem, rather than any general-purpose behavioral or information processing system. The brain, according to this viewpoint, is not the general-purpose computer often described in the cognitive literature, but rather a set of domain-specific programs designed to deal with different problems. Modern human behavior and problem solving are built on the specifics of these programs developed over the course of millions of years of hominid evolutionary history and even billions of years of animal evolution. For most psychoevolutionary emotion theorists, emotions are just such programs, each having evolved to deal with a specific problem and each emotional adaptation enlisting and integrating various physiological and cognitive subsystems in the service of that adaptation. Cosmides and Tooby (2000) are particularly clear about this structure, arguing that discrete emotions are superordinate programs designed to coordinate specific existing programs in the service of different adaptational problems. They provide an interesting discussion of the various subprograms enlisted by these superordinate programs called emotions (for example, attention, memory, and facial expressions).

From this perspective, it is clear why researchers from this position generally avoid the simplifying structures of affect dimensions. Because discrete emotions evolve to solve fundamental and unique problems of adaptation, too much is lost by simplifying along the lines of PA-NA or valence and arousal. It is also clear why the construct of emotion includes diverse physiological and experiential components. The full constellation comprises the complete program. Finally, it is clear why each discrete emotion has an action tendency associated with it. Emotions are programs designed to direct adaptive behavior. However, adaptation has to be understood in terms of the demands faced by humans throughout their evolutionary history. Adaptations developed millions of years ago may be counterproductive in the context of current circumstances.

Many psychoevolutionary theories of emotions have tried to examine these demands and describe discrete emotional systems consistent with this analysis. Izard's differential emotion theory (DET) and Plutchik's psychoevolutionary theory are examples of this approach. Recently, Izard (1993) has extended DET to discuss the different ways in which emotions can be instigated. In doing this, he has tried to integrate evolutionary, physiological, and cognitive approaches to emotion generation. Cosmides and Tooby (2000) provide an illustrative discussion of the emotion program for jealousy and how it evolved from the adaptive problems faced by what they call an "evolutionary recurrent situation," that is, a recurrent problem situation that endured over a long enough time to have selective consequences. They discuss the full constellation of the program, including situation-detection mechanisms (perceptual processes that identify the situation and elicit the emotion), physiological regulation in service of the problem solution, and programs that assign response priority when multiple problem situations are detected.

Facial Expressions

Facial expression research is relevant to the whole psychoevolutionary emotion program in at least two ways. First, the evidence for universality of emotional facial expression is taken as evidence for the universality of the emotions themselves across our species and independent of cultural differences, thus providing evidence for the development of these emotions in human evolutionary history. Second, the identification of discrete facial expression patterns is taken as evidence for the validity of particular discrete emotions. Thus, it is clear why emotion researchers working within an evolutionary framework spend so much time studying the nature and universality of facial expressions.

The history of the study of facial expressions of emotions is a long one. Most researchers trace current thinking at least to Darwin's *The Expression of the Emotions in Man and Animals* (1872), but discussions of the topic can be read in Aristotle. (See Fridlund, 1994, for a history of the study of facial expression with an emphasis on Darwin's position.) Current work on facial expressions of emotions began with the groundbreaking work of Tompkins and the follow-up research by Ekman and Izard. Tompkins's position can be found in Tompkins (1963). Izard's DET appears in a number of his writings (Izard, 1977, 1994, 1997). Ekman's position is also well described in much classic and recent work (Ekman, 1992, 1993; Ekman & Friesen, 1971; Keltner & Ekman, 2000).

Although differences among these researchers' positions exist, Russell has described a number of common elements in what he calls the Facial Expressions Program (FEP) (Russell, 1994; Russell & Fernandez-Dols, 1997). Although Russell is critical of the program, the description he gives of its basic assumptions is reasonably accurate. The essential element of the FEP can be discerned from the term *facial expression*. That is, various facial displays express underlying emotional states. More specifically, the FEP postulates that there are a small number of basic emotions, approximately seven by most accounts but varying slightly among researchers; each basic emotion is discrete, with a unique physiological, behavioral, and subjective coherence. These basic emotions are evolutionarily based, that is, they developed through natural selection to solve unique problems, and coevolving with each discrete emotion is a facial expression that serves as a signal of the emotion, with the signal itself being an evolutionary adaptation.

According to Ekman (1999) it was central to the evolution of an emotion to let other members of the species know what you were "feeling" and what you were likely to do about it. Thus, a communicative function went hand in hand with the evolution of the emotion itself. This signaling system is primarily, but not entirely, in the face. Because there are seven or so basic emotions, there should be seven or so facial configurations that express those emotions in a way that is readable to other members of the species.

The existence of these basic emotions does not imply that emotional experience is not subject to cultural processes. For example, advocates of the FEP are not so naive as to suggest that people cannot hide their basic emotional states. All agree that there are culturally determined display rules that can mask emotional expression. In addition, elicitors of particular emotions can be culture specific. Nonetheless, however elicited, basic emotions are discrete with unique display configurations, unless overridden by controlled disguise processes.

All researchers in this area, both advocates and critics of the FEP, agree that a central piece of evidence supporting the FEP is the universality of emotional expression, and by this they mean cross-cultural similarity of emotional display. As Russell and Fernandez-Doz (1997) point out, there are a number of components to the universality idea, and two of them are central. First is the proposition that observers in different cultures attribute the same underlying emotion to the same facial displays. That is, if I show a picture of a person with a particular facial display to people in the United States, Japan, New Guinea, and Mozambique, they will all agree on the emotion the person is experiencing. Evidence for this proposition is gathered using the facial judgment paradigm across cultures. The second proposition is that these facial displays are expressions of the same emotions across all cultures. That is, across cultures, people who are angry show the same facial expression, and across cultures people who are disgusted show the same facial expressions. This second proposition, seemingly more fundamental to the FEP, has been tested infrequently.

Most of the evidence for universality comes from facial judgment studies conducted in multiple cultures. Essentially, photographs of faces of people expressing various of the presumed basic emotions (happiness, anger, fear, surprise, disgust, sadness) are shown to observers in different cultures, and these observers are asked to choose which of the basic emotions is being displayed (the forced-choice format) or to indicate in their own words which emotion is being displayed (the free-response format). Supportive evidence for universality is high levels of correct attributions (the observer identifies the emotion that the person in the picture was supposed to be depicting) across cultures. This paradigm as been used for over thirty years, primarily using the set of photographs that Ekman and Friesen (1975) developed.

Readers may think that there is a consensus about the validity of the universality position, but in fact there is not. There is little disagreement over the results of the core set of studies conducted over the past thirty years. (See Russell, 1994, for a summary.) Those studies generally find high levels of accuracy across subjects in many countries as participants choose from among a list of emotions a single emotion to describe a face presented in a photograph. In these core studies, depending on the study, the country in which the data are collected and the emotion being represented, anywhere from 50 percent to 100 percent of subjects are able to label the emotion depicted correctly. If results are aggregated across studies, accuracy rates range from 63 percent (non-Western cultures identifying anger) to 96 percent (Western cultures identifying happiness). All results are above chance, and, at least on the face of it, accuracy levels appear strong across cultures, supporting the universality hypothesis.

However, some have argued that the strength of those results is suspect and the universality hypothesis is not, in fact, well supported. This has played out primarily as a debate between Russell (1994; Russell & Fernandez-Dolz, 1997) on one side and Ekman (1994b; Keltner & Ekman, 2000) and Izard (1994) on the other. Russell's critique is based on a number of points, some evidentiary and some logical. Analyses of the basic studies in aggregate indicate that accuracy varies significantly by culture (Western cultures being more accurate) and emotion type (happiness being most accurate, anger and fear being least accurate), with a significant culture-by-emotion interaction. Apparently, culture does make a difference in facial recognition, and the culture effect varies across emotions. In addition, Russell demonstrates that accuracy is reduced to substantially less impressive levels when free-response formats replace forced-choice formats (in which predetermined lists are shown to subjects) and when preliterate societies are studied instead of students potentially exposed to Western culture. Finally, he suggests that accuracy might be inflated by preselection of pictures in the standard set of photographs and the order of stimulus presentation.

A different kind of criticism of the facial expressions approach comes from Fridlund (1994, 1997). He takes issue with the idea that emotional expression would evolve as an adaptation. Coming from a behavioral ecology viewpoint, he argues that there is no adaptive advantage for the display of emotional states. In fact, there is likely to be an adaptive disadvantage to an involuntary display of internal states. He agrees that facial displays are greatly the result of selection pressures but argues that they serve a behavioral signaling function and that the signal and the ability to read the signal have coevolved. Facial expressions have evolved, but not as emotional displays, and so the commonality of display does not bear directly on the nature and structure of emotions.

It is unfortunate that the evolutionary position has become so intertwined with the facial expression position. Fridlund's work shows that the evolution of emotion programs can be understood as separate from the evolution of communicative facial expressions. Evolution is the single most important organizing concept in the biological sciences, and it makes little sense to deny its ultimate utility for psychology generally and emotions specifically. Yet thinking of emotions as evolved problem-solving modules begs the question of the triggers of those modules and the differential cognitive and behavioral responses that serve adaptive problem solving, as well as how problems that drove emotion selection differ from current problems that elicit these emotions. Answers to these kinds of questions are likely to lead to better integration of evolutionary positions with the cognitive perspective.

Cognitive Tradition

Across all areas of affect study, the use of the terms *cognition* or *cognitive* has frequently added confusion to the discourse. In the attitude literature, we commonly read about the cognitive and affective components or causes of attitudes, when in fact what is usually being expressed is the distinction between beliefs about the attitude object on the one hand and affective experiences with and reactions to the attitude object on the other. This clarification is important because for many attitude theorists, the affective component is infused with cognitive processes of various degrees of complexity.

Similarly, in the emotion literature, when we contrast the cognitive tradition with the biological or physiological tradition, we are not saying that these later positions suggest no role for cognition. In fact, a burgeoning area of research is the neuroscience of cognitive processes in emotion (Lane & Nadel, 2000). Yet neither can the differences simply be understood as ones of emphasis or focus, as if all the positions understood the same role for cognitive processes but the cognitive researchers chose to focus on exploring this component.

Two general ideas seem to be the defining characteristics of a "cognitive" position on emotion. First, the cognitive tradition gives great weight to interpretive processes in the generation of particular emotions (Lazarus, 1991). That is, the experience of one emotion instead of another is seen to be a function of the way the person interprets or appraises the triggering event. Historically, this has been the defining feature of a cognitive position, as researchers sought to describe these emotion-generating appraisals. These cognitive positions are generally referred to as appraisal theories. More recently, a second "cognitive" issue has captured the attention of researchers: the cognitive consequences of emotional experiences (such as interference, distraction, elaboration, or judgment biases). Both issues are of relevance to organizational researchers, the first having to do with the conditions of emotion generation, the second the consequences of emotional experiences. We start with a discussion of appraisal theories of emotional elicitation.

Appraisal Theories of Emotion Elicitation

Scherer (1999) has well described the key idea of appraisal theories: "A central tenet of appraisal theory is the claim that emotions are elicited and differentiated on the basis of a person's subjective evaluation or appraisal of the personal significance of a situation, object or event on a number of dimensions or criteria" (p. 637). Current interest in these interpretive processes is generally traced to the early 1960s and three seminal pieces of research. Arnold (1960a, 1960b) was the first to use the term *appraisal* in the context of emotion generation (Scherer, 1999). She described how appraisal of events using three dimensions leads to the elicitation of discrete emotions. Schachter and Singer (1962) reported that injection of adrenaline led to undifferentiated arousal (with appropriate placebo controls) that subjects then experienced as a particular discrete emotion depending on the emotional state being displayed by a confederate in the experimental room. Thus, the subjective experience of any emotion was the consequence of both the awareness of autonomic arousal and the particular cues available for interpreting the reason for the arousal. Lazarus (1966), while focusing more on stress than emotion in his early writings, talked about an appraisal process first driven by the assessment of the harm or benefit of an occurrence followed up by assessments of coping potential. These writings set the stage for current appraisal research.

Over the past decade and a half, much work has been done on the appraisal process in emotion generation. Smith and Kirby (2001) provide an excellent recent summary of this position. After discussing the basic logic of appraisal theories—that is, emotion generation being the consequence of personal interpretive analysis of emotion-generating situations—Smith and Kirby discuss two essential requirements of any appraisal theory. First, they suggest, an appraisal theory should describe the dimensions along which appraisals are made (such things as harm or benefit or attribution of responsibility). This they label the structural component of an appraisal theory. Second, any appraisal theory must be able to describe the cognitive processes that underlie the application of these dimensional evaluations. This they label the process component.

Substantially more attention has been paid to the structural component than to the process component, and numerous theories have been offered describing the particular appraisal dimensions that generate discrete emotions (Frijda, 1993; Ortony, Clore, & Collins, 1988; Roseman, 1991; Smith & Ellsworth, 1985; Smith & Lazarus, 1993). To illustrate the basic idea, I will summarize the model provided by Smith and Lazarus (1993) as described in Smith and Kirby (2001). As with all other appraisal theorists, emotion elicitation starts with an event. In their model, that event is then appraised using six dimensions: motivation relevance (How important is the event or situation to the person's goals and objectives?), motivational congruence (Is the event or situation consistent with or facilitative of those goals and objectives?), problem-focused coping potential (Can one act on the situation to change it or maintain it?), emotion-focused coping potential (Can the person adjust to the situation?), self-accountability (To what extent is the person responsible for the situation?), and future expectancy (What are the expectations of whether the situation will change?). Particular discrete emotions are generated by particular profiles of appraisals. Thus, a situation appraised as motivationally incongruent and important, with another person being judged responsible, will produce the discrete emotion of anger. The same negative state with an appraisal of low problem-focused coping potential and little possibility of change will produce sadness.

Smith and Lazarus (1993) and others distinguish between primary and secondary appraisal. Primary appraisal focuses on whether the situation is relevant to personal well-being (motivational relevance) and whether it is good or bad (motivational congruence). Secondary appraisal focuses on the additional set of dimensions (varying across researchers) like coping potential and attribution of responsibility. Primary appraisal is responsible for the intensity and direction of the emotion, while secondary appraisal results in the particulars of discrete emotions. Smith and Kirby (2001) note the similarity of the outcomes of primary appraisal to the dimensions of affect represented by the circumplex, while arguing that secondary appraisals account for the differentiation among the discrete emotions. Although the language of primary and secondary appraisal suggests a sequential nature to these two types of judgments, such a sequence is rarely discussed or tested (but see Scherer, 1999).

Most of the tests of the various versions of appraisal theories have involved similar methods. In some cases, subjects are asked to recall a specific instance of a particular emotion and then to evaluate the circumstances using the particular set of hypothesized appraisal dimensions (Roseman, Spindel, & Jose, 1990). In other studies, subjects are asked to think of either real or imaginary situations described by particular patterns of appraisal configurations and report the emotion they felt or would likely feel. These studies generally support the appraisal process; predictions of emotions from appraisal responses are well above chance levels (Smith & Kirby, 2001). However, they do not allow one to choose among the different models, since most tests do not pit one model against another, and most of the models are rather similar in their basic elements.

A particularly interesting set of discrete emotions that result from appraisals of self responsibility are the "self-conscious emotions": pride, guilt, shame, and embarrassment. Much of the work on this topic has been done by June Price Tangney and her associates and by Michael Lewis. (Good summaries of this work can be found in Tangney, 1999; Tangney & Fisher, 1995; and Lewis, 2000.) Apart from the fact that these emotions are of enormous importance for describing organizational experiences, they also illustrate the necessity of going beyond the simple positive-negative dimensional structure of affect. For example, guilt and shame are both negative affective states, located very near each other on structures defined either by pleasantness and activation or by positive and negative affectivity. Yet the behavioral consequences of these discrete emotions are substantially different. Guilt, which appears to be the result of an appraisal of self-responsibility coupled with a focus on the particular behavior enacted, tends to produce engaged, reparative responses as the person tries to make amends for his or her actions. Shame, which also is a result of an appraisal of self-responsibility but one coupled with a focus on the deficiencies of the self, tends to produce withdrawal behavior intended to hide the self from others.

Appraisal theories are not without their critics, even among cognitively oriented emotion researchers. An important critique of the logic of theories of appraisal-generated emotions is presented by Parkinson (1997). Parkinson starts his critique by noting that appraisal theories ascribe a causal role for appraisals; people's emotions are generated by their appraisals. Parkinson suggests that an alternative position is that appraisals are part of the conceptual structure of emotions. That is, it is not the blaming of others that causes us to be angry; rather, the definition of anger includes, and requires, an evaluation of external blame. It is not anger if there is not external blame: "The consensual meaning of emotion implies evaluation directed at an intentional object, and the presence of this evaluative relation is a relatively central criterion for the classification of an episode in emotional terms" (Parkinson, 1997, p. 67). Parkinson then argues that the results of research using basic appraisal research paradigm cannot distinguish between the normal "causal" view and his conceptual-definitional view, because the method does not examine appraisal processes as they play out in real time. A different criticism focuses on the speed of emotional responses, suggesting that the appraisal processes are too slow to account for the speed of emotional reactions.

Of course, appraisal theorists defend their position. In response to Parkinson's critique, Scherer (1999) argues that appraisals influence more than simply the self-reports of emotional experience, including responses like facial expressions and action tendencies independent of the cognitive system. However, he also acknowledges that more research tying appraisals to other parts of the emotion complex needs to be undertaken. Smith and Kirby (2001) defend appraisal theory from the "slowness" argument by pointing out that nothing in appraisal theory requires that the appraisals be conscious or verbally mediated, although they do acknowledge that it is incumbent on appraisal theorists to examine the process, not just the content, of appraisals. (Recent attempts at process models can be found in Smith & Kirby, 2001, and Clore & Ortony, 2000.)

Cognitive Consequences of Affect States

Appraisal theories seek to describe the cognitive processes that produce emotion generation. However, affective states themselves have substantial and varied effects on cognitions and cognitive processes. The cognitive consequences of affective states have been given a great deal of attention in the past ten to fifteen years, and a fine summary of various programs of research in this area can be found in Forgas (2001). Forgas's introductory chapter in that book provides a ready overview of this literature and distinguishes between the influence of affect on the content of cognition and the influence of affect on the processing of information; I will structure the main part of the discussion in these terms. It should be made clear at the outset that this literature is overwhelmingly about the effects of mood states rather than discrete emotions.

The general discussion of the effects of mood on cognitive content is framed in terms of what is called the congruity effect. The type of congruity effect most familiar to organizational psychologists is the evaluative bias effect illustrated in Isen's body of work (Isen, 2000; Isen & Baron, 1991). Here, being in a positive mood positively biases a wide variety of evaluative judgments. Congruity in memory processes is also well studied (see Eich, 1995; Ellis &

Moore, 1999; Parrott & Spackman, 2000). Memory congruity effects are shown when being in a certain mood facilitates either the encoding or retrieval of material that is consistent in valence with the mood. While Ellis and Moore conclude that mood-congruent encoding is a more robust finding than mood-congruent retrieval, Parrot and Spackman (2000) conclude that mood-congruent retrieval effects are well demonstrated. Mood congruency also appears with regard to the likelihood estimations of positive and negative events (Schwarz, 2000). People in positive moods overestimate the likelihood of positive events and underestimate the likelihood of negative events. The reverse is generally true for negative moods. Overall, congruity appears to be a robust finding across a number of outcomes, although there is some indication that it is more consistent for positive than negative mood states (Fiedler, 2001).

Affective influences on cognition are not limited to the content of cognition. An equally active and important area of research focuses on the effects of mood states on information processing styles. Useful recent summaries can be found in Fiedler (2001), Schwarz (2000), and Wyer, Clore, and Isbell (1999). In addition, Dalgleish and Power (1999) have a number of interesting chapters on various aspects of this issue. A general consensus appears to be that being in a positive mood seems to produce a more heuristic processing style with more reliance on existing knowledge structures, and being in a negative mood seems to foster a more systematic information processing style, more reliant on detailed examination of the information at hand (Schwarz, 2000). Forgas (2001) states that positive moods produce a more "top-down," generative processing style, while negative moods produce a more "bottom-up," externally focused style. Fiedler (2001) labels the processing strategy associated with positive affective states "assimilative" and that associated with negative affective states "accommodative." The processing strategy differences are shown empirically as more reliance on schemas and stereotypes in person perception and on peripheral cues in persuasion when in a positive mood. Positive moods generally facilitate creative problem solving, presumably because of the facilitation of integrative thinking. In contrast, people in a negative mood are more focused on individual attributes when making judgments, rely more on argument content in persuasion situations, and appear to be less constructive on memory tasks.

Forgas (1995) has presented an interesting theory about when and under what conditions affect will influence cognitive processes. His position, labeled the affect infusion model, discusses four information processing strategies that people use when dealing with judgment tasks. His argument is that judgments requiring substantive or heuristic processing will be more influenced by affective states than will judgments requiring direct access of information. Forgas's position attempts to organize the existing literature on when mood does or does not influence judgments and has important implications for organizational researchers who are studying the way affect influences immediate performance. Many of these implications are laid out in Forgas and George (2001).

Research on the cognitive consequences of affect has focused almost entirely on the effects of mood states. Fiedler (2001) provides the conceptual reasoning for this when he suggests that because moods are more diffuse and less experientially tied to specific objects and events than are discrete emotions, they are more likely to have general and diverse effects. While this may be true, one cannot help but feel that part of the overemphasis on mood effects is due to the different cadre of researchers who focus on moods and discrete emotions. In any case, research on the cognitive processing consequences of discrete emotions has begun to generate interest in the emotion literature. Keltner (Keltner, Ellsworth, & Edwards, 1993; Lerner & Keltner, 2000) and DeSteno, Petty, Wegener, and Rucker (2000) showed judgment biases that were different for different discrete emotions equivalent in simple valence (anger versus sadness, for example). These studies show that effects of affect on cognitive processes are not limited to mood states.

The research within the cognitive tradition clearly puts to rest the old distinctions between cognition and emotion. Cognitive processes both drive emotional responses and are themselves part of the response constellation. Research on the cognitive outcomes of affective states also indicates the complexity of outcome processes, a complexity that makes discussions of performance effects challenging. The disconnect between the focus on discrete emotions for causal research and moods for outcome research appears to be slowly dissipating, at least as shown by studies on the processing consequences of discrete emotions.

The Physiological Tradition

The physiology of emotion has always been a central issue in the study of affect. Given the lengthy history on the topic, the technical nature of the work, and the fact that research is moving so rapidly, it is impossible in this chapter to do justice to the full physiological tradition. Consequently, I touch on only a few themes I think will interest readers. Those desiring more detailed introductions might look at LeDoux's *The Emotional Brain* (1996) (although this has a very materialistic orientation; at one point he says that conscious experiences of emotions are "red herrings, detours, in the scientific study of emotions"); Damasio's well-known *Descartes' Error* (1994) and the more recent *The Feeling of What Happens* (1999); Cacioppo, Berntson, Larsen, Poehlman, and Ito (2000) and LeDoux and Phelps (2000) in the most recent *Handbook of Emotions;* various interesting chapters (particularly with regard to the role of the amygdala) in Lane and Nadel (2000); Panksepp (1998); and Heller, Nitschke, and Miller's review of research on hemispheric lateralization and emotion (1998).

Feedback

Within the enormity of the literature, two general questions have seemed to hold center stage. The first is what is generally referred to as the feedback question, and it can be traced to the work of William James (1884). James (and separately a Danish researcher named Lange) offered an intriguing hypothesis about the nature of emotions. He suggested that the intuitive idea that we perceive an emotional stimulus, it causes a subjective experience, which then leads to a bodily response, actually reverses the order of the emotion process. Of course, the initial event is perceived, but then an autonomic response produced by processes not at the level of awareness is generated, and it is the perception of these bodily changes that produces the experience of the emotion. James did acknowledge the importance of perceptual, even interpretive, aspects of emotion generation, and he explicitly stated that this core process was true only with regard to certain basic emotions. His focus was on the subjective experience of emotion, which he took to be a consequence of the perception of bodily changes in the autonomic nervous system (ANS). The James-Lange viewpoint might be labeled the ANS feedback position.

An important implication is that the discrete emotions we experience have unique ANS response patterns, and consequently much research has been done trying to find these unique and discrete patterns. Cacioppo et al. (2000) report a meta-analysis of this research and conclude that the evidence does not support emotion-specific ANS activity. At best, the research supports the idea that higher ANS activity is involved in high-arousal emotions and particularly negative emotions. While this and other criticisms (see Plutchik, 1994) have driven the James-Lange theory off the agenda of contemporary emotion research, the theory has had enormous influence, stimulating much research on the physiology of emotion. It also influenced cognitive approaches to emotion, as Schacter and Singer (1962) were greatly influenced by this position. In addition, as Cacioppo et al. (2000) point out, weaker versions of the ANS feedback idea are possible and supportable. One such weaker version is consistent with a Schachter and Singer logic of diffuse ANS activity being coupled with situational cues to produce discrete emotional experience.

An alternative bodily feedback position is the facial feedback hypothesis (Tomkins, 1962). Tompkins took the evolutionary position on facial expressions a step further from the idea that discrete emotions are expressed in the face. He argued that the feedback from these facial expressions induced emotional feelings. Of course, the validity of this position requires strong evidence for unique facial expressions for discrete emotions, evidence that is less than conclusive. Heilman (2000) and Cacioppo et al. (2000) have brief critiques of this position.

Emotion Centers and Systems

The second general topic of psychophysiological research on emotion, the one that has captured most research attention, is the identification of the emotion centers of the brain. Readers are probably aware of research in this tradition from discussions of, for example, the limbic system, the role of the amygdala in emotional experience, and the research on hemispheric lateralization in emotion expression and recognition. Some readers might be surprised, however, to know how divergent opinions are among psychobiologists about the data in this area. These disagreements are greatly the result of the methodological difficulties inherent in this research. Traditional research took one of two methodological approaches. First, surgical ablation of proposed centers was conducted in primates, and observations of changes in emotion responses were recorded. These results have been less than definitive because precision in the surgery can be difficult to attain. Often, brain areas not of primary interest but potentially relevant can also be destroyed. (Think of a confound in our own methods.) Second, the assumption that structures work similarly across primate species (including humans) is not always defensible. A second approach has been to look at the emotional deficiencies of humans who have had particular structures destroyed by accident or by surgery intended to correct a neurological problem (epilepsy, for example). Such research, although interesting and informative, is limited by the imprecision in the localization of damage. However, today's research has a new tool: neuroimaging. Through positron emission tomography and magnetic resonance imaging, researchers can see the activation of areas of the brain when humans are exposed to emotional stimuli. This helps account for what appears to be increasing progress being made in the area.

Interestingly, this progress seems to be pointing to the limitations of searching for emotion centers. Certainly, the relevance of the amygdala is being shown, but so is the importance of each of the frontal hemispheres of the cortex, as well as other areas of the brain. This research is not inconsistent. What it tells us is that emotional processes are not localized in particular areas but engage many different functional areas of the brain, not surprising given both the recognition that emotions are constellations of patterned responses and that they engage multiple systems in the service of adaptation. Today, more work is being done on emotion systems than emotion centers (see LeDoux, 1996, for example).

Physiological and Psychological Organization

Of what relevance is this work on the physiology of emotion centers and systems? Why should psychologically oriented emotion researchers, particularly organizational researchers, want to pay attention to these findings? The simplest answer is that knowledge of the physiological subsystems provides insight into the appropriate direction to search for psychological processes. Physiological systems can constrain psychological processes and in so doing provide another criterion in addition to prediction efficiency for gauging the reasonableness of psychological constructs. At the same time, we need to be careful in using such data, as physiological organization and psychological organization need not be isomorphic. I will use recent research on the behavioral inhibition system (BIS) and the behavioral approach system (BAS) to illustrate both points.

Gray (1987) has proposed the existence of two systems, a behavioral approach system and a behavioral inhibition system, that he believes integrates motivational, emotional, and personality findings. A large amount of work has been conducted in the past ten years using this two-system approach. Davidson has conducted much of this work, and good summaries of the nature of the systems and of his own work can be found in Davidson (1995) and Sutton and Davidson (1997). In addition, Carver and White (1994) have developed a paper-and-pencil measure of individual differences in the two systems.

Davidson (1995) well describes the nature of the two systems and physiological location and also provides a brief history of research in the area. He argues that the right hemisphere, particularly the frontal or anterior areas, is specialized for withdrawal, and the anterior area of the left hemisphere is specialized for approach behavior. He, and Carver and White (1994) as well, argues that the circuitry-mediating approach tendency is associated with sensitivity to rewards and escape from punishment and produces positive affect in response to such signals. The circuitry-mediating inhibition is sensitive to signals of punishment and nonreward and causes negative affect in response to such cues. Davidson argues that people with damage to the left frontal hemisphere (the approach areas) display signs of apathy, loss of interest, loss of pleasure in objects, and a general "lowered threshold for the experience of sadness and depression" (p. 363).

Some of Davidson's work has focused on showing that exposure to positive and negative stimuli produces the predicted effects on cortical activity in the appropriate areas. However, Davidson is particularly interested in using asymmetries in resting cortical activity between the two hemispheres as a stable individual difference measure of reactivity to positive and negative events. He has shown that such asymmetry predicts intensity of reactions to positive and negative stimuli. Interestingly, and importantly, these asymmetries correlate much better with paper-and-pencil measures of the BIS and BAS than they do with measures of positive and negative affectivity. Davidson, Carver, and White and others all point to the underlying systems as being systems of reactivity, not stable affect differences. Asymmetries are, according to Davidson, unrelated to unprovoked or resting affective states.

These data are of interest to I/O psychologists in a number of ways. They particularly point to the importance of distinguishing between affect reactivity and dispositional levels of average affect. That is, the physiological data tell us that we should be looking at differences in the way people react to events as the underlying process to account for individual differences in affect. They also point to the approach-avoidance elements of emotional experience, as the affect reactivity systems appear to be designed in the service of behavioral response. Research by Harmon-Jones and Allen (1998) illustrates this point by demonstrating that anger, a negative but approach-oriented emotion, is associated with left frontal activity.

While recognizing that knowledge of the underlying physiology can help guide our thinking about psychological processes, we also must be aware of the limitations of this logic. Physiological organization and psychological organization need not be isomorphic. Inhibition and approach illustrate this point. One might argue that the existence of these two systems helps solve the debate about the structure of momentary affect. That is, a PA-NA structure rather than a bipolar pleasantness structure better fits with the underlying physiology. However, it is equally plausible to argue that the two systems work together to produce the momentary subjective experience of bipolar pleasantness. Green et al. (1999) cogently make this argument and use the analogy of the heating and cooling system of a house to illustrate their point. Houses have separate heating and cooling systems, but the subjective experience of temperature is bipolar and unidimensional. Physiological and psychological systems need to be compatible but need not be equivalent.

Emotional Regulation

One of the hazards of any overall structure for a chapter is that important topics may not fall neatly into the categories presented. Such is the case with emotional regulation. Yet the topic is of sufficient importance to both the study of emotions and the study of emotions in organizations that I could not legitimately exclude it simply to maintain the illusion that my general structure is complete.

Gross (1999) has published a nice, if overly brief, review of the emotion regulation literature, and a recent book by Parkinson, Totterdale, Briner, and Reynolds (1996) is another useful resource. In addition, the special issue of *Psychological Inquiry* on mood regulation with the lead article by Larsen (2000) and accompanying commentaries is an important conceptual addition to the literature.

Gross makes the distinction among three uses of the term *emotional regulation*. In the first use, the term refers to the way emotions regulate or influence our thoughts and behaviors. This has already been covered in the section on the cognitive consequences of affective states. In the second use, the term refers to how we try to regulate the emotional experiences of others. Gross prefers to reserve the term *emotional regulation* for the third way it is used, referring to the processes by which we regulate the experience and expression of our own emotions. Although all three are important areas of study, they are separate issues and cannot be examined as a single topic.

Gross (1999) describes how the topic of emotional regulation grew out of research on coping, and particularly the seminal work of Lazarus and Folkman (1984) on problem-focused and emotion-focused coping with stress. Yet coping and emotional regulation are different concepts. Coping as a response to stress focuses on efforts to deal with negative and taxing situations. Emotional regulation, on the other hand, focuses on regulating affective experiences, whether they are positive or negative and taxing or not. In addition, research on emotional regulation has incorporated the concept of emotion-focused coping into a broader set of regulatory processes.

If emotions are thought to be adaptive responses to situations, why is there a need to regulate them? One reason is that the affective state itself can persist after its functional value disappears. In addition, emotional responses can be adaptive for certain problems but interfere with other important tasks. The fact that our guilt from yelling at our children at breakfast may be a functional response in the service of family harmony does not diminish the problems arising from ruminating over that guilt when we are trying to work. Finally, the overt display of emotions can be dysfunctional in certain circumstances.

Larsen (2000) presents a general model of mood regulation that is meant to account for the regulation of the subjective experience of mood, the "feeling" of affect. Using control theory as his framework, he discusses the various mechanisms involved in the "control" of mood states, including paying attention to current affect states, mechanisms for effecting change in mood states, and differences in desired affect levels. While control theory is likely to be familiar to most organizational psychologists, Larsen's discussion of it in the context of mood regulation has two components worth noting. First, he has a lengthy discussion of the way individual differences affect each stage of the regulation process. This discussion can encourage further work on the processes that mediate personality effects. Second, he discusses the various ways in which people regulate their moods. In this regard, he presents a taxonomy of mood regulation techniques that crosses two dimensions. The first dimension is cognitive (ways to think) versus behavioral (things to do) techniques. The second dimension is whether the person focuses on the mood itself or the situation. Behavioral strategies focused on the mood are such things as distraction or exercising. Cognitive strategies focused on the situation are such things as cognitive reframing or downward social comparison. This taxonomy should be particularly useful for organizational researchers as they begin to examine the way affect states directly influence momentary performance. That is, some regulation techniques may interfere with task performance, and some may actually facilitate performance.

Developing out of the coping literature, much of the work on emotion regulation focuses on changing or enhancing an existing state. However, much anticipatory work can also be done to regulate affect. Aspinwall and Taylor (1997) have reviewed the literature on proactive coping, and although their review focuses on coping rather than emotion regulation, the processes they raise are more broadly relevant.

One additional topic in this area deserves mention. Muraven and Baumeister (2000) have proposed a muscle analogy for understanding the nature of self-regulatory resources, including emotional regulation. This regulatory muscle gets depleted as it is used and requires rest for recovery. It gets stronger as it is exercised.

This conceptualization, new and controversial, helps explain some intuitive observations about self-regulatory processes (why it has been so hard to diet under stress, for example) and will no doubt generate interest among organizational researchers.

Understanding the processes of emotion regulation will help us understand the way affect influences performance in organizations. Cropanzano and I (Weiss & Cropanzano, 1996) proposed a class of performance-relevant behaviors that we called affect driven. What we meant was that affective states have immediate influences on performance by way of the manner in which these states influence a wide variety of performance-relevant behaviors and cognitive processes. We now understand that these affect-driven behaviors can themselves be broken into two categories. Some behaviors and cognitive processes are the natural consequences of the state itself. So, for example, positive affective states enhance creativity. Anger seems to provoke aggression. Other behaviors and cognitive processes are by-products of the attempt to regulate affective states. Some instances, such as distraction or socializing, are the consequence of the regulation process, not the state itself. Both types of behaviors have performance implications, but for different reasons.

Conclusion

It seems clear that the nature of affective experiences is wide ranging. Moods differ from emotions, and emotions themselves have many varieties. People can and do feel angry, sad, guilty, happy, and ashamed. The causes of these various emotional states are beginning to be understood, and so too are their cognitive and behavioral consequences. Organizational researchers need to widen their activities to capture the way emotions are actually experienced in work settings, as dimensional summaries may hide meaningful differences in emotional experiences.

People may feel angry and happy and guilty all in the same day. Affective states can and do fluctuate, and many (but not all) of their behavioral and cognitive consequences are immediate and last as long as the state itself lasts. This implies that we need to arm ourselves with methods that allow us to study work in the moment, as the affect processes play out in real time. Such techniques as momentary ecological assessment and experience sampling are just beginning to make their way into the organizational literature. They will, I believe, allow for more interesting, valid, and relevant research on affect processes at work than can now be obtained with typical methods that rely on aggregated, recollective data.

The performance implications of affective states are enormous but complicated. We recognize the limitations of the "positive affect–good, negative affect–bad" position, a holdover from the days when satisfaction and affect were considered equivalent constructs. Affective states influence behaviors and cognitions directly and indirectly through affect regulation. Full explication of all of these processes and their relationships to the demands of different tasks will allow us to make the sophisticated predictions of performance effects that are required.

In spite of the resurgence of interest in mood and emotions at work, the organizational literature has not begun to tap into the full body of basic research on affect. Reading this chapter along with Brief and Weiss (2002) will bring this point home. I hope that this brief exploration of the basic research will help produce a more productive connection between the two fields.

References

Arnold, M. B. (1960a). *Emotion and personality: Vol. 1. Psychological aspects.* New York: Columbia University Press.

Arnold, M. B. (1960b). *Emotion and personality: Vol. 2. Neurological and physiological aspects.* New York: Columbia University Press.

Aspinwall, L. G., & Taylor, S. E. (1997). A stitch in time: Self-regulation and proactive coping. *Psychological Bulletin, 121,* 417–436.

Averill, J. R. (1975). A semantic atlas of emotional concepts. *Catalog of Selected Documents in Psychology.* Vol 53.

Barkow, J. H., Cosmides, L., & Tooby, J. (1992). *The adapted mind: Evolutionary psychology and the generation of culture.* New York: Oxford University Press.

Bradburn, N. M. (1969). *The structure of psychological well-being.* Chicago: Aldine.

Brief, A. P., & Weiss, H. M. (2002). Organizational behavior: Affect in the workplace. *Annual Review of Psychology, 53,* 279–307.

Buss, D. M. (1999). *Evolutionary psychology.* Needham Heights, MA: Allyn & Bacon.

Cacioppo, J. T., Berntson, G. G., Larsen, J. T., Poehlmann, K. M., & Ito, T. A. (2000). The psychophysiology of emotion. In M. Lewis & J. M. Haviland-Jones (Eds.), *Handbook of emotions* (2nd ed., pp. 173–191). New York: Guilford Press.

Cacioppo, J. T., Gardner, W. L., & Berntson, G. G. (1999). The affect system has parallel and integrative processing components: Form follows function. *Journal of Personality and Social Psychology, 76,* 839–855.

Cartwright, J. (2000). *Evolution and human behavior: Darwinian perspectives on human nature.* Cambridge, MA: MIT Press.

Carver, C. S., & White, T. L. (1994). Behavioral-inhibition, behavioral activation, and affective responses to impending reward and punishment—The BIS BAS Scales. *Journal of Personality and Social Psychology, 67,* 319–333.

Clore, G. L., & Ortony, A. (2000). Cognition in emotion: Always, sometimes or never? In R. D. Lane & L. Nadel (Eds.), *Cognitive neuroscience of emotion* (pp. 24–61). New York: Oxford University Press.

Cosmides, L., & Tooby, J. (2000). Evolutionary psychology and the emotions. In M. Lewis & J. M. Haviland-Jones (Eds.), *Handbook of emotions* (2nd ed., pp. 91–115). New York: Guilford Press.

Crawford, C. B., & Krebs, D. L. (1997). *Handbook of evolutionary psychology.* Mahwah, NJ: Lawrence Erlbaum.

Dalgleish, T., & Power, M. (1999). *Handbook of cognition and emotion.* New York: Wiley.

Damasio, A. R. (1994). *Descartes' error: Emotion, reason and the human brain.* New York: Putnam.

Damasio, A. R. (1999). *The feeling of what happens.* New York: Harcourt, Brace.

Darwin, C. (1872). *The expression of the emotions in man and animals.* London: Murray.

Davidson, R. J. (1995). Cerebral asymmetry, emotion and affective style. In R. J. Davidson & K. Hugdahl (Eds.), *Brain asymmetry.* Cambridge, MA: MIT Press.

Diener, E., Suh, E. M., Lucas, R. E., & Smith, H. L. (1999). Subjective well-being: Three decades of progress. *Psychological Bulletin, 125,* 276–302.

Eagly, A. H., & Chaiken, S. (1993). *The psychology of attitudes.* Fort Worth, TX: Harcourt.

Eich, E. (1995). Searching for mood dependent memory. *Psychological Science, 6,* 67–75.

Ekman, P. (1994a). All emotions are basic. In P. Ekman & R. J. Davidson (Eds.), *The nature of emotion: Fundamental questions* (pp. 15–19). New York: Oxford University Press.

Ekman, P. (1994b). Strong evidence for universals in facial expressions: A reply to Russell's mistaken critique. *Psychological Bulletin, 115,* 268–287.

Ekman, P. (1999). Basic emotions. In T. Dalgleish & M. Power (Eds.), *Handbook of cognition and emotion* (pp. 45–60). New York: Guilford Press.

Ekman, P., & Davidson, R. J. (1994). *The nature of emotion: Fundamental questions.* New York: Oxford University Press.

Ekman, P., & Friesen, W. V. (1971). Constants across cultures in the face and emotions. *Journal of Personality and Social Psychology 17,* 124–129.

Ekman, P., & Friesen, W. V. (1975). *Unmasking the face.* Upper Saddle River, NJ: Prentice Hall.

Ekman, P., & Friesen, W. V. (1976). *Pictures of facial affect.* Palo Alto, CA: Consulting Psychologists Press.

Ellis, H. C., & Moore, B. A. (1999). Mood and memory. In T. Dalgleish & M. Power (Eds.), *Handbook of cognition and emotion* (pp. 193–210). New York: Wiley.

Deiner, E. (1999). Introduction to the special section on the structure of emotion. *Journal of Personality and Social Psychology, 76,* 803–804.

DeSteno, D., Petty, R. E., Wegener, D. T., & Rucker, D. D. (2000). Beyond valence in the perception of likelihood: The role of emotion specificity. *Journal of Personality and Social Psychology, 78,* 397–416.

Ekman, P. (1992). Facial expressions of emotion: new findings, new questions. *Psychological Science, 3,* 34–38.

Ekman, P. (1993). Facial expression and emotion. *American Psychologist, 48,* 384–392.

Fiedler, K. (2001). Affective influences on social information processing. In J. P. Forgas (Ed.), *Handbook of affect and social cognition* (pp. 163–185). Hillsdale, NJ: Erlbaum.

Fisher, V. E., & Hanna, J. V. (1931). *The dissatisfied worker.* New York: Macmillan.

Forgas, J. P. (1995). Mood and judgment: The affect infusion model (AIM). *Psychological Bulletin, 117,* 39–66.

Forgas, J. P. (Ed.). (2001). *Handbook of affect and social cognition.* Hillsdale, NJ: Erlbaum.

Forgas, J. P., & George, J. M. (2001). Affective influences on judgment and behavior: An information processing perspective. *Organizational Behavior and Human Decision Processes, 86,* 3–34.

Fridlund, A. J. (1994). *Human facial expression: An evolutionary view.* Orlando, FL: Academic Press.

Fridlund, A. J. (1997). The new ethology of human facial expressions. In J. A. Russell & J. M. Fernandez-Dols (Eds.), *The psychology of facial expression.* New York: Cambridge University Press.

Frijda, N. H. (1993). Moods, emotion episodes and emotions. In M. Lewis & J. M. Haviland (Eds.), *Handbook of emotions* (pp. 381–404). New York: Guilford Press.

Frijda, N. H. (2000). The psychologist's point of view. In M. Lewis & J. M. Haviland-Jones (Eds.), *Handbook of emotions* (2nd ed., pp. 59–74). New York: Guilford Press.

Gray, J. A. (1987). *The psychology of fear and stress.* (2nd ed.). Cambridge: Cambridge University Press.

Green, D. P., Goldman, S. L., & Salovey, P. (1993). Measurement error masks bipolarity in affect ratings. *Journal of Personality and Social Psychology, 64,* 1029–1041.

Green, D. P., Salovey, P., & Truax, K. M. (1999). Static, dynamic, and causative bipolarity of affect. *Journal of Personality and Social Psychology, 76,* 856–867.

Gross, J. J. (1999). Emotion regulation: Past, present, future. *Cognition and Emotion, 13,* 551–573.

Harmon-Jones, E., & Allen, J.J.B. (1998). Anger and frontal brain activity: EEG asymmetry consistent with approach motivation despite negative affective valence. *Journal of Personality and Social Psychology, 74,* 1310–1316.

Heilman, K. M. (2000). Emotional experience: A neurological model. In R. D. Lane & L. Nadel (Eds.), *Cognitive neuroscience of emotion* (pp. 328–344). New York: Oxford University Press.

Heller, W., Nitschke, J. B., & Miller, G. A. (1998). Lateralization in emotional disorders. *Current Directions in Psychological Science, 7,* 26–32.

Hersey, R. B. (1932). *Workers' emotions in shop and home.* Philadelphia: University of Pennsylvania Press.

Isen, A. M. (2000). Positive affect and decision making. In M. Lewis & J. M. Haviland-Jones (Eds.), *Handbook of emotions* (2nd ed., pp. 417–435). New York: Guilford Press.

Isen, A. M., & Baron, R. A. (1991). Positive affect as a factor in organizational-behavior. *Research in Organizational Behavior, 13,* 1–53.

Izard, C. E. (1977). *Human emotions.* New York: Plenum.

Izard, C. E. (1992). Basic emotions, relations among emotions, and emotion cognition relations. *Psychological Review, 99,* 561–565.

Izard, C. E. (1993). Four systems for emotion activation—cognitive and noncognitive processes. *Psychological Review, 100,* 68–90.

Izard, C. E. (1994). Innate and universal facial expressions—evidence from developmental and cross-cultural research. *Psychological Bulletin, 115,* 288–299.

Izard, C. E. (1997). Emotions and facial expressions: A perspective from differential emotions theory. In J. A. Russell & J. M. Fernandez-Dols

(Eds.), *The psychology of facial expression*. New York: Cambridge University Press.

James, W. (1884). What is emotion. *Mind, 19,* 188–205.

Keltner, D., & Ekman, P. (2000). Facial expressions of emotion. In M. Lewis & J. M. Haviland-Jones (Eds.), *Handbook of emotions* (2nd ed., pp. 236–249). New York: Guilford Press.

Keltner, D., Ellsworth, P. C., & Edwards, K. (1993). Beyond simple pessimism—effects of sadness and anger on social-perception. *Journal of Personality and Social Psychology, 64,* 740–752.

Kornhauser, A. W., & Sharp, A. A. (1932). Employee attitudes: Suggestions from a study in a factory. *Personnel Journal, 10,* 393–404.

Lane, R. D., & Nadel, L. (2000). *Cognitive neuroscience of emotion.* New York: Oxford University Press.

Larsen, R. J. (2000). Toward a science of mood regulation. *Psychological Inquiry, 11,* 129–141.

Lazarus, R. S. (1966). *Psychological stress and the coping process.* New York: McGraw-Hill.

Lazarus, R. S. (1991). *Emotion and adaptation.* New York: Oxford University Press.

Lazarus, R. S. (1993). From psychological stress to the emotions: A history of changing outlooks. *Annual Review of Psychology, 44,* 1–21.

Lazarus, R. S., & Folkman, S. (1984). *Stress, appraisal and coping.* New York: Springer.

LeDoux, J. E. (1996). *The emotional brain.* New York: Simon & Schuster.

LeDoux, J. E., & Phelps, E. A. (2000). Emotional networks in the brain. In M. Lewis & J. M. Haviland-Jones (Eds.), *Handbook of emotions* (2nd ed., pp. 157–172). New York: Guilford Press.

Lerner, J. S., & Keltner, D. (2000). Beyond valence: Toward a model of emotion-specific influences on judgement and choice. *Cognition and Emotion, 14,* 473–493.

Lewis, M. (2000). Self-conscious emotions: Embarrassment, pride, shame and guilt. In M. Lewis & J. M. Haviland-Jones (Eds.), *Handbook of emotions* (2nd ed., pp. 623–636). New York: Guilford Press.

Morris, W. N. (1989). *Mood: The frame of mind.* New York. Springer-Verlag.

Muraven, M., & Baumeister, R. F. (2000). Self-regulation and depletion of limited resources: Does self-control resemble a muscle? *Psychological Bulletin, 126,* 247–259.

Ortony, A., Clore, G. L., & Collins, A. (1988). *The cognitive structure of emotions.* Cambridge: Cambridge University Press.

Ortony, A., & Turner, T. J. (1990). What's basic about basic emotions. *Psychological Review, 97,* 315–331.

Panksepp, J. (1998). *Affective neuroscience: The foundations of human and animal emotions.* New York: Oxford University Press.

Parkinson, B. (1997). Untangling the appraisal-emotion connection. *Personality and Social Psychology Review, 1,* 62–79.

Parkinson, B., Totterdall, P., Briner, R. B., & Reynolds, S. (1996). *Changing moods: The psychology of mood and mood regulation.* White Plains, NY: Longman.

Parrott, W. G., & Spackman, M. P. (2000). Emotion and memory. In M. Lewis & J. M. Haviland-Jones (Eds.), *Handbook of emotions* (2nd ed., pp. 476–490). New York: Guilford Press.

Petty, R. E., Wegener, D. T., & Fabrigar, L. R. (1997). Attitudes and attitude change. *Annual Review of Psychology, 48,* 609–647.

Plutchik, R. (1980). *Emotion: A psychoevolutionary synthesis.* New York: HarperCollins.

Plutchik, R. (1984). Emotions: A general psychoevolutionary theory. In K. R. Scherer & P. Ekman (Eds.), *Approaches to emotion.* Hillsdale, NJ: Erlbaum.

Plutchik, R. (1994). *The psychology and biology of emotion.* New York: Harper-Collins.

Rosch, E. (1973). Natural categories. *Cognitive Psychology, 4,* 328–350.

Roseman, I. J. (1991). Appraisal determinants of discrete emotions. *Cognition and Emotion, 5,* 161–200.

Roseman, I. J., Spindel, M. S., & Jose, P. E. (1990). Appraisals of emotion-eliciting events—testing a theory of discrete emotions. *Journal of Personality and Social Psychology, 59,* 899–915.

Russell, J. A. (1994). Is there universal recognition of emotion from facial expression—a review of the cross-cultural studies. *Psychological Bulletin, 115,* 102–141.

Russell, J. A., & Barrett, L. F. (1999). Core affect, prototypical emotional episodes, and other things called emotion: Dissecting the elephant. *Journal of Personality and Social Psychology, 76,* 805–819.

Russell, J. A., & Carroll, J. M. (1999a). On the bipolarity of positive and negative affect. *Psychological Bulletin, 125,* 3–30.

Russell, J. A., & Carroll, J. M. (1999b). The phoenix of bipolarity: Reply to Watson and Tellegen (1999). *Psychological Bulletin, 125,* 611–617.

Russell, J. A., & Fernandez-Dols, J. M. (1997). What does a facial expression mean. In J. A. Russell & J. M. Fernandez-Dols (Eds.), *The psychology of facial expression.* Cambridge: Cambridge University Press.

Schacter, S., & Singer, J. E. (1962). Cognitive, social and physiological determinants of emotional state. *Psychological Review, 69,* 379–399.

Scherer, K. R. (1999). Appraisal theory. In T. Dalgleish & M. Power (Eds.), *Handbook of cognition and emotion* (pp. 637–665). New York: Wiley.

Schwarz, N. (2000). Emotion, cognition, and decision making. *Cognition and Emotion, 14,* 433–440.

Selye, H. (1974). *Stress without distress.* Philadelphia: Lippincott.

Shaver, P., Schwartz, J., Kirson, D., & O'Connor, C. (1987). Emotion knowledge—further exploration of a prototype approach. *Journal of Personality and Social Psychology, 52,* 1061–1086.

Smith, C. A., & Ellsworth, P. C. (1985). Patterns of cognitive appraisal in emotion. *Journal of Personality and Social Psychology, 48,* 813–838.

Smith, C. A., & Kirby, L. D. (2001). Affect and cognitive appraisal processes. In J. P. Forgas (Ed.), *Handbook of social cognition* (pp. 75–92). Hillsdale, NJ: Erlbaum.

Smith, C. A., & Lazarus, R. S. (1993). Appraisal components, core relational themes, and the emotions. *Cognition and Emotion, 7,* 233–269.

Sutton, S. K., & Davidson, R. J. (1997). Prefrontal brain asymmetry: A biological substrate of the behavioral approach and inhibition systems. *Psychological Science, 8,* 204–210.

Tangney, J. P. (1999). The self-conscious emotions: Shame, guilt, embarrassment, and pride. In T. Dalgleish & M. J. Power (Eds.), *Handbook of cognition and emotion.* Chichester, England: Wiley.

Tangney, J. P., & Fischer, K. W. (1995). *Self-conscious emotions.* New York: Guilford Press.

Tellegen, A., Watson, D., & Clark, L. A. (1999a). On the dimensional and hierarchical structure of affect. *Psychological Science, 10,* 297–303.

Tellegen, A., Watson, D., & Clark, L. A. (1999b). Further support for a hierarchical model of affect: Reply to Green and Salovey. *Psychological Science, 10,* 307–309.

Tomkins, S. S. (1962). *Affect, imagery, and consciousness: The positive affects.* New York: Springer.

Tomkins, S. S. (1963). *Affect, imagery, and consciousness: Vol. 2. The negative affects.* New York: Springer.

Tooby, J., & Cosmides, L. (1992). The psychological foundations of culture. In J. H. Barkow, L. Cosmides, & J. Tooby (Eds.), *The adapted mind: Evolutionary psychology and the generation of culture* (pp. 19–136). New York: Oxford University Press.

Watson, D., & Tellegen, A. (1999). Issues in the dimensional structure of affect—Effects of descriptors, measurement error, and response formats: Comment on Russell and Carroll (1999). *Psychological Bulletin, 125,* 601–610.

Watson, D., Wiese, D., Vaidya, J., & Tellegen, A. (1999). The two general activation systems of affect: Structural findings, evolutionary considerations, and psychobiological evidence. *Journal of Personality and Social Psychology, 76,* 820–838.

Weiss, H. M. (1999). An examination of the joint effects of affective experiences and job beliefs on job satisfaction and variations in affective experiences over time. *Organizational Behavior and Human Decision Processes, 78,* 1–24.

Weiss, H. M. (in press). Deconstructing job satisfaction: separating evaluations, beliefs, and affective experiences. *Human Resource Review.*

Weiss, H. M., and Brief, A. P. (2001). Affect at work: An historical perspective. In R. L. Payne & C. L. Cooper (Eds.), *Emotions at work: Theory, research and applications for management.* New York: Wiley.

Weiss, H. M., & Cropanzano, R. (1996). Affective events theory: A theoretical discussion of the structure, causes and consequences of affective experiences at work. *Research in Organizational Behavior, 18,* 1–74.

Wyer, R. S., Clore, G. L., & Isbell, L. (1999). Affect and information processing. In M. Zanna (Ed.), *Advances in experimental social psychology.* Orlando, FL: Academic Press.

CHAPTER 3

Emotion
Models, Measures, and Individual Differences

Randy J. Larsen
Ed Diener
Richard E. Lucas

In recent decades, we have witnessed a rapid expansion of research on emotion. Entered as a keyword in PsychINFO, the term *emotion* elicits over twenty-two thousand entries (as of this writing). For comparison, the keyword *cognition* elicits just over fourteen thousand entries. And there are additional signs that emotion has become a vibrant new area within psychology, such as the publication of handbooks (Ekman & Davidson, 1994; Lewis & Haviland, 1993), as well as textbooks (Cornelius, 1996; Reeve, 1997). Other signs of the growing popularity and impact of emotion research include specialized journals in emotion (for example, the new American Psychological Association journal *Emotion*), scientific societies dedicated to this topic (for example, International Society for the Study of Emotion), and a new program for emotion research at the National Institute of Mental Health. The zeitgeist suggests that Tomkins may have underestimated things a bit in 1981 when he penned his oft-repeated phrase, "The next decade or so belongs to affect" (1981, p. 314).

Why should industrial/organizational (I/O) psychologists be interested in emotions? One important reason is that emotions have been shown to influence a wide variety of phenomena that are highly relevant to organizational and workplace behaviors. As a sampling, emotion influences the occurrence and course of altruism, creativity, learning and memory, social perception and interaction, social comparison, resource allocation, self-evaluation, moral reasoning, attraction and liking, attributions and expectations, judgment and decision making, self-regulation and coping, irrational beliefs, and rumination (Cornelius, 1996). In addition, emotion is directly relevant to understanding specific topics central to I/O psychology, such as job satisfaction, worker motivation, and understanding how job characteristics (such as personal control) contribute to important outcomes, such as productivity (Warr, 1999). In addition, a dispositional view of emotion, along with the theories and measures developed in the area of personality and emotion (Larsen, 2000a), may help I/O psychologists better understand the personal characteristics that people bring to the workplace and how these characteristics interact with job characteristics to influence behavior on the job (Judge & Larsen, 2001).

To gain an anecdotal grasp of the importance of emotion to work, consider the case of Elliot, who, through damage to his brain, lost his ability to experience emotion (Damasio, 1994). Prior to his injury, Elliot was a successful businessman. At his firm, he was a role model for younger colleagues. His social skills were such that he often was called on to negotiate disputes at work. Elliot was highly respected, and his prosperity and professional status were enviable.

One day, Elliot began to have severe headaches, and it turned out that a small tumor was found growing on the lining of tissue that covers the brain just above his eyes and behind his forehead. The tumor was pushing against his brain and had damaged a small portion of his prefrontal cortex, which had to be removed with the tumor. Elliot tolerated the operation well and recovered quickly, with no apparent lasting damage. His IQ was tested after the operation and was found to be superior, as it was before his operation. His memory was tested and was found to be excellent. His ability to use and understand language was also unaffected by the operation. His ability to do arithmetic, memorize lists of words, visualize objects, and read a map all remained unaffected by the operation.

Elliot's family and coworkers, however, reported that he had changed. He could not seem to manage his time properly. Elliot needed lots of prompting from his wife to get off to work in the morning. Once at work, he had problems finishing tasks. If he was interrupted in a task, he had difficulty starting back up where he left off. Often, he would get sidetracked for hours; for example, in reshelving some books, he would often stop to read one of them and not return to his desk for hours. He knew his job but had trouble putting all the actions together in just the right order.

Soon Elliot lost his job. He tried various business schemes on his own and finally took his life savings and started an investment management business. He teamed up with a disreputable character, against the advice of many of his friends and family members. This business went bankrupt, and he lost all his savings. A divorce followed. Elliot quickly remarried, but to a woman whom none of his friends or family approved of. This marriage ended quickly in another divorce. Without a source of income and without a family to support him, Elliot became a drifter. He came to the attention of Antonio Damasio, a neurologist at the University of Iowa, who later described Elliot in a book about emotion and the brain (Damasio, 1994). It seems that the small bit of brain matter lost due to Elliot's tumor was essential in transmitting emotional information to the higher reasoning centers of his brain. Elliot reported that the only change in himself that he could notice was that after his operation, he did not feel any strong emotion, or much of any emotion at all. Without emotions, Damasio (1994) argues, people have difficulty making decisions. How could Elliot choose this over that if he had no preferences? How could he have a gut feeling that his new business partner was untrustworthy if he had no gut feelings? How could he know he should return to his desk and not read the book when in fact he had no preference for one activity over the other?

The case of Elliot strongly illustrates the importance of emotion or, in this case, the lack of emotion, in understanding behaviors important in the workplace. Emotions influence many processes that should be of interest to I/O psychologists. In this chapter, we provide an overview of some of the important models and measurement tools in emotion research, especially with reference to those useful for organizational psychologists. We give special attention to individual differences in emotion, the emotional characteristics that people bring to the workplace.

Models of Emotion

The most global definition of emotion draws from systems theory, identifying emotion as a multiattribute process that unfolds over time, with the attributes unfolding at different rates. Emotions attributes are manifest in multiple channels (experiential, physiological, expressive, cognitive, and behavioral), and the channels themselves are loosely coupled (Venables, 1984) such that measures of different emotion attributes (such as self-report and physiological) may not correlate highly. In an ideal world, measuring emotion would entail assessment across multiple attributes simultaneously. Data obtained on multiple attributes may converge on the latent construct of emotion and increase the confidence that we can place in the accuracy of the assessment. However, even with multiple measures synchronized in time, the latent psychological construct of "emotion" remains some inferential distance from the observed data it can produce. Emotion must be viewed as an inferred construct, and researchers should be cautioned against viewing specific operational definitions as complete and without remainder. As a scientific term, *emotion* carries surplus meaning beyond any specific emotion measure.

Primary Emotions Versus Emotion Dimensions

Two fundamental views on the nature of emotion bifurcate the field. One view—the primary emotions view—holds that the domain is best represented as a small set of fundamental (by some criterion) or basic emotions. Lists of usually between five and nine basic emotions are offered, defined by such criteria as unique facial expressions, distinct action tendencies, or adaptive significance. Sometimes called the categorical view, this perspective conceptualizes affect as consisting of nonoverlapping categories.

I/O psychologists may prefer the primary emotions view when they are interested in very specific emotions in the workplace. For example, an important topic is aggression in the workplace, and so psychologists studying this topic may prefer to focus specifically on anger and related dispositional characteristics such as hostility and impulse control. Moreover, there are specific measures of anger, in terms of self-report and measures of facial expressiveness and voice characteristics that may be indicative of anger (Larsen & Fredrickson, 1999).

The primary emotions view is especially useful as a theoretical foundation when the psychologist has a specific behavior or category of acts that he or she is interested in understanding, such as aggression in the workplace. Using theories developed by primary emotion theorists (Ekman & Rosenberg, 1997; Izard, 1977) I/O psychologists might try to understand the functional significance of specific emotions, as well as how these functions adapt to and play out in the workplace. For example, most primary emotion theorists view the function of anger as motivating behavior that will correct wrongs committed against oneself, as well as act as a social signal that one will not tolerate such wrongs in the future. Such a functional analysis of the primary emotion of anger may help explain why and how and under what conditions it is displayed in the workplace.

In contrast to the primary emotions view, a second view holds that the affect domain is best represented by a small set of underlying dimensions (two or three). This dimensional view suggests that all emotional experiences are blends of a few dimensional ingredients. Valence (from pleasant to unpleasant) and arousal are the dimensions that many researchers use who endorse the dimensional view of affect (Lang, Bradley, & Cuthbert, 1990, 1992; Russell, 1978, 1980). In this view, anger is viewed as a high-arousal, negatively valenced emotion. Anxiety, fear, disgust, and distress are similar high-arousal negative emotions. While many such high-arousal negative emotions appear quite different from each other, a couple of findings lend support to the value of a dimensional view of emotion. First, many processes that influence or are influenced by emotions are sensitive to broad classes of emotion, such as the high-arousal negative emotions, and are not diagnostic of specific emotions. For example, failure experiences, such as a severe criticism from one's supervisor at work, result in some people experiencing intense sadness, whereas others experience intense anger. So we know that a high-arousal negative emotion is likely to follow certain events, but we do not know which specific one. Many psychological processes have these general emotional effects. Another finding that supports the dimensional view draws on dispositional findings; many people who experience one high arousal negative emotion (such as anger) often also experience other high-arousal negative emotions (such as sadness). This is not to say that people experience sadness and anger at the same time, but rather people who experience a lot of anger will also experience a lot of sadness over time (Zelenski & Larsen, 2000). Findings such as these lend weight to the notion that arousal and valence may be important dimensions for understanding the emotion domain.

Within the dimensional view of affect, one model prevails. This is the circumplex model, and its essential features are presented in Figure 3.1. Discussions of the circumplex model can be found in Larsen and Diener (1992), as well as a recent issue of the *Journal of Personality and Social Psychology* devoted to the structure of affect (Diener, 1999). A few distinguishing features characterize the circumplex model. First, the model is a two-dimensional map of the affective domain. A map of the earth, for comparison, can be represented in two dimensions: longitude and latitude. All locations on earth can be uniquely specified using two reference coordinates. Similarly, by stating that the affect domain is a circumplex, we imply that all specific emotions can be described using the coordinates of two dimensions. A second feature of the circumplex model is that it lacks simple structure. Regardless of where the two reference dimensions are located in the circumplex, there will always be individual emotions that lie between those coordinates. Another characteristic of the circumplex is that two dimensions at a right angle to each other (orthogonal, as in Cartesian coordinates) will provide the maximum information about the location of individual emotions in the circumplex space. Thus, the circumplex structure provides a specific measurement model of the emotion domain.

Figure 3.1 represents the circumplex model with the primary coordinates (shown in heavy lines) of pleasure-displeasure and high-low activation (or arousal). These two reference dimensions are descriptively useful because they represent two maximally different aspects of the affect domain. The pleasure-displeasure dimension captures the hedonic continuum, with all unpleasant emotions on one side and all pleasant emotions on the other. Activation represents a continuum from sleep to extreme levels of alertness, engagement, and arousal and does not refer to hedonic content. The diagonal coordinates of the pleasure-by-arousal circumplex have received a

Figure 3.1. Affect Circumplex Model.

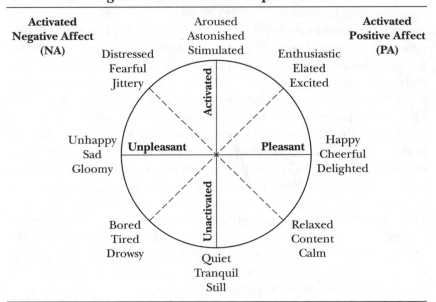

Source: Adapted from Larsen and Diener (1992).

good deal of attention. For example, the emotions at the upper left octant have been referred to as negative affect (NA), and those at the upper right octant have been referred to as positive affect (PA). A self-report measure of these emotions has been published and widely used in emotion research (the Positive and Negative Affect Schedule, or PANAS; Watson, Clark, & Tellegen, 1988). Work on the correlates of these two orthogonal affective dispositions is fast accumulating and is reviewed by Watson (2000).

A discussion of the circumplex model in relation to the workplace issues (such as job satisfaction) can be found in Warr (1999). One issue, for example, concerns the overlap of general life satisfaction (defined as frequently experiencing positive emotions) and specific work satisfaction (defined as the frequent experience of positive emotions on the job). Conceptualized in this way, researchers (Judge & Watanabe, 1993) have found evidence for mutual influence: job satisfaction appears to be an important contributor to life satisfaction, and people high in life satisfaction tend to enjoy their jobs more than people low in life satisfaction do. Other work-place issues that could be investigated with dimensional models of emotion concern how specific job characteristics might contribute to job satisfaction through the promotion of frequent positive emotions at work. For example, a job that provides opportunities for skill use or some degree of personal control may produce more frequent positive emotions in the workplace. Other issues concern emotion regulation strategies that result in the remediation of negative emotions and the promotion of positive emotions (Larsen, 2000a) and how specific strategies might be employed to regulate emotions in the workplace. For example, in a study of salespersons, Larsen and Gschwandtner (1995) examined the emotional impact of rejection and failure on the job, as well as specific strategies that the salespersons used to regulate their emotions at work.

Applied to organizational behavior, one popular view (Cropanzano, James, & Konovsky, 1993; Warr, 1999) is that the circumplex model might best be employed in terms of pleasure versus displeasure at various levels of activation. Therefore, in Figure 3.1, we have provided four emotion adjectives to anchor six octants of the emotion circumplex. Because of the measurement implications of the circumplex (for example, attributes located directly opposite from each other on the circumplex are correlated −1.0), these six octants actually represent three bipolar dimensions. Selecting the high-activation end to name the bipolar dimensions, we have a dimension of negative affect (NA), which refers to frequent experiences of distress, anxiety, or annoyance and infrequent experiences of relaxation, contentment or calm. At 90 degrees to this (and hence orthogonal) is the dimension of positive affect (PA), referring to frequent experiences of enthusiasm, elation, and excitement and infrequent experiences of boredom or feelings of dullness or sluggishness.

To summarize the issues in modeling emotion, the question of whether emotion should be modeled as two or three general dimensions or as seven or more discrete categories has a long history and continues to be discussed (Lazarus, 1991; Zelenski & Larsen, 2000). The circumplex model posits that emotions that are close to each other on the circumference (such as anger and anxiety) are similar in terms of the dimensions, whereas emotions that are 180 degrees away from each other are opposites (such as happy and sad). In contrast, supporters of the primary emotions views

(Ekman, Levenson, & Friesen, 1983; Izard, 1977) hold that the circumplex model obscures important distinctions between closely spaced emotions, such as anxiety and anger. An important issue embedded within this dimensional versus primary emotion debate concerns measurement specificity: measures designed to assess discrete emotions can be aggregated into dimensional representations after the fact. The reverse, however, is rarely possible. The implications of which model to use should be thought through ahead of time by researchers, especially with respect to whether specific discrete emotions are the target of their work or whether general valence- or arousal-based emotions, or their rotations as general positive and negative affect, are a better fit to the researcher's theoretical agenda.

Emotion States Versus Emotion Traits

Emotions are typically thought of as states. This implies that emotions are temporary, are due primarily to causes outside the person, and have distinct onsets and offsets. Although emotions are fluctuating states, they nevertheless fluctuate around some mean or average level for each person, and persons differ reliably from each other in their average level of various emotions. Emotions can also be conceptualized as having an enduring traitlike component, that this component is due primarily to causes inside the person (such as personality), and that trait conception of emotion refers to the set point or expected value for each person on that emotion, other things being equal (George, 1986). Emotions are thus hybrid phenomena, consisting of both trait and state components, allowing the researcher to focus on one or the other components in addressing various questions.

The distinction between state and trait emotion is important to the I/O researcher for four reasons. First, emotion states can influence specific behaviors that may have important work implications, such as the relation between positive emotion states and creativity (Fredrickson, 2001). I/O researchers may wish to understand how specific emotion states contribute to, moderate, or mediate the effects of specific work behaviors, such as studying how negative emotions affect future expectations or how anxiety narrows the range of attention. Second, with regard to emotional states, the other causal direction should also be considered, such as the influence of workplace behaviors and events on the emotional states of those on the job. To the extent that emotional reactions on the job spill over into other areas of life (Judge & Watanabe, 1993), the emotional effects of the workplace may have wide-ranging implications. Third, I/O researchers should be aware that people bring emotional dispositions to the workplace; that is, not everyone shows up in the same emotional state. To the extent that emotion dispositions refer to the expected value of emotion for an individual, people are likely to have predictable emotional levels and reactions to events at the workplace. Understanding how trait emotions work and the causes and consequences of these specific dispositions will help I/O psychologists predict and explain specific workplace reactions. And finally, states and traits can easily be confused, and so I/O researchers need to be aware of the distinction. It is not difficult to find publications in the emotion literature where a correlational study is done between measured emotion (say, positive affect) and some other variable (say, helping), and the authors interpret this as a state relationship: "People are more likely to help when in a positive mood." However, when measuring emotions in people off the street, the researcher is more likely to be tapping emotion traits, that is, the most likely level or expected value for each person. Consequently, it may really be that the kind of person who is most likely to be in a positive state (high trait PA) is also the most likely kind of person to be helpful. To infer state effects, the researcher must employ state manipulations and proper experimental, not correlational, designs.

Emotion traits are receiving a good deal of attention from personality researchers, as well as from psychologists interested in motivation and the biological bases of behavior. When it comes to trait emotion, PA and NA may be thought of as the "Big Two" (Tellegen, 1985). The main hedonic dimension in the circumplex, running between PA and NA, may also be empirically useful in assessing generalized trait satisfaction, as this dimension purely contrasts pleasant and unpleasant affective states. The measurement implications of the main dimensions of the emotion circumplex in dispositional terms are discussed in more detail in Larsen and Diener (1992) and Warr (1999). In the following section, we draw out some of the theoretical issues involved in conceptualizing emotions as traits.

Individual Differences in Emotion

The existence of individual differences in emotion, especially in terms of broad PA and NA dimensions, is extensively documented in both correlational (Watson, 2000) and experimental (Larsen & Ketelaar, 1991) research. An important question concerns where these individual differences come from and what their nature is. Larsen (2000c) proposes a simple but heuristically useful way to think about the origin and nature of individual differences in emotion. This view of individual differences can be expressed using the familiar stimulus-organism-response (S-O-R) model presented in Figure 3.2. This model is useful because it cleaves an emotional response into two component subprocesses: the stimulus-input side and the response-output side. In terms of trait emotion, individuals may differ from each other because of differences in sensitivity to the stimulus or because of differences in the amount of response output (or both).

Larsen (2000b) argues that this distinction between stimulus sensitivity and response modulation is useful precisely because different personality factors may influence these two component

Figure 3.2. S-O-R Model of the Role of Personality in Moderating and Mediating Affective Responses.

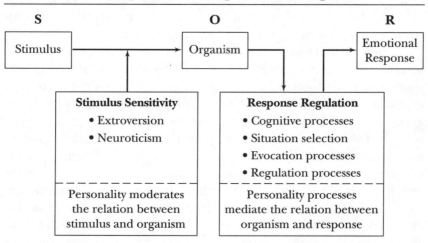

Source: Larsen (2000b).

processes independently. In the next section, we briefly review personality research that fits this S-O-R model. A useful way to interpret this model is that certain personality characteristics effect the input side by moderating sensitivity to specific hedonic stimuli, such that the same stimulus will be experienced differently by different people. On the output side, other personality characteristics may mediate emotion responses by influencing if, how, and when emotions are expressed.

For I/O psychologists interested in emotion, the distinction between sensitivity to input and control of response output can be heuristically as well as practically useful. This distinction allows the I/O psychologist to think separately about which factors make a person vulnerable to specific emotions and the processes whereby such vulnerability is created (such as attention to emotion cues in the environment), on the one hand, and, on the other, to think about the processes whereby some people come to control or self-regulate their emotions in the work environment. A rich theory in the basic emotion literature seeks to explain individual differences in sensitivity to emotional input, and so we turn first to the S-O part of the S-O-R model.

Individual Differences in Sensitivity to Hedonic Stimuli: The Input Side

More than a dozen studies have been published in the past decade showing robust correlations between extraversion (E) and average PA, and between neuroticism (N) and average NA (reviewed in Rusting & Larsen, 1997, 1998). E and N are traits that show up in almost every typology of personality, are typically the two strongest traits (in terms of accounting for the most variance), and are the focus of several biologically based theories of personality (Depue, 1996; Eysenck, 1967; Gray, 1981, 1990, 1994). While many researchers have speculated that E and N represent differential sensitivity to positive and negative affective stimuli, respectively, correlational data do not provide the necessary support for such claims. However, experimental studies also support these relations. In four separate studies to date (Larsen & Ketelaar, 1989, 1991; Rusting & Larsen, 1999; Zelenski & Larsen, 1999), Larsen and his colleagues have found that E relates to differential susceptibility to positive mood inductions and

N relates to negative mood inductions. For example, in Larsen and Ketelaar (1989), pleasant and unpleasant moods were induced using false performance feedback (success and failure, respectively). PA and NA were assessed both before and after the mood induction. Extraversion predicted significant increases in PA to the success feedback, and neuroticism predicted significant increases in NA to the failure feedback.

In terms of theoretical explanations for why E and N should relate to PA and NA, respectively, the most relevant theory is perhaps that proposed by Gray (1990, 1994). Called reinforcement sensitivity theory (RST), this theory is actually a revision of Eysenck's (1967) original theory of E and N. Eysenck proposed that E was linked to general cortical arousability (extraverts were less arousable and hence needed strong stimulation) and that N was linked to a lower threshold for activation in the limbic system. Gray proposed an alternative explanation by positing two separate brain mechanisms responsible for sensitivity to rewards and punishments. Gray suggested that extraversion is related to an enhanced sensitivity to cues of reward. Extraverts are mainly motivated by pleasure or reward, he argued, and so have a strong tendency to approach, even in novel situations. Extraverts expect rewards and are vigilant for possible sources of reward in the environment. Gray thus named the hypothesized neurological substrate for this individual difference the behavioral activation system (BAS); this system responds to incentives and generates positive affect.

Neuroticism, Gray hypothesized, is responsible for individual differences in response to cues of punishment and frustration. That is, high-N individuals are mainly motivated to avoid punishment and consequently have a strong tendency to be vigilant for threat and are ready to inhibit or interrupt their behavior, especially in novel environments. Gray thus named the hypothesized neurological substrate for this individual difference the behavioral inhibition system (BIS). High-BIS persons are attentive to signs of impending punishment or frustration and have a low threshold for noticing aversive stimuli and thus for experiencing negative emotion.

Gray's theory has implications for exploring dispositional effects in organizational settings. The theory would predict, for example, that persons with a strong BAS system (extraverted) will respond more positively to rewards and positive evaluations on the job compared to individuals with a weak BAS. Alternatively, individuals with a strong BIS (high neuroticism) would respond more aversively to workplace punishments and negative evaluations on the job compared to individuals with a weak BIS.

Job environments and organizational settings could potentially be assessed in terms of available cues of reinforcement, frustration, threat, relief, and punishment. These are the environmental cues most relevant to Gray's theoretical constructs. Several studies buttress this application of Gray's theory to organizational settings. Brief, Butcher, and Roberson (1995), for example, report that high-neuroticism individuals were less responsive to a positive mood induction (their ratings of job satisfaction were less affected by being given a small gift) than low-neuroticism individuals. On the positive emotion side, Stewart (1996) reports a link between extraversion and reward sensitivity in a study of salespersons.

An important implication of Gray's personality theory is the idea that some people may be prepared to respond with positive affect to certain stimuli, whereas others may be prepared to respond with negative affect. In an environment that is constant across persons, such as the work environment, this means that there will be individual differences in the impact of specific environmental features. Another important implication is that these two dimensions are empirically orthogonal. This implies that some people are high in both reward and punishment sensitivity, and others are relatively low in both. People with different combinations of hedonic sensitivities will react differently to hedonic features of the environment, including that of the workplace.

Understanding the implications of individual differences in BIS and BAS (or E and N, or trait PA and NA) will provide important directions for future research, especially concerning implications for job motivation, satisfaction, and management. For example, how will people differentially respond to unpleasant events at work? How will different motivation programs affect people who differ in terms of sensitivity to incentives versus punishment? Motivational programs can be phrased in terms of the gains (incentive framing) or the losses (aversive framing) associated with some specific topic. For example, getting employees to work together as a team can be phrased in terms of the benefits of doing so (increased productivity) or the losses of not doing so (being beaten by a competitor). It is likely that loss framing will motivate high-N persons and that reward framing will motivate extraverts. This hypothesis, as well as related predictions about differential behavior in the workplace and the marketplace correlating with E and N, await testing by I/O psychologists who take seriously the notion of individual differences in sensitivity to hedonic events.

Individual Differences in Response Modulation: The Output Side

Thus far, we have emphasized individual differences in sensitivity to hedonic events. These may be best understood as hedonic vulnerabilities that are stable and difficult to change (Depue, 1996). However, with regard to the output side—controlling emotional responses—there may be more flexibility for learning and training. People may be able to change or adapt to new ways of regulating their emotional responses. In fact, the concept of emotional intelligence, which is already influencing theories of organizational behavior (Goleman, 1995, 1998), views this ability as having five components. Three components of emotional intelligence refer to processes in the self: (1) self-awareness of feelings and preferences, (2) self-regulation of emotions, and (3) self-motivation to engage in appropriate behaviors. The two other aspects of emotional intelligence refer to regulating emotions in others: (4) the ability to empathize with the emotions of others (5) and relationship skills that foster interpersonal emotion management. Viewed as a general ability, emotional intelligence focuses on how people become aware of and effectively modulate their own emotions and the emotions of others. According to the model in Figure 3.2, emotional intelligence refers to those characteristics that influence the O-R or output side of the S-O-R equation.

There is a growing literature on individual differences in the self-regulation of emotion (see *Psychological Inquiry,* 2000, volume 11, which is devoted to emotion regulation). There appear to be four processes whereby people regulate (or dysregulate) their emotional responses. One process is *cognitive,* and it refers to those behaviors "in the head" that work to create differences between people in how they process hedonic information. A few examples are attributional style, optimism, repressive coping style, and social comparison processes. In terms relevant to organizational psychology, individuals with a high level of certain traits (such as disagreeableness) would be more likely to recall repeatedly (ruminate on) negative feedback from a supervisor or an unpleasant job experiences. Those who are high on other traits (such as conscientiousness) might preferentially process positive job experiences (such as successes, positive feedback). Judge and Locke (1993) report that specific dysfunctional thought processes mediated the relationship between trait emotion and job satisfaction. They also cite other studies that support the notion of differential cognitive processes that discriminated among individuals with different emotional reactions to work experiences (Brief et al., 1995; Necowitz & Roznowski, 1994).

A second process whereby personality can influence emotional responding refers to *situational selection,* or choosing to be in certain kinds of situations and not in others. The situations a person chooses to be in will, in turn, influence the kinds of emotions he or she is likely to experience. Much research has shown that we do not randomly choose our friends, our mates, our hobbies, our college classes, our jobs, or our careers. How we go about making these selections is due, at least in part, to our personality. Applied to organizational psychology, this notion refers to the classic selection issue: people should self-select into occupations that are a good match to their dispositional tendencies. For example, Judge and Cable (1997) report that individuals' culture preferences were strongly predicted by personality; for example, extraverted job seekers preferred organizations that emphasized affiliation and teamwork. More research is needed that links personality traits to choice of situations and subsequent affective experiences in organizations.

The third process whereby personality influences emotional responses is called *evocation.* This refers to those processes whereby people change or influence the situations they are in. Particularly when it comes to the social aspects of situations, people often evoke typical responses in others. For example, extraverts are more likely to get other people to like them (Watson, 2000).

Machiavellianism is a personality trait that specifically implicates strategies for evoking certain responses in others. According to a review of the literature on Machiavellianism, high and low scorers represent two alternative strategies of social evocation (Wilson, Near, & Miller, 1996). The high Machiavellian engages in an exploitative social strategy—one that betrays friendship and uses other people opportunistically. The low Machiavellian, in contrast, engages in a strategy of cooperation, sometimes called tit-for-tat, a strategy based on reciprocity (you help me, and I'll help you).

The success of influence strategies engaged in by the high Machiavellian should depend greatly on the social context (Larsen & Buss, 2002). One study examined a real-world setting by studying the sales performance of stockbrokers from two different organizational contexts (Shultz, 1993). One organizational context, the NYNEX, is highly structured and rule bound, with little room for salespeople to innovate or improvise. Employees are required to follow a two-volume manual of rules. The second organizational context, represented by corporations such as Merrill Lynch and Shearson, Lehman, and Hutton, is more loosely structured and allows more opportunities for wheeling and dealing.

The sales success of high and low Machiavellian salespersons in these two organizational contexts was evaluated by the size of the commissions earned. In the loosely structured organizations like Merrill Lynch, the high Machiavellians earned fully twice as much in commission as the low Machiavellians. However, in the more structured organizations, the low Machiavellians earned twice as much money on commissions as the high Machiavellians. Studies such as these point to the important role of socioemotional evocation, or social influence strategies, which often interact with organizational structure to produce specific outcomes.

The last process whereby personality influences emotional responses refers to direct attempts at emotion regulation. Persons may differ in the strategies they employ for emotion regulation or in the frequency or success of those affect-regulating behaviors. Some theorists have presented lists of specific strategies or behaviors for regulating mood (Morris, 1989; Morris & Reilly, 1987; Thayer, 1996). Recently, Larsen (2000a) employed an act frequency approach to develop a taxonomy of mood-regulating strategies. Participants were asked to nominate acts they use for getting out of an unpleasant mood caused by various life events. Larsen (2000a) presents twenty-five strategies and behaviors that people commonly reported using to cope with unpleasant events and feelings. The emotion regulation acts were categorized along two dimensions. Some acts were cognitive strategies (reframing, social comparison), whereas others were clearly behavioral activities (problem-directed action, making a plan to avoid problems in the future). The second dimension concerned the directedness of the acts. That is, some acts were directed at changing the person or how he or she was feeling (such as exercising, distraction, or helping others), whereas other acts were directed more at changing the situation (seeking advice or putting the situation in perspective).

Larsen and Gschwandtner (1995) used experience sampling to examine how salespersons attempt to regulate their feelings on the job, particularly in terms of responding to the stresses commonly associated with sales careers, such as high rejection rates, factory delays, and supervisor pressure. These researchers found many mood-regulating acts from lists of coping mechanisms—for example, downward social comparison, self-reward, distraction, socializing, venting, and the use of pharmacological agents. Other mood-regulating acts also were found, such as helping others, talking to a friend or mentor, future thinking, and praying. Interesting sex differences emerged in emotion-regulation behaviors. Larsen and Gschwandtner found, for example, that in the face of work stress, salesmen were much more likely than saleswomen to report exercising, whereas saleswomen were much more likely than salesmen to talk to a mentor or friend. It is likely that programs to teach mood-regulation strategies could be developed for organizations. Applications of the concept of emotional intelligence have already been made in the areas of management (Goleman, 1998).

So far, we have focused on different models of emotion (categorical versus dimensional) and have discussed important related issues (emotions as states versus traits). We followed a theoretical lead on individual differences in emotional responding and considered the separable components of sensitivity to emotional stimuli and the control of emotional responses. Wherever possible, we noted how these ideas could be connected with I/O psychology. To the I/O researcher, however, the most practical and useful advice about emotions might concern observations on their measurement. After all, researchers cannot proceed to seek answers to their questions if they do not adequately measure the important psychological constructs in their questions. For researchers interested in emotion constructs, we now turn to a consideration of measurement issues in the emotion domain.

Measuring Emotions

There are many views on the nature of emotion (Ekman & Davidson, 1994). In fact, Kleinginna and Kleinginna (1981) identified over ninety different definitions of the term *emotion*. We briefly considered the problem of definition at the outset of this chapter and pointed out that emotions are manifest in multiple systems. For example, emotions can be referenced to experiences, physiological changes, expressive behaviors, cognitive biases or changes, or changes in the probabilities of specific behaviors. A researcher could use measures that tap into one or more of these systems. However, the systems themselves are loosely coupled (Venables, 1984), such that different measures of emotion (such as expression and physiological) may not correlate highly. Issues of reliability and validity of measurement are therefore important concerns in the assessment of emotion. Just because someone is using so-called hard measures, such as behavior observation or physiology, does not mean that the measures are more reliable or valid or that he or she need not be concerned with these issues.

Reliability

Most researchers think of reliability of measurement as high test-retest correlations. However, as a measurement concept, reliability refers to the degree to which some observed score reflects the true amount of the construct being measured. Because we never have access to true scores, reliability can only be estimated. For psychological constructs referring to traits or stable characteristics of persons, a test-retest correlation is a good estimate of reliability. Here, we assume little or no meaningful within-participant variance on the construct being measured. Emotion, however, is often construed as a within-subject construct (that is, a state) or a hybrid construct between a state and a trait. Because emotion is a complicated state-trait construct, we cannot use simple test-retest correlations as estimates of measurement reliability.

Another estimate of reliability is an internal consistency estimate, such as coefficient alpha or odd-even item composite correlations. These are measures of item homogeneity and therefore assess the degree to which the various items are measuring the same underlying construct. Internal consistency works equally well for state and trait measures. However, this estimate of measurement reliability works only for multi-item scales. Single-item measures, which are common in emotion research, cannot be examined in terms of internal consistency.

One approach to single-item measures is to forget about reliability concerns altogether and focus instead on concerns of validity. As most psychologists know, measurement reliability sets the upper bound on validity correlations. If a measure is valid, then it must be reliable. Nevertheless, passing up reliability concerns is dangerous, especially when trying to figure out null findings (Was the failure due to measurement unreliability, or was it due to a faulty hypothesis? See Meehl, 1978, for more detailed discussion). Nevertheless, strong evidence for validity, with multiple converging methods and replicated patterns of association, can add credibility to the claim that a particular measure is reliable.

Validity

Emotions are theoretical constructs that are only inferentially linked to observable measures. By saying this, we mean that although emotion may be represented by many different measures, it cannot be reduced to any single one. This underscores the importance of construct validity in understanding and communicating the scientific meaning of emotion terms

Through construct validity, meaning is given to a scientific term, such as *emotion*, by the nomological network of assertions in which that term appears (Cronbach & Meehl, 1955). Theoretical and measurement models guide the researcher in building a network of associations around the construct of emotion. Theory testing and measurement development proceed in tandem.[1] Each link in a nomological network helps add to the scientific meaning of the terms in the network. Some links refer to positive associations (convergent validity) and some to negative or null associations (discriminant validity). In addition, some links specify the conditions under which emotions are likely to be evoked (predictive validity).

The sum of relationships built up around specific emotions creates something like a mosaic. When enough pieces of the mosaic (strands in the nomological network) are in place, we get the picture. Certainly, construct validity is always unfinished, and things are always true until there are new findings. Nevertheless, there comes a point where we reach some consensual agreement about the shared scientific meaning of a construct and an agreed-on set of measures of that construct. This characterizes the state of affairs in the area of emotion measurement; while the experts may debate the specifics, most researchers agree on a set of measures and terms that are useful for studying emotion. The remainder of this chapter introduces I/O researchers to a set of agreed-on measures.

Specific Measurement Techniques

Because emotion is a multicomponent construct, there are many aspects that can be measured. Deciding which aspect one is most interested in will lead researchers to select from the broad array of measurement methodologies. Self-report measures are clearly the most popular and widely used measures of emotion and probably of most use to I/O researchers, so we begin with a consideration of this category of measurement.

Self-Reports of Emotional Experience

Self-report measures rely on participants to represent their experience of emotion accurately through the use of rating scales or adjective checklists. Users of self-report measures often argue that the participants themselves are in the most privileged position to observe, assess, and synthesize information about their own feeling states. These measures allow the participants to express, in some standard format, the information about subjective feelings that only they have access to.

There are many self-report measures of emotion, and substantial similarities can be found among them. Our review here will not be exhaustive. Instead, we will describe a few exemplars and highlight certain measurement issues common in the self-report domain. (Additional instruments are reviewed in MacKay, 1980; Stone, 1995; and Larsen and Fredrickson, 1999.) We begin with single-item measures of emotion.

Single-Item Measures of Self-Reported Emotion

A measurement strategy with a good deal of face validity is simply to ask participants to rate how they are feeling on a single emotion dimension. That emotion might be a global affective dimension (such as, How unpleasant are you feeling?) or a specific emotion (How anxious do you feel?). The response scale might be unipolar (*not at all anxious* to *extremely anxious*) or bipolar (*unpleasant* to *pleasant*). Options for responding are often Likert-type scales, with five-, seven-, or nine-point formats.

Advantages of single-item measures are that they are easy to construct, easily understood by participants, and quickly administered and scored. Virtually any emotion term can anchor a single-item scale, making this self-report technique vital for researchers targeting primary or discrete emotions (Ekman, Friesen, & Ancoli, 1980; Gross & Levenson, 1993). Disadvantages are those that accrue whenever measurement is extremely brief: the report sample may no be representative, the content domain may not be adequately sampled, and the sampling error may be large, Despite disadvantages, single-item measures are very popular in the experimental and survey literatures, where brevity is a considerable concern.

A variation on the single-item theme is to make the response scale a visual analogue of the digital response options. Visual analogue scales (VAS) might present the participant with a horizontal line separating two opposing adjectives, and the participant is asked to place a mark on the line describing how he or she is feeling. Other VAS methods can be devised for unipolar response options, with the line anchored with "not at all" to "extremely much" for a specific emotion. Alternatively, an analogue of the emotion can be presented to the participant, such as a series of five cartoon faces, going from a frown expression on the face at one end to an extreme smile face on another. The participants are asked to circle the face that represents how they are feeling. This has the advantages of being useful with young children or participants from different linguistic cultures.

Single-item measures can also be useful to collect real-time reports of emotion, and these techniques may have useful applications to specific I/O contexts. The general strategy is to collect self-reports of a single emotion on a moment-by-moment basis. The self-report can be either on-line, as the emotion is being experienced, or retrospective. The most basic real-time self-report measure uses a rotating dial or a sliding meter, where respondents adjust a pointer as often as necessary so that it always reflects how they are feeling. Several researchers have described continuous rating dials of this sort (Bunce, Larsen, & Cruz, 1993; Fredrickson & Kahneman, 1993; Gottman, 1993; Gottman & Levenson, 1985). Like single-item measures more generally, rating dials may use either bipolar (*very negative* to *very positive*) or unipolar verbal anchors (*no anxiety at all* to *extreme anxiety*) and either Likert-type or VAS.

Continuous rating dials can be used to automate data acquisition. The dial itself can be connected to a potentiometer or variable resistor, which controls the voltage output from a common voltage source. The electrical output from the dial can then feed to an analogue-to-digital data-acquisition device to monitor the respondent's self-reports continuously. When the demands of an experiment are low, such as viewing emotional film clips, participants can use a rating dial to report in real time on emotion (Bunce et al., 1993; Fredrickson & Kahneman, 1993). When the demands of an experiment are high (where simultaneous reporting would be too disruptive, such as during social interaction), participants can use a rating dial during a replay of the procedure. Studies of emotion in marital interaction are examples of using continuous self-reports of emotion during a video-recall technique (Gottman & Levenson, 1985; Levenson & Gottman, 1983).

One limitation to the continuous self-report techniques is that they are limited to assessing just one or two emotion dimensions. Although it is technically feasible to create a bank of rating dials, with one dial each for anger, fear, sadness, disgust, and enjoyment, a limiting factor would be the respondent's ability to track his or her discrete emotions in real time. A solution to this problem would be to collect self-reports for multiple emotions using multiple passes through a video-recall technique. This approach would no doubt test the limits of each participant's cooperation.

Multi-Item Self-Report Measures of Emotion

The majority of multi-item measures consist of lists of adjectives describing emotional states. Some are checklists, where the participant simply checks all emotions that he or she is feeling. Some measures are rating scales, where participants rate each adjective for the intensity or frequency with which the feeling applies to him or her. Although this is a large category of instruments, they are essentially variations on these two response themes: checklists or rating scales. The differences among them have to do with response scales used, the number of emotion adjectives, scale names, and the instructions, particularly the time frame.

Among the first emotion rating scales to gain research attention was the 130-item Mood Adjective Checklist (MACL; Nowlis & Green, 1957). Despite the name, the MACL is not a checklist. Users rate how they feel on the following scale: *definitely felt it, slightly, cannot decide, definitely not*. Scoring results in twelve factor scores: aggression, anxiety, surgency, elation, concentration, fatigue, social affection, sadness, skepticism, egotism, vigor, and nonchalance. Researchers have criticized the MACL for the unbalanced response format (MacKay, 1980). Other researchers propose a simple positive-negative valence scale scoring for this instrument (Stone, 1995).

A true checklist has since eclipsed the MACL in terms of popularity. Zuckerman and Lubin's Multiple Affect Adjective Checklist (MAACL) (1965) is very similar to the MACL in length, with the MACL having 130 items and the MAACL having 132. Although many of the items are the same on the two inventories, the MACL has languished, whereas the MAACL went on to become the most widely used self-report emotion assessment instrument in the 1970s and 1980s (Larsen & Sinnett, 1991). The MAACL's success was probably due to its distribution by a professional test publisher. It comes with a user manual, annotated references, history of development, and documented psychometric properties, along with scoring keys and multiple answer sheets. Another reason for its popularity might be the checklist format, which makes administering it much faster than the MACL.

The MAACL has only three subscales: depression, anxiety, and hostility. The scales are highly intercorrelated and appear to lack discriminant validity. Gotlib and Meyer (1986) factored the original

MAACL items and report two factors, which they label positive and negative affect, consistent with the labels proposed by Watson and Tellegen (1985) a few years earlier. In 1985, Zuckerman and Lubin (1985) revised the Multiple Affect Adjective Checklist. The revision mainly concerns the scoring format, which now allows for several pleasant emotion scores, as well as global positive and negative affect.

Several researchers have argued that checklists are susceptible to response sets and other forms of nonrandom error. Bentler (1969) argued against using checklists in psychometric assessment. More recently, Green, Goldman, and Salovey (1993) demonstrated that checklist mood assessments contain significant nonrandom error and conclude, "Like Bentler before us, we advise caution when researchers analyze data obtained with a checklist format" (p. 1036).

A couple other noteworthy adjective rating scales were published, including Thayer's Activation-Deactivation Adjective Checklist (1967), designed to assess the dimensions of energetic and tense arousal, and Izard's Differential Emotions Scale (1977), aimed at assessing multiple discrete emotions. Each of these scales was designed to assess emotion from the author's particular theoretical point of view.

A more recent introduction in the list of mood adjective rating scales is the Positive and Negative Affect Schedule (PANAS; Watson et al., 1988). The PANAS is based on the circumplex model of affect (Russell, 1980; Watson & Tellegen, 1985), and its strengths and weaknesses are discussed in some detail by Larsen and Diener (1992). The PANAS contains ten items on each of its two scales: positive affect (PA; high arousal pleasant) and negative affect (NA; high arousal unpleasant). The items are mood adjectives and are rated on a five-point scale, labeled *not at all or slight, a little, moderately, quite a bit,* and *very much.* The PA and NA scales were constructed to be uncorrelated, and they generally are.

Most research on the PANAS has been correlational, and the scales correlate with external variables in ways that imply validity. For example, extraversion correlates with frequent reports of PA, and neuroticism correlates with frequent reports of NA. A few studies have used the PANAS in experimental research. For example, Larsen and Ketelaar (1991) used it in an experiment wherein pleasant and unpleasant moods were induced using guided imagery techniques. They found that the positive induction increased PA but did not lower NA, and the negative induction increased NA but did not lower PA. This differential sensitivity to positive and negative emotion inductions supports the construct validity of the PANAS.

Self-report is the most efficient and easiest technique for measuring emotion. However, this techniques relies on assumptions that research participants are both willing and able to observe and report on their own emotions. Under certain circumstances, these assumptions may not hold. For example, if some emotional episode is outside conscious awareness or is not represented in working memory, participants will be unable to report on that feeling state accurately. Certain populations, for various reasons, may have meager comprehension of semantic information; very young children fall in this category. Other populations, like the very old, may not have the concentration or attention span to complete a lengthy self-report measure like the MAACL. Language can also be a problem, as when adjectives are used with participants whose principal language is not the one in which the instrument is presented. In addition to translation issues, cultural psychologists have argued that some cultures have emotions, or at least emotion terms, that are not identifiable in other cultures (Mesquita & Frijda, 1992).

Another assumption that may not be justified is the idea that all participants are willing to report on their emotions. Participants might respond to the scale on the basis of some response set, for example. The most frequently discussed response set is socially desirable responding. Here, participants respond to items in a manner that creates a positive impression rather than on the basis of how they really feel. A different response set is extreme responding, where participants may be motivated to use end points or large numbers. While some researchers have written about this, the few studies done on extreme responding on emotional trait questionnaires have found little evidence that this is a problem (Larsen & Diener, 1987). Other researchers have argued that even a small amount of extreme responding can introduce systematic distortions that can particularly affect the covariance structure of a set of ratings (Bentler, 1969).

Another potential problem is measurement reactivity—the idea that measurement alters the thing being measured. Administering an emotion rating scale that is very long, or multiple times, may alter the emotional state of interest. A second issue is measurement independence. Often, researchers want to assess emotion frequently during an experiment, especially in within-subject designs. One potential effect of repeated emotion measurement is stereotypic responding (Stone, 1995): participants settle into a response profile that does not change much across the assessment occasions. This can be assessed by examining standard deviations across assessment occasions.

Due to their ease of administration and face validity, self-rating measures of emotion will undoubtedly remain popular. Indeed, self-report may be the best method for assessing the experiential aspect of emotion, as only the person himself or herself has access to that information. So far, self-reports of emotion, particularly using the PANAS, have been popular in I/O research. Other techniques, however, are useful for assessing other aspects of emotion that should not be overlooked by I/O psychologists.

Measures of Expressed Emotion

Having an observer rate how much emotion a target participant is feeling, based on expressive cues, is an alternative to self-report. Some observers might be experts on the target person's emotional experiences (a spouse, roommate, or coworker can fall into this category), or the observer and target might be strangers. The assessment strategy is to provide the observer with relevant information about the target, such as direct observation or video recordings. Observers then make judgments about the likely emotional state of the target person (including type and intensity). Such observer reports, however, are based on social attributions of a target's emotional state. Attributions about emotion will be limited by the information available or biased by a target's impression management strategies. As such, observer ratings of emotion are probably best used in combination with other measures.

One way to limit attributions is to use trained observers. One system for training observers is the Specific Affect Coding System (SPAFF; Gottman & Krokoff, 1989; Gottman & Levenson, 1992; for a brief review, see Gottman, 1993). This system separates expressed emotion into specific categories of positive and negative categories, such as interest, affection, humor, validation, excitement/joy, anger, belligerence, domineering, contempt, disgust, tension, sadness, whining, and defensiveness. Coders trained in this system consider the totality of expressive information available, including verbal content and tone, facial displays, gesture, and posture. SPAFF training involves training in recognizing important facial, gestural, and vocal markers of emotion.

Two significant benefits to observer ratings are that they can be unobtrusive and can be used in naturalistic settings, such as work or in organizational meetings. The techniques are also inexpensive and fast, especially when they are based on gestalt impressions or a few visible cues. One drawback of observer ratings is the training required of some coding systems. In addition, the SPAFF was developed to study marital interactions, and it may not be suitable to other types of interactions, such as those between coworkers or between supervisor and worker. Studying emotions in these contexts may require the development of new coding systems.

Some expressive coding systems are based on small but distinct observable changes in facial expression. A comprehensive system for coding emotion in the face is the Facial Action Coding System (FACS; Ekman & Friesen, 1975, 1978). The FACS consists of forty-six anatomically based action units (AUs), which refer to specific observable changes in the face. For example, AU 1 raises the inner brows, AU 9 wrinkles the nose, and AU 12 raises the outer lip corners. The system requires extensive training and certification for reliable use (Ekman & Friesen, 1975, 1978). This training program is self-paced and involves learning the anatomical basis of each AU, extensive study of the forty-six AUs in photos and videotape, and rules for specifying minimal changes for scoring and combining AUs. About forty hours of initial training are required to achieve acceptable reliability and certification (Ekman & Friesen, 1975).

Facial coding can be useful in measuring emotion that is expressed in visible facial changes. However, in some situations, people may inhibit facial displays of emotions. An additional drawback is that full use of the FACS demands a lot of time and effort. FACS scoring requires about one hour of coding for each minute of videotape (depending on the density of facial action). Some research questions may not require such detailed assessment of facial expressions, and so Ekman and others have developed more global systems for coding facial action (for example, EMFACS by Ekman & Friesen, 1978; see Fridland, Ekman, & Oster, 1986; MAX by Izard, 1979). In addition, researchers are attempting to use computer vision to undertake the tiresome task of facial action coding. As of this writing, the most advanced system is that being developed at Carnegie Mellon University under the guidance of Jeffry Cohn (see Cohn, Zlochower, Lien, & Kanade, 1999); it is able to code approximately half of the FACS action units accurately and is moderately robust to out-of-plane head movements.

Facial assessments may also be obtained using physiological measures of muscle contractions using electromyography (EMG). (Detailed descriptions of facial EMG techniques may be found in Cacioppo, Petty, Losch, & Kim, 1986.) EMG is able to assess muscular contractions that are too small to produce visible changes in the face (Cacioppo et al., 1986). Researchers interested in measuring emotions with facial EMG should have training in electophysiological technique or else collaborate with someone with this expertise.

Another expressive channel with great potential as a measure of emotion, particularly in organizational or group settings, is the voice. People in organizations and groups speak to one another, and the voice may carry information about the speaker's emotional state. Vocal analysis for emotion follows one of two possible strategies. The simpler strategy is to have humans listen to audiotaped speech and evaluate the speaker's affective state. A more technologically advanced strategy is to have audiotapes digitized and analyzed by computer. The computer decomposes the sound waves into a set of acoustic parameters.

The ability of untrained listeners to recognize or infer speakers' emotional states correctly has been evaluated in several studies (Scherer, 1986; Scherer, Banse, Wallbott, & Goldbeck, 1991; van Bezooijen, 1984). In these studies, actors are used to produce sentences in a way that imparts a specific emotional tone, such as anger, fear, disgust, joy, or sadness. The speech samples are then played for naive listeners who select which emotion is intended. Correct selection rates across these studies are about 50 percent, a rate four to five times what would be expected by chance (Pittam & Scherer, 1993).

Researchers studying digital voice analysis are still searching for the parameters that best reflect emotion. Parameters typically gathered are (1) fundamental frequency, perceived as overall voice pitch;

(2) small perturbations in the fundamental frequency; (3) intensity, indexed in decibels; and (4) speech rate or tempo (Scherer, 1986). Acoustical analysis of speech effectively identifies the arousal level associated with different emotional states (Bachorowski & Owren, 1995). However, acoustical measures fall short of identifying specific emotions.

Emotion-Sensitive Tasks

A variety of behavioral tasks have been shown to be sensitive to affective states (Mayer, 1986; Mayer & Bremer, 1985; Mayer, Mamberg, & Volanth, 1988). Many of these may be of interest to I/O psychologist due to their ease of administration and their nonobvious use as indicators of emotion. Most of these emotion-sensitive tasks started out as dependent variables in experimental studies of emotion. However, many researchers view the links between performance on these tasks and emotions as reliable enough to use performance changes on the tasks as indicators that an emotional state is present.

One task is to ask participants how much they would like to engage in various behaviors, such as talk with a good friend, engage in some exercise, or have a pleasant meal. Teasdale and colleagues (Teasdale, Taylor, & Fogarty, 1980) report that this task is sensitive to depressed mood. This task supposedly works because sadness is related to the action tendency to withdraw. When depressed, people often lose interest in activities that formerly gave them pleasure. Depressed mood is also thought to be associated with depressed psychomotor function. Tasks involving coordinated psychomotor movements should therefore be sensitive to sadness or unpleasant affective states. Writing speed, for example, is a psychomotor task thought to be influenced by depressed mood. Velten (1968) used this task as one criterion measure in the validation study of his mood induction procedure. Other psychomotor tasks that have been used in emotion research include letter cancellation and smooth-pursuit motor tasks. Performance speed is most sensitive to depressed emotional state. Pleasant moods, however, do not increase psychomotor speed.

One category of emotion-sensitive tasks consists of judgment tasks. One popular strategy is to have participants make probability estimates of the likelihood of various good and bad events happening in the future. For example, participants may be asked the probability of being killed in a car crash, dying in an airplane accident, or contracting AIDS in their lifetime. It has been shown that persons in unpleasant emotional states overestimate the probability of such bad events (Johnson & Tversky, 1983). Moreover, the events do not have to be self-referential to be sensitive to affective states (Cunningham, 1988).

Another useful task is to ask participants to generate associations to positive, neutral, and negative stimuli—for example, "Write down as many words as come to mind in sixty seconds when you hear each of the following stimulus words: *happy, disappointed, generous, destroy, peace,* and *pain.*" Mayer and Bremer (1985) show that performance on this task correlates with naturally occurring mood. Seidlitz and Diener (1993) used a variation wherein participants recalled as many happy experiences from their own life as they could in a given time period. Participants higher on trait positive affect recalled more pleasant experiences in the same time period than did participants lower on trait happiness. Teasdale and colleagues (Teasdale & Fogarty, 1979; Teasdale & Russell, 1983) have also demonstrated that emotion inductions influence recall of pleasant and unpleasant memories in predictable ways.

Another strategy of assessing emotion with task performance involves various information processing parameters. Reaction times in lexical decision tasks, for example, have been shown to be sensitive to affective states (Challis & Krane, 1988). The participant's task is to judge whether a string of letters represents a word or a nonword. On each trial, the letters represent a nonword, an emotion word (such as *anger*), or a neutral word (such as *house*). Participants in positive affective states are quicker and sometimes more accurate at judging positive words compared to participants in neutral states, and vice versa for unpleasant moods (Niedenthal & Setterlund, 1994).

Another strategy is to present participants with incomplete word stems and ask them to add letters to complete the word. Word stems are selected so that they can be completed as an emotion term or a neutral term. For example, ANG__ could be completed as ANGER, ANGLE, ANGEL, or ANGLO; JO_ could be completed as JOY or JOB (Rusting & Larsen, 1998). A related technique is the use of homophones—words that sound alike but have different meanings. With this technique, the subject hears the word (*die* or *dye*, for example) and is asked to write that word. Participants in an unpleasant mood are more likely to write or complete the word stems in a manner congruent with their mood (Halberstadt, Niedenthal, & Kushner, 1995).

Physiological Measures of Emotion

It is unlikely that I/O psychologists will find much use for physiological measures of emotion. However, one paradigm that may find its way into I/O research is based on the eyeblink startle reflex. The startle reflex involves a rapid shutting of the eyes (blink), pulling the chin down, and a rapid inhalation. It is easy to elicit through the application of a sudden and loud acoustic stimulus. Startle potentiation refers to an increase in the startle response (measured as a faster or stronger blink) when the person is startled while he or she is in an unpleasant emotional state (Vrana, Spence, & Lang, 1988). The researcher most responsible for developing this technique in humans is Lang (Lang et al., 1990), who has demonstrated startle potentiation for unpleasant emotions, as well as a slowing down of the startle during positive emotions compared to neutral states. This effect had been well documented in animals for decades. Patrick has studied individual differences in startle responses, with an emphasis on psychopaths (Patrick, 1994; Patrick, Cuthbert, & Lang, 1994). Psychopaths are thought to be deficient in fear and other self-regulating negative emotions. Patrick's research demonstrates that psychopaths do not show the expected pattern of startle potentiation in fear or anxiety conditions, even though they self-report appropriately heightened fear and anxiety to threatening stimuli. The strengths of the startle technique are that it is a nonverbal, involuntary, and extremely fast measure of affective state, especially useful for assessing the pleasantness-unpleasantness dimension. However, the laboratory equipment and expertise necessary to use this technique represent a significant cost to the researcher.

Other links between emotion and bodily reaction are more indirect. Emotions are tied to tendencies to act in specific ways (fear is associated with the tendency to fight or flee), and changes in physiology occur primarily to support those actions (the increase in heart rate in fear to support the acts of fleeing or fighting; Frijda, 1988; Lazarus, 1991). This indirect association between emotion and bodily changes is sometimes evident in autonomic nervous system (ANS) activity (Cacioppo, Klein, Berntson & Hatfield, 1993). In terms of the ANS and emotion, there are two points of view. One view sees distinct emotions being associated with distinct patterns of ANS activity (James, 1884; Levenson, Ekman, & Friesen, 1990). The other view is that distinct emotions are associated with undifferentiated ANS activity (Mandler, 1975; Schacter & Singer, 1962). Empirical support for specific autonomic patterns being associated with specific emotions has been obtained in few studies. However, the cumulative data on specific emotional signatures are mixed and therefore remain inconclusive (for reviews, see Cacioppo et al., 1993; Cacioppo & Gardner, 1999; Levenson, 1992; Zajonc & McIntosh, 1992).

Many different autonomic measures have been used to assess emotion, some more fruitful than others. Because these measures are not likely to have wide appeal to I/O psychologists, interested readers should consult Cacioppo and Tassinary (1990) for more details. A main drawback to physiological measures is their invasiveness. Attaching electrodes often requires participants to disrobe partially. Measures of blood pressure use pressurized cuffs that, when inflated, can draw attention and sometimes even cause pain. In addition to invasiveness, physiological measures typically restrict participants' mobility because they are wired to amplifiers and recording devices. Also, body movement can sometimes create errors in measurement, and so participants are often required to remain immobile. There are ambulatory physiological monitors, but their reliability does not yet match laboratory-based measures, they are very expensive, and they are still subject to movement artifacts.

Conclusion

Emotion is a topic receiving attention from all quarters of psychology. The publication of this book attests to the fact that organizational psychologists have recently found emotion to be important in describing and understanding behavior in organizations. In this chapter, we have sought to illuminate some of the key issues in the field of basic emotion research, as well as some of the important individual differences in emotion. In addition, we have provided a modest review of important techniques for assessing emotion. Some of the notable trends we touched on follow:

- An increasing adoption of the dimensional model of emotion. This model is highly applicable to dispositional approaches to emotion and is also useful for understanding emotions as states. While I/O researchers may find some uses for discrete emotion theories (such as anger), the widespread application of dimensional models attests to their utility, especially the circumplex model, which is a dimensional model.
- A focus on two dimensions. Emotion researchers often debate the existence and nature of a third emotion dimension. However, there is wide consensus on the first two dimensions, or what might be called the "Big Two" emotion dimensions: PA and NA. Alternatively, with a rotation of the circumplex, two other dimensions emerge: valence (pleasant to unpleasant) and arousal (low to high). I/O researchers are starting to adopt measures of the big two emotions in their research (Warr, 1999).
- The use of experience sampling methods is also gaining wider use. This strategy involves having participants keep records of their emotions (or other experiences) repeatedly over a specified time period, such as a month or more. A related notion is the continuous measurement of emotion using techniques such as rating dials that the participant adjusts constantly to reflect his or her emotional state. The kinds of data generated using such intensive sampling techniques can be used to address unique questions that can be addressed only with such data—for example, Do emotions lead or lag behind other variables? What is the duration of the emotional effect of some event? Do emotions synchronize with other variables over time? Do emotions habituate over time?
- The differentiation of emotional sensitivity from emotional response. This application of a simple S-O-R model usefully divides up the research on emotion into the two components of sensitivity and output control. The importance of this model is that it divides emotional individual differences into those that pertain to stimulus sensitivity (the input or S-O side) and those that pertain to response magnitude (the output or O-R side). We present some evidence that two important individual differences in emotional

sensitivity are the traits of extraversion and neuroticism. On the output, or O-R, side of the model, we stressed individual differences in behaviors that regulate or influence the magnitude of emotional responses. I/O researchers might find this distinction useful, especially as they consider the role of individual differences in emotion in the workplace.

• When it comes to measurement, it is useful to consider the five relatively distinct aspects of emotion: experience, expression, behavior, cognition, and physiology. We reviewed several measures that tap these different aspects: self-report measures for experience, observation for expression, performance tasks for behavior and cognition, and physiological measures for the physiological aspect of emotion. In our opinion, the strongest research will use more than one form of measurement. Moreover, no single emotion measure can serve as the gold standard. Each measure reflects one specific facet of emotion, has its strengths and weaknesses, and, when used in isolation, provides an incomplete picture of emotion.

Emotion is a broad topic, and it can be studied from many different perspectives. Although the findings on emotion are not as well organized or interrelated as in the area of cognition, there are nevertheless issues and measures in the emotion domain on which there is consensus. We have presented these here, and we hope we have conveyed our enthusiasm for emotion research and our belief that many research areas in I/O psychology would benefit from a consideration of the role of emotion.

Note

1. Because emotions have multiple aspects (such as facial action, autonomic activity, subjective experience, behavioral tendencies), should we expect strong correlations among measures of these different components? Most researchers believe that aspects of emotion are loosely coupled and complexly interacting systems (Frijda, Knipers, & ter Schure, 1989). The various response systems (e.g., cardiac system, brain) have multiple tasks beyond being active during an emotion. Consequently, strong correlations among measures of different aspects of emotion are neither expected nor required for construct validity. While discrepancies between component measures can represent challenges to existing theories, some discrepancies can be used to index emotional dissociation, repression or psychopathology (see Bonanno,

Keltner, Holen & Horowitz, 1995; Kring & Neale, 1996; Newton & Keenan, 1991). The strongest evidence for validity occurs when the theory of the particular emotion is used to make predictions about the conditions under which that emotion will be evoked or the type of persons for whom that emotion will be most easily evoked. Combine this with measurement theory and knowledge of specific measures, and predictions may be generated and tested in specific studies.

References

Bachorowski, J., & Owren, M. J. (1995). Vocal expression of emotion: Acoustic properties of speech are associated with emotional intensity and context. *Psychological Science, 6,* 219–224.

Bentler, P. M. (1969). Semantic space is (approximately) bipolar. *Journal of Psychology, 71,* 33–40.

Bonanno, G. A., Keltner, D., Holen, A., & Horowitz, M. J. (1995). When avoiding unpleasant emotions might not be such a bad thing: Verbal-autonomic dissociation and midlife conjugal bereavement. *Journal of Personality and Social Psychology, 69,* 975–989.

Brief, A. P., Butcher, A., & Roberson, L. (1995). Cookies, disposition, and job attitudes: The effects of positive mood inducing events and negative affectivity on job satisfaction in a field experiment. *Organizational Behavior and Human Decision Processes, 62,* 55–62.

Bunce, S. C., Larsen, R, J., & Cruz, M. (1993). Individual differences in the excitation transfer effect. *Personality and Individual Differences, 15,* 507–514.

Cacioppo, J. T., & Gardner, W. L. (1999). Emotion. *Annual Review of Psychology, 50,* 191–214.

Cacioppo, J. T., Klein, D. J., Berntson, G. G., & Hatfield, E. (1993). The psychophysiology of emotion. In M. Lewis & J. M. Haviland (Eds.), *Handbook of emotions* (pp. 119–142). New York: Guilford Press.

Cacioppo, J. T., Petty, R. E., Losch, M. E., & Kim, H. S. (1986). Electromyographic activity over facial muscle regions can differentiate the valence and intensity of affective reactions. *Journal of Personality and Social Psychology, 50,* 260–268.

Cacioppo, J. T., & Tassinary, L. G. (1990). Inferring psychological significance from physiological signals. *American Psychologist, 45,* 16–28.

Challis, B. H., & Krane, R. V. (1988). Mood induction and the priming of semantic memory in a lexical decision task: Asymmetric effects of elation and depression. *Bulletin of the Psychonomic Society, 26,* 309–312.

Cohn, J. F., Zlochower, A., Lien, J., & Kanade, T. (1999). Automated face analysis by feature point tracking has high concurrent validity with manual FACS coding. *Psychophysiology, 36,* 35–43.

Cornelius, R. R. (1996). *The science of emotion.* Upper Saddle River, NJ: Prentice Hall.

Costa, P. T., & McCrae, R. R. (1980). Influence of extraversion and neuroticism on subjective well-being: Happy and unhappy people. *Journal of Personality and Social Psychology, 38,* 668–678.

Cronbach, L. J., & Meehl, P. (1955). Construct validity in psychological tests. *Psychological Bulletin, 52,* 281–302.

Cropanzano, R., James, K., & Konovsky, M. A. (1993). Dispositional affectivity as a predictor of work attitudes and job performance. *Journal of Organizational Behavior, 14,* 595–606.

Cunningham, M. R. (1988). What do you do when you're happy or blue? Mood, expectancies, and behavioral interest. *Motivation and Emotion, 12,* 309–331.

Damasio, A. R. (1994). *Descartes' error: Emotion, reason, and the human brain.* New York: Putnam.

Depue, R. A. (1996). A neurobiological framework for the structure of personality and emotion: Implications for personality disorders. In J. F. Clarkin & M. F. Lenzenweger (Eds.), *Major theories of personality disorder* (pp. 347–390). New York: Guilford Press.

Diener, E. (1999). Introduction to the special section on the structure of emotion. *Journal of Personality and Social Psychology, 76,* 803–804.

Ekman, P., & Davidson, R. J. (1994). *The nature of emotion: Fundamental questions.* New York: Oxford University Press.

Ekman, P., & Friesen, W. V. (1975). *Unmasking the face.* Upper Saddle River, NJ: Prentice-Hall.

Ekman, P., & Friesen, W. V. (1978). *Facial action coding system.* Palo Alto, CA: Consulting Psychologists Press.

Ekman, P., Friesen, W. V., & Ancoli, S. (1980). Facial signs of emotional experience. *Journal of Personality and Social Psychology, 39,* 1124–1134.

Ekman, P., Levinson, R. W., & Friesen, W. (1983). Autonomic nervous system activity distinguishes among emotions. *Science, 221,* 1208–1210.

Ekman, P., & Rosenberg, E. L. (Eds.). (1997). *What the face reveals: Basic and applied studies of spontaneous facial expressions using the Facial Action Coding System (FACS).* New York: Oxford University Press.

Eysenck, H. J. (1967). *The biological bases of personality.* Springfield, IL: Charles C. Thomas.

Fredrickson, B. L. (2001). The role of positive emotions in positive psychology: The broaden-and-build theory of positive emotions. *American Psychologist, 56,* 218–226.

Fredrickson, B. L., & Kahneman, D. (1993). Duration neglect in retrospective evaluations of affective episodes. *Journal of Personality and Social Psychology, 65,* 45–55.

Fridland, A. J., Ekman, F., & Oster, H. (1986). Facial expressions of emotion: Review of literature, 1970–1983. In A. Siegman & S. Feldstein (Eds.), *Nonverbal behavior and communication* (pp. 143–223). Hillsdale, NJ: Erlbaum.

Frijda, N. H. (1988). The laws of emotion. *American Psychologist, 43,* 349–358.

Frijda, N. H., Kuipers, P., & ter Schure, E. (1989). Relations among emotion, appraisal, and emotional action readiness. *Journal of Personality and Social Psychology, 57,* 212–229.

George, J. M. (1996). Trait and state affect. In K. R. Murphy (Ed.), *Individual differences and behavior in organizations* (pp. 145–171). San Francisco: Jossey-Bass.

Goleman, D. (1995). *Emotional intelligence.* New York: Bantam Books.

Goleman, D. (1998). *Working with emotional intelligence.* New York: Bantam Books.

Gotlib, I., & Meyer, J. (1986). Factor analysis of the Multiple Affect Adjective Check List: A separation of positive and negative affect. *Journal of Personality and Social Psychology, 50,* 1161–1165.

Gottman, J. M. (1993). Studying emotion in social interaction. In M. Lewis & J. M. Haviland (Eds.), *Handbook of emotions* (pp. 475–487). New York: Guilford Press.

Gottman, J. M., & Krokoff, L. (1989). Marital interaction and marital satisfaction: A longitudinal view. *Journal of Consulting and Clinical Psychology, 57,* 47–52.

Gottman, J. M., & Levenson, R. W. (1985). A valid measure for obtaining self-report of affect. *Journal of Consulting and Clinical Psychology, 53,* 151–160.

Gottman, J. M., & Levenson, R. W. (1992). Marital processes predictive of later dissolution: Behavior, physiology and health. *Journal of Personality and Social Psychology, 63,* 221–233.

Gray, J. A. (1981). A critique of Eysenck's theory of personality. In H. J. Eysenck (Ed.), *A model for personality* (pp. 246–276). New York: Springer-Verlag.

Gray, J. A. (1990). Brain systems that mediate both emotion and cognition. *Motivation and Emotion, 4,* 269–288.

Gray, J. A. (1994). Personality dimensions and emotion systems. In P. Ekman & R. J. Davidson (Eds.), *The nature of emotion: Fundamental questions* (pp. 329–331). New York: Oxford University Press.

Green, D. P., Goldman, S. L., & Salovey, P. (1993). Measurement error masks bipolarity in affect ratings. *Journal of Personality and Social Psychology, 64,* 1029–1041.

Gross, J. J., & Leverson, R. W. (1993). Emotional suppression: Physiology, self-report, and expressive behavior. *Journal of Personality and Social Psychology, 64,* 970–986.

Halberstadt, J. B., Niedenthal, P. M., & Kushner, J. (1995). Resolution of lexical ambiguity by emotional state. *Psychological Science, 6,* 278–282.

Izard, C. E. (1977). *Human emotions.* New York: Plenum.

Izard, C. E. (1979). *The Maximally Discriminative Facial Movement Coding System (MAX).* Newark: Instructional Resources Center, University of Delaware.

James, W. (1884). What is an emotion? *Mind, 9,* 188–205.

Johnson, E. J., & Tversky, A. (1983). Affect, generalization, and the perception of risk. *Journal of Personality and Social Psychology, 45,* 21–31.

Judge, T. A., & Cable, D. M. (1997). Applicant personality, organizational culture, and organization attraction. *Personnel Psychology, 50,* 359–394.

Judge, T. A., & Larsen, R. J. (2001). Dispositional affect and job satisfaction: A review and theoretical extension. *Organizational Behavior and Human Decision Processes, 86,* 67–98.

Judge, T. A., & Locke, E. A. (1993). Effect of dysfunctional thought processes on subjective well-being and job satisfaction. *Journal of Applied Psychology, 78,* 475–490.

Judge, T. A., & Watanable, S. (1993). Another look at the job satisfaction/life satisfaction relationship. *Journal of Applied Psychology, 78,* 939–948.

Kleinginna, P. R., & Kleinginna, A. M. (1981). A categorized list of emotion definitions, with suggestions for a consensual definition. *Motivation and Emotion, 5,* 345–379.

Kring, A. M., & Neale, J. M. (1996). Do schizophrenic patients show a disjunctive relationship among expressive, experiential, and psychophysiological components of emotion? *Journal of Abnormal Psychology, 105,* 249–257.

Lang, P. J., Bradley, M. M., & Cuthbert, B. N. (1990). Emotion, attention, and the startle reflex. *Psychological Review, 97,* 377–395.

Lang, P. J., Bradley, M. M., & Cuthbert, B. N. (1992). A motivational analysis of emotion: Reflex-cortex connections. *Psychological Science, 3,* 44–49.

Larsen, R. J. (2000a). Emotion and personality: Introduction to the special symposium. *Personality and Social Psychology Bulletin, 26,* 651–654.

Larsen, R. J. (2000b). Toward a science of mood regulation. *Psychological Inquiry, 11,* 129–141.

Larsen, R. J. (2000c). Maintaining hedonic balance. *Psychological Inquiry, 11,* 218–225.

Larsen, R. J., & Buss, D. A. (2001). *Personality psychology: Domains of knowledge about human nature.* New York: McGraw-Hill.

Larsen, R. J., & Diener, E. (1987). Affect intensity as an individual difference characteristic: A review. *Journal of Research in Personality, 21,* 1–39.

Larsen, R. J., & Diener, E. (1992). Problems and promises with the circumplex model of emotion. *Review of Personality and Social Psychology, 13,* 25–59.

Larsen, R. J., & Fredrickson, B. L. (1999). Measurement issues in emotion research. In D. Kahneman, E. Diener, & N. Schwarz (Eds.), *Understanding quality of life: Scientific perspectives on enjoyment and suffering.* New York: Russell Sage Foundation.

Larsen, R. J., & Gschwandtner, L. B. (1995, March). A better day. *Personal Selling Power,* pp. 41–49.

Larsen, R. J., & Ketelaar, T. (1989). Extraversion, neuroticism, and susceptibility to positive and negative mood induction procedures. *Personality and Individual Differences, 10,* 1221–1228.

Larsen, R. J., & Ketelaar, T. (1991). Personality and susceptibility to positive and negative emotional states. *Journal of Personality and Social Psychology, 61,* 132–140.

Larsen, R. J., & Sinnett, L. (1991). Meta-analysis of manipulation validity: Factors affecting the Velten mood induction procedure. *Personality and Social Psychology Bulletin, 17,* 323–334.

Lazarus, R. S. (1991). *Emotion and adaptation.* New York: Oxford University Press.

Levenson, R. W. (1992). Autonomic nervous system patterning in emotion. *Psychological Science, 3,* 23–27.

Levenson, R. W., Ekman, P., & Friesen, W. V. (1990). Voluntary facial action generates emotion-specific autonomic nervous system activity. *Psychophysiology, 27,* 363–384.

Levenson, R. W., & Gottman, J. M. (1983). Marital interaction: Physiological linkage and affective exchange. *Journal of Personality and Social Psychology, 45,* 587–597.

MacKay, C. J. (1980). The measurement of mood and psychophysiological activity using self-report techniques. In I. Martin & P. Venables (Eds.), *Techniques in psychophysiology* (pp. 501–562). New York: Wiley.

Mandler, G. (1975). *Mind and emotion.* New York: Wiley.

Mayer, J. D. (1986). How mood influences cognition. In N. E. Sharkey (Ed.), *Advances in cognitive science* (pp. 290–314). Chichester, England: Ellis Horwood.

Mayer, J. D., & Bremer, D. (1985). Assessing mood with affect-sensitive tasks. *Journal of Personality Assessment, 49,* 95–99.

Mayer, J. D., Mamberg, M. M., & Volanth, A. J. (1988). Cognitive domains of the mood system. *Journal of Personality, 9,* 261–275.

Meehl, P. E. (1978). Theoretical risks and tabular asterisks: Sir Karl, Sir Ronald, and the slow progress of soft psychology. *Journal of Consulting and Clinical Psychology, 46,* 806–834.

Mesquita, B., & Frijda, N. H. (1992). Cultural variations in emotions: A review. *Psychological Bulletin, 112,* 179–204.

Morris, W. N. (1989). *Mood: The frame of mind.* New York: Springer-Verlag.

Morris, W. N., & Reilly, N. P. (1987). Toward the self-regulation of mood: Theory and research. *Motivation and Emotion, 11,* 215–249.

Necowitz, L. B., & Roznowski, M. (1994). Negative affectivity and job satisfaction: Cognitive processes underlying the relationship and effects on employee behaviors. *Journal of Vocational Behavior, 45,* 270–294.

Newton, T., & Keenan, T. (1991). Further analyses of the dispositional argument in organizational behavior. *Journal of Applied Psychology, 76,* 781–787.

Niedenthal, P. M., & Setterlund, M. B. (1994). Emotion congruence in perception. *Personality and Social Psychology Bulletin, 20,* 401–411.

Nowlis, V., & Green, R. (1957). *The experimental analysis of mood* (Tech. Rep. No. Nonr-668(12)). Washington, DC: Office of Naval Research.

Patrick, C. J. (1994). Emotion and psychopathy: Startling new insights. *Psychophysiology, 31,* 319–330.

Patrick, C. J., Cuthbert, B. N., & Lang, P. J. (1994). Emotion in the criminal psychopath: Fear image processing. *Journal of Abnormal Psychology, 103,* 523–534.

Pittam, J., & Scherer, K. R. (1993). Vocal expression and communication of emotion. In M. Lewis & J. M. Haviland (Eds.), *Handbook of emotions* (pp. 185–197). New York: Guilford Press.

Reeve, J. (1997). *Understanding motivation and emotion* (2nd ed.). Fort Worth, TX: Harcourt, Brace.

Russell, J. A. (1978). Evidence of convergent validity on the dimensions of affect. *Journal of Personality and Social Psychology, 36,* 1152–1168.

Russell, J. A. (1980). A circumplex model of affect. *Journal of Personality and Social Psychology, 39,* 1161–1178.

Rusting, C. L., & Larsen, R. J. (1997). Extraversion, neuroticism, and susceptibility to positive and negative affect: A test of two theoretical models. *Personality and Individual Differences, 22,* 607–612.

Rusting, C. L., & Larsen, R. J. (1998). Personality and cognitive processing of affective information. *Personality and Social Psychology Bulletin, 24,* 200–213.

Schachter, S., & Singer, J. E. (1962). Cognitive, social, and physiological determinants of emotional state. *Psychological Review, 69,* 379–399.

Scherer, K. R. (1986). Vocal affect expression: A review and a model for future research. *Psychological Bulletin, 99,* 143–165.

Scherer, K. R., Banse, R., Wallbott, H. G., & Goldbect, T. (1991). Vocal cues in emotion encoding and decoding. *Motivation and Emotion, 15,* 123–148.

Schultz, J. S. (1993). Situational and dispositional predictions of performance: A test of the hypothesized Machiavellianism × structure interaction among sales persons. *Journal of Applied Social Psychology, 23,* 478–498.

Seidlitz, L., & Diener, E. (1993). Memory for positive versus negative life events: Theories for the difference between happy and unhappy persons. *Journal of Personality and Social Psychology, 64,* 654–663.

Stewart, G. L. (1996). Reward structure as a moderator of the relationship between extraversion and sales performance. *Journal of Applied Psychology, 81,* 619–627.

Stone, A. A. (1995). Measures of affective response. In S. Cohen, R. Kessler, & L. Gordon (Eds.), *Measuring stress: A guide for health and social scientists* (pp. 148–171). Cambridge: Cambridge University Press.

Teasdale, J. D., & Fogarty, S. J. (1979). Differential effects of induced mood on retrieval of pleasant and unpleasant events from episodic memory. *Journal of Abnormal Psychology, 88,* 248–257.

Teasdale, J. D., & Russell, M. L. (1983). Differential effects of induced mood on the recall of positive, negative and neutral words. *British Journal of Clinical Psychology, 22,* 163–171.

Teasdale, J. D., Taylor, R., & Fogarty, S. J. (1980). Effects of induced elation-depression of the accessibility of memories of happy and unhappy experiences. *Behavior Research and Therapy, 18,* 339–346.

Tellegen, A. (1985). Structures of mood and personality and their relevance to assessing anxiety, with an emphasis on self-report. In A. H. Tuma & J. D. Maser (Eds.), *Anxiety and the anxiety disorders* (pp. 681–706). Hillsdale, NJ: Erlbaum.

Thayer, R. E. (1967). Measurement of activation through self-report. *Psychological Reports, 20,* 663–678.

Thayer, R. E. (1996). *The origin of everyday moods: Managing energy, tension, and stress.* New York: Oxford University Press.

Tomkins, S. S. (1981). The quest for primary motives: Biography and autobiography of an idea. *Journal of Personality and Social Psychology, 41,* 306–329.

van Bezooijen, R. (1984). *The characteristics and recognizability of vocal expression of emotions.* Dordrecht, Netherlands: Foris.

Velten, E. (1968). A laboratory task for the induction of mood states. *Behavior Research and Therapy, 6,* 473–482.

Venables, P. H. (1984). Arousal: An examination of its status as a concept. In M.G.H. Coles, J. R. Jennings, & J. A. Stern (Eds.), *Psychophysiological perspectives* (pp. 134–142). New York: Van Nostrand Reinhold

Vrana, S. R., Spence, E. L., & Lang, P. J. (1988). The startle probe response: A new measure of emotion? *Journal of Abnormal Psychology, 97,* 487–491.

Warr, P. (1999). Well-being in the workplace. In D. Kahneman, E. Diener, & N. Schwarz (Eds.), *Well-being: The foundations of hedonic psychology* (pp. 392–412). New York: Russell Sage Foundation.

Watson, D. (2000). *Mood and temperament.* New York: Guilford Press.

Watson, D., Clark, L. A., & Tellegen, A. (1988). Development and validation of brief measures of positive and negative affect: The PANAS Scales. *Journal of Personality and Social Psychology, 54,* 1063–1070.

Watson, D., & Tellegen, A. (1985). Toward a consensual structure of mood. *Psychological Bulletin, 98,* 219–235.

Weiss, H. M., & Cropanzano, R. (1996). Affective events theory: A theoretical discussion of the structure, causes, and consequences of affective experiences at work. *Research in Organizational Behavior, 18,* 1–74.

Wilson, D. S., Near, D., & Miller, R. R. (1996). Machiavellianism: A synthesis of the evolutionary and psychological literatures. *Psychological Bulletin, 119,* 285–299.

Zajonc, R. B., & McIntosh, D. N. (1992). Emotions research: Some promising questions and some questionable promises. *Psychological Science, 3,* 70–74.

Zelenski, J. M., & Larsen, R. J. (1999). Susceptibility to affect: A comparison of three personality taxonomies. *Journal of Personality, 67,* 761–791.

Zelenski, J. M., & Larsen, R. J. (2000). The distribution of emotions in everyday life: A state and trait perspective from experience sampling data. *Journal of Research in Personality, 34,* 178–197.

Zuckerman, M., & Lubin, B. (1965). *The Multiple Affect Adjective Check List.* San Diego, CA: Educational and Industrial Testing Service.

Zuckerman, M., & Lubin, B. (1985). *Manual for the Multiple Affect Adjective Checklist-Revised.* San Diego, CA: Educational and Industrial Testing Service.

PART 2

Individual and Multiperson Regulatory Processes

The regulation of emotions in work situations is a complex process that uses an ancient neurochemical technology tuned by modern socialization and learning processes. These capacities are then applied in rapidly changing environments that, except for face-to-face encounters, rely on communications media (print, telephone, e-mail) that are extremely new from a historical perspective. Emotional regulation generally occurs in the context of multiple work demands and may involve interactions with relatively unfamiliar individuals (customers). A further complication arises because emotions are rapidly occurring processes, and self-regulatory processes often rely on slower, deliberative cognitive activity. A final complication is that a key component of emotional communication, facial expression, may be designed by evolution to encode and decode a number of emotions automatically (Cosmides & Tooby, 2000).

Consequently, emotional regulation, particularly under trying situations, is a challenge for the human architecture. Social and organizational processes must therefore create many explicit norms and rules for feeling and displaying emotions, and individuals must effectively learn these multiple requirements for emotions at work to be regulated effectively. Emotional regulation in family situations (see MacDermid, Seery, and Weiss, Chapter Twelve, this volume) has similar requirements, which are especially challenging when emotions are negative and extreme. The following three chapters develop a basis for understanding emotions and emotional regulation at multiple levels involving intraindividual information processing (Chapter Four), personality and dyadic processes (Chapter Five), and group and organizational factors (Chapter Six). We believe this multilevel perspective is needed to understand both problems with and opportunities for effective emotional regulation at work.

In Chapter Four, Lord and Harvey adopt an information processing approach to understanding emotions and emotional regulation. They structure this topic by positing that three qualitatively different information processing architectures are involved in experiencing and regulating emotions and cognitions: emotional, connectionist, and symbolic architectures. Architectures are the fixed structures that provide the frame for cognitive processing. They are generally described in terms of functions (memory capacities, nature of units, permissible operations, learning and interpretative processes, and means for interaction with the external world) rather than underlying physical systems (neural circuits). *Emotional architectures* incorporate human learning into a genetically based memory system with very fast and reliable operating processes that rely on dedicated, domain-specific systems. Emotional architectures can rapidly orient an individual toward an external environment and quickly initiate appropriate responses, both social and individual. The emotional architecture is ideally configured to be a superordinate system for structuring other cognitive operations because it can operate faster and therefore adjust more rapidly to internal and external environments.

Connectionist architectures are based on networks of neuron-like units developed over time through consistent learning experiences. They are intermediate in processing speed because they rely on parallel processing in which all units in a network can operate at the same time. Because they learn slowly, connectionist networks are ideal for extracting statistical regularities from experienced environments. Such regularities are critical in developing appropriate perceptual (categories, schemas, norms) or behavioral (scripts, condition-action productions) systems. Thus, processes such as socialization, repetition-based learning, and extraction of linguistic or social structures may be best conceptualized as involving connectionist architectures.

Connectionist architectures provide an overlay to emotional architectures that can translate their operation into modern circumstances (fear of guns rather than snakes). Because connectionist architectures operate automatically and through multiple networks, they are ideally suited for grounding emotional systems in contemporary contexts. *Symbolic architectures* allow the conscious manipulation of symbols according to a variety of rules (such as addition or subtraction of numbers). They operate slowly and serially, with one operation and then another. Their strength is analytic, cognitive processing, and the orientation of individuals to their particular moment-to-moment circumstances. Conscious intentions can activate or deactivate specific neural networks using automatic procedures that are by-products of current goals or more resource-demanding intentional processes. Connectionist processes can also automatically prime symbolic level cognitions. Thus, there is a two-way flow of regulation between these two architectures.

Lord and Harvey explain that the experience and regulation of emotions is a joint function of all three architectures. Emotional architectures may quickly orient an individual to an important environmental event while simultaneously preparing response systems, connectionist architectures may automatically compute a primary appraisal and initiate categorical responses, and slower-acting symbolic processes may further refine reactions through secondary appraisal and attempts to modify response programs that are already being executed. The decoding of emotions and encoding of emotion-based responses using these multiple systems and characteristic time frame poses many social challenges and opportunities. Both positive and negative emotions can be socially communicated with automatic, unintentional connectionist-based processes, creating a genuine and adaptive aspect of social interactions. Yet genuine, immediate reactions may not always serve higher-level business or societal needs or even an individual's current goals. Thus, workers must often alter or suppress their more immediate emotional reactions using symbolic-level processes. Consequently, issues like emotional labor, which involve work with a strong emotional regulation component, have become popular applied topics as we move to a more service-based economy. A strength of the Lord and Harvey framework is that by translating emotional labor into the interplay between various architectures, we not only gain greater understanding of work-related emotional labor, we can also broaden our perspective to see emotional regulation as part of all intra- and interindividual self-regulatory activities.

In Chapter Five, Pugh examines emotional regulation at individual and dyadic levels. Like the stimulus-organism-response model that Larsen, Diener, and Lucas present in Chapter Three, Pugh's approach separates emotional regulation into input and output processes and stresses the difference between automatic and controlled processes, which can be equated with the effects of connectionist and symbolic-level architectures, respectively. Pugh notes that input to felt emotions may involve both automatic, unconscious processes and controlled, conscious processes such as stimulus appraisal. Response output also involves both automatic and controlled processes. Expression of emotions is subject to display rules that may involve the automatic use of well-learned social norms when in the presence of others, or when in organizational contexts, more specific organizational display rules may be used. The use of organizational display rules generally requires the conscious suppression of response tendencies, because organizational norms are not as well practiced as social norms. Pugh also reviews evidence indicating that conscious suppression has greater costs in terms of consuming cognitive resources and creating greater stress on an individual.

Pugh's framework emphasizes the task environment as an important causal factor for the generation of emotional experience. He notes that sensitivity to many aspects of task environments occurs outside conscious awareness, and thus, workers are not aware of the need to regulate such responses, a phenomenon that probably is produced by more primitive emotional and connectionist architectures. Interestingly, Pugh notes that such unconscious affective priming often has more of an effect on attitudes and behaviors than affect from a known source. Known sources of affect are more likely to be regulated through explicit, controlled processes, but as he explains, this regulation requires symbolic-level, conscious resources, and it can often have ironic rebound effects when such resources are later allocated to other tasks. One explanation for such effects may be that ironic monitoring processes co-opt emotional and connectionist architectures to detect stimuli capable of producing the suppressed emotions. When competing attentional demands decouple these processes from symbolic-level control, they continue to operate, ironically producing the to-be-suppressed emotion. Thus, as Pugh notes, a busy but inexperienced service worker engaged in emotional labor may experience precisely the type of emotions he or she is guarding against, and this ironic experience is particularly likely when a worker's task environment has many competing, symbolic-level tasks that demand attention, such as computing the correct change for a customer.

Pugh's chapter builds on his careful treatment of task environments by considering the effects of one's dyadic partner. One critical effect is *emotional contagion,* a process by which one dyadic partner automatically "catches" the emotion expressed by the other, often without either party's being aware of this process. While this means of homogenizing emotional experience may have been effective for an ancestral dyad (or group) by allowing automatic responses to emotional cues from any member of a social unit, it may have undesirable consequences in modern organizations. For example, customers may catch the negative emotions of service workers, and since this process is automatic, it may affect attitudes toward an organization or its product rather than being attributed by the customer to a service worker's bad mood. Pugh also notes that emotional contagion is particularly likely to occur under situations with high cognitive load, so that supervisor-subordinate dyads working under high demands may become infected with negative emotions, which may then be attributed to qualities of the dyad rather than the demanding task. Contagion is produced by expressed emotional responses. Pugh notes that there are stable individual differences in the tendency to express emotions, which can be expected to have widespread effects on social processes such as emotional contagion or the ability for others to perceive one's emotions accurately. Research finds that women express both positive and negative emotions to a greater extent than men do (which might be thought of in terms of genetic differences in emotional architectures), but Pugh notes that this tendency appears to be modified by socialization (implying more of a connectionist-level explanation). Men are more likely to express powerful emotions such as anger or pride, and women are more likely to express less powerful emotions such as liking or warmth. By such processes, men and women may be perceived to be more differentiated in terms of stereotypical emotions than they actually are. In sum, Pugh's treatment of emotions and emotional regulation nicely illustrates both the subtle interplay between alternative types of cognitive architectures and the generalization of individual self-regulation tendencies to the expression and regulation of social processes.

Chapter Six by George extends the treatment of social aspects of emotional regulation by examining group and organizational processes. She emphasizes that groups are the building blocks of organizations and that group dynamics and affect are reciprocally related. Like Pugh, she also emphasizes that emotions are regulated by both automatic and controlled processes, implying that multiple architectures are used to integrate affective processes and group dynamics. George stresses that affect has multiple functions in face-to-face work groups. Affect unites individuals, creating a collective meaning and clarifying group boundaries; it signals appraisals of circumstances as well as relations with other group members; it manifests and reinforces roles and status differences; and it also influences cognitive and decision-making processes by evoking shared schema. These multiple functions of face-to-face work groups are also illustrated in courageous, norm-violating actions at work (see Worline, Wrzesniewski, and Rafaeli, Chapter Nine, this volume).

Several automatic and controlled processes are associated with these functions. George notes that primitive emotional contagion is a critical process that automatically links the mimicking of facial, vocal, and postural expressions of others with one's actual felt emotions. Emotions also reflect a secondary response to common group tasks, outcomes, and events. These secondary responses generally reflect automatic processes, since controlled processing capacity tends to be focused on the primary work demands of groups. Vicarious processes associated with learning and emotional empathy comprise a third automatic means by which group affect develops. George also discusses four intentional, controlled processes that influence the affective experience of group members: (1) group composition effects, such as personality composition, attraction-selection attrition processes, and leader affect; (2) interpersonal processes related to social comparisons and socialization; (3) normative processes pertaining to feeling rules, expression rules, and surface versus deep acting; and (4) power and status relations. Although her focus is on group-level affect, George also identifies analogous organizational-level processes that affect emotional regulation.

Importantly, George explains that these multiple group and organizational processes do not always produce homogeneous group affect, because there are also powerful factors that seek to assert the primacy of an autonomous self. Variability in affective tone also exists across groups, because of differential relations with group effectiveness and also because the nature of group context may create substantial differences in the intensity of group interactions or the nature of group processes; for example, some groups may interact using technologically mediated rather than face-to-face processes. George also notes that group affect is understudied by individuals interested in organizational behavior, in part because affective processes at this level are less apparent than at individual levels. Nevertheless, group- and organizational-level processes are essential to understand because the affective culture they develop can engage a variety of cognitive and motivational processes in individuals. This point is echoed in subsequent chapters that examine courageous actions (Chapter Nine), organizational socialization processes (Chapter Ten), cross-cultural effects on emotions (Chapter Eleven), and the effects of family processes on work behavior (Chapter Twelve).

Reference

Cosmides, L., & Tooby, J. (2000). Evolutionary psychology and emotions. In M. Lewis & J. M. Haviland-Jones (Eds.), *Handbook of emotions* (2nd ed., pp. 91–115). New York: Guilford Press.

CHAPTER 4

An Information Processing Framework for Emotional Regulation

Robert G. Lord
Jennifer L. Harvey

In this chapter, we discuss how emotions and cognitive processes interact by integrating two frameworks that have been discussed by various groups of psychologists: cognitive architectures (Newell, 1990; McClelland & Rumelhart, 1986) and models of emotions (Izard, 1993) and emotional regulation (Gross, 1998). Different architectures allow for processes with differential speeds of operation and reliance on prior experience. Similarly, various components producing or regulating emotions also operate with different speeds and necessitate different types of learning. To understand how this framework translates into behavior in organizations, we follow Scherer's suggestion (1994) that strength of emotions influences the latency between releasing stimuli and behavior. Stronger emotions therefore require more rapid cognitive processing, which limits both the type of architectures that can be used and the range of potential behaviors. We begin with an example illustrating the interplay between information processing factors and emotions and the moderating aspects of context. Then we turn to discussions of cognitive architectures and models of emotional experience and regulation but first we need to explain how we are conceptualizing emotions.

Emotions have been defined in a number of ways. These definitions may emphasize underlying components (Izard, 1993; Russell

& Barrett, 1999) or short-lived response tendencies with functional importance (Frijda, 1986; James, 1884, 1894; Levenson, 1994; Scherer, 1984), or they may contrast emotions to other terms, such as *mood* or *affect* (Gross, 1998). We adopt the approach that emphasizes underlying components because of its value in understanding how components relate to emotional regulation. Other approaches also have substantial liabilities. For example, emphasizing response tendencies may work well for negative emotions, but it is less appropriate for understanding the importance of positive emotions (Fredrickson, 1998). Following Izard (1993), we conceptualize emotion as involving three basic processes: a neural substrate, an expressive or motor component, and an experiential component. Although some researchers suggest that a cognitive appraisal is a necessary precondition for emotions (Lazarus, 1984), Izard argues that this is not a necessary requirement for emotions, although he suggests that the interaction of emotions and cognitions is common.

Cognitions, Emotions, and Context

Emotions occur in context, and the relevant context establishes the intensity of emotions and the time parameters in which events and processes must occur in order to have meaning. The intensity and time parameters thereby encourage or limit the manner in which emotions can be perceived and regulated. For example, consider the well-discussed phenomenon of road rage. When driving, we are primed to respond quickly to internal and external signals, often before we can consciously evaluate such signals. Emotions, being an internal signal, help us react quickly to potential danger without having to think consciously about our actions: emotions come to the surface, and we respond. For example, someone cuts in front of us when driving, we slam on our brakes, and label the person with a name or respond with a gesture, all before we have had time to think carefully about the situation.

This example demonstrates the positive aspect of emotions in that they cue the appropriate response and prepare the body for that response—in the example, attention to the situation and strength to slam on the brake. They also illustrate the principle of

Scherer (1994) that emotions provide a flexible interface linking environments to behavior. As briefly explained in Chapter One (see Figure 1.1), strong emotions reliably and rapidly release instrumental responses, often before they can be regulated by slower cognitive processes. Road rage, by definition, is a strong emotion and should provoke a rapid response. However, the resulting emotion can also linger and become an underlying influence on subsequent cognition. As in the example, our emotions influence our cognitions of the other driver and as a result lead us to a very negative construal of this person. Yet if we subsequently reappraise the situation after the threat of an accident has passed, our cognitions may alter our emotions. For instance, suppose we notice that the driver who cut in front of us is an older person. This new information may change our thoughts from blaming the person to excusing the person, which may trigger emotions such as compassion or pity rather than anger. On the other hand, suppose we notice instead that the driver was using a cellular phone. This new information may increase blame of the individual, accentuate our anger and hostility, and produce an even worse construal of the other driver.

Thus, there is a continual interplay between cognitions and emotions, and the causal arrow between emotions and cognitions can go in either direction. Such inconsistencies in processes suggest that a simple flow diagram that sequences the effects of alternative components (stimulus → emotions → cognitions) is unlikely to be an adequate description of the interplay between cognitions and emotions as they unfold over time. Instead, we are better served by viewing stimuli, cognitions, emotions, and behavior as involving the continual interactions of various systems (perceptual, cognitive, emotional, and behavioral systems) and searching for principles that help us understand the functioning and interrelation of such systems.

Cognitive and computer scientists who have struggled with such issues have recognized that understanding information processing and intelligent behavior often requires more than just an explication of specific processes, choices, sequences, or acquired knowledge. In addition, it often requires an assessment of the nature of the technology or architecture that produces these cognitive activities.

Alternative Architectures for Regulating Emotions

Many theories of emotion or emotion regulation include cognitive processing constructs; however, a comprehensive information processing approach analyzes cognitive processing at a deeper level. Specifically, it begins with an assessment of the human information processing technology or the constraints and affordances provided by the human hardware that implements processing operations. In this section, we develop such an approach to understanding emotions.

Human Architectures

Architectures are the fixed structure that provides the frame for cognitive processing. They are generally described in terms of functions (memory capacities, nature of units, permissible operations, learning and interpretative processes, and means for interaction with the external world) rather than underlying physical systems (neural circuits). Human architectures generally specify at least three aspects of the systems that implement processing operations. First, they describe the *memory systems* and the means by which information is stored and retrieved (or recreated) from memory. For example, traditional symbolic architectures often include a long-term memory unit with very large capacity, slow input, and fast but often unreliable retrieval. They also include a short-term or working memory unit with very limited capacity, easy input and retrieval of information, and the capacity to store information for only a few seconds. Second, architectures specify *basic operations,* or operations that the system can perform with high efficiency and speed because there are dedicated mechanisms associated with these operations. For example, the interpretation of basic emotions expressed by facial expressions may be so fundamental to human existence that dedicated units have developed to perceive emotions efficiently and extremely quickly (for example, in 5 to 10 milliseconds; Edwards, 1990). Third, architectures specify the means of *sequencing cognitive operations* (often called *control mechanisms* by cognitive scientists), providing order, coherence, and purpose to information processing. For example, it is common for processing procedures to be triggered automatically whenever the contents of working memory (which include current goals, thoughts, and sensory inputs) match a unique pattern associated with that processing procedure. Control then becomes an emergent property of the entire system rather than the function of a separate executive processing unit.

We used the plural term *architectures* in the heading to this section to emphasize that human processing technology is a result of evolutionary forces that occurred in the distant past to create many specialized processing units for tasks with evolutionary importance (Churchland & Sejnowski, 1992). These multiple task-specific units may have different architectural parameters, but they also must operate as a system to achieve most contemporary processing requirements. These qualities can be seen in the operation of fear responses, which often begin with very fast-acting stimulus perception, which automatically prepares the body for extreme exertion in the form of aggression or withdrawal. These responses are implemented by relatively primitive architectures that operate in a few milliseconds and involve little conscious control or explicit reasoning. However, once initiated by primitive systems, fear responses often involve an additional component, such as cognitive appraisal (Lazarus, 1991), that involves higher-level neocortical systems that are responsible for conscious, deliberate processing. These higher-level processes interpret fear within the current task, social, and motivational context. Emotions and emotional regulation emerge through the interaction of multiple systems.

Table 4.1 specifies key qualities of three very different types of architectures—symbolic, connectionist, and emotion—that have been offered as explanations for information processing. Rather than being competing explanations, we maintain that all three are needed to understand emotions, but they may apply to different components of the processes that lead to emotions and emotion regulation.

Symbolic Architectures

This higher-level architecture is probably most familiar to scientists and corresponds most closely with lay theories of emotional regulation as well. It is the means by which conscious, purposeful information processes are used to create rule-based procedures for operating on sensory-motor information or information retrieved

Table 4.1. Parameters of Symbolic, Connectionist, and Emotional Architectures.

	Symbolic	Connectionist	Emotional
Time frame	500 milliseconds to 10 seconds	200 to 500 milliseconds	As fast as 10 milliseconds
Supporting technology	Register-based system that retrieves, transforms in rule-based manner, and restores symbol structures	Relaxation system that iteratively satisfies a large number of weak constraints by transmitting activation and inhibition among units	Functionally coherent neuroanatomical and neurochemical circuits with direct connections to expressive and motivational systems and optional connections to cognitive systems
Memory systems	Separate units	Activation (inhibition) pattern	Neurochemical
Storage/learning	New symbol structures created	Weighted connections change	Interaction of genetically coded information and cognitions
Retrieval	Access unit	Recreate pattern	Sensorimotor activation or motivational engagement
Sequencing mechanism	Executive unit, serial process, load sensitive	Emergent, parallel process, load insensitive	Stimulus and evolution based, fixed mechanisms; load insensitive

from memory. For example, it is the mechanism that implements rules such as "count to ten" before responding to anger-invoking situations that otherwise may produce emotional outbursts. Symbolic architectures conceptualize memory as a fixed location like a file drawer or bin and depend on finding and retrieving the right information from memory at exactly the right time—the "count to ten" rule when one is angry. They are quite dependent on having adequate attentional resources. That is, one needs work space to implement rules like "count to ten." Indeed, Wegner's research (1994) shows that when attentional resources are taxed, conscious attempts at emotional regulation (more specifically mood) often backfire, producing ironic effects that are the opposite of intentions.

The implementation of cognitive processes in symbolic architectures occurs in serial fashion, with operations being sequenced by a higher-order executive unit that may create an appropriate sequencing through either procedures such as means-end analysis or more exploratory processes. Alternatively, it can sometimes retrieve schemas from memory that have built-in sequences, such as scripts. Performance in such architectures is often highly dependent on learning (Newell, 1990), as knowledge can often substitute for processing operations; one applies learned rules such as counting to ten rather than developing new context-specific ways to regulate anger. Learning increases efficiency, but it is often a slow process that is dependent on context-specific experience (Anderson, 1987).

Connectionist Architectures

This type of architecture has only recently been introduced and accepted in the mainstream of cognitive psychology and thus has not typically been used in models of emotions. It is based on a biological model of the brain with networks of neuron-like processing units that continuously integrate information from input sources and pass the resulting activation (inhibition) on to connected output units. Neural networks are particularly good at modeling processes like perception and categorization, and they are likely systems for detecting many emotion-relevant stimuli or linking strong emotions and behavioral responses. This is because processing occurs in parallel in neural networks, allowing them to integrate large amounts of information in very little time using simple processes like the selective transmission of activation and inhibition among units. This parallel flow of operations is controlled by organization that emerges from the local interaction of the units themselves. Thus, there is no central "executive" unit in neural networks.

In connectionist networks, the amount of activation (inhibition) transmitted from one unit to another depends on connection weights among units, which have been determined through learning. The weights reflect the strength of positive and negative constraints between units, and meaning is created when the network simultaneously satisfies such constraints. The satisfaction of multiple constraints depends on feedback processes that allow units to interact and update activation (inhibition) (Smith, 1996). This occurs dynamically over many cycles and should result in all units' reaching an asymptote, or steady state. This dynamic, constraint satisfaction process is referred to as *settling in* or *relaxing*. When the network has settled in, generally, the most possible constraints have been satisfied, and a coherent interpretation can be made. This process can contextualize the meaning of stimuli or the production of specific responses to stimulus patterns.

Memory in neural networks depends on both the strength of connections among units and the pattern of input to a network. In neural networks, knowledge is stored or encoded in the connection weights (constraints) among units, and it can be retrieved only by reinstating the previously experienced pattern of activation. The conceptualization of memory in connectionist architectures is that it is recreated rather than being stored in a fixed location. Because learning is incremental and modifies the connection weights among units (Smith, 1996), memory is also contextualized and modified by learning that intervenes between a stimulus event and its recall.

Emotional Architectures

Architectures generally have been discussed only in terms of cognitive functioning, with the contemporary issue being whether symbolic or connectionist architectures are better suited for understanding cognitions. However, evolutionary psychologists (Cosmides & Tooby, 2000) recognize that emotional systems have computational capacities and also serve to coordinate many other processes, such as perception and motor systems, learning, goal choice, reflexes, energy level, and communications. Consistent with this recognition, we maintain that it also is desirable to think in terms of a unique architecture for representing emotions. Emotions are not necessarily activated by cognitions (Izard, 1993), which implies that they are supported in part by a different system. Emotions are also more closely associated with primitive parts of the brain (amygdala and limbic systems) than cognitive systems (hippocampal memory systems and neocortex) (LeDoux & Phelps, 2000), and emotions are developmentally earlier than cognitive responses; systems that react to pain are functional at birth, and very young infants can decode emotions from their mother's facial expressions as well as communicate appropriate emotions (Tronick, 1989). Just as connectionist architectures support symbolic-level process, emotional architectures are needed to organize sensory, somatic, motor, and cognitive (and perhaps social) systems functionally in ways that enable effective responding to situations of evolutionary importance (Levenson, 1994). Similarly, Panksepp (2000) emphasizes that emotional command circuits orchestrate coherent behavioral, physiological, cognitive, and affective consequences that can substantially outlast precipitating events. Neurological evidence indicates that basic or "Blue Ribbon" emotions (seeking-expectancy, rage-anger, fear-anxiety, care-nurturance, panic-separation, and play-joy) have unique neuroanatomical circuits and distinctive neurochemical basis for producing coordination (Globus & Arpaia, 1994; Panksepp, 2000).

As shown in Table 4.1, the supporting technology for an emotional architecture involves functionally coherent neural systems that are richly connected to hormonal, expressive, and motivational systems. Such connections are needed to tie emotions to specific behavioral systems. Connections to cognitive systems, although not required (Izard, 1993), are very useful to help interpret situations and emotions and to use emotional reactions as a basis for directing learning (Fredrickson, 1998). Memory and learning systems in emotional architectures are likely to be highly integrated with sensory-motor responses and for this reason involve neural chemical changes, such as the operation of various hormone systems. Learning in its most fundamental sense may be a very long-term activity that involves changes in genetics that occur over many generations. However, with extensive experience, connectionist and symbolic architectures can modify the expression of genetically based emotional systems. For example, although fear may be elicited through emotional architectures, our response to that fear can be changed by connectionist and symbolic architectures, as can the stimuli that elicit fear (LeDoux & Phelps, 2000).

Retrieval of emotions requires feeling these emotions again. To retrieve emotions, specific sensory-motor and motivational states are usually needed for people to feel emotions (Izard, 1993). That is, emotions are embodied in the sense that multiple physical and mental processes combine to create emotions. Emotional retrieval is not just an information access issue. Emotions also depend on context in that they frequently depend on external environmental cues, which are processed in parallel, although emotions can be cued internally as well.

Emotion-Cognition Interaction

The role of cognitions in interpreting emotions has a long history of scholarly debate (Cannon, 1927; James, 1884, 1894) with some contemporary theorists arguing that cognitions are a necessary component of emotions (Lazarus, 1984; Schacter & Singer, 1962), while others (Izard, 1993; LeDoux & Phelps, 2000) maintain that cognitions are not required to experience emotions. Our position is that emotional architectures do not require cognitive components, but there is often a close linkage between cognitions and emotions. This linkage helps us interpret emotions and emotion-eliciting stimuli, and it also uses emotions to help manage cognitions. For example, hearing a strange noise may produce a startle or orienting response, but contextual primes or cognitive appraisals may then be needed to translate this arousal into an emotional response. If the context is being home alone at night, in a neighborhood with recent burglaries, then accessing these cognitions will help translate this emotional arousal into fear. In contrast, if it is daytime and the children and dog have been roughhousing, arousal may be translated into anger with the expectation of broken furniture. Social cues, which are often processed preconsciously through connectionist architectures, can also help translate external stimuli into emotions and responses.

The interaction of cognitive and emotional components can also be seen in the sensitivity of individual to emotional stimuli that vary along a pleasant-unpleasant dimension (see Larsen, Diener, and Lucas, Chapter Three, this volume). For example, genetic differences in underlying circuitry may make some individuals (introverts) more excitable than others (extroverts), and patterns of learning may develop connectionist architectures with stronger or more numerous connections to either negative or positive stimuli (see Gray, 1990; Higgins, 1998). The combination of such factors may be responsible for important individual differences in sensitivity to positive versus negative stimuli (such as positive versus negative affectivity). Thus, connectionist architectures may have a critical role in predisposing individuals to notice positive or negative stimuli, which then produce reactions largely through emotional architectures. This is but one example of a very general process in which connectionist architectures can help develop individual differences (such as personality dimensions) that then affect sensitivity to and perception of emotional stimuli. (See Larsen Diener, and Lucas, Chapter Three, this volume, for a more detailed discussion of this process.)

The role of emotions in influencing cognitions is equally important. Indeed, many specific types of negative emotions are thought to occur because they facilitate appropriate cognitive and behavioral responses to specific types of threats (Frijda, 1986; Levenson, 1994). Although negative emotions have often been seen as influencing cognitions, less attention has been given to the effects of positive emotions on cognitions. Positive emotional responses are not as distinctive as negative emotional responses, and their associated role on cognitions is less clear, yet Fredrickson (1998) makes a compelling case that they are important for facilitating both the acquisition of cognitively based skills and the development of communal and cooperative social structures.

The interaction of emotions and cognitions can also be understood from a more physiological perspective. Globus and Arpaia (1994) note that the brain is a "wet computer" in which masses of interconnected neurons are stimulated by inputs and then transfer activation to output units. Constraints on such networks help produce differentiated patterns (meanings) from otherwise undifferentiated connections. Constraints may be relatively fixed, as by genes, or when learning modifies synaptic efficiency. In contrast, they also can be "tuned" (made more efficient) by the release of classical transmitters at low frequencies or neuropeptides at high frequencies. Thus, the type of neurotransmitter released into the synapse constrains the interaction of neurons without leaving any trace, providing a flexible, fluid-based overlay to more fixed constraints. They note that "global attunements" can be produced by motivational states such as hunger, which may predispose one to think about food or eating. Similarly, emotional states can be thought of as global attunements rather than behavioral dispositions. Fixed constraints, constraints from sensory input, current thought, and motivational or emotional attunements may combine to create relatively stable patterns of activation (attractors), which can be thought of as behavioral or cognitive tendencies.

Such a view of emotional-cognitive interaction indicates that cognitive processing occurs in a chemically tuned hardware system. As Globus and Arpaia (1994) note, "Synaptic efficacy, for example, is under exquisitive and highly complex control by neurochemical modulation of rate of neurotransmitter synthesis, release, transport and uptake; this in effect tunes the connection weights" (p. 357). They explain that the amount of transmitter available at a synapse can make connections more efficacious, and opiode peptides can narrow the shape of action potentials, thereby limiting the spread of an impulse in the axonal aborization. Environmental and bodily input also constrain organization in the brain, with high-intensity inputs from external, internal, motivational, or emotional sources dominating constraints. Through such means, the brain continually self-tunes and self-organizes. Such means also provide a system by which a variety of emotions can have differential effects on cognitions and behavior, with emotional intensity increasing the importance of emotional relative to other internal or external constraints.

In sum, in most circumstances, emotional, connectionist, and symbolic architectures interact in producing affective and behavioral responses to situations. The nature of this interaction is highly dependent on contextual factors, particularly the time pace of activities, the strength of emotions, and the intensity of other inputs. Nevertheless, we need to understand the underlying mechanisms in each architecture to grasp how these different systems can jointly participate in the stimulus appraisals and judgments that occur before actions. We suspect that the layperson's understanding of emotion and emotional regulation overemphasizes the role of symbolic factors because they are more salient and also because people lack insight into faster operating processes, which are often outside conscious awareness. As a consequence, attempts to understand or regulate emotions may be misdirected unless a more comprehensive approach is taken.

Time Parameters

Emotions also often have characteristic time courses, with different architectures having effects that can be described in terms of time-dependent parameters. While each architecture can operate on different time frames spanning a few millisecond to many seconds, these architectures also cooperate in producing affective or behavioral responses that must of necessity operate in the same timescale, which is often determined by the context and emotional intensity (Scherer, 1994). Contextual information processing requirements may exclude or permit various processes, and immediately prior events may create leading or lagging effects of specific architectures. For example, reacting to a dangerous predator involves emotions preparing the body for fighting or fleeing, which must be done so quickly in response to threatening stimuli that such responses are not mediated by symbolic architectures. Connectionist architectures are fast enough to help one recognize situations and decide whether to fight or flee and whether a situation was appropriately categorized as threatening. In such cases, emotional and connectionist architectures are leading systems, which constrain related symbolic processing, often eliciting familiar thoughts and responses as illustrated by well-known threat-rigidity effects (Staw, Sandelands, & Dutton, 1991). Such time-related aspects of emotional architectures are discussed in this section. They provide a primary basis for understanding how context constrains architectural interactions in producing emotions and emotional regulation.

Table 4.1 shows the characteristic time frame for initiating operations in each of the architectures we have described. Our estimation of somewhere between 10 and 50 milliseconds as the lower bound for emotional architectures is based on several considerations. First, several researchers have used emotional stimuli that were presented for less than 10 milliseconds and still had considerable effects on attitude formation (Edwards, 1990; Murphy & Zajonc, 1993) or recognition of emotion-related words (Girondi & Lord, 1998). Second, the evolutionally based effects in emotional perceptions have been linked to functionally coherent neural systems (Izard, 1993). Newell (1990) suggests that neural circuits operate in the range of 10 milliseconds. All of these positions are consistent with the assertion that emotional systems must of necessity operate very fast if their function is to prepare thought and physical systems for interacting with the environment. Emotions interrupt and often redirect conscious processing (Simon, 1967). Thus, their initial effects should operate faster than conscious perception of stimuli, which is in the range of 30 to 60 milliseconds, and certainly much faster than serial symbolic operations. Importantly, because they are much faster than connectionist or symbolic-level processes, processes internal to emotional architectures cannot be directly regulated by these higher-level systems. However, there are indirect ways to regulate emotions by using higher-level systems to activate or suppress specific emotions.

Our estimation that connectionist networks can generally settle in to stable states in 200 to 500 milliseconds comes directly from theorists working with those networks (Rumelhart, Smolensky, McClelland, & Hinton, 1986). As with emotional architectures, the actual processes used are unconscious, although the results may be consciously perceived. In contrast, symbolic-level processes operate on a time frame of 500 milliseconds to 10 seconds (Newell, 1990), which is slow enough for awareness and conscious selection of specific operations.

The importance of understanding time parameters is threefold. First, faster processes are generally leading systems in that they begin to create interpretations or prepare one for action before slower systems can become operational. Thus, faster systems such as emotion can provide an underlying quality or structure to processes, which is important to understand. For example, considerable research (Edwards, 1990; Fabrigar & Petty, 1999; Murphy & Zajonc, 1993) provides evidence that emotionally based attitudes can be changed more effectively with affective than with cognitively based influence attempts.

Second, understanding time parameters helps us understand what tasks can or cannot be appropriately handled by a specific architecture. For example, some aspect of social communications (particularly communications based on nonverbal behavior) may operate at a speed that is more compatible with an affective or connectionist than a symbolic medium. For example, muscle tension around a speaker's eyes may signal difficulty in formulating a thought. Such cues are not perceived in isolation, but may be part of more complex patterns that are interpreted by connectionist or emotional systems and create the basis for such processes as trust or distrust, empathy, compassion, or fear.

Third, from a more philosophical perspective, internal representations of external reality are delayed in proportion to the speed with which various systems can respond to stimuli. Emotional or connectionist representations therefore may more faithfully track some external realities (such as social processes) than our more conscious symbolic-level processes. Many times, conscious thoughts and underlying feelings may give us different messages. For example, social perceptions always involve affective reactions (Srull & Wyer, 1989), and frequently trait ascriptions or social stereotypes are automatically activated by connectionist architectures (Blair & Benaji, 1996; Kunda & Thagard, 1996; Van Overwalle, Drenth, & Mausman, 1999). However, these processes can produce interpretations that may not be consistent with later symbolic-level interpretations. Although perceivers may be aware of an uneasiness associated with such perceptions, symbolic-level introspection is likely to be misleading because it can access only the symbolic-level processes.

Applied concerns with emotions often focus on behavior. Therefore, one way to see the applied relevance of the three architectures we have described is to examine how they link emotions and behavior. As noted previously, Scherer (1994) maintained that emotional intensity moderates the linkage between emotions and behavior, with strong emotions quickly releasing behaviors but weaker emotions allowing slower and more variable behavioral responses. We suggest that as the time between emotions and responses increases, processing in more sophisticated but slower architectures can intervene, modulating the linkage between emotions and behavior. Thus, as Figure 4.1 shows, very intense emotions may trigger behavior before even connectionist architectures can function effectively, less intense emotions may allow for connectionist-based stimulus categorization and selection of previously learned responses to intervene, and even less intense emotions afford time for symbolic-level processes to construct novel situational interpretations and invent appropriate behavioral responses. Importantly, then, regulating emotional intensity may also regulate the nature of the information processing that produces behavioral responses in organizations, as well as the variability of those responses. Thus, organizational processes that reduce emotional intensity may also facilitate symbolic-level control of behavior.

Figure 4.1 also suggests why it is hard for individuals to regulate strong emotions consciously: they emerge with sufficient intensity to produce behavioral responses before conscious, symbolic-level processes can operate effectively. Emotional regulation has received extensive attention from behavioral scientists interested in emotions.

Figure 4.1. Increased Behavioral Variability as Greater Latency Between Stimulus and Response Permits More Cognitive Processing.

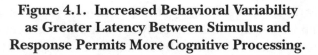
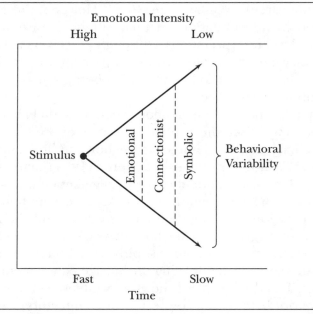

Emotional Regulation

We defined emotions in terms of three components (a neuro-anatomical-neurochemical substrate, an expressive or motor component, and an experiential component) because it helps us to define and understand emotional regulation. Emotional regulation can be defined as "the process by which individuals influence which emotions they have, when they have them, and how they experience and express these emotions" (Gross, 1998, p. 275). Emotional regulation thus affects the components that define emotions. However, these components are usually influenced indirectly by changing antecedents, such as situation selection, situation modification, attentional deployment, and cognitive change, as Gross has argued (1998). Indirect approaches are used because people do not have volitional control over the components of emotions. Gross notes that volitional control can be exercised with respect to antecedents as well as responses to emotions. We have explained that processing speed is a critical component determining volitional control, with the components comprising emotions operating too fast to be directly regulated by relatively slow conscious processes.

The interrelation of these processes is illustrated by the following example. Being yelled at by one's boss or coworker is likely to produce anxiety, which involves increased activation of neural transmitters; neuromuscular activity involving muscle tension, facial expressions, and posture; and feelings of uneasiness, desire to escape the situation, and heightened attention to social and environmental cues. These reactions happen too fast to be prevented as part of the initial experience of anxiety, but with experience, one can learn to regulate such emotions by avoiding one's boss when she appears angry (situation selection), using humor to make one's boss feel better (situation modification), focusing on nonthreatening aspects of the environment (attention deployment), or cognitively reframing the angry comments as constructive criticism or the babbling of a lunatic (cognitive change). Response modulation may also involve volitional processes (for example, counting to ten before responding or censoring verbal comments).

Applying an Information Processing Framework to Emotional Regulation

We focus on the approach to emotional regulation that Gross (1998) developed because it is based on "conceptual analyses of the regulatory processes underlying diverse emotion regulatory acts" (p. 281), which fits well with our information processing approach. Other approaches (Levenson, 1994; Walden & Smith, 1997) categorize emotional regulation in terms of the targeted emotional component. For example, Walden and Smith focus on the components of subjective experience, physiology, expressive behavior, or outcomes.

Gross's (1998) conceptual analysis focuses on four antecedent processes as well as response-focused activities in emotional regulation. The cells of Table 4.2 combine these processes with connectionist and symbolic architectures, which we have discussed previously. We had difficulty deciding whether to include a column for emotional architectures in this analytic system for several reasons. There may be instances when emotions are regulated without cognitive interventions through means that involve emotional architectures, such as when immediately prior emotional events increase or decrease the capacity of an individual to experience an inconsistent emotion or when drugs alter the physiological basis for emotions. Yet most of the time people rely on cognitive processes to modulate emotions, which is why we focus on delineating how such processes will interact with the emotional architecture.

Situation Selection

According to Gross (1998), certain people, places, or objects can be selected as a means to regulate emotions. As shown in Table 4.2, we suggest that such selection can involve either connectionist or symbolic processes. Initially, it is easy to think of explicit aspects of situation selection as involving symbolic processes. For example, Gross gives the example of changing one's route to the store to avoid an offensive neighbor, which involves explicit, conscious decisions. However, over time, the connectionist mechanisms can routinely select this alternative route. Because connectionist processes may not be explicitly understood, they may also lead one to select situations that foster unwanted emotions. Ironically, one may be unconsciously driven to avoid or approach people or situations that

Table 4.2. Connectionist and Symbolic Analogues of Emotional Regulation Process.

Regulatory Step	Connectionist	Symbolic
Situation selection	Familiar situations	Novel and slow-paced situations; unlearning
Situation modification	Habitual social actions	Purposeful change in physical or social environment
Attention deployment	Concentrating on a competing task	Conscious suppression of emotions
Cognitive change	Bolstering self-confidence; eliciting social support; redefining familiar work tasks; forming intentions or beginning tasks	Conscious redefinition (opportunity rather than threat); thinking about processes rather than outcomes
Response modulation	Habitual, situationally cued indirect means; skillful emotional labor	Novel choice of indirect means; unfamiliar emotional labor

produce undesired emotions; for instance, previously battered individuals may be unconsciously attracted to abusive individuals, or people with test anxiety may avoid studying for tests in areas where they have the least confidence, thereby making actual testing situations more threatening.

Although learning can change situation selection processes from symbolic to connectionist, unlearning often reverses this procedure by consciously examining maladaptive connectionist processes. Because people often lack reflective insight into connectionist processes, interventions of this type may require external guidance from parents, friends, coworkers, or counselors. Thus, what was solely an intrapersonal emotion regulation process can become a dyadic or even group process.

Situation Modification

This antecedent process changes aspects of the situation so as to alter the emotions it elicits. For example, a person who feels uneasy being home alone at night may cope by turning on more interior or exterior lights, locking doors, and having a burglar alarm installed. Such actions reflect symbolic-level processes. Prior learning may also evoke a desire for companionship in such situations, reflecting more of a connectionist process.

Interpersonal dynamics add another complication to situation modification in that many situations are created through social interactions, and often unintentionally. For example, as stressed by the social-functional approach to emotions, one's behavior or expressed emotions may create situations by eliciting emotional responses from others (Keltner & Kring, 1998). Some emotions (anxiety, love, gratitude) help build social bonds, while other emotions (sympathy, anger, jealousy, embarrassment) maintain, protect, and restore social relations (Keltner & Kring, 1998). Social aspects of situation modification, such as the expression and response to emotions, are likely to be so habitual that they are implemented automatically by connectionist architectures and may even be learned before symbolic architectures are fully developed (Tronick, 1989). Thus, processes such as emotional contagion (see Pugh, Chapter Five, this volume) may depend on connectionist-level processes. Nonfunctional situation modification can also occur. For example, an individual who is unhappy may unintentionally behave in overly critical ways toward others, thereby making positive social interactions less likely. Alternatively, their negative mood may be "caught" by others through the operation of connectionist-level processes for which neither party has any conscious awareness.

Attention Deployment

As Gross (1998) suggested, this process involves directing one's attention toward or away from a particular situation. People often try to regulate their emotions by trying not to think of them. This is a symbolic-level process as people explicitly try to divert their attention away from the emotion. Unfortunately, this method rarely works in the long run. As shown in the work of Wegner (1994), when we try to inhibit an emotion by diverting our attention away from it, a mechanism is engaged that continuously searches our thoughts for the to-be-suppressed emotion. While this mechanism is effective when competition for our cognitive resources is limited, it is not when there are multiple demands on our attention. With cognitive load, the to-be-suppressed emotions are often more prevalent than normal, and previously suppressed emotions often rebound, producing subsequent ironic effects (Wegner, 1994). Thus, instead of not thinking about the emotion, we find ourselves unable to think about anything else but the emotion.

Alternatively, by focusing all of our attention on a task, emotional regulation may occur effortlessly through connectionist-level processes. In a study by Girondi and Lord (1998), emotional inhibition occurred unconsciously because subjects were engaged in a task that was inconsistent with the to-be-suppressed emotion. When attention is focused on the task at hand, emotions that are inconsistent with the task will be inhibited through negative connection weights. Wenzlaff and Bates (2000) recently extended this idea in a series of three experiments in which subjects unscrambled words to create either positive or negative statements. Specifically, they found that concentration on creating positive statements from the scrambled words was as effective in inhibiting the construction of negative statements as explicit instructions to avoid making negative statements. Moreover, this concentration strategy was effective under high load and showed no subsequent rebound effect, whereas suppression instructions showed ironic effects under high load and ironic rebound effects (high levels of the previously suppressed mood when suppression instructions were no longer in force). Thus, directing attention away from an emotion is useful for short-term emotional regulation, but for long-term emotional regulation, concentration on alternative emotions may be more useful because it relies on connectionist-level processes.

Cognitive Change

Given that emotion-eliciting cues in the situation have been attended to, they must be given meaning to elicit an emotional reaction, which involves cognitive processes. A central issue in such meaning is often whether an individual has the capacity to manage the situation. Different perceptions of competence may be the difference between fear- and challenge-related emotions for different individuals who are experiencing the same external situation. Bolstering one's own perceived competence, then, may be one cognitive means to regulate emotions. External factors like social support can also have the same effect.

Another cognitive means to change one's emotional reactions to a situation involves reappraisal (Gross, 1998). For example, doctors may reappraise critical surgical situations as being intellectually challenging rather than situations where death is likely. Alternatively, changes in business environments can be redefined as opportunities rather than threats (Dutton & Jackson, 1987). Such reappraisals would initially involve symbolic-level activities because reappraisal involves transformations applied to the symbol structures representing situational features. However, with practice or experience, such transformations may become automatic, being cued directly by situational features. In such cases, reappraisal may be carried out by connectionist architectures, and reappraisal should be a much faster process.

One interesting possibility is a combination of competence-based self-evaluation and reappraisal caused by engaging in action. As Gollwitzer (1996) has demonstrated, when intentions are formed and actions are initiated (as one moves from a deliberative to an actional mind-set), one becomes more optimistic about outcomes, which should produce a more positive emotional response. In addition, actions change one's focus, emphasizing cognitive structures (scripts and schemas) involved in producing actions rather than external features of a situation. To return to our example of a critical surgery, beginning the task may then precipitate an automatic cognitive reappraisal of its emotional consequences, which is likely produced by a connectionist architecture. Similar responses are frequently reported by athletes or performers who find that they are more nervous before than after beginning a critical game or performance. In short, forming intentions and beginning actions may be an important connectionist mechanism that changes emotions.

Response Modulation

This form of emotional regulation involves altering the physiological, experiential or behavioral response (Gross, 1998) and occurs late in the emotion-generation process, after the emotion is initiated. Many studies of this phenomena focus on symbolic activities associated with explicit attempts to suppress emotions. For example, Gross and Levenson (1997) found that although people can suppress the outward signs of emotions, they were less successful at suppressing the physiological and experiential aspects of emotional responses. We suspect that this effect occurs because physiological and experiential aspects of responses are more closely tied to emotional or connectionist architectures, while behavioral responses, particularly novel responses, have a stronger symbolic element. Because it is difficult to directly regulate processes in connectionist or emotional architectures (processes in these architectures are too fast for modulation by symbolic processes), people often use indirect means, which directly affect the functioning of these architectures. For example, food, drugs (such as alcohol, caffeine, and nicotine), and exercise all have an impact on physiological or experiential aspects of emotional responses.

These basic findings from the emotions literature have direct relevance to the topic of emotional labor, which is an applied concern related to response modulation (Grandey, 2000; Morris & Feldman, 1996). Emotional labor involves controlling the outward expression of emotions to conform to situational requirements and may or may not involve changes in physiological or experiential aspects (see the discussion of this issue in Grandey and Brauburger, Chapter Eight, this volume). In emotional labor, emotions are altered for instrumental, business-oriented purposes, but an additional concern is the long-term consequences to an individual. Emotional labor may have adverse long-term consequences on health (Fredrickson, 1998; Gross & Levenson, 1997). However, there are circumstances where emotional regulation produces positive outcomes, as, for example, when actors express appropriate emotions in playing a role. Importantly, actors do this effectively in situations that are well rehearsed and have social systems comprising other actors to provide cues that support their response modulation activities. Emotional regulation also corresponds to a salient identity (being a good actor) rather than conflicting with underlying norms and values. This suggests that contextual variables like practice, social support, and identity congruence may differentiate harmful from positive effects of emotional regulation. For example, Grandey and Brauburger mention that some individuals experience a sense of pride as a result of successfully regulating their emotions. Inconsistencies between architectures may also be a source of stress, as well as an impediment to effective emotional regulation.

Emotional Regulation in Organizational Contexts

In short, as Table 4.2 illustrates, emotional regulation can involve a variety of steps that are associated with either connectionist or symbolic architectures. In using this system as a practical guide, one must also keep in mind the pace or time requirements of a particular activity and the intensity of emotions. Furthermore, emotions and emotional regulation involve the interactions of all three architectures, with emotional circuits priming cognitions, as well as cognitions influencing the operation of emotional systems. It is also important to realize that some methods of emotional regulation are externally oriented (situation selection, situation modification). Thus, they may require substantial power or discretion to apply in organizations. Other methods such as attention deployment and cognitive change are internally oriented and thus require internal self-regulatory skills rather than organizational power. Finally, response modulation pertains to an internal-external boundary and thus depends on both internal regulation and organizational factors such as norms for emotional display.

Emotional Regulation and Control of Behavioral Processes

The relevance of our framework to a broad variety of work-related areas can be seen best if we reorient our focus to viewing emotions as mediating processes in producing behavior and organizing cognitions rather than as end states to be regulated. This view is consistent with Scherer's suggestion (1994) that emotions mediate between stimuli and responses, with strong emotions producing very strong connections between stimuli and responses and weaker emotions affording time for more intervening cognitive processes (see Figure 4.1). It is also a central point in Weiss and Cropanzano's affective events theory (1996). Thus, although emotional regulation is important in its own right, it can also be seen as a critical intervening mechanism that may be used to control indirectly a number of processes that are closely related to behaviors of applied interest. For example, emotions have been found to have a direct impact on physiological and behavioral responses (Russell & Barrett, 1999), motivation (Carver & Scheier, 1998), cognitive and social skill development (Fredrickson, 1998), the scope of cognitive processes (Gohm & Clore, 2000; Isen & Baron, 1991), social communications (Tronick, 1989; Levinson, 1994), and the development of social relationships (Keltner & Kring, 1998). We suggest that such diverse processes can be indirectly regulated through their strong linkages to emotional processes. Failure to consider such emotion-based linkages therefore ignores an important determinant of individual and social processes in organizations. Furthermore, attempts to control such processes through organizational interventions or procedures that ignore emotional architectures are likely to be unsuccessful.

Our argument that emotional architectures are often lead architectures raises the practical issue of how emotions can be regulated with slower-acting connectionist or symbolic processes, which often lag emotional reactions. This generally cannot occur effectively with concurrent processes if emotions are intense (see Figure 4.1), but even with intense emotions, regulation though symbolic and connectionist processes may be quite effective if regulatory processes are in place before emotional events occur. Two examples illustrate this process. First, implementation intentions, which are intentions based on explicit plans specifying when, where, and how goals can be attained, can automatize goal-directed responses to situational cues (Gollwitzer & Schaal, 1998). Thus, symbolic-level, anticipatory thought can automatically trigger emotion-regulating responses to certain situations. Second, cultural norms regarding emotional reactions and expression can produce similar effects, albeit through connectionist architectures. For example, Mastenbroek (2000) reviews a six-hundred-year trend, arguing that emotional regulation in organizations has taken centuries to evolve to its present state and reflects important cultural changes. Early eruptions of violence and aggression have been replaced by more even-tempered, disciplined, reliable, cooperative behavior as organizational norms for emotional regulation at work have developed. Well-learned norms regarding the meaning of emotion-evoking cues and potential responses can be implemented relatively quickly when incorporated into connectionist architectures that are also linked with emotion-producing networks. Such cultural norms often require extensive training and systems of organizational sanctions to change the way emotions were regulated, and they may be an important aspect of newcomer socialization (see Ashforth and Saks, Chapter Ten, this volume), which can be viewed as one means to train the appropriate interpretation of emotional stimuli and display of emotions in new employees.

Application at Individual and Dyadic Levels

In this brief section, we provide prototypical examples of how applied issues can be approached in terms of emotional regulation and information processing. At an individual level, motivational processes are often dominated by emotional processes related to self-identifies as feared as well as desired selves often direct behavior (Carver & Scheier, 1998). Challenging situations (see Worline, Wrzesniewski, and Rafaeli, Chapter Nine, this volume) thus often depend on the ability of individuals to use connectionist and symbolic-level systems to regulate emotions in a manner that modulates both emotion-behavior linkages and the intensity-based limitations on cognitive processes (see Figure 4.1). Similar issues apply in the regulation of aggressive tendencies (see Glomb, Steel, and Arvey, Chapter Seven, this volume). In both cases, strong emotions can preclude effective cognitive control, and it may be necessary to change these emotional limitations before behavior can be effectively changed.

At dyadic levels, social-cognitive processes like performance appraisal (Robbins & DeNisi, 1994) and dyadic leadership (Liden, Wayne, & Stillwell, 1993) are often heavily influenced by emotional components. Emotions are a ubiquitous and easily processed aspect of social perceptions because there are many basic-level, hard-wired components used in perceiving emotions in others and expressing our own emotions (Keltner & Ekman, 2000). Connectionist-level architectures can also be readily applied to prototypical patterns of emotions, producing culturally specific effects. This computational ease is complemented by the linkage of communicated emotions with many appropriate responses by others, as emphasized by social-functional perspectives on emotions. Emotions are not only easily perceived and remembered; they indicate in a largely implicit manner how to respond to others in a way that moves social relations toward more favorable, mutually beneficial outcomes (Keltner & Kring, 1998).

There are two obvious additional points where such social processes can break down, causing applied problems. One is that emotionally based social perceptions and social communications are largely implicit, fast-acting processes that may not normally be processed by symbolic architectures. Hence, they may be difficult to regulate explicitly and difficult to correct when they go awry. Another weakness is that these processes may be relatively inflexible because they are grounded in hard-wired processes, learned before symbolic capacities develop (Tronick, 1989) or connectionist processes that require extensive learning. When emotionally based, social-cognitive processes do not fit with the demands of work situations (there may be ethnic culture and work culture mismatches, family and work inconsistencies, and gender and work role inconsistencies), these two difficulties are likely to accentuate problems, making self-correction a slow and difficult process. Work-family conflict (see MacDermid, Seery and Weiss, Chapter Twelve, this volume) provides a prototypical example of the conflict and tension that can arise when the expressiveness and intensity of family-based processes conflict with work-based norms for reserved and tempered emotional expression. These latter emotions may afford more symbolic-based processing, yet be deficient in creating emotions like trust or positive affect needed for cooperation and the development of intellectual and social resources (Fredrickson, 1998).

Interestingly, many individual and dyadic processes emphasize the functional value of emotions. Yet at both an individual (Globus & Arpaia, 1994) and a social level (Keltner & Kring, 1998), dysfunction or pathology can also occur in emotion-based processes. Dysfunction at an individual level can reflect the inability of individuals to maintain normal attunement of hardware because of chemical anomalies or peculiar learning histories. For example, Pugh (Chapter Five, this volume) notes that gender and dispositional affectivity can affect the capacity to regulate emotions. Inconsistencies between emotional hardware and current work tasks can also be problematic. For example, the social-functional perspectives stress that the expression of one's emotions and reaction to emotions in others is a critical basis for social communication that develops from birth (Keltner & Kring, 1998; Tronick, 1989). The disgenuine use of emotions for organizational gain as in emotional labor (see Grandey and Brauburger, Chapter Eight, this volume, on customer service) undercuts this social communication process and often pits connectionist and symbolic architectures against emotional architectures. Anticipatory intentions and extensive training may permit such regulation of emotions, but only when time demands and cognitive load are low.

Application at Multiperson Levels

There is substantial benefit from viewing multiperson processes as extensions of the same processes that exist at individual and dyadic levels, particularly because emotions ultimately are communicated, felt, and reacted to through individual-level processes. Yet this approach oversimplifies and ignores important aspects of collective emotional processes at work (for discussion of the social aspects of emotions at work, see George, Chapter Six, and Worline, Wrzesniewski, and Rafaeli, Chapter Nine, both this volume). Groups, including families, often have their own unique mood or emotional tone (George, 1990), and for many reasons, emotional tones in these larger entities are less likely to change as a function of any one member's emotional needs or expression. Emotional tones may also already be established when newcomers enter groups. Group members, then, must adjust to the emotional tone of groups rather than having it evolve in a way that meets their needs. Recruitment, selection, attraction socialization, and attrition processes (see Ashforth and Saks, Chapter Ten, this volume) thus become more critical processes when emotional regulation is considered at a multiperson level.

Multiperson processes are also likely to emphasize culturally based framing, feeling, display, and interaction rules for emotions that are learned at a connectionist level and perpetuated through implicit rules and patterns. As Mastenbroek (2000) noted, such rules may develop over very long periods of time. When newcomers lack experience with a particular culture, socialization processes are likely to be particularly difficult in the area of emotional communication and emotional regulation (see Earley and Francis, Chapter Eleven, this volume), in part because such rules may be difficult to represent or learn using symbolic-level processes.

In sum, we have seen that regulating emotions at work is actually a very complex process that brings together external constraints created by organizational and societal cultures (such as norms), more immediate face-to-face social systems associated with groups and dyads, and individual organizational members. This complexity is compounded by the fact that many aspects of group or dyadic systems operate implicitly and may be largely dependent on automatic processes (such as the facial expression and perception of emotions that have a strong genetic basis). Individuals also manifest genetically based complexity in that symbolic, connectionist, and emotional architectures reflect distinct functional and physical structures engineered by evolution for ancient tasks but which cooperate in processing information relevant to contemporary human tasks and situations. All of these interpersonal and intrapersonal systems, with their different time pace and different loci, cooperate in the continuous regulation of emotion, information processing, and behavior.

References

Anderson, J. R. (1987). Skill acquisition: Compilation of weak-method problem solutions. *Psychological Review, 94,* 192–210.

Blair, I. V., & Banaji, M. R. (1996). Automatic and controlled processes in stereotype priming. *Journal of Personality and Social Psychology, 70,* 1142–1163.

Cannon, W. B. (1927). The James-Lang theory of emotions: A critical examination and an alternative theory. *American Journal of Psychology, 39,* 106–124.

Carver, C. S., & Scheier, M. F. (1998). *On the self-regulation of behavior.* Cambridge: Cambridge University Press.

Churchland, P. S., & Sejnowski, T. J. (1992). *The computational brain.* Cambridge, MA: MIT Press.

Cosmides, L., & Tooby, J. (2000). Evolutionary psychology and emotions. In M. Lewis & J. M. Haviland-Jones (Eds.), *Handbook of emotions* (2nd ed., pp. 91–115). New York: Guilford Press.

Dutton, J. E., & Jackson, S. E. (1987). Categorizing strategic issues: Links to organizational actions. *Academy of Management Review, 12,* 76–90.

Edwards, K. (1990). The interplay of affect and cognition in attitude formation and change. *Journal of Personality and Social Psychology, 59,* 202–216.

Fabrigar, L., & Petty, R. E. (1999). The role of the affective and cognitive bases of attitudes in susceptibility to affectively and cognitively based persuasion. *Personality and Social Psychology Bulletin, 25,* 363–382.

Fredrickson, B. L. (1998). What good are positive emotions? *Review of General Psychology, 2,* 173–186.

Frijda, N. H. (1986). *The emotions.* Cambridge: Cambridge University Press.

George, J. M. (1990). Personality, affect, and behavior in groups. *Journal of Applied Psychology, 75,* 107–116.

Girondi, A. M., & Lord, R. G. (1998, May). *Nonconscious inhibition of emotions.* Paper presented at the Tenth Annual Convention of the American Psychological Society, Washington, DC.

Globus, G. G., & Arpaia, J. P. (1994). Psychiatry and the new dynamics. *Biological Psychiatry, 35,* 352–364.

Gohm, C. L., & Clore, G. L. (2000). Individual differences in emotional experience: Mapping available scales to processes. *Personality and Social Psychology Bulletin, 26,* 679–698.

Gollwitzer, P. M. (1996). The volitional benefits of planning. In P. M. Gollwitzer & J. A. Bargh (Eds.), *Linking cognition and motivation of behavior* (pp. 287–312). New York: Guilford Press.

Gollwitzer, P. M., & Schaal, B. (1998). Metacognition in action: The importance of implementation intentions. *Personality and Social Psychology Review, 2,* 124–136.

Grandey, A. A. (2000). Emotion regulation in the workplace: A new way to conceptualize emotional labor. *Journal of Occupational Health Psychology, 5,* 95–110.

Gray, J. A. (1990). Brain systems that mediate both emotions and cognition. *Motivation and Emotions, 4,* 269–288.

Gross, J. J. (1998). The emerging field of emotional regulation: An integrative review. *Review of General Psychology, 2,* 271–299.

Gross, J. J., & Levenson, R. W. (1997). Hiding feelings: The acute effects of inhibiting negative and positive emotion. *Journal of Abnormal Psychology, 106,* 95–103.

Higgins, E. T. (1998). Promotion and prevention: Regulatory focus as a motivational principle. In M. P. Zanna (Ed.), *Advances in experimental social psychology.* Orlando, FL: Academic Press.

Izard, C. E. (1993). Four systems for emotion activation: Cognitive and noncognitive processes. *Psychological Review, 100,* 68–90.

James, W. (1884). What is an emotion? *Mind, 9,* 188–205.

James, W. (1894). The physical basis of emotion. *Psychological Review, 101,* 205–210.

Keltner, D., & Ekman, P. (2000). Facial expression of emotions. In M. Lewis & J. M. Haviland-Jones (Eds.), *Handbook of emotions* (2nd ed., pp. 236–249). New York: Guilford Press.

Keltner, D., & Kring, A. M. (1998). Emotion, social function, and psychopathology. *Review of General Psychology, 2,* 320–342.

Kunda, Z., & Thagard, P. (1996). Forming impressions from stereotypes, traits, and behaviors: A parallel-constraint-satisfaction theory. *Psychological Review, 103,* 284–308.

Lazarus, R. S. (1984). On the primacy of cognition. *American Psychologist, 39,* 124–129.

Lazarus, R. S. (1991). *Emotion and adaptation.* New York: Oxford University Press.

LeDoux, J. E., & Phelps, E. A. (2000). Neural networks in the brain. In M. Lewis & J. M. Haviland-Jones (Eds.), *Handbook of emotions* (pp. 157–172). New York: Guilford Press.

Levenson, R. (1994). Human emotion: A functional view. In P. Ekman & R. J. Davidson (Eds.), *The nature of emotion* (pp. 123–126). New York: Oxford University Press.

Liden, R. C., Wayne, S. J., & Stilwell, D. (1993). A longitudinal study of the early development of leader-member exchanges. *Journal of Applied Psychology, 78,* 662–674.

Mastenbroek, W. (2000). Organizational behavior as emotion management. In N. M. Ashkanasy, C. E. Hartel, & W. J. Zerbe (Eds.), *Emotions in the workplace* (pp. 19–36). Westport, CT: Quorum Books.

McClelland, J. L., Rumelhart, D. E., and the PDP Research Group. (1986). *Parallel distributed processing: Explorations in the microstructure of cognition: Psychological and biological models.* Cambridge, MA: MIT Press.

Morris, J. A., & Feldman, D. C. (1996). The dimensions, antecedents, and consequences of emotional labor. *Academy of Management Review, 21,* 986–1010.

Murphy, S. T., & Zajonc, R. B. (1993). Affect, cognition, and awareness: Affective priming with optimal and suboptimal stimulus exposures. *Journal of Personality and Social Psychology, 64,* 723–739.

Newell, A. (1990). *Unified theories of cognition.* Cambridge, MA: Harvard University Press.

Panksepp, J. (2000). Emotions as natural kinds within the mammalian brain. In M. Lewis & J. M. Haviland-Jones (Eds.), *Handbook of emotions* (pp. 137–156). New York: Guilford Press.

Robbins, T. L., & DeNisi, A. S. (1994). A closer look at interpersonal affect as a distinct influence on cognitive processing in performance evaluations. *Journal of Applied Psychology, 79,* 341–353.

Rumelhart, D. E., Smolensky, P. M., McClelland, J. L., & Hinton, G. E. (1986). Schemata and sequential thought processes in PDP models. In J. L. McClelland, D. E. Rumelhart, and the PDP Research Group. (Eds.), *Parallel distributed processing: Explorations in the microstructure of cognition: Psychological and biological models* (pp. 7–57). Cambridge, MA: MIT Press.

Russell, J. A., & Barrett, L. F. (1999). Core affect, prototypical emotional episodes, and other things called *emotion*: Dissecting the elephant. *Journal of Personality and Social Psychology, 76,* 805–819.

Schacter, S., & Singer, J. (1962). Cognitive, social and physiological determinants of the emotional state. *Psychological Review, 69,* 379–399.

Scherer, K. (1984). On the nature and function of emotion: A component process approach. In K. R. Scherer & P. E. Ekman (Eds.), *Approaches to emotion* (pp. 293–317). Hillsdale, NJ: Erlbaum.

Scherer, K. (1994). Emotion serves to decouple stimulus and responses. *The nature of emotion.* New York. Oxford University Press.

Simon, H. A. (1967). Motivational and emotional controls of cognition. *Psychological Review, 74,* 29–39.

Smith, E. R. (1996). What do connectionism and social psychology offer each other? *Journal of Personality and Social Psychology, 70,* 893–912.

Srull, T. K., & Wyer, R. S. (1989). Person memory and judgment. *Psychological Review, 96,* 58–83.

Staw, B. M., Sandelands, L. E., & Dutton, J. E. (1991). Threat-rigidity effects in organizational behavior: A multilevel analysis. *Administrative Science Quarterly, 26,* 501–524.

Tronick, E. Z. (1989). Emotions and emotional communication in infants. *American Psychologist, 44,* 112–119.

Van Overwalle, F., Drenth, T., & Mausman, G. (1999). Spontaneous trait inference. *Personality and Social Psychology Bulletin, 25,* 450–462.

Walden, T. A., & Smith, M. C. (1997). Emotional regulation. *Motivation and Emotion, 21,* 7–25.

Wegner, D. M. (1994). Ironic processes of mental control. *Psychological Review, 101,* 34–52.

Weiss, H. M., & Cropanzano, R. (1996). Affective events theory: A theoretical discussion of the structure, causes and consequences of affective experiences at work. In B. M. Staw & L. L. Cummings (Eds.), *Research in organizational behavior* (Vol. 18, pp. 1–74). Greenwich, CT: JAI Press.

Wenzlaff, R. M., & Bates, D. E. (2000). The relative efficacy of concentration and suppression strategies of mental control. *Personality and Social Psychology Bulletin, 26,* 1200–1212.

CHAPTER 5

Emotional Regulation in Individuals and Dyads
Causes, Costs, and Consequences
S. Douglas Pugh

Chapters One through Three have laid the groundwork for understanding the role of emotions at work; they have described conceptualizations of affect, mood, and emotion, how emotion can be measured and manipulated, and how individuals regulate the emotions they feel and express. As Lord and Harvey noted in Chapter Four, however, emotions and their regulation are strongly affected by context: the environment an individual finds himself or herself in helps determine the adoption and the effectiveness of a variety of emotion-regulation strategies. What occurs when emotion regulation is attempted in busy task environments? How do the emotions of interaction partners (an angry coworker or an enthusiastic boss, for example) affect one's own emotions and emotion regulation? Are certain people more willing or more able to regulate their emotions? These and other questions are addressed in this chapter, which examines those factors that constrain, facilitate, or otherwise affect the regulation of emotion at the individual and dyadic levels of analysis.

The Process of Emotion Regulation

A useful starting point for understanding influences on emotion regulation at the individual, task, and dyadic level of analysis is Gross's model of emotion generation (1998, 1999). (Also see the stimulus-organism-response model presented by Larsen, Diener, and Lucas in Chapter Three, this volume, which also captures the essence of this framework.) As Larsen and colleagues note, these models provide a useful heuristic for approaching individual differences in emotion, because they subdivide the process of emotion generation into two components: inputs into the system and responses from the system. According to this model, the experience of emotion begins with an emotional stimulus input into the system. The input then triggers emotion-response tendencies, which may include behavioral, physiological, and experiential changes; these three components together represent the initial experience of emotion for the individual. Response tendencies do not, however, necessarily translate into visible emotional responses; various types of automatic and controlled processes determine whether the generated emotion experience translates into a visible emotional response. An adaptation of Gross's (1998) model is presented in Figure 5.1.

The focus of this chapter is the process of emotion regulation, which Gross (1999) defined as "the ways individuals influence which emotions they have, when they have them, and how they experience or express these emotions" (p. 542). In general terms, emotion regulation occurs at two points in the process depicted in Figure 5.1: antecedent to the activation of emotional response tendencies and after the emotion has been generated. Antecedent-focused emotion regulation techniques act on the stimuli coming into the system before emotional response tendencies are activated. For example, physicians cognitively transform patients from real peo-

Figure 5.1. Process Model of Emotion Regulation.

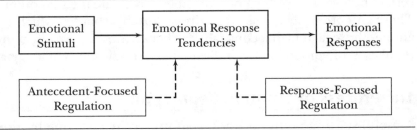

Source: Adapted from Gross (1998).

ple into analytic and clinical objects in order to ward off any inappropriate feelings that might interfere with their neutral affective displays (Smith & Kleinman, 1989). In contrast, response-focused techniques such as suppression act only on the outward expression of emotion, after emotion response tendencies have arisen.

This framework will be used to examine how contextual factors and individual differences affect emotion regulation in organizations. Each of the factors examined in this chapter can be framed in terms of its influence on inputs into the system depicted in Figure 5.1 and in terms of its influence on the responses from the system. Task environments differ, for example, in the affective inputs they provide to the system, and they also affect responses from the system because they differ in the types of emotions that are viewed as appropriate to express. The points at which the task environment, dyadic interactions, and individual differences influence emotion regulation are represented graphically in Figure 5.2.

Figure 5.2. Effects of Task Environment, Dyadic Interaction, and Individual Differences on Emotion Regulation.

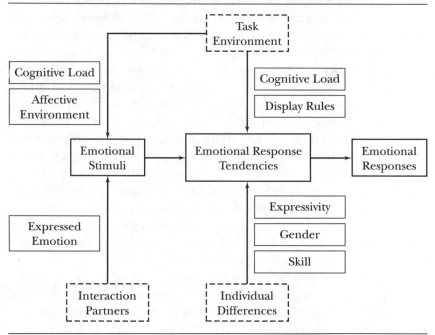

The Cost of Emotion Regulation

People regulate emotions through antecedent-focused coping, such as cognitively reappraising a situation, or response-focused coping, such as suppressing undesired affective states. Research now shows that although the effects of antecedent- and response-focused coping may appear similar in terms of expressive behavior, other effects may be quite different. Specifically, Gross (1998) had participants view films of medical procedures designed to elicit feelings of disgust while being instructed to regulate their emotional responses either through reappraisal or suppression. Gross found that both reappraisal and suppression were successful in reducing expressive behavior, but only reappraisal decreased subjective feelings of disgust. Furthermore, suppression, but not reappraisal, led to increased sympathetic nervous system activation, as recorded by measures such as finger pulse, finger temperature, and skin conductance. Other research by Gross and his colleagues supports the finding of suppression extracting physiological costs (Gross & Levinson, 1993, 1997).

Recently, Richards and Gross (1999, 2000) extended these findings by demonstrating that in addition to physiological costs, suppression has cognitive costs as well. In two experiments, Richards and Gross (1999) show that suppressing the expression of emotion impairs memory performance on a concurrent task. Richards and Gross (2000) replicated and extended these findings by showing that when comparing suppression with reappraisal, only suppression hurts memory performance. They propose that suppression, because it occurs relatively late in the emotion-generation processes, consumes greater resources than does reappraisal. As a result, fewer cognitive resources are available for the concurrent memory task, resulting in impaired performance. Complementing these findings, recent work by Baumeister and colleagues (Baumeister, Bratslavsky, Muraven, & Tice, 1998) shows that the self-regulation of emotion depletes mental resources, as indexed by measures of perseverance and performance on subsequent tasks.

The costs of emotion regulation can be best understood by placing emotion regulation within the context of more general models of self-regulation (Carver & Scheier, 1981; Kanfer & Ackerman, 1989). Richards and Gross (2000) note that emotion regulation implies the existence of a negative feedback loop. One's existing state (say, anger) is compared with a referent standard (say, pleasantness), and if a discrepancy is noted, an operating process will be engaged to reduce the discrepancy. Both monitoring and taking corrective action, however, require effort and may deplete cognitive resources available for other tasks. Baumeister and colleagues (1998) make a similar point with their ego depletion model, which posits that all acts of self-regulation deplete limited resources within the individual and will thus affect subsequent performance on a range of unrelated acts.

These findings in the emotions realm appear to have a close parallel with Kanfer and Ackerman's cognitive resources model of self-regulation. Kanfer and Ackerman proposed that self-regulatory activities such as self-monitoring require cognitive resources. Because cognitive resources are finite, the benefits of self-regulatory activities can be realized only when there are sufficient resources for engaging in the self-regulatory activity itself. Otherwise, cognitive resources that would have been allocated to task performance may be diverted to the service of self-regulation, resulting in impaired task performance and learning. In a series of experiments, the authors demonstrated that goal setting, a self-regulatory activity, improved performance when tasks were well learned, but on novel, resource-dependent tasks, goal setting led to impaired task performance. These findings complement those of Richards and Gross (2000), where suppression, a cognitively demanding emotion regulation strategy, led to impaired performance on a memory task. In both cases, the cognitive resources required by the self-regulatory activity appear to be diverted from the concurrent tasks, with a negative impact on task performance.

Automatic and Controlled Processes in Emotion Regulation

The model presented in Figure 5.1 is not an exact replication of Gross's framework (1998, 1999). In his original model, Gross posits that an evaluation of an emotional stimulus mediates between the stimulus input and the individual's emotional response tendencies. The evaluation requirement was dropped in the model to broaden the framework to allow for the many influences on affect that fall outside conscious awareness and attention (Zajonc, 1980). Including nonconscious, automatic influences on affect is useful for this chapter because it allows for the examination of when emotional regulation occurs and when it does not. Specifically, a stimulus that is not consciously perceived may influence emotional experience, and subsequently emotional expression, precisely because its effects occur outside conscious awareness and the resultant emotions are not regulated. A consideration of both conscious and nonconscious influences on emotion and emotion regulation is important because automatic processes may affect us precisely because we are less likely to guard against them.

Task Environment Effects on Emotion Regulation

In an early study of cross-cultural differences in the expression of emotion, Ekman (1972) recorded the facial expression of emotion in Japanese and American subjects while they watched emotion-eliciting film clips. The facial displays of emotion for the Japanese and American subjects were nearly identical when they were watching the films alone, but when they were watching the film clips in the presence of another individual of the same ethnicity, there were marked differences in the expression of emotion between American and Japanese subjects, with Japanese subjects hiding their negative feelings to a greater extent than the Americans. This example illustrates the importance of considering context in any discussion of emotion regulation. Had context not been manipulated in this work, no differences would have been detected between Japanese and American study participants. But by considering the norms and meanings attached to context, it can be seen that for the Japanese participants, the presence of another individual mandates the regulation of negative emotional expression. Ekman (1972) originally used the term *display rules* to describe societal norms about appropriate emotional displays, and organizational researchers have demonstrated that organizations also place powerful constraints on the emotions experienced and expressed within their boundaries (Hochschild, 1983; Rafaeli & Sutton, 1989; Van Maanen & Kunda, 1989). I explore three ways in which the organizational task environment affects emotion regulation: through norms affecting the need to regulate emotion, through inputs into the emotion system, and by affecting the ability to regulate emotion.

The Need to Regulate: Display Rules

Ekman (1972) refers to norms about which emotions a member of a social system should express as display rules. Emotion management in response to display rules may include processes that are so well learned that they operate outside conscious awareness, as well as more controlled processes. As an example of more automatic processes, there is significant evidence that the presence of others causes us to attenuate the expression of emotion (Buck, 1984). This fact likely is due to strong socialization against the unregulated expression of emotion by adults (Friedman & Miller-Herringer, 1991); children can be expected to gloat when they triumph and throw temper tantrums when they lose, but the same behaviors are frowned on in adults. There also is evidence that people engage in antecedent-focused emotion regulation by attempting to put themselves in appropriate moods prior to social interactions (Erber, Wegner, & Therriault, 1996). Given the ubiquity of socialized norms governing emotion regulation when interacting with others, it is likely that emotion regulation in the service of societal display rules is automatic (Wegner & Bargh, 1998); that is, the regulation strategies are so well rehearsed that they can be deployed at will and with little conscious effort.

A different picture emerges in organizations where display rules serve organizational or professional goals. A number of qualitative and quantitative studies show that employees frequently are socialized to display particular emotions and sanctioned when their emotional displays violate group or organizational norms. Flight attendants, for example, are taught to express good cheer even to rude passengers (Hochschild, 1983), and bill collectors are trained to express feelings of tension, urgency, and slight irritation toward debtors (Sutton, 1991). Frequently, display rules also require the suppression of emotional responses. Starting in medical school, for example, doctors learn that affective neutrality is the appropriate rule for emotional display while interacting with patients. Feelings such as disgust over the patient's condition do arise but are to be suppressed (Smith & Kleinman, 1989). Although eventually these display rules may be so well learned that they are enacted automatically, conforming to them initially requires a great deal of planning and conscious effort, and many of the emotional displays required of physicians in their daily practice are highly scripted and effortful (Locke, 1996; Smith & Kleinman, 1989).

Display rules therefore make the regulation of emotion an important element of job performance. As a form of self-regulation in the service of organizational goals, conforming to display rules is a controlled process that requires planning and effort on the part of the employee. Research shows that bill collectors, physicians, flight attendants, and others develop specific coping strategies in response to demands of the task environment. Yet the task environment can complicate attempts at emotion regulation at both the input and response sides of the model. Task environments generate more or less affective stimuli as an input into the system, and some of the stimuli may be outside conscious awareness, hindering the effectiveness of controlled emotion regulation. Cognitive demands in the task environment also may hamper the ability to regulate emotions successfully.

Inputs: The Affect of the Task Environment

In many cases, the task environment supplies the stimulus that begins the process of emotion generation (Weiss & Cropanzano, 1996). Consider physicians. The environment where they work, such as a hospital room, provides an abundance of negative emotional stimuli: the human body in various stages of disease and decay. The stimuli cause negative emotional reactions in the physicians, which interfere with professional display rules; thus, physicians develop a variety of emotion regulation strategies to cope with the effects of the environment. The task environment, then, is an important causal factor for the generation of emotional experience and, subsequently, the need for emotion regulation strategies.

Because task environments are important for supplying affective stimuli, it may be fruitful to describe environments in terms of their potential to generate affective experiences. Despite frequent conceptualizations of the environment in terms of organizational climate, organizational culture, and task characteristics, few organizational scholars have modeled environments in terms of affective stimuli, although recent research has begun to move in this direction (Weiss & Cropanzano, 1996). Researchers in consumer behavior and environmental psychology, however, have a long history of thinking of organizational environments in affective terms. Over twenty-five years ago, Kotler (1974) encouraged the study of atmospherics, or the deliberate design of an organization's environment to produce specific emotional effects in customers. To Kotler, the environment was an affect-creating medium, and he conceptualized the environment in terms of four dimensions: visual, aural, olfactory, and tactile. Kotler's work was largely speculative, but Russell and Snodgrass (1987) document extensive evidence that characteristics of the environment have a substantial impact on the affective experiences of those within it. These characteristics range from the completely imperceptible, such as the presence of chemicals (for example, environmental pollutants such as pesticides) that have well-established effects on mood, to sensory stimuli such as sunlight, temperature, and sounds. Similarly, in the marketing literature, Bitner's concept of servicescapes (1992) describes the environment along the dimensions of ambient conditions, space and function, and signs, symbols, and artifacts. Bitner proposes that these dimensions affect employee and customer cognitive, emotional, and physiological responding.

The literature just reviewed is a small sampling of a large body of work, mostly in marketing, consumer behavior, and environmental psychology, on the affect-producing qualities of environments. This work shows that the affect associated with particular environments is related to outcomes relevant to organizational researchers, such as customer affect, time spent in the environment, and ratings of employee friendliness and competence (Darden & Babin, 1994). The marketing and environmental psychology perspectives go beyond existing organizational research on affect in organizations, however, because they emphasize the more subtle impact of affect that may occur outside conscious awareness. Russell and Snodgrass (1987) note, "We may be affected in an emotional way by almost any aspect of the physical environment—from chemicals we breathe to its symbolic meaning. The person affected may be aware of some of these influences, *but more often is not*" [emphasis added] (p. 259). Russell and Snodgrass illustrate this point with an example of an early experiment by Winslow and Herrington (1936). In this research, workers were exposed to the odor of burned dust. The odor was strong enough to be noticed by anyone entering the room where the experiment occurred, but because its level was increased gradually, workers were unaware of its presence. Despite workers' lack of awareness, their appetites were affected by the odor, as measured by the amount of food they consumed during the experiment. The notion that affective changes can be brought about without conscious awareness is well established in more recent research as well (Wegner & Bargh, 1998). Social psychologists have demonstrated that small incidents of minor relevance (Isen, 1984), the weather (Schwarz & Clore, 1983), mere exposure to object or event (Zajonc, 1980), and even facial expressions and bodily postures (Adelmann & Zajonc, 1989; Stepper & Strack, 1993) can have an impact on affective states. Importantly, these effects do not depend on the conscious processing of the emotional stimuli.

For those who work in affectively charged environments, the existence of stimuli that make emotion regulation necessary likely are obvious. The flight attendants whom Hochschild (1983) studied, for example, were quite aware that customers who drank too much and made sexual advances were the source of tension and anger and that this anger interfered with their job performance. They were able to describe clearly specific emotion-regulation strategies that help mitigate felt anger. In environments where there are obvious emotional inputs that are incongruent with display and feeling rules, therefore, employees develop emotion regulation strategies that help thwart the effects of the environmental stimuli (see Rafaeli & Sutton, 1990; Sutton, 1991; Van Maanen & Kunda, 1989; Locke, 1996; Smith & Kleinman, 1989). In contrast, in other environments, the subtle influences on affect may be more insidious. Because affect may be influenced without conscious awareness, emotion regulation strategies may not be put into place to guard against the impact of the environment. That is, if the employee is unaware that the place where she works is influencing her affective state, one would not expect her to have developed an efficient emotion regulation strategy. It is not a far stretch to generalize from the workers whom Winslow and Herrington (1936) studied to a twenty-first-century office worker laboring under conditions of poor lighting, stale air, and distracting ambient noise. Unlike the police officer or physician who takes conscious steps to regulate emotion for work, the office worker, less aware of the causal antecedents to his or her affective states, takes no steps to guard against the impact of the environment.

Furthermore, research suggests that unappraised affect may actually have more of an impact on outcomes than when the source of the affect is known. In their work on affective priming, for example, Murphy and Zajonc (1993) find that an affective prime presented below the threshold of conscious awareness (4 milliseconds) influences preferences for novel stimuli, but the same effects do not emerge when the affective primes are presented for longer durations. Wegner and Bargh (1998) have interpreted this finding as suggesting that emotional priming may be more effective when it occurs without consciousness, and this position also is supported by Schwarz and Clore's "affect as information" model of judgment formation (1983). Simply stated, it appears that affective inputs may affect us the most when we are the least aware of them. As such, potential sources of unappraised affect in the environment should be accorded as much research attention as the more obvious sources found in unruly customers and menacing bosses.

The Ability to Regulate: Cognitive Demands in the Environment

Research on the expressed emotion of customer service personnel has consistently shown that when stores are busy, employees express less positive emotion toward customers. A negative relationship between store pace and employees' display of positive emotion has been demonstrated in supermarkets in Israel (Rafaeli & Sutton, 1990), convenience stores in the United States and Canada (Sutton & Rafaeli, 1988; Rafaeli, 1989), and banks in the United States (Pugh, 2001). One explanation for this relationship is that store busyness creates tension and stress, which is then reflected in verbal and nonverbal behavior (Rafaeli & Sutton, 1990; Pugh, 2001). Rafaeli and Sutton note that the clerks they studied were "tense during busy times, apparently due to the cognitive overload evoked by the crowded setting and the stress of serving customers who were irritated from navigating the busy store and from waiting in line" (1990, p. 625). Recently, findings from Wegner's work on ironic processes have emerged that provide strong support for Rafaeli and Sutton's speculation that the failure to display positive emotion is tied to cognitive load.

When we try to suppress a thought, why does that thought persistently intrude into our consciousness? This issue is addressed by Wegner's research (1994) on the ironic processes of mental control. Ironic processes in Wegner's work refer to counterintentional effects that result from efforts at self-control of mental states. Wegner reviews research showing a variety of ironic effects: attempts at thought suppression lead to the frequent reoccurrence of the unwanted thought, attempts at relaxation can lead to increased stress levels, and, most important for this chapter, attempts at gaining a positive mood can lead to higher negative moods.

Wegner (1994) proposes that attempts at mental control initiate two processes. First, an operating process searches for mental contents consistent with the desired state. At the same time, a monitoring process is initiated that searches for any sensations or thoughts that are inconsistent with the desired state. If the desired state is one of happiness, an operating process searches for mental contents consistent with happiness, while the monitoring process searches for the intrusion of any thoughts inconsistent with happiness. Ironic effects occur because the monitoring process heightens sensitivity to those things that are not part of the desired mental state. These effects are most likely under conditions of mental load, where the search for undesired thoughts or sensations is enough to invite them into consciousness and thus activate precisely the state one was trying to avoid.

There is substantial evidence that ironic monitoring processes usually occur when conscious control processes are overwhelmed by distractions or stress (Wegner & Bargh, 1998). For example, Wegner, Erber, and Zanakos (1993) asked participants to put themselves in a particular mood state (for example, try to be happy, try not to be happy, or no instructions) while writing about a past life event that had emotional significance. When participants were under no cognitive load, they could perform as requested: those asked to be happy actually were happy, and those asked not to be happy evidenced less positive mood. When the participants were placed under cognitive load by performing a distracting mental task, however, they failed to achieve their desired mood states. In fact, their subsequent moods were in the opposite direction to what they had attempted to achieve: those attempting to achieve positive mood were the most sad, and those seeking negative mood were the most happy. Wegner concludes from his research that "the central variable dividing successful control from ironic effects is the availability of mental capacity. . . . Mental control exerted during mental load will often produce ironic effects, resulting in mental states that go beyond 'no change' to become the opposite of what is desired" (p. 35).

Based on this evidence, it appears that the causal link between cognitive load and ironic effects is one key to understanding the negative busyness–display of emotion relationship. Service workers engage in a constant process of regulating their emotional experiences and expressions in order to conform to organizational display rules (Grandey, 2000). As the busyness increases in store environments, employees begin to experience greater feelings of tension and stress (Sutton & Rafaeli, 1988). As internal feelings turn more negative, service workers have to suppress those feelings more in order to conform to display rules that generally prohibit the expression of negative emotion. Yet at the same time that they are attempting to suppress their gradually increasing negative affect, the busyness of the store environment and demands of customers are contributing to the workers' cognitive overload (Rafaeli & Sutton, 1990). Furthermore, as the work of Richards and Gross (1999, 2000) has shown, attempts at suppression also consume cognitive resources. The result, as Wegner (1994) would predict, is an increasing display of negative affect—precisely the type of display that service workers typically guard against.

The link between busyness in the task environment and the failure to maintain positive emotional displays highlights the fact that emotion regulation is a form of self-regulation, and self-regulation has a cost: it consumes mental resources (Baumeister et al., 1998; Kanfer & Ackerman, 1989). As the availability of cognitive resources diminishes, the likelihood of ironic effects increases. Importantly, the display of positive emotion is only one small aspect of an employee's job performance. In banks, for example, workers are expected to process financial transactions accurately concurrent with maintaining the desired emotional display. As the work of Kanfer and Ackerman (1989), and more recently Richards and Gross (1999,

2000), has shown, an emphasis on the regulation of emotion may divert cognitive resources from concurrent tasks, which will negatively affect performance if the task is resource dependent. Practically, this suggests that organizations at times may face a trade-off: desired emotional displays by employees versus performance on cognitively demanding tasks. Training employees in antecedent-focused regulation strategies may make this trade-off less necessary because these likely consume fewer cognitive resources than response-focused strategies such as suppression.

Summary: The Task Environment and Emotion Regulation

In sum, the task environment has been conceptualized as affecting emotion regulation by providing affective inputs into the emotion system, imposing display rules, and influencing cognitive load. I now shift to an examination of emotion regulation in dyads, but many of the processes already outlined remain relevant for understanding dyadic processes. Specifically, whereas the task environment has been proposed as an important source of affective inputs, the focus now turns to one's interaction partner as a source of affective inputs (see Figure 5.2). Similar to the affect of task environments, the affect of interaction partners is proposed to influence one's own affect outside conscious awareness, although the process in dyads is more powerful due to emotional contagion (Hatfield, Cacioppo, & Rapson, 1994). The role of cognitive load in emotion regulation also is revisited by considering the relative independence of the automatic process of contagion from the effects of cognitive load and then examining load as a potential mediator linking emotion regulation to common social cognitive processes in dyads such as persuasion and stereotyping.

Emotion Regulation in Dyads

Dyads are the foundation for a variety of processes that social and organizational psychologists study, and frequently researchers hypothesize connections between the affect and emotions of dyad members. Lord, Brown, and Freiberg (1999), for example, propose that initial relationships between superiors and subordinates are influenced largely by affective information, and this affective information is transmitted from superiors through subtle means that are outside conscious awareness. Similarly, Sutton and Rafaeli (1988) suggest that negative affect in customers influences the felt and expressed emotions of service employees. Below, I review evidence for the concept of emotional contagion, which provides a theoretically grounded explanation for how affect is transmitted between dyad members. In addition, the introduction of dyadic processes in emotion regulation moves the discussion into the social cognitive arena, where processes such as persuasion, stereotyping, and attribution are commonly studied within dyads. Under the theme of the costs of emotion regulation, this section also examines how emotion regulation may affect some common social cognitive processes.

Emotional Contagion

Lord et al. (1999) propose that supervisors may influence employees by "subtle affective messages that are communicated outside of conscious awareness" (p. 171). Recent research on the concept of emotional contagion—the idea that the observation of another's emotional expression induces a congruent affective state in the observer (Neumann & Strack, 2000)—helps clarify the mechanisms of this affective exchange. Defined formally, emotional contagion is "the tendency to automatically mimic and synchronize facial expressions, vocalizations, postures, and movements with those of another person and, consequently, to converge emotionally" (Hatfield, Cacioppo, & Rapson, 1992, p. 153). Through our interactions with other people, we catch their emotions. Meeting with a depressed student, for example, may leave a professor tired, lethargic, and somewhat depressed herself, although there appears to be nothing objectively causing this affective state. Typically, contagion is modeled as occurring in two steps (Hatfield et al.,1994; Neumann & Strack, 2000). First, in interactions, people come to synchronize and mimic the other person's emotional expressions, as conveyed by voice, posture, facial expressions, gestures, and other means. Support for this proposition comes from a long history of research, mostly associated with the study of the process of empathy (Bavelas, Black, Lemery, & Mullett, 1987). Researchers have demonstrated that viewing pictures of happy or angry faces evokes differential, congruent responses in the facial expressions of subjects (Dimberg, 1982). For example, McHugo and colleagues (McHugo, Lanzetta, Sullivan, Masters, & Englis, 1985) presented subjects with images (videotapes without sound) of President Reagan expressing happiness-reassurance, anger-threat, and fear-evasion. Analyses of facial displays showed subjects smiling when presented with the happiness-reassurance image and frowning with the anger-threat and fear-evasion images. Recent research by Chartrand and Bargh (1999) has demonstrated that interaction partners also mimic behavioral mannerisms such as foot shaking and face rubbing, and Neumann and Strack (2000) find evidence of mimicry in the vocal expression of emotion.

There are two important points to consider with regard to these well-established mimicry processes. First, mimicry appears to be functional, in that it facilitates social interaction. Chartrand and Bargh (1999) demonstrate that when a confederate mimicked the movements and postures of an interaction partner, that partner reported that the interaction went more smoothly and reported greater liking for the experimental partner. Second, considerable evidence indicates that mimicry is an automatic, unintentional process (Bavelas et al., 1987; Chartrand & Bargh, 1999; Neumann & Strack, 2000). In addition to the behavioral mimicry reviewed above, there is evidence that even less controlled processes such as autonomic nervous system activity become synchronized in dyads including therapists and patients, mothers and infants, and spouses (Levenson & Ruef, 1997). Chartrand and Bargh (1999) assert that behavioral mimicry, which they refer to as the chameleon effect, is "an entirely passive and preconsciously automatic process" (p. 896).

Mimicry of expressive behavior therefore occurs automatically during interactions and appears to facilitate the interaction. Unintentional imitation of another's expressive behavior also does more: it activates a congruent mood state in the observer (Neumann & Strack, 2000). This is the second step of contagion: an individual's affective state is influenced by the activation or feedback resulting from the mimicry of emotional expression (Hatfield et al., 1994). One way that expressive behavior affects the experience of emotion is described by the facial feedback hypothesis. In its simplest form, the facial feedback hypothesis proposes that there will be a correspondence between facial efference and subjective experience. Research by Strack, Martin, and Stepper (1988) shows, for example, that artificially created facial expressions can produce corresponding changes in affective states. As reviewed by Adelmann and Zajonc (1989), the evidence for the facial feedback hypothesis is quite strong; one's reported affect and emotions to some extent appear to be influenced by facial efference. Furthermore, these effects are found for other expressive behaviors, including posture and vocalizations (Stepper & Strack, 1993).

Given that interactions produce mimicry of expressive behaviors and the mimicked behaviors produce corresponding affective states, Hatfield et al. (1994) proposed that people catch the emotions of their interaction partners. Recent research supports their theory. Neumann and Strack (2000) found that listening to a speech spoken in a slightly happy or sad voice produced corresponding mood states in listeners. Similar effects have been found by Gump and Kulik (1997), Hsee, Hatfield, Carlson, and Chemtob (1990), and Sullins (1991), among others. Furthermore, a recent meta-analysis of thirty-six studies in the clinical psychology literature finds substantial support for the contagion of depressive mood (Joiner & Katz, 1999). Researchers also have found evidence for emotional contagion in the workplace. In a study of emotional contagion in employee-customer interactions, Pugh (2001) found that positive displays of emotion by bank tellers were associated with higher levels of positive affect among their customers, and a recent study by Lewis (2000) demonstrates that a leader's expression of negative emotion produces a corresponding negative affective state in observers.

Similar to the affect of the task environment, the relevance of the emotional contagion phenomenon for emotion regulation hinges largely on the fact that contagion is automatic and outside conscious awareness. The affect of one's interaction partner acts as an input into one's emotional system (Gross, 1998). As a result, affective states and resultant behaviors may change in response to the stimuli, but these changes likely will be subtle and outside conscious awareness. The independence of conscious, cognitive processes and more automatic contagion processes is perhaps best seen in the study by McHugo et al. (1986) on affective responses to the facial displays of President Reagan. For self-reported emotions, participants with negative attitudes toward Reagan reported uniformly negative emotional responses to all of his facial displays, whereas his supporters reported emotions congruent with his displayed emotion. For less controllable physiological responses, such as facial electromyography (EMG), however, there were no differences between supporters and opponents in response to Reagan's facial displays. That is, Reagan's opponents tended to smile when Reagan smiled, whether they intended to or not.

Contagion therefore can hinder emotion regulation because the process is largely uncontrollable, and, as with the subtle effects of task environment, if the affective input is not realized, proper steps for emotion regulation may not be taken. Consider as an example the process of emotion regulation that a supervisor uses during a disciplinary meeting with a subordinate. The supervisor may be working hard to conduct a proper meeting by maintaining a calm, neutral demeanor, concentrating on the facts of the case and carefully planning his or her words. Yet while the supervisor is consciously working to maintain the appropriate emotional display, nonconscious contagion processes may be undermining these efforts, leading the supervisor to experience the tension, anxiety, and anger the employee is feeling and reflect these feelings back to the employee. Because the motor-mimicry processes causing contagion operate outside conscious awareness, the supervisor likely is doing nothing to guard against this less obvious influence on his or her emotion; emotional experience may be affected because adequate emotion regulation is not taking place.

Load and Emotion Regulation Revisited

Previously, certain techniques of emotion regulation were proposed to have a cost in terms of mental resources. As a form of self-regulation, emotion regulation consumes cognitive resources that may be diverted from concurrent tasks (Kanfer & Ackerman, 1989), and relatedly, if demands in the task environment drain cognitive resources, one is likely to have difficulty regulating emotion (Wegner, 1994). Emotional contagion, however, appropriates little or no cognitive resources and functions relatively independently from cognitive processes. This can be seen, for example, in Neumann and Strack's finding (2000) that distraction while listening to a speech impairs recognition of the content of the speech but has no impact on contagion from the speaker's vocal tone. Under load, those processes not activated automatically typically suffer, whereas automatic processes do not (Wegner & Bargh, 1998). Because emotion regulation is hindered by cognitive load but contagion is not, it is reasonable to expect that the catching of another's emotion will increase as cognitive load increases. Moreover, because of the effects of load on the ability to regulate emotion, individuals under load are more likely to express undesired emotions. This sets up a potentially vicious pattern in dyads working under intense pressure: as one individual finds it more difficult to regulate his or her emotions, the partner in the dyad is simultaneously more susceptible to catching that emotion and reflecting it back through mimicry processes. The expected result would be an escalation of undesired emotions in the dyad.

The idea that there is an interplay between emotions and social cognitive processes has been treated implicitly thus far, as seen in, for example, the discussion of Chartrand and Bargh's (1999) finding that emotional synchronization in dyads facilitates social interactions. In fact, the discussion of dyadic processes brings to the front a host of social cognitive processes (such as attribution, persuasion, and stereotyping) that have a bidirectional relationship with emotion regulation; they influence emotion regulation and are affected by attempts at emotion regulation. One example of the effects of social cognitions on emotion regulation is given by Lord and Harvey in Chapter Four of this volume in discussing the emotional responses that may arise from being cut off in traffic. The attributions one makes for the cause of the other driver's actions (Was the action deliberate or due to unavoidable circumstances?) give rise to very different emotions. Similarly, unfavorable stereotypes of certain groups may generate negative emotions when in their presence, prompting the need for suppression of those emotions. The effects of emotions on social cognitive processes also are fairly straightforward. For example, mood effects on judgment formation are well established in the social psychology literature (see Forgas, 1995). What is perhaps less obvious is that attempts at emotion regulation may also affect a variety of social cognitive processes through effects on cognitive load; these are presented here as additional hidden costs or consequences of emotion regulation.

For a variety of social cognitive processes, a key question is the extent to which people use effortful, systematic processes in forming judgments and impressions versus employing heuristics or shortcuts. In the domain of persuasion, Chaiken's (1980) heuristic-systematic model and Petty and Cacioppo's (1986) elaboration likelihood model distinguish between arriving at attitude judgments by considering the quality and logic of the arguments (the systematic or central route to persuasion) versus arriving at judgments by using rules of thumb or features unrelated to the message (the heuristic or peripheral route to persuasion). Similar distinctions are made in person perception research (Fiske & Neuberg, 1990) and attribution research (Gilbert, Pelham, & Krull, 1988). In general, findings show that more effortful processing strategies require both sufficient processing motivation and sufficient cognitive resources (Bless & Schwarz, 1999). For example, Gilbert et al. (1988) demonstrated that when participants were cognitively busy, they ignored situational factors and instead made dispositional attributions for a target's behavior, but situational factors were given due consideration when participants were not under cognitive load. Wegner and Bargh (1988) refer to it as a general rule that "conscious, deliberate forms of processing information about attitude issues as well as about people are not used unless the individual has both the attention and the intention to give the matter full consideration. . . . In their stead, stereotypic and heuristic shortcuts are taken" (p. 467).

Because response-focused emotion regulation consumes cognitive resources, individuals attempting to regulate their emotions through suppression can be expected to engage in more heuristic processing of information. That is, while attempting to suppress emotion, a person would be expected to engage in more stereotypic thinking about others, make more dispositional attributions, and be influenced by more peripheral cues (Petty & Cacioppo, 1986). Although to date I am aware of no research explicitly testing these propositions, there is a body of research that finds an association between affect and persuasion and stereotyping (Bless & Schwarz, 1999). This research shows a negative association between positive mood and effortful processing, possibly due to either decreased motivation to process information carefully when in a positive mood or the limits that positive mood place on processing capacity (these explanations have recently been questioned by Bless & Schwarz, 1999). Regardless of the cause, the association between emotion regulation, cognitive load, and load-dependent social cognitive processes again makes the point that the benefits of emotion regulation must be weighed in the light of the costs.

Individual Differences in Emotion Regulation

To this point, the discussion has focused on contextual factors that influence emotion regulation, but even the most casual observation of individuals will reveal differences in emotion that appear consistent regardless of the context. Certain individuals are pleasantly engaged with their environment in work and nonwork settings; they are active, enthusiastic, and upbeat in a variety of situations. Other individuals typically appear dull, lethargic, anxious, or afraid. The prevailing wisdom in the literature is that these observable differences reflect stable differences in an individual's experienced affect; substantial evidence exists documenting these differences (see Larson, Diener, and Lucas, Chapter Three, this volume). The alternative perspective I present suggests that these clearly observable differences in people may not always reflect differences in experienced emotion.

Consider first that we typically make judgments of another's emotional state based on that person's expressive behavior: the facial expressions, vocalizations, body posture, and other movements that serve as outward indicators of emotional experience (Ambady & Rosenthal, 1992). Perhaps what we take to be observed differences in emotional experience really reflect differences in emotional expression, or the "behavioral changes that accompany emotion, including the face, voice, gestures, posture, and body movement" (Gross, John, & Richards, 2000, p. 712). To make this example concrete, think about two clerks at the local division of the state motor vehicles office. Referring back to Figure 5.1, assume that both receive the same amount of negative inputs from the environment (such as angry customers), and both are equally sensitive to the negative emotional stimuli. Yet the emotional responses observed by customers and coworkers may be quite different for the two clerks. For Clerk A, the negative affect caused by the environment has a barely perceivable influence, but for Clerk B, a scowl and aggressive body language leave no doubt as to his negative affective state. For both clerks, the internal experience of emotion may be the same, yet Clerk B appears to an observer to be experiencing greater negative affect because more obvious behavioral changes accompany his emotional states.

In terms of Gross's model (see Figure 5.1), the two clerks differ in terms of their response-focused emotion regulation, that is, in the extent to which emotional response tendencies actually manifest themselves as outwardly expressed emotion. This stable individual difference has been termed *emotional expressivity* (Gross & John, 1997). Although there are several individual differences relevant for understanding emotion regulation, such as differences in sensitivity to emotional inputs, expressivity is given nearly exclusive focus here due to the relative inattention it has received in the literature relative to variables on the input side of Figure 5.1 (see Larsen, Diener, and Lucas, Chapter Three, this volume, for a coverage of these). Furthermore, expressivity has shown strong links to gender, the role of which also is examined below. Finally, this section concludes with a brief treatment of individual differences in skill at emotion regulation.

Emotional Expressivity

Gross and John (1997) define emotional expressivity as the extent to which individuals manifest emotional impulses behaviorally. Psychologists have long had an interest in the behavioral expression of emotion, as emotions expressed through somewhat less controlled channels of facial expressions and posture are seen as providing particularly accurate insights into actual emotional experience (Ambady & Rosenthal, 1992). An emerging body of research on individual differences in emotional expressivity suggests that visible signs of emotion may be a more accurate indicator of inner emotional experience for some individuals than for others.

The current interest in emotional expressivity can most readily be traced to Friedman and colleagues' development of their measure of expressivity, the affective communication test (ACT; Friedman, Prince, Riggio, & DiMatteo, 1980). Their conceptualization of expressivity, defined as "the use of facial expressions, voice, gestures, and body movements to transmit emotions" (p. 333), stressed positively valenced emotions and their application for the purpose of influencing others. Their view of expressiveness was rooted in ideas of charisma; highly expressive people are able to "move, inspire, and captivate others" (p. 333). The construct has obvious links to outcomes of interest to industrial/organizational psychologists. For example, researchers (Morris & Feldman, 1996; Pugh, 2001) have suggested that measures of expressiveness may be useful for selection purposes in jobs where the expression of emotion is a crucial component of job performance (Hochschild, 1983). Although evidence from the workplace is scarce, a handful of studies support this idea. Pugh (2001) demonstrated a modest association ($r = .22$) between scores on a modified version of the ACT and the extent to which bank tellers expressed positive emotion during interactions with customers. In addition, a study by DiMatteo, Teranta, Friedman, and Prince (1980) found that physicians' ability to express emotions in nonverbal communication was positively associated with their patients' satisfaction with the medical care they received.

Recently, researchers in this area have expressed dissatisfaction with the ACT measure because it is an overly broad construct, encompassing not just expressiveness but the use of emotions for the purpose of social influence. More recent effort by researchers has been directed toward developing and validating more pure measures of emotional expressiveness. Recent examples are King and Emmons's emotional expressivity questionnaire (1990), Kring, Smith, and Neal's emotional expressivity scale (1994), and the measure with the greatest empirical support, Gross and John's Berkeley Expressivity Questionnaire (BEQ; 1997). Gross and John's research has shown that three factors emerge in self and peer ratings of expressivity: (1) impulse strength, or the general strength of emotion-response tendencies; (2) negative expressivity, or the degree to which negative emotional response tendencies are expressed behaviorally; and (3) positive expressivity, or the degree to which positive emotional response tendencies are expressed behaviorally (Gross & John, 1997). Later research (Gross & John, 1998) indicates the presence of two additional factors: expressive confidence, or confidence and comfort in public displays of emotion, and masking, which refers to attempts to conceal discrepancies between inner feelings and outward expressions. The three dimensions of impulse strength and positive and negative expressivity load on a higher-order factor of core emotional expressivity and capture the essence of the expressivity construct (Gross & John, 1998). Note also that measures of dispositional emotional expressivity have been shown to be distinct from indicators of emotional experience and personality traits such as extraversion and neuroticism (Friedman et al., 1980; Gross & John, 1997, 1998).

The three-factor model of core emotional expressivity has several advantages over the unifactoral models previously advanced (Friedman et al., 1980; Kring et al., 1994) in terms of discriminant validity with a number of criteria. Specifically, Gross and John (1997) find that in response to a positive mood induction, positive expressivity predicted displays of positive emotion (as evidence in facial expressions and upper body movement), but negative expressivity did not. Similarly, following a negative mood induction, negative expressivity predicted expression of negative emotion, but positive expressivity did not. Although weaker than the effects for either negative or positive expressivity, impulse strength is positively related to both positive and negative emotional displays, indicating that this factor is capturing the general tendency to have stronger or weaker emotional responses following stimuli, regardless of the valence of the emotions.

The practical implication of the three-factor model is that if one wishes to anticipate the type of emotions that an individual will express, the factor with the greatest predictive validity may depend on the type of stimuli input into the system. If keeping one's composure in an environment full of negative emotional stimuli, such as angry customers, is important, then the negative expressivity subscale of the BEQ (Gross & John, 1997) will be the most informative for predicating which employees will reciprocate an angry customer with their own negative emotions. According to Gross and John's findings, the measure of positive expressivity will provide little information regarding the likelihood of negative displayed emotions. Similarly, in an environment generally characterized by positive inputs, positive expressivity will be the strongest predictor of an employee's display of positive emotion.

In sum, emotional expressivity acts as a type of output filter between emotional experience and expressive behavior, and research documents stable individual differences in expressivity; for some individuals, the experience of emotion is accompanied by substantial behavioral changes—postural or facial, for example—whereas with others, the behavioral changes associated with emotion are slight. Returning to the topic of dyads, note that because emotionally expressive individuals manifest greater behavioral changes with emotion than do low expressives, highly expressive people should cause greater contagion in their interaction partners (Hatfield et al., 1994). Indeed, the greatest contagion would be expected in a dyad with two highly expressive individuals each feeding of the other's emotions (and this effect should be magnified if the dyad is under pressure). Friedman and Riggio (1981) found some evidence for the power of highly expressive people to influence the emotions of others. In groups of three, with one person high on expressivity and two lower on the construct (as measured with the ACT; Friedman et al., 1980), the mood of the highly expressive person had the greatest influence on the moods of the other group participants. Interestingly, this effect appeared to hold only for negative moods, perhaps anticipating the need to distinguish between positive and negative expressivity (see Gross & John, 1997).

Although evidence for the dispositional construct of expressivity is plentiful, the causes of differences in expressivity are less well researched. The research of Cacioppo and colleagues (1992) suggests that the cause is partly physiological, with individuals differing in system gain, that is, the increment in a response (output) of a system per unit of stimulation (input). Cacioppo and colleagues also stress that physiology is only part of the picture and that social, cultural, and developmental factors must also be considered. One individual difference that likely has its origin in all of the above is observed with gender differences in emotional expressiveness. A substantial body of research consistently finds females to be more emotionally expressive than males.

Gender Differences and Emotion Regulation

A common stereotype is that females are more "emotional" than males. Returning to the theme that observed differences in emotionality might not accurately reflect differences in experienced emotion, research demonstrates that males and females do not differ reliably in terms of emotional experience. There are significant differences, however, between males and females in the emotions expressed (LaFrance & Banaji, 1992): women are more emotionally expressive than men (Hall, 1984; La France & Banaji, 1992; Shields, 1987). Evidence for these differences comes from a variety of sources: for example, women relative to men exhibit greater movement in facial muscles, measured using EMG, in response to affective stimuli (Schwartz, Ahern, & Brown, 1979). Females also are better emotion senders: compared to males, females' spontaneous facial responses to emotional stimuli are more accurately decoded by receivers (Manstead, 1991). A meta-analysis by Hall (1984) shows that females express more emotion through nonverbal means, including smiles and laughs, eye contact, touching, and body movement. Hall's analysis shows that this applies to expression of negative emotion as well. Finally, Gross and John's research on self-reported emotional expressivity consistently shows females scoring higher than males on all three dimensions of core emotional expressivity: positive expressivity, negative expressivity, and impulse intensity (Gross & John, 1995, 1997, 1998).

Male-female differences in expressiveness are well established; however, the origins of these differences are more open to question. Some evidence for differences in facial EMG suggests origins in physiology (Cacioppo et al., 1992), but most research points to global display rules that dictate appropriate emotion displays for male and females. Typically, females are afforded greater latitude in emotions deemed appropriate for display than are males. Consistent with this observation, male subjects in Gross and John's study (1997) report more masking of their emotions than do females. The notion that differences in emotional expressiveness are learned through sex role socialization is supported by Manstead (1991), who notes that the reliable gender differences in expressivity found in adults are not consistently found in studies involving infants and children. This suggests that display rules are not fully active until late childhood, as sex role orientation becomes firmly socialized.

Application of these findings to the workplace may have the effect of reinforcing some common stereotypes about the superior abilities of women in jobs that require the display of positive emotion. Sociologists have long been interested in the idea of gendered work—that women and men play out gender roles in organizations and that organizations create, justify, and reinforce gender distinctions (Acker, 1990). Service work, in particular, frequently is regarded as gendered; scripts for good service include stereotyped feminine behaviors such as friendliness, deference, and flirting (Hall, 1993; Hochschild, 1983). Although there is much debate over whether different gender roles in organizations simply are manifestations of societal gender roles that are brought into the organization, or whether organizations structure and promote gendered performances as part of the work role (Hall, 1993), the fact that women and men do differ in their nonverbal emotional expressiveness and the types of expressive behaviors associated more with women, such as warmth and friendliness, also are the types of behaviors that conform to notions of good service (Hochschild, 1983), is well established.

Application of research on emotional expressiveness to workplace issues also will benefit from more recent efforts to refine measures of expressiveness to focus on specific emotions rather than global negative and positive expressivity. For example, Gross and John's findings that women score higher on positive and negative expressivity than do men suggests that women will display both more positive and more negative emotions during service transactions. From an organizational perspective, the display of positive emotion toward customers usually is encouraged, but the display of such negative emotions as anger toward an irritating customer certainly is not (Van Maanen & Kunda, 1989). Recent research by Timmers, Fischer, and Manstead (1998) suggests a slightly different pattern than found in Gross and John's work. The authors found that men are more likely to display powerful emotions (anger, pride) while women are more likely to display less powerful emotions (warmth, liking). Again, this pattern conforms to notions of the desirable attributes of customer service workers: the ability to express positive emotion toward customers and restraint or unwillingness to display negative emotions such as anger or frustration, even when provoked (Van Maanen & Kunda, 1989).

I caution readers against interpreting these findings as suggesting that gender be used as a selection criterion for service jobs. Both males and females have been shown to display a full range of positive and negative emotions in service jobs (Rafaeli, 1989). Furthermore, although displayed emotion is important in shaping customer perceptions of service (Pugh, 2001), its importance relative to other factors, such as speed and reliability, is unknown, and gender differences on other dimensions of service performance have not been established. Most important, however, such an interpretation might unfairly segregate women into customer contact positions, which frequently are some of the lowest-paid and least stable jobs in an organization.

Skill and Emotion Regulation

Emotion regulation has been presented here as a technique of self-regulation that is conscious and controlled, and when suppression is the regulatory technique employed, emotion regulation consumes cognitive resources. With repeated practice, however, even emotion regulation that is conscious and initiated intentionally can take on characteristics of an automatic process (Bargh, 1989). Wegner and Bargh (1998) note that the effectiveness of emotion control processes varies due to two key factors: strategy choice and control expertise. Strategy choice involves learning which techniques for emotion regulation work and which do not; expertise, according to Wegner and Bargh, often just comes down to the amount of practice an individual has in regulating his or her emotions. Conceptualizing skill as this combination of efficient strategy selection and expertise at applying the strategy, increasing skill at emotion regulation moves the process from an effortful and demanding one to a process that is nearly automatic. Importantly, emotion regulation as an automatic process does not imply that it is completely outside conscious awareness. Well-learned emotion regulation may be initiated consciously, but once initiated, it operates without the need for conscious guidance, attention, or monitoring (Wegner & Bargh, 1998).

The implication is that as skill at emotion regulation increases, the cognitive demands of emotion regulation decrease. Thus, with increasing skill, the possibility of ironic effects and impaired performance on other tasks performed while regulating emotion decreases. Relatedly, if attentional resources are viewed as a finite reserve from which both self-regulation and task performance processes draw, then as skill at task performance increases to where the task is nearly automatic (the procedural knowledge phase; Kanfer & Ackerman, 1989), the effectiveness of emotion regulation should increase because more resources will be free for emotion regulation.

Conclusion

In this chapter, I have focused on issues relevant to emotion regulation in individuals and dyads. Using Gross's model (1998) as an orienting framework, several diverse influences on emotion regulation have been integrated using three general themes. First, each influence on emotion regulation presented here can be modeled as affecting either inputs into the system in Figure 5.1 or the emotional responses from the system. Inputs into the system that were considered were the affect of the task environment and the affect of one's interaction partner in a dyad. Inputs into the system begin the process of emotion generation and necessitate the need for emotion regulation. Of course, these two inputs are only a sampling of the myriad influences on emotion encountered in organizations and were selected due to their less-than-obvious nature; other inputs might include, for example, antecedents to workplace aggression (see Chapter Seven) or work-family conflict (see Chapter Twelve). On the output side, the link between emotional response tendencies and expressed emotion is affected by display rules, cognitive load, and differences in expressivity, gender, and skill at regulating emotion. Each of these variables modulates the link between experienced and expressed emotion and helps emphasize that the observable emotional responses of an individual may not be an accurate reflection of that person's experienced emotion.

The second theme was that emotion regulation is largely a conscious, controlled process, yet emotions can be affected with or without conscious awareness. When inputs into the system affect emotions outside conscious awareness, as with emotional contagion processes or the subtle affect of the task environment, problems with emotion regulation may emerge because steps are not taken to guard against these influences.

Third, and perhaps most important, there is value in thinking of emotion regulation in terms of more general processes of self-regulation, which allows for the observation that emotion regulation does not come without a cost. Certain techniques of emotion regulation, most notably suppression, place demands on cognitive resources just as do other forms of self-regulation (Kanfer & Ackerman, 1989). As such, when several resource-dependent processes compete for scarce attentional resources, performance on one or more of the processes may suffer. Increasing skill at emotion regulation moves emotion regulation toward more of an automatic process (Bargh, 1989) and in so doing reduces the amount of resources it consumes. Part of increasing skill at emotion regulation may be learning to use antecedent-focused techniques (see Lord & Harvey, Chapter Four, this volume) that consume fewer resources than do response-focused regulation techniques.

Space limitations prohibit exploring all of the possible interactions between the individual, environmental, and dyadic processes discussed, and interested readers can likely identify a number of questions and additional links in Figure 5.2. For example, if individuals low on expressivity show their emotions less, is suppression less cognitively taxing for these persons? If so, one would expect that these individuals would show fewer detriments in either emotion regulation (ironic processes) or performance of a simultaneous task while under cognitive load. Furthermore, numerous additional features in the environment and dyads may moderate the relationships discussed in this chapter. The discussion of dyads, for example, was fairly rudimentary; the fact that dyads differ in type and purpose was not explored. For example, there is some evidence that power differentials in dyads influence emotion regulation; powerful parties have more freedom to express their felt emotions, and less powerful parties are expected to keep their emotions in check and therefore must engage in greater emotion regulation (Morris & Feldman, 1996). Power therefore imposes its own display rules and could be incorporated into this chapter's framework as affecting the link between emotional response tendencies and emotional expression. The self-concept may also play a role in emotional contagion in dyads. Hatfield et al. (1994) suggest that when the self is construed as fundamentally related to others, one will be more vulnerable to emotional contagion.

The ready availability of these and other research questions illustrates that the model presented here is a simplified representation of reality. Gross's foundation is useful as a starting point, and perhaps future research will reduce the gaps between this model and more general frameworks of self-regulation (such as Carver & Scheier, 1981). Such an integration would be valuable in terms of parsimony and would lead to a better understanding of both success and failures in emotion regulation.

References

Acker, J. (1990). Hierarchies, jobs, bodies: A theory of gendered organizations. *Gender and Society, 4,* 139–158.

Adelmann, P. K., & Zajonc, R. B. (1989). Facial efference and the experience of emotion. *Annual Review of Psychology, 40,* 249–280.

Ambady, N., & Rosenthal, R. (1992). Thin slices of expressive behavior as predictors of interpersonal consequences: A meta-analysis. *Psychological Bulletin, 111,* 256–274.

Bargh, J. A. (1989). Conditional automaticity: Varieties of automatic influence in social perception and cognition. In J. S. Uleman & J. A. Bargh (Eds.), *Unintended thought* (pp. 3–51). New York: Guilford Press.

Baumeister, R. F., Bratslavsky, E., Muraven, M., & Tice, D. M. (1998). Ego depletion: Is the active self a limited resource? *Journal of Personality and Social Psychology, 74,* 1252–1265.

Bavelas, J. B., Black, A., Lemery, C. R., & Mullett, J. (1987). Motor mimicry as primitive empathy. In N. Eisenberg & J. Strayer (Eds.), *Empathy and its development* (pp. 317–338). Cambridge: Cambridge University Press.

Bitner, M. J. (1992). Servicescapes: The impact of physical surroundings on customer and employees. *Journal of Marketing, 56,* 57–71.

Bless, H., & Schwarz, N. (1999). Sufficient and necessary conditions in dual-process models: The case of mood and information processing. In S. Chaiken & Y. Trope (Eds.), *Dual-process theories in social psychology* (pp. 423–440). New York: Guilford Press.

Buck, R. (1984). *The communication of emotion.* New York: Guilford Press.

Cacioppo, J. T., Uchino, B. N., Crites, S. L., Snydersmith, M. A., Smith, G., Berntson, G. G., & Lang, P. J. (1992). Relationship between facial expressiveness and sympathetic activation in emotion: A critical review, with emphasis on modeling underlying mechanisms and individual differences. *Journal of Personality and Social Psychology, 62,* 110–128.

Carver, C. S., & Scheier, M. F. (1981). *Attention and self-regulation: A control-theory approach to human behavior.* New York: Springer-Verlag.

Chaiken, S. (1980). Heuristic versus systematic information processing and the use of source versus message cues in persuasion. *Journal of Personality and Social Psychology, 64,* 759–765.

Chartrand, T. L., & Bargh, J. A. (1999). The chameleon effect: The perception-behavior link and social interaction. *Journal of Personality and Social Psychology, 76,* 893–910.

Darden, W. R., & Babin, B. J. (1994). Exploring the concept of affective quality: Expanding the concept of retail personality. *Journal of Business Research, 29,* 101–109.

DiMatteo, M. R., Taranta, A., Friedman, H. S., & Prince, L. M. (1980). Predicting patient satisfaction from physicians' nonverbal communication skills. *Medical Care, 18,* 376–387.

Dimberg, U. (1982). Facial reactions to facial expressions. *Psychophysiology, 19,* 643–647.

Ekman, P. (1972). Universals and cultural differences in facial expression of emotion. In J. Cole (Ed.), *Nebraska Symposium on Motivation* (pp. 207–283). Lincoln: University of Nebraska Press.

Erber, R., Wegner, D. M., & Therriault, N. (1996). On being cool and collected: Mood regulation in anticipation of social interaction. *Journal of Personality and Social Psychology, 70,* 757–766.

Fiske, S. T., & Neuberg, S. E. (1990). A continuum of impression formation, from category-based to individuating processes: Influences of information and motivation on attention and interpretation. In M. P. Zanna (Ed.), *Advances in experimental social psychology* (Vol. 23, pp. 1–74). Orlando, FL: Academic Press.

Forgas, J. P. (1995). Mood and judgment: The affect infusion model (AIM). *Psychological Bulletin, 117,* 39–66.

Friedman, H. S., & Miller-Herringer, T. (1991). Nonverbal display of emotion in public and in private: Self-monitoring, personality, and expressive cues. *Journal of Personality and Social Psychology, 61,* 766–775.

Friedman, H. S., Prince, L. M., Riggio, R. E., & DiMatteo, M. R. (1980). Understanding and assessing nonverbal expressiveness: The affective communication test. *Journal of Personality and Social Psychology, 39,* 333–351.

Friedman, H. S., & Riggio, R. E. (1981). Effect of individual differences in nonverbal expressiveness on transmission of emotion. *Journal of Nonverbal Behavior, 6,* 96–101.

Gilbert, D. T., Pelham, B. W., & Krull, D. S. (1988). On cognitive busyness: When person perceivers meet persons perceived. *Journal of Personality and Social Psychology, 54,* 733–740.

Grandey, A. A. (2000). Emotion regulation in the workplace: A new way to conceptualize emotional labor. *Journal of Occupational Health Psychology, 1,* 95–110.

Gross, J. J. (1998). Antecedent- and response-focused emotion regulation: Divergent consequences for experience, expression, and physiology. *Journal of Personality and Social Psychology, 74,* 224–237.

Gross, J. J. (1999). Emotion and emotion regulation. In L. A. Pervin & O. P. John (Eds.), *Handbook of personality* (2nd ed.). New York: Guilford Press.

Gross, J. J., & John, O. P. (1995). Facets of emotional expressivity: Three self-report factors and their correlates. *Personality and Individual Differences, 19,* 555–568.

Gross, J. J., & John, O. P. (1997). Revealing feelings: Facets of emotional expressivity in self-reports, peer ratings, and behavior. *Journal of Personality and Social Psychology, 72,* 435–448.

Gross, J. J., & John, O. P. (1998). Mapping the domain of expressivity: Multimethod evidence for a hierarchical model. *Journal of Personality and Social Psychology, 74,* 170–191.

Gross, J. J., John, O. P., & Richards, J. M. (2000). The dissociation of emotion expression from emotion experience: A personality perspective. *Personality and Social Psychology Bulletin, 26,* 712–726.

Gross, J. J., & Levinson, R. W. (1993). Emotional suppression: Physiology, self-report, and expressive behavior. *Journal of Personality and Social Psychology, 64,* 970–986.

Gross, J. J., & Levinson, R. W. (1997). Hiding feelings: The acute effects of inhibiting negative and positive emotion. *Journal of Abnormal Psychology, 106,* 95–103.

Gump, B. B., & Kulik, J. A. (1997). Stress, affiliation, and emotional contagion. *Journal of Personality and Social Psychology, 72,* 305–319.

Hall, E. J. (1993). Smiling, deferring, and flirting: Doing gender by giving "good service." *Work and Occupations, 20,* 452–471.

Hall, J. A. (1984). *Nonverbal sex differences.* Baltimore, MD: Johns Hopkins University Press.

Hatfield, E., Cacioppo, J. T., & Rapson, R. L. (1992). Primitive emotional contagion. In M. S. Clark (Ed.), *Review of personality and social psychology: Vol. 14. Emotion and social behavior* (pp. 151–177). Thousand Oaks, CA: Sage.

Hatfield, E., Cacioppo, J. T., & Rapson, R. L. (1994). *Emotional contagion.* Cambridge: Cambridge University Press.

Hochschild, A. R. (1983). *The managed heart.* Berkeley: University of California Press.

Hsee, C. K., Hatfield, E., Carlson, J. G., & Chemtob, C. (1990). The effect of power on susceptibility to emotional contagion. *Cognition and Emotion, 4,* 327–340.

Isen, A. M. (1984). Toward understanding the role of affect in cognition. In R. Wyer & T. Srull (Eds.), *Handbook of social cognition* (pp. 179–236). Hillsdale, NJ: Erlbaum.

Joiner, T. E., & Katz, J. (1999). Contagion of depressive symptoms and mood: Meta-analytic review and explanations from cognitive, behavioral, and interpersonal viewpoints. *Clinical Psychology: Science and Practice, 6,* 149–164.

Kanfer, R., & Ackerman, P. L. (1989). Motivation and cognitive abilities: An integrative aptitude-treatment interaction approach to skill acquisition. *Journal of Applied Psychology, 74,* 657–690.

King, L. A., & Emmons, R. A. (1990). Conflict over emotional expression: Psychological and physical correlates. *Journal of Personality and Social Psychology, 58,* 864–877.

Kotler, P. (1974). Atmospherics as a marketing tool. *Journal of Retailing, 49,* 49–64.

Kring, A. M., Smith, D. A., & Neale, J. M. (1994). Individual differences in dispositional expressiveness: Development and validation of the emotional expressivity scale. *Journal of Personality and Social Psychology, 66,* 934–949.

LaFrance, M., & Banaji, M. (1992). Toward a reconsideration of the gender-emotion relationship. In M. S. Clark (Ed.), *Review of personality and social psychology* (Vol. 14, pp. 178–202). Thousand Oaks, CA: Sage.

Levenson, R. W., & Ruef, A. M. (1997). Physiological aspects of emotional knowledge and rapport. In W. Ickes (Ed.), *Empathic accuracy.* New York: Guilford Press.

Lewis, K. M. (2000). When leaders display emotion: How followers respond to negative emotional expression of male and female leaders. *Journal of Organizational Behavior, 21,* 221–234.

Locke, K. (1996). A funny thing happened! The management of consumer emotions in service encounters. *Organization Science, 7,* 40–58.

Lord, R. G., Brown, D. J., & Freiberg, S. J. (1999). Understanding the dynamics of leadership: The role of follower self-concepts in the leader/follower relationship. *Organizational Behavior and Human Decision Processes, 78,* 167–203.

Manstead, A.S.R. (1991). Expressiveness as an individual difference. In R. S. Feldman & B. Rime (Eds.), *Fundamentals of nonverbal behavior.* New York: Cambridge University Press.

McHugo, G. J., Lanzetta, J. T., Sullivan, D. G., Masters, R. D., & Englis, B. G. (1985). Emotional reactions to a political leader's expressive displays. *Journal of Personality and Social Psychology, 49,* 1513–1529.

Morris, J. A., & Feldman, D. C. (1996). The dimensions, antecedents, and consequences of emotional labor. *Academy of Management Review, 21,* 986–1010.

Murphy, S. T., & Zajonc, R. B. (1993). Affect, cognition, and awareness: Affective priming with optimal and suboptimal stimulus exposures. *Journal of Personality and Social Psychology, 64,* 723–739.

Neumann, R., & Strack, F. (2000). Mood contagion: The automatic transfer of mood between persons. *Journal of Personality and Social Psychology, 79,* 211–223.

Petty, R. E., & Cacioppo, J. T. (1986). The elaboration likelihood model of persuasion. In L. Berkowitz (Ed.), *Advances in experimental social psychology* (Vol. 19, pp. 124–203). Orlando, FL: Academic Press.

Pugh, S. D. (2001). Service with a smile: Emotional contagion in the service encounter. *Academy of Management Journal, 44,* 1018–1027.

Rafaeli, A. (1989). When cashiers meet customers: An analysis of the role of supermarket cashiers. *Academy of Management Journal, 32,* 245–273.

Rafaeli, A., & Sutton, R. I. (1989). The expression of emotion in organizational life. In L. L. Cummings & B. M. Staw (Eds.), *Research in organizational behavior* (Vol. 11, pp. 1–42). Greenwich, CT: JAI Press.

Rafaeli, A., & Sutton, R. I. (1990). Busy stores and demanding customers: How do they affect the display of positive emotion? *Academy of Management Journal, 33,* 623–637.

Richards, J. M., & Gross, J. J. (1999). Composure at any cost? The cognitive consequences of emotion suppression. *Personality and Social Psychology Bulletin, 25,* 1033–1044.

Richards, J. M., & Gross, J. J. (2000). Emotion regulation and memory: The cognitive costs of keeping one's cool. *Journal of Personality and Social Psychology, 79,* 410–424.

Russell, J. A., & Snodgrass, J. (1987). Emotion and the environment. In D. Stokols & I. Altman (Eds.), *Handbook of environmental psychology* (pp. 245–280). New York: Wiley.

Schwartz, G. E., Ahern, G. L., & Brown, S. L. (1979). Lateralized facial muscle response to positive versus negative emotional stimuli. *Psychophysiology, 16,* 561–571.

Schwarz, N., & Clore, G. L. (1983). Mood, misattribution, and judgments of well-being: Informative and directive functions of affective states. *Journal of Personality and Social Psychology, 45,* 513–523.

Shields, S. A. (1987). Women, men and the dilemma of emotion. In P. R. Shaver & C. Hendrick (Eds.), *Review of personality and social psychology* (Vol. 7, pp. 229–250). Thousand Oaks, CA: Sage.

Smith, A. C., & Kleinman, S. (1989). Managing emotions in medical school: Students' contacts with the living and the dead. *Social Psychology Quarterly, 52,* 56–69.

Stepper, S., & Strack, F. (1993). Proprioceptive determinants of emotional and nonemotional feelings. *Journal of Personality and Social Psychology, 64,* 211–220.

Strack, F., Martin, L., & Stepper, S. (1988). Inhibiting and facilitating conditions of the human smile: A nonobtrusive test of the facial feedback hypothesis. *Journal of Personality and Social Psychology, 54,* 768–777.

Sullins, E. S. (1991). Emotional contagion revisited: Effects of social comparison and expressive style on mood convergence. *Personality and Social Psychology Bulletin, 17,* 166–174.

Sutton, R. I. (1991). Maintaining norms about expressed emotions: The case of bill collectors. *Administrative Science Quarterly, 36,* 245–268.

Sutton, R. I., & Rafaeli, A. (1988). Untangling the relationship between displayed emotions and organizational sales: The case of convenience stores. *Academy of Management Journal, 31,* 461–487.

Timmers, M., Fischer, A. H., & Manstead, A.S.R. (1998). Gender differences in motives for regulating emotions. *Personality and Social Psychology Bulletin, 24,* 974–985.

Van Maanen, J., & Kunda, G. (1989). Real feelings: Emotional expression and organizational culture. In L. L. Cummings & B. M. Staw (Eds.), *Research in organizational behavior* (Vol. 11, pp. 43–103). Greenwich, CT: JAI Press.

Wegner, D. M. (1994). Ironic processes of mental control. *Psychological Review, 101,* 34–52.

Wegner, D. M., & Bargh, J. A. (1998). Control and automaticity in social life. In D. T. Gilbert, S. T. Fiske, & G. Lindzey (Eds.), *The handbook of social psychology* (4th ed., Vol. 1, pp. 446–496). New York: McGraw-Hill.

Wegner, D. M., Erber, R., & Zanakos, S. (1993). Ironic processes in the mental control of mood and mood-related thought. *Journal of Personality and Social Psychology, 65,* 1093–1104.

Weiss, H. M., & Cropanzano, R. (1996). Affective events theory: A theoretical discussion of the structure, causes, and consequences of affective experiences at work. In L. L. Cummings & B. M. Staw (Eds.), *Research in organizational behavior* (pp. 1–74). Greenwich, CT: JAI Press.

Winslow, C. A., & Herrington, L. P. (1936). The influence of odor upon appetite. *American Journal of Hygiene, 23,* 143–156.

Zajonc, R. B. (1980). Feeling and thinking: Preferences need no inferences. *American Psychologist, 35,* 151–175.

CHAPTER 6

Affect Regulation in Groups and Teams

Jennifer M. George

Work groups are a basic building block of organizations. Thus, it is not surprising that attention has focused on numerous aspects of group functioning, such as roles, rules and norms, group identity, group processes and dynamics, and decision making in groups. A commonality among research on diverse topics related to work group functioning is a focus on how members of work groups come to make sense of and define their membership in the group, their group's tasks and responsibilities, the environment and conditions under which they are working, and the desirability of remaining in the group.

Traditionally, these accompaniments of group life have been viewed from a cognitive perspective. A grossly simplified paradigm of research in the area is as follows. A researcher identifies some focal topic related to work groups and then seeks to uncover the determinants and consequences of the cognitive and motivational processes surrounding the group phenomenon of interest. For example, research on social loafing in work groups has looked at the extent to which extrinsic factors such as task visibility and rewards and punishments and intrinsic factors such as interesting work (George, 1992, 1995a) may influence the occurrence of social loafing in work groups.

As another example, attention has focused on how members of groups make sense of their surroundings and the wider environment through the use of shared schemas, mental models, or knowledge structures (Klimoski & Mohammed, 1994; Walsh & Fahey, 1986; Walsh, 1995). While a focus on cognitive and motivational processes in groups has no doubt contributed to our understanding of group-based phenomena, it has also contributed to a relative neglect of the affective or emotional side of work group life.

A large and diverse body of literature in social psychology and related fields attests to the fact that cognition and affect are highly interdependent (Forgas, 2000; Forgas & George, 2001; Martin & Tesser, 1996). Each has the potential to and does influence the other in multiple ways. Cognitive processes are intimately connected to affect, and affect is linked to and gives meaning to cognition. Moreover, in the absence of affect, the significance and implications of information generated by cognitive processes become ambiguous at best (Damasio, 1994; George, 2000). To put it simply, thinking and feeling are inextricably bound up with each other; one does not exist without the other.

Hence, understanding any aspect of human behavior in work organizations—whether leadership (George, 2000), work motivation (George & Brief, 1996), or group functioning—can be enriched by consideration of the multiple potential roles of affect or emotion. In this chapter, I focus on affect regulation in groups and teams or the processes that give rise to the emotional lives of groups.

The Context of Affect Regulation in Groups and Teams

To this point, I have used the terms *group* and *team* interchangeably, and this is not uncommon in the literature. However, the term *team* implies something more than, for example, a group of employees who report to the same supervisor. Hence, it is useful to distinguish conceptually between groups and teams: a group is commonly defined as two or more individuals who interact with each other to achieve certain goals or meet certain needs; a team is a group in which there is a high level of interaction among members, and members work intensively together to achieve a common goal (George & Jones, 2002). Thus, all teams are also groups, but not all groups are necessarily teams. Groups can also be distinguished in terms of whether they are formal groups established by an organization to help achieve organizational goals, such as task forces and self-managed work teams, or informal groups established by organizational members to help achieve their own goals or needs, such as friendship groups and interest groups.

Considerable attention has been focused on group development over time and group dynamics (for example, see Gersick, 1988; Shaw, 1981; Tuckman & Jensen, 1977). A review of this literature is beyond the scope of this chapter and could be the subject of an entire book. However, it is important to keep in mind that both group development and group dynamics are likely to be reciprocally related to affect regulation in groups. Thus, for example, in considering aspects of group dynamics such as group cohesion and establishment and conformity to group norms, affect experienced in the context of group membership is likely to play a key role as well as be a subsequent consequence. Thus, researching group dynamics necessarily requires attention to the affective dimension of group life in addition to the relatively exclusive focus on cognitions and beliefs, such as how attractive group membership is and how important group norms are.

Many of the challenges that groups face necessarily are interrelated, and most likely in a complex way, with affect regulation. Challenges such as the effective management of diversity, managing conflict and keeping it task based rather than personalized, and minimizing performance problems such as social loafing are affect laden. Thus, it is surprising that the study of affect regulation in groups has not been the focus of scholarly attention until recently (Barsade, 2000; George, 1990).

Moreover, groups necessarily are required to interact with other groups inside an organization and, increasingly, outside an organization's boundaries as well. The focus and nature of these interactions are likely to be affect laden (as when intergroup conflict occurs, for example), and the interactions themselves are likely to influence affect regulation. At a higher level of analysis, organizational factors also impinge on groups and influence affect regulation within them, such as degrees of formalization and centralization, organizational culture, and the physical work environment.

Rapid advances in information technology and the prevalence of e-mail and Web-based forms of communication in organizations also have implications for affect regulation in work groups. For example, virtual teams, in which a significant amount of communication and interaction takes place electronically rather than face-to-face, are increasingly relied on to overcome barriers of time and distance, as well as more efficiently manage group tasks (Finholt & Sproull, 1990; Lipnack, 1999; Strauss, 1997). Clearly, one could imagine how affect regulation in virtual teams and groups might differ in significant ways from affect regulation in groups whose members meet face-to-face and also serve different functions and meet different needs.

These and other facets of the context within which work groups are embedded are important to consider in understanding affect regulation in work groups. However, given the overall focus of this chapter and book, as well as the fact that affect regulation in work groups has received scant attention in the literature until recently, I focus primarily on affect regulation as it occurs within groups, side-stepping the wider issues of the context in which it takes place. This by no means reflects on the importance of the latter.

One way to keep the wider context in mind might be to think in terms of a simplified yet useful generic guide to understanding work groups: input—process—output (Guzzo & Shea, 1992; Hackman & Morris, 1975). Inputs here can include members' knowledge and skills, effort, and personalities and other individual differences; processes can include motivation, learning, conflict management, and conformity or deviance; and outcomes can include group performance, group effectiveness, and member well-being and satisfaction (Hackman, 1992). The wider organizational context in which a group operates can affect each of these factors (potentially, in a reciprocal fashion). Similarly, affect regulation may be a potential cause and consequence of each of these factors (again, in a reciprocal manner).

This guide can be refined by the distinctions among actual group performance, potential group performance, process losses, and process gains. Steiner (1972) suggested that actual group performance often differs from a group's potential performance by process losses arising from coordination problems, such as duplication of effort, and motivation problems, such as social loafing (Guzzo & Shea, 1992). This perspective can be augmented by the consideration of process gains: increases in potential performance over time due to discovery and implementation of new and improved means of coordinating and motivating group members (Guzzo & Shea, 1992). A focus on process gains takes into account that potential performance is not static but can increase; research on group synergies, creativity, and innovation explicitly acknowledges the potential for performance increases over time.

Once again, we can consider affect regulation in groups from the perspective of actual and potential performance and process losses and gains. Affect regulation can be a potential cause and consequence of each of these phenomena, and reciprocal relations are again likely. Hence, future research in this tradition should take into account affect regulation and its potential influences on performance outcomes.

The Multiple Roles of Affect in Group Life

Given the highly interdependent nature of affect and cognition, as well as interdependencies between affect and motivation (Martin & Tesser, 1996), affect pervades group life and plays multiple roles in group functioning. It is beyond the scope of this chapter to elucidate these many roles. Rather, I provide a sampling of just a few of the many roles of affect in group life.

Before proceeding, however, it is useful to distinguish between affect, emotions, and moods. In this chapter, I am using the term *affect* generically to refer to a wide variety of feeling states that include emotions and moods. *Emotions* are relatively intense feeling states that have recognizable antecedent causes; emotions interrupt ongoing thought processes and behaviors and demand attention (Forgas, 1992; Morris, 1989; Simon, 1982). *Moods* are generalized and pervasive feeling states that do not necessarily have recognizable antecedent causes (Morris, 1989). Emotions and moods change over time, but emotions tend to be more short-lived due to their intensity. Emotions can also feed into moods such that once the emotion and its cause have been dealt with, it leads to a similarly valenced mood state. Moods subtly influence ongoing thought processes and behaviors, whereas emotions demand and often redirect attention.

At a basic level, one of the major functions of affect in groups is to unite individuals in such a way that even though each individual member is unique, with his or her own aspirations and desires, the group is collectively meaningful for its members as a single entity (Sandelands & St. Clair, 1993). Affect imbues events, choices, and decisions with meaning (Damasio, 1994), and the affect that group members experience in the context of their group membership provides a sense of collective meaning and purpose.

Affect's role in creating group entity has been expressed implicitly and explicitly in the literature in a number of ways. For example, it has been suggested that emotions have the potential to clarify the boundaries of a group and signify the members of a group (Durkheim, 1915/1965; Keltner & Haidt, 1999). Positive emotions experienced in a group may contribute to the sense of the group as a single collective entity, and negative emotions toward others outside the group may serve to reinforce group boundaries (Frijda & Mesquita, 1994; Heise & O'Brien, 1993). Consistent with this reasoning, affect is linked to group identity and identification processes (Brickson, 2000).

As another example, the literature on group cohesiveness suggests that affect or emotion helps to bind group members together and promotes desires to remain a member of the group (Barsade & Gibson, 1998; Festinger, 1950; Seashore, 1954). Interestingly enough, when one looks at the content of popular measures of group cohesiveness, they appear to be emphasizing cognitive content, yet one would venture to guess that "forces which are acting on the members to stay in a group" (Festinger, 1950, p. 274) have a large affective component.

In addition to helping to establish group entity, emotions also play an important informational and signaling role (Frijda, 1988) in groups. Experienced and conveyed emotions provide group members with information about how other members of the group are feeling, how they appraise circumstances and events affecting the group, and how they perceive their relationships with other group members (Hess & Kirouac, 2000).

Experienced emotions signal significant events that have the potential to affect the well-being of the group and its members and direct their attention to pressing concerns. For example, the positive emotions that members of a group experience after a significant success can direct members to their collective capabilities and potential for future success while reinforcing the group as a collective entity that is attractive to belong to. Similarly, experienced negative emotions can signal threats or problems in need of attention and redirect group members' attention to factors that may threaten the well-being of a group. For example, negative emotions arising from disappointing results on a project that a group spearheaded may direct members' attention to their shortcomings and ways to overcome them. Similarly, negative emotions arising from disagreements or conflicts within a group may focus attention on interpersonal processes in the group and how group members treat each other. In essence, the emotions experienced in groups in response to internal and external stimuli and events imbue those stimuli and events with meaning and significance for group members.

Emotions also serve to make manifest and reinforce roles and status differences within groups (Keltner & Haidt, 1999). The experience and expression of certain emotions in groups are linked to relative status within the group (Clark, 1990; Collins, 1990; Coser, 1960). For example, research has found that having high status within a group, such as being the group leader, is associated with the experience of positive emotions (Lovaglia & Houser, 1996; Lucas & Lovaglia, 1998). As another example, the experience and expression of anger provide cues as to relative positions of dominance and power in a group (Coats & Feldman, 1996; Knutson, 1996).

Moreover, the moods that group members experience are likely to influence their information processing and behavior. For example, when members of a group experience negative moods, they may be more critical and discerning, and when they experience positive moods, they may be more helpful to each other, as well as to people outside the group (George, 1991, 1996a; Isen & Baron, 1991; Salovey, Hsee, & Mayer, 1993; Sinclair & Mark, 1992). It also is likely that affect is linked to shared schemas or mental maps in groups and thus influences cognitive processes and decision making (George, 1996b).

Just as groups clearly experience broad dimensions of affect such as positive and negative mood (George, 1996), they also experience more specific emotions nested underneath these broad dimensions. For example, group members may collectively experience shame on learning of a missed opportunity, pride for a job well done, anxiety in an uncertain situation when the stakes are high, and enthusiasm while working on an intrinsically interesting task.

These are just a sampling of the many significant roles that affect plays in work groups. The existence and diversity of these many roles underscore the importance of understanding affect regulation in groups.

Unconscious, Relatively Automatic, or Passive Affect Regulation in Groups

Some affect regulation that takes place in groups is relatively passive. It may be unconscious or automatic and is not the result of group members' taking active steps to regulate or manage their own or each other's feelings. This does not necessarily imply that people are unaware of the fact that their moods and emotions are being influenced, but rather that the influence process is carried out without deliberate intentions or interventions. Here, I discuss three potential mechanisms by which affect is regulated in a passive manner in groups: primitive emotional contagion, exposure to common events and tasks, and vicarious processes.

Primitive Emotional Contagion

Early studies of groups, mobs, and crowds suggest that sometimes members of groups are highly susceptible to contagious feelings, with an accompanying deindividuation of the self leading to a lack of self-awareness and self-regulation and total absorption into the group as a collective (Diener, 1980). In such circumstances, emotions are often generated that are strong and contagious and not consciously controlled or managed, with accompanying behavioral manifestations (Diener, 1980). More recently, research and writings in a variety of areas suggest that moods and emotions can indeed be contagious in groups (e.g., Barsade, 2000).

This relatively automatic and unconscious regulation or sharing of affect across individuals has been referred to as primitive emotion contagion by Hatfield and her colleagues (Hatfield, Cacioppo, & Rapson, 1994).[1] Hatfield, Cacioppo, and Rapson (1992) define primitive emotional contagion as "the tendency to automatically mimic and synchronize facial expressions, vocalizations, postures, and movements with those of another person and, consequently, to converge emotionally" (pp. 153–154). These authors emphasize that while primitive emotional contagion is multiply determined, it often originates with the mimicking and synchronization of the emotional expressions and manifestations of others, including their facial expressions, tone of voice, stance or posture, and behaviors (Bavelas, Black, Lemery, & Mullet, 1987; Bernieri, Reznick, & Rosenthal, 1988), often without conscious awareness (O'Toole & Dubin, 1968). This mimicking and synchronization have been observed in a variety of settings and contexts, such as when infants or very young children cry when they see and hear others cry (Goleman, 1989), therapists "feel" the feelings of their clients (Jung, 1968; Reik, 1948), and waves of hysteria and accompanying inexplicable symptoms sweep through a town or village (Tseng & Hsu, 1980).

In primitive emotional contagion, the mimicking of the expression of emotion serves to promote emotional experience consistent with the emotions expressed. This linkage between the expression of emotion and the experience of emotion has been studied in a number of ways (Hatfield et al., 1992). First, research suggests that facial expressions that correspond to different emotions can induce the corresponding experienced emotions in those making the expressions. Although this facial feedback hypothesis has been the subject of some controversy (Adelmann & Zajonc, 1989; Izard, 1977; Tomkins, 1982), research does suggest that facial expressions of emotions and experienced emotions are linked, that the former can precede the latter, and that linkages are specific at the level of discrete emotions (Hatfield et al., 1992).

For example, Duclos et al. (1989) had students make facial expressions that corresponded to four discrete emotions—fear, anger, disgust, and sadness—in an experiment whose purpose was disguised so that the students were unaware of the focus on emotions. The instructions for the facial expressions were neutrally and unemotionally provided (for example, for fear, "Raise your eyebrows. And open your eyes wide. Move your whole head back, so that your chin is tucked in a little bit, and let your mouth relax and hang open a little"; Duclos et al., 1989, p. 101). After students made the facial expressions and performed a distracter task to disguise the purposes of the study, they completed an affect rating scale. Consistent with the premises of primitive emotional contagion, participants reported experiencing the specific emotion corresponding to the facial expression they made. In the organizational literature, preliminary research also suggests that emotional contagion can and does take place in work groups (Barsade, 2000; Bartel & Saavedra, 2000).

Exposure to Common Tasks, Outcomes, and Events

George (1996b) proposed that affective regulation can occur in groups through exposure to common tasks and outcomes. To the extent that members of a group perform similar or analogous tasks, their affect may come to be regulated not through any deliberate means but rather through the affect-generating potential of their common tasks. For example, performing intrinsically satisfying work may result in the experience of positive moods, performing boring work may result in low levels of positive affect (such as feeling sleepy and sluggish), working in a hot, noisy factory may generate negative affect, and being a member of a top management team overseeing a major downsizing may result in team members' feeling sad or nervous.

Affect generated in work groups from exposure to common tasks can be thought of as secondary responses, with the primary responses being the actual behaviors performed to accomplish work tasks (Humphrey, 1985, 2000). Humphrey (1985) found that the kinds of tasks workers performed influenced the kind of affect they experienced, consistent with this reasoning. For example, workers performing jobs higher in complexity expressed more positive moods and emotions such as enthusiasm, while those performing jobs lower in complexity exhibited boredom.

Tschan and von Cranach (1996) suggest that it is useful to differentiate the kinds of group tasks in terms of the actions taken or behaviors performed to accomplish group objectives or goals and the regulation of these actions. Their action-oriented approach may be particularly useful for exploring affect as a secondary response to common group tasks since it is the actions taken to perform tasks that are most likely to generate affect rather than more general descriptions of tasks along abstract dimensions (for example, complexity, uncertainty, or clarity).

Actions and their regulation can be described along at least three dimensions: hierarchical organization, sequential organization, and cyclical organization (Frese & Zapf, 1994; Tschan & von Cranach, 1996; von Cranach, 1996). Hierarchical organization refers to the extent to which a group's work entails subtasks or subgoals that are performed in the interest of an overall goal or objective. More specifically, a group's overall objective or goals may entail a hierarchy of subgoals that need to be accomplished to reach the overall objective. Tasks or actions performed in the service of goals lower in the hierarchy and the regulation of such actions may be fundamentally different from actions performed and the regulation of such actions in the service of goals at higher levels in the hierarchy (Tschan & von Cranach, 1996). In fact, different classification schemes have been proposed to describe different levels of action regulation depending on the extent to which action regulation entails relatively automatic and quick processes (found at low levels in the hierarchy) or controlled and slow processes (found at high levels in the hierarchy) (Rasmussen, 1987; Semmer & Frese, 1985; Shiffrin & Schneider, 1977).

Sequential organization refers to the extent to which actions need to be performed in a predetermined order (Tschan & von Cranach, 1996). Group tasks differ in the extent to which actions need to be taken in a certain sequence and the flexibility of that sequence. Cyclical organization refers to the action cycles used to perform subgoals or subtasks such as a generic sequence of setting a goal, developing an action plan to achieve the goal, executing the plan, and evaluating the results (Tschan & von Cranach, 1996).

It is likely that each of these three ways of classifying or distinguishing among groups tasks has implications for the generation of affect as a secondary response. For example, members of groups whose work is low in hierarchical organization may have different affective reactions accompanying their actions than members of groups whose work is high in hierarchical organization. Moreover, when a group's work is high in hierarchical organization, one might expect there to be more variance in affect experienced by group members. For example, group members performing actions to accomplish goals low in the hierarchy might be more likely to feel bored or listless because their actions are relatively automatic and predetermined, while group members performing actions to accomplish goals at higher levels in the hierarchy might experience more enthusiasm but also perhaps be more anxious or nervous.

Sequential and cyclical organization might also influence affect as a secondary response to actions taken. Not only may affective reactions differ depending on whether sequential organization is high or low, but they also may vary depending on where each group member's actions fall within the sequence. Similarly, the steps, flexibility or rigidity, and duration of work cycles are likely to influence affective responses.

Clearly, however, the causal arrow can go in the opposite direction as well. That is, affect and, in particular, emotions can be the triggers for action and the initiators of tasks (Frijda, 1988). For example, negative emotions signal that the status quo is problematic and redirect attention to the emotion-precipitating circumstances or events. The anger that members of an R&D team experience on learning that their budget has been cut by 50 percent, for instance, may redirect their attention from ongoing tasks to lobbying managers for additional resources, documenting the need for these resources, and publicizing the many important contributions the team has made to the organization.

At a more microlevel, and based on affective events theory (Weiss & Cropanzano, 1996), to the extent that members of work groups experience or encounter similar kinds of events in the workplace, their affect may come to be regulated. Basch and Fisher (2000) describe a variety of kinds of events that may have the potential to generate positive and negative affect in the workplace. To the extent that members of work groups experience the same kinds of events, their affect may be regulated in a similar fashion by these events. For example, involvement in decision making, planning, and problem solving is proposed to have the potential to generate positive affect, and task problems, lack of influence or control, and acts of customers are proposed to have the potential to generate negative affect (Basch & Fisher, 2000). To the extent that members of work groups have similar exposure to these affect-generating events, they might experience the concomitant affective states that accompany the events.

In addition to common sets of tasks, actions, or events, members of work groups are often exposed to common kinds of outcomes. Katz (1964) distinguishes between two kinds of outcomes: individualized and membership. Individualized outcomes are rewards such as money, recognition, and positive feedback that are given or withheld based on the actions and performance of group members (George & Brief, 1992). In addition to such positive outcomes, it is important to consider potential negative individualized outcomes, such as critical and nonconstructive feedback and threats of job insecurity.

Research suggests that the availability of both positively and negatively valenced outcomes has the potential to influence or regulate the experience of positive and negative affect by group members. For example, Gray (1971, 1981, 1987) suggests that different parts of the brain are sensitive to signals of rewards and punishments, which in turn generate positive and negative moods and emotions, respectively, when such signals have been detected. The behavioral activation system (BAS) is that part of the central nervous system that responds to signals of rewards; when rewards are present and detected by this system, positive affect is experienced. Analogously, the behavioral inhibition system (BIS) is sensitive to signals of punishment, and when punishment or negative-valenced outcomes are present and detected by this system, negative affect is experienced (Gray, 1981; Larsen & Katelaar, 1991). Hence, the BAS and BIS regulate positive and negative affect in the presence of rewards (or positive outcomes) and punishments (or negative outcomes), respectively. (For more on the BAS and the BIS and their links to extraversion and neuroticism, see Larsen, Diener, and Lucas, Chapter Three, this volume.) Others have linked rewards to positive moods and emotions (Clark & Watson, 1988; George, 1995b).

Affect in work groups is likely to be influenced by several features of individualized outcomes. For example, outcomes that are distributed at the individual level will likely have differential effects on the affect of the outcome recipient and other group members than will outcomes that are distributed at the team level (for example, everyone in a team receives a bonus depending on team performance). Outcomes distributed at the individual level may have further differential effects on affect regulation in groups depending on perceptions of distributive and procedural justice and the extent to which zero-sum conditions prevail. Consistent with this reasoning, outcomes such as incentive compensation may be reacted to differently depending on a number of factors (George, Brief, Webster, & Burke, 1989).

Membership outcomes are equally available to all members of a work group by virtue of their membership in the wider organization (George & Brief, 1992; Katz, 1964). While Katz focused on positively valenced membership outcomes or rewards, at least in some organizations, both positive and negative membership outcomes may be present. Examples of positive membership outcomes include family-friendly policies, flexible work schedules, a pleasant work environment, benefits, and availability of snacks and drinks.

As Katz (1964, p. 138) indicates, the availability of such member-ship rewards may result in the creation of a "more favorable mood" in an organization. Examples of negative membership outcomes include a punitive leadership style that may pervade an organiza-tion; unpleasant, uncomfortable, or dangerous working conditions; or chronic job insecurity. Hence, affect in work groups may be reg-ulated by the wider organizational context and the extent to which it provides positive or negative membership outcomes.

Vicarious Processes

Affect regulation can also occur in groups through vicarious pro-cesses (Kelly & Barsade, 2001). Bandura (1986) suggests that when observers see and hear the emotional expressions of others (that is, models in social learning theory terms), these expressions can cre-ate similar affective experiences in the observers. For example, ob-serving teammates' expressions of anger and frustration over a lack of management support might provoke in observers similar feelings of anger and frustration even if the observers' initial reactions to the same stimuli were more neutral. While it can be debated whether such vicarious processes are conscious or relatively unconscious, they are somewhat passive and may involve some kind of associative learn-ing akin to classical conditioning (Kelly & Barsade, 2001).

Whether these vicarious processes are analogous to the processes responsible for primitive emotional contagion is an interesting theoretical and empirical question. To the extent that vicarious processes are consciously engaged, then this would be a point of distinction between vicariously spread affect and emotional con-tagion. Moreover, the emotional contagion literature focuses more on the effects of the mimicry of facial expressions, whereas the lit-erature on vicariously spread affect is less focused on this potential causal mechanism. Having said this, however, it also is likely that sometimes affect that spreads among members of a group can be explained from both a primitive emotional contagion perspective and a vicarious learning perspective, and it may prove difficult to distinguish the two. Hence, I suggest that these mechanisms may be overlapping but also are distinct enough to be considered sep-arate processes. However, this is clearly a question in need of fur-ther theorizing and research.

In a related vein, emotional empathy or the experience of the observed emotions of other group members (Bandura, 1986; Davis, 1983; Hoffman, 1975) can play a role in affect regulation in groups. In fact, empathy may be particularly relevant to affect regulation in teams, especially those with close ties or bonds between their members. Empathy is a complicated and multidimensional construct (Davis, 1983) and in a sense exemplifies emotion as a socially transmitted phenomenon. As Batson (1998) indicates, "Empathetic emotions do not fit easily within current social psychological conceptions of emotion, yet they are profoundly—even quintessentially—social" (p. 304).

The distinction between vicarious affect and emotional empathy is perhaps most apparent in the case of negative emotions. For example, when feelings of distress are experienced vicariously, individuals are motivated to alleviate their own negative feelings, but when empathetic distress is experienced, individuals are motivated to alleviate the negative feelings of others (Batson, 1998; Batson, Duncan, Ackerman, Buckley, & Birch, 1981). For instance, in a work team, a member might experience negative affect vicariously on learning that a fellow team member has been laid off; however, the member still employed might rationalize the firing by downgrading her perceptions of the contributions of the just-departed member or reminding herself that this person has generous financial resources to tide her over until she finds another position. In this same scenario, empathetic negative affect might lead to the team member's commiserating with her laid-off colleague and providing social and more tangible forms of support, such as suggesting contacts or leads for alternative employment. Hence, emotional empathy might be a more powerful force in regulating affect in groups than vicarious affect, particularly in the case of negative affect, because the latter prompts efforts to alter the affect vicariously experienced while the former focuses on the feelings of others.

Conscious, More Deliberate, or Intentional Affect Regulation in Groups

A growing body of literature attests to the fact that affect is also regulated in groups through more conscious or deliberate means. The distinction between conscious and unconscious affect regulation in groups is relatively arbitrary. The boundary between the two is necessarily fuzzy and ambiguous, and one could reasonably argue that some of the unconscious mechanisms are conscious, and vice versa. In this chapter, I rely on this distinction for convenience of organization, as well as to make the basic point that affect is regulated in groups intentionally and unintentionally.

The literature pertaining to the relatively intentional regulation of affect in groups points to a number of mechanisms by which affective experience is influenced by group membership and processes. I have grouped these mechanisms into four generic categories: group composition effects (includes personality composition, attraction-selection-attrition processes, leader affect, and emotional intelligence), interpersonal influence effects (includes social comparison processes and socialization), normative pressures (includes feeling rules, expression rules, surface acting, and deep acting), and power and status relations.

Group Composition Effects

Based in part on the attraction-selection-attrition model (Schneider, 1987; Schneider, Goldstein, & Smith, 1995), George (1990, 1996b) reasoned that affect may be regulated in work groups due to personality similarity among group members. More specifically, given that personality or disposition is a significant determinant of affective states, to the extent that members of work groups have similar standings on traits underlying affective experience (such as positive affectivity or extraversion and negative affectivity or neuroticism; Watson, 2000), affective states experienced at work may come to be regulated by the modal personality of the group.

The attraction-selection-attrition framework suggests that individuals with similar personalities tend to be attracted to and selected by work settings, and those with dissimilar personalities are likely to leave work settings through attrition, resulting in homogeneity in personality within settings (Schneider, 1987). Although this model and the research that supports it have been articulated at the organizational level of analysis, George (1996b) reasoned that analogous processes might operate at the work group level. More specifically, prospective group members may find work groups more or less appealing depending on the extent to which their personalities are similar to the personalities of current group members because personality similarity is a basis for attraction (Bryne, Griffitt, & Stefaniak, 1967; Griffitt, 1966). Moreover, work groups themselves or group leaders may select new members based on their perceptions of the extent to which prospective members will fit in or get along with existing members. For example, self-managed work teams and R&D teams often have the autonomy to select their members, and team leaders often play an important role in this process. When teams and their leaders are making selection decisions, their impressions of the extent to which potential new members will fit in with the group might be influenced by the extent of perceived personality congruence between the applicant's personality and the dominant personality profile in the group (to the extent that one exists). Moreover, when group members find themselves in a group whose members have dissimilar personalities, they may seek a transfer to a different group. These are just a few examples of some of the ways in which groups might come to be composed of individuals with similar personalities. Again, given the well-documented causal linkage between personality traits and the experience of affective states (Watson, 2000), affect may be regulated in groups by forces leading to similarity in personality within the groups.

Another potential compositional mechanism by which affect may be regulated in groups revolves around the role of leader traits or dispositions. Leaders often play a decisive role in the selection of new members of work groups, as well as in the placement of new and existing organizational members on important teams, task forces, and committees. In terms of the selection of new members, leaders may be likely to select new members whose personalities are similar to their own. Given the heightened attraction that leaders are likely to have for organizational members whose personalities are similar to their own, leaders may also be more likely to place such individuals on important teams, task forces, and committees because they may be more likely to perceive that these individuals will be effective in decisive roles. For example, consider the case of a leader who is high on extraversion and forming an important new team to head up a newly negotiated alliance with a major supplier. Other considerations being equal, this leader may be more likely to appoint members to this committee who are high on extraversion because they may be perceived to be more attractive and effective.

In addition, the personality traits of leaders, in particular, extraversion or positive affectivity and neuroticism or negative affectivity, influence the moods and emotions leaders experience at work (George, 1995b, 1996a). Leader moods and emotions are likely to influence the moods and emotions of group members through diverse mechanisms because leader affect influences leaders' cognitions and behaviors. For example, leader affect may infect group members through primitive emotional contagion (Hatfield et al., 1994). As another example, leader affect may influence group members' affect through the kind of work environment that leaders who experience certain kinds of affective states at work are likely to create for their followers. For instance, leaders who tend to experience positive moods and emotions at work may be instrumental in creating a pleasant work environment; they may be nice to be around, they may be more likely to notice and reward positive behaviors, they may express confidence in their followers and set a positive tone for them, and they may make group membership a rewarding experience (George & Bettenhausen, 1990). To the extent that a pleasant work environment is created and sustained by leaders in positive moods, their followers may also experience positive moods. More generally, given that extraversion and neuroticism have been linked to reactivity of the brain to positive and negative stimuli, respectively, in localized regions, these traits have the potential to have far-reaching effects on leaders and how they influence their followers (Canli et al., 2001).

A final composition mechanism by which affect may come to be regulated within groups revolves around the emotional intelligence levels of group members. Emotional intelligence is an individual difference reflecting the ability to know, understand, and regulate moods and emotions in the self and others (Mayer & Salovey, 1997). More specifically, emotional intelligence encompasses the following capabilities: the ability to appraise and express moods and emotions, the ability to use moods and emotions to enhance cognitive processes and decision making, having accurate knowledge about emotions, and having the ability to manage one's own and other people's moods and emotions (Mayer & Salovey, 1993, 1995, 1997; Mayer, DiPaolo, & Salovey, 1990; Salovey & Mayer, 1989–1990, 1994; Salovey et al., 1993; Salovey, Mayer, Goldman, Turvey, & Palfai, 1995).

To the extent that members of a work group are high on emotional intelligence, they may be able to generate and maintain excitement, enthusiasm, confidence, and optimism in the group, as well as a sense of cooperation and trust (George, 2000). When groups are composed of members who are high on emotional intelligence, members will be aware of their own feelings and the feelings of others and will also be able to influence these feelings to enhance effectiveness (broadly defined). I do not mean to imply that emotional intelligence will result in group members' being blindly optimistic or naively excited and confident. Rather, emotional intelligence may result in group members' being aware of problems but confident and optimistic about being able to address them effectively. Moreover, group members will be able to anticipate and manage their own and others' reactions to both positive and negative stimuli. They may also be more likely to realize the potential benefits of negative moods and emotions, such as their signaling function, that is, alerting group members to problems and threats (Frijda, 1988; George & Brief, 1996), as well as their potential to trigger critical thinking and deductive reasoning (George, 2000) and even creativity under certain conditions (George & Zhou, in press).

More generally, emotional intelligence may regulate emotions through promoting constructive thinking, or the capacity to address and solve problems with a minimum of stress in groups (Epstein, 1990; Epstein & Meier, 1989; George, 2000; Katz & Epstein, 1991). Rather than getting mired in escalating conflicts and win-lose scenarios, groups whose members are high on emotional intelligence may be better able to devise creative solutions to problems and disagreements, engender a win-win mentality, and instill a sense of mutual cooperation and trust while being able to approach problems, opportunities, and decision making flexibly; generate a variety of alternatives; and have a broadened perspective (George, 2000; Mayer, 1986; Salovey & Mayer, 1989–1990).

Interpersonal Influence Effects

Interpersonal influence effects on affect regulation include both social comparison processes and socialization processes. Although these means of social influence are necessarily interrelated, for ease of exposition, I discuss each in turn.

Social comparison theory suggests that people are motivated to evaluate the appropriateness of their feelings, thoughts, and behaviors, and they do so by comparing themselves to others (Festinger, 1954; Taylor, 1998). For comparison purposes, these others should be similar and relevant to the focal person (Festinger, 1954; Sullins, 1991). The results of social comparison processes in groups can be convergence or relative uniformity in feelings, thoughts, and behaviors (Sullins, 1991).

Relevant here is the fact that emotion can be regulated in groups through social comparison processes. In fact, a number of studies suggest that social comparison of affective states and resultant convergence in feelings does occur in small groups (Sullins, 1991; Wrightsman, 1960). Moreover, the patterns of results obtained in such studies tend to be consistent with the tenets of social comparison theory.

For example, social comparison theory emphasizes the importance of comparison others being similar and relevant to a focal person (Festinger, 1954; Sullins, 1991). In existing work groups, there may be a sufficient level of perceived similarity and relevance in order for social comparisons to take place. However, it may also be the case that some individuals may perceive the other members of their work group to be more similar and relevant to them personally than do other individuals. For example, individuals who are committed to their work groups and evaluate their groups positively may be more likely to view other group members as similar and relevant to themselves and rely on them for social comparison processes than those who have less positive perceptions and attitudes. Consistent with this reasoning, Totterdell, Kellett, Teuchmann, and Briner (1998) found that convergence between the mood of a focal nurse and the moods of his or her teammates tended to be higher when commitment to the team was high, perceptions of team climate were favorable, and the nurses reported having fewer hassles with their teammates. Another example of research illustrating the importance of perceived relevance for emotional comparison in groups is a recent study of affect convergence in sports teams. More specifically, Totterdell (2000) found that the mood of a focal person on the team was more likely to converge with the mood of his teammates on the same occasion rather than on a different occasion and also more likely to occur when the focal person and the team were engaged in interdependent activities. In a final example of research consistent with a social comparison interpretation of affect convergence in groups, Bartel and Saavedra (2000) found mood convergence to be more prevalent in work groups whose members interacted with each other frequently, had social connections with each other, and perceived a certain degree of task interdependence in the group's work.

In addition to the ongoing effects of social comparison, affect may be regulated in groups through socialization. Socialization refers to the learning process that occurs when new members of an organization gain knowledge of important organizational values, objectives, norms, and expectations (Fisher, 1986). Often, a newcomer's immediate work group is influential in the socialization process because group members are readily accessible, more likely to be perceived as similar to oneself, and also have some degree of reward power (Fisher, 1986; Rakestraw & Weiss, 1981; Weiss & Nowicki, 1981). While socialization in groups often entails learning appropriate on-the-job behaviors (George & Bettenhausen, 1990), newcomers also may observe the affective experiences of their team members and infer desired or modal affective experiences. As an anecdotal example, Southwest Airlines is well known for its emphasis on fun and positive affect (Quick, 1992); when newcomers join Southwest, their immediate work group may play a key role in socializing this affective orientation. Clearly, socialization also can entail communicating and enforcing feeling rules. However, the point is that even when feeling rules are not very salient in a work setting, newcomers to groups may nonetheless learn the kinds of affective states other group members experience or do not experience on the job and thus come to have their affect regulated by this aspect of socialization (Kelly & Barsade, 2001).

Normative Pressure

Normative pressure as a mechanism of affect regulation in groups is probably best captured by Hochschild's work on emotion management (Hochschild, 1975, 1979, 1983). In particular, Hochschild focuses on how social structures and normative pressures relate to multiple aspects of feelings including "the way we wish we felt, the way we try to feel, the way we feel, the way we show what we feel, and the way we pay attention to, label, and make sense of what we feel" (Hochschild, 1990, p. 117). Emotion management includes both emotion work (the regulation of feelings and their expression in one's personal life) and emotional labor (the regulation of feelings and their expression at work).

Feeling rules dictate how one should feel in a certain setting and what feelings are inappropriate, whereas expression rules dictate what emotions should be expressed in a setting and how they should be expressed (Kemper, 2000). Hochschild (1990) further distinguishes between surface acting and deep acting. Surface acting entails controlling and managing emotional expressions to modify experienced feelings, whereas deep acting entails modifying experienced feelings more directly (for example, by using relaxation techniques, cognitive restructuring, or visualization of alternative scenarios).

Morris and Feldman (1996) suggest that emotional labor varies along four dimensions: frequency of normative expressed emotion, duration and intensity of emotional displays, variety of emotions to be expressed, and extent of emotional dissonance (expressing emotions that are at odds with how one really feels; Middleton, 1989). While it is clearly an empirical question, it is likely that as each of these dimensions of emotional labor increases, the extent of affect regulation in groups may also increase.

Power and Status Relations

In contrast to approaches such as social comparison, which focus on similarities across members of a group and the convergence of their experienced affect, consideration of the effects of power and status relations on affect regulation focuses on differences between members of a work group and, in particular, power and status relations. As Clark (1990) puts it, "One of the most interesting paradoxes of social existence is that while we share group life together, we are also separated and divided by hierarchies based on gender, race, social class, age, ethnicity, occupation, beauty, intelligence, competence, interpersonal skills, and so forth. We find hierarchy virtually everywhere, permeating the social structure and everyday interaction" (p. 306).

Kemper (1978, 2000) suggests that a good portion of these differences and manifestations of hierarchy can be captured by the constructs of power and status. From this perspective, emotions are experienced and regulated by the meanings conveyed by power and status relations embedded in situations (Kemper, 2000). Based on the existing empirical literature, Kemper (2000) proposes distinct kinds of feelings that are experienced in situations differing in power and status dynamics. For example, increases in one's own power relative to others are proposed to lead to feelings of security, whereas decreases in one's own relative power are proposed to lead to fear and anxiety. As another example, increases in one's own relative status are proposed to lead to happiness and contentment, whereas decreases in one's own relative status can lead to anger, shame, or depression depending on attributions of the cause of loss of status and its changeability (Kemper, 2000). Other structural approaches to the sociology of emotions are consistent with Kemper's logic in that they show how differences in groups influence emotional experience. For example, Lucas and Lovaglia (1998) found in two experiments that high-status leaders reported experiencing more positive affect during a group task than did nonleaders.

Interestingly enough, while many of the mechanisms of affect regulation in groups I have discussed thus far would seem to lead to relatively consistent or homogeneous affective reactions in groups or the existence of a group affective tone (George, 1990, 1996b), social structural approaches such as Kemper's (1978, 2000) focus on how differences inherent in social groups lead to different affective experiences depending on one's relative position in the group. Are these two approaches contradictory or complementary? I would argue the latter for several reasons.

First, not all groups have affective tones, and affect can and does vary within groups (George, 1996b). Second, forces for homogeneity and heterogeneity in affect within groups can coexist and may actually promote group effectiveness. Whether an affective tone exists or not may depend on the relative strength of these forces. Third, real structural differences do exist in groups with concomitant effects on affective reactions. Finally, the fact that desires for self-control and self-determination (Deci & Ryan, 1980), as well as a need to feel connected with others in meaningful relationships, coexist as important drivers of human behavior suggest that group life may be permeated by forces that both seek to assert the primacy of the self as an autonomous, self-determined agent and seek to see the self as an accepted and integrated member of a collective entity. The extent to which affective reactions are homogeneous in a group may depend on the relative strength of these forces, as well as the interaction of the various mechanisms (both unconscious and conscious) by which affect comes to be regulated within groups.

Conclusion

In this chapter, I have reflected on diverse potential mechanisms by which affect may be regulated in groups. Given these and other mechanisms of affect regulation and the highly interdependent nature of affect and cognition, it is surprising, and also somewhat disconcerting, that affect regulation in groups has not received more attention in the literature. Groups and teams are affect generators through multiple mechanisms, and the affect experienced in the context of group membership can have far-reaching effects on group development over time, group dynamics, group performance, and group effectiveness (broadly defined to include member well-being).

Given changes in technology, economic structure, and the competitive landscape, teams increasingly are being relied on in organizations in place of more traditional kinds of work groups. The intensity of interactions and interdependence in teams, in conjunction with their goal orientation, is likely to amplify both the affect regulation that takes place in teams and the consequences of such affect regulation for team functioning. It is imperative for researchers to incorporate the causes and consequences of both the relatively intense emotions experienced in the context of group membership, as well as the more subtle and pervasive mood states, into studies of group functioning and effectiveness. Just as it is misleading to study individual cognition in an affective void, so too is it misleading to study group functioning from an exclusive cognitive or behavioral perspective. I hope that the resurgence of interest in affect in the workplace in general (as evidenced by the publication of this book), as well as this chapter in particular and other research on affect regulation in work groups and teams, will spur group researchers to incorporate the affective side of group life into their theories and empirical studies.

The study of affect regulation in groups necessarily evokes consideration of factors at both higher and lower levels of analysis. For example, in the beginning of the chapter, I noted how the wider organizational context within which groups are nested plays a significant role in multiple aspects of their functioning. Similarly, those of us who study work groups are continually reminded of the fact that while we hope work groups are more than the some of their parts, groups *are* composed of individuals, and understanding group functioning necessitates understanding the functioning of the individuals who make up a group.

While factors at the individual level of analysis that impinge on understanding affect regulation in groups are somewhat readily apparent based on the nature of the mechanism under consideration, factors at the organizational level are somewhat less apparent. In an effort to highlight some of these contextual factors as well as pose some questions for future research, in Table 6.1 I review the affect regulation mechanisms, speculate on the contextual influences on each mechanism, and pose some questions for future research.

There are certain implicit caveats in this chapter that I would like to make explicit. First, my treatment of proposed mechanisms of affect regulation in groups is by no means exhaustive. Given the highly interdependent nature of affect, cognition, motivation, and social interaction, other mechanisms can and should be identified and studied. Second, I view affect regulation in groups broadly to encompass any of the ways in which workers' affective experiences on the job come to be influenced by their work groups. Thus, affective regulation can lead to homogeneous affective experiences in a group or heterogeneous affective reactions within a group, depending on the mechanisms in operation. Third, the classification scheme I have relied on is crude at best and subject to debate. Clearly, one could convincingly argue that some of the affect regulation mechanisms I classified as conscious or deliberate might be better viewed as unconscious or relatively passive, and vice versa. Moreover, some mechanisms might entail both relatively conscious

Table 6.1. Group and Contextual Influences on Affect Regulation.

Group Level: Affect Regulation	Organizational Level: Potential Contextual Influences	Sample Research Questions
Automatic/passive regulation		
Emotional contagion	Culture, symbols, ceremonies	How do person, group, and contextual factors interact to affect susceptibility to, and extent of, emotional contagion in groups?
Common tasks and events	Organizational structure, policies and procedures, work environment, benefits	What kinds of group tasks are most likely to be influential in affect regulation, and why? What role do different forms of individualized and membership outcomes play in affect regulation in groups?
Vicarious processes	Stories and myths, recreational and social activities	When and why is vicarious affect most likely to be experienced? What are the varying roles that emotional empathy plays in groups?
Intentional regulation		
Group composition	Organizational composition, organizational leadership	How long does it take for attraction, selection, and attrition processes to operate, and how are these processes constrained? How do different dimensions of composition interact with each other?
Interpersonal influence	Socialization	When might emotional social comparison not take place, and why?
Normative pressure	Organizational norms and values	To what extent does affect regulation depend on the specific affective state in question, and why?
Power and status	Organizational politics, organizational networks	How do forces resulting in differential affective reactions interact with forces result-

or intentional and unconscious or unintentional effects. I relied on this scheme because it helped to clarify my own thinking about these diverse mechanisms and for ease of exposition purposes. To the extent that this scheme muddies rather than clears the water, I hope it will stimulate more in-depth consideration of the complexities and potential inherent contradictions surrounding affect regulation in groups and more research in this dynamic, important, and fascinating area.

Note

1. It is important to note that the term *emotional* in *emotional contagion* is used quite broadly to refer to the full range of affective states, including moods and emotions. So as to be consistent with the relevant literature, *emotional contagion* in this chapter refers to the contagion of affective states in general, including both moods and emotions.

References

Adelmann, P. K., & Zajonc, R. B. (1989). Facial efference and the experience of emotion. *Annual Review of Psychology, 40,* 249–280.

Bandura, A. (1986). *Social foundations of thought and action.* Upper Saddle River, NJ: Prentice-Hall.

Barsade, S. G. (2000). *The ripple effect: Emotional contagion in groups.* Working Paper 91, Yale School of Management.

Barsade, S. G., & Gibson, D. E. (1998). Group emotion: A view from top and bottom. *Research on managing groups and teams* (Vol. 1, pp. 81–102). Greenwich, CT: JAI Press.

Bartel, C. A., & Saavedra, R. (2000). The collective construction of work group moods. *Administrative Science Quarterly, 45,* 197–231.

Basch, J., & Fisher, C. D. (2000). Affective events-emotions matrix: A classification of work events and associated emotions. In N. M. Ashkanasy, C.E.J. Hartel, & W. J. Zerbe (Eds.), *Emotions in the workplace: Research, theory, and practice* (pp. 36–48). Westport, CT: Quorum Books.

Batson, C. D. (1998). Altruism and prosocial behavior. In D. T. Gilbert, S. T. Fiske, & G. Lindzey (Eds.), *The handbook of social psychology* (4th ed., Vol. 2, pp. 282–316). New York: McGraw-Hill.

Batson, C. D., Duncan, B., Ackerman, P., Buckley, T., & Birch, K. (1981). Is empathetic emotion a source of altruistic motivation? *Journal of Personality and Social Psychology, 40,* 290–302.

Bavelas, J. B., Black, A., Lemery, C. R., & Mullet, J. (1987). Motor mimicry as primitive empathy. In N. Eisenberg & J. Strayer (Eds.), *Empathy and its development* (pp. 317–338). Cambridge: Cambridge University Press.

Bernieri, F. J., Reznick, J. S., & Rosenthal, R. (1988). Synchrony, pseudo-synchrony, and dissynchrony: Measuring the entrainment process in mother-infant interactions. *Journal of Personality and Social Psychology, 54,* 243–253.

Brickson, S. (2000). The impact of identity organization on individual and organizational outcomes in demographically diverse settings. *Academy of Management Review, 25,* 82–101.

Bryne, D., Griffitt, W., & Stefaniak, D. (1967). Attraction and similarity of personality characteristics. *Journal of Personality and Social Psychology, 5,* 82–90.

Canli, T., Zhao, Z., Desmond, J. E., Kang, E., Gross, J., & Gabrieli, J.D.E. (2001). An fMRI study of personality influences on brain reactivity to emotional stimuli. *Behavioral Neuroscience, 115,* 33–42.

Clark, C. (1990). Emotions and micropolitics in everyday life: Some patterns and paradoxes of "place." In T. D. Kemper (Ed.), *Research agendas in the sociology of emotions* (pp. 305–333). Albany: State University of New York Press.

Clark, L., & Watson, D. (1988). Mood and the mundane: Relations between daily life events and self-reported mood. *Journal of Personality and Social Psychology, 54,* 296–308.

Coats, E. J., & Feldman, R. S. (1996). Gender differences in nonverbal correlates of social status. *Personality and Social Psychology Bulletin, 22,* 1014–1022.

Collins, R. (1990). Stratification, emotional energy, and the transient emotions. In T. D. Kemper (Ed.), *Research agendas in the sociology of emotions* (pp. 27–57). Albany: State University of New York.

Coser, R. L. (1960). Laughter among colleagues. *Psychiatry, 23,* 81–95.

Damasio, A. R. (1994). *Descartes' error: Emotion, reason, and the human brain.* New York: Avon Books.

Davis, M. H. (1983). Measuring individual differences in empathy: Evidence for a multidimensional approach. *Journal of Personality and Social Psychology, 44,* 113–126.

Deci, E. L., & Ryan, R. M. (1980). The empirical exploration of intrinsic motivational processes. In L. Berkowitz (Ed.), *Advances in experimental social psychology* (Vol. 13). Orlando, FL: Academic Press.

Diener, E. (1980). Deindividuation: The absence of self-awareness and self-regulation in group members. In P. B. Paulus (Ed.), *Psychology of group influence* (pp. 209–242). Hillsdale, NJ: Erlbaum.

Duclos, S. E., Laird, J. D., Schneider, E., Sexter, M., Stern, L., & Van Lighten, O. (1989). Emotion-specific effects of facial expressions and postures on emotional experience. *Journal of Personality and Social Psychology, 57,* 100–108.

Durkheim, E. (1915/1965). *The elementary forms of the religious life* (J. W. Swain, Trans.). New York: Free Press. (Original work published 1915).

Epstein, S. (1990). Cognitive-experiential self-theory. In L. Pervin (Ed.), *Handbook of personality theory and research* (pp. 165–191). New York: Guilford Press.

Epstein, S., & Meier, P. (1989). Constructive thinking: A broad coping variable with specific components. *Journal of Personality and Social Psychology, 57,* 332–350.

Festinger, L. (1950). Informal social communication. *Psychological Review, 57,* 271–282.

Festinger, L. A. (1954). Theory of social comparison processes. *Human Relations, 7,* 117–140.

Finholt, T., & Sproull, L. S. (1990). Electronic groups at work. *Organizational Science, 1,* 41–64.

Fisher, C. D. (1986). Organizational socialization: An integrative review. In K. M. Rowland & G. R. Ferris (Eds.), *Research in personnel and human resources management* (Vol. 4, pp. 101–145). Greenwich, CT: JAI Press.

Forgas, J. P. (1992). Affect in social judgments and decisions: A multiprocess model. In M. Zanna (Ed.), *Advances in experimental and social psychology* (Vol. 25, pp. 227–275). Orlando, FL: Academic Press.

Forgas, J. P. (Ed.) (2000). *Feeling and thinking: The role of affect in social cognition.* Cambridge: Cambridge University Press.

Forgas, J. P., & George, J. M. (2001). Affective influences on judgments and behavior in organizations: An information processing perspective. *Organizational Behavior and Human Decision Processes, 86,* 3–34.

Frese, M., & Zapf, D. (1994). Action as the core of work psychology: A German approach. In H. C. Triandis, M. D. Dunnette, & L. M. Hough (Eds.), *Handbook of industrial and organizational psychology* (2nd ed., Vol. 4, pp. 271–340). Palo Alto, CA: Consulting Psychologists Press.

Frijda, N. H. (1988). The laws of emotion. *American Psychologist, 43,* 349–358.

Frijda, N. H., & Mesquita, B. (1994). The social roles and functions of emotions. In S. Kitayama & H. Marcus (Eds.), *Emotion and culture: Empirical studies of mutual influence* (pp. 51–87). Washington, DC: American Psychological Association.

George, J. M. (1990). Personality, affect, and behavior in groups. *Journal of Applied Psychology, 75,* 107–116.

George, J. M. (1991). State or trait: Effects of positive mood on prosocial behaviors at work. *Journal of Applied Psychology, 76,* 299–307.

George, J. M. (1992). Extrinsic and intrinsic origins of perceived social loafing in organizations. *Academy of Management Journal, 35,* 191–202.

George, J. M. (1995a). Asymmetrical effects of rewards and punishments: The case of social loafing. *Journal of Occupational and Organizational Psychology, 68,* 327–338.

George, J. M. (1995b). Leader positive mood and group performance: The case of customer service. *Journal of Applied Social Psychology, 25,* 778–794.

George, J. M. (1996a). State and trait affect. In K. Murphy (Ed.), *Individual differences and behavior in organizations* (pp. 145–171). San Francisco: Jossey-Bass.

George, J. M. (1996b). Group affective tone. In M. West (Ed.), *Handbook of work group psychology* (pp. 77–93). New York: Wiley.

George, J. M. (2000). Emotions and leadership: The role of emotional intelligence. *Human Relations, 53,* 1027–1055.

George, J. M., & Bettenhausen, K. (1990). Understanding prosocial behavior, sales performance, turnover: A group level analysis in a service context. *Journal of Applied Psychology, 75,* 698–709.

George, J. M., & Brief, A. P. (1992). Feeling good-doing good: A conceptual analysis of the mood at work-organizational spontaneity relationship. *Psychological Bulletin, 112,* 310–329.

George, J. M., & Brief, A. P. (1996). Motivational agendas in the workplace: The effects of feelings on focus of attention and work motivation. In B. M. Staw & L. L. Cummings (Eds.), *Research in organizational behavior* (Vol. 18, pp. 75–109). Greenwich, CT: JAI Press.

George, J. M., Brief, A. P., Webster, J., & Burke, M. (1989). Incentive compensation as an injurious condition of work: A study of labeling. *Journal of Organizational Behavior, 10,* 155–167.

George, J. M., & Jones, G. R. (2002). *Understanding and managing organizational behavior* (3rd ed.). Upper Saddle River, NJ: Prentice Hall.

George, J. M., & Zhou, J. (in press). Understanding when bad moods foster creativity and good ones don't: The role of context and clarity of feelings. *Journal of Applied Psychology.*

Gersick, C.J.G. (1988). Time and transition in work teams: Toward a new model of group development. *Academy of Management Journal, 31,* 9–41.

Goleman, D. (1989, March 28). The roots of empathy are traced to infancy. *New York Times,* pp. B1, B10.

Gray, J. A. (1971). The psychophysiological basis of introversion/extraversion. *Behavior Research and Therapy, 8,* 249–266.

Gray, J. A. (1981). A critique of Eysenck's theory of personality. In H. J. Eysenck (Ed.), *A model of personality* (pp. 246–276). New York: Springer-Verlag.

Gray, J. A. (1987). Perspectives on anxiety and impulsivity: A commentary. *Journal of Research in Personality, 21,* 493–509.

Griffitt, W. (1966). Interpersonal attraction as a function of self-concept and personality similarity-dissimilarity. *Journal of Personality and Social Psychology, 4,* 581–584.

Guzzo, R. A., & Shea, G. P. (1992). Group performance and intergroup relations in organizations. In M. D. Dunnette & L. M. Hough (Eds.), *Handbook of industrial and organizational psychology* (2nd ed., Vol. 3, pp. 269–313). Palo Alto, CA: Consulting Psychologists Press.

Hackman, J. R. (1992). Group influences on individuals in organizations. In M. D. Dunnette & L. M. Hough (Eds.), *Handbook of industrial and organizational psychology* (2nd ed., Vol. 3, pp. 199–267). Palo Alto, CA: Consulting Psychologists Press.

Hackman, J. R., & Morris, C. G. (1975). Group tasks, group interaction process, and group performance effectiveness: A review and proposed integration. In L. Berkowitz (Ed.), *Advances in experimental social psychology* (Vol. 9, pp. 45–99). Orlando, FL: Academic Press.

Hatfield, E., Cacioppo, J., & Rapson, R. L. (1992). Primitive emotional contagion. In M. S. Clark (Ed.), *Review of personality and social psychology: Vol. 14. Emotion and social behavior* (pp. 151–177). Thousand Oaks, CA: Sage.

Hatfield, E., Cacioppo, J. T., & Rapson, R. L. (1994). *Emotional contagion.* Cambridge: Cambridge University Press.

Heise, D. R., & O'Brien, J. (1993). Emotion expression in groups. In M. Lewis & J. M. Haviland (Eds.), *Handbook of emotions* (pp. 489–498). New York: Guilford Press.

Hess, U., & Kirouac, G. (2000). Emotion expression in groups. In M. Lewis & J. M. Haviland-Jones (Eds.), *Handbook of emotions* (2nd ed., pp. 368–381). New York: Guilford Press.

Hochschild, A. R. (1975). The sociology of feeling and emotion: Selected possibilities. In M. Millman & R. Kanter (Eds.), *Another voice* (pp. 280–307). New York: Anchor.

Hochschild, A. R. (1979). Emotion work, feelings rules, and social structure. *American Journal of Sociology, 85,* 551–575.

Hochschild, A. R. (1983). *The managed heart: The commercialization of human feeling.* Berkeley: University of California Press.

Hochschild, A. R. (1990). Ideology and emotion management: A perspective and path for future research. In T. D. Kemper (Ed.), *Research agendas in the sociology of emotions* (pp. 117–142). Albany: State University of New York Press.

Hoffman, M. L. (1975). Developmental synthesis of affect and cognition and its implications for altruistic motivation. *Developmental Psychology, 11,* 607–622.

Humphrey, R. H. (1985). How work roles influence perception: Structural-cognitive processes and organizational behavior. *American Sociological Review, 50,* 242–252.

Humphrey, R. H. (2000). The importance of job characteristics to emotional displays. In N. M. Ashkanasy, C.E.J. Hartel, & W. J. Zerbe

(Eds.), *Emotions in the workplace: Research, theory, and practice* (pp. 236–249). Westport, CT: Quorum Books.

Isen, A. M., & Baron, R. A. (1991). Positive affect as a factor in organizational behavior. In B. M. Staw & L. L. Cummings (Eds.), *Research in organizational behavior* (Vol. 13, pp. 1–54). Greenwich, CT: JAI Press.

Izard, C. E. (1977). *Human emotions.* New York: Plenum.

Jung, C. G. (1968). *Analytical psychology: Its theory and practice.* New York: Random House.

Katz, D. (1964). The motivational basis of organizational behavior. *Behavioral Science, 9,* 131–146.

Katz, L., & Epstein, S. (1991). Constructive thinking and coping with laboratory-induced stress. *Journal of Personality and Social Psychology, 61,* 789–800.

Kelly, J. R., & Barsade, S. G. (2001). Mood and emotions in small groups and work teams. *Organizational Behavior and Human Decision Processes, 86,* 99–130.

Keltner, D., & Haidt, J. (1999). Social functions of emotions at four levels of analysis. *Cognition and Emotion, 13,* 505–521.

Kemper, T. D. (1978). *A social interactional theory of emotions.* New York: Wiley.

Kemper, T. D. (2000). Social models in the explanation of emotions. In M. Lewis & J. M. Haviland-Jones (Eds.), *Handbook of emotions* (2nd ed., pp. 45–58). New York: Guilford Press.

Klimoski, R., & Mohammed, S. (1994). Team mental model: Construct or metaphor? *Journal of Management, 20,* 403–437.

Knutson, B. (1996). Facial expressions of emotion influence interpersonal trait inferences. *Journal of Nonverbal Behavior, 20,* 165–182.

Larsen, R. J., & Katelaar, T. (1991). Personality and susceptibility to positive and negative emotional states. *Journal of Personality and Social Psychology, 61,* 132–140.

Lipnack, J. (1999). Virtual teams. *Executive Excellence, 16,* 14–15.

Lovaglia, M. J., & Houser, J. A. (1996). Emotional reactions and status in groups. *American Sociological Review, 61,* 867–883.

Lucas, J. W., & Lovaglia, M. J. (1998). Leadership status, gender, group size, and emotion in face-to-face groups. *Sociological Perspectives, 41,* 617–637.

Martin, L. L., & Tesser, A. (Eds.). (1996). *Striving and feeling: Interactions among goals, affect, and self-regulation.* Hillsdale, NJ: Erlbaum.

Mayer, J. D. (1986). How mood influences cognition. In N. E. Sharkey (Ed.), *Advances in cognitive science* (Vol. 1, pp. 290–314). Chichester: Ellis Horwood.

Mayer, J. D., DiPaolo, M., & Salovey, P. (1990). Perceiving affective content in ambiguous visual stimuli: A component of emotional intelligence. *Journal of Personality Assessment, 54,* 772–781.

Mayer, J. D., & Salovey, P. (1993). The intelligence of emotional intelligence. *Intelligence, 17,* 433–442.

Mayer, J. D., & Salovey, P. (1995). Emotional intelligence and the construction and regulation of feelings. *Applied and Preventive Psychology, 4,* 197–208.

Mayer, J. D., & Salovey, P. (1997). What is emotional intelligence: Implications for educators. In P. Salovey & D. Sluyter (Eds.), *Emotional development, emotional literacy, and emotional intelligence* (pp. 3–31). New York: Basic Books.

Middleton, D. R. (1989). Emotional style: The cultural ordering of emotions. *Ethos, 17(2),* 187–201.

Morris, J. A., & Feldman, D. C. (1996). The dimensions, antecedents, and consequences of emotional labor. *Academy of Management Review, 21,* 986–1010.

Morris, W. N. (1989). *Mood: The frame of mind.* New York: Springer-Verlag.

O'Toole, R., & Dubin, R. (1968). Baby feeding and body sway: An experiment in George Herbert Mead's "taking the role of the other." *Journal of Personality and Social Psychology, 10,* 59–65.

Quick, J. C. (1992, Autumn). Crafting an organizational culture: Herb's hand at Southwest Airlines. *Organizational Dynamics,* pp. 45–56.

Rakestraw, T. L., & Weiss, H. M. (1981). The interaction of social influences and task experience on goals, performance, and performance satisfaction. *Organizational Behavior and Human Performance, 27,* 326–344.

Rasmussen, J. (1987). Cognitive control and human error mechanisms. In J. Rasmussen, K. Duncan, & J. Leplat (Eds.), *New technology and human error* (pp. 53–61). New York: Wiley.

Reik, T. (1948). *Listening with the third ear: The inner experience of a psychoanalyst.* New York: Farrar, Straus, & Giroux.

Salovey, P., Hsee, C. K., & Mayer, J. D. (1993). Emotional intelligence and the self-regulation of affect. In D. M. Wegner & J. W. Pennebaker (Eds.), *Handbook of mental control* (pp. 258–277). Upper Saddle River, NJ: Prentice Hall.

Salovey, P., & Mayer, J. D. (1989–1990). Emotional intelligence. *Imagination, Cognition, and Personality, 9,* 185–211.

Salovey, P., & Mayer, J. D. (1994). Some final thoughts about personality and intelligence. In R. J. Sternberg & P. Ruzgis (Eds.), *Personality and intelligence* (pp. 303–318). Cambridge: Cambridge University Press.

Salovey, P., Mayer, J. D., Goldman, S. L., Turvey, C., & Palfai, T. P. (1995). Emotional attention, clarity, and repair: Exploring emotional intelligence using the trait meta-mood scale. In J. W. Pennebaker (Ed.), *Emotion, disclosure, and health* (pp. 125–154). Washington, DC: American Psychological Association.

Sandelands, L., & St. Clair, L. (1993). Toward an empirical concept of group. *Journal for the Theory of Social Behaviour, 23,* 423–458.

Schneider, B. (1987). The people make the place. *Personnel Psychology, 40,* 437–454.

Schneider, B., Goldstein, H. W., & Smith, D. B. (1995). The ASA framework: An update. *Personnel Psychology, 48,* 747–773.

Seashore, S. E. (1954). *Group cohesiveness in the industrial work group.* Ann Arbor: University of Michigan, Institute for Social Research.

Semmer, N., & Frese, M. (1985). Action theory in clinical psychology. In M. Frese & J. Sabini (Eds.), *Goal directed behavior* (pp. 296–310). Hillsdale, NJ: Erlbaum.

Shaw, M. E. (1981). *Group dynamics: The psychology of small group behavior* (3rd ed.). New York: McGraw-Hill.

Shiffrin, R. M., & Schneider, W. (1977). Controlled and automatic information processing. II. Perceptual learning, automatic attending and a general theory. *Psychological Review, 84,* 127–190.

Simon, H. A. (1982). Comments. In M. S. Clark & S. T. Fiske (Eds.), *Affect and cognition: The Seventeenth Annual Carnegie Symposium on Cognition* (pp. 333–342). Hillsdale, NJ: Erlbaum.

Sinclair, R. C., & Mark, M. M. (1992). The influence of mood state on judgment and action: Effects on persuasion, categorization, social justice, person perception, and judgmental accuracy. In L. L. Martin & A. Tesser (Eds.), *The construction of social judgments.* Hillsdale, NJ: Erlbaum.

Steiner, I. D. (1972). *Group process and productivity.* New York: Academic Press.

Strauss, S. G. (1997). Technology, group process, and group outcomes: Testing the connections in computer-mediated and face-to-face groups. *Human-Computer Interaction, 12,* 227–266.

Sullins, E. S. (1991). Emotional contagion revisited: Effects of social comparison and expressive style on mood convergence. *Personality and Social Psychology Bulletin, 17,* 166–174.

Taylor, S. E. (1998). The social being in social psychology. In D. T. Gilbert, S. T. Fiske, & G. Lindzey (Eds.), *The handbook of social psychology* (4th ed., Vol. 1, pp. 58–95).

Tomkins, S. S. (1982). Affect theory. In P. Ekman (Ed.), *Emotion in the human face* (2nd ed., pp. 353–395). Cambridge: Cambridge University Press.

Totterdell, P. (2000). Catching moods and hitting runs: Mood linkage and subjective performance in professional sports teams. *Journal of Applied Psychology, 85,* 848–859.

Totterdell, P., Kellett, S., Teuchmann, K., & Briner, R. B. (1998). Evidence of mood linkage in work groups. *Journal of Personality and Social Psychology, 74,* 1504–1515.

Tschan, F., & von Cranach, M. (1996). Group task structure, processes and outcomes. In M. A. West (Ed.), *Handbook of work group psychology* (pp. 95–121). New York: Wiley.

Tseng, W. S., & Hsu, J. (1980). Minor psychological disturbances of everyday life. In H. C. Triandis & J. D. Draguns (Eds.), *Handbook of cross-cultural psychology, Vol. 6: Psychopathology* (pp. 61–97). Needham Heights, MA: Allyn & Bacon.

Tuckman, B. W., & Jensen, M. C. (1977). Stages of small group development. *Group and Organizational Studies, 2,* 419–427.

von Cranach, M. (1996). Toward a theory of the acting group. In E. Witte & J. H. Davis (Eds.), *Understanding group behavior: Small group processes and interpersonal relations* (Vol. 2, pp. 147–187). Hillsdale, NJ: Erlbaum.

Walsh, J. P. (1995). Managerial and organizational cognition: Notes from a trip down memory lane. *Organizational Science, 6,* 280–321.

Walsh, J. P., & Fahey, L. (1986). The role of negotiated belief structures in strategy making. *Journal of Management, 12,* 325–338.

Watson, D. (2000). *Mood and temperament.* New York: Guilford Press.

Weiss, H. M., & Cropanzano, R. (1996). Affective events theory: A theoretical discussion of the structure, causes, and consequences of affective experiences at work. In B. M. Staw & L. L. Cummings (Eds.), *Research in organizational behavior* (Vol. 18, pp. 1–74). Greenwich, CT: JAI Press.

Weiss, H. M., & Nowicki, C. E. (1981). Social influences on task satisfaction: Model competence and observer field dependence. *Organizational Behavior and Human Decision Processes, 27,* 345–366.

Wrightsman, L. (1960). Effects of waiting with others on changes in the level of felt anxiety. *Journal of Abnormal and Social Psychology, 61,* 216–222.

PART 3

Applications to Applied Problems

Two common themes underlie the chapters in Part Three, which focus on a variety of specific applied problems. One is that emotions at work (and home) are reactions to the affective events that provide emotional shocks to individuals. This idea originates in Weiss and Cropanzano's (1996) affective events theory (AET), which maintains that events, not environments, are proximal causes of reactions in organizations and that affective reactions are mediational processes in the generation of work behaviors. Thus, the emotional structure of affective events is important in understanding behavior. Events provoke different emotions in individuals—anger, frustration, joy, pride, fear—and these different emotions have behavioral implications because emotions have associated action tendencies. Emotions are produced by a primary appraisal of an event as being good or bad for an individual and consistent or inconsistent with current goals, and they are generated in part by a primitive emotional architecture (see Lord and Harvey, Chapter Four, this volume).

Several applied issues discussed in the upcoming chapters–emotional labor, violence at work, courage—involve attempts to control immediate, automatic emotional reactions to affective events using deliberate, conscious, symbolic architectures. These chapters focus on the process and value of controlling reactions to specific emotions, such as anger or fear, illustrating the applied utility of thinking in terms of basic emotions and their associated action tendencies. Organizations can also help control emotions through socialization processes (see Ashforth and Saks, Chapter Ten) that build appropriate interpretive structures and responses to affective events. Emotional regulation processes occurring in the family can also cross the work-family boundary, influencing reactions to emotional events at work (or vice versa) as MacDermid, Seery, and Weiss explain (Chapter Twelve).

The second common theme running through several applied issues is that emotions at work (and in the family) involve social processes. Thus, emotions reflect both automatic and controlled aspects of social processes that may occur at dyadic, group, or organizational levels. Social perception processes are important components of courage at work, emotional regulation, and aggression: courage at work often involves the perceptions that actors handle challenging situations with less fear than observers; the goal of emotional regulation is often to portray a specific type of emotional reaction to customers; and aggression is defined in terms of an actor's intent, which depends on a social inference process. This theme illustrates that reactions to affective events also include assessments of the social context, the qualities and intentions of other individuals, and norms for appropriate social reaction. These individual-based social-cognitive processes are often combined with dyadic or group-based processes such as social contagion, as already discussed in Chapters Five and Six. For example, the anger associated with aggression may be contagious, increasing the likelihood of aggressive responses to experienced aggression at work. The interpretation of affect also reflects the effects of even larger social units such as culture, which Early and Francis discuss in Chapter Eleven. They note that devices engineered for socially communicating emotions (faces) convey expressions that are meaningful cross-culturally, although important social differences have also been found.

Part Three begins with the Glomb, Steel, and Arvey chapter on workplace violence and aggression. Like other aggression researchers, they conceptualize aggression as interpersonal behaviors perpetrated with an intent to harm others, but it is often unclear whether this intent is inferred by observers of aggression or is consciously held by the perpetrator. Building on AET, Glomb, Steel, and Arvey identify two types of aggressive behavior. Affect-driven behaviors, which tend to be impulsive and spontaneous, may not involve conscious intent by actors, but observers may infer intent and may also generalize from an aggressive act, drawing inferences about a perpetrator's personality. Judgment-driven behaviors, in contrast, are premeditated, attitude-based aggressive acts that reflect the indirect effects of affective events as operating through attitudinal processes.

Glomb, Steel, and Arvey's framework also examines antecedents to affective events, paying particular attention to the role of individual differences. For example, they note that individuals high on trait anger react more to ambiguous situations, tending to interpret them in terms of threat or attack. Impulsivity, another trait that they note has a strong association with aggression, reflects the tendency to act without thought. These two traits reflect the input and output sides, respectively, of the stimulus-organism-response (S-O-R) individual difference model that Larsen, Diener, and Lucas developed in Chapter Three. When these two traits combine, affect-driven reactions to events are more likely because there is little time for the more conscious emotional regulation processes that Glomb, Steel, and Arvey discuss to intervene in regulating aggression.

Glomb, Steel, and Arvey also discuss several situational factors that can undermine intentional control of emotions, such as stress or cognitive load (which reduce cognitive resources), substance and alcohol abuse (which increase attention to immediate situational cues), and aggressive organizational cultures (which may strengthen the link between angry reactions and aggressive behaviors). By distinguishing multiple pathways to aggression and identifying a variety of antecedents, the authors create a conceptual framework with several applied implications that they use to discuss multiple options such as selection, training, and organizational-level practices that may alter the likelihood and nature of aggression at work.

In Chapter Eight, Grandey and Brauburger also use AET and Gross's model (1998) of emotional regulation as the basis for explaining reactions to anger, but their focus is on effective emotional regulation in the production of "service with a smile." They see context as influencing the frequency of affective events and the amount of autonomy employees have to deal with such affective shocks. Following Gross, they note that given sufficient power over context, employees could regulate emotions through two externally focused strategies, situation selection and situation modification. However, more typically, employees providing customer service must use internally focused strategies, which involve changing one's attentional focus or cognitively reinterpreting an interaction. Both of these "deep-acting" strategies create cognitive demands on workers, but if they induce actual feelings that are consistent with required emotional displays, they may create a source of pride and accomplishment for employees. In contrast, when employees must use response modulation to fake positive emotional responses (surface acting), negative outcomes such as stress and burnout may result. Because emotional labor has important consequences for both employees and customers, Grandey and Brauburger maintain that it should be managed more effectively by organizations through developing appropriate selection, training, and empowerment strategies.

In Chapter Nine, Worline, Wrzesniewski, and Rafaeli address the role of courage in breaking organizational routines to improve performance. Courage, which is commonly defined as the ability to persist in spite of fear, often involves an explicit choice to suppress fear-related flight responses. Like emotional labor, courage reflects effective behavior made possible by the regulation of emotions, but in this case, the emotion is fear rather than anger, and the social embeddedness of courageous behavior and regulatory processes is the focus of this chapter. The chapter authors propose that courage "occurs within a regulatory system operating at a social level, with cognition, emotion and action intertwined to mutually constitute work performance." Courage thus involves a dynamic social process, in which both risks and the speed of progress toward desired goals are assessed as part of a sense-making and monitoring process.

Courage is often easier to observe in others than in oneself. Assessment of courage may often be created through social observations, as observers infer that an actor behaved bravely, seemingly experiencing less emotion than observers experienced. Interestingly, Worline, Wrzesniewski, and Rafaeli also note that courage is often described by observers in terms of stories rather than abstract qualities, suggesting that it is encoded by observers in episodic memory, which is more closely integrated with emotions than semantic memory (Allen, Kaut, Kopera-Frye, Bowie, & Lord, 2001).

The social embeddedness of courage is also shown by these authors' assertion that courageous acts often upset social routines and interaction patterns in organizations. Emotional reactions are key mediators of this process: negative or distress-related emotions in response to courageous acts can narrow observers' personal agency, while positive emotions can expand their sense of agency; courageous behaviors can also diminish or strengthen social connections depending on whether approach- or avoidance-related emotions are evoked in observers; and collective rather than self-motivated courageous behavior can inspire observers to feel a sense of connection to the organization as a whole, evoking collective rather than individual identities. In sum, Worline, Wrzesniewski, and Rafaeli illustrate that work performance is interwoven with emotions in a dynamic social process, in which courageous disruptions of organizational routines can promote both individual growth and an expansion of organizational routines and meaning. In a postscript, these authors apply their framework to understanding courage and work after September 11, 2001.

In Chapter Eleven, Ashforth and Saks focus on emotion-related processes pertaining to organizational entry. Preentry processes related to recruitment and selection often have a strong emotional component. They note that potential employees are often recruited and attracted to organizations through emotional processes, which may involve the transmission of emotions from initial contacts in an organization (such as emotional contagion from interviewers). These informal processes are complemented by more formal processes in which individuals are selected for emotional competencies. Here, Ashforth and Saks note that like any other desired skill, selection for emotional competencies must be integrated with careful job analysis, needs to reflect effective measurement of specific skills, and should show incremental validity compared to other selection measures.

Postentry processes concern socialization through emotions and the socialization of emotions. Ashforth and Saks build on AET to explain socialization through emotions. They argue that socialization involves appraisal and learning from events that are often explicitly orchestrated by organizations to produce relatively homogeneous, institutionalized socialization. Alternatively, appraisal and learning may stem from spontaneous individualized events, which tend to produce a haphazard socialization experience with greater variability among individuals and greater role ambiguity.

In either case, emotions are key mediating processes that motivate and influence the nature of the information processes used in learning. The socialization of emotions attempts to create appropriate occupational, organizational, or subunit competencies in managing emotions. The pervasive effect of emotions on organizational entry processes is summed up in Ashforth and Saks's observation that individuals may "feel rather than think their way into a new job and organization."

Earley and Francis, in Chapter Eleven, adopt an international perspective on emotions in addressing a variety of cross-cultural issues pertaining to emotions in the workplace. They approach cross-cultural analysis from a processing perspective, emphasizing that encoding, appraisal, and display are key steps in generating emotions at work and that culture can have different effects on these specific steps. After carefully reviewing the literature on cross-cultural differences in core emotions, they conclude that the universal aspect of emotions is contained in the dimensions underlying appraisal, but that the display of emotions varies across cultures, a conclusion that dovetails with the S-O-R model of Chapter Three.

Earley and Francis develop a broader framework for organizing information regarding cross-cultural influences on emotions. In this framework, influences from four separate types of social units—societal context, industry and organizational context, work unit and group characteristics, and employee experience—have cascading effects on emotion-related processes. They suggest that these cultural influences operate like hidden prompters that are sending response cues to actors. Although not developed in such terms, this model is quite consistent with the operation of multilayered neural networks (see Lord and Harvey, Chapter Four, this volume) in which different layers correspond to the units that Earley and Francis identify. In such a network, each layer could successively transform hidden prompts to fit better with the unit-specific context. Earley and Francis's framework nicely organizes a wide variety of literature, helping us to understand many salient examples of cross-cultural differences, such as how the presence of others is a powerful moderator of emotional reactions in collectively oriented cultures. Earley and Francis also review the limited literature on cross-cultural differences in emotional reactions at work. The very limited amount of such research suggests that their framework will be valuable in generating future studies on this topic.

In Chapter Twelve, MacDermid, Seery, and Weiss examine the effects on emotions of another cultural unit–the family–as well as examine the carryover of emotional processes, experiences, and effects from work to family and family to work. Building on AET, they address a number of factors that can affect emotional reactions to events. They also partition the behavioral effects of emotional responses into attitude-driven and affect-driven categories. Attitudes can generalize across the work-family boundary, affecting behaviors in either domain, and attitudes can reflect both antecedent cognitive and emotional processes. Similarly, factors associated with affect-driven behavior such as emotional labor, self-management of emotions through various types of coping, and emotional by-products (for example, memory, risk-taking, creativity, and aggression) can generalize across work-family boundaries. Through such processes, affective events in one domain can influence the response to affective events in the other.

Although MacDermid, Seery, and Weiss develop a model showing responses to specific events, they also emphasize that the more collective family or work context must also be considered. By providing a coherent model of how emotion-related events and processes traverse the work-family boundary, this chapter can expand and integrate our notion of applied research. It ends by considering three areas of application that reflect these authors' expanded view of the work-family interface: the day-to-day process of emotional transmission, managing one's own emotions, and managing the emotions of others (emotion of labor).

By expanding the conceptualization of emotional effects across cultures and families, the final two chapters in Part Three create a rich notion of emotions and emotional regulation processes. Emotions are central in human lives. Emotion-related processes reflect our human heritage, the consequences of the social systems we have developed, and the biological and learning factors that differentiate one individual from another. To improve both human welfare and organizational functioning, applied practice and research need to be grounded in these multiple perspectives.

References

Allen, P. A., Kaut, K., Kopera-Frye, Bowie, T., & Lord, R. G. (2001). *An emotional mediational theory of age differences in episodic and semantic memory*. Working paper, University of Akron.

Gross, J. J. (1988). The emerging field of emotional regulation: An integrative review. *Review of General Psychology, 2,* 271–299.

Weiss, H. M., & Cropanzano, R. (1996). Affective events theory: A theoretical discussion of the structure, causes and consequences of affective experiences at work. In B. M. Staw & L. L. Cummings (Eds.), *Research in organizational behavior* (Vol. 18, pp. 1–74). Greenwich, CT: JAI Press.

CHAPTER 7

Office Sneers, Snipes, and Stab Wounds

Antecedents, Consequences, and Implications of Workplace Violence and Aggression

Theresa M. Glomb
Piers D. G. Steel
Richard D. Arvey

Newington, Connecticut—Angered about a salary dispute and his failure to win a promotion, a Connecticut Lottery accountant reported promptly to his job this morning, hung up his coat and then methodically stabbed and gunned down four of his bosses, one of whom he chased through a parking lot, before turning the gun on himself [Rabinovitz, 1998].

Santa Ana, California—A dismissed state highway employee armed with an AK-47 assault rifle killed four of his former co-workers at a maintenance yard yesterday in Orange, a Los Angeles suburb, before being shot to death by the police in a fierce gun battle [Dismissed worker kills four and then is slain, 1997].

In recent years, stories like these have become a staple for the American media. Workplace aggression has crept into our organizations (U.S. Department of Labor, 1998; Northwestern National Life Insurance Company, 1993), capturing the attention of employees who fear aggression from coworkers and organizational outsiders, and the general public who fear becoming innocent victims of workplace aggression. Homicide was the second leading cause of job-related deaths in 1996 (Toscano & Windau, 1998). That same year, over eighteen thousand workers suffered nonfatal injuries resulting in days away from work due to assaults and violent acts (U.S. Department of Labor, 1998). As unfortunate as it may be, the phrase "going postal" has entered our vernacular, inspired by the alarming incidents in which current or former employees of the U.S. Postal Service violently attack current or former coworkers. Given the visibility of and media attention to acts of workplace aggression, it is not surprising that organizations and researchers are interested in investigating factors related to workplace aggression and the development of prevention strategies to combat this growing workplace threat.

Despite this organizational and societal interest, a research base for workplace aggression and violence is only beginning to accumulate. This research is limited in a number of ways. First, early research on workplace violence and aggression defined the concept narrowly, focusing on extreme acts of violence, such as physical assault and homicide, at the expense of more frequent types of aggressive behaviors, such as verbal assaults. Second, much of the existing research has not investigated the complex interplay of job, organizational, and individual factors related to workplace aggression (for exceptions, see Folger & Baron, 1996; Glomb, 2002; Neuman & Baron, 1997, 1998; O'Leary-Kelly, Griffin, & Glew, 1996). Many of the theoretical models available (Barling, 1996; Neuman & Baron, 1998; O'Leary-Kelly et al., 1996) have not been empirically tested. Third, many of the theoretical models and empirical studies on aggression do not include affective or emotional variables in their frameworks. This neglect of affective and emotional variables in the study of workplace aggression seems imprudent given that aggression is closely linked to the emotion of anger. The neglect of emotion and affect in the study of workplace aggression is not unusual; organizational research in general has ignored emotion and affective experiences at work (Weiss & Cropanzano, 1996).

Given the pervasive effect of affective and emotional reactions of individuals in a variety of contexts, ignoring them in worklife is both unrealistic and unwise. Emotions and affect are important given that aggression is a frequent behavioral manifestation of emotional reactions such as anger. Consequently, this chapter examines workplace aggression and anger within a larger framework of the nature, causes, and consequences of emotional and affective work experiences and problems with emotion regulation. We integrate research investigating workplace aggression within that of broader theoretical frameworks useful for examining the role of emotions in organizations, specifically, affective events theory (Weiss & Cropanzano, 1996) and emotion regulation theory. We use these general approaches, along with empirical work on antecedents of aggression, to understand better the interplay of emotion and aggression, propose a model of aggression based on a broader theory of affect at work, and posit preventative measures.

Conceptualizing Aggression

Early attention to workplace aggression focused largely on violent and extreme examples of aggressive behavior, particularly workplace homicide. However, most workplace homicides (80 percent) occur during the course of a robbery or other crime (Toscano & Windau, 1998) and are clustered in certain high-risk occupations, such as taxi driver and convenience store clerk. A relatively small number of homicides are perpetrated by current or former coworkers over work-related issues (129, or 14 percent of all job-related homicides in 1996). Furthermore, physical aggression is less frequent than other forms of nonphysical aggression (Greenberg & Barling, 1999; Glomb, 2002; Neuman & Baron, 1998). Although the seriousness of workplace homicides and physical violence cannot be dismissed, the low base rate of these extreme forms of aggressive behaviors supports the rationale for examining workplace aggression using a broader conceptualization that includes less extreme forms of aggressive behaviors. In addition, mildly aggressive acts can have great impact when they are experienced in quantity. As mild aggressive acts increase in frequency, subsequent aggressions can occur before the effects of earlier ones have fully dissipated (Zillman, 1993). These overlapping effects build on each other, augmenting their impact. Eventually, repeated mild aggression can create considerable distress and aggression itself, such as that seen after periods of prolonged provocation or threat (Berkowitz, 1993).

Our conceptualization of workplace aggression is similar to that of Neuman and Baron (1998), who define workplace aggression as "efforts by individuals to harm others with whom they work, or have worked, or the organizations in which they are presently, or were previously, employed" (p. 395) with the exception that we focus more on interpersonal forms of aggression rather than aggression directed at the organization. Aggression directed at the organization overlaps considerably with other constructs, such as organizational retaliation, work withdrawal, and organizational workplace deviance (see Skarlicki & Folger, 1997, 1999; Hanisch & Hulin, 1990, 1991; Robinson & Bennett, 1995) and is not considered here. Note also that the focus is on aggression from others working within the organization rather than from persons outside the organizations, such as that displayed during the course of a robbery attempt. Others have suggested that aggression from organizational outsiders may be predicted by a different set of antecedents, such as working hours and occupation (see Budd, Arvey, & Lawless, 1996), from those discussed here.

The component of intent to harm is one of the most critical and complex issues in defining aggression. Defining aggression solely by the behavior (without the qualification of intentionality) may misrepresent the construct. For example, yelling at another employee is a behavior commonly included in the aggressive behaviors construct; without the qualification of intentionality, yelling to be heard over the loud noise of machinery in a plant would be considered aggressive. Constructs such as political influence behaviors are particularly difficult because the primary intentions are self-serving (Ferris, Russ, & Fandt, 1989); harming another in the process is often an unfortunate by-product. Similarly, workplace incivility is defined as having "ambiguous intent to harm" (Anderson & Pearson, 1999, p. 457). Thus, the intent to harm condition may be fuzzy at the margins of the behavioral construct space. The conceptualization in this chapter follows that taken by previous aggression researchers (Baron & Neuman, 1998; Folger & Baron, 1996; Neuman & Baron, 1998) by conceptualizing aggression broadly as a variety of interpersonal aggressive acts perpetrated with an intent to harm.

Aggressive behaviors have been classified by Buss (1961) according to three facets: physical or verbal, active or passive, and direct or indirect. The physical-verbal facet is defined by whether aggression is exhibited through physical (for example, hitting) or verbal acts (for example, threats). The active-passive facet is determined by whether harm is inflicted by engaging in some behavior (for example yelling at another) or withholding some action (for example, withholding needed job information). The direct-indirect facet deals with whether harm is expressed directly at the target (for example, swearing at another or making obscene gestures) or through some intermediary or object that the target values (for example, destroying property or spreading rumors). Note that aggressive behaviors are defined by their placement on all three of these dimensions; yelling at a coworker is verbal, active, and direct. Within the realm of workplace aggression, Neuman and Baron (1998) proposed the three-factor model of workplace aggression composed of expressions of hostility (for example, dirty looks, spreading rumors), obstructionism (for example, failure to return telephone calls, refusal to provide needed resources or equipment), and overt aggression (for example, assault, destroying property). Most research has focused on direct, active, physical, and verbal behaviors (Folger & Baron, 1996). However, the desire to inflict harm can be expressed through various forms of aggression; ignoring other dimensions may fail to conceptualize workplace aggression accurately.

Prevalence of Workplace Aggression

Although national data exist on extreme forms of aggression, such as physical assault and homicide, few data exist on the frequency of more mild aggressive behaviors. Baron and Neuman (1996, 1998; Neuman & Baron, 1998) provide data on the relative frequencies of employees' being the targets of a broad array of behaviors classified as workplace aggression. These data indicate that the most frequent manifestations of aggression are those considered to be relatively mild forms of verbal harm, such as talking behind others' backs and interrupting others when speaking; among those least frequent are forms of overt physical aggression such as physical assault and attack with a weapon. These results are consistent with Glomb (2002) and Greenberg and Barling (1999), who also report that respondents are most frequently the targets of relatively mild aggressive behaviors, such as speaking with an angry tone of voice or giving another person dirty looks.

Scant information is available on employees' self-reports of perpetrating aggression. Baron, Neuman, and Geddes (1999) asked respondents whether they had engaged in aggression toward five different targets. Results indicated that employees report engaging in aggression more frequently toward coworkers and immediate supervisors than subordinates, other supervisors, or the organization. Glomb (2001) investigated employees' self-reports of engaging in a set of twenty-four aggressive behaviors. Consistent with the self-reports from recipients of aggression, she found that relatively mild aggressive behaviors, such as using an angry tone of voice or giving another dirty looks, were most commonly reported. This consistency in the behaviors reported by both targets and perpetrators suggests that workplace aggression should be examined as a broad set of interrelated behaviors varying in severity. To predict these behaviors, we turn now to theoretical explanations for workplace aggression.

Theoretical Perspectives of Workplace Aggression

Aggression has been extensively studied in general contexts (for an overview of aggression theory, see Baron & Richardson, 1994; Berkowitz, 1993; Geen, 1990), yet there have been few comprehensive models of workplace aggression and violence. Theories of workplace aggression often give minimal attention to the affective or emotional components of the aggressive experience, whereas in theories of general aggression, the role of affect and emotion is more central.

Neuman and Baron's model (1997) proposes that antecedent events, such as frustration, stressors, and norm violations, result in a variety of cognitive, affective, and arousal reactions, which lead to primary and secondary appraisal processes. These appraisal processes include considerations regarding the aggressive act, such as whether it was intentional and the level of harm, as well as considerations regarding the appropriate response, such as the consequences of aggression and coping strategies. As a result of these cognitive appraisal processes, an individual chooses aggression or nonaggression. This model is largely concerned with the intrapsychic processes that occur between a stimulus event and aggression, with a focus on the prediction of a specific aggressive or nonaggressive reaction to an event, rather than the antecedents of frequent aggression, as is the case with other models (O'Leary-Kelly et al., 1996). This model does include affect, but the role of the cognitive appraisal of the stimulus seems paramount in predicting whether aggression will occur. The role of individual differences, such as an individual's emotional regulation, is not explicitly considered but is likely intertwined with the appraisal process whereby the individual interprets the stimuli and determines how to respond.

Barling's model (1996) attempts to predict physical aggression or violence rather than the less severe forms of aggression and, like the Neuman and Baron model, focuses on the prediction of particular instances of violence. Like many other models, Barling proposes both workplace factors, such as injustice and job insecurity, and personal factors, such as aggressive history, alcohol use, and psychological aggression, as contributing to workplace violence. Unlike other models, Barling's model includes outcomes. However, the outcomes proposed—psychological, psychosomatic, and organizational—are outcomes for the target of the violence, not the aggressor. Missing is an explicit consideration of the role of the negative affect or anger in the aggression process. Similarly absent is attention to emotional regulation processes that influence the likelihood and type of aggression.

O'Leary-Kelly et al.'s model (1996) of organizational motivated aggression and violence also posits both organizational and individual factors as contributors to workplace aggression. These authors differ in their terminology from other researchers (for example, Neuman & Baron, 1998) by terming the harmful behavior or intent *organization-motivated aggression* (OMA) and the result of such behavior *organization-motivated violence* (OMV). OMA is aggression ultimately caused by the organization but predicted by both individual and organizational antecedents. Whether OMA will result in OMV is determined by the organizational response. The organizational response is also theorized to feed back to influence the organizational and individual characteristics. In this theory, the potential consequences of the OMV are not delineated. Neither negative affect and anger nor their regulation plays a primary role in this theory.

These models of workplace aggression have not been empirically tested in their totality. However, specific relationships between antecedents and outcomes of aggression have been explored.

Antecedents and Consequences of Workplace Aggression

Antecedents of workplace aggression loosely group into three broad categories: aspects of the situation or organization that may give rise to aggression, individual differences associated with aggression, and emotional self-regulatory skills (Gross, 1998), which we consider separately from other individual differences because they are likely more trainable skills rather than innate characteristics.

Situational Antecedents of Engaging in Aggression

Given the primary role of negative affect in theories of aggression (Berkowitz, 1993, 1994) and empirical data associating negative affect with increased aggression (Baron & Bell, 1976; Berkowitz & Turner, 1974), we would expect situational antecedents to be those in a workplace environment that precipitate negative affect among employees and consequently elevate levels of workplace aggression. Any number of workplace characteristics might create negative affect. We discuss potential organizational antecedents, specifically, organizational justice, job stress, reciprocal aggression, and tolerance for aggression.

Organizational Justice
Both anecdotal evidence (Barling, 1996) and theoretical work (Folger & Baron, 1996; Neuman & Baron, 1998) suggest that violent acts by employees or former employees can be attributed to organizational decisions that the perpetrator perceives as unfair. However, results from empirical research testing a link between aggression and organizational justice and its distinct components (procedural, distributive, and interactional justice; Folger & Cropanzano, 1998) have been somewhat mixed. In work by Folger et al. (1998), procedural justice predicted assaults, but not threats, in one organization; distributive justice was not predictive of assaults or threats. Similarly, Greenberg and Barling (1999) found that procedural and interactional justice, but not distributive justice, predicted aggression against one's supervisor but not against subordinates and coworkers. Baron et al. (1999) found that fair treatment from one's supervisor was related to a one-item assessment of aggression toward one's

supervisor and the organization (but not toward coworkers, subordinates, and other superiors). Baron and Neuman (1996, 1998) found relationships between the frequency of organizational changes such as layoffs, compensation cutbacks, and outsourcing, which frequently bring issues of justice to the fore, and being the target of, witnessing, and engaging in aggression. Glomb (2001) failed to support a strong relationship between the three types of justice and engaging in aggression; zero-order relations between justice and aggression dissipated once individual differences variables were taken into account. Others have suggested that the interaction among types of justice is critical in predicting behavior (Brockner & Siegel, 1996; Skarlicki & Folger, 1997, 1999); however, an interaction effect predicting workplace aggression has not been empirically supported (Glomb, 2001).

As is evident from the research, the links between organizational justice and aggression are somewhat inconsistent and may depend on the type of justice and the target of the aggression; in particular, organizational justice, especially procedural and interactional justice, seems to be related to acts directed at the organization or agents of the organization such as one's supervisor, but not to other targets.

Organizational and Job-Related Stress

One of the key findings of the Northwestern National Life Insurance Company (1993) survey on workplace violence and aggression was the link between job stress and aggression. However, this finding suggested that stress could be both a cause and an effect of workplace violence. The link between stress and engaging in aggressive behaviors may be explained using the frustration-aggression hypothesis (Dollard, Doob, Miller, Mowrer, & Sears, 1939), due to the conceptual overlap between stress and organizational frustration (see Chen & Spector, 1992, for a discussion). Relationships between both organizational frustration (Spector, 1997; Storms & Spector, 1987) and job stressors such as role ambiguity, role conflict, interpersonal conflict, and situational constraints (Chen & Spector, 1992; Spector, 1997) and interpersonal aggression, sabotage, and hostility have been reported. Other research has suggested linkages between job stressors and the emotional reactions of anger (Hodapp, Neuser, & Weyer, 1988), feelings of hostility (Houston & Kelly, 1989), and a self-report assessment of the trait of aggression (Bedeian, Armenakis, & Curran, 1980). Thus, the literature on organizational stress and frustration suggests both a theoretical and empirical link between stress and workplace aggression. However, the causal direction of such a relationship is questionable, and indeed the relationship may be dynamic.

Reciprocal Aggression

A particularly insidious effect of aggression is that it fosters more of the same. Bandura (1973) suggested that the most reliable way of eliciting aggression is by assaulting or threatening another. Researchers have long suggested that aggression is reciprocal in nature, such that if one individual engages in an aggressive behavior, he or she may become the target of aggression from the person against whom he or she aggressed (see Andersson & Pearson, 1999, for a discussion of the incivility spiral; see Tripp & Bies, 1997, for evidence of reciprocal vengeance). However, despite the strong effects of being the target of aggression on eliciting a similar or more serious response, there is little empirical evidence accounting for the influence of these reciprocal processes in research on workplace aggression. Research by Glomb (2001) suggests a strong relationship between self-reports of being the target of aggression and engaging in aggression. A reciprocal relationship is also supported in qualitative accounts of specific aggressive incidents (Callister, 2000; Glomb, 2002). The operation of reciprocal aggression underscores the importance of preventing even mild aggressive acts to prevent "incivility spirals" (Andersson & Pearson, 1999).

Organizational Tolerance for Aggressive Behaviors

Bandura (1973) recognized the importance of individuals' beliefs regarding the outcomes of aggression when he proposed that these beliefs could explain contradictory empirical findings concerning the link between anger and physiological tension. Borrowing from the social learning framework, O'Leary-Kelly et al. (1996) suggest that the organizational response toward aggression will not only moderate the relationship between aggression and whether it results in violence, but will also influence the individual and organizational factors that precede aggression. In certain organizations and occupations, a permissive climate for aggressive behaviors may exist (Brown, Cron, & Slocum, 1998; Morrill, 1995). Individuals' perceptions of the contingencies between engaging in workplace aggression and the subsequent consequences are likely to be based on their direct and vicarious experiences in the organization. Tripp and Bies (1997) argue that revenge behaviors may be considered functional by an individual, and the functionality of the revenge is often dependent on the outcomes that ensue. Neuman and Baron's theory includes "aggressive norms" as an influence on workplace aggression, and Robinson and O'Leary-Kelly's (1998) work on group antisocial behavior seems to support the existence of group norms, as well as the presence of organizational norms, regarding punishment for antisocial behavior. However, Glomb (2001) failed to find a direct or indirect effect of organizational tolerance regarding aggression once other situational and personal variables were taken into account.

Thus, the theoretical proposition that the organizational climate for aggressive behaviors may contribute to the variance in the frequency and severity of aggressive behaviors among organizations awaits strong and consistent empirical support. However, it is possible that the organizational climate for aggression operates in complex and multiple ways. If employees perceive that engaging in aggressive behavior results in experiencing negative outcomes, then the frequency of aggression may be reduced, behaviors that are less severely punished or unobservable (such as passive or indirect behaviors) may be enacted as substitutes for other aggressive behaviors, or if climate operates as a moderator, it may attenuate the relationships between antecedents and aggression.

Individual Antecedents of Engaging in Aggression

Because the organizational environment is largely shared, situational effects cannot entirely explain aggression. Otherwise, we would find pockets of aggression where all individuals exposed to the same set of situational characteristics were aggressors. Individual differences have an impact, a statement that is not only consistent with several theories of aggression (Berkowitz, 1994; Neuman & Baron, 1997) but is also supported by considerable research. At a broad level of analysis, twin studies have been used to tease apart the typical amount of variance in aggression that is genetically determined and environmentally determined (Lykken, 1995). Results show that in the long term, genes are of paramount importance, accounting for about 80 percent of the stable component of aggression. Similarly, past aggressive behavior is a good predictor of future transgressions, with those who have a history of aggression being more likely to aggress against others (Berkowitz, 1978), including their coworkers (Greenberg & Barling, 1999).

However, *individual differences* is a catch-all term, and it obscures the many different components involved, each with its own contribution. Here, we consider several that have been specifically connected to workplace aggression in multiple studies: trait anger, impulsiveness, and substance abuse.

Trait Anger

Trait anger is "the disposition to perceive a wide range of situations as annoying or frustrating, and the tendency to respond to such situations with more frequent elevations in state anger" (Spielberger, 1991, p. 1). When people high in trait anger encounter an ambiguous situation, their default interpretation is one of threat or attack. Also, the anger they feel tends to be more intense and may not easily dissipate. Trait anger is often viewed as interchangeable with trait hostility (Spielberger, Sydeman, Owen, & Marsh, 1999), and we treat the two as equivalent here. Unsurprisingly, the relationship between trait anger and aggression is well established, supported by research using both self-report and observed behavior, as well as conducted in both nonwork (Biaggio, Supplee, & Curtis, 1981; Lemerise & Dodge, 2000; van Elderen, Verkes, Arkesteign, & Komproe, 1996) and workplace settings. In the workplace, researchers have suggested significant relations between trait anger or hostility and the frequency of employees engaging in minor and major aggressive interpersonal acts (Fox & Spector, 1999; Glomb, 2001), showing anger (Houston & Kelly, 1989), and self-reports of both passive and active, as well as both physical and verbal, aggression (Holland & Shelton, 1999).

In addition, trait anger has been suggested as a component of Type A personality (Berkowitz, 1993; Friedman & Rosenman, 1974). The Type A behavior pattern is related to self-reports of engaging in workplace aggression (Baron et al., 1999; Glomb, 2001). Individuals with the Type A behavior pattern lose their tempers more frequently (Holmes & Will, 1985), report more conflict with coworkers than Type B's (Baron, 1989), and demonstrate tendencies toward aggression and irritability in organizational contexts (Evans, Palsane, & Carrere, 1987). Furthermore, Type A's not only report engaging in more aggressive behaviors than Type B's, they also report being the target of aggression more often (Holmes & Will, 1985).

Several other personality traits that may be related to trait anger have also been linked to aggressive behaviors, including low agreeableness and high neuroticism (Ones, Viswesvaran, Schmidt, & Reiss, 1994) and negative affectivity (Frone, 1998). In summary, trait anger has been found to be a strong and consistent predictor of engaging in aggression.

Impulsiveness

Impulsiveness or low control is to act quickly without thought or concern for the future, reacting on emotions with little reflection. The role of impulsiveness is considered so predominant in aggressive acts that Gottfredson and Hirschi (1990) argue that most criminality reflects this one aspect (Baumeister, Heatherton, & Tice, 1994). Berkowitz (1993) reports, however, that impulsiveness is typically and wrongly ignored in most theories and research on aggression.

Empirically, the connection between impulsiveness and aggression has not been confirmed as extensively as trait anger, but the results obtained are stronger. Holland and Shelton (1999) found that impulsiveness was the strongest personality predictor from more than forty tested (including hostility) in predicting workplace physical and verbal aggression of both an active and a passive nature. Similar results have been found among workplace adolescents (Frone, 1998), employees in mental retardation facilities (Latham & Perlow, 1996), and a large diverse sample of employed men (Jockin, Arvey, & McGue, in press). Even psychopaths and sociopaths show a strong tendency to be impulsively aggressive, although they often complement this violent predilection with a more premeditated predatory approach (Hart & Dempster, 1997; Lykken, 1995).[1]

However, it also seems possible to inhibit impulses too much. Pennebaker (1992) suggests that although inhibition can be healthy and adaptive most of the time, when maintained over long periods it can adversely affect psychological health. Consistent with work by Megargee (1966), Cox and Leather (1994), in a review of violence at work, as well as Verona and Carbonell (2000), in a study of one-time violent females, note that exceptionally assaultive offenders were actually extremely conscientious and controlled. Similarly, Dutton (1997) speaks of avoidant batterers whose "violence is typically a response to long-stored negative affect, which is itself generated by their deficits in assertiveness" (p. 40). All of these researchers are describing an aggressor who has little experience at being aggressive and typically remains passive even to moderately strong provocations. Consistent with the ironic process theory of suppression (Wenzlaff & Wegner, 2000), they hypothesize that when under extremely harsh provocation or mental stress, or perhaps under more moderate but more prolonged conditions, these offenders literally explode and show far more violence than their impulsive counterparts. It is possible that some of the more serious workplace violence may be due to the mild-mannered and extremely self-controlled employee whose eventual brutal actions surprise all.

Substance and Alcohol Abuse

The full effects of substance abuse on aggressive behavior are incredibly complex given the pharmacological choices available. However, since alcohol abuse is by far the most prevalent, we explore its effects here in greater detail. Berkowitz (1993) reviews research indicating that the critical effect of drinking on aggression is "alcoholic myopia." When drinking, one pays attention only to the most immediate and obvious cues of the situation. In addition, one is less able to process effectively and understand the cues one does perceive. This will result in a condition very close to impulsiveness as one becomes shortsighted (myopic) and starts reacting based solely on the immediate situation and feelings. Other researchers argue similarly. Alcohol does not so much increase violent feelings as reduce the long-term inhibitions against their expression (Steele & Southwick, 1985; Zillman, 1993). Baumeister et al. (1994) offer an interesting example of this: soldiers were issued rations of "grog" before battles during World War I, ostensibly to ease the task of killing.

Empirically, the relationship between substance abuse and workplace aggression is not entirely clear. Greenberg and Barling

(1999) report a moderate relationship between alcohol consumption and aggression against a coworker, though not against a supervisor or subordinate. Frone (1998) found a relatively strong relationship between substance abuse and interpersonal aggression at the workplace. In addition, McFarlin, Fals-Stewart, Major, and Freitas (1999) found that extreme substance abusers (those who had been medically treated for their abuse) were five times more likely to engage in workplace violence than nonabusers. However, Chen and Spector (1992) reported a nonsignificant relationship between substance abuse and interpersonal aggression. Substance abuse is significantly confounded with other individual differences related to aggression. Because both impulsiveness and trait anger are related to substance abuse (Johnson, Malo, Corrigan, & West, 1993; Morissette, 1994), it could be that the actual effects of substance abuse alone may not be as strong after controlling for inherent impulsiveness and anger.

Emotional Regulation

Consistent with Lord and Harvey's review in Chapter Four of this volume, we focus on Gross's approach (1998) to emotional regulation. Gross defines emotional regulation as "the process by which individuals influence which emotions they have, when they have them, and how they experience and express these emotions" (p. 275). Emotional regulation can be either antecedent focused or response focused. As it applies to workplace aggression, antecedent-focused attempts try to prevent negative affect, particularly that of anger, from occurring, while response-focused attempts try to alter the physiological, experiential, or behavioral responses, particularly that of aggression, to the negative affect. There are four antecedent-focused categories. First, there is *situation selection:* individuals avoid (or seek out) situations expected to create an undesirable (or desirable) emotional response. For our workplace aggression example, employees might seek a transfer to another work team or department to avoid a coworker who incites anger. Second, there is *situational modification:* an existing situation is modified or adapted to control the emotional impact. For example, employees may convert much of their face-to-face interactions with a coworker who incites anger to e-mail exchanges. Third, there is *attentional deployment:*

individuals may use distraction to shift their focus from the emotion-eliciting event, or, conversely, they may use rumination to direct attention toward the emotion experienced (Gross, 1998). Employees may, for example, throw all their energies into their work to prevent becoming aware of the hostile situation. Fourth, there is *cognitive change:* one reinterprets the situation so as to alter one's emotions. Employees who perceive hostility from a coworker may reframe the situation so that the hostility is considered amusing and ineffectual rather than anger eliciting. All of these forms of emotional regulation are considered antecedent focused because they intervene before the emotion is experienced. Finally, there is the response-focused strategy of *response modulation:* individuals attempt to influence the physiological, experiential, or behavioral responses to the emotion (Gross, 1998). For example, an employee who is feeling angry toward an unreasonable client can control his or her emotionally expressive behavior to avoid showing anger or behaving aggressively.

Doubtless, these methods of emotional regulation are effective in preventing workplace aggression, but it is difficult to assess systematically to what extent. Most regulatory strategies have been studied only with regard to anxiety and depression, with very little consideration of anger and aggression. In addition, what work has been done has typically used child, clinical, or criminal populations—groups that may not generalize to the workplace. Finally, the use of emotional regulation strategies can be partially predicted by personality traits (Kardum & Hudek-Knezevic, 1996; Thayer, Newman, & McClain, 1994). Thus, it is possible that any relationship between emotional regulation strategies and aggression or anger may be captured by personality characteristics like impulsiveness.

Still, some organizational research indicates that emotional regulation skills matter in controlling anger. Mearns and Mauch (1998) found a fairly strong correlation between police officers' anger and a variety of emotional regulation strategies that they labeled active coping. Also studying police officers, Gerzina and Drummond (2000) showed experimentally that emotional regulation skills in general could be useful for decreasing anger. They trained police officers in a variety of emotional regulation techniques, such as relaxation skills and cognitive reappraisals, for six weeks, and then eight weeks later assessed employees on several anger measures. They found that the trained officers felt significantly less angry in comparison to a waiting-list control group. Beck and Fernandez (1998) obtained a similar result with a small group of college students.

Some research has been conducted specific to one of the categories of emotion regulation. With respect to the cognitive change category, Larsen, Diener, and Cropanzano (1987) found that those who respond intensely to negative stimuli tend to elaborate on the worst part of the event; they overgeneralize the event, as well as focus on how the event relates to themselves.

A few studies have been conducted regarding the attentional deployment category, particularly rumination and distraction. Presumably, those who ruminate and are unable to redirect their attention should be more aggressive. Rusting and Nolen-Hoeksema (1998) conducted a series of experiments on anger, distraction, and rumination. Those who were unable to stop ruminating increased in anger, while those who tried to distract themselves (for example, by thinking about happier thoughts) tended to show a decrease. Also, King, Emmons, and Woodley (1992) found that behavioral inhibition correlated negatively with rumination; those who keep thinking about an incident become more impulsive. To stop rumination, Wenzlaff and Bates (2000) conclude that attempts to suppress aggressive thoughts directly often backfire (according to ironic process theory). Much more effective is a concentrative strategy of mental control, where one focuses on other more desirable thoughts.

Finally, some research has been done with response modulation, diminishing the feelings of anger without expressing aggressiveness. Thayer et al. (1994), exploring a variety of emotional regulation strategies, found that a combination of relaxation techniques and exercise is the most effective way of managing a bad mood. Brown et al. (1995), investigating the same strategies for anger specifically, did not find support for the exercise component though concluded that the relaxation techniques did have some value. Also, Deffenbacher and Stark (1992), comparing relaxation and cognitive coping skills, found that relaxation training alone reduced anger with little or no benefit from incorporating cognitive training.

Given the multitude of emotion regulation strategies, it is easy to see how improving the emotional regulation processes of employees may serve to reduce negative affect or anger or its resultant aggressive behavior.

Outcomes of Aggressive Behaviors

The outcomes of experiencing aggressive behaviors in the workplace have received modest empirical research attention (see for exceptions Budd et al. 1996; Glomb, 2002; Tepper, 2000; Tripp & Bies, 1997). This may be because workplace aggression is often the outcome of interest. Many theoretical models end at workplace aggression (Neuman & Baron, 1998; O'Leary-Kelly et al., 1996), failing to recognize the potential repercussions of being the target of and engaging in aggression on job and personal outcomes. Although there is evidence of positive consequences of aggressive acts (Tripp & Bies, 1997), most research suggests primarily negative consequences of experiencing aggressive behaviors, such as job dissatisfaction, job stress, and intentions to change jobs (Budd et al., 1996; Glomb, 2002); psychological (for example, depression), psychosomatic (for example, headaches, sleep problems), and organizational (for example, absence, turnover intentions, job performance) consequences (Barling, 1996; Glomb, 2002); reciprocal aggression and unforeseen negative consequences (Glomb, 2002; Tripp & Bies, 1997); job dissatisfaction, worsened working relations, and increased job stress (Glomb, 2002). Glomb (2002) suggests that the negative outcomes can occur for both the targets and the perpetrators of aggressive acts. Given these negative outcomes, organizations that attempt to reduce workplace aggression will likely enjoy improvements in a variety of organization and employee-relevant outcomes.

Affective Events Theory

Although workplace aggression and anger have been studied, general theories of organizational behaviors and attitudes have largely neglected the areas of emotional and affective experiences in organizations. Weiss and Cropanzano's (1996) affective events theory (AET) stimulated much of the discussion about affective experiences at work. AET focuses on the structure, causes, and consequences of affective experiences at work by examining the antecedents of employees' experiences of affective work events and the affective, attitudinal, and behavioral reactions to these events.

The antecedents and mediating relationships of the aggressive behaviors that are the focus of this chapter could be easily placed within this general framework. We posit that many of the relations proposed in theoretical work and tested in empirical studies could be integrated into the context of a broader framework of affective experience at work; specifically, we use AET (see Figure 7.1).

According to AET, work environment features influence the occurrence of positive or negative affective work events. Experiencing these events leads to affective reactions that in turn lead to affect-driven behaviors and work attitudes. Work attitudes influence judgment-driven behaviors. The affect-driven behaviors are direct responses to affective experiences. The judgment-driven

Figure 7.1. An Affective Events Theory–Based Model of Workplace Aggression.

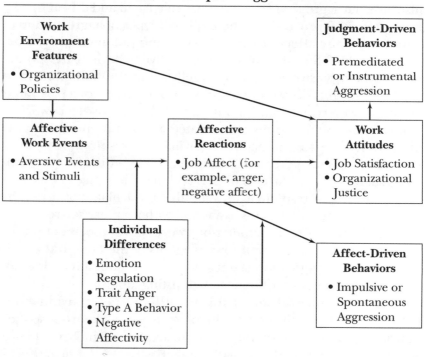

behaviors are mediated by work attitudes. Individual differences also play a role.

If we apply this framework to workplace aggression, we can envision a large number of work environment features, such as organizational policies or job structure, that would lead to negative affective events, such as a disagreement with a coworker, unfair feedback from one's supervisor, or being passed over for a promotion. These negative affective events would lead to negative affect experienced on the job. This broad negative affect would include emotions such as anger and frustration. According to AET, this affect would have two types of effects: (1) affect would lead directly to affect-driven behaviors and (2) affect would influence work attitudes that ultimately result in judgment-driven behaviors. We posit that both paths from affect on the job may lead to workplace aggression, albeit by slightly different means.

Aggression has often been subdivided into impulsive aggression, which is relatively unplanned or spontaneous, and premeditated or instrumental aggression, which is more calculated and driven by cognitive, effortful processing. These distinct types of aggression map closely onto the affect-driven behaviors and judgment-driven behaviors in AET. Specifically, some aggressive behaviors are spontaneous and impulsive and driven largely by the emotion or affect in the present. This description conjures up the vision of a frustrated employee who is angry and spontaneously lashes out at a coworker. Such a response would be uncalculated and not premeditated. At other times, negative affect or anger may not result in behavioral manifestations of aggression, but instead may influence work attitudes such as job satisfaction or perceptions of injustice. These attitudes may in turn result in aggression that is calculated or driven by judgment, such as when dissatisfaction with a supervisor results in attempts to sabotage the supervisor's work or when perceptions of injustice result in aggression toward agents of the organization. In both cases, the aggression is not solely the result of affect or emotion, but rather is also influenced by existing attitudes.

Furthermore, AET allows for the influence of individual differences at multiple points in the process. Here we propose that individual differences will influence the extent to which a negative affective event will lead to negative affect, whether the negative affect will result in aggressive behaviors, and whether these behaviors will be judgment or affect driven. For example, antecedent-focused emotional regulation skills will influence whether negative affect follows from a negative affective event, and response-focused skills will determine whether negative affect results in attitudinal and behavioral outcomes (that is, aggression).

We believe that this AET-based model provides insight into workplace aggression by distinguishing multiple pathways to aggression and positing a variety of antecedents. Furthermore, the broad framework allows for integration and, possibly, clarification of the existing literature. For example, distinguishing aggression that is affect driven or more spontaneous from aggression that is judgment driven or more calculative may shed light on some of the mixed results regarding the antecedents of aggression.

Implications for Organizations

The preceding discussion and model of how situational, organizational, and individual differences antecedents and emotion regulation strategies influence violence and aggression in workplace settings suggests a variety of interventions aimed at reducing aggression. These fall roughly into implications for selection, training, and policy and practice issues.

Selection

There is consistent evidence that individual differences, especially the traits of hostility and impulsiveness, are good predictors of workplace aggression. Consequently, selecting out those who are notably both hostile and impulsive should be considered. To this end, several clinical measures, such as the Minnesota Multiphasic Personality Inventory and the California Personality Inventory, show "substantial relationships to violence report measures" (Slora, Joy, & Terris, 1991, p. 423). Also, nonclinical personality inventories, such as the Hogan Personality Inventory or the Personal Reaction Blank, have been meta-analytically shown to be similarly valuable (Ones et al., 1994). In addition, and perhaps more relevant for this discussion concerning emotions and individual differences, is that there may be selection tools more specifically targeted to assessing emotionality and emotion regulation skills. Labig (1995) and Arvey, Renz, and Watson (1998) have suggested that employers could assess emotionality among applicants by developing role-playing and other simulations to induce emotions among applicants. Although such methods are fraught with ethical and possible legal problems, an alternative strategy could be to use an experienced-based situational interview (see Pulakos & Schmitt, 1995), where applicants are asked to recall emotions or events where emotional reactions and behavioral responses occurred. Arvey et al. (1998) also reviewed a number of self-report measures directly assessing specific facets of emotions (including the Emotional Expressiveness Questionnaire; King & Emmons, 1990) and called for research to establish their validity in predicting job outcomes, including the display of aggression in the workplace.

The research record on relationships between specific measures of individual differences of emotionality and incidences of workplace aggression and violence is minimal. Problems of such screening methods include overidentification of applicants as aggression "prone," faking, potential adverse impact, and negative applicant reactions. Nevertheless, using selection tools to screen out potentially aggressive individuals is a potential aggression-reduction method. However, this approach addresses only potential individual differences antecedents of workplace aggression, neglecting situational precursors.

Training

Selecting out particularly violent individuals may reduce aggression from a number of individuals, yet the majority of employees report engaging in some type of aggressive behaviors. Selection alone will not eliminate aggression from the workplace. For many employees, emotional self-regulation training is an option for reducing workplace aggression. Many companies are already acknowledging this and, with increasing frequency, provide training designed to help employees handle or manage their emotions (Tevlin, 1997; Coles, 1996). Available programs are quite varied, ranging widely in the skills trained as well as workplace conditions for their implementation. Some programs emphasize the role of cognitive components involved in aggressive acts (such as getting employees to think about their reactions and behavior), and others emphasize the role that affect and emotions play in aggression. For example, Cox and Leather (1994) outline several interventions, each specific to different stages in an episode of violence. Unfortunately, the research base has not been sufficiently developed to assess which of these techniques are more effective and in what situations. Consequently, we recommend that training take a broad-based approach, using both antecedent-focused and response-focused strategies. At a minimum, any program should provide relaxation techniques as well as ones that reduce anger rumination. Yates (1985) provides a good summary of theoretical approaches and practical techniques using such self-management methods that can provide a foundation for emotion management programs. This approach to aggression reduction will be particularly useful in addressing many of the lower-level forms of aggression that result from common situational antecedents such as stress and frustration.

Policies and Practices

At the organizational level, there are several steps in preventing workplace aggression, with the initial one being assessment. Is workplace aggression a problem for your company or department? Preferably, this can be determined by surveying employees regarding the frequency with which they initiate or are the recipients of different aggressive acts that range in severity. More typically, companies assess only employee attitudes or job dissatisfaction, though these can still serve as more distal indicators of aggression in the workplace. If there is a significant amount of hostility, either observed or felt, then it is necessary to determine its source. We have already discussed typical culprits, such as organizational justice, a climate permissive of aggression, and job stress, though any work environment feature that leads to aversive events or negative affect may be a cause. Finally, once an unacceptable work feature has been identified in sufficient detail, an appropriate intervention should be undertaken. For example, given an excessively permissive climate for aggression, organizations should institute a formal policy declaring their intolerance of workplace aggression, find ways of effectively informing employees of this policy, and determine how they will enforce it. The presence of these policies and perceptions of behavior-outcome contingencies may create a strong organizational climate that reduces workplace aggression and violence by addressing situational precursors to aggression.

Future Research Directions

Given the complexities inherent in studying anger and aggression in organizations, future research should consider aggression as a behavioral construct influenced by a dynamic pattern of relations. The behavioral construct must be further specified to consider the role of intentionality and to distinguish hostile aggression from instrumental aggression and political influence behaviors.

Although research suggests that aggressive behaviors are prevalent in organizations, we know little about the patterns among aggressive behaviors and their functioning over time. Data on specific aggressive encounters have suggested a progression of aggression model in which the enactment of extreme behaviors is preceded by the enactment of less severe types of behaviors (for example, giving dirty looks precedes yelling or raising your voice, which precedes physical aggression; Glomb, 2002). Future research should investigate the ordering and patterning among aggressive behaviors.

Future research should provide adequate consideration of the psychological and cognitive processes underlying the linkage between antecedents and aggression. It is often assumed that the emotion of anger or cognitive appraisals accompany aggressive behaviors; however, the presence or absence of these features is rarely measured. Research designed to take into account the mediating negative affective state, emotion regulation, and cognitive appraisal processes may be better able to explain the phenomenon of workplace aggression.

The reciprocal nature of aggression requires increased attention. The neglect of reciprocity in aggression may be due to the tendency to measure aggression in the aggregate (rather than in the context of a specific incident), where aggression that is reciprocal is difficult to identify. Future research must be cognizant of the multiple methods necessary to capture both the general levels of aggression and the nature of aggression as it operates in specific aggressive encounters. Longitudinal research may aid in exploration of the reciprocal nature of aggression, as well as allow inferences about causal relationships.

Consideration of reciprocal aggression highlights the issue of the targets of workplace aggression, a group we know little about. Although the literature on specific instances of workplace bullying and harassment may provide insight (for review, see Keashley & Jagatic, in press), the characteristics of targets are currently not well known. Consistent with the victimization literature in other areas, future research that explores the characteristics of targets will assist in advancing our knowledge of aggression at work.

Researchers should consider aggression within the larger external context. The stressors and frustrations that precede workplace aggression need not necessarily occur at work. In particular, researchers might focus on the interplay between workplace and domestic violence. Many relationships could be explored as the potential links between the two are varied. Violent relationships may spill over into the workplace; indeed, in 1996, one-sixth of workplace homicides for female employees were the result of domestic disputes (Toscano & Windau, 1998). Alternatively, a predisposition to aggression and violence may manifest itself both at home and at work such that the same individual differences variables may explain variance in both types of aggression. Suppression of aggression or the negative emotions or affect underlying them could be released at home instead of at work (displacement). These possibilities warrant attention; advancements in one research area may inform the other.

Careful evaluation of interventions and trainings should be undertaken. There are few empirical data available on the effectiveness of alternative strategies to combat workplace aggression. Although the interventions discussed above seem reasonable in targeting the antecedents of aggression and coping with its occurrence, absent rigorous evaluation we cannot be certain of their utility.

Conclusion

Although it is unlikely that workplace aggression will be eradicated, acknowledging and understanding the complex interplay of precursors to aggression will lead to more effective interventions. Emphasizing the role of affect and the multiple paths to aggression allows for interventions designed to target the process at a number of critical points; interventions can be targeted to control the individual differences characteristics of employees, the situational characteristics of organizations, employees' affective work experiences, and employee cognitions surrounding aggressive episodes. Only by taking a multipronged approach to aggression and violence reduction can we hope to reduce its prevalence in organizations.

Note
1. These two forms of antisocial personality disorder differ; psychopathy is primarily due to hereditable causes, and sociopathy has its roots in poor parenting and socialization.

References
Andersson L. M. & Pearson C. M. (1999). Tit for tat? The spiraling effect of incivility in the workplace. *Academy of Management Review, 24,* 452–471.

Arvey, R. D., Renz, G. L., & Watson, T. W. (1998). Emotionality and job performance: Implication for personnel selection. *Research in Human Resource Management, 16,* 103–147.

Bandura, A. (1973). *Aggression: A social learning analysis.* Upper Saddle River, NJ: Prentice Hall.

Barling, J. (1996). The prediction, experience, and consequences of workplace violence. In E. Q. Bulatao & G. R. VandenBos (Eds.), *Violence on the job: Identifying risks and developing solutions* (pp. 29–49). Washington, DC: American Psychological Association.

Baron, R. A. (1989). Personality and organizational conflict: Effects of the Type A behavior pattern and self-monitoring. *Organizational Behavior and Human Decision Processes, 44,* 281–296.

Baron, R. A., & Bell, P. A. (1976). Aggression and heat: The influence of ambient temperature, negative affect, and a cooling drink on physical aggression. *Journal of Personality and Social Psychology, 33,* 245–255.

Baron, R. A., & Neuman, J. H. (1996). Workplace violence and workplace aggression: Evidence of their relative frequency and potential causes. *Aggressive Behavior, 22,* 161–173.

Baron, R. A., & Neuman, J. H. (1998). Workplace aggression—the iceberg beneath the tip of workplace violence: Evidence of its forms, frequency and targets. *Public Administration Quarterly, 21,* 446–464.

Baron, R. A., Neuman, J. H., & Geddes, D. (1999). Social and personal determinants of workplace aggression: Evidence of the impact of perceived injustice and the Type A behaviors pattern. *Aggressive Behavior, 25,* 281–296.

Baron, R. A., & Richardson, D. R. (1994). *Human aggression.* New York: Plenum Press.

Baumeister, R. F., Heatherton, T. F., & Tice, D. M. (1994). *Losing control: How and why people fail at self-regulation.* Orlando, FL: Academic Press.

Beck, R., & Fernandez, E. (1998). Cognitive-behavioral self-regulation of the frequency, duration, and intensity of anger. *Journal of Psychopathology and Behavioral Assessment, 20,* 217–229.

Bedeian, A. G., Armenakis, A. A., & Curran, S. M. (1980). Personality correlates of role stress. *Psychological Reports, 46,* 627–632.

Berkowitz, L. (1978). Is criminal violence normative behavior? Hostile and instrumental aggression in violent incidents. *Journal of Research in Crime and Delinquency, 15,* 148–161.

Berkowitz, L. (1993). *Aggression: Its causes, consequences, and control.* New York: McGraw-Hill.

Berkowitz, L. (1994). Is something missing? Some observations prompted by the cognitive-neoassociationist view of anger and emotional aggression. In L. R. Huesmann (Ed.), *Aggressive behavior: Current perspectives.* New York: Plenum Press.

Berkowitz, L., & Turner, C. W. (1974). Perceived anger level, instigating agent, and aggression. In H. London & R. E. Nisbett (Eds.), *Thought and feeling: Cognitive alteration of feeling states.* Chicago: Aldine.

Biaggio, M. K., Supplee, K., & Curtis, N. (1981). Reliability and validity of four anger scales. *Journal of Personality Assessment, 45,* 639–648.

Brockner, J., & Siegel, P. A. (1996). Understanding the interaction between procedural and distributive justice: The role of trust. In R. M. Kramer & T. R. Tyler (Eds.), *Trust in organizations: Frontiers of theory and research* (pp. 390–413). Thousand Oaks, CA: Sage.

Brown, S., Cron, W., & Slocum, W. (1998). Effect of trait competitiveness and perceived intraorganizational competition on salesperson goal setting and performance. *Journal of Marketing, 62,* 88–98.

Brown, D. R., Wang, Y., Ward, A., Ebbeling, C. B., Fortlage, L., Puleo, E., Benson, H., & Rippe, J. M. (1995). Chronic psychological effects of exercise and exercise plus cognitive strategies. *Medicine and Science in Sports and Exercise, 27,* 765–775.

Budd, J. W., Arvey, R. D., & Lawless, P. (1996). Correlates and consequences of workplace violence. *Journal of Occupational Health Psychology, 1,* 197–210.

Buss, A. H. (1961). *The psychology of aggression.* New York: Wiley.

Callister, R. (2000, August). Anger episodes at work: An Approach to the study of anger in organizations. In T. M. Glomb (Chair) Anger at Work: Conceptual and Methodological Extensions. Symposium conducted at the Second International Conference on Emotions in Organizational Life, Toronto.

Chen, P. Y., & Spector, P. E. (1992). Relationships of work stressors with aggression, withdrawal, theft and substance use: An exploratory study. *Journal of Occupational and Organizational Psychology, 65,* 177–184.

Coles, D. M. (1996, February 5). Trained to teach control. *Fort Collins Coloradoan,* p. C1.

Cox, T., & Leather, P. (1994). The prevention of violence at work: Application of a cognitive behavioral theory. *International Review of Industrial and Organizational Psychology, 9,* 213–245.

Deffenbacher, J. L., & Stark, R. S. (1992). Relaxation and cognitive-relaxation treatments of general anger. *Journal of Counseling Psychology, 39,* 158–167.

Dismissed worker kills four and then is slain. (1997, December 20). *New York Times,* p. A8.

Dollard, J., Doob, L. W., Miller, N. E., Mowrer, O. H., & Sears, R. R. (1939). *Frustration and aggression.* New Haven, CT: Yale University Press.

Dutton, D. G. (1997). A social psychological perspective on impulsivity/intimate violence. In C. D. Webster & M. A. Jackson (Eds.), *Impulsivity: Theory, assessment, and treatment* (pp. 32–41). New York: Guilford Press.

Evans, G. W., Palsane, M. N., & Carrere, S. (1987). Type A behavior and occupational stress: A cross-cultural study of blue-collar workers. *Journal of Personality and Social Psychology, 52,* 1002–1007.

Ferris, G. R., Russ, G. S., & Fandt, P. M. (1989). Politics in organizations. In R. A. Giacalone & P. Rosenfeld (Eds.), *Impression management in the organization.* Hillsdale, NJ: Erlbaum.

Folger, R., & Baron, R. A. (1996). Violence and hostility at work: A model of reactions to perceived injustice. In E. Q. Bulatao & G. R. VandenBos (Eds.), *Violence on the job: Identifying risks and developing solutions* (pp. 51–85). Washington, DC: American Psychological Association.

Folger, R., & Cropanzano, R. (1998). *Organizational justice and human resource management.* Thousand Oaks, CA: Sage.

Folger, R., Robinson, S. L., Dietz, J., McLean Parks, J., & Baron, R. A. (1998). When colleagues become violent: Employee threats and assaults as a function of societal violence and organizational justice. *Proceedings of the Academy of Management, Organizational Behavior Division,* pp. A1–A7.

Fox, S., & Spector, P. E. (1999). A model of work frustration-aggression. *Journal of Organizational Behavior, 20,* 915–931.

Friedman, M., & Rosenman, R. (1974). *Type A behavior and your heart.* New York: Knopf.

Frone, M. R. (1998). *Predictors of workplace deviance among employed adolescents.* Paper presented at the annual meeting of the Society for Industrial and Organizational Psychology, Dallas, Texas.

Geen, R. G. (1990). *Human aggression.* Pacific Grove, CA: Brooks/Cole.

Gerzina, M. A., & Drummond, P. D. (2000). A multimodal cognitive-behavioural approach to anger reduction in an occupational sample. *Journal of Occupational and Organizational Psychology, 73,* 181–194.

Glomb, T. M. (2001). *Workplace aggression: Antecedents, behavioral components, and consequences.* Manuscript submitted for publication.

Glomb, T. M. (2002). Workplace anger and aggression: Informing conceptual models with data from specific encounters. *Journal of Occupational Health Psychology.*

Gottfredson, M. R., & Hirschi, T. (1990). *A general theory of crime.* Stanford, CA: Stanford University Press.

Greenberg, L., & Barling, J. (1999). Predicting employee aggression against coworkers, subordinates and supervisors: The roles of person behaviors and perceived workplace factors. *Journal of Organizational Behavior, 20,* 897–913.

Gross, J. (1998). The emerging field of emotion regulation: An integrative review. *Review of General Psychology, 2,* 271–299.

Hanisch, K. A., & Hulin, C. L. (1990). Job attitudes and organizational withdrawal: An examination of retirement and other voluntary withdrawal behaviors. *Journal of Vocational Behavior, 37,* 60–78.

Hanisch, K. A., & Hulin, C. L. (1991). General attitudes and organizational withdrawal: An evaluation of a causal model. *Journal of Vocational Behavior, 39,* 110–128.

Hart, S. D., & Dempster, R. J. (1997). Impulsivity and psychopathy. In C. D. Webster & M. A. Jackson (Eds.), *Impulsivity: Theory, assessment, and treatment* (pp. 212–232). New York: Guilford Press.

Hodapp, V., Neuser, K. W., & Weyer, G. (1988). Job stress, emotion, and work environment: Toward a causal model. *Personality and Individual Differences, 9,* 851–859.

Holland, B., & Shelton, D. (1999). *Shining a light in the dark: Exposing workplace aggression.* Paper presented at the annual meeting of the Society for Industrial and Organizational Psychology, Atlanta, GA.

Holmes, D. S., & Will, M. J. (1985). Expression of interpersonal aggression by angered and nonangered persons with Type A and Type B behavior patterns. *Journal of Personality and Social Psychology, 48,* 723–727.

Houston, B. K., & Kelly, K. E. (1989). Hostility in employed women: Relation to work and marital experiences, social support, stress, and anger expression. *Personality and Social Psychology Bulletin, 15,* 175–182.

Jockin, V., Arvey, R. D., & McGue, M. (2001). Perceived victimization moderates self-reports of workplace aggression and conflict. *Journal of Applied Psychology, 86,* 1262–1269.

Johnson, W. L., Malow, R. M., Corrigan, S. A., & West, J. A. (1993). Impulse behavior and substance abuse. In W. G. McCown, J. L. Johnson, & M. B. Shure (Eds.), *The impulsive client: Theory, research, and treatment* (pp. 225–246). Washington, DC: American Psychological Association.

Kardum, I., & Hudek-Knezevic, J. (1996). The relationship between Eysenck's personality traits, coping styles and moods. *Personality and Individual Differences, 20,* 341–350.

Keashly, L., & Jagatic, K. (in press). By any other name: American perspectives on workplace bullying. In S. Einarsen, H. Hoel, D. Zapf, & C. Cooper (Eds.), *Bullying and emotional abuse in the workplace: International perspectives on research and practice.* London: Taylor Francis.

King, L. A., & Emmons, R. A. (1990). Conflict over emotional expression: Psychological and physical correlates. *Journal of Personality and Social Psychology, 58,* 864–877.

King, L. A., Emmons, R. A., & Woodley, S. (1992). The structure of inhibition. *Journal of Research in Personality, 26,* 85–102.

Labig, C. E. (1995). *Preventing violence in the workplace.* New York: AMACOM.

Larsen, R. J., Diener, E., & Cropanzano, R. S. (1987). Cognitive operations associated with individual differences in affect intensity. *Journal of Personality and Social Psychology, 53,* 767–774.

Latham, L. L., & Perlow, R. (1996). The relationship of client-directed aggressive and nonclient-directed aggressive work behavior with self-control. *Journal of Applied Social Psychology, 26,* 1027–1041.

Lemerise, E. A., & Dodge, K. A. (2000). The development of anger and hostile interactions. In M. Lewis & M. Haviland-Jones (Eds.), *Handbook of emotions* (2nd ed., pp. 594–606). New York: Guilford Press.

Lykken, D. T. (1995). *The antisocial personalities.* Hillsdale, NJ: Erlbaum.

McFarlin, S. K., Fals-Stewart, W., Major, D. A., & Frietas, T. T. (1999). *Prevalence of workplace violence among substance abusers.* Paper presented at the annual meeting of the Society of Industrial Organizational Psychology, Atlanta, Georgia.

Mearns, J., & Mauch, T. G. (1998). Negative mood regulation expectancies predict anger among police officers and buffer the effects of job stress. *Journal of Nervous and Mental Disease, 186,* 120–125.

Megargee, E. (1966). Undercontrolled and overcontrolled personality types in extreme antisocial aggression. *Psychological Monographs, 80*(3) (Whole No. 611).

Morissette, P. (1994). At risk alcohol consumption habits of female professionals and white-collar workers. *Employee Assistance Quarterly, 10,* 47–62.

Morrill, C. (1995). *The executive way: Conflict management in corporations.* Chicago: University of Chicago Press.

Neuman, J. H., & Baron, R. A. (1997). Aggression in the workplace. In R.
A. Giacalone & J. Greenberg (Eds.), *Antisocial behavior in organizations.* Thousand Oaks, CA: Sage.

Neuman, J. H., & Baron, R. A. (1998). Workplace violence and workplace
aggression: Evidence concerning specific forms, potential causes,
and preferred targets. *Journal of Management, 24,* 391–419.

Northwestern National Life, Employee Benefits Division. (1993). *Fear and
violence in the workplace: A survey documenting the experience of American
workers.* Minneapolis, MN: Author.

O'Leary-Kelly, A. M., Griffin, R. W., & Glew, D. J. (1996). Organization-
motivated aggression: A research framework. *Academy of Management
Review, 21,* 225–253.

Ones, D. S., Viswesvaran, C., Schmidt, F. L., & Reis, A. D. (1994, April).
*The validity of honesty and violence scales of integrity tests in predicting vi-
olence at work.* Paper presented at the annual meeting of the Academy of Management, Dallas.

Pennebaker, J. W. (1992). Inhibition as the linchpin of health. In H. S.
Friedman (Ed.), *Hostility, coping, and health* (pp. 127–140). Washington, DC: American Psychological Association.

Pulakos, E. D., & Schmitt, N. (1995). Experience-based and structured
interview questions: Studies of validity. *Personnel Psychology, 48,*
289–308.

Rabinovitz, J. (1998, March 7). Rampage in Connecticut: The overview;
Connecticut lottery worker kills four bosses, then himself. *New York
Times,* p. A1.

Robinson, S. L., & Bennett, R. J. (1995). A typology of deviant workplace
behaviors: A multidimensional scaling study. *Academy of Management
Journal, 38,* 555–572.

Robinson, S. L., & O'Leary-Kelly, A. M. (1998). Monkey see, monkey do:
The influence of work groups on the antisocial behavior of employees. *Academy of Management Journal, 41,* 658–672.

Rusting, C. L., & Nolen-Hoeksema, S. (1998). Regulating responses to
anger: Effects of rumination and distraction on angry mood. *Journal of Personality and Social Psychology, 74,* 790–803.

Skarlicki, D. P., & Folger, R. (1997). Retaliation in the workplace: The
roles of distributive, procedural, and interactional justice. *Journal
of Applied Psychology, 82,* 434–443.

Skarlicki, D. P., & Folger, R. (1999). Personality as a moderator in the relationship between fairness and retaliation. *Academy of Management
Journal, 42,* 100–108.

Slora, K. B., Joy, D. S., & Terris, W. (1991). Personnel selection to control
employee violence. *Journal of Business and Psychology, 5,* 417–426.

Spector, P. E. (1997). The role of frustration in antisocial behavior at work. In R. A. Giacalone & J. Greenberg (Eds.), *Antisocial behavior in organizations* (pp. 1–17). Thousand Oaks, CA: Sage.

Spielberger, C. D. (1991). *State-Trait Anger Expression Inventory (Professional Manual)*. Odessa, FL: Psychological Assessment Resources.

Spielberger, C. D., Sydeman, S. J., Owen, A. E., & Marsh, B. J. (1999). Measuring anxiety and anger with the State-Trait Anxiety Inventory (STAI) and the State-Trait Anger Expression Inventory (STAXI). In M. E. Maruish (Ed.), *The use of psychological testing for treatment planning and outcomes assessment* (2nd ed., pp. 993–1021). Hillsdale, NJ: Erlbaum.

Steele, C. M., & Southwick, L. (1985). Alcohol and social behavior: I. The psychology of drunken excess. *Journal of Personality & Social Psychology, 48,* 18–34.

Storms, P. L., & Spector, P. E. (1987). Relationship of organizational frustration with reported behavioral reactions: The moderating effect of locus of control. *Journal of Occupational Psychology, 60,* 227–234.

Tepper, B. J. (2000). Consequences of abusive supervision. *Academy of Management Journal, 43,* 178–190.

Tevlin, J. (1997, September 16). They don't get mad, they get a consultant. *Minneapolis Star Tribune,* p. D1.

Thayer, R. E., Newman, J., Robert, & McClain, T. M. (1994). Self-regulation of mood: Strategies for changing a bad mood, raising energy, and reducing tension. *Journal of Personality and Social Psychology, 67,* 910–925.

Toscano, G. A., & Windau, J. A. (1998, Spring). Profile of fatal work injuries in 1996. *Compensation and Working Conditions,* pp. 37–45.

Tripp, T. M., & Bies, R. J. (1997). What's good about revenge? The avenger's perspective. In R. J. Lewicki, R. J. Bies, & B. H. Sheppard (Eds.), *Research on negotiation in organizations* (Vol. 6, pp. 145–160). Greenwich, CT: JAI Press.

U.S. Department of Labor. Bureau of Labor Statistics. (1998, April 8). *Lost-worktime injuries and illnesses: Characteristics and resulting time away from work, 1996* [news release]. Washington, DC: Author.

van Elderen, T., Verkes, R. J., Arkesteijn, J., & Komproe, I. (1996). Psychometric characteristics of the Self-Expression and Control Scale in a sample of recurrent suicide attempters. *Personality and Individual Differences, 21,* 489–496.

Verona, E., & Carbonell, J. L. (2000). Female violence and personality: Evidence for a pattern of overcontrolled hostility among one-time violent female offenders. *Criminal Justice & Behavior, 27,* 176–195.

Weiss, H. M., & Cropanzano, R. (1996). Affective events theory: A theoretical discussion of the structure, causes and consequences of affective experiences at work. In B. M. Staw & L. L. Cummings (Eds.), *Research in organizational behavior* (Vol. 19, pp. 1–74). Greenwich, CT: JAI Press.

Wenzlaff, R. M., & Bates, D. E. (2000). The relative efficacy of concentration and suppression strategies of mental control. *Society of Personality and Social Psychology, 26,* 1200–1212.

Wenzlaff, R. M., & Wegner, D. M. (2000). Thought repression. *Annual Review of Psychology, 51,* 59–91.

Yates, B. T. (1985). *Self-management: The science and art of helping yourself.* Belmont, CA: Wadsworth.

Zillman, D. (1993). The mental control of angry aggression. In D. M. Wegner & J. W. Pennebaker (Eds.), *Handbook of mental control* (pp. 370–392). Upper Saddle River, NJ: Prentice Hall.

CHAPTER 8

The Emotion Regulation Behind the Customer Service Smile

Alicia A. Grandey
Analea L. Brauburger

There has been much touting of the new service economy of the twenty-first century (Offermann & Gowing, 1990). In order to distinguish one's company from those selling similar products, organizations advertise "service with a smile," which is thought to contribute to customers' perceptions of quality service, satisfaction, loyalty, and their overall impression of the organization (Albrecht & Zemke, 1985; Parasuraman, Zeithaml, & Berry, 1985). According to Hochschild (1979, 1983), service employees are getting paid for emotional control and expressions and thus are engaging in "emotional labor." Customer service employees constantly regulate their emotions and emotional expressions while interacting with customers. Hochschild (1983) mentions this form of work as having positive outcomes for the organization, but requiring effort from the employee that is often overlooked. Front-line service workers expend more effort when they have feelings that are incongruent with the friendly displays required of them. Thus, identifying the situations that create this dissonance and methods of coping with these situations may help with developing training modules and reduce stress of front-line employees.

Two theoretical frameworks were integrated to help explain the emotion-eliciting events and outcomes, as well as the different approaches of emotion regulation in the service setting. First, the affective events theory (AET) is a general framework involving the effect of work events and emotional reactions on work attitudes and behaviors (Weiss & Cropanzano, 1996). It considers the work characteristics as a driver of the affective events and affective behaviors—in this case, the interpersonal and affective demands of the service job and the affect-driven behaviors of interest, include helping (George, 1991), harming, or hiding from customers in service encounters. Affective events such as interpersonal stressors or conflicts can create incongruent emotions with the service job requirements. This chapter incorporates the second framework, emotion regulation, into different phases of the AET (see Figure 8.1). Emotion regulation is defined as "the processes by which individuals influence which emotions they have, when they have them, and how they experience and express these emotions" (Gross, 1998b, p. 275). Gross's (1998b) emotion management approaches emerged from the integration of previous work on emotion coping and management from a variety of fields and recently has been applied to work situations (Grandey, 2000). Service employees can regulate the external context, their internal processes, or their behavioral response and can do so proactively (antecedent-focused emotion regulation) or reactively (response-focused emotion regulation (Grandey, 2000; Gross, 1998a).

This chapter uses the integrated model shown in Figure 8.1 to answer the following questions: (1) What are the characteristics of customer service settings that influence the likelihood of affective events and behaviors? (2) What types of work events are most likely to create the need to perform emotion regulation? (3) How can employees proactively and reactively regulate their emotions in these service settings? (4) How effective are these techniques of regulation for both service performance and employee well-being? (5) How can this knowledge translate into applications in workplace settings?

Customer Service Work Demands and Service Behaviors

Hochschild's (1983) three main characteristics of emotional labor jobs provide a useful guideline for identifying relevant customer service job characteristics. One characteristic is that the job requires

Figure 8.1. Emotion Regulation in the Customer Service Setting.

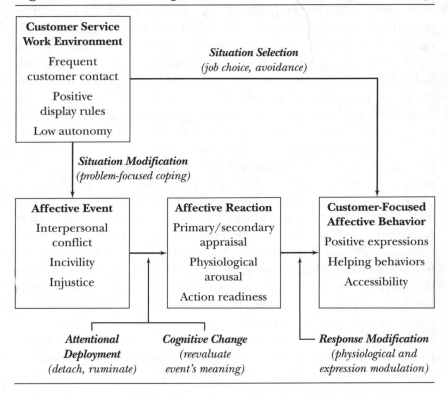

high levels of customer contact in terms of frequency, intensity, or duration of interactions (Morris & Feldman, 1996). The second is that the job requires using emotional displays to evoke affective reactions from customers. Organizational control over employees' emotional displays, or a lack of emotional autonomy, is the third characteristic of emotional labor jobs.

Frequency of Customer Contact

Customer service jobs, by their nature, require employees to interact with customers regularly, meeting their needs by offering both tangible and intangible products (Albrecht & Zemke, 1985;

Parasuraman et al., 1985). Whereas some employees interact mainly with other employees and supervisors, the customer service employee is a boundary spanner, with a third source of interaction in the workday. The continuous availability of employees to the public is one of the dimensions of good customer service (Parasuraman et al., 1985).

Hochschild's (1983) description of flight attendants pointed out the difficulty of providing personal service to every passenger—hundreds of them. Previous research on service and caring health professions has considered customer contact frequency, duration, and intensity as predictors of work attitudes and burnout with mixed results (Brotheridge & Grandey, in press; Cordes, Dougherty, & Blum, 1997; Maslach, 1978; Morris & Feldman, 1997; Singh, Goolsby, & Rhoades, 1994). As proposed by AET (Weiss & Cropanzano, 1996) and other models (Brotheridge & Grandey, in press; Grandey, 2000), a more proximal predictor of work outcomes than the work characteristics themselves may be how these work characteristics create affective events and reactions.

Gutek and colleagues have proposed a specific dimension of high-contact service work that may influence the affective tone of the work. Frequent interactions with the public can be either service *encounters,* where the employee is unlikely to see that particular individual again, or service *relationships,* where the employee and customer interact regularly (Gutek, Bhappu, Liao-Troth, & Cherry, 1999; Gutek, Cherry, Bhappu, Schneider, & Woolf, 2000). Work motivation has been proposed to be different for the employee depending on whether the service is an encounter or a relationship. The service relationship provider is "motivated to provide good service in order to retain customers" (Gutek et al., 1999, p. 220). Gutek and colleagues also state that a service relationship may go beyond the objective outcomes and satisfy the customers' expressive needs (social and emotional), which may also be true for the employee. It is likely that a service relationship would assist employees in providing authentic expressions to customers they see regularly, provided they are on good terms with those people. This dichotomy has not been used in the emotional labor literature, but it makes an important distinction about the motivation for different customer service employees.

Display Rules

Emotional labor researchers have explored the variation of emotional displays expected in different jobs and have proposed three types of emotional work requirements: integrative, differentiating, and suppression (Wharton & Erickson, 1993; Jones & Best, 1995). Front-line service employees are generally expected to express integrative emotions such as friendliness and sympathy (Parasuraman et al., 1995). Employees in other job types, such as bill collectors or bouncers, are expected to inspire differentiating emotions, such as fear, perhaps by portraying anger (Hochshild, 1979; Sutton, 1991). The third type, suppression, is descriptive of jobs where neutralizing emotions are required, such as therapists or judges. These work characteristics are display rules of the job, which may be communicated as informal norms or formal requirements (Ekman & Friesen, 1975; Goffman, 1959; Hochschild, 1983).

Customer service employees typically perceive that there are integrative display rules (Brotheridge & Grandey, in press; Jones & Best, 1995). The employee's role is to create positive feelings in the customers, so that they will leave with a positive impression of this company and therefore return. Not only are these positive expressions to be maintained across time and customer situation, but they also should be authentic and sincere expressions (Ashforth & Humphrey, 1995). The assumption made is that if the employee is smiling and being genuinely friendly, these positive expressions will be "caught" by the customer, who will then form a positive impression of the establishment. Support for the idea of emotional contagion (Hatfield, Cacioppo, & Rapson, 1994) has been demonstrated in actual service settings (Pugh, 2001) and is discussed in Chapter Five. Others have also found that positive expressions relate to customer service outcomes such as customer satisfaction, tips, and sales (George, 1991; George & Bettenhausen, 1990; Kelley & Hoffman, 1997; Parkinson, 1991; Tidd & Lockhard, 1978).

This research regarding positive displays and service outcomes provides a rationale for the enforcement of display rules but has typically ignored the true feelings and emotion regulation that service representatives need. In fact, researchers suggest that just the emotional display rules of the job act as a work stressor by controlling employees' personal feelings (Jones & Best, 1995). Schaubroeck and Jones (2000) found that the display rules to express positive emotions and suppress negative were both positively related to physical symptoms of stress, although only positive display rules were significant when the effects of age, gender, and negative affectivity were considered. On the contrary, Brotheridge and Grandey (in press) found that the perceived rule to express positive emotions related positively to a sense of personal accomplishment, but having to hide negative displays to customers related to emotional exhaustion. Given that these studies all employed self-report techniques, the mixed results may speak to the need for identifying the actual events and emotional experiences occurring at work, which may make the display rules more or less onerous.

Finally, it has not been unequivocally established how these affective display rules fit into performance expectations as they are traditionally considered in industrial/organizational (I/O) psychology. The debate over what is considered technical performance versus contextual performance continues in the field in general (Borman & Motowidlo, 1993; Organ, 1997) and is confused in the service setting. Contextual performance has typically encompassed "playing nice with others," which could certainly include being friendly to customers. However, in customer service contexts, these positive displays may be an explicit, trained, and rewarded part of the job, and hence part of in-role performance. Although being friendly to customers may be an in-role expectation, it is probably not part of technical performance, since it is intangible and subjective. Nonetheless, this is mainly conjecture. Job analyses are needed that include dimensions of emotional expressions in order to determine if they would emerge as required behaviors that can be evaluated and compensated (Arvey, Renz, & Watson, 1998). One job analysis of the work demands of call center employees demonstrated that employees provided examples of positive affective displays as part of effective performance (Shiarella, 1999). Subject matter experts rated some of these positive display behaviors as contextual performance ("extra effort" or "supporting" dimensions), but some could not be categorized into the known dimensions of technical and contextual performance. Applying I/O knowledge of performance to display rules and affective performance would allow for the emotional effort of service work to be recognized as in-role and compensated accordingly. If affective displays are in-role, employees are more likely to perform that behavior (Morrison, 1994). However, these displays may not be sincere, as discussed in a later section.

Autonomy

Display rules are often enforced through secret shoppers, manager evaluations, and customer comments, to name a few (Fuller & Smith, 1996; Rafaeli & Sutton, 1987). "Hiring smiling faces" and training employees to "smile!" is one part of human resource processes (Hochschild, 1983; Rafaeli & Sutton, 1987; VanMaanen & Kunda, 1989). These display rules decrease emotional autonomy, or freedom of expression of one's true feelings. General work autonomy also tends to be low for customer service jobs. Research has found that a sense of autonomy tends to be an important factor in work attitudes and stress (Hackman & Oldham, 1976; Spector, 1998), and in emotional labor articles, this variable has been a strong (negative) predictor of burnout beyond emotional demands (Wharton, 1993). Organizational control over emotional displays may create less intrinsic motivation and less authentic displays to customers, with detrimental results (Grandey, 2000; Hackman & Oldham, 1976). This lack of autonomy over emotions may also create difficulty in coping with work events and personal life due to a sense of estrangement from one's true feelings (Erickson & Wharton, 1997; Hochschild, 1983). In addition, this lack of emotional and behavioral autonomy for service workers has implications for the choices available to them in terms of emotion regulation.

Externally Focused Emotion Regulation

Service workers have frequent interactions with customers when they are expected to show positive displays, and they have little autonomy over their expressions and the situation. In the ideal situation, these job characteristics contribute directly to engaging in affective service behaviors (smiling) and experiencing positive affective events (see Figure 8.1). This ideal situation may be more likely if the employee is a good fit for these demands. Two externally focused emotion regulation tactics are situation selection and situation modification (Gross, 1998b), whereby individuals choose or modify their interactions with people and places in ways that may maximize the pleasantness of the experience and thus regulate their emotional state (Diener, Larson, & Emmons, 1984).

Situation Selection

An individual's disposition, values, and needs contribute to the type of situation that is most desirable for that person. In the case of customer service, individuals may self-select into jobs where they can interact with many people because they are extroverted and desire interacting with and helping others. They may select jobs that require positive expressions (flight attendants) or negative expressions (bill collectors) because these fit their natural emotional expressivity (Arvey et al., 1998). They may choose jobs that have low levels of autonomy because they lack experience or knowledge or they have low growth needs (Hackman & Oldham, 1976). If the individual's needs and personality are matched to the job, suggesting a good person-job fit (Edwards, 1991), he or she should be satisfied with the job and show more authentic expressions toward customers (Arvey et al., 1998; Steel, Arvey, & Kyllonen, 1999).

Another way to regulate emotions by situation selection, once the job has been selected, would be to select working with people or in contexts that are pleasant or fit the individual's affective state. For example, a retail clerk may opt to work in the back room hanging and pressing new garments, because he or she is having a bad day, or ask another employee to help a customer who is known to be unpleasant. However, because good customer service means availability to customers (Parasuraman et al., 1985) and customer service employees may have low autonomy to choose their work tasks, it may be difficult for employees to use situation selection in ongoing work situations.

Situational Modification

Situational modification is a regulatory strategy that works by changing a potential emotion-eliciting situation, thus having an impact on the link between job characteristics and affective events (see Figure 8.1). This category resembles active problem-focused coping (Folkman & Lazarus, 1985), which attempts to change the situation. For example, a customer service employee may talk with a difficult person to keep a stressful event from happening in the future or may arrange the work schedule to avoid interacting with certain people. This strategy is preventative and antecedent focused by attempting to change the situation to avoid the evocation of certain emotions.

Effectiveness of Externally Focused Emotion Regulation

Situation selection may help employees choose jobs for which they are dispositionally suited, thus lessening the regulation needed on a regular basis. However, even with the most ideal person-job fit, the interpersonal nature and display rules of customer service jobs make it likely that regulation would be needed in acute situations. While situational modification such as directly confronting an individual may be suitable for dealing with coworkers or others with similar organizational power, this may be less feasible for interactions with customers. Modifying the situation in order to avoid such acute events may be difficult in settings where "the customer is always right" or there is little chance for problem solving or in-depth discussion whereby the interaction can be improved. In such cases, workers may hide in the back room when certain customers approach (regulating by situation selection), thus lowering their availability to customers. Particularly in customer interactions, the script for what is said, done, and expressed (Leidner, 1996; Rafaeli & Sutton, 1987) may be so explicit that changing that particular encounter is either impossible or highly discouraged. In fact, coping studies have found that problem-focused coping predominates when stressful conditions are viewed as controllable by action, and emotion-focused coping (internal emotion regulation) is prevalent when conditions are viewed as hard to change (Carver, Scheier, & Weintraub, 1989; Folkman & Lazarus, 1985). In other words, internal, rather than external, emotion regulation may be more likely used by service representatives with low autonomy. These internal emotion regulation techniques will be discussed within the context of the affective events and reactions link of Figure 8.1.

Affective Events and Reactions

In customer service settings, the characteristics of the job and the need for affective behaviors with customers create special emotional demands on the employee. Selection of a job that fits one's natural emotional expression acts as a preemptive, or antecedent-focused, emotion regulation technique. However, once in the service job, even employees with great person-job fit may find themselves in situations that require emotion regulation. In particular, affective events that create a negative emotion create dissonance between the display rules and true feelings. Emotional dissonance, where the feeling state is discrepant from the display (Hochschild, 1983), has consistently been related to stress outcomes (Abraham, 1998; Erickson & Wharton, 1997; Grandey, 2000b; Morris & Feldman, 1997; Pugliesi, 1999). In order to cope with the emotional events that may occur and minimize dissonance, we need to understand the types of events that may create negative emotions and how employees can regulate these reactions.

Emotions are usually characterized as affective, short-lived, relatively intense, and typically interruptive of thought processes (Fiske & Taylor, 1991; Frijda, 1993; George, 1996). Thus, events may occur within work environments that act as affective shocks to the existing system (Weiss & Cropanzano, 1996). Of course, as is well known in the emotions literature, objective events may not have a direct relationship with an emotional response; many factors contribute to whether the event creates an emotional response. Emotions themselves are multifaceted, involving cognitive processes, physiological arousal, and behavioral predispositions. An employee can regulate emotions and change behaviors by cognitively refocusing or reevaluating in several ways, as shown in Figure 8.1. Especially since much previous work has examined positive affect (George & Brief, 1996; Isen & Baron, 1991; Staw, Sutton, & Pelled, 1994), this section focuses on events that create negative emotional responses, as well as how employees can regulate emotions to these events while in the service setting.

To identify work-related affective events, researchers often depend on the recall method: they ask participants to recall a work situation (a critical incident) when they felt a specific emotional reaction, such as anger or fear. This has allowed organizational researchers to identify emotions felt at work and has provided a sense of what types of events are occurring that contribute to emotional responses, on average. For example, in one study, M.B.A. students wrote descriptions about events that induced eight basic emotions, and these descriptions were content-analyzed to describe general types of affective events for each emotion (Gibson, 1997). Basch and Fisher (2000) used a similar process with international hotel employees, who identified work events that created specific emotions. These were sorted into categories of events that instigated positive emotions (such as goal progress) and negative emotions (such as making mistakes), with interpersonal categories (such as acts of customers or coworkers) being implicated in both. However, providing a single emotion and asking participants about a past work event that evoked that emotion is based on recall memory and post hoc appraisals, and it does not allow for the complex concurrence of multiple and conflicting emotions (Arvey et al., 1998; Folkman & Lazarus, 1988). Diary and experience-sampling methodology studies have also been recently undertaken to explore the experience of emotions at work (Grandey, Tam, & Brauburger, in press; Kurek, Le, & Weiss, 2001). Because emotions of negative valence, like anger and sadness, are more likely to result in emotion regulation (Gross, 1998b), particularly in the service setting where integrative displays are required, we review negative affective events.

Affective Events Eliciting Negative Emotions in Service Settings

Negative emotions are generally felt when individuals perceive that an event holds some harm for the individual or impedes goals (Lazarus, 1991). Although different people may appraise the same events as more or less harmful, certain types of events may be more likely than others to evoke negative emotions such as anger, anxiety, or sadness. Interpersonal events are of most interest for this chapter, because regulating negative emotions becomes particularly important when the employee is constantly interacting with the public. In one study of international hotel employees (Basch & Fisher, 2000), the service representatives reported 736 events as causes of discrete work emotions; 44 percent of the total affective events (positive and negative) referred to acts by management

(198), customers (97), and coworkers (27), with the vast majority of these events associated with negative emotions. The ubiquity of interpersonal exchanges resulting in negative emotions, combined with the potential for emotional dissonance, makes such exchanges important to discuss in the light of emotion regulation. Due to the perception that they harm one's sense of self or personal goals, this chapter identifies three interpersonal events that relate to negative work reactions: interpersonal conflict, incivility, and injustice.

Interpersonal Conflict

Stress and coping studies have identified interpersonal conflict as a source of negative reactions (Hepburn, Loughlin, & Barling, 1997; Peeters, Buunk, & Schaufeli, 1995; Terry, Tonge, & Callan, 1995). In one study, university employees indicated that interpersonal conflicts between and among staff were common and a source of negative reactions such as stress (Pugliesi & Shook, 1997). In another study, the frequency of interpersonal conflict related positively to the affective reactions of anxiety, frustration, and job dissatisfaction (Spector & Jex, 1998). In a similar vein, interpersonal conflict with supervisors related to negative work attitudes, while conflict with coworkers related to personal and psychological stress (Frone, 2000). A recent diary study found that "personal attacks" from supervisors, customers, and coworkers was a commonly reported category of events creating intense anger (Grandey et al., in press). These negative affective reactions from interpersonal conflict are discrepant from the required positive displays to customers. Workplace interpersonal conflict refers to ongoing difficult relationships, which can create a climate that makes positive expressions difficult and emotion regulation necessary.

Incivility Events

Even more insidious for a brief employee-customer exchange is workplace incivility, defined as "low-intensity deviant behavior with ambiguous intent to harm the target, in violation of workplace norms for mutual respect. Uncivil behaviors are characteristically rude and discourteous, displaying a lack of regard for others" (Andersson & Pearson, 1999, p. 457). Although the previous literature has focused on coworker and supervisors as a source of incivility, the customer needs to be considered as well (Cortina,

Magley, Williams, & Langhout, 2001). Customers have more social power than the front-line employee in the service encounter, so that they do not need to respond to an employee's smile and friendly "hello" or may feel justified in personally attacking the service employee (Goffman, 1959; Hochschild, 1983). A spiral may ensue involving incivility from customer A to the employee, and the employee's unregulated anger may affect how the employee treats customer B, who may respond negatively, and so on. In fact, a diary study with working students found that the most common source of anger was customer incivility (Grandey et al., in press). Employees in another study reported that they dealt with difficult customers as often as once or twice a day (Bailey & McCollough, 2000). In a survey study, Cortina et al. (2001) found that 71 percent of participants reported some experience with workplace incivility in the past five years and that these experiences were linked with job dissatisfaction and work withdrawal. Given these affective and behavioral responses, how one copes with these events through different regulation techniques is worthy of future study and has implications for training (Cortina et al., 2001; Grandey et al., in press).

Injustice Events

Incivility events and interpersonal conflict may be a source of negative emotions because they are seen as a violation of justice norms (Andersson & Pearson, 1999). The organizational justice literature suggests that when employees perceive an injustice, negative emotions and the need to "make things even" emerge (Adams, 1965; Cropanzano & Greenberg, 1997). Injustice perceptions occur when outcomes or procedures are seen as unfair in comparison to certain standards and when interpersonal treatment is discourteous or disrespectful without justification (Cropanzano & Greenberg, 1997). In particular, the affective response of anger is associated with perceiving unjust treatment. In an interview study with community residents, unjust treatment was the most commonly reported event that produced anger (Fitness, 2000). In a recent laboratory study, high levels of anger were reported when both the outcome and the process were unfair as perceived by the participant (Weiss, Suckow, & Cropanzano, 1999).

Interactional injustice interacts with the fairness perceptions of the outcome and process to produce organizational retaliation and deviant behaviors (Aquino, Lewis, & Bradfield, 1999; Skarlicki & Folger, 1997). The service retailing and marketing literature has shown that when customers are upset or complain about a product, if the employee reacts to them with rudeness, this interactional injustice may undermine the effects of the compensation (Blodgett, Hill, & Tax, 1997; Tax, Brown, & Chandrashkedaran, 1998). In other words, there are important reasons for employees to regulate their emotions while interacting with customers, even when things seem unfair. Because the injustice literature focuses on the perception or appraisal of events, emotion regulation may involve the employee's attempting to reappraise what has happened in order to modify emotions (Cropanzano, Weiss, Suckow, & Grandey, 2000). Such modification of actual feeling states is discussed next as internally focused emotion regulation.

Internally Focused Emotion Regulation

The affective events of interpersonal conflict, incivility, and injustice require emotion regulation because they arouse negative emotions that do not fit the display rules of the job and may occur with people with whom there may be high costs due to the power differential (customers) if true feelings are shown. Emotions research has noted that emotional arousal can interfere with performance, taking precedence above cognitive and social processes (Fiske & Taylor, 1991; Isen & Baron, 1991; Weiss & Cropanzano, 1996). This may be especially true in the service setting, when the affective display is part of the work performance. As stated earlier, customer service employees may respond by using emotion-focused coping, defined as efforts to change either the way the stressful relationship with the environment is attended to or to change the meaning of what is happening (Lazarus & Folkman, 1984; Walden & Smith, 1997) rather than changing the situation. Two examples of internally focused emotion regulation techniques are attentional deployment and cognitive change (Gross, 1998a).

Attentional Deployment

The technique of attentional deployment refers to a broad category also known as cognitive refocusing. Gross (1998b) discusses how in any situation there are multiple components, and the individual can decide to focus attention on any one of them to regulate his or her emotions. In a difficult customer situation, the employee may engage in *distraction,* thinking about something nonemotional or pleasant and unrelated to the encounter. For example, the employee who has just had a nasty interaction with someone at work may think about plans for the evening that are fun or look at pictures of the family vacation in order to lift her mood (Parkinson & Totterdell, 1999). Conversely, this employee could practice *rumination* and focus on the incivility event and her emotional reaction to the event.

Another identified technique of attentional deployment that customer service representatives may use is disengagement, or *detachment* (Folkman & Lazarus, 1991; Parkinson & Totterdell, 1999). Here, rather than changing feelings by actively thinking about more positive events (as in distraction) or about the emotional event itself (rumination), the employee may try to regulate emotional reactions by cognitively distancing herself from her feelings or the situation. Examples of such practices may be attempting to think of nothing at all, mentally switching off, waiting passively for something to change, or engaging in the wishful thinking that things would be different (Folkman & Lazarus, 1985; Parkinson & Totterdell, 1999). Some researchers have studied humor as a way of regulating negative emotions in the workplace (Avolio, Howell, & Sosik, 1999; Parrish & Quinn, 1999). Humor, or making light of the situation, may act to distance the individual from the situation and has been discussed as a technique of caring professionals who deal with life-or-death situations (Maslach, 1978). However, in the customer service setting, the use of humor during a negative work encounter could be potentially detrimental to the service interaction if the customer felt the employee was mocking him or her.

Cognitive Change

Cognitive change is another example of internally focused emotion regulation as a response to affective events. As stated by early theories of emotions and stress, how individuals evaluate a situation, rather than the objective situation itself, influences the emotions felt (Lazarus, 1991). Primary appraisal consists of deciding whether the event is personally relevant to the individual and his or her goals, resulting in positive or negative emotion states. Secondary appraisal consists of determining blame or credit attributions and evaluating coping resources, which result in more specific emotional states (Lazarus, 1991). However, if that same event has uncertain meaning and an individual cannot necessarily tell what is going to happen or what should be done about it, anxiety may occur.

In short, the way in which an individual cognitively processes what is happening will alter the emotions felt (Folkman & Lazarus, 1991; Lazarus, 1991). For example, a customer service representative who has just been yelled at by her supervisor may appraise the situation in several ways. A gut-level response may be sadness or shame if she believes that she has done something very wrong and deserves to be punished, or anger or disgust if she decides that her supervisor is a jerk and is acting in a completely unfair manner. She may reevaluate this situation to dull her negative reaction, perhaps deciding that her supervisor was having a bad day and could not totally be held accountable for this unfair response (Cropanzano et al., 2000). Hochschild (1983) described flight attendants' learning to regulate emotional reactions to difficult passengers by thinking of them as small children who need help. Appraising them in this way would minimize anger and aggressive tendencies, thus helping the employee to cope with the work situation effectively. As William Shakespeare's Hamlet said, "There is nothing either good or bad but thinking makes it so" (act II, scene 2, line 259).

Effectiveness of Internally Focused Emotion Regulation

Emotion regulation through modifying attention or cognitions, also known as "deep acting" (Grandey, 2000; Hochschild, 1983), seems to be effective in modifying the individual's experience of emotion (Lazarus & Alfert, 1964). According to laboratory studies using videos to elicit emotions, viewing the situation in a detached manner (attention deployment) was found to result in lower reports of emotional experience and less expression of negative emotions (Gross, 1998a; Gross & Levenson, 1997). In the workplace, studies using varied methods have supported these laboratory findings. A field intervention study using an experience sampling methodology found that cognitive distraction (attentional deployment) was the most often used strategy of trainee teachers, but that cognitive reappraisal was more effective at changing reported mood (Totterdell & Parkinson, 1999). One survey study with administrative assistants found that a higher level of deep acting, or internal emotion regulation, was associated with a higher coworker rating of affective delivery to customers (Grandey, in press). Reappraisals of the blame and controllability of circumstances have been found to diminish stress reactions (Stemmler, 1997), presumably because the emotion is lessened by this reappraisal and thus interferes less with attentional resources (Baumeister, Heatherton, & Tice, 1994).

In the coping literature, effectiveness has not been extensively examined. In general, however, emotion-focused coping efforts are identified as maladaptive, while problem-focused approaches are viewed as adaptive or more effective (Billings & Moos, 1984; Headey & Wearing, 1990). However, as Folkman, Lazarus, Gruen, and DeLongis (1986) point out, "It is important not to value a particular form of coping without reference to the context in which it is used" (p. 578). It may be that in the service setting where more direct regulation methods are constrained, emotion-focused or internal-focused regulation is the more effective method. Coping research within the service setting is needed to pursue this possibility.

Affective Reactions and Affective Behaviors

Affective reactions and resulting behaviors have been studied mainly in terms of moods and task-related performance. Social and organizational psychologists have studied how positive and negative moods affect task-related behaviors such as goal setting, decision making, cognitive performance, performance ratings, and sales performance (George & Bettenhausen, 1990; George & Brief, 1996; Isen & Baron, 1991; Staw & Barsade, 1993). In this chapter, we have been focusing on affective reactions as emotional responses, where the affect felt is due to a specific target, as opposed to generalized mood states. In addition, we are interested in affective reactions that are inconsistent with the required affective displays to customers. Whereas feeling pride or happiness in response to work events (such as supervisor praise or a job well done) may improve customer service behaviors due to their motivational aspects (George & Brief, 1996; Hackman & Oldham, 1976), feeling anger, or anxiety in response to work events push one toward behaviors that typically are not condoned in jobs with integrative or positive display rules.

Frijda (1988) and others have discussed the idea of "action readiness," where the emotional state prepares the individual to approach or avoid the stimulus. The clenching of the fist and the heart racing provide action tendencies for the individual to respond to a situation. Regulating emotions means regulating or controlling such behavioral tendencies due to social norms, higher-order goals, and the display rules of the job. As Averill (1983) points out, the experience of anger generally results not in violence or aggression but rather in subtler forms, such as sarcasm. In other words, despite feeling anger due to an incivility event, the customer service representative needs to clench his or her teeth and still say, "Have a nice day." Not only does this need to occur with that customer, but also to the next customer in line, and the next, all with sincerity (Ashforth & Humphrey, 1995; Tax et al., 1998). How can the employee regulate behavioral tendencies, and how effective is this response-focused emotion regulation?

Response-Focused Emotion Regulation

In response-focused emotion regulation, the individual manipulates the expression of emotion by influencing physiological or behavioral responses to the event (Gross, 1998b). Individuals can modify the physiological tension that accompanies anger and anxiety and suppress or hide expressions from public viewing.

Physiological Modification

Physiological modification is the attempt to regulate one aspect of emotional responding: the physiological arousal state (Lazarus, 1991). There are several ways this can be accomplished. Removal from any social interaction for a brief period (a "time-out") allows an arousal state to have a chance to return to baseline levels (Repetti, 1992). For example, a call center for an international phone company requires fifteen seconds to pass between every call before the next one is allowed through the queue. Another technique used to regulate the body's arousal is the intake of chemicals (Grandey, 2000; Gross, 1998a). A regular smoker may take a smoke break (the nicotine calms anxiety rather than stimulating the individual if they are already addicted), others may drink coffee to improve positive mood, or they may attend happy hours where alcohol is served. In addition to the physiological effects on emotion regulation, these functions are often socially embedded, providing the opportunity for social support. This social support can result in advice for future situational modification or rumination or distraction, or it can offer ideas for cognitive reappraisal (Carver et al., 1989; Folkman & Lazarus, 1991). The literature on social support as a coping tool is too broad to cover here and is kept separate in other taxonomies of emotion regulation (Gross, 1998b) or stress and coping (Hobfoll, 1989).

Expression Modulation

In expression modulation, a person has a tendency toward an emotional response but manipulates the expression of that response (Frijda, 1988; Gross, 1998b). An individual may suppress authentic feelings, enhance the intensity of an authentic emotion, or fake an emotional expression (Grandey, 2000). In the customer service setting, these approaches may be commonly used to interact with customers and meet the display rules of the job. Hochschild (1983) wrote about customer service employees' engaging in "surface acting." For example, a flight attendant may mask a bad mood and paste a smile on her face to her airline passengers, or a waiter may suppress disgust and remain polite and helpful toward the customer who is eating too much. In one study, M.B.A. students recalled emotional events at work, and in 62 percent of negative emotional experiences, the true emotions were not expressed to the instigators of those emotions (Gibson, 1997). One study with working students who had mostly service jobs found they reported faking their feelings 50 percent of the time when feeling anger (Grandey et al., in press). A study with Canadian full-time employees coded into five job categories found that those with service jobs were more likely than clerical workers and physical laborers to report surface acting or faking expressions (Brotheridge & Grandey, in press). Thus, response modulation is used at work, particularly for those with explicit display rules to show positive expressions.

Effectiveness of Response-Focused Regulation

Methods of physiological modulation, if available to the employee, are effective in that they calm one of the main signs that one is experiencing a strong emotion (Frijda, 1993). An effective way for employees to calm the body's arousal state is through social withdrawal, as demonstrated by research with air traffic controllers returning home and taking time alone before joining the family (Repetti, 1992). Similarly, meditation and relaxation techniques have been introduced to work environments and found to calm the body's stress reactions (Alexander, Langer, Newman, Chandler, & Davies, 1989; Ivancevich, Matteson, Freedman, & Phillips, 1990). However, such possibilities may not be available for entry-level customer service representatives. Studies have found main effects of social support and sharing emotions (a form of rumination) as decreasing stress and negative emotions (Cropanzano, Howes, Grandey, & Toth, 1997; Pennebaker, 1985).

The effectiveness of response modulation by faking expressions has been tested with multiple outcome variables. According to one theory, enhancing expressions or putting on a smile should have positive effects. In short-term laboratory studies, some studies have found that modifying the facial muscles into certain emotional expressions changed the experience of emotions (Adelmann & Zajonc, 1989; Stepper & Strack, 1993), otherwise known as the facial-feedback effect. This effect suggests that customer service representatives who show positive expressions at work should be very happy employees. This is overly simplified, as more recent tests of this facial-feedback effect have shown. When individuals are aware of the source of their expressions (in this case, the awareness of display rules or customer expectations), this effect has been found to diminish (Wegener & Petty, 1996). Survey studies did not find support for the facial-feedback model predicting job satisfaction (Adelmann, 1995) or work tension (Côté & Morgan, 2000). Thus, faking expressions should not be effective for employee stress management or service delivery.

Laboratory studies have found evidence for the stressful nature of suppressing true emotions as well, which corresponds to Hochschild's (1983) thesis. In two studies, subjects were asked to respond naturally or suppress their emotions of sadness or disgust in response to a video (Gross, 1998a; Gross & Levenson, 1997). The suppression condition resulted in decreased observable signs of emotion, but the levels of the self-reported experience of emotion and the physiological measures of emotional arousal did not decrease. The effects of chronic response-focused emotional regulation are not known from these studies. In addition, these studies focus on the inhibition of negative emotions, but do not explore the expression of positive emotions. Perhaps it takes even more effort to suppress anger while also expressing friendliness, as may occur in service encounters.

Recent research has found that being expected to show positive expression is not as stressful as the experience of faking or surface-level acting (Brotheridge & Grandey, in press; Côté & Morgan, 2001). This is consistent with research suggesting that framing emotional regulation requirements in positive terms makes the suppression of negative emotions automatic and less likely to produce ironic or rebound effects later (Wenzlaff & Bates, 2000). However, when people are aware of suppressing negative emotions to meet demands and they are in a high-demand situation (such as a busy store), having a negative response may be more likely due to later rebound effects. In support of this idea, field research has consistently shown that employees who report higher levels of expression modulation (measured as emotional dissonance or surface acting) reported more stress and burnout (Abraham, 1998; Adelmann, 1995; Brotheridge & Grandey, in press; Côté & Morgan, 2000; Grandey, 2000b; Morris & Feldman, 1997; Pugliesi, 1999), including non-self-reported measures of coronary heart disease risk factors (Härenstam, Theorell, & Kaijser, 2000).

Not only has faking been found to be stressful, but it may be detrimental to organizational goals as well. Early work on faking emotions suggested that people could discern an authentic smile, called a Duchenne smile, from a faked one, due to certain muscles around the eye (Ekman, 1992). Field research has supported that faking emotions is not only reported as stressful by employees, but also as less effective based on coworker ratings of affective displays toward customers (Grandey, in press). Lab research has found that recall memory and problem-solving ability were impaired when participants were told to hide from view evoked emotions like sadness and disgust (Baumeister, Bratslavsky, Muraven, & Tice, 1998;

Richards & Gross, 1999). Suppressing emotions requires resources that are then not available for other tasks and may have the ironic effect of thinking about the situation even more (Baumeister et al., 1998; Baumeister et al., 1994; Wegner, 1994); this could certainly have costs for employee interactions with customers. Thus, faking positive emotions and hiding negative emotions, forms of expression modulation in the service setting have detrimental outcomes for the organization and the employee.

Overview of Emotion Regulation

One descriptive study provides evidence of the use of all of the above regulation tactics in a customer service setting. Bailey and McCollough (2000) obtained descriptions from employees about how they coped with difficult customers. Responses included leaving the work floor (situation selection), thinking of something funny (attention deployment), realizing some people are never happy no matter what (cognitive change), and trying to stay calm and taking deep breaths (response modulation). These qualitative findings are supportive of how work events may create more emotional labor and how employees may use externally focused or internally focused tactics to regulate emotions. Obviously, some are counter to desirable customer service dimensions, such as situation selection resulting in a lack of availability (Parasuraman et al., 1985). In addition, laboratory and field studies that have focused on the use of response-focused regulation, such as suppression and faking, have found detrimental health and performance effects for the employee and the organization. In response to unexpected negative events, response modulation may be the only approach that is used, although externally and internally focused regulation may be used with the next customers in order to cope with the first event. This "spiral of incivility" (Anderson & Pearson, 1999) needs to be broken by effective emotion regulation.

The question then is, Does internally focused emotion regulation have similar costs? Does putting resources into attentional deployment or cognitive appraisal diminish resources from the self or the work performance? This is less well known. Research on the effects of emotion regulation in work settings, or with cognitive performance outcomes in laboratory settings, is slowly emerging.

Emotion regulation strategies such as engaging in diversionary tactics (attentional deployment) were effective with teachers in terms of mood regulation (Totterdell & Parkinson, 1999), although work outcomes were not assessed.

One such outcome of interest is burnout. In an unpublished pilot study by the first author, 111 part-time working students rated the extent to which they did emotion regulation tactics in response to a negative emotional situation at work, such as an angry customer. Although all of the tactics were reported being used an average of "sometimes," the frequency of response-focused emotional regulation (faking) was independent of the levels reported of positive reappraisal, distraction, or seeking social support. More interesting, this response-focused emotion regulation related positively to emotional exhaustion, while the other forms of regulation did not.

This result is consistent with research using other work samples. Modifying internal states is less detrimental than high levels of faking expressions, and in fact doing this deeper, more internal regulation may be a predictor of a sense of personal accomplishment (Brotheridge & Grandey, in press). This effect is borne out in the service recovery literature, showing that when employees handle a difficult situation or angry customer successfully (which includes *not* showing their own frustration), this can result in a very positive customer experience (Bitner, Booms, & Tetreault, 1990). Similarly, this semantic distinction between requiring positive expressions versus negative suppression is consistent with other emotion researchers who have used these as framing techniques to create motivational tendencies (Crowe & Higgins, 1997). Research on emotional labor needs to consider these different emotional demands separately.

Implications of Emotion Regulation Perspective for Customer Service

AET suggests that ongoing emotional events that have negative affective reactions may have short-term effects on affect-driven behaviors such as customer service encounters and long-term effects on work attitudes and withdrawal behaviors (Weiss & Cropanzano, 1996). A chronic lack of fit between display rules and personal style, or an acute lack of fit between display rules and affective reactions to work, may have such costs as employee stress and poor customer service. Thus, the guiding framework shown in Figure 8.1, which identifies causes of these mismatches and ways to regulate oneself effectively when mismatches occur, suggests implications for human resource processes. In Chapter Ten of this volume, Ashforth and Saks discuss the broader organizational context and implications of emotion regulation within that context. In this chapter, we have focused on customer service contexts and coping with dissonant emotions in particular. Within that focus, effective emotion regulation is regulation where employees choose and modify their situations, monitor and adjust their cognitions, and respond appropriately to customers in ways that do not result in dissonance and stress for extended periods of time. Although much empirical research is still needed before work interventions should be adopted, the following implications are suggested.

Selection

At the entry level, person-job fit is needed such that the individual's natural emotional and expressive style matches the display rules of the job (Arvey et al., 1998). Although positive affectivity has been shown to have positive impact on helping behaviors, managerial potential, and sales performance (George & Bettenhausen, 1990; Isen & Baron, 1991; Staw & Barsade, 1993; Staw et al., 1994), other research suggests that those who report intensely high positive affect may also be more reactive to negative stimuli (Diener, Colvin, Pavot, & Allman, 1991; Larsen & Diener, 1987). This idea of affect intensity suggests that seeking employees high in positive affectivity may not be the best approach for customer service representatives because they may also react strongly to negative affective events (see Chapter Three, this volume, by Larsen, Diener, and Lucas). The use of personality dimensions from the Big Five dimensions of personality, which include affectively loaded dimensions such as agreeableness and emotional stability, has also been found to predict service performance (Hogan, Hogan, & Busch, 1984; Mount, Barrick, & Stewart, 1998). Other variables such as positive and negative expressivity and emotional frustration to work events are being pursued (Pugh, 2001; Steel et al., 1999), and may provide information beyond the Big Five dimensions (Binning &

Adorno, 2001). Applications of these issues may involve validating and using selection tools that account for such individual differences, as reviewed in Arvey et al. (1998) and Grandey (2000). The selection process should also provide realistic job previews about display rules and affective events. Realistic job previews may help potential employees to practice self-selection as an emotion regulation strategy by selecting themselves into jobs appropriate for their emotional skills and minimizing potential emotional dissonance.

Training

As Bitner et al. (1990) stated, "Exemplary firms understand that managing the service encounter involves more than training employees to say 'have a nice day'" (p. 71). Service marketing research has suggested that employees be trained in recognizing how best to respond to customers in ways that will result in customer satisfaction (Blodgett et al., 1997). Because faked expressions are detrimental, employees need to learn how to respond to customers with empathy, even when the customer is angry or upset. Hochschild (1983) talked about the detriment of turning feelings into a commodity when organizations train workers to engage in deeper-level emotion regulation. But recent research on emotional intelligence and emotion regulation also suggests that employees can learn how to modify their emotional responses at work for both personal and organizational benefit (Goleman, 1995). A recent study by Totterdell and Parkinson (1999) demonstrated that teachers could be trained to be aware of their coping styles and to modify their style of coping in order to alter their mood at work. Such findings could be applied to the service setting if employers were willing to invest the resources in these front-line workers. For example, training materials such as videotapes and role playing could be developed that not only show appropriate interactions with customers, but how employees can regulate themselves in that encounter without losing their own sense of self in the process.

Policy and Structural Change

Is management aware of what events are creating dissonant emotional reactions in employees on the front line? Given the potential of an incivility spiral, whereby employees may carry their sense of unjust treatment and anger with them until it escalates into work-place aggression (Andersson & Pearson, 1999), employers may be moved to recognize such situations and attempt to change them. If events are occurring due to customer situations, management may want to decrease the negative-inducing events through policies that give employees the power to respond appropriately to complaining customers. Service representatives and the organization benefit from a system that provides employees with the resources and autonomy to offer more than an apology to difficult customers (Bitner, Booms, & Mohr, 1994; Bitner et al., 1990; Levesque & McDougall, 2000). Even more revolutionary would be giving the employees the auton-omy to respond to rude customers as deemed appropriate, rather than blindly demanding friendly smiles despite sexual harassment or other incivility, as seen in recent events (Curtis, 1998). Research has also supported the value of supportive policies and work climate in order to decrease stress responses and improve affective states (Cropanzano et al., 1997; Eisenburger, Huntington, Hutchison, & Sowa, 1986; Howes, Cropanzano, Grandey, & Mohler, 2000).

Conclusion

Current directions in the economy and I/O research provide a ripe environment to study emotion regulation in customer service settings. As service orientation becomes important for almost any industry to maintain viability, recognition of the difficulties facing service representatives in maintaining the customer's positive im-pression needs to be recognized. I/O psychology has also begun to embrace emotions and emotional regulation as acceptable top-ics of study, as shown by recent conference symposia, books, and journal articles. In settings such as customer service, understand-ing the events that create negative emotions and the ways in which it is effective to cope with these emotions is crucial for both service performance and employee well-being.

More broadly, these emotion regulation skills may help in many life domains beyond service settings. One theoretical piece proposed that people who have service jobs, who are more likely to be women, may also be more likely to manage their own and others' emotions at home. This work-nonwork crossover effect has the potential for certain people to experience higher stress but also to be more skilled at such regulation (Wharton & Erickson, 1993).

If individuals were trained to regulate their emotions in the work setting, perhaps this would result in positive spillover between work and home. In turn, social relationships at work and at home could be aided by one's skill at managing one's emotions, as suggested by the emotional intelligence literature (Goleman, 1995; Mayer & Salovey, 1995). Rather than suppressing or ignoring emotional actions in the workplace, as was previously encouraged (Ashforth & Humphrey, 1995), emotion regulation can be integrated into our thinking about effective work (and life) functioning.

References

Abraham, R. (1998). Emotional dissonance in organizations: Antecedents, consequences, and moderators. *Genetic, Social, and General Psychology Monographs, 124,* 229–246.

Adams, J. S. (1965). Inequity in social exchange. In L. Berkowitz (Ed.), *Advances in experimental social psychology* (pp. 267–299). Orlando, FL: Academic Press.

Adelmann, P. K. (1995). Emotional labor as a potential source of job stress. In S. L. Sauter & L. R Murphy (Eds.). *Organizational risk factors for job stress.* Washington, DC: American Psychological Association.

Adelmann, P. K., & Zajonc, R. B. (1989). Facial efference and the experience of emotion. *Annual Review of Psychology, 40,* 249–280.

Albrecht, K., & Zemke, R. (1985). *Service America! Doing business in the new economy.* Homewood, IL: Dow Jones-Irwin.

Alexander, C. N., Langer, E. J., Newman, R. I., Chandler, H. M., & Davies, J. L. (1989). Transcendental meditation, mindfulness, and longevity: An experimental study with the elderly. *Journal of Personality and Social Psychology, 57,* 950–964.

Andersson, L. M., & Pearson, C. M. (1999). Tit for tat? The spiraling effect of incivility in the workplace. *Academy of Management Review, 24,* 452–471.

Aquino, K., Lewis, M., & Bradfield, M. (1999). Justice constructs, negative affectivity, and employee deviance: A proposed model and empirical test. *Journal of Organizational Behavior, 20,* 1073–1091.

Arvey, R. D., Renz, G. L., & Watson, W. W. (1998). Emotionality and job performance: Implications for personnel selection. *Research in Personnel and Human Resources Management, 16,* 103–147.

Ashforth, B. E., & Humphrey, R. H. (1995). Emotion in the workplace: A reappraisal. *Human Relations, 48,* 97–125.

Averill, J. R. (1983). Studies on anger and aggression: Implications for a theory of emotion. *American Psychologist, 38,* 1145–1160.

Avolio, B. J., Howell, J. M., & Sosik, J. J. (1999). A funny thing happened on the way to the bottom line: Humor as a moderator of leadership style effects. *Academy of Management Journal, 42,* 219–227.

Bailey, J. J., & McCollough, M. A. (2000). Emotional labor and the difficult customer: Coping strategies of service agents and organizational consequences. *Journal of Professional Services Marketing, 20,* 51–72.

Basch, J., & Fisher, C. D. (2000). Affective events-emotions matrix: A classification of work events and associated emotions. In N. Ashkanasy, C. Härtel, & W. Zerbe (Eds.), *Emotions in the workplace: Research, theory, and practice* (pp. 36–48). Westport, CT: Quorum Books.

Baumeister, R., Bratslavsky, E., Muraven, M., & Tice, D. (1998). Ego depletion: Is the active self a limited resource? *Journal of Personality and Social Psychology, 74,* 1252–1265.

Baumeister, R. F., Heatherton, T. F., & Tice, D. M. (1994). *Losing control: How and why people fail at self-regulation.* Orlando, FL: Academic Press.

Billings, A. G., & Moos, R. H. (1984). Coping, stress and social resources among adults with unipolar depression. *Journal of Personality and Social Psychology, 46,* 877–891.

Binning, J. F., & Adorno, A. J. (2001). *Personality and emotional labor as predictors of turnover in call center customer service.* Paper presented at the Sixteenth Annual Meeting of the Society for Industrial and Organizational Psychology, San Diego, CA.

Bitner, M. J., Booms, B. H., & Mohr, L. A. (1994). Critical service encounters: The employee's viewpoint. *Journal of Marketing, 58,* 95–106.

Bitner, M., Booms, B. H., & Tetrault, M. S. (1990). The service encounter: Diagnosing favorable and unfavorable incidents. *Journal of Marketing, 54,* 71–84.

Blodgett, J. G., Hill, D. J., & Tax, S. S. (1997). The effects of distributive, procedural and interactional justice on postcomplaint behavior. *Journal of Retailing, 73,* 185–210.

Borman, W. C., & Motowidlo, S. J. (1993). Expanding the criterion domain to include elements of contextual performance. In N. Schmitt & W. C. Borman (Eds.), *Personnel selection in organizations.* San Francisco: Jossey-Bass.

Brotheridge, C. M., & Grandey, A. (in press). Emotional labor and burnout: Merging two literatures on "people work." *Journal of Vocational Behavior.*

Carver, C. S., Scheier, M. F., & Weintraub J. K. (1989). Assessing coping strategies: A theoretically based approach. *Journal of Personality and Social Psychology, 56,* 267–283.

Cordes, C. L., Dougherty, T. W., & Blum, M. (1997). Patterns of burnout among managers and professionals: A comparison of models. *Journal of Organizational Behavior, 18,* 685–701.

Cortina, L. M., Magley, V. J., Williams, J. H., & Langhout, R. D. (2001). Incivility in the workplace: Incidence and impact. *Journal of Occupational Health Psychology, 6,* 64–80.

Côté, S., & Morgan, L. M. (2001, August). *Put on a happy face! Stress implications of emotional labor at work.* Paper presented at the annual meeting of the Academy of Management, Toronto, Canada.

Cropanzano, R., & Greenberg, J. (1997). Progress in organizational justice: Tunneling through the maze. In C. L. Cooper & I. T. Robertson (Eds.), *International review of industrial and organizational psychology* (Vol. 12, pp. 317–372). New York: Wiley.

Cropanzano, R., Howes, J., Grandey, A., & Toth, P. (1997). The relationship of organizational politics and support to work behaviors, attitudes, and stress. *Journal of Organizational Behavior, 18,* 159–180.

Cropanzano, R., Weiss, H. M., Suckow, K., & Grandey, A. (2000). Doing justice to workplace emotion. In N. Ashkanasy, C. Härtel, & W. Zerbe (Eds.), *Emotions in the workplace: Research, theory, and practice.* Westport, CT: Quorum Books.

Crowe, E., & Higgins, E. T. (1997). Regulatory focus and strategic inclinations: Promotion and prevention in decision-making. *Organizational Behavior and Human Decision Processes, 69,* 117–132.

Curtis, K. (1998, September 3). Smiley face out of place at Safeway, workers say. *Oregonian,* p. B-4.

Diener, E., Colvin, R., Pavot, W., & Allman, A. (1991). The psychic costs of intense positive affect. *Journal of Personality and Social Psychology, 61,* 492–503.

Diener, E., Larsen, R., & Emmons, R. (1984). Person × situation interactions: Choice of situations and congruence response models. *Journal of Personality and Social Psychology, 47,* 580–592.

Edwards, J. (1991). Person-job fit: A conceptual integration, literature review, and methodological critique. In C. L. Cooper & I. T. Robertson (Eds.), *International review of industrial and organizational psychology* (Vol. 6, pp. 283–357). New York: Wiley.

Ekman, P. (1992). Facial expressions of emotion: New findings, new questions. *Psychological Science, 3,* 34–38.

Ekman, P., & Friesen, W. V. (1975). *Unmasking the face: A guide to recognizing emotions from facial clues.* Upper Saddle River, NJ: Prentice-Hall.

Eisenburger, R., Huntington, R., Hutchison, R., & Sowa, D. (1986). Perceived organizational support. *Journal of Applied Psychology, 71,* 500–507.

Erickson, R. J., & Wharton, A. S. (1997). Inauthenticity and depression: Assessing the consequences of interactive service work. *Work and Occupations, 24,* 188–213.

Fiske, S. T., & Taylor, S. E. (1991). *Social cognition* (2nd ed.). New York: McGraw-Hill.

Fitness, J. (2000). Anger in the workplace: An emotion script approach to anger episodes between workers and their superiors, co-workers and subordinates. *Journal of Organizational Behavior, 21,* 147–162.

Folkman, S., & Lazarus, R. S. (1985). If it changes it must be a process: Study of emotion and coping during three stages of a college examination. *Journal of Personality and Social Psychology, 48,* 150–170.

Folkman, S., & Lazarus, R. S. (1988). Coping as a mediator of emotion. *Journal of Personality and Social Psychology, 54,* 466–475.

Folkman, S., & Lazarus, R. S. (1991). Coping and emotion. In A. Monat & R. S. Lazarus, et al. (Eds.), *Stress and coping: An anthology* (3rd ed., pp. 207–227). New York: Columbia University Press.

Folkman, S., Lazarus, R. S., Gruen, R. J., & DeLongis, A. (1986). Appraisal, coping, health status, and psychological symptoms. *Journal of Personality and Social Psychology, 50,* 571–579.

Frijda, N. H. (1988). The laws of emotion. *American Psychologist, 43,* 349–358.

Frijda, N. H. (1993). Moods, emotion episodes, and emotions. In M. Lewis & I. M. Haviland (Eds.), *Handbook of emotions* (pp. 381–403). New York: Guilford Press.

Frone, M. R. (2000). Interpersonal conflict at work and psychological outcomes: Testing a model among young workers. *Journal of Occupational Health Psychology, 5,* 246–255.

Fuller, L., & Smith, V. (1996). Consumers' reports: Management by customers in a changing economy. In C. L. Macdonald & C. Sirianni (Eds.), *Working in the service society* (pp. 29–49). Philadelphia: Temple University Press.

George, J. M. (1991). State or trait: Effects of positive mood on prosocial behaviors at work. *Journal of Applied Psychology, 76,* 299–307.

George, J. M. (1996). Trait and state affect. In K. R. Murphy (Ed.), *Individual differences and behavior in organizations* (pp. 145–171). San Francisco: Jossey-Bass.

George, J. M., and Bettenhausen, K. (1990). Understanding prosocial behavior, sales performance, and turnover: A group level analysis in a service context. *Journal of Applied Psychology, 75,* 698–709.

George, J. M., & Brief, A. P. (1996). Motivational agendas in the workplace: The effects of feelings on focus of attention and work motivation. In B. M. Staw & L. L. Cummings (Eds.), *Research in organizational behavior* (Vol. 18, pp. 75–109). Greenwich, CT: JAI Press.

Gibson, D. E. (1997). The struggle for reason: The sociology of emotions in organizations. *Social Perspectives on Emotion, 4,* 211–256.

Goffman, E. (1959). *Presentation of self in everyday life*. New York: Overlook Press.

Goleman, D. (1995). *Emotional intelligence*. New York: Bantam Books.

Grandey, A. (2000). Emotion regulation in the workplace: A new way to conceptualize emotional labor. *Journal of Occupational Health Psychology, 5*, 95–110.

Grandey, A. (in press). When the "show must go on": Surface and deep acting as determinants of emotional exhaustion and peer-rated service delivery. *Academy of Management Journal.*

Grandey, A., Tam, A., & Brauburger, A. (in press). Affective events at work: A diary study of part-time workers. *Motivation and Emotion.*

Gross, J. (1998a). Antecedent- and response-focused emotion regulation: Divergent consequences for experience, expression, and physiology. *Journal of Personality and Social Psychology, 74*, 224–237.

Gross, J. (1998b). The emerging field of emotion regulation: An integrative review. *Review of General Psychology, 2*, 271–299.

Gross, J., & Levenson, R. (1997). Hiding feelings: The acute effects of inhibiting negative and positive emotions. *Journal of Abnormal Psychology, 106*, 95–103.

Gutek, B. A., Bhappu, A. D., Liao-Troth, M. A., & Cherry, B. (1999). Distinguishing between service relationships and encounters. *Journal of Applied Psychology, 84*, 218–233.

Gutek, B. A., Cherry, B., Bhappu, A. D., Schneider, S., & Woolf, L. (2000). Features of service relationships and encounters. *Work and Occupations, 27*, 319–352.

Hackman, J. R., & Oldham, G. R. (1976). Motivation through the design of work: Test of a theory. *Organizational Behavior and Human Performance, 16*, 250–279.

Härenstam, A., Theorell, T., & Kaijser, L. (2000). Coping with anger-provoking situations, psychosocial working conditions, and ECG-detected signs of coronary heart disease. *Journal of Occupational Health Psychology, 5*, 191–203.

Hatfield, E., Cacioppo, J., & Rapson, R. L. (1994). *Emotional contagion*. Cambridge: Cambridge University Press.

Headey, B., & Wearing, A. J. (1990). Subjective well-being and coping with adversity. *Social Indicators Research, 22*, 327–349.

Hepburn, C. G., Loughlin, C. A., & Barling, J. (1997). Coping with chronic work stress. In B. H. Gottlieb (Ed.), *Coping with chronic stress* (pp. 343–366). New York: Plenum Press.

Hobfoll, S. E. (1989). Conservation of resources: A new attempt at conceptualizing stress. *American Psychologist, 44*, 513–524.

Hochschild, A. R. (1979). Emotion work, feeling rules, and social structure. *American Journal of Sociology, 85*, 551–575.

Hochschild, A. R. (1983). *The managed heart: Commercialization of human feeling.* Berkeley: University of California Press.

Hogan, J., Hogan, R., & Busch, C. (1984). How to measure service orientation. *Journal of Applied Psychology, 69,* 167–173.

Howes, J., Cropanzano, R., Grandey, A., & Mohler, C. (2000). Who is supporting whom? Quality team effectiveness and perceived organizational support. *Journal of Quality Management, 5,* 207–223.

Isen, A. M., & Baron, R. A. (1991). Positive affect as a factor in organizational behavior. In L. L. Cummings & B. M. Staw (Eds.), *Research in organizational behavior* (Vol. 13, pp. 1–53). Greenwich, CT: JAI Press.

Ivancevich, J. M., Matteson, M. T., Freedman, S. M., & Phillips, J. S. (1990). Worksite stress management interventions. *American Psychologist, 45,* 252–261.

Jones, R. G., & Best, R. G. (1995). *A further examination of the nature and impact of emotional work requirements on individuals and organizations.* Paper presented at the annual meeting of the Academy of Management, Vancouver, B.C.

Kelley, S. W., & Hoffman, K. D. (1997). An investigation of positive affect, prosocial behaviors, and service quality. *Journal of Retailing, 73,* 407–427.

Kurek, K. E., Le, B., & Weiss, H. M. (2001). *Studying affective climates using web-based experience-sampling methods.* Paper presented at the Sixteenth Annual Conference of the Society for Industrial and Organizational Psychology, San Diego, CA.

Larsen, R., & Diener, E. (1987). Affect intensity as an individual difference characteristic: A review. *Journal of Research in Personality, 21,* 1–39.

Lazarus, R. S. (1991). Progress on a cognitive-motivational-relational theory of emotion. *American Psychologist, 46,* 819–834.

Lazarus, R. S., & Alfert, E. (1964). Short-circuiting of threat by experimentally altering cognitive appraisal. *Journal of Abnormal and Social Psychology, 69,* 195–205.

Lazarus, R. S., & Folkman, S. (1984). *Stress, appraisal, and coping.* New York: Springer.

Leidner, R. (1996). Rethinking questions of control: Lessons from McDonald's. In C. L. Macdonald & C. Sirianni (Eds.), *Working in the service society* (pp. 29–49). Philadelphia: Temple University Press.

Levesque, T. J., & McDougall, G. H. (2000). Service problems and recovery strategies: An experiment. *Canadian Journal of Administrative Sciences, 17,* 20–37.

Maslach, C. (1978). The client role in staff burn-out. *Journal of Social Issues, 34,* 111–124.

Mayer, J. D., & Salovey, P. (1995). Emotional intelligence and the construction and regulation of feelings. *Applied and Preventive Psychology, 4,* 197–208.

Morris, J. A., & Feldman, D. C. (1996). The dimensions, antecedents, and consequences of emotional labor. *Academy of Management Review, 21,* 986–1010.

Morris, J. A., & Feldman, D. C. (1997). Managing emotions in the workplace. *Journal of Managerial Issues, 9,* 257–274.

Morrison, E. W. (1994). Role definition and organizational citizenship behaviors: The importance of the employee's perspective. *Academy of Management Journal, 37,* 1543–1567.

Mount, M. K., Barrick, M. R., & Stewart, G. L. (1998). Five-factor model of personality and performance in jobs involving interpersonal interactions. *Human Performance, 11,* 145–165.

Offermann, L. R., & Gowing, M. K. (1990). Organizations of the future: Changes and challenges. *American Psychologist, 45,* 95–108.

Organ, D. W. (1997). Organizational citizenship behavior: It's construct clean-up time. *Human Performance, 10,* 85–97.

Parasuraman, A., Zeithaml, V. A., & Berry, L. L. (1985). A conceptual model of service quality and its implications for future research. *Journal of Marketing, 49,* 41–50.

Parkinson, B. (1991). Emotional stylists: Strategies of expressive management among trainee hairdressers. *Cognition and Emotion, 5,* 419–434.

Parkinson, B., & Totterdell, P. (1999). Classifying affect-regulation strategies. *Cognition and Emotion, 13,* 277–303.

Parrish, M. M., & Quinn, P. (1999). Laughing your way to peace of mind: How a little humor helps caregivers survive. *Clinical Social Work Journal, 27,* 203–211.

Peeters, M. C., Buunk, B. P., & Schaufeli, W. B. (1995). A micro-analytic exploration of the cognitive appraisal of daily stressful events at work: The role of controllability. *Anxiety, Stress, and Coping, 8,* 127–139.

Pennebaker, J. (1985). Traumatic experience and psychosomatic disease: Exploring the roles of behavioral inhibition, obsession, and confiding. *Canadian Psychology, 26,* 82–95.

Pugh, S. D. (2001). Service with a smile: Emotional contagion in the service encounter. *Academy of Management Journal, 44,* 1018–1027.

Pugliesi, K. (1999). The consequences of emotional labor: Effects on work stress, job satisfaction, and well-being. *Motivation and Emotion, 23,* 125–154.

Pugliesi, K., & Shook, S. L. (1997). Gender, jobs, and emotional labor in a complex organization. *Social Perspectives on Emotion, 4,* 283–316.

Rafaeli, A., & Sutton, R. I. (1987). Expression of emotion as part of the work role. *Academy of Management Journal, 12,* 23–37.

Repetti, R. L. (1992). Social withdrawal as a short-term coping response to daily stressors. In H. S. Friedman (Ed.), *Hostility, coping, and health* (pp. 151–165). Washington, DC: American Psychological Association.

Richards, J. M., & Gross, J. J. (1999). Composure at any cost? The cognitive consequences of emotion suppression. *Personality and Social Psychology Bulletin, 25,* 1033–1044.

Schaubroeck, J., & Jones, J. R. (2000). Antecedents of workplace emotional labor dimensions and moderators of their effects on physical symptoms. *Journal of Organizational Behavior, 21,* 163–183

Shiarella, A. H. (1999). *Conceptualizations of job behaviors: Do they match the contextual job performance domain?* Unpublished master's thesis, Colorado State University, Fort Collins.

Singh, J., Goolsby, J. R., & Rhoades, G. K. (1994). Behavioral and psychological consequences of boundary spanning burnout for customer service representatives. *Journal of Marketing Research, 16,* 558–569.

Skarlicki, D. P., & Folger, R. (1997). Retaliation in the workplace: The roles of distributive, procedural, and interactional justice. *Journal of Applied Psychology, 82,* 434–443.

Spector, P. E. (1998). A control theory of the job stress process. In C. L. Cooper (Ed.), *Theories of organizational stress* (pp. 153–169). New York: Oxford University Press.

Spector, P. E., & Jex, S. M. (1998). Development of four self-report measures of job stressors and strain: Interpersonal Conflict at Work Scale, Organizational Constraints Scale, Quantitative Workload Inventory, and Physical Symptoms Inventory. *Journal of Occupational Health Psychology, 3,* 356–367.

Staw, B. M., & Barsade, S. G. (1993). Affect and managerial performance: A test of the sadder-but-wiser vs. happier-and-smarter hypotheses. *Administrative Science Quarterly, 38,* 304–331.

Staw, B. M., Sutton, R. I., & Pelled, L. H. (1994). Employee positive emotion and favorable outcomes at the workplace. *Organization Science, 5,* 51–71.

Steel, P., Arvey, R., & Kyllonen, P. (1999). *Factor structure of emotional expressiveness: Genuine vs. masked emotions.* Paper presented at the annual meeting of the Society of Industrial and Organizational Psychologists, Atlanta, GA.

Stemmler, G. (1997). Selective activation of traits: Boundary conditions for the activation of anger. *Personality and Individual Differences, 22,* 213–233.

Stepper, S., & Strack, F. (1993). Proprioceptive determinants of emotional and nonemotional feelings. *Journal of Personality and Social Psychology, 64,* 211–220.

Sutton, R. I. (1991). Maintaining norms about expressed emotions: The case of bill collectors. *Administrative Science Quarterly, 36,* 245–268.

Tax, S. S., Brown, S. W., & Chandrashekaran, M. (1998). Customer evaluations of service complaint experiences: Implications for relationship marketing. *Journal of Marketing, 62,* 60–76.

Terry, D. J., Tonge, L., & Callan, V. J. (1995). Employee adjustment to stress: The role of coping resources, situational factors, and coping responses. *Anxiety, Stress, and Coping, 8,* 1–24.

Tidd, K. L., & Lockhard, J. S. (1978). Monetary significance of the affiliative smile: A case for reciprocal altruism. *Bulletin of the Psychonomic Society, 11,* 344–346.

Totterdell, P., & Parkinson, B. (1999). Use and effectiveness of self-regulation strategies for improving mood in a group of trainee teachers. *Journal of Occupational Health Psychology, 4,* 219–232.

Van Maanen, J., & Kunda, G. (1989). Real feelings: Emotional expression and organizational culture. In L. L. Cummings & B. M. Staw (Eds.), *Research in organizational behavior* (Vol. 11, pp. 43–103). Greenwich, CT: JAI Press.

Wegener, D. T., & Petty, R. E. (1996). Effects of mood on persuasion processes: Enhancing, reducing, and biasing scrutiny of attitude-relevant information. In L. L. Martin & A. Tesseret (Eds.), *Striving and feeling: Interactions among goals, affect, and self-regulation* (pp. 329–362). Hillsdale, NJ: Erlbaum.

Wegner, D. M. (1994). Ironic processes of mental control. *Psychological Review, 101,* 34–52.

Weiss, H., & Cropanzano, R. (1996). An affective events approach to job satisfaction. In B. M. Staw & L.L. Cummings (Eds.), *Research in organizational behavior* (Vol. 18, pp. 1–74). Greenwich, CT: JAI Press.

Weiss, H., Suckow, K., & Cropanzano, R. (1999). Effects of justice conditions on discrete emotions. *Journal of Applied Psychology, 84,* 786–794.

Wenzlaff, R., & Bates, D. E. (2000). The relative efficacy of concentration and suppression strategies of mental control. *Personality and Social Psychology Bulletin, 26,* 1200–1212.

Wharton, A. S. (1993). The affective consequences of service work. *Work and Occupations, 20,* 205–232.

Wharton, A. S., & Erickson, R. J. (1993). Managing emotions on the job and at home: Understanding the consequences of multiple emotional roles. *Academy of Management Review, 18,* 457–486.

CHAPTER 9

Courage and Work

Breaking Routines to Improve Performance

Monica C. Worline
Amy Wrzesniewski
Anat Rafaeli

Organizations are social systems designed to preserve themselves and their status quo. The pervasive influence of norms provides a ready means of control over what people think, say, and do (Hackman, 1992; Gersick & Hackman, 1990). Routines for doing work proscribe the possibilities for accomplishment (Bourdieu, 1990; Cyert & March, 1963; March & Simon, 1958; Nelson & Winter, 1982). Roles create strong scripts for how people behave toward one another (Goffman, 1959). Divisions of labor give rise to divisions of power that enforce subtle rules for relating to one another and to work (Sandelands, 2001; Tiedens, 2000). Expectations for appropriate behavior are formed from the ongoing pattern of routines, norms, roles, and scripts (Bourdieu, 1990; Cohen & Bacdayan, 1994). Given that organizational systems are designed on such pervasive and scripted control, where does courage fit into organizational life? Is courage a meaningful concept in work performance?

In his indictment of the morality of managerial cultures, Jackall (1988) illuminated ways in which managers, dependent on an organization for their economic means and social stature, suppressed their personal morality and courage in the work context. In Jackall's portrait of organizations, managers rely on expectations, scripts, roles, and routines to sabotage the common good and preserve the status quo. All in all, when scholars think about organizations, they do not often think of them as places that can bring out the best in people. Yet as emotion researchers have begun to point out, organizations are sites of life, with all of its richness and variety (Ashkenasy, Hartel, & Zerbe 2000; Fineman, 1993, 2000). High-quality performance in organizations often requires people to be at their best. In this chapter, we argue that sustaining high-quality performance in organizational contexts requires employees to act with courage. Building from stories taken from over two hundred employees in the high-technology sector, we create a model of courage in organizations. We propose that courageous action in an organizational system results in changes in the enactment of agency in one's work, the connections between people in the workplace, and the collectively shared conception of the organization as a whole.

Defining Courage for Organization Studies

Courage has been the topic of centuries of philosophical debate, poetic treatment, and political treatise. Becker (1973) proposed that the whole development of social science was a clarification of human heroism, and Tillich (1952) wrote of courage that "few concepts are as useful for the analysis of the human situation" (p. 1). These centuries of writings, however, have not resolved some central questions about the definition of courage. Miller (2000) opens *The Mystery of Courage* with an illustrative quotation from a soldier's autobiography: "It is hard to be brave. It is hard to know what bravery is" (p. xiii). Courage has been most interesting to psychologists because of its intimate relationship with fear. William James thought of courage as energizing the will to allow people to face fear (Connell, 1997). In James's view, courage gave humanity the ability to persist against the unknown.

Although courage has not received much empirical attention in psychology since James, most psychologists have defined it as the ability to persist in spite of fear (Rachman, 1990). The notion of courage implicitly relies on the presence of danger, loss, risk, or potential injury. Without a sense of danger, risk, or vulnerability, there is no courage in an act; hence, we tend to think of courage together with the emotion of fear (Finfgeld, 1999; Shelp, 1984; Van Eynde, 1998). Fear is an emotional response to danger, risk, and vulnerability that theorists have proposed sparks a flight response (Frijda, 1986). Courage is valuable in that it allows us to dampen our immediate response to danger, halting the flight response in order to evaluate the appropriate course of action (Szagun & Schauble, 1997). A courageous person has a proper respect for fear and is able to act or persist in the face of fear (Pears, 1978; Walton, 1986; Yearley, 1990).

Shelp (1984) proposed an extended definition of courage that comes as close to a consensual definition as exists in the psychological, medical, and philosophical traditions: "Courage is the disposition to voluntarily act, perhaps fearfully, in a dangerous circumstance, where the relevant risks are reasonably appraised, in an effort to obtain or preserve some perceived good for oneself or others, recognizing that the desired perceived good may not be realized" (p. 354). Using the insights distilled in this definition, to understand an act or a person as courageous, we must take into account whether (1) free choice is involved in taking the action, (2) some sort of risk is present in the situation, (3) the risk has been adequately appraised, and (4) the action serves worthy aims. In this definition, courage is different from a "pure" emotional state because it must involve certain kinds of cognitive judgments. Szagun (1992) defines courage as an emotion-related mental construct that involves multifaceted emotional experience along with an understanding of risk taking. Szagun finds that by the age of eleven or twelve, children share a belief that something courageous must be somewhat reflective, freely chosen, and not automatic.

In accord with this definition, a courageous person must have a disposition to take risks (Shelp, 1984) yet must also overcome a disposition to take unconsidered risks (Yearley, 1990; Szagun & Schauble, 1997). In philosophy, Aquinas concluded that disregarding fear would hinder the development of courage because it would lead one into foolhardy situations (Yearley, 1990). Little empirical work addresses individual differences in courage due to the difficulty of creating and controlling courage in typical psychological studies. In a study comparing whistleblowers to people who do not object to organizational wrongdoing, Rothschild and Miethe (1999) find no significant individual differences between these groups. However, Rachman and his colleagues (Cox, Hallam, O'Connor, & Rachman, 1983; O'Connor, Hallam, & Rachman, 1985) found subtle evidence for physiological differences in the ability to suppress fear when they studied bomb disposal operators. Their studies showed that soldiers who had received medals of honor, when asked to undergo severe stress in a laboratory task, exhibited lower heart rates than did nondecorated soldiers (Cox et al., 1983; O'Connor et al., 1985). However, these physiological differences did not translate into behavioral differences in the laboratory situations, such that even under extreme stress, all of the bomb disposal operators performed their duties, although some of them were less physiologically aroused by the circumstances (Cox et al., 1983; O'Connor et al., 1985).

Because courage includes an emotional dimension accompanied by an aspect of judgment, scholars have imbued the concept with a moral quality. Goldberg and Simon (1982) portray courage as a "moral deed with an imperative aim" (p. 108). In everyday circumstances, people usually regard courage as "doing what is right," including confronting the status quo or opposing an unhealthy idea (Deutsch, 1961; Van Eynde, 1998; Walton, 1986). Empirical tests show that people perceive action toward worthy ends as more courageous than simply risky action (Szagun, 1992). Hence, people have a reluctance to designate a murderer as courageous, even when the murderer takes great risks to accomplish the crime (Shelp, 1984).

In developing a definition of courage that will adequately apply in the study of organizations, we suggest that it is important to consider the social embeddedness of people's activity, including the purposes of their actions. This is a slightly different approach from that taken by scholars of ethics, where courage is purely a moral quality (Pybus, 1991). Walton (1986) defines courage as "an excellence of practical action," indicating that in everyday settings, courage must be considered in the light of the ordinary activities in which people are engaged. In this chapter, we adopt Walton's approach, regarding as courageous the kinds of everyday work activities that are featured in stories we collected from people in organizations. Walton emphasizes that courage is a valued quality because in the midst of uncertainty, courageousness puts an emphasis on judgment and helps to tip a situation toward worthy ends. Organizational scholars have pointed out that managing uncertainty is a prime consideration in organizational processes (Galbraith, 1973), making this approach to courage highly applicable in studies of organization.

When we address courage in organizational settings, we are addressing everyday action that involves risk, has been freely chosen, demonstrates considered assessment of consequences, and pursues excellence within the circumstances where it occurs. One implication of such a definition is that courageous action will stand out from the routine flow of activity in an organization. Courageous activity, being freely chosen, worthy, practical action in the face of risk, is likely to call for effortful interruption of the scripts, norms, roles, and routines that pattern organizational life. This kind of exceptional action is likely to trigger strong emotions in organizational settings (Weiss & Cropanzano, 1996). We propose that emotions are crucial mediating factors between courageous activity and the transformation of agency at work, connections between people, and the organization as a whole.

Courageous Actors Influence Observers

In order to explore courage in the workplace, we rely on an analysis of accounts that were solicited from 201 managers and employees in high-technology companies who were attending training sessions on critical thinking skills. At the beginning of each training session, a one-page questionnaire was given to the participants that contained the following four open-ended questions, modeled after Szagun and Schauble's study (1997) of the experience of courage:

1. Have you ever seen courage at work? If yes, please tell a story about what happened.
2. What made the event or situation seem courageous to you?
3. How did you feel during the event or situation?
4. Did anything in your work change as a result of the event or situation you described?

In response to these open-ended questions, we received 184 stories about events in the workplace that our participants would identify as courageous in some way. Of these stories, 83 percent are interpersonal, in the sense that they were stories about someone else's action; 17 percent were intrapersonal, with a focus on action undertaken by the storyteller. The high percentage of people who offered stories about other people in their organization calls up a question about the unit of analysis at which to examine courage in organizations. Although we were careful to design questions and solicit stories in such a way that people could write about themselves or about others, the vast majority of responses were stories about another person. This high percentage may be due to a response bias, in that people are reluctant to identify themselves as having qualities such as courage. We hold this possibility open and do not debate the fact that people can be courageous on their own. However, we suggest that this trend illuminates something of the nature of courage in organizations. Because, by its definition, courage requires judgment, we propose that courage is often easier to discern in another than in oneself. Discerning courageous activity within oneself draws on what William James (1909) called "the knower and the known" (see Greenwald & Breckler, 1985). James poetically named the unique human ability to present the self to the self (Greenwald & Breckler, 1985) or, in other words, to be both actor and observer at the same time. We suggest that this quality is at the heart of courage because it is the heart of self-reflexive judgment and the ability to persist in the face of fear.

In order for courage to be present, a courageous actor and an influenced observer must be present—even within the same person. Courage requires engaging in a difficult or dangerous situation while actively assessing the risks and consequences. Although this analysis seems to require that we treat courage as a dyadic phenomenon, this is not necessarily so. Psychology has long understood people as capable of and motivated by monitoring their own behavior (Carver & Scheier, 1990; Carver, Sutton, & Scheier, 2000; Higgins, 1997). Carver and Scheier (1990, 1998) and others in psychology have proposed that human experience is largely powered by goals toward which people progress, along with a constant self-regulation system that checks current states in relation to goal-determined reference values. According to this theory, people's rate of progress toward goals is monitored through the self-regulation system as well, and the rate of progress toward goals gives rise to affect (Carver & Scheier, 1990, 1998). At the individual level, Carver and Scheier (1990, 1998) propose a dynamic system in which cognition, emotion, and action are intertwined to mutually constitute performance.

We propose an analogous regulation system operating at a social level, with cognition, emotion, and action intertwined to mutually constitute work performance. As depicted in Figure 9.1, our model takes into account that people in organizations motivate and regulate their behavior based in part on the norms, roles, scripts, and routines that come to be taken for granted in the organization. When people encounter behavior that is discrepant from the taken-for-granted norms, roles, scripts, and routines, they emotionally sense and cognitively monitor features of the exceptional action to determine progress toward worthy goals and feelings and values that are important in the organization (Brissett & Edgley, 1990; Gardner & Avolio, 1998; Grove & Fisk, 1989; Rosen, 1985). This monitoring process is part of ascribing courage to exceptional organizational activity, as people make inferences about the risk involved, the amount of free choice available to the actor, and the quality of judgment that motivates the behavior, along with the purposes of the exceptional action.

In Carver and Scheier's (1990) psychological model, it is the movement toward a goal, and the speed of that movement, that determine affective response. In developing a dynamic model of work performance that weaves threads of cognition, emotion, and action into a social fabric, it is important to remind ourselves that workplace sense-making processes are both emotional and cognitive, created through work cultures, routines, values, and interactions that are not solely individual (Bartel & Saavedra, 2000; Huy, 1999; Katz, 1999; Salancik & Pfeffer, 1978; Rafaeli & Worline, 2001;

**Figure 9.1. Courageous Activity Disrupts
Norms and Sparks Sense-Making.**

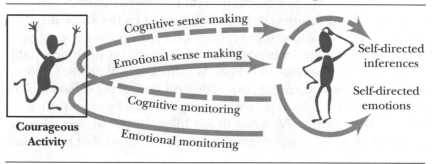

Weick, 1995). Thus, in our model, people use their emotional and cognitive presence to monitor the social world, and violations of norms, roles, scripts, or routines prompt sense-making processes regarding meaning, as well as progress and speed toward desired goals.

Since discerning courage requires an ability to be both actor and observer, it is not surprising that we can more readily see courage in others than we can in ourselves. Especially in organizations, where action is at a premium, people can easily observe others' performances (Brissett & Edgley, 1990; Gardner & Avolio, 1998; Giacalone & Rosenfeld, 1989; Goffman, 1959; Rosen, 1985; Rosenfeld, Giacalone, & Riordan, 1995). The stories of courage that we gathered demonstrate that people feel strong emotion when behavior is outside normative bounds and use their inferences about levels of risk, free choice, quality of judgment, and worth of the activity to determine whether exceptional action is courageous. The combination of emotional response and cognitive inference about exceptional activity in the organization creates the possibility for changes in self-directed thoughts and feelings. The dynamics described here and depicted in Figure 9.1 provide the basis for our proposition that courage in organizations transforms people's enactment of agency in their work, their connections with others in the organization, and their sense of the organization as a whole.

Courage Changes the Possibilities for Agency in Organizations

An influenced observer, in our analysis, is someone who sees courage in an organizational environment, experiences the emotions that are sparked by the courageous action, and is changed by the experience. We believe these actor-observer dynamics can take place in regard to oneself, but as evidenced by the large number of interpersonal responses to requests for stories about courage, it is easier for employees to observe such things as risk, choice, judgment, and worthy ends in others. We think it is likely that people who have witnessed courageous action on the part of others in similar roles will be able to act with courage themselves in a future situation (Bandura, 1977; Nemeth & Chiles, 1988), in part because they may be able to perceive more clearly the effort that they could take on behalf of worthy ends in the organization. A quintessential example of this dynamic in the stories we collected comes from Sonja, a graphic designer in a software firm (all names of research participants have been changed):

> My manager had the courage to tell the corporate branding people that the visual direction they had chosen for packaging and advertising was not good. He went on to tell them that we wouldn't be following their direction and that we would ship our own designs. If they wanted everything to match, they would have to follow our lead. He explained why this was better for the company. This seemed courageous to me because it was very bold and in some ways seemed "inappropriate." The branding people are hired because they are experts, and here we were telling them that their entire effort was going to fail.
>
> I felt two things during this event. One, I felt very proud of my manager and proud to be on his team. I also felt a bit exposed, because it was my design skills that he was gambling on. I felt scared because the tension in the room was extremely high, and I didn't want to be part of a controversy. After this event, I realized that my job and responsibilities are so much larger than I see them. It also made me realize that if you believe in what you are doing or designing, then it doesn't matter who you need to defend the design to or how high you want to push it because it is okay to do that. It made me feel very qualified and capable to do this work, where before I felt like there were so many other people who could do a better job than me.

Sonja experiences this incident as a violation of the corporate routine. In noting that the "branding people" are "experts," she reveals her expectation that their opinions will hold weight and usually win out in such decisions. The fact that the "experts" are made to change their usual mode of operating is a violation of routines in the design world. In response to this exceptional action, Sonja senses and monitors the situation for the kinds of elements we have already described that will help her determine whether her manager is acting with courage. For example, she notes that the manager is doing something risky, as marked by her description of it as "bold" and her feeling that something is "inappropriate." In addition, she infers that the manager is using wise judgment in pressing this issue, which she notes by stating that the manager can explain why his decision is better for the company.

In response to this incident of everyday courage in the organization, Sonja's agency in her role is changed. She reports that her responsibilities feel enlarged and that she has a heightened sense of willingness to push for the validity of her own designs. After witnessing this incident, Sonja describes herself as feeling increasingly qualified and capable, indicating a renewed sense of self-efficacy and worth in regard to her role. Sonja's feelings of efficacy go hand in hand with her realization that she can enact a larger role for herself in the organization. Sonja's sense of agency is buoyed by this incident, building her ability to carry out her work competently.

Creed and Scully (2001) use the term *situated embedded agency* to describe how people engage in competent behavior in organizations. Rather than seeing employees as passive actors or prisoners of organizational scripts, they note the ways in which people navigate within institutional norms and routines and use their discretion to make a difference in collective outcomes. Sonja's story relates to Creed and Scully's notion of competence in that it demonstrates how Sonja and her manager move within the routines of the organization to get their work done. Experiencing courage in an organization changes people's views of the expanse of action available to them. This widened vision of the discretionary room within the institutional practices enhances people's agency in their work roles. For instance, Sonja's realization that it does not matter "who you need to defend the design to or how high you want to push it" is a re-visioning of her discretion within the institutional practices of the design world. Her way of noting this is that "it's okay to do that." Her widened view of discretion in the organization is accompanied by emotions that buoy her confidence and sense of competence, helping to create a dramatically enlarged picture of what is possible in her role. The process by which the experience of courage changes the enactment of agency is depicted in frame 1 of Figure 9.2.

Our claim that experiencing courage changes the possibilities for agency is not intended to imply that such changes are always positive. Seeing activity that is outside expected roles, norms, scripts, or routines can also trigger a dampening of vision about what is possible in a role, as illustrated in a story told by Juan, a programmer in a software company:

Figure 9.2. Courageous Activity Changes Agency, Connections, and Sense of the Organizational Whole.

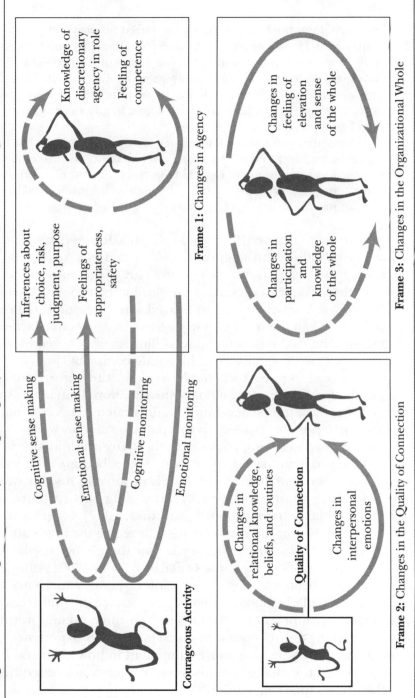

Years ago, I was working for a guy who started his own company out of his home. He was new to the business and made a fixed bid on a consulting job without knowing the full extent of the problem. The customer insisted on extra work that wasn't explicitly spelled out. This guy could have found some way to get out of the situation, but instead he spent many hours of unpaid time to give the customer what he agreed on.

Doing that extra work almost killed his young company, but he insisted on doing it, even after being offered an out. He risked his company to keep his word. I would have taken the out if it were me at the time. This probably made me extremely cautious in making my own promises for years afterward.

As Juan experiences the emotional pull between keeping a commitment and the vast amount of work created by a mistake, he is discerning that the perseverance on the part of the entrepreneur is courageous. The perseverance of the entrepreneur violated Juan's scripts for work activity, as he indicated when he noted that he would have "taken the out." In response to this exceptional action, Juan senses the risk to the company, as illustrated in his comment that the "extra work almost killed his young company." Juan infers that the choice to persist was made freely by the entrepreneur, even in the face of ways to opt out of the situation. Juan also monitors the worth of the perseverance, as illustrated in his comment that the entrepreneur "risked his company to keep his word."

In response to seeing courage in the entrepreneur's persistence, however, Juan writes that his own choices became more cautious. Juan's sense of agency and what is possible in his role were limited rather than expanded by witnessing this instance of courage. Social learning theory (Bandura, 1977) suggests that Juan's view of making choices is changed by seeing the implications of another's choices. In Juan's story, we see this change accompanied by a feeling of cautiousness. Creed and Scully (2001) offer an addition to a social learning explanation of Juan's experience in their view of skilled embedded agency as a source of competence. Juan creates competence within his role through taking precautions in making a work commitment. Through his experience of courage, Juan may become more competent in how he enacts his role, although the changes in his sense of agency are very different than those that Sonja described.

Emotion Mediates Changes in Agency

Sonja's and Juan's stories are accounts of changing agency in response to experiencing courage at work. The striking difference in tone and impact between Sonja's story and Juan's story highlights the mediating role of emotion in these experiences. Juan does not use many emotion terms to describe his feelings at the time, yet the overall tone of the story is cautious, anxious, and dejected. In contrast, Sonja writes that she feels proud of her manager and her position in the group. Although her pride is tinged with fear, the overall tone of her story is positive and upbeat. The affective tone and emotional response to experiences of courage at work is an important determinant of the resulting changes in agency.

We have discovered through these stories of courage at work that modern technological work involves deep and powerful emotions. In relying on stories, we call on a psychological tradition that values the conversational nature of our social lives (Edwards & Potter, 1992; Harre & Gillett, 1994). Stories are powerful modes through which we make sense of our experiences of and with others (Veroff, Chadiha, Leber, & Sutherland, 1993; Weick, 1995). Stories are also a dominant medium for storing and communicating information to others about things that have occurred, reasons for success or failure, and general principles of behavior (Baumeister & Newman, 1994). By describing the nature of courage in a story form, our respondents were "closer to the experience itself" (Baumeister & Newman, 1994, p. 677) and thus were more connected to the emotional content of the event they were recalling. Stories of courage are a particularly good method to reveal the holistic, dynamic, emotional nature of work performance. Because emotion is so prominent and influential in these stories, they clarify the ways in which work performance is constituted in and through emotion.

Emotion researchers argue that the experience of emotion goes along with specific action tendencies (Frijda, 1986; Lazarus, 1991; Levenson, 1994). Essentially, the idea is that when we experience an emotion, we are simultaneously moved toward an action, such as fear creating the impulse to flee (Frijda, 1986). Fredrickson (1998), in what she calls the broaden-and-build model of positive emotion, has expanded this idea into "thought-action repertoires," in which both positive and negative emotions are accompanied by an impulse toward specific thoughts and actions, such that fear is associated with the urge to escape, anger with the urge to attack, joy with the urge to play, pride with the urge to achieve, contentment with the urge to savor, and so on (Fredrickson, 1998, in press). The association of emotion with specific thought-action repertoires is important to the experience of courage in organizations. When solely negative emotion is generated by the experience of courage at work, it will generate particular thought-action repertoires that limit activity, close the range of options, and dampen creativity. And when positive emotion is generated by the experience of courage at work, it will generate particular thought-action repertoires that expand activity, broaden the range of options, and heighten creativity.

It may be rare that people experience solely positive emotion in response to organizational events. Researchers looking into the role of emotion in sport have discovered that high performance is often accompanied by a mix of positive and negative emotions (Hanin, 2000), similar to that described by Sonja. It appears that a combination of positive feelings about an activity and negative feelings related to the demands of the situation seem to result in heightened performance (Hanin, 2000). Juan, in contrast to Sonja, does not report any positive emotions in response to the entrepreneur's courageous persistence. That Juan experienced solely anxiety or distress when observing courage implies that his thought-action repertoire would involve limiting his engagement, escaping from the situation, and carefully avoiding a similar situation in the future. In contrast, Sonja's positive emotion of pride may have triggered a different thought-action repertoire such that she was moved to expand her activity, heighten her creativity, and strive to accomplish more in the organization. Pride, in particular, Fredrickson (in press) suggests, is an emotion that opens the door for the advancement of achievement-related goals.

Carver and Scheier's (1990, 1998) theory of self-regulation further suggests that emotion arises from a sense of the rate of progress toward desired goals. Analogizing this process at a social level and assuming that monitoring can be an interpersonal process, Juan would sense that the entrepreneur is not quickly moving toward his desired goals, giving rise to negative affect in relation to his perseverance. According to Carver and Scheier (1998), this negative affect would signal to Juan that the entrepreneur should disengage from this activity and that continuing it may be destructive. Sonja, on the other hand, would sense her manager's and her own movement toward valued goals at a rate faster than expected, due to the manager's unexpected leap-frogging of the expert designers, giving rise to positive affect. In turn, this positive affect acts as a cue for Sonja to engage in further activity in accord with these goals (Carver & Scheier, 1998).

In organizational settings, this observed relationship between emotion and activity appears as a constant performance stream that is continually interwoven with feeling (Sandelands, 1988). Moments when norms, roles, scripts, and routines are violated, however, give rise to powerful emotional responses. These exceptional actions have the ability to create change in organizational performance. When people experience negatively valenced emotions in response to courageous activity, agency may be narrowed, decision making may become more cautious, and creativity may be limited. In contrast, when positively valenced emotions are experienced in response to courageous activity, agency may be broadened, decision making may be less cautious, and creativity may be enhanced.

Courage Changes the Quality of Connection in Organizations

Many accounts of work performance focus on individual outcomes. Yet organizations are composed of relationships and connections (Bradbury & Lichtenstein, 2000; Feldman & Rafaeli, 2001; Simon, 1981; Sandelands & Stablein, 1987), suggesting that performance is often more interpersonal than our theories allow. Because we can see organizations as networks of connected people (Burt, 1982, 1992; Dacin, Vantresca, & Beal, 1999) and as compositions of relationships (Bradbury & Lichtenstein, 2000; Kahn, 1998), a large portion of work performance is tied to the establishment and maintenance of interpersonal connections. The quality of these connections has a great deal of impact on people's ability to get work accomplished and on the functioning of the organization as a whole (Gersick, Bartunek, & Dutton, 2000; Kahn, 1998).

High-quality connections between people develop from a combination of knowledge, emotion, and interaction (Miller & Stiver,

1991). Some researchers describe the quality of connections in terms of knowledge and emotional attunement (Benner, Tanner, & Chesla, 1996; Fletcher, 1998; Jacques, 1993). Knowing when to create rapport and when not to, when to initiate creative activity and when to make quick decisions are part of what constitutes valuable, high-quality connections (Benner et al., 1996; Fletcher, 1998; Jacques, 1993). Connections are also created and maintained through interaction within organizational routines. Feldman and Rafaeli (2001) argue that routines create connections between people that facilitate shared understandings about tasks and the larger organizational mission. When courageous activity in organizations upsets routines and disrupts taken-for-granted roles and scripts, it may also disrupt the emotion, knowledge, and interaction patterns that sustain connections between people.

Siri, a new employee in a software firm, offers an example of the way in which a courageous action can change the quality of a connection between people:

> At school, after having an argument with a teacher that was clearly my fault, he apologized to me for his part in the argument. It seemed courageous to me because it was against the run of authority and something that was above his moral right. It taught me the concept of responsibility for a person's part in any incident, and made me feel very admiring and respectful.

For Siri, this apology is outside his expectations for the role of teacher and outside the routine activity for someone on the winning side of an argument. Siri senses and monitors the situation for the factors that are important in ascribing courage. He infers that the teacher freely chooses to apologize, which he notes by indicating that there was no fault on the teacher's part. He similarly infers worthy ends on the part of the teacher, describing the activity as above his "moral right." He captures some of the feeling experience of this exceptional action when he describes the apology as "against the run of authority." In the wake of Siri's interpretation of this activity as courageous, he experiences feelings such as respect and admiration for the teacher. He writes that this interaction taught him basic lessons about accepting personal responsibility and resolving conflicts.

As a result of a courageous apology, the quality of the connection between Siri and his teacher is changed. Knowledge between the interactants is changed, as Siri now understands the teacher differently and thinks differently about his own moral responsibility (Benner et al., 1996). Emotions between the interactants are changed, with enhanced respect and admiration offering Siri and the teacher emotional resources to build a higher-quality connection (Miller & Stiver, 1991). Routines for interaction are also changed, as evidenced by Siri's reexamination of responsibility and its implications for how to handle conflict resolution in the future (Feldman & Rafaeli, 2001). As a result of the combination of changes in knowledge, emotion, and routine, the connection between Siri and the teacher is strengthened. Siri is drawn toward the teacher and may come to regard him as a kind of intellectual role model (Cavanagh & Moberg, 1999; Nemeth & Chiles, 1988). The process by which courage in an organization changes the quality of connection between people is depicted in frame 2 of Figure 9.2.

As with potential changes in agency, changes in the quality of connection between people in response to an experience of courage are not always positive. Sara, an engineer in a software firm, offered an example of connections being both diminished and strengthened through observing courage:

A coworker was called in to meet with a new vice president for our group. The employee had approximately two years of experience with the company, while the vice president had approximately three weeks of experience. The vice president accused the engineer of not doing her job and outlined her ineptitude in general. Shocked by the accusations, the engineer listed her work and education, qualifications, and experience. She then asked the vice president for specific examples to support her opinion. The vice president had no examples.

This seemed courageous to me because the engineer could have simply taken the "abuse" and apologized, although she was not in fact guilty of such behavior. Rather, she questioned the basis of the vice president's assumptions. This decision set the tone for their future working relationship. I felt shocked and disbelieving as this was happening. Afterward, I worked harder to prove myself to this vice president and to document my own activities for a similar encounter. I lost respect for the vice president and gained respect for the engineer.

For Sara, the behavior of the vice president was unexpected due to her senior role and for her level of experience in the organization. The vice president's attack was also a violation of the "get to know you" routines that exist in most organizations. The violation of the roles and routines transforms the quality of the connection between Sara and the vice president. While Sara discerns courage on the part of her coworker, her response to the vice president's action in this incident is one of shock and disbelief. Her immediate reaction is to engage defensive routines in the connection, such as preparing for confrontation and documenting her abilities and activities (Argyris, 1982; Miller & Stiver, 1991). The negative emotion that Sara feels in response to the initial incident is carried into a lasting change in the emotional tone of the connection, as represented by her comment that she "lost respect" for the vice president. The loss of respect between Sara and the vice president diminishes their emotional resourcefulness and weakens the quality of the connection (Miller & Stiver, 1991).

The multiple connections that compose organizations are evident in Sara's story. In addition to the change in quality of connection between Sara and the vice president, Sara's connection with her coworker is enhanced through this incident. Sara sees her coworker as courageous and takes her response to the vice president as a kind of model for her future behavior (Nemeth & Chiles, 1988). The quality of the coworker's connection to the vice president is also changed by this incident, as illustrated in Sara's comment that this interaction "set the tone for their future working relationship." As illustrated by both Siri's and Sara's stories, witnessing a courageous incident in everyday organizational life has the potential to transform the quality of connections between coworkers and between employees and managers.

Emotion Mediates Changes in the Quality of Connections Between People

Evans and White (1981), setting out to create an empirical definition of courage, found a potential actor-observer difference in the perception of courage. Regardless of age level, people seem to use their own sense of fear of a situation to understand how brave another person is being. Whether the same sense of fear is present in the courageous actor, people seem to use their own feelings as a guide to understanding others. This research brings into relief the organizational reality that emotions such as fear and qualities such as courage are created as much through social observation as they are through individual difference (Fineman, 1993; Katz, 1999; Rafaeli & Worline, 2001). In fact, few researchers grapple with the quandary that an action may be perceived as courageous yet the person carrying it out will deny having courage. This paradox seems to be common in everyday settings (Finfgeld, 1999; Worline & Wrzesniewski, 2001). Understanding how courage transforms the quality of connections in organizations reveals the ways in which emotion transcends individual-level analysis and social realities are interpersonally and mutually created (Edwards & Potter, 1992; Gergen, 1994; Harre & Gillett, 1994; Rafaeli & Worline, 2001; Sampson, 1993).

Instances of courage in organizations spark emotion in many people—onlookers as well as those involved. The multiple audiences in organizations create, as Rafaeli and Worline (2001) recently argued, the virtual impossibility of treating emotion as an individual force in social organization. Exploring the history of emotion research in organizational scholarship, Rafaeli and Worline point out that the inability to distinguish between individually "felt" emotion and organizationally required "displayed" emotion, along with the multiple audiences who participate in emotional interactions, creates situations in which emotion seems to be generated and sustained by the life of the organization. Socially created emotion generated in work interactions has a mediating role in transforming the quality of connections between people. Siri's and Sara's constructions of their own and others' emotions affect the quality of their connections with others in their work organizations.

Emotions that mediate changes in the quality of connection are vital to work performance. Such emotions may enhance or diminish work engagement (Kahn, 1990), respect (Lawrence-Lightfoot, 1999) and trust (Kramer, 1999; Uzzi, 1997), which have been shown to be crucial to organizational performance. Baumeister and Leary (1995) suggest that forging high-quality connections with others is a way to introduce meaning into work life. Benner and her colleagues

(1996) argue that emotion is a primary way in which people attune to one another, develop expertise, and accomplish their work. Emotions are critical to the creation of high-level work performance through their impact on the creation of meaning and high-quality connections at work.

Emotion may also have a role in modifying work routines by modifying the quality of connections between people. Many organizational researchers have emphasized that routines contribute to the stability of organizations (Cyert & March, 1963; Hannan & Freeman, 1983; Kerr & Slocum, 1981; Nelson & Winter, 1982), but others have noted that routines allow for adaptation (Feldman, 2000). Examining the mechanisms that allow for routines to be sources of both stability and change, Feldman and Rafaeli (2001) argue that routines facilitate connections between people. When emotions disrupt or change connections between people, changes in routines may ensue. Carver et al. (2000) argue that most behavior can be traced to basic patterns of approach and avoidance that are highly affected by affective processes. Following their logic at a social level, as demonstrated clearly in Sara's story, when strong emotions accompany violations of routines, new patterns of interpersonal approach or avoidance may be established (Carver et al., 2000; Feldman & Rafaeli, 2001).

Courage Transforms Possibilities for the Organization as a Whole

Rollo May (1978) argues that each act of courage raises the moral and social conscience of a society. Because courage has a link to constructions of moral action (Rorty, 1988; Shelp, 1984; Walton, 1986), it is often connected to a sense of what is "right" or "good." In turn, what is "right" or "good" is usually construed as that which serves a social whole (Goldberg & Simon, 1981; Finfgeld, 1999). The connection between action that serves the whole and courage is evident in a variety of contexts, from studies of soldiers (Rachman, 1990), to whistle-blowers and Holocaust resistors (Glazer & Glazer, 1989; Rothschild & Miethe, 1999; Shepela et al., 1999), to people who are terminally ill (Finfgeld, 1999). For instance, among soldiers, Rachman (1990) finds that service to a small group or unit is the prime way in which courageous action is sustained.

Whistle-blowers often feel strongly connected to their organizations and talk about their action as serving the overarching purposes of the organization or of society (Glazer & Glazer, 1989; Rothschild & Miethe, 1999). Shepela and her colleagues (1999) note that courageous resistors such as those who sheltered potential Holocaust victims are distinguished by a strong sense of "we-ness" with humanity, and hence may be inclined to take risky action in order to serve the whole of society. Finfgeld (1999) finds that people who are terminally ill sustain their courageous persistence by engaging in community service. Across numerous contexts, courageous action is connected to perceptions of service to a social whole.

In the stories we gathered from employees and managers in the high-technology sector, courageous activity is often tied to the broader aims of the organization. When assumptions about work norms, routines, roles, and scripts are disrupted, attempts to understand and make sense of the disruption ensue (Weick, 1995). One of the factors that people consider is the worth of the action, whether or not disruptive activity is directed to aims that serve a broader purpose or an aim espoused by the organization as a whole. Our analysis of courage stories suggests that behavior "outside the grooves" of routines seems to be evaluated for not only its punishment potential (Deutsch, 1961), as psychologists have suggested, but also for its service to the group or organization.

An example of a courageous activity that serves the broader mission of the organization is offered in Kurt's account of a test manager who was working with his team of engineers:

> The test manager took a stand for his position to not let any new features creep into the product, despite the entire war team against him, even his manager's opposition. One could say he's inflexible, but in this case, the inflexibility was ultimately needed to ship the product on time, which was by far more important than the new features.
>
> This seemed courageous to me because against all odds, against authority, and against the majority, he made his point and did the best for the product. It felt confrontational, I felt a little sympathy for him, and he gained a lot of respect from me afterwards. After this, I try to take a stronger stand whenever needed and whenever I believe I'm right and the results matter to the bottom line.

Kurt sees his coworker's ability to take a stand against pressure to expand a product as courageous. Kurt monitors the violations of the routines and role responsibilities in the organization for unreasonable or self-serving behavior, as noted by his admission that this could simply be "inflexibility" on the part of the test manager. Kurt also senses the risk in his coworker's action, as noted by his description of it as "against all odds, against authority, and against the majority." Because Kurt concludes that this risky violation of organizational protocol serves the broader purposes of the whole organization, he comes to see the test manager as courageous. Kurt describes the test manager as a kind of hero, protecting the overarching goals of the organization against the whims of people who would jeopardize it. When Kurt observes this instance of courage, his feeling of respect for the test manager is heightened, and he finds in himself a renewed sense that he too can serve the best interests of the organization. The process by which courage changes the possibilities for the organization as a whole is depicted in frame 3 of Figure 9.2.

Wrzesniewski and Dutton (2001) have recently argued that people use the organizational mission as a part of how they craft the accomplishment of their work. In their example, when hospital cleaners see themselves as connected to the organizational mandate of healing, they do their job tasks differently so as to help patients and visitors heal. Experiencing courage in an organization may be one way in which the mission and mandate of the organization become visible and viable as a part of people's everyday work. In order for people to craft their work according to the mission and goals of the organization, a vision of the mission must be accessible even to people in positions that are removed from the formal leadership. In Kurt's story, courageous work performance is one way in which people see, feel, and experience the values, standards, and possibilities of the organization in action. When people experience the organization's mission and vision in relation to themselves, their resources for action change. Kurt is prompted to attend to ways in which his silence affects the organization's goals. As a result, he comes to view his own opinions and skills as important to the organization's overall performance.

Courageous work performance may be a kind of informal leadership that has the potential to affect formal leadership as well. Max, a software developer, offers an example of courage that created interaction between formal and informal leadership:

A colleague of mine questioned the complete product line and direction of the product. He was a software developer with less than two years of experience. He told our manager (and later the chief technical officer directly) that the technology was all wrongly focused.

It was courageous to stand up and question the purpose of the whole product line, to question a senior manager. He prepared data, articles, reviews, and market research to back up his claim. He did this just a month before the company's initial public offering.

I felt inspired and motivated to stand up and vocalize my thoughts and doubts. For any question or issue, it is important to have backup information to validate the stand. It also changed my thinking that upper management knows everything. I learned to ask good questions and prepare supporting data.

In my workplace, management acknowledged that the technology and product lines needed revisiting, and a number of reviews and follow-up alignments of product line and technology followed.

Max finds courage in a junior member of the organization risking confrontation with the senior leadership in order to make the organization's vision and product line more successful. Max sees his coworker's action as a strong violation of the role of junior engineer and the routines of carrying out orders that accompany hierarchical organizations (Mintzberg, 1979; Sandelands, 2001). Max monitors the exceptional action of his coworker for good judgment, as he indicates when he describes that the engineer is well prepared with multiple sources of evidence to support his claims. Max reveals the tension he sensed in this experience when he notes that this was just a month prior to the company's initial public offering, a time of great stress and urgency when people are expected to fall in line in support of the organization. Max experiences strong emotions of inspiration and motivation in response to this incident. Inspiration is an emotion related to a sense of the whole, similar to "elevation" that Haidt (2000) described. Inspiration and elevation are sparked by seeing someone go beyond what is expected or beyond what seems humanly possible (Haidt, 2000). The feeling of inspiration changes Max's connection to the organization as a whole, changing his view of the role of management, how the organization should be run, and how he should participate.

Max further indicates that the organization's technology and strategy are transformed through this interaction of informal and formal leadership. For Max, and potentially for many others who witnessed this incident, the organization is both materially and socially changed. It is materially transformed, as the technology and product line changes, and socially transformed as the "management knows everything" myth vanishes. This courageous act that brings the informal leadership into interaction with the formal leadership sparks strong emotions that may be related to an organization's overall emotional capability (Huy, 1999). Through the action of his coworker, Max not only sees his ability to participate in the organization differently, but also witnesses the transformation of the direction, mission, and mandate of the organization.

Emotion Mediates Changes in People's Sense of the Organization as a Whole

In Kurt's and Max's stories of courageous work performance, strong emotions are interwoven with the "doing" of the work and the mission of the organization. These emotions play an important mediating role between the experience of courage and a changed sense of organization. Kurt writes that he feels confrontation, sympathy, and increased respect as he experiences his coworker's courageous resistance. Max writes that he feels inspired and motivated as he sees his coworker influence the organization's strategy and product line. These emotions help facilitate a changed sense of participation in the organization as a whole and a deepened connection to the aims of the organization. In keeping with scholars who have proposed that we perceive social wholes largely through feeling (Sandelands, 1998), we propose that violations of routines are often interpreted through a feeling of the whole. Actions that violate routines in order to serve the group or the organization's larger purpose are felt as courageous. Merely self-serving behavior, however, is not felt in the same way (Finfgeld, 1999). Accounts of courage in organizations, like those from Kurt and Max, tend to emphasize feelings such as confrontation and inspiration, which are emotional responses to seeing "good" or "moral" activity (Haidt, 2000). Courageous activity makes the social whole present through feeling.

Emotions sparked by the experience of courage in organizations help people interpret action in the organization (Fineman,

1993; Weick, 1995). As an important feature of the organization's culture and context, emotion is one factor that shapes what people notice and helps determine how they will interpret what they notice (Daft & Weick, 1984; Starbuck & Milliken, 1988; Rafaeli & Worline, 2001). When people feel inspired by action in an organization, they interpret their own and others' actions as important contributions to the organization as a whole. In addition, emotions in response to courageous activity become part of the feeling of the whole that guides future thought and action. The construal of feelings in response to exceptional action—that is, whether the observer experiences a courageous incident as inspirational or defeating—has a direct impact on the accomplishment of work and the interpretations of the whole that are sustained over time (Harre & Gillett, 1994; Katz, 1999).

As with changes in agency and connection, changes in the organization in response to courageous action may not be positive. In some instances, seeing courageous activity in the organization generates feelings of guilt or displeasure rather than feelings of awe or admiration. As we have argued, when people experience negative emotions in response to the experience of courage, the negative emotion triggers avoidance patterns (Carver et al., 2000) and narrowed thought-action repertoires (Fredrickson, 1998). In relation to participation in the organization, when people experience courage and feel emotions such as inspiration and admiration, approach routines and broadening thought-action repertoires ensue, and people are likely to invest in the organization. In contrast, when people experience courage in the organization and feel emotions such an anxiety, despair, or guilt, avoidance routines and dampening thought-action repertoires ensue, and people are likely to withdraw from participation in the organization.

Conclusion

Courage is part of the texture of the workplace. Tight deadlines, difficult relationships, admitting mistakes, accepting failures—these are the kinds of challenges that people in organizations face daily. In contemporary work, courage is not simply the greatness of leadership or the goodness of moral authority, but rather is a lens into strength, skill, and agency in organizations. Courage contains a destructive edge, of which we cannot lose sight (Rorty,

1988). Yet demanding work situations also create the possibility for challenge, growth, and resilience (Dweck & Leggett, 1988). This chapter makes a case that understanding how people respond to challenging work environments requires organizational scholars to explore understudied human qualities such as courage.

Seeing courage in work performance reveals a deep emotional current in everyday work life. Performance is interwoven with emotion. Hodson (1998) finds that emotions such as pride and shame are highly important in promoting desirable organizational outcomes. Pratt and Barnett (1997) report that Amway distributors rely on emotion to produce organizational learning. Hirokawa, DeGooyer, and Valde (2000) find that emotions figure as a major reason that people cite for the failure or success of small groups. More clearly than ever before, research is documenting the importance of emotion in organizational performance. Emotion is integral to organizational life (Rafaeli & Worline, 2001).

In this chapter, we have used the concept of courage in organizations to build a dynamic model of work performance from interwoven threads of thought, feeling, and action. This model demonstrates that moments of high-level performance in the organization disrupt taken-for-granted roles, scripts, norms, and routines and prompt cognitive and emotional sense-making processes that create the meanings attached to the disruption of taken-for-granted patterns. When exceptional action in an organization involves free choice, risk, or vulnerability, features accurate assessment of the consequences, and is directed at worthy aims, it is interpreted as courageous. Courageous activity has the potential to transform people's sense of agency in their work by widening their vision of the discretionary action available within their role and triggering emotions that buoy feelings of competence. Courageous activity has the potential to transform the quality of connections between people in organizations by changing the relational knowledge, beliefs, and routines that people use in their work, as well as triggering emotions that sustain resourcefulness between people. Courageous activity has the potential to transform the organization as a whole through changing people's participation and felt connection to the organization's mission and goals.

A recent study of the introduction of new technology in a large midwestern health care organization revealed that employees who fear making mistakes are less likely to experiment with new technology systems and by extension are less likely to become proficient with the technology (Lee, 2001). The failure of courage in organizations is directly tied to failures in organizational performance. In order to meet the challenges of the contemporary marketplace, organizations across all types of industries are going to have to find ways to foster courage. Our model of courage at work suggests that the emotion created by disruption in routines in the organization is critical to the agency and adaptive capability that people exhibit in the wake of change. Broadened possibility, expanded agency, higher-quality connections, and a vital sense of the organizational whole are possible when courage is an accepted part of the organizational landscape.

As organizational scholars, we will not fully understand the highest levels of organizational performance until we examine factors in the organization that foster an ability to respond to challenge with courage and generate positive emotion that inspires others to see broadened possibilities for agency, connection, and change.

Postscript: Courage and Work After September 11

This research was completed prior to the terrorist attacks in the United States on September 11, 2001. It will be read through new eyes after the events of that day. Before September 11, we were too often guilty of thinking of courage as irrelevant to the workplace or simply a concept that mattered for the study of leadership. Events in the world have reminded us of the shortsightedness of such a perspective. Too often, organizational research disregards work that serves the public, such as that done by firefighters and postal workers. Too often, organizational scholars ignore public servants such as politicians and soldiers who spend their time in service of creating and sustaining a free and democratic society. The events of September 11 and afterward remind us that courage is a staple of all such work, and it deserves our time, care, and attention.

September 11 brought us more stories of courage on the part of bond traders and business managers and corporate secretaries too—different from those featured in the bulk of this chapter yet similar in their themes. One of the moving stories in the wake of the events at the World Trade Center, featured in the September 16 edition of the *New York Times,* was that of a corporate manager, Harry Ramos, who gathered people from his floor into the stairwell and began leading them down the seventy flights of stairs that they would have to descend to safety. Along the way, Ramos and his companions picked up others, strangers, who were also trying to find a way out of the building. One of these strangers, Victor, stopped on the thirty-sixth floor and could go no further. Harry Ramos sent the others ahead to continue down the stairs, turning back as Victor pleaded not to be alone. The last words that his coworkers heard from Harry Ramos were, "Victor, don't worry. I'm with you." Harry Ramos understood the power of human connection and chose to give comfort to a fellow human being, even in the midst of terror and destruction. Stories such as this one demonstrate that courage is indeed born from and sustained within human connections. They give us a terrible and powerful view of how courage can transform human relationship.

When we read the stories from September 11, we privately ask ourselves if we could have acted in the same way. In that private questioning is the seed of the reflective process of courage we have proposed in this chapter. We cannot know, of course, how we would act. The philosopher Thomas Aquinas wrote that it was impossible, through schooling or even through faith, to instill courage. The best we can do, Aquinas concluded, is to prepare ourselves daily for moments that involve fear by cultivating wise judgment and valuing the shared humanity of others. We know that work such as firefighting is an example of daily practice in preparation for situations that involve fear, discerning judgment, and the value of shared humanity. The November 2001 edition of *Men's Journal* features stories from firefighters about their experiences on September 11. In introducing their stories, the journalist writes that the firefighters' most common response to questions was, "We're just doing our job." This response echoes the responses from our research on courage in all kinds of workplaces—that daily preparation for difficult situations changes one's perspective on what comprises courageous activity. Given this difference in perspective between onlookers and actors, between firefighters and laypeople, it becomes even more necessary to develop models of courage that take into account the social and interpersonal dimensions of this most human virtue.

As we slowly begin to gather and tell all of the stories of courage from September 11, those stories will undoubtedly buoy us and help us to heal. They will offer us additional lessons about the nature of courage and work, lessons we have only begun to explore in this chapter. One such lesson is that courage is not the opposite of fear. September 11 shows us that only insanity could produce fearlessness in the wake of such a tragedy. Quoted in the *New York Times Magazine* on September 23, 2001, a New York City firefighter says, "Every fire is scary. That's the way it is. You're a damned liar if you say you're not scared." Firefighters, and probably many other workers as well, develop an intimacy with fear so that it becomes a guide to doing work on the edge of what is possible. The Mohawk tribe of Native Americans, who are famous for their ability to walk tightrope-thin beams of steel to build skyscrapers, refuse to work with anyone who is not afraid. In such situations, with such training, fear becomes a way to remain mindful and not lose focus. Organizational theory often loses this emotional perspective on demanding work. Working heedfully and mindfully (Weick & Roberts, 1993; Weick, Sutcliffe, & Obstfeld, 1999) must in some way involve this relationship of courage and fear. Complex emotional processes such as these certainly deserve more attention in our research on all kinds of organizations.

September 11 presents the world with a great leadership challenge. Our leaders now need courage too. They must be mindful, walking the cliff edge of danger. They must honor the connections between people. And they must find a way to use their judgment to sustain a sense of the society as a whole. In order to sustain a society's courage, our leaders need a richer vision of the social dimensions of courageous activity. Organizational scholars might contribute to the response to September 11 by uncovering how leaders in the twenty-first century sustain courage in their societies and in their organizations. Our theories and research have usually focused on the leader as a separate entity, looking for courage as an internal attribute that distinguishes one leader from the next or influences some limited task. In the wake of September 11, we see that leaders must summon up their courage and that as they do so, the rest of us are changed as well.

Courage is wise action in the face of danger that honors the visceral connection of human being to human being. The firefighters who gave their lives demonstrate this. The story of Harry Ramos is a tribute to it. The leadership choices that our society makes must reflect as much. Organizational scholars are called, more than ever before, to understand how we can build wise, effective, courageous organizations and how such organizations can develop, sustain, and support wise, effective, and courageous people.

References

Argyris, C. (1982). *Reasoning, learning and action*. San Francisco: Jossey-Bass.

Ashkenasy, N., Hartel, C.E.J., & Zerbe, W. J. (Eds.). (2000). *Emotions in the workplace: Theory, research, and practice*. Westport, CT: Quorum Books.

Bandura, A. (1977). *Social learning theory*. Upper Saddle River, NJ: Prentice-Hall.

Bartel, C., & Saavedra, R. (2000). The collective construction of work group moods. *Administrative Science Quarterly, 45*, 197–231.

Baumeister, R. F., & Leary, M. R. (1995). The need to belong: Desire for interpersonal attachments as a fundamental human motivation. *Psychological Bulletin, 117*, 497–529.

Baumeister, R. F., & Newman, L. S. (1994). How stories make sense of personal experiences: Motives that shape autobiographical narratives. *Personality and Social Psychology Bulletin, 20*, 676–690.

Becker, E. (1973). *The denial of death*. New York: Free Press.

Benner, P., Tanner, C., & Chesla, C. (1996). *Expertise in nursing practice: Caring, clinical judgment, and ethics*. New York: Springer.

Bourdieu, P. (1990). *The logic of practice*. Stanford: Stanford University Press.

Bradbury, H., & Lichtenstein, B. M. (2000). Relationality in organizational research: Exploring the space between. *Organization Science, 11*, 551–564.

Brissett, D., & Edgley, C. (1990). *Life as theater: A dramaturgical sourcebook*. New York: Aldine de Gruyter.

Burt, R. S. (1982). *Toward a structural theory of action: Network models of social structure, perception and action*. Orlando, FL: Academic Press.

Burt, R. S. (1992). *Structural holes: The social structure of competition*. Cambridge, MA: Harvard University Press.

Carver, C. S., & Scheier, M. F. (1990). Origins and functions of positive and negative affect: A control-process view. *Psychological Review, 97*, 19–35.

Carver, C. S., & Scheier, M. F. (1998). *On the self-regulation of behavior*. Cambridge: Cambridge University Press.

Carver, C. S., Sutton, S. K., & Scheier, M. F. (2000). Action, emotion, and personality: Emerging conceptual integration. *Personality and Social Psychology Bulletin, 26*, 741–751.

Cavanagh, G. F., & Moberg, D. J. (1999). The virtue of courage within the organization. In M. L. Pava (Ed.), *Research in ethical issues in organizations* (pp. 1–25). Greenwich, CT: JAI Press.

Cohen, M., & Bacdayan, P. (1994). Organizational routines are stored as procedural memory: Evidence from a laboratory study. *Organization Science, 5,* 554–568.

Connell, R. J. (1997). *William James on the courage to believe* (2nd ed.). New York: Fordham University Press.

Cox, D., Hallam, R., O'Connor, K., & Rachman, S. (1983). An experimental analysis of fearlessness and courage. *British Journal of Psychology, 74,* 107–117.

Creed, W.E.D., & Scully, M. A. (2001). Songs of ourselves: Employees' deployment of social identity in everyday workplace encounters. *Journal of Management Inquiry, 9,* 391–412.

Cyert, R. M., & March, J. G. (1963). *A behavioral theory of the firm.* Upper Saddle River, NJ: Prentice Hall.

Dacin, M. T., Vantresca, M. J., & Beal, B. D. (1999). The embeddedness of organizations: Dialogue and directions. *Journal of Management, 25,* 317–356.

Daft, R. L., & Weick, K. E. (1984). Toward a model of organizations and interpretation systems. *Academy of Management Review, 9,* 284–295.

Deutsch, M. (1961). Courage as a concept in social psychology. *Journal of Social Psychology, 55,* 49–58.

Dweck, C., & Leggett, E. (1988). A social-cognitive approach to motivation and personality. *Psychological Review, 95,* 256–273.

Edwards, D., & Potter, J. (1992). *Discursive psychology.* Thousand Oaks, CA: Sage.

Evans, P. D., & White, D. G. (1981). Towards an empirical definition of courage. *Behaviour Research and Therapy, 19,* 419–424.

Feldman, M. S. (2000). Organizational routines as a source of continuous change. *Organization Science, 11,* 611–629.

Feldman, M. S., & Rafaeli, A. (2001). Organizational routines as sources of connections and understandings. Manuscript submitted for publication.

Fineman, S. (1993). Organizations as emotional arenas. In S. Fineman (Ed.), *Emotion in organizations* (pp. 9–35). Thousand Oaks, CA: Sage.

Fineman, S. (Ed.). (2000). *Emotion in organizations* (2nd ed.). Thousand Oaks, CA: Sage.

Finfgeld, D. L. (1999). Courage as a process of pushing beyond the struggle. *Qualitative Health Research, 9,* 803–814.

Fletcher, J. K. (1998). Relational practice: A feminist reconstruction of work. *Journal of Management Inquiry, 7,* 163–186.

Fredrickson, B. L. (1998). What good are positive emotions? *Review of General Psychology, 2,* 300–319.

Fredrickson, B. L. (in press). Why positive emotions matter in organizations: Lessons from the Broaden-and-Build model. *Psychologist-Manager's Journal.*

Frijda, N. H. (1986). *The emotions.* Cambridge: Cambridge University Press.

Galbraith, J. R. (1973). *Designing complex organizations.* Reading, MA: Addison-Wesley.

Gardner, W. L., & Avolio, B. J. (1998). The charismatic relationship: A dramaturgical perspective. *Academy of Management Review, 23,* 32–59.

Gergen, K. J. (1994). *Realities and relationships: Soundings in social construction.* Cambridge, MA: Harvard University Press.

Gersick, C.J.G., Bartunek, J. M., & Dutton, J. E. (2000). Learning from academia: The importance of relationships in professional life. *Academy of Management Journal, 43,* 1026–1044.

Gersick, C.J.G., & Hackman, J. R. (1990). Habitual routines in task-performing groups. *Organizational Behavior and Human Decision Processes, 47,* 65–97.

Giacalone, R. A., & Rosenfeld, P. (Eds.). (1989). *Impression management in the organization.* Hillsdale, NJ: Erlbaum.

Glazer, M. P., & Glazer, P. M. (1989). *The whistleblowers: Exposing corruption in government and industry.* New York: Basic Books.

Goffman, E. (1959). *The presentation of self in everyday life.* New York: Doubleday.

Goldberg, C., & Simon, J. (1982). Toward a psychology of courage: Implications for the change (healing) process. *Journal of Contemporary Psychotherapy, 13,* 107–128.

Greenwald, A., & Breckler, A. (1985). To whom is the self presented? In B. R. Schlenker (Ed.), *The self in social life.* New York: McGraw-Hill.

Grove, S. J., & Fiske, R. P. (1989). Impression management in marketing: A dramaturgical perspective. In R. A. Giacalone & P. Rosenfeld (Eds.), *Impression management in the organization* (pp. 427–439). Hillsdale, NJ: Erlbaum.

Hackman, J. R. (1992). Group influences on individuals in organizations. M. D. Dunnette & L. M. Hough (Eds.), *Handbook of industrial and organizational psychology* (2nd ed., pp. 199–267). Palo Alto, CA: Consulting Psychologists Press.

Haidt, J. (2000). The positive emotion of elevation. *Prevention and Treatment, 3.* Available: http://journals.apa.org/prevention/volume3/pre0030003c.html.

Hanin, Y. L. (2000). Successful and poor performance and emotions. In Y. L. Hanin (Ed.), *Emotions in sport.* Champaign, IL: Human Kinetics.

Hannan, M. T., & Freeman, J. R. (1983). Structural inertia and organizational change. *American Sociological Review, 29,* 149–164.

Harre, R., & Gillett, G. (1994). *The discursive mind.* Thousand Oaks, CA: Sage.

Higgins, E. T. (1997). Beyond pleasure and pain. *American Psychologist, 52,* 1280–1300.

Hirokawa, R. Y., DeGooyer, D., & Valde, K. (2000). Using narratives to study task group effectiveness. *Small Group Research, 31,* 573–591.

Hodson, R. (1998). Pride in task completion and organizational citizenship behaviour: Evidence from the ethnographic literature. *Work and Stress, 12,* 307–321.

Huy, Q. N. (1999). Emotional capability, emotional intelligence, and radical change. *Academy of Management Review, 24,* 325–345.

Jackall, R. (1988). *Moral mazes: The world of corporate managers.* New York: Oxford University Press.

Jacques, R. (1993). Untheorized dimensions of caring work: Caring as structural practice and caring as a way of seeing. *Nursing Administration Quarterly, 17,* 1–10.

James, W. (1909). *The meaning of truth.* White Plains, NY: Longman.

Kahn, W. A. (1990). Psychological conditions of personal engagement and disengagement at work. *Academy of Management Journal, 33,* 692–724.

Kahn, W. A. (1998). Relational systems at work, *Research in organizational behavior* (Vol. 20, pp. 39–76). Greenwich, CT: JAI Press.

Katz, J. (1999). *How emotions work.* Chicago: University of Chicago Press.

Kerr, S., & Slocum, J. W. (1981). Controlling the performances of people in organizations. In P. C. Nystrom & W. H. Starbuck (Eds.), *The handbook of organizational design* (Vol. 2). New York: Oxford University Press.

Kramer, R. M. (1999). Trust and distrust in organizations: Emerging perspectives, enduring questions. *Annual Review of Psychology, 50,* 569–598.

Lawrence-Lightfoot, S. (1999). *Respect: An exploration.* Reading, MA: Perseus Books.

Lazarus, R. S. (1991). Progress on a cognitive-motivational-relational theory of emotion. *American Psychologist, 46,* 819–834.

Lee, F. (2001). The fear factor. *Harvard Business Review, 79,* 29–30.

Levenson, R. W. (1994). Human emotions: A functional view. In P. Ekman & R. Davidson (Eds.), *The nature of emotion: Fundamental questions* (pp. 123–126). New York: Oxford University Press.

March, J. G., & Simon, H. A. (1958). *Organizations.* New York: Wiley.

May, R. (1978). *The courage to create.* New York: Bantam Books.

Miller, J. B., & Stiver, I. (1991). *The healing connection.* Boston: Beacon Press.

Miller, W. I. (2000). *The mystery of courage*. Cambridge, MA: Harvard University Press.

Mintzberg, H. (1979). *The structuring of organizations: A synthesis of the research*. Upper Saddle River, NJ: Prentice Hall.

Nelson, R., & Winter, S. G. (1982). *An evolutionary theory of economic change*. Cambridge, MA: Harvard University Press.

Nemeth, C., & Chiles, C. (1988). Modelling courage: The role of dissent in fostering independence. *European Journal of Social Psychology, 18*, 275–280.

O'Connor, K., Hallam, R., & Rachman, S. (1985). Fearlessness and courage: A replication experiment. *British Journal of Psychology, 76*, 187–197.

Pears, D. F. (1978). Aristotle's analysis of courage. *Midwestern Studies in Philosophy, 3*, 273–285.

Pratt, M. G., & Barnett, C. K. (1997). Emotions and unlearning in Amway recruiting techniques: Promoting change through "safe" ambivalence. *Management Learning, 28*, 65–88.

Pybus, E. (1991). *Human goodness: Generosity and courage*. New York: Harvester Wheatsheaf.

Rachman, S. J. (1990). *Fear and courage* (2nd ed.). New York: Freeman.

Rafaeli, A., & Worline, M. C. (2001). Individual emotion in work organizations. *Social Science Information, 40*, 95–123.

Rorty, A. O. (1988). *Mind in action: Essays in the philosophy of mind*. Boston: Beacon Press.

Rosen, M. (1985). Breakfast at Spiro's: Dramaturgy and dominance. *Journal of Management, 11*, 31–48.

Rosenfeld, P., Giacalone, R. A., & Riordan, C. A. (1995). *Impression management in organizational life*. New York: Routledge.

Rothschild, J., & Miethe, T. D. (1999). Whistle-blower disclosures and management retaliation: The battle to control information about organization corruption. *Work and Occupations, 26*, 107–128.

Salancik, G. R., & Pfeffer, J. (1978). A social information processing approach to job attitudes and task design. *Administrative Science Quarterly, 23*, 224–253.

Sampson, E. E. (1993). *Celebrating the other: A dialogic account of human nature*. Boulder, CO: Westview Press.

Sandelands, L. E. (1988). The concept of work feeling. *Journal for the Theory of Social Behaviour, 18*, 437–457.

Sandelands, L. E. (1998). Feeling and form in groups. *Visual Sociology, 13*, 5–23.

Sandelands, L. E. (2001). *Male and female in social life*. New Brunswick, NJ: Transaction Publishers.

Sandelands, L., & Stablein, R. (1987). The concept of organization mind. *Research in the Sociology of Organizations, 5*, 135–161.

Scherer, K. (2001). The future of emotion: Foreword. *Social Science Information, 40*, 5–10.

Shelp, E. E. (1984). Courage: A neglected virtue in the patient-physician relationship. *Social Science and Medicine, 18*, 351–360.

Shepela, S. T., Cook, J., Horlitz, E., Leal, R., Luciano, S., Lutfy, E., Miller, C., Mitchell, G., & Worden, E. (1999). Courageous resistance: A special case of altruism. *Theory and Psychology, 9*, 787–805.

Simon, H. A. (1981). *Sciences of the artificial*. Cambridge, MA: MIT Press.

Starbuck, W. H., & Milliken, F. J. (1988). Executives' perceptual filters: What they notice and how they make sense. In D. C. Hambrick (Ed.), *The executive effect: Concepts and methods for studying top managers* (pp. 35–65). Greenwich, CT: JAI Press.

Szagun, G. (1992). Age-related changes in children's understanding of courage. *Journal of Genetic Psychology, 153*, 405–420.

Szagun, G., & Schauble, M. (1997). Children's and adults' understanding of the feeling experience of courage. *Cognition and Emotion, 11*, 291–306.

Tiedens, L. Z. (2000). Powerful emotions: The vicious cycle of social status positions and emotions. In N. M. Ashkanasy (Ed.), *Emotions in the workplace: Research, theory, and practice* (pp. 72–81). Westport, CT: Quorum Books.

Tillich, P. (1952). *The courage to be*. New Haven, CT: Yale University Press.

Uzzi, B. (1997). Social structure and competition in interfirm networks: The paradox of embeddedness. *Administrative Science Quarterly, 42*, 35–67.

Van Eynde, D. F. (1998). A case for courage in organizations. *Management Review, 87*, 62.

Veroff, J., Chadiha, L., Leber, D., & Sutherland, L. (1993). Affects and interactions in newlyweds' narratives: Black and white couples compared. *Journal of Narrative and Life History, 3*, 361–390.

Walton, D. N. (1986). *Courage: A philosophical investigation*. Berkeley: University of California Press.

Weick, K. E. (1995). *Sensemaking in organizations*. Thousand Oaks, CA: Sage.

Weick, K. E., & Roberts, K. H. (1993). Collective mind in organizations: Heedful interrelating on flight decks. *Administrative Science Quarterly, 38*, 357–381.

Weick, K. E., Sutcliffe, K. M., & Obstfeld, D. (1999). Organizing for high reliability: Processes of collective mindfulness. *Research in Organizational Behavior, 21*, 81–123.

Weiss, H. M., & Cropanzano, R. (1996). Affective events theory: A theoretical discussion of the structure, cause and consequences of affective experiences at work. In B. Staw & L. Cummings (Eds.),

Research in organizational behavior (Vol. 18, pp. 1–74). Greenwich, CT: JAI Press.

Worline, M. C., & Wrzesniewski, A. (2001). *Why tell courage stories? Toward a relational view of courage.* Paper presented at the Western Academy of Management, Sun Valley, ID.

Wrzesniewski, A., & Dutton, J. E. (2001). Crafting a job: Revisioning employees as active crafters of their work. *Academy of Management Review, 26,* 179–201.

Yearley, L. H. (1990). *Mencius and Aquinas: Theories of virtue and conceptions of courage.* Albany: State University of New York Press.

CHAPTER 10

Feeling Your Way
Emotion and Organizational Entry

Blake E. Ashforth
Alan M. Saks

Theory and research on organizational entry have focused mainly on newcomers' cognitions and behaviors—how they think and act their way into a new job and organization—rather than on newcomers' emotions—how they *feel* their way. As Kidd (1998) put it, emotion is "an absent presence in career theory" (p. 275). However, given the stress of recruitment and selection and the personal upheaval that subsequent organizational entry often entails, it seems likely that emotions are inevitably and often intensely experienced during this time.

This chapter explores the role of emotion during organizational entry. It discusses how entry is saturated with emotion and how emotion is not only an outcome of entry processes but how it at least partly mediates the impact of these processes on the attractiveness of the organization and on individual learning and adjustment. The first section examines the preentry phase, encompassing recruitment and selection processes. We argue that organizations often recruit and select at least partly *for* emotion and

This chapter was supported by a grant from the Australian Research Council (A79801016). We thank Rich Klimoski and Bob Lord for their very helpful comments on an earlier draft.

via emotion. The next section examines the postentry phase, encompassing socialization processes. We argue that socialization occurs at least partly *via* emotion, and we discuss the socialization *of* emotion.

Preentry: Recruitment and Selection Processes

Although the role of emotions in the workplace has received increasing interest (Ashkanasy, Härtel, & Zerbe, 2000), relatively little attention has been given to the role of recruitment and selection (see Arvey, Renz, & Watson, 1998, for an exception). In this section, we explore two areas that have particularly important implications for recruitment and selection. The first area is recruitment and selection *for* emotion, that is, how to assess the emotional demands of a job and the construction of selection methods to test job applicants' emotional skills. In particular, we consider the link between emotions and work behavior and outcomes, individual differences in emotion, and some approaches for assessing applicants' emotional skills during recruitment and selection. The second topic is recruitment and selection *via* emotion, that is, how emotion and self-appraisals of emotion at least partially mediate the effect of recruitment and selection practices on recruitment outcomes. In particular, we describe how recruitment and selection practices can be orchestrated to provoke desired emotions in applicants that will influence their cognitions, behavior, and recruitment outcomes.

Recruitment and Selection *for* Emotion

According to Rafaeli and Sutton (1989), organizations have three means of maintaining formal and informal norms about expressed emotions: recruitment and selection, socialization, and rewards and punishments. However, if recruitment and selection are to be used for maintaining display norms, it is necessary to answer three questions: (1) Are emotions related to work behavior and outcomes? (2) Are there individual differences in emotionality? (3) If so, how can individual differences in emotionality be measured vis-à-vis recruitment and selection?

Are Emotions Related to Work Behavior and Outcomes?

Anecdotal and empirical evidence indicates that emotions are indeed related to work behaviors, attitudes, performance, and other outcomes (Arvey et al., 1998; Staw, Sutton, & Pelled, 1994; Weiss & Cropanzano, 1996). In fact, emotions appear to have both positive and negative effects on work behavior and outcomes. For example, many dysfunctional workplace behaviors such as fraud, sabotage, sexual harassment, and violence appear to be at least partially caused by maladaptive emotional responses (Arvey et al., 1998; Griffin, O'Leary-Kelly, & Collins, 1998).

Although emotions are often stereotypically viewed as the antithesis of more rational conceptualizations of work, it remains that the display of emotion in many jobs is in fact job-related behavior (Arvey et al., 1998) and should therefore be treated like other job requirements. There are many examples of jobs (nurse, funeral director) and organizations (Mary Kay Cosmetics, Disney World) with strong requirements for displays of emotion (Rafaeli & Sutton, 1989).

Emotionality can also be considered in terms of both person-job (P-J) and person-organization (P-O) fit. According to Arvey et al. (1998), an individual's emotionality should be congruent with the emotions required in a job and organization, and emotional P-J and P-O fit likely contributes to job performance.

Thus, there appears to be sufficient evidence to conclude that emotionality is related to work behaviors and outcomes. However, in order to consider emotionality for recruitment and selection purposes, it is also necessary to determine if there are individual differences in emotionality.

Are There Individual Differences in Emotionality?

In their model of workplace emotionality, Arvey et al. (1998) argue that stable individual differences along with job demands and social and organizational factors combine to trigger felt emotions, which in turn trigger displayed emotions and behaviors that influence job performance. Individuals are said to differ in the types of emotion experienced, the intensity of emotional experiences, and how emotions change over time. Also, individuals differ in their display of emotion, behavioral responses to felt emotions, and the level of discomfort associated with the suppression of felt emotions and the display of emotions not felt. Thus, "individuals have stable, consistent patterns of emotional responses that generalize across stimuli and environments" (pp. 105–106).

With respect to the experience of emotion, one of the most important individual difference variables appears to be trait affect. Larsen, Diener, and Lucas (Chapter Three, this volume) suggest that individuals with trait-negative affect are more likely to dwell on negative feedback and unpleasant work experiences, whereas those with trait-positive affect tend to focus more on positive feedback and work experiences. Furthermore, emotional reactions influence behavior. Thus, trait affect helps to explain how people react and respond to affective events.

Rafaeli and Sutton (1989) note three key individual difference variables related to the display of emotions: gender, self-monitoring, and emotional stamina. Regarding gender, women are more likely than men to display warmth and liking in their transactions with others. Individuals who score high on self-monitoring have been found to regulate the display of emotions better: they have more control over the display of emotions and conform more closely to *display rules,* the prescriptions governing the display of emotion in a given situation (Ekman, 1973). Finally, individuals with high emotional stamina are able to display desired emotions over longer periods of time.

There is also evidence that individual differences influence one's ability to regulate displayed emotions (Larsen, Diener, and Lucas, this volume). Two individual differences that appear to be particularly important are emotional adaptability and emotional intelligence. Schaubroeck and Jones (2000) define adaptability as being able to "naturally adapt [one's] emotions to the situational context" (p. 167). They found that emotional labor was not related to physical symptoms for persons who were emotionally adaptive and conclude that emotionally adaptable persons are more "self-aware emotionally" (p. 180) and better able to separate their authentic self from their role-required self. Thus, emotional adaptability may be particularly important for jobs that require much emotional labor.

Emotional intelligence (EI) also has implications for the ability to regulate emotions. As Larsen, Diener, and Lucas note in Chapter Three, three of the purported dimensions of EI (self-awareness, self-regulation, and self-motivation) involve one's own emotional processes, and the other two dimensions (empathy and social skills) refer to regulating the emotions of others. As a general ability, people with high EI are better able to sense their own and other's emotions and to regulate their emotions. Thus, EI appears to be a particularly important individual difference in situations where it is necessary to regulate the display of felt emotions.

In sum, there is evidence that there are stable individual differences in terms of felt and displayed emotions, as well as emotional regulation, and these differences are distinct from related concepts such as moods, personality, stress, and job satisfaction (Arvey et al., 1998; Weiss & Cropanzano, 1996). Thus, it should be possible to predict individuals' emotional responses to job demands, as well as their subsequent behavior and job performance. However, it is first necessary to determine if, what, and when emotions are relevant for a particular job and organization, as well as how to measure individual differences in emotionality vis-à-vis recruitment and selection.

How Can Individual Differences in Emotionality Be Measured Vis-à-Vis Recruitment and Selection?

Before we consider how to measure emotional propensities, it is necessary to identify jobs where this would in fact be useful in terms of selection validity and utility. In this regard, it makes sense to focus on jobs where tasks are emotionally demanding and there are clear requirements for the expression of emotions, positive or negative. Typical examples are jobs that involve stressful interpersonal interactions and client contact and where there are strong display rules (such as bill collector, flight attendant, and salesperson; Arvey et al., 1998; Hochschild, 1983; Rafaeli & Sutton, 1989). However, a job analysis will still be necessary to determine the nature of the emotional demands made by the job or organization.

Job analysis for emotions. Although job analysis methods have not been developed for identifying emotional demands, it should not be too difficult to adapt existing job analysis methods for this purpose. For example, the critical incident technique could be used to generate effective and ineffective displays of emotion with respect to particular tasks. The examples can then be grouped into dimensions of job-relevant emotions and used to develop interview questions or verbal performance tests. Another approach, suggested by Arvey et al. (1998), is to identify critical tasks and work events that trigger various emotional reactions. In addition, job analysis techniques such as interviews and questionnaires can be used to identify the emotional demands and tasks along with other job-relevant tasks and knowledge, skills, and abilities (KSAs) required to perform a job. For instance, the Position Analysis Questionnaire is a computerized instrument that assesses the emotionality associated with jobs (Arvey et al., 1998).

A good example of how existing job analysis procedures can be used to identify emotional demands is described by Schmitt and Ostroff (1986), who used a behavioral consistency approach to develop selection tests for emergency telephone operators. A job analysis generated a comprehensive list of task statements, the KSAs required to perform each task, and the identification of the most critical task dimensions and KSAs. This resulted in six dimensions, including emotional control. Examples of the task statements for emotional control include: "Remains calm even in emergency situations when a caller is hysterical or upset" and "Controls emotions in emergency to gather and transmit appropriate information" (p. 94).

Selection for emotions. Among the various methods of assessing emotionality, self-report measures are the most popular, feasible, and widely used, especially when done using a questionnaire (Arvey et al., 1998; Larsen, Diener, and Lucas, this volume). Arvey et al. describe a number of self-report measures of emotionality, most consisting of adjective checklists or rating scales and often including what appear to be personality traits rather than emotions. Although these measures might serve research purposes, they have limited use for selection because most were designed to test a specific theory. Self-report measures of emotionality are also susceptible to social desirability bias and faking. In addition, job applicants may view such measures as intrusive and may respond with negative emotions, which, as described below, can be detrimental to recruitment outcomes. Finally, it is unclear to what extent emotionality is related to a particular job without first conducting a job analysis.

Although self-report measures of emotionality have limited utility for selection, measures of personality and EI are promising. The use of personality tests for selection has become more acceptable thanks largely to research linking the Big Five Dimensions of Personality to job performance. Among the dimensions, emotional stability appears to be the most relevant. Individuals with high emotional stability are more stable and confident and better able to control their emotions. Emotional stability has been found to be positively related to job performance in service jobs (Hogan, Hogan, & Roberts, 1996), perhaps because of the need for emotional control when interacting with customers. For the purpose of selection, the NEO-Personality Inventory and the Personality Characteristics Inventory (PCI) are reported to be the most often used measures of the Big Five (Gatewood & Feild, 1998).

Although still in its infancy, the use of EI for selection has been gaining momentum in organizations (Martinez, 1997). A group known as the Consortium on Social and Emotional Competence in the Workplace has been studying how employers can identify and develop the EI skills of employees and has developed tools to measure EI. However, there are serious concerns regarding the construct validity of EI, as well as its measurement. For example, Davies, Stankov, and Roberts (1998) concluded that "the empirical status of emotional intelligence is questionable" (p. 1012), and the results of three studies indicate that "little remains of emotional intelligence that is unique and psychometrically sound" (p. 1013). A key debate that echoes throughout the recent *Handbook of Emotional Intelligence* (Bar-On & Parker, 2000) concerns not only the operationalization of EI but its very conceptualization. Thus, although EI appears promising, more conceptual and empirical work is needed on the nature and measurement of EI and its incremental predictive validity in selection.

Ultimately, the development of selection measures for emotions requires a methodology for converting the emotional demands of a job into selection tests. For example, Schmitt and Ostroff (1986) demonstrate how to transform specific job behaviors associated with emotional control into selection tests. Two particularly promising methods for measuring emotion-related criteria are verbal performance tests and structured behavioral or situational interviews. Verbal performance tests require job applicants to perform some aspect of a job that typically involves tasks that are language or people oriented (Gatewood & Feild, 1998). Such tests can be designed to reproduce work situations that require emotional displays and regulation. Schmitt and Ostroff (1986) designed a telephone call simulation to select emergency telephone operators. It required applicants to participate in a role-playing exercise in which they took calls from complainants who could be emotional or hysterical. The performance test was designed to assess applicants' emotional control as well as communication skills and judgment. Such verbal performance tests provide an excellent means of placing applicants in work-related situations in which they must demonstrate their ability to regulate their emotions. In addition, performance tests provide applicants with a very realistic preview of the job (Schmitt & Ostroff, 1986).

Structured employment interviews can also be used to assess applicants' skills in emotional regulation. Schmitt and Ostroff (1986) designed a situational interview to measure emotional control among emergency telephone operators. Interview questions can be designed to measure job-relevant displays of emotion in the same way that questions are designed using critical incidents from a job analysis. For example, if one wanted to measure how job applicants would react to irate and rude customers, a behavioral interview question might be, "Tell me about a time when a customer was rude to you and insulted you or the organization" (this could be altered to a situational interview question by changing, "Tell me about a time . . . " to "What would you do if . . . "). Follow-up probes might then identify felt emotion ("How did this incident make you feel?"), displayed emotions ("How did you react to the customer?"), and behavior ("What did you do after the customer was rude to you?"), providing grist for evaluation. In addition, by comparing the felt emotion to the displayed emotion, it is possible to evaluate an applicant's ability to regulate his or her emotions.

Interview questions could also be designed to measure an individual's previous experience and general ability to regulate emotions rather than how that person would respond to hypothetical work incidents. An interview question to measure emotional regulation might be, "Individuals [or employees] often have to change their emotions in response to the demands of the situation. Tell me about a time when you had to change your emotions quickly in order to deal with a situation [or work situation]." Probe questions might include, "What was the situation?" "How did you feel?" "How did you change your emotions?" "How did the change in emotions make you feel?" and "What was the outcome?"

In sum, job analysis procedures and test construction methodology can be used to identify emotion-related skills and criteria along with other job-relevant KSAs (perhaps leading to a revised acronym, KSAEs). Furthermore, existing selection practices such as measures of emotional stability, verbal performance tests, and behavioral or situational interviews can be designed with high content and face validity to assess job applicants' skills in emotional regulation.

However, even if a job analysis has been used to develop job-related selection tests and emotionality can be adequately measured for selection purposes, one still has to be concerned about the predictive and incremental validity of the measures. If emotionality is to become part of selection criteria, one needs to know the expected gain in predictive validity beyond that of cognitive ability tests, structured interviews, personality tests, and so on. Thus, although a strong case has been made that emotion is related to job performance (Arvey et al., 1998), the real issue is whether emotional constructs can explain *unique* variance in job performance and increase the predictive validity of existing selection systems.

Finally, it is worth noting that although our focus has been on P-J fit in terms of the emotional demands of a *job,* the display of emotions has also been linked to organizational culture and policies such that organizations often vary in the type and level of emotionality that is desired (Arvey et al., 1998). Thus, one can also talk about P-O fit in terms of the emotional demands of an *organization.* However, for selection purposes, the organization is on much stronger ground, legal and otherwise, when measuring emotion for P-J fit rather than P-O fit. P-O fit and emotion can be more adequately managed by an organization's socialization processes, as described later. What is perhaps most important is that individuals have the capacity to regulate their emotions according to the demands of a job and organization. The emotions that are expected to be displayed or suppressed can be learned and reinforced during socialization.

Recruitment and Selection *via* Emotion

Research indicates that recruitment and selection practices influence applicant reactions and recruitment outcomes. For example, recruiters who are perceived by job applicants to be informative and knowledgeable, as well as warm, personable, and friendly, have been found to elicit more positive reactions (for example, job and organization attractiveness) and outcomes (for example, job offer acceptance; Barber, 1998; Rynes, 1990). Applicants have been found to react more favorably to selection procedures perceived as nonintrusive as well as fair in terms of procedural and distributive justice (Gilliland, 1994, 1995; Ployhart & Ryan, 1998). Applicants' reactions to selection methods are related to their attitudes toward a job and organization, as well as their job acceptance decisions (Macan, Avedon, Paese, & Smith, 1994).

In this section, we argue that emotions and self-appraisals of emotions at least partly mediate the effect of recruitment and selection practices on applicant attitudes, behavior, and recruitment outcomes. Weiss and Cropanzano's (1996) affective events theory (AET) provides a useful way for understanding the effect of recruitment and selection. According to AET, organizational events give rise to specific affective reactions and emotions. These emotions then lead to various attitudinal and behavioral outcomes. Thus, emotions are considered to be a mediating mechanism for the influence of organizational events on outcomes.

This perspective suggests that organizations can orchestrate recruitment and selection practices to evoke desired emotions toward the job and organization. For instance, recruiters who appear enthusiastic and friendly through their language and nonverbal behavior can influence the emotions of applicants through *emotional contagion* (Hatfield, Cacioppo, & Rapson, 1994). Contagion refers to the tendency to mimic and synchronize emotional cues automatically such that one comes to actually experience the implied feelings. By eliciting positive emotions, recruiters can increase perceptions of job and organization attractiveness and job acceptance rates. Recruitment materials and events such as brochures, videos, job fairs, and on-site visits, as well as selection procedures that incorporate rules of procedural justice (Gilliland, 1995), can also be designed to elicit such emotions.

In an insightful analysis, Pratt and Barnett (1997) describe how Amway recruiters provoke multiple and conflicting emotions during recruitment to change recruits' cognitions and behavior. Recruiters stimulate strong positive (excitement and desire) and negative emotions (dissatisfaction and fear) as well as feelings of trust and safety through the use of emotive language (for example, "excitement," "dreams") and labels (for example, Amway "winners" versus non-Amway "losers"), eliciting and co-opting individuals' aspirations, disparaging the status quo, using personal testimonials, and so on. The conflicting emotions galvanize some recruits to "unlearn" conventional ways of working that are antithetical to Amway and to develop a zealous attachment to the organization and its unique ideology. Amway recruitment thus also becomes a socialization device that enhances P-O fit and postentry attitudes and behavior.

Although this example demonstrates how recruitment activities can influence emotions and cognitions, an interesting stream of research on persuasion and attitude change suggests that there exists an affective-cognitive persuasion matching effect (Fabrigar & Petty, 1999). In other words, affective persuasion is most effective for changing affective attitudes, whereas cognitive persuasion is most effective for changing cognitive attitudes. Thus, recruitment efforts need to be designed carefully so that they match the attitude component that one wants to influence.

In summary, emotions have an important role to play in understanding how recruitment and selection practices influence job applicants' attitudes and behavior. Our main argument is that recruitment and selection procedures can be designed to elicit certain emotions, and these emotions may at least partially mediate the impact of recruitment and selection on pre- and postentry attitudes and behavior. This also means that emotions can be stimulated during anticipatory socialization, thereby paving the way for postentry socialization.

Postentry: Socialization Processes

Emotion has generally been treated as a dependent variable in quantitative socialization research, as an outcome of work adjustment processes. Research has examined the role of socialization practices in reducing anxiety and other aversive affective states and in enhancing a positive sense of well-being. And research has examined the link between socialization and work attitudes, principally job satisfaction and organizational commitment, that are assumed to include an affective component.[1]

What is less evident in these studies—but is the sine qua non of *qualitative* socialization research—is a sense of how emotion saturates the very experience of "learning the ropes" in an organization. Accordingly, our purpose here is to expand the focus beyond socialization *for* emotion to socialization *via* emotion, that is, how emotion and self-appraisals of emotion help mediate the impact of socialization events on newcomers' learning and behavior, and socialization *of* emotion, that is, how newcomers learn about the organization's or subunit's emotional culture through socialization practices. As Lutz (1983) notes, "Emotions can be seen as both the medium and the message of socialization. Their uniqueness, and their crucial importance for understanding development, lies in this dual and encompassing role" (p. 260).

Socialization *via* Emotion

Socialization is realized largely through specific events, and the emotional arousal and cognitive appraisal stimulated by these events at least partly mediate the impact of socialization on newcomer learning and behavior. Our model is adapted from AET and is summarized in Figure 10.1. Given our interest in socialization via emotion, we will pay particular attention to the links between events and emotions.

Figure 10.1. Socialization *via* Emotion.

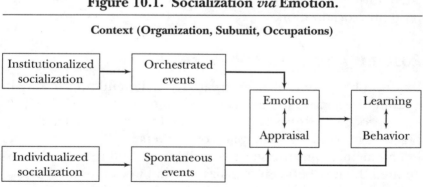

Institutionalized Versus Individualized Socialization Tactics.
Van Maanen and Schein (1979) proposed six bipolar tactics that
are typically used to socialize newcomers. The *collective (versus individual)* tactic involves grouping newcomers and exposing them
to common experiences instead of treating each newcomer individually and exposing him or her to idiosyncratic experiences. *Formal (versus informal)* socialization involves separating a newcomer
from his or her more experienced peers for a limited period, versus not separating him or her. The *sequential (versus random)* tactic
refers to a fixed series of steps leading to the desired role, rather
than an ambiguous or dynamic series. *Fixed (versus variable)* socialization consists of a timetable for assuming the role rather than no
timetable. *Serial (versus disjunctive)* socialization involves the use of
role models versus no role models. Finally, *investiture (versus divestiture)* involves affirming a newcomer's incoming identity and attributes rather than denying and tearing them away.

Jones (1986) argued that these tactics—collective, formal, sequential, fixed, serial, and investiture—cluster together and encourage newcomers to accept prefabricated roles passively, thereby
reinforcing the status quo. Thus, Jones dubbed this set of tactics
institutionalized socialization. Conversely, at the other end of the six
continua, the tactics encourage newcomers to explore the status
quo and develop their own approaches to their roles. Jones termed
this cluster *individualized socialization.* Ashforth, Saks, and Lee
(1997) argued that institutionalized socialization reflects a structured indoctrination program, whereas individualized socialization
reflects a relative absence of structure; indeed, newcomers appear
to be socialized more by default than design.[2] Accordingly, Ashforth et al. found that the individualized end of the socialization
continuum was positively associated with role ambiguity, role conflict, and stress symptoms—in short, negative emotions—among
newcomers.

Orchestrated Versus Spontaneous Events

The socialization tactics are conceptual abstractions that are made
real through specific events in specific settings. As Figure 10.1
shows, the tactics of institutionalized socialization, as a structured
program, are more likely to be associated with orchestrated or

planned events rather than spontaneous or unplanned events. Orientation sessions (collective tactic), training programs at headquarters (formal and fixed), developmental assignments (sequential), regular advice from a coworker (serial), welcome rituals (investiture) or ritualized insults (divestiture), and myriad other events provide the platform for learning and adjustment. Conversely, the tactics of individualized socialization are more likely to be associated with spontaneous events. Phrases like "sink or swim" and "flying by the seat of your pants" convey the haphazard and opportunistic nature of individualized socialization.

Emotion ↔ Appraisal

As Weiss and Cropanzano (1996) remark, "Implicit in all definitions [of emotion] is that an emotion is a reaction to an event" (p. 18). As Figure 10.1 depicts, orchestrated and spontaneous events trigger emotion and appraisal as the newcomer struggles to make sense of events and discern their personal relevance and importance (Lord and Harvey, Chapter Four, this volume). As such, emotion serves a *signal function* (Darwin, 1965), directing and motivating the newcomer to attend more to some events and less to others. Although some theorists award causal primacy to emotion and others to appraisal, most would agree that emotion and appraisal are tightly coupled. As Fineman (1997) puts it, "We have feelings about what we think and thoughts about what we feel" (p. 16).

Primary and secondary appraisal. Following AET, an event triggers an initial or *primary appraisal* where one assesses the relevance of the event to one's goals (Lazarus, 1991). The greater the perceived relevance and the more important the goals, the more intense the emotional response will be. Furthermore, if the event is perceived as enabling one's goals, the emotions tend to be positive, whereas if the event is perceived as blocking one's goals, the emotions tend to be negative. Weiss and Cropanzano (1996) note that goal-incongruent events tend to provoke stronger emotions than do congruent events.

Following Ashforth's (2001) model of organizational entry, newcomers tend to have four major goals or "motives": (1) meaning (sense making and meaningfulness), (2) identity (self-definition), (3) competence and control, and (4) belonging. Thus, events that are perceived to be relevant to one or more of these motives may be potent catalysts for emotion. For example, Mansfield (1972) describes the angst experienced by recruits who were subjected to a series of training assignments in various departments; in the absence of a permanent position, they found it difficult to define themselves and feel attached. And Fiebig and Kramer (1998), although not focusing on newcomers, found that organizational events involving external recognition and stress relief were frequent catalysts for positive emotions, whereas events involving relational problems, task problems, and being challenged were frequent catalysts for negative emotions (also see Basch & Fisher, 2000).

In *secondary appraisal,* the newcomer evaluates the particulars of the event and his or her personal resources and options and decides what, if any, response is desirable (Lazarus, 1999; Weiss & Cropanzano, 1996). In so doing, the molar experience of positive versus negative feelings and intense versus mild feelings is refined into more specific emotions. Gibson (1995) asked M.B.A. students to describe an emotional event from their work experience. A perception that one was ignored or criticized—that is, deliberately wronged—triggered anger, whereas a perception that one failed or faced a threat external to the organization triggered fear. In short, an event that blocked one's goals (and presumably aroused negative and intense feelings) precipitated, through secondary appraisal, anger or fear. As Weiss and Cropanzano (1996) note, however, differing cognitive theories of emotion have proposed that differing event and personal dimensions are evaluated (Power & Dalgleish, 1997). Smith and Pope (1992) propose that appraisal and emotion are tightly coupled such that a given appraisal necessarily generates a specific emotion.

In sum, the critical point of the emotion ↔ appraisal dialectic is that goal-relevant events trigger arousal and the meaning one derives from the events shapes the specific emotional form that the arousal takes. Lazarus (1999) adds that the appraisal process may occur instantaneously and include both conscious and unconscious evaluation (also see Lord and Harvey, Chapter Four, this volume, regarding symbolic, connectionist, and emotional architectures).

Before leaving this section, we wish to expand on three key issues regarding the interaction of emotion and appraisal: negative versus positive emotion signals, events and emotions, and the social construction of events and emotions.

Negative versus positive emotion signals. It is often argued that organizational entry is anxiety provoking (Katz, 1985). First, newcomers face "disorientation, foreignness, and a kind of sensory overload" (Louis, 1980, p. 230). They must navigate their way in an ambiguous world and may be concerned that their motives for meaning, identity, control, and belonging will not be realized. Second, given the naiveté of newcomers and the tendency of recruiters to oversell their organizations, organizational entry tends to be associated with *surprise,* which Louis defined as "one's affective reactions to any difference [between expectations and experiences]" (p. 237) or to "discrepant events" (p. 245). The literatures on reality shock, unmet expectations, and psychological contract violations imply that surprises are usually quite unpleasant (Morrison & Robinson, 1997; Wanous, Poland, Premack, & Davis, 1992).

The implication of the view that entry is anxiety provoking is that the emotion signals that partially mediate the impact of socialization events tend to be negative and, perhaps, that the emotional tone of the entry process is negative (or at least characterized by the pursuit of relief). However, socialization may also be characterized by affirmation of important expectations, pleasant surprises rather than unpleasant ones, and the experience of positive rather than negative emotional arousal (such as curiosity, delight, or hope) in the face of uncertainty. For example, Arnold (1985) found that 45 percent of the surprises reported by newcomers were pleasant ones, versus 40 percent negative and 15 percent neutral. The friendliness of coworkers and the informality of the workplace garnered the highest proportion of pleasant surprises, whereas the "handling of communication and decisions" (for example, inefficient, political) and "life-style outside of work" (p. 312; for example, lack of free time, decrease in quality of social life) garnered the most unpleasant surprises. Similarly, reviews by Nicholson and West (1989) and Bruce and Scott (1994) suggest that the stress associated with organizational entry is often not pronounced or fades relatively quickly after entry. Indeed, Nicholson and West conclude that there is "little support for generality of the stress model; people actively seek out the 'stress' of desirable moves" (p. 185).

In sum, organizational entry is likely characterized by a variety of emotion signals, with the relative proportion (and importance) of positive and negative signals affecting the overall tone of the process.

Events and emotions. As noted, events range from orchestrated to spontaneous. Orchestrated events have been studied under various rubrics, including socialization tactics, organizational and occupational/work group cultures, transformational leadership, and symbolic management (Kunda, 1992; Pfeffer, 1981; Trice, 1993; Van Maanen & Schein, 1979). Typically, orchestrated events are designed to accomplish one or more of the following three affective objectives.

The first objective is to arouse positive emotion that can be attached to the organization, subunit, leader, coworkers, task, self, and so on or to specific facets associated with these entities, such as goals and beliefs, thus making them more attractive. Miracle and Rees (1994) describe a high school pep rally for a football game. The student body convened in a gym festooned with banners and pictures of the school mascot, and members of the football team, wearing their red and white school jackets, sat on a raised platform. The school band played rousing music, cheerleaders led students through ritualized chants and cheers, and the principal offered a brief speech extolling the school's quality and sense of tradition and pride and then introduced the coach, who spoke about the importance of the upcoming game and introduced the players. The rally, in short, aroused emotions that could be generalized to the school itself and its pursuit of achievement.

The second objective is to arouse negative emotion that can be attached to the status quo, rivals, past actions, and so on or to specific facets associated with them, thus galvanizing movement away from a disparaged object. Bourassa and Ashforth (1998) describe how new fishers on a trawler were routinely disparaged and harassed by veterans and supervisors, thus motivating the newcomers to forget their stigmatized incoming identities and become accepted as bona-fide fishers.

The third objective is to quell negative emotions, such as anxiety and anger, that may interfere with task performance and impair trust in the organization. (A fourth objective, to quell positive emotions that may interfere with future performance, appears to be relatively rare.) Ashforth and Kreiner (in press) note that organizations often employ the techniques of habituation (where repeated exposure to the same stimulus lessens its emotional impact) and desensitization (where exposure to different stimuli of increasing aversiveness lessens their impact) to "normalize" extraordinary situations, that is, to render them seemingly ordinary so that they do not arouse disruptive emotions. Hafferty (1991) argues that medical students are required to dissect cadavers so that they will become habituated to handling human bodies and death.

Because the effectiveness of an orchestrated event is often dependent on the evocation of particular emotions, it is essential that the event foster verisimilitude—a compelling sense of authenticity. Thus, orchestrated events often include settings, props, costumes, roles, and scripts, and the actors and audience alike may suspend their disbelief and engage in "mutual face-work" (Ball, 1972, p. 181) to sustain the performance. In practice, however, many orchestrated events are choreographed and delivered rather clumsily, such that the performance is experienced as insincere and coercive (Kunda, 1992). Furthermore, organizational members may develop cynical attitudes toward the emotional manipulation inherent in orchestrated events, even if the events are well intended and well managed.

Spontaneous events associated with socialization have been studied in many workplace ethnographies, from the work life of kitchen workers (Fine, 1996) to that of weapons scientists in a nuclear laboratory (Gusterson, 1998). A common denominator of these ethnographies is the succession of more or less loosely coupled events that punctuate organizational life. A new assignment, an argument with a coworker, an overheard remark, and so forth may trigger the emotion ↔ appraisal dialectic. Thus, Bullis and Bach (1989) describe work adjustment as a series of "socialization turning points" (p. 273)—whether spontaneous or orchestrated. Indeed, this episodic quality is reflected in some models of socialization that are loosely organized around formative events such as job assignments and performance appraisals (Wanous, 1992).

The notion of turning points suggests several implications for organizational entry (Ashforth, 2001). First, a given event becomes a turning point when it raises or resolves an important issue. Because the newcomer must be receptive to the possibility of learning, the timing and nature of the event are critical. Second, the sequence of turning points strongly affects work adjustment. Lennox Terrion and Ashforth (2002) concluded from a study of police executives in an off-site development course that humorous put-downs offered early in the life of the course would have seriously undermined the emergent cohesion but that the same put-downs offered later served to symbolize and cement the cohesion. Third, the more a newcomer's learning is predicated on spontaneous events, the more erratic his or her trajectory of learning may appear, perhaps fostering misattributions about his or her adjustment (for example, "He's a slow learner" versus "He's had few learning opportunities"). Indeed, the touch of randomness in spontaneous events may undermine adjustment, as when a chance string of negative events undermines a newcomer's fragile confidence. Fourth, as suggested by the pep rally example, the transformational power of an event may be increased via emotional contagion, whereby arousal is amplified.

Social construction of events and emotion. Because organizational events are often complex and have multiple causes, their meaning tends to be equivocal (Weick, 1995). Newcomers often resolve equivocality by looking to others for cues on how to decode "the" meaning. And because management has a vested interest in the meaning that newcomers derive, managers often attempt to regulate the appraisal process through institutionalized socialization. In particular, role models (serial tactic) shape the lessons that are drawn from early experiences, and like-minded peers (collective tactic) may reinforce the lessons. Thus, the orchestrated events associated with institutionalized socialization often occur in a "social cocoon" (Greil & Rudy, 1984, p. 260), where newcomers are subjected to a strong and consistent informational context such that mixed messages are absent and managers and peers model the desired lessons. Ricks (1997) describes a U.S. Marine Corps boot camp where recruits were induced to interpret the harassment they routinely endured as character building.

At least four emotional phenomena are at work during socialization. First, as described later under "Socialization *of* Emotion," newcomers may be explicitly and implicitly taught to understand the emotional culture (defined later). Second, as in the pep rally example, newcomers may "catch" emotions from others through emotional contagion. Third, institutionalized socialization fosters common experiences and feelings and helps induce identification and cohesion (Ashforth et al., 1997). Thus, newcomers may come to feel warmth and empathy toward others, creating a positive and supportive emotional climate (also defined later). Drawing on Bowlby (1979), Andersen and Guerrero (1998) contend that "most intense emotions arise when people are forming, maintaining, disrupting, terminating, or renewing close relational ties with others" (p. 57). Fourth, newcomers may engage in *emotional comparison*, gauging the meaning of their own arousal from the verbal and nonverbal cues of others (Bartel & Saavedra, 2000). Emotion is thus said, at such times, to be socially constructed (Averill, 1980). Rosenberg (1990) adds that because individuals are strongly motivated to avoid emotional interpretations that imply threatening consequences, their interpretations tend to be biased. For instance, newcomers may be predisposed to interpret their stimulation in the new setting as excitement (confirming the desirability of their job choice) rather than fear or disappointment. This motivational bias may help account for the "honeymoon effect" among newcomers (Fichman & Levinthal, 1991).

However, because newcomers are not blank slates awaiting management's inscription, the meanings and emotions derived from events may nonetheless deviate from management's prescriptions. For example, a former IBM employee described the company's intensive socialization process this way: "What they call loyalty, I call exploitation" (from a discussion with the first author). In such cases, the presence of like-minded newcomers may, through emotional comparison and contagion, actually exacerbate the disaffection (Van Maanen & Schein, 1979).

Learning ↔ Behavior

As Figure 10.1 shows, the emotion ↔ appraisal dialectic fosters a learning ↔ behavior dialectic. The appraisal of emotion signals may suggest important lessons about oneself (for example, who one is, what one values, what one is capable of) and one's environment (who can be trusted, what tasks are desirable, whether the organization deserves respect). Arnold (1985) describes how workplace surprises triggered various revelations for newcomers. One commented, "When I started, I wasn't sure I would like it, but I never thought I would react so negatively. I know now that I appreciate day-to-day living much more than a routine, and I feel no urgency to make plans for my future" (p. 316). Indeed, job satisfaction and organizational commitment, as attitudes to work, can be seen as outcomes of this learning process.

The learning ↔ behavior dialectic tends to unfold both proactively and reactively. On the proactive side, the emotion ↔ appraisal process may spur one to engage the work environment actively through information and feedback seeking (such as questioning, observing, and testing limits), networking, negotiating job changes, and self-management (such as goal setting, self-observation, and self-reward; Ashforth, 2001). On the more reactive side, the emotion ↔ appraisal process may spur what the stress literature refers to as coping (Lazarus, 1999), where the newcomer seeks to deal with pressing demands through a mix of problem-focused and emotion-focused tactics. For example, Folkman and Lazarus's (1988) coping questionnaire has eight factors: confrontive coping, distancing, self-controlling, seeking social support, accepting responsibility, escape avoidance, planful problem solving, and positive reappraisal. As these tactics suggest, coping is not necessarily reactive and may involve modifying external demands or internal states. However, the less control the individual has over work demands, the greater the reliance on reactive coping is (Lazarus, 1999).

Feedback loop. Figure 10.1 also depicts a feedback loop between the learning ↔ behavior and the emotion ↔ appraisal dialectics. Learning and action generate iterations of emotion ↔ appraisal and subsequent learning ↔ behavior as the newcomer struggles to come to grips with the work environment and his or her place within it.

In particular, actually *doing* one's job is a fundamental and ongoing means of affectively and cognitively experiencing the job and one's organization, learning the job, and gaining self and social validation for one's progress. In a real sense, newcomers "feel their way," using affective antennas to gauge their progress and fit with the work environment.

How deterministic is the emotion-behavior link? Frijda (1993) argues that a component of emotion is "action readiness" (p. 383), comprising general activation and a readiness for certain classes of behavior and cognition. Frijda notes that different emotions tend to involve a readiness for different behaviors (such as disgust → avoidance or joy → approach), and the stronger the emotion, the greater the impact on behavior (also see Lord and Kanfer, this volume). Gibson (1995), for instance, found that anger was actually expressed in 53 percent of the anger episodes reported by M.B.A. students regarding their work experience, despite the strong prohibitions in most organizations against anger expression.

Although the emotion ↔ appraisal dialectic predicts gross behaviors (such as approach versus avoidance), the principle of equifinality suggests that the dialectic may lead to one or more of a variety of specific, functionally equivalent acts (Smith & Pope, 1992). For example, disappointment with a coworker's performance may induce one to confront the coworker, take future tasks to a different coworker, or have the coworker removed from the group. Consistent with interactionism, specific behavioral choices likely result from the interplay of personal and situational factors, such as self-efficacy and work group culture.

Context

Finally, Figure 10.1 shows that socialization unfolds with an organizational, subunit (for example, department, work group), and occupational context (indeed, demographics, industry, national culture, and so on could also be included as contextual factors). The impact of the context is felt in several ways. First, the context affects the patterning of orchestrated and simultaneous events. For example, Ashforth, Saks, and Lee (1998) found that institutionalized (versus individualized) socialization was more likely to be used in large mechanistic organizations and for jobs with relatively high motivating potential. Second, as discussed below under "Socialization *of* Emotion," the context affects the social construction of meaning. Trice (1993) describes the varied ideologies that occupations provide for their members so that events can be construed in ways that affirm the worth of the occupations. Third, as also discussed below, the context shapes the very way that emotions are experienced and expressed.

In sum, orchestrated and spontaneous events may serve as socialization turning points, whereby the emotions, appraisal, learning, and behaviors generated by events foster dramatic changes in oneself, one's environment, and the fit between the two. Indeed,

Denzin's (1989) notion of *epiphanies* suggests that seemingly minor events may trigger major changes.

Socialization *of* Emotion

Eisenberg, Cumberland, and Spinrad (1998) define *emotional competence* as "an understanding of one's own and others' emotions, the tendency to display emotion in a situationally and culturally appropriate manner, and the ability to inhibit or modulate experienced and expressed emotion and emotionally derived behavior as needed to achieve goals in a socially acceptable manner" (p. 242; cf. Saarni, 1993). In organizational contexts, emotional competence is reflected in (1) understanding the emotional culture and climate associated with one's work role and organization; (2) accurately appraising one's own emotions and being able and willing to regulate them and their expression, as necessary, for personal and organizational goals; and (3) accurately appraising the emotions of superordinates, coworkers, clients, and others and being able and willing to respond appropriately for others', personal, and organizational goals (typically, by dispelling negative emotions and fostering positive ones).

We will focus primarily on how newcomers are socialized to understand the emotional culture and to regulate the experience and expression of their own and others' emotions. As outlined in Figure 10.2, we argue that socialization via substantive and symbolic management and off-site and on-the-job training imparts the emotional culture to newcomers. The relationship is partially mediated through the construction of social identities.

Emotional Culture

Emotional culture refers to the dominant values, beliefs, assumptions, and norms of the organization or a given subunit regarding affective issues, together with the symbolic vehicles for conveying these attributes, such as vocabulary and metaphors (cf. Gordon, 1989). For example, Plas and Hoover-Dempsey (1988, pp. 219–221) contrast conservative organizations where the display of emotion is discouraged with the "macho culture" in one software development company where managers were expected to defend their views aggressively,

Figure 10.2. Socialization *of* Emotion.

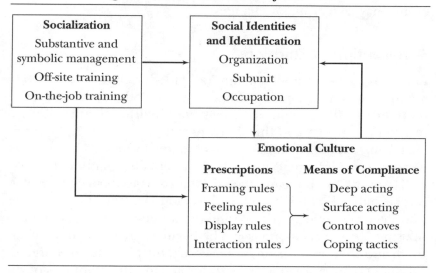

and "yelling, gesturing, and calling each other obscene names" were condoned. In contrast, *emotional climate* refers to the dominant affective tones, if any, of the organization or a given subunit. Following the circumplex model of affect (Russell, 1980; see Larsen, Diener, and Lucas, this volume), the emotional climate can be assessed on two orthogonal dimensions: pleasant-unpleasant and high-low arousal. For instance, George (1990) found that work groups could be characterized by their positive and negative affective tones. Emotional culture and climate are mutually reinforcing as values, beliefs, assumptions, and norms pertaining to emotion influence the prevailing affective tone, and the tone tends to reinforce the values, beliefs, and so on.

Prescriptions. Newcomers are socialized to understand at least four components of the emotional culture. Each component is a set of prescriptions. The first set, *framing rules,* refers to prescriptions "governing how to ascribe meanings to situations" (Hafferty, 1991, p. 15). Framing rules are recipes for sense making, guiding, and perhaps determining how events and other stimuli are interpreted. As Mills and Kleinman (1988) note, "Taking on any new ideology involves learning how to feel differently about things" (p. 1020).

For example, framing rules may guide the decoding of the emotional climate, the appraisal of others' emotions, and even the interpretation of one's own arousal. The U.S. Army, like most military institutions, places a huge premium on self-control and group coordination. Accordingly, army drill sergeants, who socialize recruits, are taught in drill sergeant school that most emotional expression, from smiling to conveying anger, is a sign of weakness and that the only legitimate way of talking about emotion is to use the terms *motivation* and *attitude*—terms that convey that emotion is *controllable* and is either high or low (motivation) or good or bad (attitude) (Katz, 1990).

The second set of prescriptions is *feeling rules,* defined as norms that specify the range, intensity, duration, and object of emotions that should be experienced in a given situation (Hochschild, 1983). Bill collectors, for instance, are expected to feel some arousal and irritation when dealing with debtors (Sutton, 1991). The third set, *display rules,* was already defined as prescriptions governing the *expression* of emotion. Whereas feeling rules pertain to what is actually felt, that is, one's inner emotions, display rules pertain to what is shown, that is, one's outward behavior—behavior that may or may not reflect one's actual emotions. High-steel ironworkers are expected to display confidence rather than fear in the face of occupational dangers (Haas, 1977).

The fourth set is *interaction rules,* defined as the strategic use of emotional expression to achieve task and relational goals (cf. heuristic rules, Averill, 1986; Waldron, 1994). Emotional cultures often include institutionalized recipes for using emotion and emotion-related thought and behavior as a resource for organizational ends. Emotion in this sense is a performance. For example, an organization may encourage the use of fear or guilt to motivate employees.

Framing rules tend to shape feeling, display, and interaction rules. Hafferty (1991) describes how medical students are implicitly taught that emotions are a sign of weakness because they compromise objectivity (framing rule). Thus, students learn to mask feelings such as anxiety or disgust (display rule) or to suppress them altogether (feeling rule) and to approach patients with some detachment (interaction rule). It should be noted that as with most other norms, there tends to be some latitude in the enactment of framing, feeling, display, and interaction rules.

Means of compliance. Even if one is generally able and willing to comply with the four sets of prescriptions, a host of factors may impede compliance in a particular situation. A situation may be novel, ambiguous, or cue conflicting rules; emotions may be involuntary, may lag behind situational cues, may be blunted by task repetition, may be loosely coupled to behavior, may be affected by stressors, fatigue, and other factors, and so on.

To facilitate compliance in problematic situations, emotional cultures typically include several means of *regulating* emotion and emotion-related thought and behavior (see Grandey and Brauburger, Chapter Eight, this volume). Compliance with framing and feeling rules may be facilitated via *deep acting*, where one attempts to actually feel the prescribed emotions (Hochschild, 1983). Hochschild discusses two deep acting techniques: (1) trained imagination, where one invokes thoughts, images, and memories to induce the associated emotion, perhaps drawing on framing rules; and (2) exhorting feeling, where one attempts to evoke or suppress an emotion. Tracy and Tracy (1998) describe how emergency call takers engage in self-talk to imagine how they would feel if they were in the caller's shoes.

Compliance with display rules may be facilitated via *surface acting*, where one attempts to portray the prescribed emotions without necessarily experiencing them (Hochschild, 1983). Facial expression, body posture, gestures, voice tone, and so on may be carefully choreographed to convey particular emotional states. Surface acting may involve simulating an emotion that is not felt, neutralizing an emotion that is felt, intensifying or deintensifying the apparent strength of a felt emotion, or substituting an emotion that is not felt for one that is (Andersen & Guerrero, 1998). Haas (1977) describes how high-steel ironworkers act with bravado to mask their fear. (Surface acting may also facilitate compliance with framing and feeling rules through self-perception and cognitive dissonance processes. One's behavior is often a potent cue for inferring one's beliefs and feelings, particularly if external control is subtle; Ashforth, 2001.)

Compliance with interaction rules may be facilitated by *control moves*, where one attempts to appraise and manipulate the emotions and behaviors of others during social interactions (cf. Goffman, 1969). Control moves are the specific tactics through which the strategic interaction rules are implemented. For instance, Fitness (2000) discusses the use of feigned anger to intimidate and thereby control others.

Finally, compliance with all four sets of prescriptions may be facilitated by the coping tactics already discussed. As noted, coping is not necessarily reactive and may involve modifying the environment or oneself. The net effect is that one negotiates a better fit with the emotional culture or learns how to accommodate the culture. Pogrebin and Poole (1995) describe how police officers use humor and denial to cope with expectations that they act fearless, calm, and objective in the face of stressful situations.

Social Identities and Identification

A social identity is a socially constructed definition of a prototypical or exemplary member of a given social category. It connotes a certain persona, including specific goals, ideologies, interaction styles, and time horizons (Ashforth, 2001). Affect control theory indicates that a social identity implies certain "fundamental sentiments" (Heise, 1977, p. 164) that individuals seek to experience through their behavior, thereby confirming their fit with the identity. For instance, managers are typically expected to convey the impression that they are cool and rational, that is, in command, regardless of how perilous a situation may be. Indeed, affect control theory maintains that individuals attempt to manage situations so as to experience the "appropriate" sentiments, particularly if their identity confirmation has been threatened by "inappropriate" sentiments (Smith-Lovin, 1990). Thus, a social identity provides recipes not only for thought and action but for *feeling* (Weick, 1995).

The most critical organization-based social identities regarding the socialization of emotion tend to be vested at the level of the organization, subunit, and occupation (see Earley and Francis, Chapter Eleven, this volume, for a discussion of the impact of *national* identities on workplace emotion). Because the lower-level identities are nested within the organizational identity, the contents of the identities tend to be more or less consistent. Regarding emotion, the organizational identity embodies the emotional culture, whereas the subunit and occupational identities embody more concrete renditions of the emotional culture. For example, drill sergeants subscribe to a somewhat different rendering of an army's emotional culture than supply or mess sergeants do. It is important to note that because lower-level identities are more concrete, as well as more exclusive and proximal, they tend to be more *salient* and therefore exert a greater impact on the individual (Ashforth & Johnson, 2001).

Members of a social category are expected to adopt the corresponding social identity, to "identify with" the persona. The greater the identification, the more likely it is that the individual will perceive and respond to organizational events through the prism of the identity. Thus, social identities and identification provide definitions of the newcomer ("I am a toy designer for Mattel") that shape feeling, thought, and behavior.

Socialization

Organizations are more likely to emphasize explicitly the socialization of emotion if the emotional culture (or climate) is strong and distinctive, members are highly interdependent (as in teamwork), or members routinely deal with clients (whether external or internal to the organization) or outside parties. Newcomers tend to learn about the emotional culture and the social identities that inform it through three major channels: substantive and symbolic management, off-site training programs, and on-the-job training.

Substantive and symbolic management. These practices span the actual structuring and processes of the organization (substantive management) and the way the organization and its members are portrayed (symbolic management) (Pfeffer, 1981). Substantive and symbolic management foster a normative context that shapes social identities and identification as well as the emotional culture.

Common practices include articulating central, distinctive, and enduring organization-based identities; developing a mission statement that embodies these identities; framing goals, strategies, and actions in terms of valued identities; relating stories and myths and building traditions and rituals that glorify valued identities; creating a distinctive physical setting, dress norms, and language; invoking metaphors such as "family" to characterize the organization; arranging social events for the communal expression of emotion; championing individuals who exemplify valued identities; celebrating achievements; picking fights with external "enemies"; recruiting individuals deemed compatible with valued identities; and punishing individuals who deviate from the emotional culture (Ashforth & Mael, 1996; O'Reilly & Chatman, 1996; Van Maanen & Kunda, 1989). In short, substantive and symbolic management are designed to foster identification with the organization, subunits, and occupations and internalization of the emotional culture. Indeed, the stronger the identifications are, the greater are the internalization of framing, feeling, display, and interaction rules and the more likely is one either to feel and express the desired emotions spontaneously or to willingly engage in surface and deep acting (Schaubroeck & Jones, 2000).

Paules (1991) describes the substantive and symbolic means through which a restaurant cued waitresses to conceive of themselves as servants and thus provide friendly and deferential service. Waitresses were referred to as servers; were required to dress in maid-like costumes and to introduce themselves by their first name; were not allowed to eat, drink, or rest in the presence of customers; and were not allowed to talk back to customers: "In preserving the conventions of servitude the company encourages the waitress to internalize an image of self as servant and to adopt an interactive stance consistent with this image" (p. 138). (However, as Paules also reports, organizational members may resist identities that are imposed in a coercive manner or appear insincere or demeaning.)

Off-site training. Off-site training includes formal credentialing programs, such as in professional and trade schools, and formal training programs, such as in human resource management departments and police academies. Oakes (1990) describes how life insurance salespeople undergo a four- to six-week training program that focuses largely on the control moves associated with prospecting for clients, approaching and interviewing them, closing sales, and subsequently servicing clients. How-to manuals, videos, lecture-demonstrations, role plays, and joint fieldwork with supervisors focus on practical techniques that work: on scripted behaviors that build client interest and trust and make polite refusal difficult.

However, given that social identities cut to the very conception of self, the full internalization of an identity takes longer than the acquisition of emotional prescriptions and the means of compliance. Thus, off-site programs may span years partly because the acquisition of a certain identity is the subtext of the program. Haas and Shaffir (1987) describe how medical students learn to adopt "a cloak of competence" (p. 53) and gradually come to feel comfortable in their role of medical expert.

On-the-job training. On-the-job training involves social learning processes (Bandura, 1977) through observation, imitation, instruction, trial and error, feedback, and rewards and punishments. The training focuses largely on behavior as an indicator of feelings and thought processes and as an instrument in its own right for task, relational, and personal goals.

Ibarra (1999) describes how neophyte investment bankers and management consultants observed multiple role models and inferred the occupational identity and emotional culture, particularly display rules and control moves. The newcomers recognized there was latitude for personalizing the identity and the enactment of the emotional culture, and they experimented with "provisional selves" (p. 776). Consistent with our discussion of socialization via emotion, the newcomers were more likely to imitate role models whom they admired and felt comfortable emulating. The newcomers used feedback from self-assessments (such as, "Does this feel right?") and role-set members to evaluate and tinker with their enactments. Newcomers were likely to reject enactments that aroused emotional dissonance. The tight coupling of emotion, appraisal, learning, behavior, and identity is evident in the following quotation from a consultant: "I was not open to exploring what the client believed, nor did I show I cared about their response. It was enlightening—and depressing—to see evidence that I did this. It didn't fit with who I am. . . . I realized it was better to stick to my normal style, but modify it slightly. My perception of myself is changing. It's scary and painful but I'm learning a lot" (p. 780).

Although Figure 10.2 depicts deep and surface acting as means of complying with emotional prescriptions as outcomes of socialization, both forms of acting are also often essential to the *process* of socialization. In addition to Ibarra's work (1999), studies of medical students (Hafferty, 1991) and neophyte managers (Hill, 1992) suggest that newcomers often feel their way into a role: they engage in deep and surface acting as ways of trying on the role and use their affective reactions to gauge their emotional resonance with the role. In this sense, the short-term inauthenticity implied by acting actually serves the longer-term cause of authenticity (Ashforth & Tomiuk, 2000). Furthermore, acting may provide the behavioral cues that trigger emotional contagion such that incipient emotions are reinforced. Sutton (1991) speculates that bill collectors in an open office reinforced one another's level of intensity and irritation—the feeling rules, as noted, of debt collection.

In sum, substantive and symbolic management and off-site and on-the-job training provide potent means for imparting the nuances of the emotional culture and valued social identities. Figure 10.2 also includes a feedback loop from emotional culture to the social identities and identification. As newcomers learn and internalize the emotional culture, they develop a more nuanced understanding of organization-based identities, and if they resonate with the identities, they may internalize them more deeply as (partial) definitions of self.

Conclusion

Although organizational entry is suffused with emotion, organizational scholars are only beginning to realize the integral role that emotion plays in entry dynamics. Emotion is not simply an outcome of recruitment, selection, and socialization processes; it is a major vehicle through which these processes influence the individual. Emotion, in short, at least partly *mediates* the impact of entry processes on the newcomer. In a real sense, newcomers must feel their way into an organization.

Our analysis suggests various directions for future research. With respect to recruitment and selection, there are at least three issues worth pursuing. First, there is a need to develop and refine job analysis techniques and procedures that focus on the emotional demands and requirements of jobs. This is a critical step in the development of valid selection methods for emotion-related constructs. Second, there is a need to develop and test emotion-based selection methods. We have suggested a number of methods that appear to be fruitful. However, research is needed to assess and enhance the predictive validity of various methods across a diversity of occupations, organizations, and industries. Finally, research on the influence of various recruitment (such as recruiter behavior) and selection practices (such as different methods) on the emotional experiences of job applicants would also be worthwhile.

Regarding socialization via emotion (see Figure 10.1), research is needed on the nature, variety, and sequencing of both orchestrated and spontaneous events across occupations, organizations, and industries. What are the critical episodes through which key lessons are disseminated and emotional climates are partially determined? How does the occupational and organizational context affect the mix and emotional experience of those episodes? Research is also needed on the role of emotion as a catalyst for appraisal, learning, and behavior. In what ways does emotion both facilitate and inhibit work adjustment? What mix and intensity of emotions are most conducive to learning?

Finally, regarding the socialization of emotion (see Figure 10.2), research might focus on the socialization practices through which different emotional cultures are imparted. What mix of practices is most likely to be effective and efficient while respecting newcomers' dignity? Research might also focus on the role of social identities (and identification) as a mediator and outcome of the socialization process. To what extent must one identify with a role or organization in order to internalize and respect the emotional culture? Can one overidentify with an organization and its emotional culture?

In sum, although newcomers must feel their way through organizational entry, organizational scholars can help ensure that they do not do so in the dark.

Notes

1. However, as Weiss and Cropanzano (1996) argue with regard to job satisfaction, these attitudes, as typically operationalized, are not so much an emotional reaction as an evaluative judgment. They reflect global appraisals *about* work and the workplace more so than the immediate experience *of* work, that is, cool cognitions rather than hot emotions.

2. The tactic of investiture (versus divestiture) appears to be an exception to these arguments. Factor analyses suggest that investiture is not strongly related to the other five institutionalized tactics (Ashforth et al., 1997). Ashforth (2001) argues that the association between investiture and the other tactics depends on the nature of the organization and occupation: the more unique (and strong) the associated identities, the greater the use of divestiture relative to investiture.

Thus, divestiture is used alongside institutionalized socialization in such distinctive settings as military boot camps, organized religion, and commercial fishing. As such, divestiture processes may be as structured as the institutionalized tactics.

References

Andersen, P. A., & Guerrero, L. K. (1998). Principles of communication and emotion in social interaction. In P. A. Andersen & L. K. Guerrero (Eds.), *Handbook of communication and emotion: Research, theory, applications, and contexts* (pp. 49–96). Orlando, FL: Academic Press.

Arnold, J. (1985). Tales of the unexpected: Surprises experienced by graduates in the early months of employment. *British Journal of Guidance and Counselling, 13,* 308–319.

Arvey, R. D., Renz, G. L., & Watson, T. W. (1998). Emotionality and job performance: Implications for personnel selection. In G. R. Ferris (Ed.), *Research in personnel and human resources management* (Vol. 16, pp. 103–147). Stamford, CT: JAI Press.

Ashforth, B. E. (2001). *Role transitions in organizational life: An identity-based perspective.* Hillside, NJ: Erlbaum.

Ashforth, B. E., & Johnson, S. A. (2001). Which hat to wear? The relative salience of multiple identities in organizational contexts. In M. A. Hogg & D. J. Terry (Eds.), *Social identity processes in organizational contexts* (pp. 31–48). Philadelphia: Psychology Press.

Ashforth, B. E., & Kreiner, G. E. (in press). Normalizing emotions in organizations: Making the extraordinary appear ordinary. *Human Resource Management Review.*

Ashforth, B. E., & Mael, F. A. (1996). Organizational identity and strategy as a context for the individual. In J.A.C. Baum & J. E. Dutton (Eds.), *Advances in strategic management* (Vol. 13, pp. 19–64). Stamford, CT: JAI Press.

Ashforth, B. E., Saks, A. M., & Lee, R. T. (1997). On the dimensionality of Jones' (1986) measures of organizational socialization tactics. *International Journal of Selection and Assessment, 5,* 200–214.

Ashforth, B. E., Saks, A. M., & Lee, R. T. (1998). Socialization and newcomer adjustment: The role of organizational context. *Human Relations, 51,* 897–926.

Ashforth, B. E., & Tomiuk, M. A. (2000). Emotional labor and authenticity: Views from service agents. In S. Fineman (Ed.), *Emotion in organizations* (2nd ed., pp. 184–203). Thousand Oaks, CA: Sage.

Ashkanasy, N. M., Härtel, C.E.J., & Zerbe, W. J. (2000). Emotions in the workplace: Research, theory, and practice. In N. M. Ashkanasy, C.E.J. Härtel, & W. J. Zerbe (Eds.), *Emotions in the workplace: Research, theory, and practice* (pp. 3–18). Westport, CT: Quorum Books.

Averill, J. R. (1980). A constructivist view of emotion. In R. Plutchik & H. Kellerman (Eds.), *Emotion: Theory, research, and experience* (Vol. 1, pp. 305–339). Orlando, FL: Academic Press.

Averill, J. R. (1986). The acquisition of emotions during adulthood. In R. Harré (Ed.), *The social construction of emotions* (pp. 98–118). Cambridge, MA: Blackwell.

Ball, D. W. (1972). Self and identity in the context of deviance: The case of criminal abortion. In R. A. Scott & J. D. Douglas (Eds.), *Theoretical perspectives on deviance* (pp. 158–186). New York: Basic Books.

Bandura, A. (1977). *Social learning theory.* Upper Saddle River, NJ: Prentice-Hall.

Barber, A. E. (1998). *Recruiting employees: Individual and organizational perspectives.* Thousand Oaks, CA: Sage.

Bar-On, R., & Parker, J.D.A. (Eds.). (2000). *The handbook of emotional intelligence: Theory, development, assessment, and application at home, school, and in the workplace.* San Francisco: Jossey-Bass.

Bartel, C. A., & Saavedra, R. (2000). The collective construction of work group moods. *Administrative Science Quarterly, 45,* 197–231.

Basch, J., & Fisher, C. D. (2000). Affective events-emotions matrix: A classification of work events and associated emotions. In N. M. Ashkanasy, C.E.J. Härtel, & W. J. Zerbe (Eds.), *Emotions in the workplace: Research, theory, and practice* (pp. 36–48). Westport, CT: Quorum Books.

Bourassa, L., & Ashforth, B. E. (1998). You are about to party *Defiant* style: Socialization and identity onboard an Alaskan fishing boat. *Journal of Contemporary Ethnography, 27,* 171–196.

Bowlby, J. (1979). *The making and breaking of affectional bonds.* New York: Tavistock.

Bruce, R. A., & Scott, S. G. (1994). Varieties and commonalities of career transitions: Louis' typology revisited. *Journal of Vocational Behavior, 45,* 17–40.

Bullis, C., & Bach, B. W. (1989). Socialization turning points: An examination of change in organizational identification. *Western Journal of Speech Communication, 53,* 273–293.

Darwin, C. (1965). *The expression of the emotions in man and animals.* Chicago: University of Chicago Press. (Original work published 1872)

Davies, M., Stankov, L., & Roberts, R. D. (1998). Emotional intelligence: In search of an elusive construct. *Journal of Personality and Social Psychology, 75,* 989–1015.

Denzin, N. K. (1989). *Interpretive interactionism.* Thousand Oaks, CA: Sage.

Eisenberg, N., Cumberland, A., & Spinrad, T. L. (1998). Parental socialization of emotion. *Psychological Inquiry, 9,* 241–273.

Ekman, P. (1973). Cross-cultural studies of facial expression. In P. Ekman (Ed.), *Darwin and facial expression: A century of research in review* (pp. 169–222). Orlando, FL: Academic Press.

Fabrigar, L. R., & Petty, R. E. (1999). The role of the affective and cognitive bases of attitudes in susceptibility to affectively and cognitively based persuasion. *Personality and Social Psychology Bulletin, 25,* 363–381.

Fichman, M., & Levinthal, D. A. (1991). Honeymoons and the liability of adolescence: A new perspective on duration dependence in social and organizational relationships. *Academy of Management Review, 16,* 442–468.

Fiebig, G. V., & Kramer, M. W. (1998). A framework for the study of emotions in organizational contexts. *Management Communication Quarterly, 11,* 536–572.

Fine, G. A. (1996). *Kitchens: The culture of restaurant work.* Berkeley: University of California Press.

Fineman, S. (1997). Emotion and management learning. *Management Learning, 28,* 13–25.

Fitness, J. (2000). Anger in the workplace: An emotion script approach to anger episodes between workers and their superiors, co-workers and subordinates. *Journal of Organizational Behavior, 21,* 147–162.

Folkman, S., & Lazarus, R. S. (1988). *Manual for the ways of coping questionnaire.* Palo Alto, CA: Consulting Psychologists Press.

Frijda, N. H. (1993). Moods, emotion episodes, and emotions. In M. Lewis & J. M. Haviland (Eds.), *Handbook of emotions* (pp. 381–403). New York: Guilford Press.

Gatewood, R. D., & Feild, H. S. (1998). *Human resource selection* (4th ed.). Orlando, FL: Dryden Press.

George, J. M. (1990). Personality, affect, and behavior in groups. *Journal of Applied Psychology, 75,* 107–116.

Gibson, D. E. (1995). Emotional scripts and change in organizations. In F. Massarik (Ed.), *Advances in organization development* (Vol. 3, pp. 32–62). Norwood, NJ: Ablex.

Gilliland, S. W. (1994). Effects of procedural and distributive justice on reactions to a selection system. *Journal of Applied Psychology, 79,* 691–701.

Gilliland, S. W. (1995). Fairness from the applicant's perspective: Reactions to employee selection procedures. *International Journal of Selection and Assessment, 3,* 11–19.

Goffman, E. (1969). *Strategic interaction.* Philadelphia: University of Pennsylvania Press.

Gordon, S. L. (1989). The socialization of children's emotions: Emotional culture, competence, and exposure. In C. Saarni & P. L. Harris (Eds.), *Children's understanding of emotion* (pp. 319–349). Cambridge: Cambridge University Press.

Greil, A. L., & Rudy, D. R. (1984). Social cocoons: Encapsulation and identity transformation organizations. *Sociological Inquiry, 54,* 260–278.

Griffin, R. W., O'Leary-Kelly, A., & Collins, J. M. (Eds.). (1998). *Dysfunctional behavior in organizations* (Vols. 1 & 2). Stamford, CT: JAI Press.

Gusterson, H. (1998). *Nuclear rites: A weapons laboratory at the end of the Cold War.* Berkeley: University of California Press.

Haas, J. (1977). Learning real feelings: A study of high steel ironworkers' reactions to fear and danger. *Sociology of Work and Occupations, 4,* 147–170.

Haas, J., & Shaffir, W. (1987). *Becoming doctors: The adoption of a cloak of competence.* Stamford, CT: JAI Press.

Hafferty, F. W. (1991). *Into the valley: Death and the socialization of medical students.* New Haven, CT: Yale University Press.

Hatfield, E., Cacioppo, J. T., & Rapson, R. L. (1994). *Emotional contagion.* Cambridge: Cambridge University Press.

Heise, D. R. (1977). Social action as the control of affect. *Behavioral Science, 22,* 163–177.

Hill, L. A. (1992). *Becoming a manager: Mastery of a new identity.* Boston: Harvard Business School Press.

Hochschild, A. R. (1983). *The managed heart: Commercialization of human feeling.* Berkeley: University of California Press.

Hogan, R., Hogan, J., & Roberts, B. W. (1996). Personality measurement and employment decisions: Questions and answers. *American Psychologist, 51,* 469–477.

Ibarra, H. (1999). Provisional selves: Experimenting with image and identity in professional adaptation. *Administrative Science Quarterly, 44,* 764–791.

Jones, G. R. (1986). Socialization tactics, self-efficacy, and newcomers' adjustments to organizations. *Academy of Management Journal, 29,* 262–279.

Katz, P. (1990). Emotional metaphors, socialization, and roles of drill sergeants. *Ethos, 18,* 457–480.

Katz, R. (1985). Organizational stress and early socialization experiences. In T. A. Beehr & R. S. Bhagat (Eds.), *Human stress and cognition in organizations* (pp. 117–139). New York: Wiley.

Kidd, J. M. (1998). Emotion: An absent presence in career theory. *Journal of Vocational Behavior, 52,* 275–288.

Kunda, G. (1992). *Engineering culture: Control and commitment in a high-tech corporation.* Philadelphia: Temple University Press.

Lazarus, R. S. (1991). *Emotion and adaptation.* New York: Oxford University Press.

Lazarus, R. S. (1999). *Stress and emotion: A new synthesis.* New York: Springer.

Lennox Terrion, J., & Ashforth, B. E. (2002). From I to we: The role of putdown humor and identity in the development of a temporary group. *Human Relations, 55,* 55–88.

Louis, M. R. (1980). Surprise and sense making: What newcomers experience in entering unfamiliar organizational settings. *Administrative Science Quarterly, 25,* 226–251.

Lutz, C. (1983). Parental goals, ethnopsychology, and the development of emotional meaning. *Ethos, 11,* 246–262.

Macan, T. H., Avedon, M. J., Paese, M., & Smith, D. E. (1994). The effects of applicants' reactions to cognitive ability tests and an assessment center. *Personnel Psychology, 47,* 715–738.

Mansfield, R. (1972). The initiation of graduates in industry: The resolution of identity-stress as a determinant of job satisfaction in the early months of work. *Human Relations, 25,* 77–86.

Martinez, M. N. (1997). The smarts that count. *HRMagazine, 42*(11), 72–78.

Mills, T., & Kleinman, S. (1988). Emotions, reflexivity, and action: An interactionist analysis. *Social Forces, 66,* 1009–1027.

Miracle, A. W., Jr., & Rees, C. R. (1994). *Lessons of the locker room: The myth of school sports.* Amherst, NY: Prometheus.

Morrison, E. W., & Robinson, S. L. (1997). When employees feel betrayed: A model of how psychological contract violation develops. *Academy of Management Review, 22,* 226–256.

Nicholson, N., & West, M. (1989). Transitions, work histories, and careers. In M. B. Arthur, D. T. Hall, & B. S. Lawrence (Eds.), *Handbook of career theory* (pp. 181–201). Cambridge: Cambridge University Press.

Oakes, G. (1990). *The soul of the salesman: The moral ethos of personal sales.* Atlantic Highlands, NJ: Humanities Press International.

O'Reilly, C. A., & Chatman, J. A. (1996). Culture as social control: Corporations, cults, and commitment. In B. M. Staw & L. L. Cummings (Eds.), *Research in organizational behavior* (Vol. 18, pp. 157–200). Stamford, CT: JAI Press.

Paules, G. F. (1991). *Dishing it out: Power and resistance among waitresses in a New Jersey restaurant.* Philadelphia: Temple University Press.

Pfeffer, J. (1981). Management as symbolic action: The creation and maintenance of organizational paradigms. In L. L. Cummings & B. M. Staw (Eds.), *Research in organizational behavior* (Vol. 3, pp. 1–52). Stamford, CT: JAI Press.

Plas, J. M., & Hoover-Dempsey, K. V. (1988). *Working up a storm: Anger, anxiety, joy, and tears on the job.* New York: Norton.

Ployhart, R. E., & Ryan, A. M. (1998). Applicants' reactions to the fairness of selection procedures: The effects of positive rule violations and time of measurement. *Journal of Applied Psychology, 83,* 3–16.

Pogrebin, M. R., & Poole, E. D. (1995). Emotion management: A study of police response to tragic events. In M. G. Flaherty & C. Ellis (Eds.), *Social perspectives on emotion* (Vol. 3, pp. 149–168). Stamford, CT: JAI Press.

Power, M., & Dalgleish, T. (1997). *Cognition and emotion: From order to disorder.* East Sussex, UK: Psychology Press.

Pratt, M. G., & Barnett, C. K. (1997). Emotions and unlearning in Amway recruiting techniques: Promoting change through "safe" ambivalence. *Management Learning, 28,* 65–88.

Rafaeli, A., & Sutton, R. I. (1989). The expression of emotion in organizational life. In L. L. Cummings & B. M. Staw (Eds.), *Research in organizational behavior* (Vol. 11, pp. 1–42). Stamford, CT: JAI Press.

Ricks, T. E. (1997). *Making the corps.* New York: Scribner.

Rosenberg, M. (1990). Reflexivity and emotions. *Social Psychology Quarterly, 53,* 3–12.

Russell, J. A. (1980). A circumplex model of affect. *Journal of Personality and Social Psychology, 39,* 1161–1178.

Rynes, S. L. (1990). Recruitment, job choice, and post-hire consequences: A call for new research directions. In M. D. Dunnette & L. M. Hough (Eds.), *Handbook of industrial and organizational psychology* (2nd ed., Vol. 2, pp. 399–444). Palo Alto, CA: Consulting Psychologists Press.

Saarni, C. (1993). Socialization of emotion. In M. Lewis & J. M. Haviland (Eds.), *Handbook of emotions* (pp. 435–446). New York: Guilford Press.

Schaubroeck, J., & Jones, J. R. (2000). Antecedents of workplace emotional labor dimensions and moderators of their effects on physical symptoms. *Journal of Organizational Behavior, 21,* 163–183.

Schmitt, N., & Ostroff, C. (1986). Operationalizing the "behavioral consistency" approach: Selection test development based on a content-oriented strategy. *Personnel Psychology, 39,* 91–108.

Smith, C. A., & Pope, L. K. (1992). Appraisal and emotion: The interactional contributions of dispositional and situational factors. In M. S. Clark (Ed.), *Review of personality and social psychology* (Vol. 14, pp. 32–62). Thousand Oaks, CA: Sage.

Smith-Lovin, L. (1990). Emotion as the confirmation and disconfirmation of identity: An affect control model. In T. D. Kemper (Ed.), *Research agendas in the sociology of emotions* (pp. 238–270). Albany: State University of New York Press.

Staw, B. M., Sutton, R. I., & Pelled, L. H. (1994). Employee positive emotion and favorable outcomes at the workplace. *Organization Science, 5,* 51–71.

Sutton, R. I. (1991). Maintaining norms about expressed emotions: The case of bill collectors. *Administrative Science Quarterly, 36,* 245–268.

Tracy, S. J., & Tracy, K. (1998). Emotion labor at 911: A case study and theoretical critique. *Journal of Applied Communication Research, 26,* 390–411.

Trice, H. M. (1993). *Occupational subcultures in the workplace.* Ithaca, NY: ILR Press.

Van Maanen, J., & Kunda, G. (1989). "Real feelings": Emotional expression and organizational culture. In L. L. Cummings & B. M. Staw

(Eds.), *Research in organizational behavior* (Vol. 11, pp. 43–103). Stamford, CT: JAI Press.

Van Maanen, J., & Schein, E. H. (1979). Toward a theory of organizational socialization. In B. M. Staw (Ed.), *Research in organizational behavior* (Vol. 1, pp. 209–264). Stamford, CT: JAI Press.

Waldron, V. R. (1994). Once more, *with feeling:* Reconsidering the role of emotion in work. In S. A. Deetz (Ed.), *Communication yearbook* (Vol. 17, pp. 388–416). Thousand Oaks, CA: Sage.

Wanous, J. P. (1992). *Organizational entry: Recruitment, selection, orientation, and socialization of newcomers* (2nd ed.). Reading, MA: Addison-Wesley.

Wanous, J. P., Poland, T. D., Premack, S. L., & Davis, K. S. (1992). The effects of met expectations on newcomer attitudes and behaviors: A review and meta-analysis. *Journal of Applied Psychology, 77,* 288–297.

Weick, K. E. (1995). *Sensemaking in organizations.* Thousand Oaks, CA: Sage.

Weiss, H. M., & Cropanzano, R. (1996). Affective events theory: A theoretical discussion of the structure, causes and consequences of affective experiences at work. In B. M. Staw & L. L. Cummings (Eds.), *Research in organizational behavior* (Vol. 18, pp. 1–74). Stamford, CT: JAI Press.

CHAPTER 11

International Perspectives on Emotion and Work

P. Christopher Earley
Clare Anne Francis

Few other topics are as critical and fundamental to human activity in all organizations as that of emotion and its display. As an example, in a Thai cement factory, it is determined that the last day's output is waste because an incorrect mix has been used. The factory manager, an Australian expatriate, visits the shop floor and shows a strong emotional display of anger and frustration. His chief supervisor, a Thai manager, responds by remaining relatively silent but smiling as a result. This experience further frustrates the Australian, who turns his anger toward the Thai manager who "doesn't seem to take this problem seriously." The following day, the Thai manager has left his position to move to a new company. What the Australian manager fails to realize is that there are over twenty different types of "smiles" in Thai culture, each having subtle but different meanings. He misinterpreted this emotional display, with unfortunate consequences.

Just as we question the meaning of managerial interventions across cultural settings, so we must realize that the display and experience of emotion in the workplace vary tremendously across societies. What is the nature of emotion across cultures? Are emotions culturally unique or universals? How does the unique nature of organizational setting across cultures impinge on the emotion process? These are a few of the questions that we explore in this chapter.

Cross-Cultural Approaches to Emotion

The topic of understanding emotion from a cross-cultural perspective has a long history in psychology and anthropology. Much of this traditional work has focused on the identification of universals in emotional display (Ekman, 1972) and emotional experience (Mesquita & Frijda, 1992; Russell, 1994). In this section, we provide a brief review of this literature by focusing on three issues: emotional display, emotion categories, and appraisal processes.

The best-developed and -researched area on cross-cultural emotion is without doubt the seminal work by Ekman and his colleagues concerning emotional display and facial expressions (Ekman, 1973, 1980). In its simplest form, the argument for universality of emotional display is derived from work by Charles Darwin on the expression of emotions in man and animals (1872/1965). (Universality of emotion and its expression predates Darwin, but his theory was the first to provide a unifying reason for such a possible etic characteristic.) In the twentieth century, emotional expression and the experience of emotion was the center of much discussion by scholars. For example, Klineberg (1940) focused on the universality of display, although he noted a number of examples for which some cultures varied from one another. For example, the Maori of New Zealand express anger and threat by opening the mouth and extending their tongues. This expression is inconsistent with a number of other cultures.

Ekman, who has presented the largest body of work on emotional expression, summed up the dominant views of the literature in this way: "For more than 100 years scientists argued about whether facial expressions are universal or specific to each culture. On the one side Darwin, and, more recently, Lorenz . . . argued that facial expressions are innate, evolved behavior. On the other side, Birdwhistell [and] Klineberg . . . argued that facial expressions are instead like a language, socially learned, culturally controlled, and variable in meaning from one setting to another" (1984, p. 319).

Ekman and his colleagues (and related researchers) focused on identifying emotional expression as indicative of emotional experience. In his prototypic research paradigm, subjects are presented with photographs showing face and shoulder shots with a person depicting a particular facial expression (often posed by a professional actor). These photographs are selected to portray a wide array of facial expressions, and the subject is then asked to identify the expression. Based on this work, there appears to be overwhelming evidence suggesting that people can universally recognize facial expressions and make accurate inferences concerning underlying emotional states of the person portrayed in the photograph despite differences in race, ethnicity, and gender. Various methods of identifying the underlying characteristic have been employed, including a fixed-choice set of descriptors (short list of emotions from which one is chosen), ratings on a fixed set of emotions scales, self-generated (by the subject) emotion description, and matching the emotion displayed with a story describing an emotional event. This research has demonstrated a relatively strong set of core emotions that are easily identified across both literate and preliterate cultures, including anger, happiness, sadness, and disgust (Ekman, 1973).

This stream of work is not without substantial criticism and qualification. For example, the traditional viewpoint expressed by anthropologists such as Mead (1975) and Klineberg (1940) suggests that emotional display is a culturally based and socially constructed behavior rather than a universal one. Recent critiques of Ekman's facial expression work are presented by Russell (1994) and Mequita, Frijda, and Scherer (1997), who have questioned the universality notion that Ekman and others (Izard, 1980) have expressed. Russell provided a reanalysis of Ekman's research program on a number of bases, including subject selection, response format for expression attribution, statistical analysis, and forced choice versus free selection of responses, among others. Although Russell's critique is not without fault (see Ekman, 1994; Izard, 1994, for rebuttals), it raises a point that Mesquita and Frijda (1992) addressed in their review of this literature. Although it seems somewhat fashionable to discount the idea of universal facial expression, work as recently as 1987 by Ekman et al. has supported the universality thesis. To our reading, it appears fully warranted to suggest that there are aspects of emotional display that are universal, but with Ekman's (1994) own caveat that universality does not mean complete homogeneity of display. That is, variation across and within cultures is likely to occur (Pennebaker, Rime, & Blankenship, 1996).

Another approach taken in the study of emotions from a cross-cultural perspective is referred to as a categorical approach. This simply refers to the categorization of emotions into fundamental categories (Boucher, 1979; Levy, 1984; Mesquita et al., 1997; Ortony, Clore, & Collins, 1988; Russell, 1991; Wierzbicka, 1986). The most common set of general categories refers to five dimensions: anger, fear, happiness, sadness, and disgust (Boucher, 1979). To this basic list, a number of other categories might be added, including surprise, contempt, shame, and interest. As with the idea of emotional display, the general idea is that there is a set of fundamental emotions that are experienced in all cultures along with others that are more culture specific.

Boucher (1979) views emotional categories as hierarchically arranged with the basic emotions (such as anger or sadness) as superordinate and universal. As one travels further down the hierarchy, additional emotion categories arise as a subset of these superordinate characteristics and that are culture specific. For example, the Malaysian concept of anger differs from that in American culture in a number of ways, although the core concept appears to be the same (Russell, 1991). Similarly, there are some emotions that do not appear to exist in certain cultures to the same degree of differentiation as they do in others. For example, the Ilongot (Rosaldo, 1978) use a single word to represent what Americans collectively describe as shame, embarrassment, respect, obedience, and awe. Boucher's approach suggests that this is a perfectly compatible (with his theory) observation because the superordinate characteristic is shame, with the concept being more highly differentiated by Americans than the Ilongot.

Levy (1984) provides a slight variation on the approach that Boucher takes in suggesting that the emotion hierarchy consists of specific focal points that capture the core to an emotion at a given hierarchical level. That is, an emotion such as anger may differ from one culture to another, but it has at its base an overlapping, focal point (such as a furious reaction) that is in common. This type of lexical hierarchy is evident in work by Hupka, Lenton, and Hutchison (1999), as well as in their work on sixty language and lexical groupings derived from the Human Relations Area Files (HRAF). They found support for the notion of a hierarchy of categories and group them into roughly five stages of increasing specificity.

Wierzbicka (1986, 1994) takes this notion one step further by asserting that it may not be the emotions that are in common, but the underlying dimensions of the emotion. She suggested that the various emotions that exist across societies may not be universal, but they are all based on the same set of fundamental semantic primitives such as want, think, good, and bad. This approach has a general similarity to work done by Triandis, Osgood, and others on the development of the semantic differential (Triandis & Lambert, 1958). In this work, it was argued that all concepts could be universally defined using three underlying dimensions: evaluation (good-bad), potency (weak-strong), and activity (fast-slow). Thus, the idea presented is not that emotions form universal categories but that emotions are based on universal dimensions of semantic primitives. Wierzbicka (1994) argues that rather than positing universal emotions, it is more useful to think in terms of cultural scripts that are written in lexical universals. The specificity of these scripts is illustrated with an example:

Polish
    It is good to say something like this to someone: "I feel something very good toward you"

Australian English
    It is not good to say something like this to someone: "I feel something very good toward you."

    If I feel something very good toward someone (or something), I can say something bad [Wierzbicka, 1994, p. 163].

This quotation illustrates that the script for expressing experienced emotions differs from the Polish to the Australian samples. In the case of the Poles, it is expected for people to display emotions of liking and friendship openly. In contrast, the Australians reflect an understatement and reserve such that it demonstrates toughness and defiance.

A flurry of activity in the study of emotions has been focused on the notion that universality lies in the appraisal rather than display of emotions (Ellsworth, 1994; Mesquita & Frijda, 1992). This perspective is best demonstrated through an illustration of a typical framework employed by researchers in the area, and for this we draw from work by Frijda and Mesquita (1994). In their model,

Frijda and Mesquita describe the idea of emotion as a process rather than a state. Their model consists of the following sequence: event → event coding → appraisal → action readiness → physiological changes, behavior. Furthermore, these stages are influenced by self-regulatory processes and concerns. Concerns denote the short- and long-term dispositions to prefer certain states over others. The chief contribution of this approach is the movement of attention away from emotion as a category or display to emotion as an attribution and evaluation based on experience. The question becomes, then, whether there exists a cultural significance to the way people encode and appraise emotion-relevant events.

The appraisal process itself is largely viewed as a relatively automatic and unconscious process guided by personal experience and cultural background. Research on appraisal has revealed a number of underlying dimensions of appraisal, including attention to change (novelty-attention), pleasure or distaste (unpleasantness-pleasantness), a sense of certainty, perception of obstacles, controllability, attribution of agency (human versus nonhuman), impact on self-concept (enhance or decrease self-esteem), status maintenance, and overall judgment of value or fit with existing norms (Mesquita et al., 1997). As Mesquita et al. (1997) point out, these appraisal dimensions show a great deal of convergence across a wide range of studies conducted in cross-cultural work (Matsumoto, Kudoh, Scherer, & Wallbott, 1988; Wallbott & Scherer, 1988).

These appraisal dimensions show that individuals use a relatively modest number of underlying dimensions to understand various emotion-relevant events across cultures. In addition, a common set of appraisal dimensions can be used to capture the ways that emotions are expressed across languages. Taken together, these findings suggest that although emotional experience and display may differ across cultures, the dimensions underlying appraisal are universal.

The Role of Emotion in Cross-Cultural Work

Despite what seems to be a highly salient and obvious focus for research, surprisingly little attention has been focused on the nature of emotion in the workplace from a cross-cultural perspective. That is, how might the display and experience of emotion lead to meaningful differences and similarities across cultural boundaries?

In the workplace (even if that workplace happens to be a factory), the display of emotion and its experience is of obvious significance for a manager. These interpretations and experiences are of central importance when crossing cultural boundaries and warrant serious scrutiny.

We provide a simple, and preliminary, framework for investigating the significance of culture in understanding the role of emotion in the workplace across the globe. We emphasize a model intended as a complement to the other chapters in this volume inasmuch as our focus is on the relevant factors antecedent to emotional experience from a cross-cultural and organizational perspective. (Readers who are interested in a more complete review of the literature on cross-cultural aspects of emotion are referred to Ekman & Freisen, 1971, 1975, 1976; Ellsworth, 1994; Ellsworth & Smith, 1988; Izard, 1971, 1977, 1994; Markus & Kitayama 1991; Kitayama & Markus, 1994; Mesquita & Frijda, 1992; Mesquita et al., 1997; Russell, 1994; and Russell & Fernandez-Dols, 1997.)

We have identified a number of cultural characteristics that have relevance to emotional experience and emotional display in organizations. Some of these, such as individualism-collectivism, have received a great deal of attention in the literature from a general cross-cultural perspective (Markus & Kitayama, 1991; Triandis, 1994), while others have not. Regardless, these cultural dimensions have not been tied to emotion and emotional display within the context of organizational behavior to our knowledge in a comprehensive fashion. Thus, we focus on the explication of a framework looking at how various cultural dimensions influence the display, experience, and consequence of emotions in an organizational setting.

Overview of the Framework

Our framework consists of four general parts with cascading influences on one another (see Figure 11.1): societal context, industry and organizational context, work unit and group characteristics, and employee emotional display and experience. Quite intentionally, we have not provided an extensive and detailed model of each general part because our purpose is to use this framework for organizational purposes and highlight major spheres of influence rather than the detail of emotion display and experience from an individual's perspective. (For such a detailed approach, we recommend the previously cited authors such as Ekman, Ellsworth, or Markus and Kitayama.)

General Societal Context

We begin by focusing on the first general part of the framework, societal context, by limiting our discussion to cultural dimensions of society alone. Specifically, we focus on shame versus guilt (Mead, 1934), tight versus loose (and the individual related construct of psychological differentiation), masculinity versus femininity, and individualism versus collectivism. These dimensions were chosen to represent those cultural dimensions having obvious applicability to emotional experience and display. Our purpose is to illustrate

Figure 11.1. Cross-Cultural Perspectives of Emotion and Work.

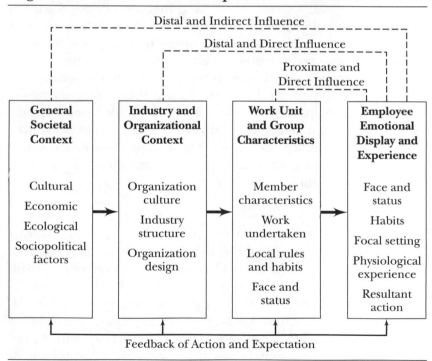

the logic of how cultural context influences emotional experience and display rather than definitively to bind the realm of societal context for the cross-cultural study of emotion.

Shame Versus Guilt

Shame refers to a situation in which a person has failed to fulfill personal or community ideals for behavior and personal states, and guilt reflects a situation in which a person transgresses the moral imperatives of a society (Lazarus & Lazarus, 1994). For example, we might say that a person who has a physical deformity experiences shame, but we would not necessarily conclude that this unfortunate person feels guilty about his appearance. However, if someone steals from his employer but is not caught, he may experience guilt but not shame. Thus, a critical dimension of these complex emotions is the degree of explicitness in the experience. Shame is a socially oriented experience, and guilt is a personal one. The origins of shame versus guilt from an anthropological perspective can be traced to a number of scholars, including Benedict (1946), Levy (1973), Lynd (1958), and Rosaldo (1978). Shame is essentially a socially based experience, whereas guilt is an individually based experience, and such a distinction maps on nicely to distinctions of societies based on self versus community.

The relationship of shame versus guilt to emotion is likely in the appraisal that occurs. What we assert is that appraisals involving personal attribution are more likely in a guilt-based culture, whereas appraisals involving group attribution are more likely in a shame-based culture. Thus, an event leading to various displays is likely to arise in a guilt-based culture because appraisals are self-based and self-regulatory.

Tight Versus Loose

Tight versus loose refers to the extent to which rules and norms are present and enforced within a society (Witkin & Berry, 1975). In a tight culture, characterized by many rules governing individuals' actions (Glenn & Glenn, 1981; Triandis, 1990), individuals conform to existing practices, and deviation from those rules is discouraged or condemned. Loose societies are characterized by a number of factors—for example, norms are expressed with a wide range of alternative channels; deviant behavior is widely tolerated;

values of group organization formality are underdeveloped; and values such as stability, duration, and solidarity are underemphasized. Tight societies are characterized by the opposite situation. Japan and the Israeli kibbutzim are tight societies, and Thailand is a loose one.

Work on tight versus loose cultures was undertaken by Witkin, Berry, and their colleagues (Berry, Kim, Minde, & Mok, 1987; Berry, 1991; Witkin & Berry, 1975). The dimension of tight versus loose is best understood within the context of an ecological-cultural-behavioral framework encompassing multilevel influences on individuals within societies. The model accounts for psychological diversity (individual and group contrasts and similarities) by taking into account two general sources of influence: ecological and sociopolitical context. These general exogenous factors influence the psychological outcomes of cognitive-style development through two classes of process variables. The first of these macrolevel influences are process variables, including biological and cultural adaptation. Process variables include ecological influences, genetic transmission, cultural transmission, and acculturation. The elements of the model are arranged on two levels: a general ecological flow having its primary effect on ecological influences, biological adaptation, and genetic transmission, and a general sociopolitical context having its primary effect on cultural adaptation, cultural transmission, and acculturation.

Cognitive styles based on field dependence and independence can be understood as manifesting the differing styles of information seeking that people engage in. When people seek information, field-dependent people look to others for this information just as they look to an external field in perceptual tasks as evidenced in the various measures used to assess field independence and dependence. Field-independent people look to themselves more than to external referents. Therefore, there are a number of social behaviors that one might expect to be associated with field dependence and independence. First, people who are field independent tend to use external referent information for attitude and judgment change less than do people who are field dependent. Second, the degree to which people monitor responses is related to field dependence and independence. Third, people who are field dependent are better able to recall and process social information and cues than people who are field independent, and finally, field-dependent people are typically judged by others to be more social, gregarious, and interested in people, while field-independent people are often characterized as self-interested, cold, distant, and task oriented.

Masculinity Versus Femininity

A number of norms are associated with masculinity and femininity. In a more masculine culture, there is an emphasis on norms that include money and objects (accumulation), performance and growth, "live to work," an achievement ideal, independence and decisiveness, excelling and trying to be the best at something, and an admiration of things that are big and fast. Sex roles in society are clearly differentiated, with men being more assertive and women more caring, and males dominate in various settings. In a more feminine culture, there is an emphasis on norms that include a people orientation, a stress on the quality of life and environment, "work to live," a service ideal, the importance of interdependence and intuition, the importance of leveling (that is, not trying to be better than others), and a view that small and slow are beautiful. Sex roles are less differentiated and more fluid, androgyny is an ideal, and sex roles are not associated with differential levels of power (Hofstede, 1980).

Hofstede stresses the relevance of masculinity and femininity for organizations primarily in terms of industrial strife, conflict, high growth, work stress, achievement, and aggression. That is, masculine cultures are essentially fast paced and aggressive and emphasize growth and development over stability and harmony. In contrast, people from a feminine culture are concerned with proper social functioning and interaction among people. A nurturing and caring perspective focusing on people and their welfare is threatened if individuals place personal gain over interpersonal harmony and functioning. This suggests that the moral character of people is of central concern because such a focus helps to determine the potential of an individual to contribute to interpersonal welfare, and it reflects a person's likely balance point. By a balance point, we mean that in a feminine culture, it is important that people know each other's moral perspective in order to understand their true needs and wants fully. It reflects a desire to understand another person in a fundamental and personal way that is not attainable through a cursory examination of a person's wealth or position (that is, to get to know the person and not just his or her role).

Individualism Versus Collectivism

The concept of individualism versus collectivism is one of the most widely discussed cultural dimensions in the literature; literally hundreds of studies have been conducted on the topic (for reviews, see Earley & Gibson, 1998; Triandis, 1995).

There are a number of varying views concerning the concept of individualism and collectivism. The distinction that Parsons and Shils (1951) used concerning how individuals relate to one another with regard to shared interests is called self-orientation versus collectivity orientation. The definition Kluckhohn and Strodtbeck (1961) used depicts the relational aspect of value orientation as individualism versus collaterality versus lineal. Individualism refers to the autonomy over action afforded to the individual. If a culture is individualistic, this suggests that individual goals have primacy over the goals of specific collateral or lineal groups. A strong collateral orientation refers to an emphasis on goals and welfare of the extended group over those of the individual. Finally, a lineal orientation refers to a prioritization of group goals (as with collateral) over time. A widespread view of individualism and collectivism is presented by Hofstede (1980, 1991) in his seminal works. According to Hofstede, individualism is a collection of values concerning the relation of an individual to his or her collectivity in society. An individualistic society is one in which people think in terms of themselves, or trait terms, and a collectivistic society is one in which an individual is defined with reference to a cultural context. Individualism is related to a number of organizational characteristics as well. Individuals from a collectivistic society call for greater emotional dependence on one another than individuals from individualistic societies, and their organizations are expected to play a stronger role in their lives.

The conceptual work by Triandis (1989, 1995) appears to be the most extensive discussion focusing on the nature of the in-group and individualism and collectivism. In his recent work, Triandis has extended and developed an interesting two-way analysis of individualism and collectivism using a distinction made by Chen, Meindl, and Hunt (1997) to define four attributes of individualism and collectivism: definition of self (independent versus interdependent), structure of goals (individual goals as independent versus compatible with group goals), emphasis on norms versus attitudes (social behavior is most directly to attitudes versus norms, duty, and obligations), and emphasis on rationality versus relatedness (computation of costs and benefits versus prioritization given to relationships regardless of costs/benefits).

Cultural Factors and Emotional Experience

If we return to our earlier presentation concerning the emotional experience as a sequence of stages and events, it is possible to understand the direct influence of cultural context on workplace emotion. In one sense, these direct effects are no different than are those effects for a nonworkplace context since we are focusing on the role of context in the appraisal and display aspects of emotion. As we discuss in the next few sections, the unique addition of a work environment provides a somewhat different perspective (from traditional cross-cultural work on emotion) inasmuch as each cascading level (organizational, work unit) has interactive effects with the societal context.

If we draw from a general appraisal model such as that presented by Frijda and Mesquita (1994), we can see that cultural factors will influence various stages of the emotion process, including event coding, appraisal, and behavior (emotion display). For example, people from a shame culture focus on events emphasizing reflecting personal status in the social context of others. Feedback suggesting a failure in public will result in negative emotional experiences for people in a shame culture. More important, a social presence is needed for regulatory behavior in a strong shame culture, whereas this social context is not as crucial for such experiences in a guilt culture. Thus, for a shame versus guilt culture, event coding and appraisal are moderated by the presence of others.

In a tight versus a loose culture, the most obvious impact of culture on emotion processes is that event coding and appraisal are based on many subtle cues in a tight culture but not a loose one. That is, inferences made concerning the emotive value of situations are more complex and subtle in a tight culture, but this does not mean that display follows as being more direct and obvious. That is, in a tight culture, there is an inherent tension between sensitivity to ascertain emotional content and the opportunity for display. As an example, in a tight culture such as Japanese society, we suggest that people are readily able to infer emotional content from a very subtle context, but this does not mean that they can display these emotions. Quite to the contrary, in a tight society, the expectation is that people will suppress their emotional display. Thus, in a tight culture, there is a contradiction that likely leads to frustration: a high sensitivity to experience and inferring emotion with little opportunity for a relief valve. Perhaps this is why emotional display becomes institutionalized in such practices as the "after work hours" venting with one's superiors in Japan (Earley & Erez, 1997).

Cultural values such as masculinity versus femininity or individualism versus collectivism have been the subject of much discussion in the literature. (For a fine review of how emotional processes are related to individualism versus collectivism, see Triandis, 1994. With regard to masculinity versus femininity, we recommend Hofstede, 1980.) As we have illustrated in the prior two examples of cultural influence, the key to predicting these effects is how cultural context influences event coding, appraisal, and display (behavior). As an example, Triandis (1994) suggests that collectivists are more likely than individualists to empathize with others and are more likely to restrain their emotional display so as not to impose on others with the in-group. Hofstede suggests that people from masculine cultures are more likely to be stoic and show restraint in experiencing and displaying emotion than people from feminine cultures.

Industry and Organizational Context

Institutions and an institutional analysis are very important in understanding the role of emotion in an organization. Institutional theory applied to organizations can be thought of as the study of functioning through an analysis of persistent rules and procedures underlying action. Organizations are viewed as dependent on a wide environment that is the product of rational and nonrational impulses and "less as a coherent rational super actor (e.g., a tightly integrated state or a highly coordinated invisible hand) than as an evolving set of rationalized patterns, models, or cultural schemes. . . . These may be built into the public polity, in the laws, or into modernized society through professional and scientific analyses or the models set by exemplary organizations" (Scott & Meyer, 1994, p. 33).

Scott and Meyer (1994) present a useful overview of a prototypical institutional model consisting of several facets. First, the origins of environmental rationalization reflect sociological influences on the nature of organizing. Second, these origins give rise to dimensions of a rationalized environment such that rules or ideologies describing or prescribing certain organizational practices create consistent changes in and across organizations. Third, these general rules and ideologies give rise to the specific mechanisms that shape organizational functioning. That is, organizations develop and perpetuate policies and rules, ideas and beliefs, and myths and rituals in the organizational identities taken on. Finally, the specific nature of an organization with its peculiar identity and activity patterns exists as a product of institutional forces. The identity, structures, and activity patterns of an organization are the result of institutionalized patterns derived from a rationalized environment.

Although there might be a wide variety of ways to approach the study of cross-cultural emotions in organizations, our emphasis has been on the nature of institutional rules and roles and how they influence emotional appraisal. For example, the dominant culture for an organization will influence and affect the style of interaction among members. In a highly networked organization (Goffee & Jones, 1996), the emphasis is on communication, friendships, and camaraderie. This suggests that individuals will generally focus on one another as a referent in making inferences concerning their emotions, and they will use these referents as a means of sense making as well. The institutional influences extend as well to providing a general context for establishing an ambience for emotion and display. The myths and rituals that exist within an organization influence the way that people interpret emotive circumstances and shape their expectations for how to react. For example, in an industry such as financial investments and stock trading, a strong culture of stoicism and restraint inhibits the strong display of emotion and attenuates the emotional experience as well. These institutional practices reflect societal culture as well as industry- and company-specific characteristics, and all of these influences shape an individual's reactions to a given situation through a variety of means.

Work Unit and Group Characteristics

The work group or team is the most proximate social influence on an employee and has a number of significant ramifications for the display, interpretation, and experience of emotion for an employee. Obviously, the work team represents a strong source of reference for an employee, and it guides and regulates immediate action (Hackman, 1990).

A group refers to two or more individuals who interact directly or indirectly for the accomplishment of a common goal. In addition, a group shares a common set of beliefs and values, and these characteristics form the basis for membership, although selection into (or out of) a group is not necessarily a voluntary action on the part of a member. For example, an individualist may choose to leave a family group, severing all ties with a critical parent or disowning the family, whereas such an option does not exist for a collectivist (Triandis, 1995). Also, our definition does not require a particular size or age of an aggregate to constitute a group, although groups will vary qualitatively according to these dimensions. Finally, our definition requires that we consider the nature and structure of a group separate from the individual members. This final point seems necessary because much research on groups takes an individualistic perspective focusing on individual needs and motives (Turner, 1985).

The immediacy of a person's work team influences how people perceive themselves as group members in a hierarchical structure of groups (Turner, 1985). At the most general level, people distinguish themselves from nonhumans, and within humans, groups are based on intraclass similarities and interclass differences. Self-categorization theory (SCT; Turner, 1985) assumes that individuals are motivated to maintain a positive self-evaluation of self-categories through a comparison of self and other member characteristics with prototypes of the next higher level of categorization. From our perspective, SCT has several interesting features that can be used to describe cultural influences. Turner argues that group formation occurs for several reasons. First, groups can form as a result of spontaneous or emergent social categorizations from the immediate situation. Second, they occur as a result of some preformed, internalized categorization scheme available from cultural sources, such as work class, gender, or race. The basic premise that individuals use preformed categories in forming in-groups as well as making judgments about out-groups seems to be crucial in understanding group processes in various cultures. The nature of group membership (categorization) implies different responses in terms of cultural characteristics. For example, collectivists will remain active with their in-group even if it places great demands on them, although individualists will exit from a particular in-group in favor of a less demanding in-group under these circumstances. This suggests that the nature of group membership, that is, what norms emerge for member behavior, varies across cultures, and so must the critical features that define self-categorization and group formation.

The immediacy of a work group affects the nature of emotional experience and its display in a number of ways. First, team members are a strong referent for appraisal (cues for how one might and should react to a given situation). Second, fellow employees make up the social context including a general sense of the mood of the workplace. Third, team members provide one another with an enacted version of what they believe to be the appropriate societal, organizational, and work culture for one another. Fourth, issues of face and status are enacted at a team level (Earley, 1997) that guide particular emotional displays over others. That is, for reasons of face and status, team members may engage in and enact certain emotional displays over others (examples are the stoicism of the investment banker and the empathy of the collectivist for in-group members). Finally, team members collectively feed back to the general cultural context the nature of emotional experience and display such that a feedback loop is formed and the environment is shaped.

Employee Emotional Display and Experience

The final aspect of our model concerns the actual interpretation and display of an emotional event by an employee, the subject of much research on the topic of emotion. In our framework, we focus on emotional experience and display using face and status, habits, focal setting, physiological experience, and resultant action (see Earley, 1997 for a more extensive discussion of these constructs and their mutual interplay).

Examples of Research in the Workplace

Although there is a long and detailed history of emotion in cross-cultural psychology, this topic has received relatively little attention in the literature on organizations. This is the case despite the attention stimulated by early work on emotional display by Sutton and Rafaeli (1988), as well as more recent work by George, Jones, and Gonzalez (1998) and Brief, Burke, George, Robinson, and Webster (1988) among others, and the interest their work stimulated. However, this fascinating and important work has not been mirrored by the work conducted by cross-cultural management research. In a review of the literature, we were able to find few studies directly examining emotion in a cross-cultural work context, although we identified a number of areas tangentially addressing such issues. For convenience, we have grouped these studies into several general categories: work and role stress, conflict and negotiation, expatriate adjustment, and other work.

Work and Role Stress

Emotion in a cross-cultural management perspective can be thought of as a reaction to work and role stresses experienced. Although there is a paucity of research on the cross-cultural aspects of emotions in the workplace, there is a reasonable literature on cross-cultural aspects of work and role stress. For example, Peterson, Smith and colleagues (1995) examined role conflict and ambiguity in a wide range of nations. They found that role stresses varied by country to a larger degree than personal and organizational factors and that role ambiguity and overload were related to cultural concepts of individualism and power distance.

Van de Vliert and Van Yperen (1996) presented an interesting debate concerning role stress: that ambient temperature explained the relation of national values to role stress based on a reanalysis of Peterson et al. (1995). More recently, Peterson and Smith (1997) refute these assertions and again state the importance of national culture for the understanding of reactions to stress and role conflict.

In their study of collective and personal efficacy, Schaubroeck, Lam, and Xie (2000) discussed the topic of job control as a coping mechanism for job stressors. They looked at the importance of job control as a coping mechanism in samples from Hong Kong and the United States and found that perceived control was related to coping for personal efficacy in the United States but collective efficacy in Hong Kong. They relate their findings to the literature on individualism defined at an individual level of analysis.

Smulders, Kompler, and Paoli (1996) looked at the general work environment of twelve European Union countries and found clusters of similarity in reactions and overall levels of job stress. A northern cluster consisted of Denmark, Germany, Netherlands, and Great Britain; a southern cluster consisted of Spain, Portugal, France, Italy, and Ireland; a middle cluster consisted of Belgium and Luxembourg; and an isolated southern cluster consisted of Greece. In general, the quality of life was highest for the northern and lowest for the southern clusters. Xie (1996) looked at the nature of job demands and control in a sample of twelve hundred employees from five Chinese cities and found that anxiety and depression were related to high job demands and low control, whereas the highest satisfaction was related to high control. Yoon and Lim (1999) examined the role of positive affectivity in relation to organizational support in a sample of hospital employees from South Korea. They found that contrary to the positive affectivity hypothesis (that good mood for employees leads to higher likeability and more support), employees' positive disposition worked against the bringing forth of organizational support. Chang and Holt (1996) looked at the importance of cultural and personal relationship patterns in relation to workplace adjustment for two Taiwanese computer firms using extensive ethnographies. Evans, Palsane, and Carrere (1987) looked at Type A behavior and occupational stress using a sample of U.S. American and Indian bus drivers.

Cooper and his colleagues (summarized nicely in Cooper & Payne, 1992) have looked at various aspects of workplace stress, well-being, stress management, and emotional experience. Cooper and Payne draw from Hofstede's cultural dimensions of power distance and masculinity and femininity as a way of organizing their thoughts concerning work and role stress across cultures. Their framework consists of interventions related to outcomes across three levels of stress experience, and they provide a number of interesting comments along these lines. In another study, Kirkcaldy and Cooper (1993) looked at the relation of work stress to leisure style for a British and German sample of managers.

An additional stream of work having great significance is that by Frese and his colleagues (Frese & Zapf, 1988; Garst, Frese, & Molenaar, 2000). Frese has looked at dynamics of stressor-strain relationships in various European samples. His stressor-strain trend model reflects both stable and dynamic stress elements such that acute stressors lead to an impact on strain through linked processes.

Finally, we would be remiss if we did not specifically single out the work by Bhagat and his colleagues (Bhagat & McQuaid, 1982; Bhagat et al., 1994). This work in the 1980s was the first to provide a fully integrative model of how subjective culture influences individual reactions to workplace characteristics including role constraints. In Bhagat et al. (1994), organizational stress was related to psychological strain using three moderator variables: problem-focused coping, emotion-focused coping, and decision latitude.

Conflict and Negotiation

Another popular topic of research with relevance for the study of emotion in the cross-cultural workplace is that of negotiation and conflict management. Although emotion is not a central focus for this work, it crops up in a number of instances as an important variable (see Pilutla & Murnighan, 1996, for a useful presentation of emotion in the general negotiation process).

Some of the most interesting work on this topic from a work perspective was presented by Ting-Toomey and her colleagues (Ting-Toomey & Cocroft, 1994; Ting-Toomey, 1985, 1988). Her theoretical perspective focuses on individualistic and collectivistic cultures using concepts of face and self-identity (also see Earley, 1997, for a further discussion). Although emotion is not a specific component of her framework, its regulation is clearly central for face-related behavior (Ting-Toomey, 1988).

Cropanzano, Aguinis, Schminke, and Denham (1999) looked at the disputant reactions to managerial conflict resolution tactics in Argentina, the Dominican Republic, Mexico, and the United States. They found that managers stimulated the most positive responses when they acted as either impartial facilitators or inquisitorial judges. Using the Miles and Snow strategy typology, Dyer and Song (1997) looked at U.S. and Japanese managers' reactions to strategy on conflict. Cropanzano et al. (1999) evaluated conflict tactics on three dimensions: fairness, likelihood of reducing future conflict, and an overall assessment. All nations responded favorably to facilitation; however, the U.S. participants rated it more positively than did the participants from the Dominican Republic and Argentina. Americans evaluated the inquisitorial style more negatively than the Dominicans and also saw it as less fair; however, the Dominicans and the Americans did not differ in their assessment regarding future conflict. The researchers suggest that culture appears to be a moderator of these positive responses. Power distance, that is, the extent to which the powerless members of society accept the unequal distribution of power, may be operative in the differences between the Dominican Republic and the United States and their respective assessments of the facilitative versus the inquisitorial styles. Participants from the Dominican Republic, a Latin American country with generally higher power distance values than the United States, may feel stressed by leaders who take a more participative approach versus a forceful and directive approach.

Morris et al. (1998) have looked at various aspects of conflict management styles across cultures. With regard to the specific overlap with emotion, they find that Asian managers use an avoidance of conflict style with reserved display of emotions in contrast to their American counterparts. Their findings in the distinction between conflict management styles of Asian and American managers also highlight the cultural impact on the display of emotion. Their review included measures of value dimensions. Social conservatism with emphasis on the values of conformity and tradition was found to undergird the Asian behavior pattern of avoiding explicit negotiation of workplace conflict, whereas the competitive style of the Americans was viewed as supported by the values of self-enhancement defined in terms of achievement.

Perhaps the most relevant and well-developed integration of affect in cross-cultural negotiations is presented by George and her colleagues (George et al., 1998). In their model, they look at how individual differences, cross-cultural differences, and context influence negotiator affect during cross-cultural negotiations and the subsequent outcomes. They provide the best conceptualization on this topic to date in our view.

Tinsley (1997) discussed the role of conflict in a Chinese cultural context. She suggests that a dual-concerns perspective (self versus other) helps differentiate between emphases for American and Hong Kong Chinese negotiators. Finally, Erez and Earley (1993) apply their self-identity model of work to negotiation and suggest that self-concept is a driver that leads some individuals to experience greater or lesser emotionality as a result of conflict.

Expatriate Adjustment

To a large extent, the literature on expatriate work assignments mirrors that of work and job stress from our perspective in this chapter. (See Black, Gregerson, & Mendenhall, 1992, on expatriate work assignments, and Schuler, Dowling, & DeCieri, 1993, on international aspects of human resource management.) In this section, we illustrate the potential role of emotionality and display from an expatriate's perspective with a few exemplar studies.

Black and Gregersen (1991) examined job, personal, and general factors affecting expatriate adjustment to work. They used a sample of managers from Americans engaged in Asia Pacific assignments in Japan, Hong Kong, South Korea, and Taiwan. They found that various aspects of training and preparation were related to individual reactions such as role discretion, ambiguity, and conflict.

Shaffer and Harrison (1998) looked at expatriates' psychological withdrawal from international assignments using work, nonwork, and family influences. Their model argues that various aspects of cross-cultural adjustment are related to withdrawal cognitions through cognitive and affective mediators such as satisfaction and affective organization commitment. Doucet and Jehn (1997) looked at the nature of harsh language used in a high-context setting. They examined the impact of American expatriates working in mainland China using various textual analyses. They also considered the experience of conflict as they compared two types of behavior for expatriate managers: intracultural conflict (between two Americans) and intercultural conflict (between an American and a Chinese).

The findings indicate a strong cultural link to this emotion experience. Americans, as members of an individualistic culture, tend to exhibit characteristic traits such as aggression and direct language in conflict interactions. Chinese, as members of a collectivistic culture, avoid confrontation in the interest of preserving harmony in the group. The findings are consistent with these expected traits in that American intracultural conflict was found to involve more hostile and aggressive behaviors consistent with their shared cultural norms than their intercultural conflicts. These were described as less hostile and aggressive interactions. In contrast to Americans in conflict, the Chinese adopt a more pleasant demeanor in the interest of social harmony and saving face.

Other Related Work

A few other studies are related to understanding emotion and work from a cross-cultural perspective. For example, Shaw, Duffy, Abdulla, and Singh (2000) studied the nature of affectivity in a sample of United Arab Emirates' bank employees. They proposed that job satisfaction would be negatively related to frustration and intention to quit for employees who were high, but not low, in positive affectivity. Pillai, Scandura, and Williams (1999) looked at the nature of transformational leadership behavior and display across cultures. Their framework is useful for understanding the role of emotional display from a cross-cultural leadership perspective. They indicate cultural influences on emotion display relative to the finding that transformational leadership was not related to job satisfaction in any non-Western cultures. They relate this specifically to low-power-distance cultures such as India, the Middle East, and Latin America. The suggestion is that the intellectual and emotional demands of transformational leaders who operate in a participative mode may be seen as manipulative and eroding trust with subordinates, and thus contributing to increased stress levels in workers.

Conclusion

The model presented in this chapter provides a preliminary framework for exploring the importance of culture in understanding the role of emotion in the workplace. Let us return to earlier questions posed. That is, is there a cultural significance in the encoding and appraisal process relative to emotion events, and how does the unique nature of the cross-cultural work setting affect the emotion process? The focus has been on antecedent factors of the emotion experience in cross-cultural work settings, and for that purpose, several cultural characteristics relevant to the emotion experience in organizations have been identified, such as tight versus loose cultures. Thus, the framework presented here provides a view of how cultural dimensions influence the emotion process and related consequences in organizations.

Frijda and Mesquita (1994) offer a model that views the emotion experience as a process, which includes event coding and appraisal stages. Related to this are the findings of Mesquita et al. (1997) of a small number of common dimensions of the appraisal process underlying the emotion experience, such as attention to change, a sense of certainty, perception of obstacles, impact on self-concept, and overall judgment of fit with existing norms. In view of these important insights and the examples of research in the workplace, we continue to conclude, consistent with their model, that the universal aspect of emotion is contained in the underlying dimensions of appraisal, while the display of emotions varies across cultures. The focal point thus becomes how the cultural dimensions influence the emotion experience, specifically the display phase, and the related consequences in the cross-cultural organizational context.

If we consider the cross-cultural work setting as a set of actors on a stage, we see that the cultural influences are similar to the hidden prompters sending response cues to the actors. Complications arise in the interactive effects of the cascading levels (the organizational context, work unit) as actors with unique prompters encounter and respond to each other in an environment that has high personal stakes for the individual employees and managers, as well as for the organization as a whole. The implications of these varying cultural influences are far reaching in the consequences that may unfold, that is, varying outcomes for managers and employees and sometimes a process of misunderstanding and compromised relationships.

The literature provides illustrations of the consequences of the hidden prompters and the varying and often challenging situations that arise in the cross-cultural organizational context. For example, two studies (Peterson et al., 1995; Smulders et al., 1996) illustrate a larger country effect relative to role and job stress than from organizational factors or from personal factors. This suggests the higher-level influence of culture on emotion display, in this case, role stress, than that of the organization and the work group as depicted by the model with the cascading layers of influence. Schaubroeck et al. (2000) also demonstrate the implications of culture on emotion as stress in terms of coping mechanisms. Job control as a coping mechanism for stressors was found to relate to personal efficacy in the United States and collective efficacy in Hong Kong. This is consistent with the cultural dimension of individualism. That is, the more individualistic culture of the United States defines the person in terms of individual traits, whereas Hong Kong, which is relatively more collectivistic compared to the United States, defines the person in terms of the in-group or the collective.

There are cultural implications in the findings of Yoon and Lim (1999) relative to positive disposition working against employees in generating organizational support in South Korea. These findings are in contrast to findings of Western researchers where good mood led to greater organizational support. Korea, a more collectivistic culture than most Western cultures, seldom includes free individual expression of dispositions. Rather, there is, as the researchers state, "encouragement of collective expression of sentiments, while individual emotions are subsumed." Thus, there is a cultural influence on display of emotion in the form of affectivity and the related consequence of organizational support.

Next steps in the research process should include empirical tests of the concepts presented in relation to the key aspects of employee management: attendance, performance, and satisfaction. Furthermore, research should attend to the matter of designing and testing appropriate elements of training on the dimensions and implications of emotion for members of the local culture and the assigned expatriates. We advocate an approach that assumes that the understanding of both the expatriates and local employees will result in mutual gain and shared accommodation to facilitate attendance, productivity, and satisfaction. Implicit in all of the findings are the varying displays of emotion as sources of potential misunderstanding and conflict in the cross-cultural work setting. These potentialities may compromise not only the individual experience relative to attendance, performance, and satisfaction but also with the obvious negative implications for the organization's operating results.

References

Benedict, R. (1946). *The chrysanthemum and the sword: Patterns of Japanese culture*. Boston: Houghton Mifflin.

Berry, J. W. (1991). Understanding and managing multiculturalism: Some possible implications of research in Canada. *Psychology and Developing Societies, 3,* 17–49.

Berry, J. W., Kim, U., Minde, T., & Mok, D. (1987). Comparative studies of acculturative stress. *International Migration Review, 21,* 491–511.

Bhagat, R. S., & McQuaid, S. J. (1982). Role of subjective culture in organizations: A review and directions for future research. *Journal of Applied Psychology, 67,* 653–686.

Bhagat, R. S., O'Driscoll, M. P., Babakus, E., Frey, L., Chokkar, J., Ninokumar, B. H., Pate, L. E., Ryder, P. A., Fernandez, M.J.G., Ford, D. L. Jr., & Mahanyele, M. (1994). Organizational stress and coping in seven national contexts: A cross-cultural investigation. In G. P. Keita & J. J. Hurrell, Jr. (Eds.), *Job stress in a changing workforce: Investigating gender, diversity, and family issues.* Washington, DC: American Psychological Association.

Birdwhistell, R. L. (1970). *Kinesics and context*. Philadelphia: University of Pennsylvania Press.

Black, J. S , & Gregersen, H. B., (1991). Antecedents to cross-cultural adjustment for expatriates in Pacific rim assignments. *Human Relations, 44,* 497–515.

Black, J. S., Gregerson, H. B., & Mendenhall, M. E. (1992). *Global assignments: Successfully expatriating and repatriating international managers.* San Francisco: Jossey-Bass.

Boucher, J. D. (1979). Culture and emotion. In A. J. Marsella, R. G. Tharp, & T. V. Ciborowksi (Eds.), *Perspectives on cross-cultural psychology* (pp. 159–178). Orlando, FL: Academic Press.

Brief, A. P., Burke, M. J., George, J. M., Robinson, B., & Webster, J. (1988). Should negative affectivity remain an unmeasured variable in the study of job stress? *Journal of Applied Psychology, 73,* 193–198.

Chang, H., & Holt, G. R. (1996). An exploration of interpersonal relationships in two Taiwanese computer firms. *Human Relations, 49,* 1489–1517.

Chen, C. C., Meindl, J. R., & Hunt, R. G. (1997). Testing the effects of vertical and horizontal collectivism: A study of reward allocation preferences in China. *Journal of Cross-Cultural Psychology, 28,* 44–70.

Cooper, C. L., & Payne, R. L. (1992). International perspectives on research into work, well-being, and stress management. In J. C. Quick, L. R. Murphy, & J. J. Hurrell, Jr. (Eds.), *Stress and well-being at work: Assessments and interventions for occupational mental health.* Washington, DC: American Psychological Association.

Cropanzano, R., Aguinis, H., Schminke, M., & Denham, D. L. (1999). Disputant reactions to managerial conflict resolution tactics: A comparison among Argentina, the Dominican Republic, Mexico, and the United States. *Group and Organization Management, 24,* 124–154.

Darwin, C. (1965). *The expression of emotions in man and animals.* Chicago: University of Chicago Press. (Original work published 1872)

Doucet, L., & Jehn, K. A. (1997). Analyzing harsh words in a sensitive setting: American expatriates in communist China. *Journal of Organizational Behavior, 18,* 559–582.

Dyer, B., & Song, X. M. (1997). The impact of strategy on conflict: A cross-national comparative study of U.S. and Japanese firms. *Journal of International Business Studies, 28,* 467–493

Earley, P. C. (1997). Doing an about-face: Social motivation and cross-cultural currents. In P. C. Earley & M. Erez (Eds.), *New perspectives on international industrial/organizational psychology.* San Francisco: New Lexington Press.

Earley, P. C., & Erez, M. (1997). *The transplanted executive.* New York: Oxford University Press.

Earley, P. C., & Gibson, C. B. (1998). Taking stock in our progress on individualism-collectivism: 100 years solidarity and community. *Journal of Management, 24,* 265–304.

Ekman, P. (1972). Universals and cultural differences in facial expressions of emotions. In J. Cole (Ed.), *Nebraska Symposium on Motivation* (pp. 207–283). Lincoln: University of Nebraska Press.

Ekman, P. (1973). *Darwin and facial expression: A century of research in review.* Orlando, FL: Academic Press

Ekman, P. (1980). *The face of man: Expressions of universal emotions in a New Guinea village.* New York: Garland.

Ekman, P. (1984). Expression and the nature of emotion. In K. R. Scherer & P. Ekman (Eds.), *Approaches to emotion* (pp. 319–344). Hillsdale, NJ: Erlbaum.

Ekman, P. (1994). Strong evidence for universals in facial expressions: A reply to Russell's mistaken critique. *Psychological Bulletin, 115,* 268–287.

Ekman, P., & Freisen, W. V. (1971). Constants across cultures in the face and emotion. *Journal of Personality and Social Psychology, 17,* 124–129.

Ekman, P., & Freisen, W. V. (1975). *Unmasking the face.* Upper Saddle River, NJ: Prentice Hall.

Ekman, P., & Freisen, W. V. (1976). *Pictures of facial affect.* Palo Alto, CA: Consulting Psychologists Press.

Ekman, P., Friesen, W. V., O'Sullivan, M., Chan, A., Diacoyanni-Tarlatzis, I., Heider, K., Krause, R., LeCompte, W. A., Pitcarin, T., Ricci-Bitti, P. E., Scherer, K., Tomita, M., & Tzavaras, A. (1987). Universals and cultural differences in the judgments of facial expressions of emotion. *Journal of Personality and Social Psychology, 53,* 712–717.

Ellsworth, P., (1994). Sense, culture, and sensibility. In S. Kitayama & H. Markus (Eds.), *Emotion and culture: Empirical studies of mutual influence* (pp. 23–50). Washington, DC: American Psychological Association.

Ellsworth, P. C., & Smith, C. (1988). From appraisal to emotion: Differences among unpleasant feelings. *Motivation and Emotion, 12,* 271–302.

Erez, M., & Earley, P. C. (1993). *Culture, self-identity, and work.* New York: Oxford University Press.

Evans, G. W., Palsane, M. N., & Carrere, S. (1987). Type-A behavior and occupational stress: A cross-cultural study of blue-collar workers. *Journal of Personality and Social Psychology, 52,* 1002–1007.

Frese, M. & Zapf, D. (1988). Methodological issues in the study of work stress: Objective vs. subjective measurement of work stress and the question of longitudinal studies. In C. L. Cooper & R. Payne (Eds.), *Causes, coping and consequences of stress at work* (pp. 375–411). New York: Wiley.

Frijda, N. H., & Mesquita, B. (1994). The social roles and functions of emotions. In S. Kitayama & H. Markus (Eds.), *Emotion and culture: Empirical studies of mutual influence* (pp. 51–88). Washington, DC: American Psychological Association.

Garst, H., Frese, M., & Molenaar, P. C. (2000). The temporal factor of change in stressor-strain relationships: A growth curve model on a longitudinal study in East Germany. *Journal of Applied Psychology, 85,* 417–438.

George, J. M., Jones, G. R., & Gonzalez, J. A. (1998). The role of affect in cross-cultural negotiations. *Journal of International Business Studies, 29,* 749–772.

Glenn, E. S., & Glenn, C. G. (1981). *Man and mankind: conflict and communication between cultures.* Norwood, NJ: Ablex.

Goffee. R., & Jones, G., (1996) What holds the modern company together? *Harvard Business Review, 74,* 133–142.

Hackman, J. R. (1990). *Groups that work (and those that don't): Creating conditions for effective teamwork.* San Francisco: Jossey-Bass.

Hofstede, G. (1980). *Culture's consequences: International differences in work-related values.* Thousand Oaks, CA: Sage.

Hofstede, G. (1991). *Cultures and organizations.* New York: McGraw-Hill.

Hofstede, G. (1997). *Cultures and organizations: Software of the mind.* New York: McGraw-Hill.

Hupka, R. B., Lenton, A. P., & Hutchison, K. A. (1999). Universal development of emotion categories in natural language. *Journal of Personality and Social Psychology, 77,* 247–278.

Izard, C. E. (1971). *The face of emotion.* New York: Appleton-Century-Crofts.

Izard, C. (1977). *Human emotion.* New York: Plenum Press.

Izard, C. E. (1980). Cross-cultural perspectives on emotion and emotion communications. In H. B. Triandis & W. Lonner (Eds.), *Handbook of cross-cultural psychology* (Vol. 3, pp. 185–221). Needham Heights, MA: Allyn and Bacon.

Izard, C. E. (1994). Innate and universal facial expressions: Evidence from developmental and cross-cultural research. *Psychological Bulletin, 115,* 288–299.

Kirkcaldy, B. D., & Cooper, C. L. (1993). The relationship between work stress and leisure style: British and German managers. *Human Relations, 46,* 669–680.

Kitayama, S., & Markus, H. R. (Eds.). (1994). *Emotion and culture: Empirical studies of mutual influence.* Washington, DC: American Psychological Association.

Klineberg, O. (1940). *Social psychology.* New York: Holt.

Kluckhohn, F. R., & Strodtbeck, F. (1961). *Variations in value orientations.* New York: HarperCollins.

Lazarus, R. S., & Lazarus, B. N. (1994). *Passion and reason: Making sense of our emotions.* New York: Oxford University Press.

Levy, R. I. (1973). *The Tahitians.* Chicago: University of Chicago Press.

Levy, R. I. (1984). Emotions in comparative perspective. In K. R. Scherer & P. Ekman (Eds.), *Approaches to emotion: A book of readings* (pp. 397–412). Hillsdale, NJ: Erlbaum.

Lorenz, K. (1965). *Evolution and modification of behavior.* Chicago: University of Chicago Press.

Lynd, H. M. (1958). *On shame and the search for identity.* New York: Harcourt, Brace and World.

Markus, H., & Kitayama, S. (1991). Culture and the self: Implications for cognition, motivation, and emotion. *Psychological Review, 98,* 224–253.

Matsumoto, D., Kudoh, T., Scherer, K., & Wallbott, H. G. (1988). Antecedents of and reactions to emotions in the United States and Japan. *Journal of Cross-Cultural Psychology, 19,* 267–286.

Mead, G. H. (1934). *Mind, self and society.* Chicago: University of Chicago Press.

Mead, M. (1975). Review of Darwin and facial expression. *Journal of Communication, 25,* 209–213.

Mesquita, B., & Frijda, N. H. (1992). Cultural variations in emotions: A review. *Psychological Bulletin, 412,* 179–204.

Mesquita, B., Frijda, N. H., & Scherer, K. R. (1997). Culture and emotion. In J. W. Berry, P. R. Dasen, & T. S. Saraswathi (Eds.), *Handbook of cross-cultural psychology* (Vol. 2, pp. 255–297). Needham Heights, MA: Allyn & Bacon.

Morris, M. W., Williams, K. Y., Leung, L., Larrick, R., Mendoza, M. T., Bhatnagar, D., Li, J., Kondo, M., Luo, J., & Hu, J. (1998). Conflict management style: Accounting for cross-national differences. *Journal of International Business Studies, 29,* 729–748.

Ortony, A., Clore, G., & Collins, A. (1988). *The cognitive structure of emotions.* Cambridge: Cambridge University Press.

Parsons, T., & Shils, E. A. (1951). *Toward a general theory of action.* Cambridge, MA: Harvard University Press.

Pennebaker, J. W., Rime, B., & Blankenship, V. E. (1996). Stereotypes of emotional expressiveness of northerners and southerners: A cross-cultural test of Montesquieu's hypothesis. *Journal of Personality and Social Psychology, 70,* 372–380.

Peterson, M. F., & Smith, P. B. (1997). Does national culture or ambient temperature explain cross-national differences in role stress? No sweat! *Academy of Management Journal, 40,* 930–946.

Peterson, M. F., & Smith, P. B. et al. (1995). Role conflict, ambiguity, and overload: A twenty-one-nation study. *Academy of Management Journal, 38,* 429–452.

Pillai, R., Scandura, T. A., & Williams, E. A. (1999). Leadership and organizational justice: Similarities and differences across cultures. *Journal of International Business Studies, 30,* 763–779.

Pilutla, M. M., & Murnighan, J. K. (1996). Unfairness, anger, and spite: Emotional rejections of ultimatum offers. *Organizational Behavior and Human Decision Processes, 68,* 208–225.

Rosaldo, R. (1978). The rhetoric of control: Ilongots viewed as natural bandits and wild Indians. In B. Babcock (Ed.), *The reversible world: Symbolic inversion in art and society* (pp. 240–257). Ithaca, NY: Cornell University Press.

Russell, J. A. (1991). Culture and the categorization of emotions. *Psychological Bulletin, 110,* 426–450.

Russell, J. A. (1994). Is there universal recognition of emotion from facial expression? A review of the cross-cultural studies. *Psychological Bulletin, 115,* 102–141.

Russell, J. A., & Fernandez-Dols, J. M. (1997). *The psychology of facial expression.* New York: Cambridge University Press.

Schaubroeck, J., Lam, S.S.K., & Xie, J. L. (2000). Collective efficacy versus self-efficacy in coping responses to stressors and control: A cross-cultural study. *Journal of Applied Psychology, 85,* 512–525.

Schuler, R. S., Dowling, P. J., & DeCieri, H. (1993). An integrative framework of strategic international human resource management. *Journal of Management, 19,* 419–459.

Scott, W. R., & Meyer, J. W. (1994). *Institutional environments and organizations: Structural complexity and individualism.* Thousand Oaks, CA: Sage.

Shaffer, M. A., & Harrison, D. A. (1998). Expatriates' psychological withdrawal from international assignments: Work, nonwork, and family influences. *Personnel Psychology, 51,* 87–118.

Shaw, J. D., Duffy, M. K., Abdulla, M.H.A., & Singh, R. (2000). The moderating role of positive affectivity: Empirical evidence from bank employees in the United Arab Emirates. *Journal of Management, 26,* 139–155.

Smulders, P.G.W., Kompier, M.A.J., & Paoli, P. (1996). The work environment in the twelve EU-countries: Differences and similarities. *Human Relations, 49,* 1291–1313.

Sutton, R. I., & Rafaeli, A. (1988). Untangling the relationship between displayed emotions and organizational sales: The case of convenience stores. *Academy of Management Journal, 31,* 461–487.

Ting-Toomey, S. (1985). Toward a theory of conflict and culture. In W. B. Gudykunst, L. P. Steward, & S. Ting-Toomey (Eds.), *Communication, culture, and organization processes.* (pp. 71–86). Thousand Oaks, CA: Sage.

Ting-Toomey, S. (1988). Intercultural conflict styles: A face negotiation theory. In Y. Kim & W. Gudykunst (Eds.), *Theories in intercultural communications* (pp. 213–235). Thousand Oaks, CA: Sage.

Ting-Toomey, S., & Cocroft, B. (1994). Face and facework: Theoretical and research issues. In S. Ting-Toomey (Ed.) *The challenge of facework: Cross-cultural and interpersonal issues* (pp. 1–36). Albany: State University of New York Press.

Tinsley, C. (1997). Understanding conflict in a Chinese cultural context. In R. Lewicki, R. Bies, & B. H. Sheppard (Eds), *Research on negotiations in organizations* (Vol. 6, pp. 209–225). Thousand Oaks, CA: Sage.

Triandis, H. C. (1989). The self and social behavior in differing cultural contexts. *Psychological Review, 96,* 506–520.

Triandis, H. C. (1990). Cross-cultural studies of individualism and collectivism. In J. Berman (Ed.), *Nebraska Symposium on Motivation, 1989* (pp. 41–133). Lincoln: University of Nebraska Press.

Triandis, H. C. (1994). Major cultural syndromes and emotion. In S. Kitayama & H. Markus (Eds.), *Emotion and culture: Empirical studies of mutual influence* (pp. 133–196). Washington, DC: American Psychological Association.

Triandis, H. C. (1995). *Individualism and collectivism.* Boulder, CO: Westview.

Triandis, H. C., & Lambert, W. W. (1958). A restatement and test of Schlosberg's theory of emotion with two kinds of subjects from Greece. *Journal of Abnormal and Social Psychology, 56,* 321–328.

Turner, J. C. (1985). Social categorization and the self-concept: A social-cognitive theory of group behavior. In E. J. Lawler (Ed.), *Advances in group processes: Theory and research* (Vol. 2, pp. 324–362). Greenwich, CT: JAI Press.

Van de Vliert, E., & Van Yperen, N. C. (1996). Why cross-national differences in role overload? Don't overlook ambient temperature! *Academy of Management Journal, 39,* 986–1004.

Wallbott, H. G., & Scherer, K. R. (1988). How universal and specific is emotional experience? Evidence from twenty-seven countries on five continents. In A. R. Scherer (Ed.), *Facets of emotion: Recent research* (pp. 226–283). Hillsdale, NJ: Erlbaum.

Wiezbicka, A. (1986). Does language reflect culture? Evidence from Australian English. *Language in Society, 5,* 349–374.

Wierzbicka, A. (1994). Emotion, language, and cultural scripts. In S. Kitayama & H. Markus (Eds.), *Emotion and culture: Empirical studies of mutual influence* (pp. 133–196). Washington, DC: American Psychological Association.

Witkin, H., & Berry, J. (1975). Psychological differentiation in cross-cultural perspective. *Journal of Cross-Cultural Psychology, 6,* 4–87.

Xie, J. L. (1996). Karasek's model in the People's Republic of China: Effects of job demands, control, and individual differences. *Academy of Management Journal, 39,* 1594–1618.

Yoon, J., & Lim, J. (1999). Organizational support in the workplace: The case of Korean hospital employees. *Human Relations, 52,* 923–945.

CHAPTER 12

An Emotional Examination of the Work-Family Interface

Shelley M. MacDermid
Brenda L. Seery
Howard M. Weiss

Connections between work conditions and family life are an increasingly popular topic of research, the focus of at least four national scientific conferences in the past five years (sponsored by the Kunz Center for the Study of Work and Family, the Business and Professional Women's Foundation, and the Alfred P. Sloan Foundation). Despite a proliferation of empirical studies, however, theoretical sophistication has lagged (Edwards & Rothbard, 2000; Grzywacz & Marks, 2000). In an effort to spur progress, we focus this chapter on the work-family interface, with particular attention to the central constructs in the existing literature: conflict and spillover. Our perspective is motivated by two elements of our own experience. First, while most traditional standards would say that as academic researchers we experience high levels of work-family conflict on most days because our jobs make time demands that interfere with family activities, we perceive ourselves as experiencing high levels of conflict on only some days. Second, when we do perceive high levels of work-family conflict, the experience is not just cognitive but also emotional. That is, although we cognitively recognize the presence of conflict most of the time, we feel it only some of the time. When we reflected on our experiences in the light of existing research and theory, we realized that the role of feelings at the work-family interface remains ambiguous. And so in this chapter, we embark on an emotional reexamination of that interface. (Readers should note that we define the term *family* broadly, to include "one or more adults related by blood, marriage or affiliation who cooperate economically, who may share a common dwelling place, and who may rear children"; Strong, DeVault, & Sayad, 1998, p. 14.)

Core Constructs in Existing Literature

A vast number of studies in the work-family literature include as key variables work-family conflict or work-family spillover or both. In this section, we consider the genesis of these constructs.

Work-Family Conflict

At the core of the literature on multiple roles, the construct of work-family conflict is firmly grounded in the role theory-based work of Robert Kahn and colleagues (Kahn, Wolfe, Quinn, & Snoek 1964), an organizational psychologist, and William Goode (1960), a family sociologist. During the first half of the twentieth century, many scholars, among them Mertons, Parsons, and Durkheim, were preoccupied with the implications of the massive organizations spawned by the industrial revolution. Following in their footsteps, Kahn and Goode took a functionalist stance toward the relationship between individuals and organizations, assuming that organizations would function best when their members developed specialized tasks and skills:

> Whether or not the corporation deserves to be called the greatest invention of the twentieth century, as some have alleged, it is an eminently rational solution to a massive problem of human and technological organization. Rationality is especially manifest in the fitting together of component parts and in the carefully planned pattern of related functions in the service of an over-all goal. To bring that plan to life requires only the appropriate behavior of people as members of organizations [Kahn et al., 1964, pp. 4–5].

Kahn and Goode further asserted (separately) that organizations would pose more demands than members could fulfill (Goode, 1960) and that those demands would conflict. This became the scarcity hypothesis, which has dominated the work-family research literature for the past forty years. Its popularity was spurred in 1985 by Greenhaus and Beutell's rearticulation and elaboration of three major forms of work-family conflict: time based, when time pressures associated with one role interfere with physical or psychological involvement in another; strain based, when symptoms such as tension, anxiety, fatigue, depression, apathy, or irritability in one role affect performance in another role; and behavior based, when behavior required in one role interferes with fulfilling the requirements of another (Greenhaus & Beutell, 1985). Items characteristic of those used to measure work-family conflict include: "Because my work is demanding, at times I am irritable at home" (Kopelman, Greenhaus, & Connolly, 1983, p. 204) and "Due to all the pressures at work, sometimes when I come home I am too stressed to do the things I enjoy" (Carlson, Kacmar, & Williams, 2000, p. 260).

Work-Family Spillover

The second core construct in the work-family literature is spillover. Like work-family conflict, spillover is conceptualized as a mechanism linking the work and family domains. In a now-classic study, Evans and Bartolomé (1980) examined the work and private lives of forty-two British and French managers and their wives, asking which of the following patterns characterized the relationship between their work and private lives (p. 286):

Spillover—one affects the other in a positive or negative way.

Independent—they exist side by side and for all practical purposes are independent of each other.

Conflict—they are in conflict with each other and cannot be easily reconciled

Instrumental—one is primarily a means to obtain something desired in the other.

Compensation—one is a way of making up for what is missing in the other.

Based on their interviews, Evans and Bartolomé concluded that spillover was the most prominent pattern displayed by these managers, and furthermore that it was primarily worry and stress, not time demands, that overflowed from work to family.

The Problem with Conflict and Spillover

Despite enthusiastic interest from researchers, the theoretical lens remains clouded by a fog of imprecision. For example, the definitions of conflict and spillover vary across studies. We consulted twelve studies and found that strain-based conflict was variously indicated as one or more of the following: stress, strain, tension, or worry; fatigue; irritability or anger; preoccupation or difficulty with relaxation; and difficulty maintaining relationships (Bond, Galinsky, & Swanberg, 1998; Frone, Russell, & Cooper, 1992; Frone, Yardley & Markel, 1997; Grzywacz & Marks, 1998; Gutek, Searle, & Klepa, 1991; Kirchmeyer, 1992; Kopelman et al., 1983; Netemeyer, Boles, & McMurrian, 1996; O'Driscoll, Ilgen, & Hildreth, 1992; Small & Riley, 1990; Stephens & Sommers, 1996; Wiley, 1987). Some of these descriptors ask respondents to make a general appraisal (stress or strain), others request reports on a specific affective experiences (angry); still others tap cognitive or behavioral challenges (tired, preoccupied, difficulty maintaining relationships). Definitions of spillover also vary. For Greenhaus and Beutell (1985), strain-based conflict was very like Evans and Bartolomé's (1980) "negative emotional spillover." But while Evans and Bartolomé decided that it was almost exclusively stress that spilled over, Lambert (1990) and others supported a much more inclusive definition: "Workers carry the emotions, attitudes, skills, and behaviors that they establish at work into their family life" (p. 242).

Today, the terms *conflict, spillover,* and *interference* are sometimes used interchangeably. Leiter and Durup (1996), for example, apply the label *interference* to a measure they borrowed from Kopelman et al. (1983), who originally developed it to measure conflict. Grzywacz and Marks (2000) use items to measure spillover that would fit equally well in measures of work-family conflict: "Stress at work makes you irritable at home" (p. 114).

A second source of theoretical confusion is the conflation of stressors and the experience of stress (Perry-Jenkins, Repetti, & Crouter, 2000). While Kahn acknowledged that the relationship between sent and received role conflict was substantially less than perfect, most existing measures seem to assume that if the stressor is recognized, such as time demands from work that compete with family responsibilities, stress is invariably experienced. As Greenhaus and Powell (2000, p. 5) put it, "Most of the scale items that assess WFC [work-family conflict] measure the extent to which one role interferes with the other role, rather than the internal conflict, uncertainty, or turmoil that is experienced in the process of choosing to participate in one role over another. In effect, most research has examined objective (or sent) role conflict rather than psychological (or experienced) role conflict" (p. 5).

Finally, relatively little progress has been made in understanding the processes through which conflict and spillover occur. Traditionally, the identification of conflict or spillover was based on the statistical relationship observed between the work and family domains, with positive and negative correlations, respectively, indicating the presence of spillover and conflict (Tenbrunsel, Brett, Maoz, Stroh, & Reilly, 1995). The problem is that simple correlations reveal little about how spillover and conflict occur. In existing theoretical models and (mostly cross-sectional) empirical studies, conflict and spillover are variously portrayed as processes, mediating variables, and outcomes in the relationship between work conditions and family life.

It is unlikely that we can resolve all of these inconsistencies in this single chapter. But for the purposes of this discussion (and possibly future ones with our colleagues), we define each construct here and elaborate our definitions in succeeding sections. We define *conflict* as a circumstance or event that has the potential to generate a negative emotional response, which occurs as a function of the interaction of two or more domains. Conversely, *enhancement* is a circumstance or event that has the potential to generate a positive emotional response, which occurs as a function of the interaction of two or more domains. *Spillover* (we prefer the term *carryover*) occurs when an emotional response in one domain is carried to another.

Taking a Closer Look at Emotions

Before explaining our model, we define some relevant terms. (We do not presume to educate those readers already expert in research on emotions, but those whose primary expertise may lie elsewhere.) An *emotion* is an affective state that occurs in reaction to an event (Frijda, 1999). Although also affective states, *moods* are less intense, of longer duration, and, unlike emotions, are not specific to an event or an object (Weiss & Cropanzano, 1996). Finally, *dispositions* are affective tendencies that persist across situations, such as relatively stable tendencies toward positive or negative affect. Discrete emotions can be plausibly organized into families, although there is still considerable debate as to the structure and content of those families. Most models include at least anger, disgust, joy, fear, and sadness.

Emotional experiences are thought to have four main components: the experiential component of affect, followed by cognitive appraisal of that affect, physiological changes, and action readiness (Frijda, 1999; Hearn, 1994). Because emotions are provoked by events and responded to through cognitive appraisal, it follows that any theory of emotion must also be a theory of how people adapt to events in their environment. Thus, specific emotions will prove especially useful for the prediction of specific behaviors (such as sad versus disappointed versus guilty). We believe that ultimately the environment-emotion-behavior chain will include a situation-emotion matrix comprising the key situational features conducive to specific emotional reactions. It seems to us that analysis of the structure of work emotions is at least as important as the analysis of the dimensions of job satisfaction.

Our particular road map for emotional processes is shown in Figure 12.1. Actually, we present two road maps: one for family emotional processes and one for work emotional processes. These are mirror images of each other, reflecting the view that the basic processes of emotion generation and response are equivalent, regardless of the domain. Although they run in parallel, they can influence each other (hence the permeable boundary in the figure), reflecting the view that elements in each domain can affect processes in the other, even when those elements are not specifically related to the interface between domains. We say more about this later.

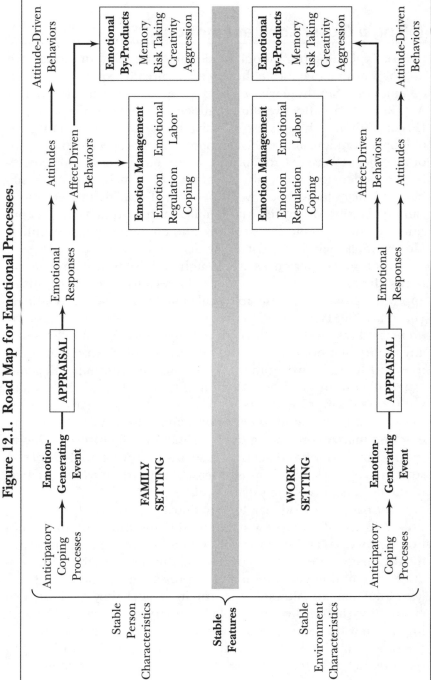

Figure 12.1. Road Map for Emotional Processes.

All emotion researchers implicitly or explicitly suggest that emotional reactions start with events or changing conditions, and so at the heart of Figure 12.1 is the emotion-generating event. However, temporally prior to this event is the possibility of anticipatory coping processes. People engage in many behaviors designed to manage their emotional states (Aspinwall & Taylor, 1997). Students avoid their advisers, and professors switch on their answering machines when expecting calls from editors for overdue material. These illustrate ways in which we manage the emotional events of our lives.

Events instigate emotional responses. However, most emotion researchers suggest that events are filtered through an appraisal process or meaning analysis (see Weiss, Chapter Two, this volume.) That is, the emotional significance of an event, that is, its valenced direction, intensity, and discrete experiential properties, is the result of a process in which the event is evaluated in terms of its significance to personal well-being, who is responsible for the event, its novelty or unexpectedness, and so forth. Different appraisal theorists postulate different evaluative dimensions (Lawler & Thye, 1999), but the overall structure of the process is similar.

The consequences of emotional states are many and varied. Some are particular to particular emotions (for example, anger, but not depression, generally causes aggression), and others are the result of processes that cut across many different emotions (for example, emotion regulation can consume regulatory resources, regardless of the emotion being regulated). Attitudinal consequences accrue from emotional experiences with objects and people. This has been demonstrated in the organizational literature (Weiss, Nicholas & Daus, 1999) wherein daily affective states have been shown to influence job satisfaction. We assume attitudes toward marital partners can be influenced by similar affective experiences. These attitudes influence certain classes of behaviors, particularly those behaviors reflecting approach-avoidance tendencies toward the object, such as turnover and marital stability (Bolger, DeLongis, Kessler, & Wethington, 1989).

Nonattitudinal consequences also result from experiencing particular affective states. For purposes of discussion, we break these into two categories. Some consequences seem best characterized as emotional by-products. That is, they seem to be natural, nonvolitional results of being in a particular state. Positive affect enhances creativity but reduces depth of processing. Some negative affective states, particularly anger, increase the likelihood of aggression. Anger biases attributional judgments (Keltner, Ellsworth, & Edwards, 1993). Other consequences can be traced to people's attempts to manage their own emotions (emotion regulation) or the emotions of others (emotional labor). Emotion management processes deplete resources that might be used for other self-regulatory activities or for performance on tasks with high cognitive load. Helping behavior appears to be driven by emotional regulation processes, as people in positive states engage in helping—but not if they perceive the helping as reducing that affect.

These processes play out at work and at home. Emotional events at home produce emotional states with behavioral and cognitive consequences of relevance to family functioning (see number 1 in Figure 12.2). Emotional events at work produce emotional states with behavioral and cognitive consequences of relevance to work attitudes and performance (see number 2 in Figure 12.2). This is obvious and not central to our thesis. Our central argument really has two points. First, processes in each domain are influenced by factors from the other. These influences are not limited to those factors defined by the interface of the two life roles (such as conflict), and a productive examination of how work influences family and how family influences work will need to look at how factors in each domain can and does influence the emotion processes in the other. Second, emotional states generated in one domain can continue to have influence in the other domain, even if the cause of the state is purely a function of events and circumstances relevant to the first.

Where do conflict and spillover fit into our model? Generally, we believe there is some utility in distinguishing between two categories or classes of processes. Once class involves the transmission of emotional states from one domain to another (see number 3 in Figure 12.2), this is emotional spillover or carryover (we prefer the latter term because it reminds us that emotions are carried in the minds of individuals). It refers to the situation in which an emotional state, generated in one domain and by events and issues of that domain, carries over to be experienced in the other domain. So, for example, an argument with a spouse for reasons having nothing to do with work might influence the mood state of the person at work.

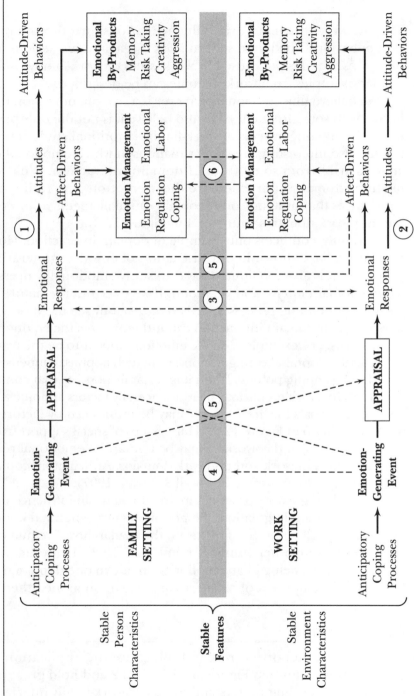

Figure 12.2. Pathways of Influence Between Domains.

This mood state can, in turn, influence various sorts of work-relevant behaviors. The mood state at work is real and has serious implications, but it is not caused by work issues or work-family issues. Similar examples from work to home can be described.

We believe that emotional carryover is a real phenomenon that occurs with some frequency. We also believe it is not the only place where interesting aspects of work-family emotional study can be found. Also interesting are those situations in which emotional reactions arise from some form of domain interaction. What we mean by domain interaction are those emotion-generating circumstances that simultaneously contain causal elements from work and nonwork domains (number 4 in Figure 12.2).

Certainly, conflict is one example of domain interaction. However, as we have shown in our discussion of emotion-generating processes, it is also too limited a way to study emotional processes from a domain interaction viewpoint. If we trace out the nature of emotion-generating processes, we can more easily see the variety of ways in which domain interaction can influence specific emotional experiences. For example, discrete emotions appear to be the result of particular appraisal configurations. One such appraisal dimension is said to be coping potential, and it is certainly possible that coping appraisals for work events may be influenced by factors at home and coping appraisals for home events may be influenced by factors at work (number 5 in Figure 12.2). Here, issues of social support from spouses, friends, and coworkers may be relevant to emotional reactions to events in work and nonwork domains. Anticipatory coping may also be relevant here (Aspinwall & Taylor, 1997).

Similarly, regulatory processes in one domain can influence outcomes in another. Regulation of emotional states generated in one domain may affect, in the short term, the availability of regulatory resources for the other (number 6 in Figure 12.2). However, over the longer term, being in an emotional climate in one domain may foster the development of resources for regulation in the other.

Applications

Three areas of emotions research illustrate the application of road maps like those in Figures 12.1 and 12.2 and hold great potential for expanding understanding of the work-family interface.

We begin with day-to-day processes of emotional transmission, move to processes of regulating one's own emotions, and then consider processes of managing the emotions of others. These illustrative examples show how the consideration of emotions enlarges our understanding of links between work conditions and family life.

Day-to-Day Processes of Emotional Transmission

Most studies of the work-family interface are cross-sectional and are either ambiguous in their treatment of time (that is, they do not specify a time frame), or focus on a middle time range, such as the past one to three months. The problem for emotion researchers is that emotional experiences may be less evident at this midrange than at intervals that are much longer (over several years) or much shorter (over several hours; Williams & Alliger, 1994). Imprecision regarding temporal order and duration may mask the effect of emotions by collapsing chronic and immediate effect, thus confounding discrete emotions, general moods, and dispositions or traits. For example, dispositional aspects of emotion such as temperament or optimism tend to be quite stable over periods of several years. In contrast, transmission or transfer of emotions across persons or settings tends to occur over very short intervals, lasting no more than a few hours or a few day. Greenhaus and Parasuraman (1999) encourage researchers to consider episodes of work-family conflict as they unfold over time, a framework consistent with the model we have proposed.

Studies led by Bolger, Larson, and Repetti (Bolger et al., 1989; Larson & Almeida, 1999; Repetti & Wood, 1997) elegantly illustrate the daily processes linking emotional experiences across domains. Repetti (1994), for example, found that male air traffic controllers who experienced emotionally taxing days at work tended to withdraw from interaction with their spouses and young children at home in the evening. This is the process known as emotional carryover (see number 3 in Figure 12.2); notice that the influence of the emotion is pronounced in family interactions even though the emotion was not generated by family issues or issues having to due with work and family. We know that emotional transmission from home to work can also occur (Williams & Alliger, 1994).

Managing One's Own Emotions

Another facet of research on emotions that relates to the work-family interface is the regulation of personal emotional experiences, which we call emotion management. In this chapter, we consider separately the management of one's own emotions, which we label emotion regulation, and attempts to manage the emotional experiences of others, which we call emotional labor (see number 6 in Figure 12.2).

Recall the four components of emotional experiences: experience, appraisal, physiological change, and action readiness. Emotion regulation thus consists of goal-directed efforts to govern the intensity and duration of each of these processes as they unfold. The goals of emotion regulation can include both dampening and heightening emotional reactions to reduce unfavorable experiences and maximize favorable ones (Keiley & Seery, 2001). Each component of emotional experience is a potential target for regulation efforts. That is, individuals may try to alter their attention to, appraisal of, and reactions to their emotional experiences (Dodge & Garber, 1991; Thompson, 1994). The resources for emotion regulation may be drawn from within, such as personal fortitude, or they may come from outside the individual, such as social pressure. Emotion regulation is unlikely, however, to change the specific emotion experienced (Thompson, 1994).

Specific strategies for emotion regulation may be classified as physiological, cognitive, or behavioral (Masters, 1991). Physiological strategies are often exercised unconsciously and may include changes in vagal tone or involuntary hyperventilation. Cognitive strategies include distracting oneself with intentional thoughts about a pleasant place. Behavioral strategies include seeking self-gratification, deep breathing, or physically leaving the field.

Regulation efforts vary in their success. Unsuccessful attempts may result in under-control—impulsive reactions, violence, or inappropriate expressions of emotion—or over-control, where individuals shut down their affective experience and do nothing to solve the difficulty. Disorders of overregulation include depression, addictions, and anxiety disorders. Parents' internal working models of attachment shape the emotional environment they create for their children, which may socialize children to use ineffective emotion management strategies (Keiley & Seery, 2001).

Emotion regulation has not yet received much attention as an aspect of coping with work-family conflict and carryover. Such research should proceed with caution on two points. First, despite contradicting evidence, negative emotions such as stress or strain have been emphasized over positive emotions in the study of both emotion regulation and conflict or spillover. Second, researchers should hesitate to accept unconditionally the "hydraulic" or "scarcity" model that undergirds much existing research on emotion regulation and conflict or spillover; this model assumes finite resources that are unavailable in one domain once expended in another and may be poorly suited to documenting the emergent properties of emotional experiences (Lazarus, 1993).

In 1977, Marks noted that the scarcity hypothesis was based on an economic metaphor he labeled a "drain" theory. He questioned the finiteness of energy based on the observation that physiological processes in the human body typically produce more energy than is needed or used at any given moment. He called attention to the "social construction" of human energy—social processes that constrain energy or make it more readily available—by proposing an "enhancement" or "expansion" hypothesis whereby roles create resources such as time, energy, or commitment for one another.

Sieber (1974) also argued for recognition of positive effects of multiple roles (including paid work): "Apparently out of deference to the assumption that multiplicity of role partners yields few benefits that might compensate for the burden of manifold or discrepant obligations, researchers and theorists alike have failed to weigh the possible rewards of role accumulation" (p. 569).

Initial studies bolster Marks's and Sieber's suspicions. In a study of business school alumni, Kirchmeyer (1992) documented not only the presence of perceptions of enhancing effects, but also a sense among the respondents that the enhancing effects were more powerful than the negative or conflicting effects. A key contribution of Barnett and colleagues, who have been particularly active in this area of research, is their operationalization of quality of experience within specific roles. For example, Barnett, Marshall, and Sayer (1992) observed that employed mothers experienced positive spillover from work to home as a function of the rewards generated by challenging work. In turn, the positive spillover helped to compensate for certain types of distress in the mothers' relationships with their children.

Muraven and Baumeister (2000) have used the muscle as a way to model the way regulatory resources, used to regulate emotions, stress, performance focus, and so forth, are weakened and strengthened. They argue that such resources get depleted when exercised and are therefore unavailable for new immediate tasks requiring regulation, but then get strengthened through exercise over a longer time frame. This refinement of the scarcity-expansion debate raises interesting questions about both short- and long-term processes of emotion regulation in relation to work-family conflict, enhancement, and carryover.

Emotional Labor: Managing the Emotions of Others

We use the term *emotional labor* to refer to intentional attempts to manage others' emotions, including attempts that are required or expected as part of one's paid work role. As Figure 12.1 shows, emotional labor is the second class of emotion management behaviors that are driven by emotional responses to events. Emotional labor includes intentionally doing or avoiding various physical, mental, verbal, and emotional activities for the purpose of creating, reducing, preventing, or regulating others' emotions (Seery, 2001).

"Doing" strategies of emotional labor involve deliberate actions to shape the emotions of another. These include strategies of:

- Mental activity (such as thinking about someone, noticing what she likes, and remembering this for future reference)
- Verbal activity (such as talking to someone and problem solving with him; inviting guests to a birthday party)
- Physical activity (such as making the food someone likes most to cheer her up, keeping one's children's favorite clothes clean because they want to wear them often, rubbing a child's back, decorating the home for a holiday, playing games with children)
- Emotional activity (such as making oneself feel happy in order to benefit another or do one's job)

"Not-doing" strategies usually involve deliberately not feeling or expressing certain emotions, such as anger, annoyance, or anxiety.

Emotional labor is often combined with or embedded in other activities. For example, talking with children about their favorite and preferred foods, shopping for ingredients, and preparing food together simultaneously serve the goals of providing pleasure (emotional labor) and ensuring that children will eat (physical maintenance). In studies of family life, emotional labor has been conceptualized as "caring," "kinwork," or "nurturance" (DeVault, 1991; di Leonardo, 1987; Dressel & Clark, 1990). In workplaces, studies of emotional labor have typically focused on specific occupations, usually those involving service or "people" work such as nurses, flight attendants (Hochschild, 1983), or food service workers (Paules, 1991).

Studies of workers have examined burnout, job satisfaction, and "emotive dissonance" (that is, workers feel compelled to display certain emotions despite experiencing quite different ones during their interactions with customers and clients; Hochschild, 1983). In general, workers whose jobs do and do not require emotional labor differ in the correlates but not their mean levels of burnout (Wharton, 1993; Wharton & Erickson, 1995). For example, unlike other workers, those who are expected to perform emotional labor as part of their jobs do not appear to be protected from burnout or job dissatisfaction by high job involvement (Wharton, 1993). The effects of emotional labor also are gendered: men whose jobs require "handling people well" may be more likely to experience emotive dissonance than men whose jobs do not require it, at least according to the results of one study (Wharton, 1993). In contrast, women whose jobs require little interaction with others and have low job involvement experience more emotive dissonance (Erickson & Wharton, 1997).

One study examined emotional labor both at home and in the workplace for women who worked in hospitals (Wharton & Erickson, 1995). An especially interesting feature of this study was its attempt to test the relevance of role scarcity and role expansion perspectives regarding the availability of human energy. Consistent with the scarcity perspective, job-related burnout was positively related to emotional labor at home. Contrary to expectations, burnout was not a function of emotional labor at work.

Instead, consistent with the expansion hypothesis, women whose jobs required moderate amounts of emotional labor performed more emotional labor at home than other women did. More important, women's job-related well-being appeared to be influenced less by their emotional labor at work than by their own and their partners' involvement in emotional labor at home. Partners' involvement in family emotional labor, more than women's own beliefs in the importance of such labor, appeared to moderate the positive association between women's emotional labor in the family and burnout at work.

Wharton and Erickson (1995) concluded that emotional labor at home is a greater threat to women's well-being at work than emotional labor on the job. Hence, the scarcity perspective seems to do a better job explaining the relations between women's family work and their job-related well-being than it does explaining the effects of emotional labor at work. The expansion perspective was supported by a positive relationship between the performance of emotional labor at work and at home. These provocative preliminary findings are qualified, however, by limitations in the measurement of emotional labor at work—simple indicators of the percentage of time spent at work in interaction with others, particularly with customers and clients—especially in relation to the measurement of such labor at home in this study, which used fifteen specific indicators of the content of emotional labor at home.

One of the aspects of prior research opened up by Wharton and Erickson's work is the pervasive but lightly tested assumption that workplaces affect families much more powerfully than the reverse. Possible exceptions have been documented by Crouter (1984), who conducted one of the first detailed studies of family-to-work effects. During face-to-face interviews, manufacturing workers reported that support they received from family members and skills they had learned at home had helped them at work. They also reported being negatively affected at work by complaints from family members about the demands of their jobs and frustrations from home.

Kirchmeyer (1992) studied the perceived effects of parenting, community work, and recreation on work. The nature of positive spillover appeared to vary according to the nonwork domain under consideration. Parenting provided unique rewards, buffered work problems, and fostered the development of self-management skills such as time management and patience. Community work was perceived as increasing one's value, providing ideas, and developing managerial skills, such as delegation and teamwork, that would be useful at the workplace. Recreation was energizing and helped workers to forget work problems.

Bolger et al. (1989) tested both family-to-work and work-to-family effects in their innovative analysis of the daily reverberations of spouses' experiences at work and at home. Their analyses revealed that statistically significant findings were more numerous for effects emanating from work, but that the statistically significant relationships were stronger for effects emanating from home.

Implications for Future Research on Work-Family Conflict and Spillover

To conclude this chapter, we return to where we began. Our premise throughout the chapter has been that theories (*conceptualizations* might be a better word) about work-family conflict and spillover pay too little attention to the emotional layer of the interface between family and work settings. We identified several of these gaps in theory, offered some suggestions for refining understanding of work-family conflict and spillover, and suggested three ways that these ideas have begun to be applied to the study of conflict and spillover. Here, we speculate on the implications for future studies of conflict and spillover.

Even a superficial comparison of the topics covered in this book and our brief examination of the work-family literature reveals narrowness in the way the emotional elements of the work-family interface have been examined. We have noted several examples of this narrowness. First, conceptualizations have been unclear, and the primary focus has been on stress, not emotion. Stress is a psychological state tapping into the extent to which primarily negative situations tax resources. It is related to but conceptually distinguishable from discrete emotional states (Lazarus, 1993). Second, researchers have been preoccupied with conflict and negative spillover from work to family, possibly overlooking a much broader range of emotional experiences. Third, the study of work-family relationships has focused almost exclusively on variables having to do with structural and psychological connections between work and family. Work-family conflict is a prime example of what we mean, referencing, as it does, an element of the interface itself. This focus on interface variables has led to the relative neglect of studies of the mechanisms through which elements of one domain influence emotion processes in the other over time in response to issues and events not directly related to the first. For example, how does family support affect emotion responses to work events at work? How do emotions generated by work events influence family interactions? Our objective for this chapter is to help researchers (and ourselves) think beyond the conflict-stress paradigm. We believe this can be accomplished by first laying out the basic nature of emotional processes and then by using these processes as a road map to point to areas where the emotional aspects of work life and the emotional aspects of family life intersect.

We endorse the continuation and expansion of explicit attention to the received element of the work-family interface: workers' and family members' affective experiences within and across settings. Researchers should stop conflating the cognitive recognition of conflict with emotional experiences of distress. To continue to do so in the face of the strong evidence of discrepancies between cognitive and affective experiences will unnecessarily prolong substantial measurement error in future results.

Work-family researchers should expand their repertoire of emotions of interest. So far, we (speaking as researchers) have been not only preoccupied with negative affective experiences but also not very discriminating about those. We (now speaking as authors) cannot recall any studies of the work-family interface, for example, that draw distinctions between guilt and resentment among workers—both affective states, both indications of the nature of the work-family interface, but probably with quite different implications for workers and for interventions because the former is directed inward and the latter is directed toward others. On the side of positive emotions, a similar observation might be made about contentment and enthusiasm.

More sophisticated understanding of diverse emotional experiences will likely yield not only better understanding of experiences within a given setting, but also of the relationships between settings. In particular, the speed, amplitude, and content of the influences flowing from family life to the work domain may be more visible when examined through an emotions lens. Alternatively, researchers may confirm their current impression that the influences of work on family are stronger than the reverse, also a useful clarification.

Researchers should pursue greater understanding of the reasons for discrepancies between cognitive judgments and subjective affective experiences. Here the appraisal process seems key. How do work experiences translate into emotional strain? In particular, what individual and contextual factors mediate these processes? For example, flexibility and control over work demands have been suggested as possible mediators, but few studies map the relevant cognitive processes in detail. What are the variations among groups of people, such as workers who perform certain tasks (for example, emotional labor), in the links between cognition and emotion? How do personality traits bound emotional responses to particular events?

Thinking about emotion regulation in relation to the work-family interface raises several possible research questions. How do individuals with different levels of skill and different strategies for emotion management respond to similar chronic stressors? What emotion management strategies are most effective in modulating the flow of affective states between work and family? When is emotion-focused coping with work-family stressors appropriate and effective? How does emotion management relate to the kinds of appraisals individuals make of their experiences? And how does emotion regulation relate to other affect-driven behaviors labeled "emotional by-products" in our model? One could postulate that the positive affect generated by a family event or circumstance could enhance work creativity or helping behavior. One could also postulate that rumination over a negative family-relevant emotional event would distract and deplete resources. How are resources for emotion management created, depleted, and deployed?

Another aspect of the emotion process that deserves study is anticipatory coping. Grandey and Brauburger (Chapter Eight, this volume) discuss situation selection and situation modification as examples of anticipatory or preemptive coping. Although it is well known that workers are not randomly assigned to jobs, the role of affective experience in the selection of work environments and subsequent experiences of conflict, enhancement, and carryover could be better understood.

Our model also is consistent with questions regarding level of analysis. Goode (1960) originally defined role strain as "difficulty in meeting given role demands" going on to specify that "the individual's total role obligations are over-demanding" (p. 485). More than just excluding mention of any specific domains, this definition targets an entirely different level of analysis—the level of the entire system of role involvements. Despite the breadth of Goode's definition, Marks and MacDermid (1996) note that "much of the literature since then has reverted to an atomistic framework. Each role is seen as a thing in itself, separable from its embeddedness in an organized system of roles" (p. 417).

Marks and MacDermid (1996), for example, have conducted research on individuals' approaches to their role systems as a whole. Questioning the well-established view that individuals organize their identities hierarchically according to the salience of particular roles, they suggested that individuals vary in the degree to which their identities are balanced or hierarchical. Balance means tending to approach every role with an attitude of attentiveness and care (though not necessarily time) rather than prioritizing roles in a more hierarchical way. Analyses of several samples have revealed consistent differences in well-being between groups of individuals who characterize their role systems as more or less balanced despite comparable levels of functioning (for example, equally busy and successful). Similarly, both Barnett (1999) and Kossek, Noe, and DeMarr (1999) have proposed theoretical models targeting the functioning of the overall role system.

Not surprisingly, multiple levels of analysis present additional challenges. One is temporal: the continuum of moment-to-moment to day-to-day to much longer-term emotional experiences. So far, the very short- or very long-term aspects of the work-family interface have received little attention, probably muddying the precision of estimates of relationships among important constructs. Another "levels" issue concerns the number of individuals involved in emotional connections between work and family. Although we have recognized emotional carryover as one way that emotions in one setting can influence emotional processes in the other, spouses provide support to one another that may influence their respective appraisals of events in both settings. Activities with friends or children may hinder or facilitate processes of emotion regulation. These in turn may affect the anticipatory coping and the instigation of emotional events in both settings.

Perhaps our most urgent admonition is that researchers should continue to work hard to understand the mechanisms through which work and family affect one another. The days of using the valence of simple correlations between work and family characteristics as firm indicators of a certain type of process should be long over. Better understanding of the conditions under which certain mechanisms operate not only drives basic knowledge forward, but also refines the opportunities available to those who want to eradicate friction between work and family life. Better understanding of the factors that stress and support the work-family interface will lead to better understanding of resilience and coping.

Finally—and here we speak as both authors and researchers—all of us face the challenge of constantly seeking to maximize the rigor of our research. The work-family literature is rife with studies that rely exclusively on cross-sectional self-reports of all variables, which then are interpreted as favoring causal flow in a particular direction. The theoretical gaps that prompted the development of this chapter are unlikely to close unless researchers make concerted efforts to strengthen their methods, measures, and designs. We already have seen some innovative examples and look forward to more.

References

Aspinwall, L. G., & Taylor, S. E. (1997). A stitch in time: Self-regulation and proactive coping. *Psychological Bulletin, 121,* 417–436.

Barnett, R. C. (1999). A new work-life model for the twenty-first century. *Annals of the American Academy of Political and Social Science, 562,* 143–158.

Barnett, R. C., Marshall, N. L., & Sayer, A. (1992). Positive-spillover effects from job to home: A closer look. *Women and Health, 19,* 13–41.

Bolger, N., DeLongis, A., Kessler, R. C., & Schilling, E. A. (1989). Effects of daily stress on negative mood. *Journal of Personality and Social Psychology, 57,* 808–818.

Bolger, N., DeLongis, A., Kessler, R. C., & Wethington, E. (1989). The contagion of stress across multiple roles. *Journal of Marriage and the Family, 51,* 175–184.

Bond, J. T., Galinsky, E., & Swanberg, J. E. (1998). *The 1997 National Study of the Changing Workforce.* New York: Families and Work Institute.

Carlson, D. S., Kacmar, K. M., & Williams, L. J. (2000). Construction and initial validation of a multidimensional measure of work-family conflict. *Journal of Vocational Behavior, 56,* 249–276.

Crouter, A. C. (1984). Spillover from family to work: The neglected side of the work-family interface. *Human Relations, 37,* 425–442.

DeVault, M. L. (1991). *Feeding the family: The social organization of caring as gendered work.* Chicago: University of Chicago Press.

di Leonardo, M. (1987). The female world of cards and holidays: Women, families, and the work of kinship. *Signs, 12,* 440–453.

Dodge, K. A., & Garber, J. (1991). Domains of emotion regulation. In J. Garber & K. A. Dodge (Eds.), *The development of emotion regulation and dysregulation* (pp. 3–11). Cambridge: Cambridge University Press.

Dressel, P. L., & Clark, A. (1990). A critical look at family care. *Journal of Marriage and the Family, 52,* 769–782.

Edwards, J. R., & Rothbard, N. P. (2000). Mechanisms linking work and family: Clarifying the relationship between work and family constructs. *Academy of Management Review, 25,* 178–199.

Erickson, R. J., & Wharton, A. S. (1997). Inauthenticity and depression: Assessing the consequences of interactive service work. *Work and Occupations, 24.* 188–213.

Evans, P.A.L., & Bartolomé, F. (1980). The relationship between professional life and private life. In B. C. Derr (Ed.), *Work, family, and the career* (pp. 281–317). New York: Praeger.

Frijda, N. H. (1999). Emotions and hedonic experience. In D. Kahneman, E. Diener, & N. Schwarz (Eds.), *Well-being: The foundations of hedonic psychology* (pp. 190–212). New York: Russell Sage Foundation.

Frone, M. R., Russell, M., & Cooper, M. L. (1992). Antecedents and outcomes of work-family conflict: Testing a model of the work-family interface. *Journal of Applied Psychology, 77,* 65–78.

Frone, M. R., Yardley, J. K., & Markel, K. S. (1997). Developing and testing an integrative model of the work-family interface. *Journal of Vocational Behavior, 50,* 145–167.

Goode, W. J. (1960). A theory of role strain. *American Sociological Review, 25,* 483–496.

Greenhaus, J. H., & Beutell, N. J. (1985). Sources of conflict between work and family roles. *Academy of Management Review, 10,* 76–88.

Greenhaus, J. H., & Parasuraman, S. (1999). Research on work, family, and gender: Current status and future directions. In G. N. Powell (Ed.), *Handbook of gender in organizations.* Thousand Oaks, CA: Sage.

Greenhaus, J. H., & Powell, G. N. (2000, August). *When work and family collide.* Paper presented at the annual meeting of the Academy of Management, Toronto, Canada.

Grzywacz, J. G., & Marks, N. F. (1998). *Family, work, work-family spillover and alcohol abuse during midlife.* Madison: Center for Demography and Ecology, University of Wisconsin.

Grzywacz, J. G., & Marks, N. F. (2000). Reconceptualizing the work-family interface: An ecological perspective on the correlates of positive and negative spillover between work and family. *Journal of Occupational Health Psychology, 5,* 111–126.

Gutek, B. A., Searle, S., & Klepa, L. (1991). Rational versus gender role explanations for work-family conflict. *Journal of Applied Psychology, 76,* 560–568.

Hearn, J. (1994). Emotive subjects: Organizational men, organizational masculinities and the (de)construction of "emotions." In S. Fineman (Ed.), *Emotion in organizations* (pp. 142–166). Thousand Oaks, CA: Sage.

Hochschild, A. R. (1983). *The managed heart: Commercialization of human feeling.* Berkeley: University of California Press.

Kahn, R. L., Wolfe, D. M., Quinn, R. P., & Snoek, J. D. (1964). *Organizational stress: Studies in role conflict and ambiguity.* New York: Wiley.

Keiley, M. K., & Seery, B. L. (2001). Affect regulation and attachment strategies of adjudicated and non-adjudicated adolescents and their parents. *Contemporary Family Therapy, 23,* 343–365.

Keltner, D., Ellsworth, P. C., & Edwards, K. (1993). Beyond simple pessimism—Effects of sadness and anger on social perception. *Journal of Personality and Social Psychology, 64,* 740–752.

Kirchmeyer, C. (1992). Perceptions of nonwork-to-work spillover: Challenging the common view of conflict-ridden domain relationships. *Basic and Applied Social Psychology, 13,* 231–249.

Kopelman, R. E., Greenhaus, J. H., & Connolly, T. F. (1983). A model of work, family, and interrole conflict: A construct validation study. *Organizational Behavior and Human Performance, 32,* 198–215.

Kossek, E. E., Noe, R. A., & DeMarr, B. J. (1999). Work-family role synthesis: Individual, family, and organizational determinants. *International Journal of Conflict Resolution, 10,* 102–129.

Lambert, S. J. (1990). Processes linking work and family: A critical review and research agenda. *Human Relations, 43,* 239–257.

Larson, R. W., & Almeida, D. M. (1999). Emotional transmission in the daily lives of families: A new paradigm for studying family process. *Journal of Marriage and the Family, 61,* 5–20.

Lawler, E. J., & Thye, S. R. (1999). Bringing emotions into social exchange theory. *American Review of Sociology, 25,* 217–244.

Lazarus, R. S. (1993). From psychological stress to the emotions: A history of changing outlooks. *Annual Review of Psychology, 44,* 1–21.

Leiter, M. P., & Durup, M. J. (1996). Work, home, and in-between: A longitudinal study of spillover. *Journal of Applied Behavioral Science, 32,* 29–47.

Marks, S. R. (1977). Multiple roles and role strain: Some notes on human energy, time, and commitment. *American Sociological Review, 42,* 921–936.

Marks, S. R., & MacDermid, S. M. (1996). Multiple roles, role balance, and role ease. *Journal of Marriage and the Family, 85,* 417–432.

Masters, J. C. (1991). Strategies and mechanisms for the personal and social control of emotion. In J. Garber & K. A. Dodge (Eds.), *The development of emotion regulation and dysregulation* (pp. 182–207). Cambridge: Cambridge University Press.

Muraven, M., & Baumeister, R. F. (2000). Self-regulation and depletion of limited resources: Does self-control resemble a muscle? *Psychological Bulletin , 126.* 247–259.

Netemeyer, R. G., Boles, J. S., & McMurrian, R. (1996). Development and validation of work-family conflict and family-work conflict scales. *Journal of Applied Psychology, 81,* 400–410.

O'Driscoll, M. P., Ilgen, D. R., & Hildreth, K. (1992). Time devoted to job and off-job activities, interrole conflict, and affective experiences. *Journal of Applied Psychology, 7,* 272–279.

Paules, G. F. (1991). *Dishing it out: Power and resistance among waitresses in a New Jersey restaurant.* Philadelphia: Temple University Press.

Perry-Jenkins, M., Repetti, R. L., & Crouter, A. C. (2000). Work and family in the 1990s. *Journal of Marriage and the Family, 62,* 981–999.

Repetti, R. L. (1994). Short-term and long-term processes linking job stressors to father-child interaction. *Social Development, 3,* 1–15.

Repetti, R. L., & Wood, J. (1997). Families accommodating to chronic stress: Unintended and unnoticed processes. In B. H. Gottlieb (Ed.), *Coping with chronic stress* (pp. 191–220). New York: Plenum.

Seery, B. L. (2001). *Four types of mothering emotion work: Distress management, ego work, relationship management and pleasure/enjoyment work.* Unpublished manuscript.

Sieber, S. D. (1974). Toward a theory of role accumulation. *American Sociological Review, 39,* 567–578.

Small, S. A., & Riley, D. (1990). Toward a multidimensional assessment of work spillover into family life. *Journal of Marriage and the Family, 52,* 51–61.

Stephens, G. K., & Sommer, S. M. (1996). The measurement of work-to-family conflict. *Educational and Psychological Measurement, 56,* 475–486.

Strong, B., DeVault, C., & Sayad, B. W. (1998). *The marriage and family experience* (7th ed.). Belmont, CA: Wadsworth.

Tenbrunsel, A. E., Brett, J. M., Maoz, E., Stroh, L. K., & Reilly, A. H. (1995). Dynamic and static work-family relationships. *Organizational Behavior and Human Decision Processes, 63,* 233–246.

Thompson, R. A. (1994). Emotion regulation: A theme in search of definition. *Monographs of the Society for Research in Child Development,* 59 (2–3), 25–52.

Weiss, H. M., & Cropanzano, R. (1996). Affective events theory: A theoretical discussion of the structure, causes, and consequences of affective experiences at work. *Research in Organizational Behavior, 18,* 1–74.

Weiss, H. M., Nicholas, J. P., & Daus, C. S. (1999). An examination of the joint effects of affective experiences and job beliefs on job satisfaction and variations in affective experiences over time. *Organizational Behavior and Human Decision Processes, 78,* 1–24.

Wharton, A. S. (1993) The affective consequences of service work. *Work and Occupations, 20,* 205–232.

Wharton, A. S., & Erickson, R. J. (1995). The consequences of caring: Exploring the links between women's job and family emotion work. *Sociological Quarterly, 36,* 273–296.

Wiley, D. L. (1987). The relationship between work/nonwork role conflict and job-related outcomes: Some unanticipated findings. *Journal of Management, 13,* 467–472.

Williams, K. J., & Alliger, G. M. (1994). Role stressors, mood spillover, and perceptions of work-family conflict in employed parents. *Academy of Management Journal, 37,* 837–868.

PART 4

Integration and Future Research

In Chapter Thirteen, Kanfer and Kantrowitz address several issues with broad relevance to emotional regulation, and they also develop an organizing framework for emotional regulation strategies. Their three-dimensional system distinguishes among the form (cognitive or behavioral), the direction (self or situation), and the focus (antecedent conditions or response to events) of emotional regulation activities. They use this framework to differentiate two types of emotional regulation strategies: primary, situation-oriented strategies that attempt to change work environments so as to produce more positive and less negative emotional events, and secondary, self-oriented strategies that change cognitions and behaviors. In terms of their three-dimensional organizing framework, primary strategies tend to have a behavioral form, are situationally directed, and focus on antecedent conditions, while secondary strategies have a more cognitive form, are directed at the self, and focus on responses to events. Importantly, secondary strategies often have costs associated with greater cognitive load or physiological stress, while primary strategies require greater foresight and power over situational factors.

Kanfer and Kantrowitz also discuss age-related changes in emotional regulation. As employees age and their organizational tenure increases, they become more adept at managing their social environment as a means to regulate emotions, and they also become more skilled in the use of cognitive emotion regulation strategies. Kanfer and Kantrowitz stress that emotional regulation has a strong functional and motivational underpinning, which can be used to understand age-related changes. Research based on a life span approach to emotions suggests that reorganization of affect and cognition becomes a central life task for older adults, so that greater capacity to regulate emotions may reflect an age-related shift in priorities, as well as proceduralization of self-regulatory skills and greater position power and control over organizational resources.

An important distinction with relevance to contemporary historical circumstances is the distinction Kanfer and Kantrowitz make between emotion regulation and coping. Emotion regulation typically focuses on a specific event and addresses specific emotions (such as anger or fear) and associated responses that occur within a relatively short time period. Coping, in contrast, focuses on negative moods and stress, as well as emotional regulation that occurs over the extended time frames associated with events such as job loss or skill obsolescence. Applied to contemporary historical events, the September 11, 2001, terrorist attacks on the World Trade Center and the Pentagon were likely to have triggered many emotional regulation responses as workers and organizations responded to an immediate threat of unknown magnitude. Fear and anger needed to be managed so instrumental responses were possible, particularly for police, firefighters, rescue workers, and government officials. The enduring consequences of this and subsequent events, however, produce longer-lasting adjustment demands. Rescue workers, police and fire personnel, postal employees, airline crews, and military personnel all have had to cope with enduring job-related stress.

An important integrative point that Kanfer and Kantrowitz make that reinforces themes from many chapters in this book is that emotional regulation (and coping) requires an interactionist perspective that looks at organizational policies and practices, group-level effects, and individual responses. Individual-level responses have been studied extensively, but we know less about the effects of groups and organizations on emotional regulation. Their chapter brings together many critical points from prior chapters to help describe the "situation" side of their interactionist perspective. As they look to the future of emotional regulation at work, Kanfer and Kantrowitz maintain that effective organizations should develop policies and practices that facilitate primary emotion regulation strategies while minimizing the costs to individuals and organizations of secondary, internally directed emotion regulation. Applied to our current context, this recommendation implies that one of the ways that organizations need to adjust to a post–September 11 world is to develop strategies that promote primary as compared to secondary emotional regulation activities by employees.

The final chapter, by Kanfer and Klimoski, develops a broad perspective on affect at work and also identifies key themes for future research. Kanfer and Klimoski argue that no grand theory of emotions at work is yet possible. Instead, they provide a heuristic meta-framework that shows how individual- and environmental-level factors affect three core processes: cognition, conation (motivation), and affect. These processes then provide a basis for organizing the contributions of prior chapters and discussing several areas where future research is needed to fill gaps in our knowledge of how emotions influence workers and work behavior. Importantly, many of these gaps pertain to potential interactions of core processes. Kanfer and Klimoski see the interaction of conative and affective processes as the new frontier for research.

Kanfer and Klimoski also comment on the complexity involved in examining motivational processes. They note that core processes of affect, cognition, and motivation may all unfold at different rates, complicating measurement and empirical investigation. Nevertheless, they maintain that because affect operates in the context of cognition and conation, all three of these variables need to be incorporated into practically useful theories of emotions at work. Kanfer and Klimoski also maintain that researchers need to consider both isolated emotional events and the organization of multiple events into thematic episodes. Isolated organization events produce discrete emotions, whereas episodes (such as those associated with socialization or leadership) are more likely to affect employees' moods.

CHAPTER 13

Emotion Regulation
Command and Control of Emotion in Work Life

Ruth Kanfer
Tracy M. Kantrowitz

The ubiquity and variety of human emotions have long been admired and cursed by writers, poets, and other observers of the human condition. Not surprisingly, psychologists and social scientists have also accorded emotions a prominent role in human functioning and adjustment, although the scientific study of emotions has waxed and waned over the past century. During the past two decades, scientific activity and interest in emotions and related constructs (for example, moods, emotional traits, affective states) have burgeoned (see, for example, reviews by Brief & Weiss, in press; Gross, 1998b; Smith & Kirby, 2001). As a consequence, theory and research on emotion regulation, defined broadly as the processes by which individuals and environments influence the experience, expression, and control of an individual's emotions, are also again on the rise (see Gross, 1999). This is particularly the case in organizational psychology (see Pugh, Chapter Five, this volume), where emotion regulation is considered crucial for effective organizational command over the environment and control of internal functions.

This chapter cuts across a variety of psychological and organizational research literatures in order to focus on one aspect of recent developments in the field: the study of individual emotion regulation as related to workplace behaviors and across a work life that often spans four or more decades. To put our topic in perspective, we suggest that contemporary studies of emotion regulation be roughly organized into two distinct but related categories: (1) investigations of the ways in which organizations (and individuals in organizations, such as supervisors) attempt to modify and regulate an employee's emotions and emotion-related behaviors, and (2) research on the determinants, processes, and consequences of an employee's efforts to manage his or her emotions and emotion-related behaviors related to work. Theory and research in the first category highlight the role of organizational procedures, dynamics, and social processes as inputs to emotional processing and as a means of regulating employee emotions. Ashforth and Saks (Chapter Ten, this volume) and George (Chapter Six, this volume), for example, describe a number of institutional practices and tactics that organizations use to develop and enforce organizational preferences for the experience, display, and regulation of emotion-related behavior in the workplace. In this line of research, person factors, such as individual differences in emotional traits, mediate relationships between organizational practices and employee emotions and behaviors.

The second category of emotion regulation research, with which this chapter is primarily concerned, focuses on the determinants and consequences of self-managed psychological and behavioral processes that initiate, direct, alter, and sustain emotion regulation as it occurs in the workplace and in work life contexts, such as job transitions, career planning, and retirement. In this person-oriented framework, organizational practices provide one class of inputs to emotion and emotion regulation. In addition, individual differences in emotional traits, motives and goals, maturational changes, and capabilities are accorded an equally important role in determining the character, intensity, and effectiveness of emotion regulation efforts.

In this chapter on self-managed emotion regulation related to the workplace and work life, we consider emotion regulation as a topic of study in terms of breadth, scope, mechanisms, and overlap with disparate research traditions; develop an interactionist (person-situation) perspective on the topic; and discuss emotion regulation as part of work life, identify abiding issues, and propose a broad agenda of potentially fruitful directions for future research on emotion regulation related to work.

Emotion Regulation in Context

Personality and clinical psychologists have long been interested in emotion regulation, and a wide variety of perspectives exist for understanding individual differences in emotional responding and psychological and behavioral adjustment. In these perspectives, the focus has typically been on the origins and development of dysfunctional regulation and clinical disorders. During the past two decades, however, research interest has shifted away from pathology and toward an understanding of adaptive emotion processes and their role in the normal range of functioning. In particular, advances in physiological, cognitive, and personality psychology have converged on a multilevel approach to understanding the salient factors and processes underlying the elicitation of emotional states, that is, the experience, expression, and regulation of emotions. Using these new conceptualizations, researchers have demonstrated the various adaptive, functional, informational, and communicative functions of both positive and negative emotions.

Several elaborated process models of emotion have been proposed, including models by Gross (1998a, 1999), Larsen, Diener, and Lucas (Chapter Three, this volume), Lord and Harvey (Chapter Four, this volume), Weiss (Chapter Two, this volume), and Lazarus (1984, 1991). As Weiss notes, most process models subscribe to a view that encompasses the interplay of physiological, cognitive, and behavioral systems. There is also widespread agreement that emotion processes involve nonconscious as well as conscious processes (see Lord and Harvey, this volume).

At the risk of oversimplification, we summarize contemporary perspectives on emotion processes in terms of two interrelated but distinct phases (Gross, 1998a). In the first phase, biological and hormonal changes in the individual and relatively stable individual differences in dispositions, select personality traits, or moods sensitize the individual to emotion-triggering events or circumstances—that is, to specific events or circumstances that have functional and motivational significance for the individual. Lazarus (1991), for example describes this first phase as involving a cognitive appraisal of circumstances or events that are interpreted as having motivational significance or relevance for the individual. This primary appraisal, occasioned by the interaction of internal and external forces, yields an interpretation of the situation that sets the stage for the experienced emotion, emotional expression, and emotion regulation.

The second, overlapping phase of the emotion process pertains to the experience, expression, and regulation of emotion. Although questions remain about the reciprocal influence of emotions and dispositional tendencies, most theorists agree that the factors that influence the experience of emotion may be distinguished from the mechanisms and determinants of emotional expression. That is, felt emotions represent the resultant process of appraisal and may or may not find expression in cognitions and behavior.

Experienced emotions represent inputs from physiological, cognitive, and behavioral systems. The particular configuration of system inputs gives rise to the nature of the felt emotion and provides part of the motivational stimulus for emotion regulation. Nonemotion motives, associated with achievement goals, social norms, and situational constraints, also contribute to the nature and intensity of felt emotions and emotion regulation. Regulatory strategies also typically involve some combination of physiological, cognitive, or behavioral activities and may range from largely nonconscious, automatized responses, such as change in heart rate, to effortful, controlled cognitive activities, such as active distraction. Regulation may be directed toward determinants of the generative emotion process or to management of emotion response tendencies. Affective clinical disorders, such as exogenous depression, are often considered common sequelae of problems in the coordination or operation of emotion regulation response systems.

Adaptation represents the hallmark by which emotion regulation processes are typically evaluated. That is, from the viewpoint of the individual, the selection and implementation of emotion regulation processes are considered in terms of the extent to which the processes facilitate personal adaptation in accord with the individual's goals and environment. However, this broad criterion is not without its difficulties. For example, adaptation encompasses a temporal perspective such that what may be effective in regulating emotions in the short run may be maladaptive in the long run or over the course of a career. Indeed, in many instances, regulation strategies that reduce immediate emotional distress, such as drinking alcohol or work withdrawal, come at a significant longer-term cost. Changing one's job to reduce felt anger toward a coworker or boss may be adaptive in the sense of reducing immediate emotional distress, but maladaptive in the long run if the factors that evoked the anger are present in future jobs. On the other hand, situational modification by an employee who changes her job to reduce feelings of job disappointment represents a potentially adaptive emotion regulation strategy in its potential for reducing felt emotion and enhancing long-term career goals. We consider adaptive regulation to encompass strategies that involve either short-term cost and long-term gain or short-term and long-term gains. Strategies that involve short-term gain but long-term costs appear to be better conceptualized as problems in self-control.

From an employer's point of view, the primary criterion for evaluating effective emotion regulation is often the extent of an employee's conformance to organizational norms for the nondisplay of what is deemed inappropriate (largely negative) emotion-related behaviors, such as fear, anxiety, guilt, and anger. Obviously, personal criteria for adaptive functioning and behaviorally based organizational criteria have substantial overlap. Nonetheless, it is not difficult to identify circumstances when organizational goals related to the regulation of emotion-related behaviors may conflict with employee goals. Survivors of organizational downsizing who cope with fear of job loss by avoiding discussion of the topic with supervisors, for example, may behave in accord with organizational norms but experience personally maladaptive emotions.

In summary, there is relatively little disagreement about basic emotion processes or the importance of emotion regulation in adaptation and effective psychological and workplace functioning. In the workplace, however, it is clear that employers and employees may differ in the value they place on various regulatory styles and strategies. As such, emotion regulation in the workplace cannot be assessed independent of the employee's goals or the organizational context. In the next section we take a closer look at emotion regulation in terms of the domain, mechanisms, and methods of assessment.

Delineating the Emotion Regulation Domain

At the broadest level, emotion regulation refers to the psychological and behavioral processes involved in the (self) management of affective response tendencies (Frijda, 1986; Thompson, 1994).

Given the saturation of affect in life activities, emotion regulation is thus implied throughout a wide range of human functioning and for a variety of purposes. Regulatory activities implemented at a nonconscious level may manifest in emotional traits and tendencies (see Lord and Harvey, this volume; Larsen, Diener, and Lucas, this volume). In this chapter, however, we limit our discussion to more deliberative emotion regulation activities—that is, actions that involve some attentional effort to activate or implement.

Several researchers provide more specific definitions of emotion regulation that delineate different aspects of the domain. Eisenberg, Fabes, Guthrie, and Reiser (2000), for example, define emotion regulation as "the process of initiating, maintaining, modulating, or managing the occurrence, intensity, or duration of internal feeling states and emotion-related physiological processes, often in the service of accomplishing one's goals" (p. 167). Gross (1998a) defines emotion regulation as the processes by which individuals influence which emotions they have, when they have them, and how they experience and express these emotions.

Several features of these two definitions warrant special attention. First, in both definitions, the focus of regulation is the contextualized self. That is, emotion regulation pertains to modulation of one's emotional processes in the context of physiological, cognitive, motivational, and environmental presses. Second, both Eisenberg et al. (2000) and Gross (1998a) regard emotion regulation as a complex phenomenon that involves management of the process by which emotions are generated, the dynamics governing intensity of felt emotion, and the expression of emotion-based behaviors. Although emotion regulation may be conceptualized as how individuals influence the emotions of others (see Grandey and Brauburger, Chapter Eight, this volume), the definitions of Eisenberg et al. (2000) and Gross (1998a) emphasize how individuals influence their own felt emotions and responses to enhance subjective well-being and accomplish valued goals.

Many insightful discussions of the domain, scope, and set of processes involved in emotion regulation have been provided, including work by Gross (1998b), Dodge (1989), Fox (1989), Lazarus (1991), and Smith and Kirby (2001). In the following section, we discuss three aspects of the emotion regulation research domain that have particular significance for the study of emotion regulation pertaining to work.

Regulation of Emotion Processes Versus Emotion-Related Behaviors

Emotion regulation may refer to either the emotion generative process or the regulation of behaviors that follow from felt emotions, that is, emotion-related behaviors. Eisenberg et al. (2000), for example, define emotion-related behavior regulation as "the process of initiating, maintaining, inhibiting, modulating, or changing the occurrence, form, and duration of behavioral concomitants of emotion" (p. 167).

Gross (1998a) makes a similar distinction in terms of antecedent-focused emotion regulation (that is, regulation of the precursors of emotion, such as the situation or the appraisal) and response-focused emotion regulation (that is, regulation of the physiological or observable signs of emotions). For example, an employee who feels anger toward a coworker and attempts to reduce his feelings of anger by reframing the situation would be regarded by Eisenberg et al. (2000) to be engaged in emotion regulation and by Gross (1998a) to be engaged in antecedent-focused emotion regulation. In contrast, Eisenberg et al. (2000) would regard efforts to prevent verbal expressions of anger toward the coworker as regulation of emotion-related behavior and by Gross (1998a) to be engaged in a form of response-focused emotional regulation.

Eisenberg et al. (2000) note that emotion regulation and regulation of emotion-related behavior are closely related processes. The effectiveness of emotion regulation often affects the demand on emotion-related behavioral regulation (that is, lapses in emotion regulation typically require greater emotion-related behavioral regulation). Some approaches to emotion regulation emphasize factors affecting regulation of the affective state; others emphasize regulation of the processes or conditions associated with the selection and abandonment of different strategies.

Emotion Regulation in Service of Goals

Emotion regulation may be undertaken for a number of goals or purposes. The most obvious purposes are reduction of subjective distress and reduction in the frequency of unacceptable emotion-related behaviors, such as physical and verbal acts of aggression. However, emotion regulation may also be undertaken to accomplish nonemotional or instrumental goals. For example, individuals may seek to reduce the experience of negative emotions that yield response tendencies that are no longer useful in the environment or in accomplishment of the individual's nonemotional goals (Gross, 1999). Attempts to regulate one's anger over a job loss because of the detrimental effect of associated response tendencies in job interviews represent one example of the instantiation of emotion regulation processes for a nonemotional goal.

Emotion regulation may also be initiated to replace one emotion with a more productive one, such as when individuals reframe task threats into challenges and so support task motivation. In these instances, emotion regulation operates to contain unacceptable response tendencies by displacing them. Individuals may also regulate their emotions for the purposes related to self-processes. In the workplace, employees may regulate emotions as a means of increasing or decreasing particular behavior patterns that are more consistent with organizational norms and job-specific work identities. Air traffic controllers, for example, may regulate anxiety as a means of increasing behavior patterns more consistent with widely held views of controllers as calm and composed.

Gross (1999) points out that little is known about the cognized goals that individuals seek to accomplish during emotion regulation. He notes, however, that emotion regulation encompasses both the increase and decrease of positive and negative emotions. As such, emotion regulation may be instantiated for the purpose of increasing emotional expressions in appropriate situations or, as is more common in work settings, to reduce the display of socially unacceptable negative emotions.

Emotion Regulation as a Set of Self-Processes

Consistent with theories of self-regulation, emotion regulation appears to involve monitoring, evaluation (appraisal), and action (regulation). Monitoring pertains to the individual's awareness of and sensitivity to external and internal events. This process may be importantly influenced by individual differences in nonability traits. Research by Gramzow, Sedikides, Panter, and Insko (2000), for example, found that individual differences in self-regulatory elasticity (composed in part of ego resiliency and ego strength) were strongly and negatively related to self-reports of emotional distress. Similarly, research by Salovey, Mayer, Goldman, Turvey, and Palfai (1995) found that a composite individual difference trait factor they termed clarity in the discrimination of feelings was significantly related to ruminative thought and mood persistence. These findings suggest an important association between self-related traits and emotion regulatory processes.

Another line of research on the self-managed process employs a cybernetic perspective (see Lord and Harvey, this volume). In this framework, emotion regulatory strategies, whether conscious or nonconscious, occur in response to the detection of a discrepancy between a desired state and the detected current state. Determinants of the desired state may be derived from internal or environmental stimuli and may be motivated by felt emotions or nonemotional goals. Determinants of the current state may arise from physiological, cognitive, or behavioral systems. Individual differences in sensitivity to event-triggering stimuli may cause differential activation or termination of emotion regulatory processes. Individuals who are high in negative affectivity, for example, may maintain lower sensitivities to negative emotion-triggering events and as a result engage in faster or more intense emotion regulation than persons low in negative affectivity.

Trait and cybernetic approaches suggest two implications for the study of emotion regulation. First, individual differences in emotion sensitivity and personality traits (such as negative affectivity and elasticity) are likely to play an important role in the instantiation of emotion regulation through their influence on monitoring. Second, in cybernetic perspectives, individual differences in nonemotional goals may influence emotion regulation through their effect on desired states. During test taking, for example, individuals may attempt to control feelings of anxiety for the purpose of improving their performance rather than reducing subjective distress.

Emotion Regulation Strategies: Toward a Taxonomy of Operations

Strategies represent the primary mechanism by which individuals regulate their emotions and emotion-related behaviors. Strategies refer to covert or overt acts involving physiological, cognitive, and behavioral systems. Acts may be directed toward modifying the events and processes that precede the felt emotion or toward regulating emotional response tendencies. Strategies may be implemented for dealing with a specific event or for regulation of emotional responses that occur repeatedly over time.

The assessment of emotion regulation represents a growing area of research. Several methodologies have been used to assess emotion regulation strategies and processes for a variety of different purposes. For example, a small number of studies investigating the operation of a specific emotion regulation strategy, such as suppression, have used multilevel physiological, behavioral, and self-report measures. The bulk of research, however, has examined the types and frequency of different emotion regulation strategies in different contexts and their association to individual differences in traits and attributes of the situation. Although these approaches provide greater breadth in the study of emotion regulation strategies, they rarely employ physiological or behavioral measures and so are heavily reliant on self-report methods of assessment.

Emotion regulation strategies as they occur in natural settings have been assessed in several ways. A number of studies have asked individuals to list, describe, or report their emotion regulation strategies over time and settings (Larsen, 2000b; Morris, 1999; Morris & Reilly, 1987; Parkinson & Totterdell, 1999; Thayer, 1996). The findings indicate the existence of literally hundreds of ways in which people manage their emotions and emotion-related behaviors. Reported strategies include physiologically oriented acts such as meditation, cognitive processing directed toward mood repair, self-efficacy enhancement, suppression, downward social comparison, and reappraisal and behavioral acts such as venting, altering the environment, and seeking social support.

Other researchers have examined individual differences in the use of specific types of emotion regulation strategies based on responses to a standardized self-report measure. Examples of self-report measures include the Ways of Coping Checklist (Lazarus & Folkman, 1984), Cognitive Emotion Regulation Questionnaire (Garnefski, Kraaij, & Spinhoven, 2001), the Emotional Control Questionnaire (Roger & Hesshoever, 1987), the Meta-Regulation Scale (Kokkonen & Pulkkinen, 1999), the Academic Volitional Strategy Inventory (McCann & Garcia, 1999), the Negative Mood Regulation Scale (Surmann, 1999), the Generalized Expectancies for Negative Mood Regulation (Catanzaro & Mearns, 1990), and the Emotion Control Scale (Roger & Najarian, 1989). Items from these measures typically ask respondents to indicate the frequency or extent of agreement with statements that describe various types of emotion regulation strategies—for example, "talked to someone about how I was feeling" (Lazarus & Folkman, 1984, p. 331), "telling myself it will pass will help me calm down (Catanzaro & Mearns, 1990, p. 552), and "I seldom show how I feel about things" (Roger & Hesshoever, 1987, p. 534).

The assessment of emotion regulation has also been conducted as part of efforts to capture individual differences in level of emotion regulation control rather than individual differences in the use of various emotion regulation strategies. For example, emotion regulation has also been assessed in the context of research on emotional intelligence. Salovey et al. (1995), for example, developed the Trait Meta-Mood Scale, a trait-based self-report measure designed to assess individual differences in attentiveness to feelings, emotion clarity, and emotion regulation, defined in terms of individual differences in modulation of negative moods (mood repair; for example, "When I become very upset, I remind myself of all the little pleasures in life.").

In the organizational domain, several researchers have developed global self-report measures of emotion control and emotion-focused coping for use in specific work contexts such as learning (McConatha & Huba, 1999; Warr & Downing, 2000), decision making (Epstein & Meier, 1989), and job search following job loss (Wanberg, Kanfer, & Rotundo, 1999). In most of these measures, items from existing scales were modified for use in the specific context, and new items were created using a rational procedure. Reliability data for these measures are generally limited to indexes of internal consistency.

The measurement of emotion regulation strategies is closely associated with the way that researchers have conceptualized the emotion process and organized emotion regulation strategies. Lazarus and Folkman (1984), for example, distinguish between emotion-focused and problem-focused coping strategies. In this scheme, problem-focused coping refers to cognitions and behaviors that alter the generation of stress-related emotions and emotional response tendencies, including, for example, problem-solving tactics aimed at both the environment and the self. In contrast, emotion-focused coping encompasses cognitive and behavioral strategies that seek to modify felt emotional distress. Examples in this category include cognitive reappraisal, avoidance, selective attention, and positive comparisons. The Ways of Coping Checklist was designed to assess use of problem-focused and emotion-focused coping strategies.

Those who have used a more open-ended format for assessing emotion regulation strategies have emphasized the difference between cognitive and behavioral emotion regulation strategies (Larsen, 2000b; Parkinson & Totterdell, 1999). Using an act frequency approach, Larsen (see Judge & Larsen, 2001; Larsen, 2000b), for example, proposed a two-dimensional taxonomy that organizes strategies according to mode of regulation (cognitive versus behavioral) and what Larsen (2000b) terms the "directedness" of acts, that is, the target of the action (changing self or feelings versus changing the situation).

The "directedness" dimension that Larsen (2000b) described has received less attention than the other two dimensions but may be usefully distinguished from focal (antecedent versus response) and format (cognitive versus behavioral) dimensions. Self-oriented strategies, whether they focus on the antecedents or responses to emotions, aim at regulation of self-variables, such as ego control, self-efficacy, and self-esteem. Individuals may engage in self-talk to enhance ego control, engage in positive social comparisons to increase self-esteem, avoid job tasks that lower self-efficacy, or engage in helping behaviors in order to increase positive self-concept. That is, these strategies seek to enhance emotional well-being and outcomes through changes in the person rather than the environment.

Self-oriented strategies typically involve cognitive processes, but not all cognitive processes are aimed at the self. Attentional deployment (Gross, 1999), for example, involves cognitive processing, but without reference to self-variables. In contrast, cognitive reappraisal also involves cognitive processing but is more likely to affect self-esteem. This distinction between self versus situational strategies seems useful for considering when cognitively costly strategies may be most effective. For example, in the regulation of felt sadness, cognitive change strategies directed toward modulating displays of sadness may be phased out as self-esteem increases and promotes a reappraisal of events. In contrast, regulation strategies that do not have self-variable implications may require sustained attentional effort.

In contrast to self-oriented strategies, situation-focused strategies are directed toward external control and modulation of emotions, regardless of any associated changes in internal variables, such as self-esteem. Environment-oriented strategies, such as situational selection, situational modification, and attentional deployment (Gross, 1999), involve actions taken for the purpose of changing the environment or for changing perceptions of the environment in a way that alters the likelihood of emotion experience or work demands on modulation of response tendencies. Strategies may also involve a single act (such as leaving a job) or repeated acts over time (such as redirecting attention away from maddening events). Environmentally oriented strategies may be behavioral or cognitive. Examples of behavioral strategies include avoiding contact with disliked coworkers to reduce feelings of anger, changing work assignments to reduce jealousy or increase job pride, changing work assignments or careers to reduce emotional labor, or implementing an exercise program to reduce subjective distress. Examples of cognitive strategies include reinterpreting the meaning of a coworker's comments and focusing attention on one's work rather than social features of the work context.

Toward a Taxonomy of Emotion Regulation Strategies

The various approaches to the assessment of emotion regulation suggest that strategies may be differentiated in terms of their direction (to alter self-processes or environmental conditions), form (physiological, cognitive, behavioral), and focus or purpose (to prevent the elicitation of felt emotions versus to modulate emotional response tendencies), their cost to the individual (automatized or demanding attentional effort), their temporal duration (one-time, brief versus repeated, long term), and their effectiveness.

Based on prior research by Gross (1999), Larsen (2000b), and Parkinson and Totterdell (1999), Figure 13.1 presents an integrative heuristic framework for the organization of purposive emotion regulation strategies based on three dimensions: direction (self versus situation), form (cognitive versus behavioral), and focus (prevention versus modulation). The framework treats emotion regulation strategies as distinct, multidimensional action patterns. Different emotion regulation strategies may be implemented in different contexts and as a single strategy or in a pattern of strategies employed over time. The organization of emotion regulation strategies in terms of multiple attributes provides a means for coordinating extant conceptual approaches and identifying new implications for emotion regulation research.

The Primacy of Situation-Oriented Strategies

Strategies that entail actions designed to change or modify the environment in order to change or control felt emotions are well represented in the popular and scientific literatures. People commonly seek to change and modify their work environments in order to reduce feelings of anger or sadness, increase feelings of joy or contentment, and control feelings of shame. A number of findings support the notion that such strategies are positively associated with improved regulation of undesirable, negative emotion-related behaviors.

Figure 13.1. An Organizational Framework of Emotion Regulation Strategies, by Direction, Form, and Focus.

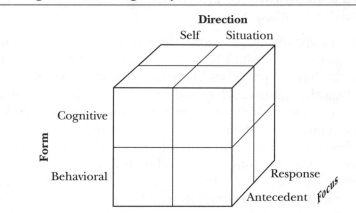

The apparent primacy of environmentally directed strategies in everyday life may be understood in the context of recent theorizing by Heckhausen and Schulz (1999). According to these authors, individuals manage their well-being through two control processes: primary control and secondary control. Primary control processes involve actions taken to change or modify the environment. In contrast, secondary control processes involve internally directed actions taken to facilitate the individual's adjustment to the environment. Heckhausen and Schulz propose that individuals employ secondary control mechanisms only when primary control mechanisms are not possible to implement or fail. From this perspective, situation-oriented strategies, directed toward modifying the environment, represent the first line of defense in emotion regulation.

It is important to note, however, that situation-oriented strategies may be antecedent or response focused. Antecedent-focused strategies, such as changing one's job to reduce anxiety in performance of particular job tasks, often entail little cognitive or conative cost to the individual beyond that of securing a new position. If the strategy is successful (a new job is found), the personal cost of regulation is minimized. In contrast, situation-oriented, response-focused strategies, such as trying to avoid performing anxiety-evoking job tasks each time they are assigned, entail sustained cognitive and conative effort. Thus, situation-oriented, antecedent-focused strategies may be preferred over response-focused strategies as the most efficient way to bring about desired changes in felt emotion and emotional response tendencies.

In many instances, situation-oriented, antecedent-focused strategies can be easily implemented and over time may become proceduralized in the form of stylistic action tendencies, such as action orientation. For example, individuals who experience undesired negative self-emotions, such as guilt or anger, in association with group membership may habitually reduce felt emotions by leaving or reducing interactions with the group. Such strategies are frequently employed in the workplace and represent a generally acceptable means of emotion regulation in many dyadic interactions. Over time, emotion regulation strategies developed in the workplace may come to represent important attributes of the person shaped by his or her work history.

Boundary Conditions on the Use of Situation-Oriented Strategies

The effectiveness of externally oriented strategies to reduce felt emotion or emotional response tendencies depends on a number of individual and environmental factors. Often such strategies may be impractical, unworkable, or unsuccessful. For example, economic, family, and job skill constraints may prevent an individual from leaving a job that provokes intense, frequent feelings of distress or boredom. Medical students who experience strong negative emotions or anxiety during surgical procedures cannot eliminate or avoid this component of training without sacrificing their career goals. Managers who experience anxiety when making a group presentation may be unsuccessful in attempts to reduce the frequency of presentations they are required to make. In person-situation contexts where situation-oriented, antecedent-focused strategies are likely to be ineffective, individuals must adopt other methods of emotion regulation.

Self-Oriented Strategies Aimed at Emotion Prevention

Self-oriented strategies operate to modify felt emotion or response tendencies by altering internal variables or processes. Although many of the most common self-strategies involve manipulation of one's cognitive processes to modulate subjective distress or response tendencies (for example, self-talk), individuals may also engage in cognitive change strategies or behaviors aimed at altering self-processes to preclude or alter emotion elicitation. Exercise programs, participation in religious events, social activities, choosing easy task assignments, and suppression represent potential strategies by which individuals may enhance their sense of self-control, self-esteem, and self-efficacy for the ultimate purpose of altering their perceptions of the environment and reducing the emotional impact of unalterable situations. We suggest that the lesser personal costs associated with antecedent-focused, self-oriented strategies make them an attractive choice for the second line of defense in workplace emotion regulation.

The Personal Costs of Self-Oriented Strategies Aimed at Emotion Modulation

The most common reference to self-oriented strategies relates to the regulation of emotional response tendencies, that is, for response-focused regulation (Gross, 1999). In comparison to other classes of strategies, these are likely to entail the greatest amount of cognitive and conative processing and to be most difficult to implement effectively. In these strategies, individuals seek to change or modulate emotion-related behaviors indirectly by changing self-variables presumed to underlie expression tendencies. For example, in the regulation of felt sadness, an individual might remind himself or herself of a happy time as a means of reducing sadness-related behavior. In contrast to situational-oriented strategies, which remove emotion response triggers, self-oriented, response-focused, cognitive strategies require the ultimate in self-control: imposition of behavior change in opposition to prevailing contingencies.

Summary

In summary, emotion regulation refers to the universe of physiological, cognitive, and behavioral strategies aimed at increasing or decreasing the experience or expression of positive and negative emotions. The underlying structure of emotion regulation strategies is an important issue for understanding who might use which strategies, under which conditions, and with what degree of success. Based on the literature, we suggest an organizational framework that distinguishes between effortful strategies in terms of their direction (self versus situation), form (cognitive versus behavior), and focus (antecedent versus response). We suggest that individuals select strategies based on historical experiences and anticipated personal costs, such that primary control strategies (those that change the environment) are preferred and proceduralized over time in terms of individual differences in action styles and coping preferences. However, in many instances, secondary control strategies (those that change the self or control emotional response tendencies) may be necessary and are likely to entail nontrivial cognitive and conative costs. The effectiveness of these secondary control strategies will depend on both person and situation factors, with failure more likely to have negative repercussions for the self.

Coordinating Concepts and Constructs

The proposed organization of emotion regulation strategies also provides a common foundation for mapping of related constructs and concepts within and across the research domains of emotion, coping, and emotional intelligence. We use the organizational framework to identify communalities and differences between concepts and constructs in these research traditions and to consider a few implications of these distinctions for emotion regulation related to work.

Moods and Emotions

Affect typically refers to the superordinate domain that encompasses both moods and emotions (see Weiss, this volume). Furthermore, both moods and emotions are multicomponential, meaning that both constructs entail physiological, experiential, cognitive, and expressive aspects (cf. Larsen, 2000a).

Distinctions between moods and emotions typically emphasize differences in the focus, duration, or directedness of each construct. In contrast to emotions, moods tend to be diffuse, pervasive, absent of a readily identifiable precipitating event, and of longer duration than emotions. Moods and emotions may also be distinguished in terms of their informational value. Emotions provide more information about the environment than moods, though moods are likely to provide more information about one's internal state (Morris & Feldman, 1997). Perhaps the most important distinction pertains to the stronger action tendencies associated with emotions in comparison to moods. As Underwood (1997) notes, "Emotions are often powerful, urgent, passionate" (p. 127). Moods are rarely described in these action-oriented terms.

Although most researchers regard the division between emotions and moods as fuzzy (see Weiss, this volume), we believe that the distinction holds potentially important implications for the study of affect regulation related to work. Building on our proposed framework, for example, we suggest that emotions are associated with greater use of situation-oriented, behavioral regulation strategies than moods. That is, because emotion episodes involve an appraisal of a specific precipitating event or circumstance, subsequent emotion regulation may be directed toward modifying the situation or event or modulating emotional responses. In contrast, mood regulation focuses primarily on altering the (usually negative) mood state of the individual (Larsen, 2000a). Because moods are not typically associated with specific events or circumstances, emotion regulation strategies aimed at situation alteration may not be employed as frequently as strategies aimed at modulation of response tendencies. That is, the individual may perceive no obvious event or circumstance to alter. But as clinical outcome studies for the treatment of exogenous depression suggest, situation modification is often an effective strategy for lessening the intensity of negative moods. In the workplace, emotion regulation to deal with moods may similarly be naturally biased toward the use of self-oriented, cognitive, response-focused strategies. Additional research is needed to investigate the similarity of regulatory patterns for related workplace emotions and moods.

Emotion Regulation and Coping

Although emotion regulation and coping developed out of different research traditions, the overlap between these concepts has been frequently noted. Clearly, both function to reduce emotional distress and facilitate adaptive functioning, and both are associated with appraisals of specific events or circumstances that evoke emotions. However, Gross (1999) suggests several distinctions between the two concepts. In particular, Gross notes that coping research typically focuses on efforts to reduce emotional distress associated with appraisal of an event as negative, whereas models of emotion regulation may be used to understand responses to events appraised as positive or negative. Although the preponderance of research on stress and coping does focus on events that elicit negative emotions, Lazarus and Folkman (1984) allow for appraisals of challenge that may foster positive as well as negative felt emotions. Nonetheless, in this sense, models of emotion regulation are clearly intended to explore a broader range of emotion change processes than have been typically examined in the stress-coping literature.

Alternatively, coping can be argued to include a wider range of self-regulatory strategies because it includes problem-focused responses, that is, nonemotional actions taken to achieve non-emotional goals (Scheier, Weintraub, & Carver, 1986). Lazarus and Folkman (1984) describe such strategies as a form of problem solving—self- or environment-directed actions taken to resolve the appraised stress. For example, individuals who lose their job during an organizational downsizing may experience emotional distress following the event but engage in problem-focused coping aimed at finding new employment (for example, making applications, revising a resumé, or learning a new job skill), rather than in emotion-focused coping aimed at reducing the subjective distress associated with job loss (such as talking about the loss or taking a vacation). This is not to say that individuals who use problem-focused coping strategies do not experience negative emotions in connection with job loss, but rather that a nonemotional goal (finding reemployment) provides the direction for regulatory activities. Indeed, failure to regulate felt emotions, coupled with early failure in job search, may ultimately undermine problem-focused coping efforts and intensify feelings of sadness and depression. In contrast to extant emotion regulation frameworks, coping paradigms are explicit in their recognition of the integral role of motivation in allocation of effort across different types of regulatory strategies. (Evidence for the role of this person factor in affect regulation is discussed later in this chapter.)

Finally, coping typically involves a longer time frame than emotion regulation (Gross, 1998a). In emotion regulation, regulatory activities are described in terms of occurring over minutes or hours. In contrast, coping is often described as occurring anywhere from minutes to months. As Lazarus and Folkman (1984) note, events interpreted as stressful may occur more or less quickly and endure hours (a test) or months (role conflict). The longer time frame for coping, and its measurement in terms of the relative frequency of types of coping over time, emphasizes the notion that coping reflects a pattern of strategies that unfold over some period of time rather than a choice or preference for a particular strategy at a particular point in time.

Differences between emotion, mood, and stress-coping models of regulation have both theoretical and practical implications.

Theoretically, emotion models permit investigation of multilevel regulation of emotions, as well as both increases and decreases in positive and negative emotions. Both mood and coping models are slanted toward regulation (reduction) of negative affective states. In the context of affect regulation related to work, emotion regulation models may be particularly useful for studying how individuals regulate specific but highly disruptive emotions, such as anger or guilt, or intensify emotions that facilitate job performance, such as pride. In contrast, stress-coping models of regulation may be more useful for investigating the determinants and consequences of broad repertoires of self-regulatory strategies to address more pervasive work-related and career stresses, such as role problems, job loss, and skill obsolescence. The choice between models depends largely on the investigator's objectives. From an organizational perspective, emotion regulation models may provide a better mapping to organizational methods aimed at regulating emotion-related behaviors. In contrast, stress-coping models may be more useful for practitioners concerned with employee development and career progress.

Emotion Regulation and Emotional Intelligence

The controversy over the validity and incompleteness of general cognitive ability measures for predicting job performance and career success helped to spawn scientific interest in the concept of emotional intelligence. Over the past fifteen years, a small group of researchers have developed measures of emotional intelligence with the intent of providing incremental predictive validity (above that of general cognitive ability) for interpersonal and managerial aspects of job performance (Bar-On, 2000; Goleman, 1995; Mayer & Salovey, 1995, 1997).

Mayer and his colleagues (for example, Mayer & Salovey, 1997), for example, describe emotional intelligence as the ability to perceive and express emotion, assimilate emotion in thought, understand and reason about emotions, and regulate emotion in the self and others. As this definition suggests, emotional intelligence entails a broad interrelated set of processes by which individuals identify, evaluate, and regulate their feelings for purposes of adaptive social functioning.

The Mayer and Salovey (1997) description includes self-oriented emotion regulation as one component of emotional intelligence, just as definitions of emotion regulation often include components of emotional intelligence. Walden and Smith (1997), for example, define emotion regulation as a process that "requires the individual to be able to assess the demands of a situation and to respond flexibly and adaptively to those demands" (p. 15). Nonetheless, research on emotion regulation and emotional intelligence differs in several important ways. First, most research on emotion regulation to date has focused on the development and use of general emotion regulation strategies, particularly among children and older adults. The focus of these efforts is on delineation of the scope and use of adaptive regulatory strategies: who uses them and their association with particular features of person-situation transactions and types of emotions. In contrast, emotion intelligence researchers have followed the abilities research pathway, focusing on the development of valid measures for the assessment of relatively stable individual differences in a general factor of emotional intelligence. To date, interest in these measures has been greatest in industry, where such measures are argued to have potential for improving personnel selection, diagnosing nonability skill deficits among job incumbents, and serving a prescriptive use in career counseling. Evidence pertaining to the validity of these measures and their incremental predictive validity for performance remains controversial (Davies, Stankov, & Roberts, 1998).

By definition, emotion regulation pertains to only part of the broad emotional intelligence construct. Indeed, even emotional intelligence researchers differ in the extent to which they perceive emotion regulation as an integral part of the emotion intelligence construct. Although several measures of emotional intelligence contain subscales aimed at assessment of emotion management or regulation—examples are the Multifactor Emotional Intelligence Scale (Mayer & Salovey, 1995) and the Bar-On Emotional Quotient Inventory (Bar-On, 2000)—most measures are designed as skill or ability tests that yield a total emotional intelligence score.

The overlap between models of emotion regulation and emotional intelligence has been noted recently by several researchers, including Fox and Spector (2000) and Martinez-Pons (1999–2000). Martinez-Pons (1999–2000) suggests that emotional intelligence may be conceptualized as the self-regulatory routines by which individuals engage in emotion and behavioral control. In his view, individual differences in emotional intelligence represent individual differences in self-regulatory effectiveness. Fox and Spector (2000) examined the predictive validity of cognitive and emotional intelligence variables on interview hiring judgments. They found support for the distinction between general and noncognitive measures of intelligence, but mixed results with respect to the influence of noncognitive measures of intelligence on hire judgments. It is noteworthy, however, that Fox and Spector (2000) did find consistent support for the influence of the mood regulation subscale on hire judgments.

Determinants of Emotion Regulation

In the previous section, we delineated the breadth and scope of the emotion regulation domain and the types of strategies by which individuals regulate their emotions. In this section, we turn to the determinants of emotion regulation related to work.

Person Influences

Emotion regulation occurs in individuals who differ in motives and goals, personality traits, cognitive abilities, and self-regulatory capabilities. The influence of these diverse person factors on the generative emotion process, as well as the selection, development, and use of emotion regulation strategies, is likely to be substantial. Higher levels of negative affectivity, for example, may place heavier demands on the individual for emotion regulation as a result of increased sensitivity to emotionally evocative events. Such traits may also influence the selection of emotion regulation strategies. Individuals high in negative affectivity may show preference for self-oriented, response-focused strategies that exacerbate rather than attenuate felt emotion and need for emotion control. In short, it is likely that person factors mediate multiple aspects of the emotion process in a way that exacerbates positive or negative trends in adaptive functioning.

For clarity, we organized the research literature and our discussion of person influences on emotion regulation into two distinct but related streams of inquiry: research on interindividual differences in personality and affective traits and tendencies and intraindividual differences in factors that influence the elicitation and regulation of emotions.

Interindividual Differences

The bulk of research on interindividual differences in emotions and emotion regulation has been conducted in the personality domain. A rapidly growing body of research attests to the relationship between select personality dimensions, such as positive and negative affectivity, and the appraisal of events, experienced emotions, and emotional response tendencies (see Larsen, Diener, and Lucas, this volume). As Gross (1999) notes, however, most research to date has focused on the relationship between individual differences in emotion antecedents and responses rather than on the relationship of traits to individual differences in the use, scope, or development of emotion regulation strategies.

A few recent studies have examined the relationship between Five Factor Model personality traits and emotion regulation strategy use (Kokkonen & Pulkkinen, 1999; O'Brien & DeLongis, 1996; Tobin, Graziano, Vanman, & Tassinary, 2000). Results of these studies are generally concordant with findings in the antecedent and response domain in demonstrating a negative relationship between neuroticism and the use of adaptive emotion regulation strategies. However, as Duclos and Laird (2001) note, it is likely that certain individuals will benefit more from some emotion regulation strategies than others. That is, the question is not simply the relationships of traits to use of adaptive or maladaptive strategies, but rather how and why traits relate to differential strategy use.

Another very recent line of inquiry in the personality–social psychology domain pertains to the influence of individual differences in motive variables on emotional processing (Brockner & Higgins, 2001; Carver, Sutton, & Scheier, 2000; Forgas & Vargas, 1999; Higgins, 2001; also see Martin & Tesser, 1996). In this work, emphasis is placed on individual differences in motives and goals that are distinct from personality or emotional traits. Martin and Tesser (1996), for example, note that the direction and strength of goals may importantly affect emotional processing. That is, differences in intrinsic and extrinsic motivational orientation, regulatory focus, approach and avoidance orientation, and self-concepts may affect antecedents, response tendencies, and regulation of emotions and mood states.

Consistent with this notion, Higgins (2001) has recently shown that regulatory focus, a motivational variable distinguishing individual differences in promotion and prevention modes of achievement motivation, exerts a direct influence on felt emotions. Additional research, to determine the incremental influence of these and other motive and goal states on emotion regulation processes, represents an important next step in this area.

In summary, personality research indicates that select affect-saturated traits mediate emotional processes in multiple ways. Evidence for the role of these traits in the activation of emotional processing, felt emotion, and emotion response tendencies is well documented, and findings on the influence of motivational variables on these processes are also emerging. But research has yet to be done demonstrating the influence of these traits on the initiation, intensity, or persistence of different types of emotion regulation strategies. In the context of work, future evidence linking traits to the particulars of emotion regulation can be helpful in the development of more finely tuned programs to remediate emotion-related behavior problems.

Intraindividual Differences

Contemporary process theories of adult affect tend to highlight the influence of interindividual differences on emotional processes. However, theory and research from developmental and aging literatures suggest that individual differences in emotional experience and emotion regulation may change over time as a function of maturation, changing goals, and experience (Eisenberg et al., 2000; Carstensen, 1992). In this section, we review the literature on age-related changes in goals, personality, and emotion regulation. Examining aspects of emotions with regard to other personal characteristics is important to elucidate the nature of age-related changes in emotions. Consistent with our strategy framework, we discuss research investigating the relationship between age and emotion regulation strategy selection and use.

Life span and aging researchers generally agree that age serves as an imperfect proxy for the developmental changes brought about by changes in biology, cognition, and environment. That is, age-related changes in emotions and emotion regulation are viewed as the result of changes in physiological, cognitive, and conative systems. Several studies in the developmental and aging literature provide interesting evidence on age-related changes in emotions and emotion regulation (Carstensen, 1992).

Research examining age and emotions has focused broadly on three aspects of emotions: emotional expressivity, emotional experience, and emotional control (Gross et al., 1997). The evidence for age-related changes in these aspects of emotional functioning suggests that while the strength of felt emotions may decrease, emotion regulatory processes may improve. For example, Diener, Sandvik, and Larsen (1985) found age-related decreases in the frequency and intensity of self-regulated emotional experience, while Lawton, Kleban, Rajagopal, and Dean (1992) found that emotional control increased with age. Results of research investigating the relationship between age and emotional expressivity has also been mixed (Gross et al., 1997; Malatesta & Kalnok, 1984). Gross et al. (1997) suggest that age-related declines in emotional expressivity may be limited to negative emotions and that aging is associated with improvement in emotion regulation, particularly in terms of the use of cognitive emotion regulation strategies.

Investigations of changes in felt emotions across the life span (Carstensen & Charles, 1994) generally show a linear relationship between emotion salience and age. Life span approaches to emotion (Carstensen, 1992; Labouvie-Vief, Hakim-Larson, DeVoe, & Schoeberlein, 1989) posit that reorganization of affect and cognition represents a central life task in adulthood, such that older adults are superior to younger adults in understanding emotional states and emotion regulation. In particular, older adults employ more mature use of emotion-focused coping strategies, make less frequent use of blame-oriented strategies, and engage in less frequent expressions of hostility than younger adults do (Blanchard-Fields & Irion, 1988). In an experience sampling study, Carstensen, Paspuathi, Mayr, and Nesselroade (2000) examined age differences in frequency, intensity, complexity, and consistency of emotional experience in everyday life. They found that age was unrelated to frequency of positive emotional experience but was curvilinearly related to negative emotional experience. These findings indicate that older adults experience positive emotions just as often as younger adults but fewer negative emotions (until age sixty). In addition, they found that both positive and negative emotions were felt as intensely in later adulthood as in early adulthood, indicating that the findings were not explainable due to a general age-related decrease in emotional intensity. Taken together, these findings suggest that contrary to general declines in physical and intellectual capabilities, general emotional functioning improves with age.

Drawing on such findings, Carstensen (1992, 1998) proposed a theory of socioemotional selectivity that highlights the role of motives in emotional functioning. Specifically, she proposed that the purpose of social interaction changes over the life span and that these changes influence the development and use of different emotion regulation strategies. According to socioemotional selectivity theory, adolescents and young adults seek social interactions primarily for their informational value. Regulatory strategies aimed at modifying the environment or modulating emotion-related behaviors are likely to be more useful during this life phase than cognitive change or reappraisal strategies. During later adulthood, however, the informational value of social interaction declines and the motive for social interactions shifts to obtaining affective rewards and supporting one's identity. These changed motives for social interaction promote the use of cognitive change and reappraisal strategies for modulating the generative emotion process. Goals in later adulthood are reorganized and tend to be characterized as emotion based (Carstensen, 1998). That is, developmental shifts in the goal of social interactions produce age-related differences in how individuals respond to social-emotional events. Drawing on notions set forth by socioemotional selectivity theory, Carstensen's theory suggests that strategy use changes with age, where younger adults tend to aim for changing the environment and older adults use internal and cognitively focused strategies, with the aim of regulating their interpretation of events and internal reactions.

Changes in Emotion Regulation

From a developmental perspective, people learn to manage their social environments in ways that regulate affect (Carstensen, 1992). Fundamental to discussing age-related changes in emotion regulation is recognizing how social motives change across the life span. Guided by the notion that a strongly held motive or set of goals affects perceptions of situations (Griner & Smith, 2000), motives guide, energize, and direct behavior. Consistent with appraisal theories of emotion (Lazarus, 1991), emotions are elicited as a function of evaluations of what an individual's circumstances imply for personal well-being. Although less research has focused on the individual differences in responsivity to similar circumstances, one stream of research has looked at the motives, needs, and goals that influence emotional reactions (Griner & Smith, 2000). Griner and Smith investigated the affiliative motive and pointed out its stability on a population level across ages and over time.

In contrast, accumulated evidence from Carstensen and colleagues (Carstensen, 1992, 1998; Carstensen & Charles, 1994) suggests that emotional functioning changes over the life span as a function of perceived time. Implicit in the notion that emotion regulation improves with age (Carstensen, 1992) is that the nature of emotion regulation changes over the life span. According to socioemotional selectivity theory (Carstensen, 1992), decreased social contact in adulthood brings about a change in goals in response to decreased competencies.

In a related line of theorizing about the developmental nature of emotions, Lebouvie-Vief and colleagues (Diehl, Coyle, & Labouvie-Vief, 1996; Labouvie-Vief et al., 1989) posit that the hallmark of developmentally mature adults' coping strategies is the absence of impulsive and outwardly aggressive reactions and the presence of strategies that involve impulse control, acceptance, and cognitive reassessment. In contrast, adolescents and young adults use strategies that are outwardly aggressive and psychologically undifferentiated, including lower levels of impulse control and self-awareness. These two modes of emotional self-regulation as a function of developmental maturity are characterized as relating to (1) intuition, subjectivity, and emotionality (younger adults) and (2) rational, objective, logical strategies (older adults).

Support for this formulation is provided by several studies showing age-related changes in work-related goals and emotion regulation strategy use. Heckhausen (2000), for example, found that work goals and concerns declined with age and that health-related goals increased with age. These results suggest that circumstances, events, or individuals that impede accomplishment of work objectives are not as likely to generate emotional responses and trigger emotion regulation as are events that impede health-related goals. Similar results indicating age-related differences in the use of problem-focused coping strategies have also been reported by McConatha and Huba (1999) and Blanchard-Fields (1996).

In summary, the results of aging theory and research suggest that intraindividual differences in age-associated motives play an important role in the elicitation of emotions at work and their regulation. In contrast to young adults, middle-aged and older adult employees are likely to show a different pattern of emotional sensitivity to the workplace and to employ a different pattern of emotion regulation strategies to address emotion-related issues. In particular, the literature suggests that older employees may employ antecedent-focused, situation-oriented strategies in contexts that trigger emotions related to self-esteem and self-concept but response-focused, self-oriented strategies in contexts that trigger non-self-related emotions such as anger. That is, when faced with the introduction of a new word processing system into the workplace, older secretaries may cope with emotional distress by taking early retirement. Younger workers, in contrast, may experience different emotional responses to the workplace change and are more likely to regard the change as a challenge and opportunity for growth. In contrast, in the context of an unpleasant dyadic relationship, older workers are more likely than younger workers to engage effective cognitive reappraisal strategies to attenuate anger. Research investigating age-emotion regulation strategy preferences has important implications for maximizing the talents of a graying American workforce.

Organizational Influences

Basic theory and research on emotion regulation cut across the life span to consider the general features of persons and environments and their transactions that give rise to emotion and its outcomes. In this broad approach, the particulars of emotion regulation are difficult to study due to the extremely broad range of antecedents and responses. Our interest in emotion regulation related to work, however, enables a narrowing of the domain. Several approaches may be taken within this context. Several chapters in this book, for example, focus on classes of emotions that are of particular interest to organizations. Glomb, Steel, and Arvey (Chapter Seven, this volume), for example, discuss antecedents and responses to workplace anger. Another perspective is to examine features of the workplace environment and work life transactions that are likely to give rise to emotions and emotion regulation. Organizational researchers have devoted substantial effort to identifying the characteristics of jobs, organizational procedures, and norms that contribute to the evocation of positive and negative emotions (see in this volume, Grandey and Brauburger, Chapter Eight; Ashforth and Saks, Chapter Ten). Similarly, in the career literature, a number of researchers have identified key career events associated with emotional functioning (London, 1998; Feldman, 1996). For purposes of this chapter, this research is particularly useful in enabling us to flesh out the details of the "situation" side of an interactionist perspective. We discuss some of these findings and their implications below.

In the workplace, organizational concerns for the appropriate display of emotion-related behaviors have led to the development of procedures specifically designed to influence the expression of emotions and emotion-related behaviors. Ashforth and Humphrey (1995) identify four general strategies by which organizations seek to reduce the expression of negative employee emotions and emotion-related behaviors. Neutralization strategies are designed to prevent the emergence of emotions that are either unavoidable or inherent in role performance. Organizational buffering strategies seek to encapsulate and segregate potentially disruptive emotions from ongoing activities. Prescribing emotions refers to an organizational strategy used to specify socially acceptable means of experiencing and expressing emotions. Normalizing emotion strategies are used to diffuse or reframe unacceptable emotions to preserve the status quo. Neutralization, buffering, and normalizing strategies appear to operate as an organizational analogue to individual antecedent-focused emotion regulation strategies. That is, their purpose is to alter the employee's cognitive appraisal of the event or situation in a way that reduces the generation of emotions. In contrast, prescribing emotions provides an organizational parallel to individual response-focused emotion regulation strategies that control the display of undesirable emotions.

Ashforth and Saks (this volume) note that organizations implement emotion regulation strategies in a variety of ways for a variety of objectives. For example, prescribing strategies may be used to reduce expressions of specific emotion-related behaviors, such as verbal abusiveness, to increase verbal expressions of positive emotions, such as pride, or to train new entrants in organizational display norms. Organizational strategies may also be used alone or in combination to attenuate or heighten specific employee emotions that arise in conjunction with organizational change programs. Buffering strategies, for example, may be used to reduce subjective distress among job layoff survivors.

On the one hand, research on organizational regulation demonstrates the feasibility of mapping job task elements, social interaction processes, and organizational procedures and policies to employee emotion regulation. On the other hand, the influence of organizational regulation strategies on employee emotion regulation processes is largely unknown, and the effectiveness of organizational interventions may be mediated by employee characteristics. For example, job redesign interventions aimed at increasing worker productivity by increasing employee job pride may also evoke feelings of anxiety and fear among employees high in negative affectivity. These feelings place a demand on emotion regulation that may cancel out the beneficial effects of the intervention. Research is needed to examine how organizational emotion control strategies may interact with employee traits and regulatory capabilities to affect performance and subjective well-being.

Emotion Regulation in Work Life

Just as the workplace is replete with events that may give rise to emotions, an individual's work life over the course of four or more decades may involve multiple events that elicit emotion and demand emotion regulation. London (1998) has identified a number of career barriers, such as job loss, disability, work demands, and underemployment that may arise from environmental, organizational, situational, or individual changes or conditions that have substantial emotional impact. Most of these events are likely to involve regulatory strategies directed toward reducing negative emotions, but events such as early job promotion or team accomplishments may also occur and evoke positive emotions. Again, relatively little attention has been given to identifying the effect of these circumstances on emotion regulation. For example, work barriers can have different antecedents and outcomes, ranging from barriers such as underemployment that arise slowly and produce little emotional reaction to those such as discrimination or job loss that are sudden and devastating. The temporal dynamics of events represent one of several important dimensions that may influence emotion regulation with respect to work life.

Person factors, such as the individual's goals, traits, and regulatory capabilities, are also likely to influence emotion regulation in response to work barriers and successes. For example, adaptive emotion regulation may be less difficult in general following the occurrence of a physical disability for an older adult than a younger adult, since older adults show higher levels of emotion-focused coping skill than younger adults. That is, older adults may be more likely to employ cognitive reappraisal strategies that reduce the intensity of the felt emotion. Similarly, emotion regulation effectiveness may be lower among persons high in negative affectivity than persons low in negative affectivity, such that persons high in negative affectivity tend to use more demanding cognitive suppression or response-focused emotion regulation strategies.

Given the substantial portion of an individual's life spent in the workplace and the importance of work to psychological functioning and social adjustment, it is also reasonable to consider how organizational practices that regulate the expression of employee emotions and emotion-related behaviors generalize to emotion regulation pertaining to work role transitions and career progress. Long periods of tenure in firms that prescribe strict rules on the display of negative emotions, such as the military, for example, may also entrain individual emotion regulation strategies for use in extraorganizational work life events, such as job search and new job training. That is, just as job experience increases technical job skills, organizational tenure may shape the individual's affect regulation history. The role of this environmental factor on the use of emotion regulation strategies in work life adaptation represents an intriguing direction for future research.

Our discussion of emotion regulation in work life identifies only a few of the many directions for future research in this area. Demographic and work trends in the American labor force, together with a turbulent economic landscape, provide an excellent opportunity for interdisciplinary research investigating the independent and interaction effects of person and organization influences on emotion regulation for career success and adjustment.

Conclusion

Substantial progress has been made in emotion research and theory. This work has led the way to a sea of change in the way we conceptualize emotion in organizations and renewed interest in identifying person and organizational influences on the emotion process. This chapter reviews the tentative first steps in what we think represents the second phase of this revolution in emotion research: a more complete understanding of the person and situation determinants and consequences of emotion regulation and its relationship to job performance and psychological adjustment.

Although emotion regulation occurs at nonconscious levels, many studies document the potential malleability of emotion processes and their outcomes through application of consciously mediated emotion regulation strategies. This appears to be particularly true in the work domain, where emotion regulation may be learned for specific transactions or tasks, and millions of dollars are spent yearly in training ostensibly for this purpose.

Nonetheless, our current knowledge about the antecedents and consequences of emotion regulation strategy development, use, and effectiveness related to work is rudimentary. There is general agreement about the importance of distinguishing between strategies in terms of their target in the emotion process (antecedent or response), their directional target (self or situation), and their mode of operation (cognitive or behavioral). Personality research findings further suggest that individual differences in emotional traits influence not only emotion generation but also emotion regulation. In a somewhat separate line of inquiry, emotional intelligence researchers propose a constellation of individual differences in "meta-cognitive-like" traits, such as clarity, that likely serve to influence the deployment of particular emotion regulation strategies in specific situations. Research on aging suggests that motives and goals represent another important determinant of emotion regulation strategy use, and researchers in this area have shown how motive changes may underlie age-related changes in the pattern of emotion regulation strategies employed. Finally, organizational research provides evidence on the active role that organizations play in the regulation of employee emotion and emotion-related behaviors. Although theory and research to date provide an excellent conceptual foundation, what is needed most now is empirical research delineating the influence of these factors on employee use and development of distinct emotion regulation strategies.

Several issues also warrant note. First, as Heckhausen (2000) has argued, individuals of all ages appear to engage in emotion self-regulation as a secondary means of control—that is, when environmental means of regulation are blocked or ineffective. These findings are fully consistent with resource allocation perspectives that indicate the potentially substantial attentional costs associated with cognitive and behavioral regulation strategies. In the context of our organizing framework, Heckhausen's approach suggests that individuals may prefer situation-oriented, antecedent-focused strategies over self-focused, response-focused strategies (which require sustained or more intense attentional effort). Obviously, in many work settings, individuals cannot escape or modify the situation sufficiently to preclude generation of a disruptive or undesirable emotion. Under these conditions, what determines the emotion regulation strategy an individual will use? Two lines of study to address this question are suggested. First, research is needed to identify the influence of traits on the choice of avoidance and suppression strategies versus response-focused coping strategies and the trainability of nonpreferred emotion regulation strategies. The second area for study relates to further specifying the relative cognitive costs and benefits of various emotion regulation strategies. Evidence on these issues will help to clarify the determinants, relative effectiveness, and malleability of emotion regulation in the context of work.

A second issue pertains to implications of emotion research findings for personnel and human resource management. Advances in personality research have been used to support the use of personality assessment for personnel selection on the grounds that persons high in emotional stability make more effective employees. Although recent findings on the role of personality traits on emotion processes might be interpreted to support this line of reasoning, it appears premature to draw conclusions at this point. In particular, it is still unclear how such traits influence the implementation of emotion regulatory processes and their consequences in specific contexts. Obviously, very high levels of negative affectivity are difficult to overcome, and organizations have long used such information for screening out maladjusted individuals. However, it is not unreasonable to expect some domain specificity in trait levels. That is, individuals in the high-normal range on the trans-situational trait could be trained or develop highly effective coping strategies for specific work-related events, such as emergencies in air traffic control and other public safety jobs. Evidence for the full range of trait influences on emotion regulation processes as well as the relative malleability of these processes in work contexts is needed to address this issue.

Emotion regulation is fundamental to psychological and social adjustment. The simultaneous and coordinated development of physiological, developmental, process, content, and organizational approaches presents an unusual and promising opportunity. Our review of research and trends identifies only a few of the many organizational psychology research possibilities and implications. Over the next decade, we expect many more to emerge.

References

Ashforth, B. E., & Humphrey, R. H. (1995). Emotion in the workplace: A reappraisal. *Human Relations, 48,* 97–125.

Bar-On, R. (2000). Emotional and social intelligence: Insights from the Emotional Quotient Inventory. In R. Bar-On & J. D. Parker (Eds.), *The handbook of emotional intelligence: Theory, development, assessment, and application at home, school, and in the workplace.* San Francisco: Jossey-Bass.

Blanchard-Fields, F. (1996). Emotion and everyday problem solving in adult development. In C. Magai & S. H. McFadden (Eds.), *Handbook of emotion, adult development, and aging.* Orlando, FL: Academic Press.

Blanchard-Fields, F., & Irion, J. (1988). The relation between locus of control and coping in two contexts: Age as a moderator variable. *Psychology and Aging, 3,* 197–203.

Brief, A. P., & Weiss, H. M. (in press). Organizational behavior: Affect in the workplace. *Annual Review of Psychology.*

Brockner, J., & Higgins, E. T. (2001). Regulatory focus theory: Implications for the study of emotions at work. *Organizational Behavior and Human Decision Processes, 86,* 35–66. [Special issue]

Carstensen, L. L. (1992). Social and emotional patterns in adulthood: Support for socioemotional selectivity theory. *Psychology and Aging, 7,* 331–338.

Carstensen, L. L. (1998). A life-span approach to social motivation. In J. Heckhausen & C. Dweck (Eds.), *Motivation and self-regulation across the life span.* Cambridge: Cambridge University Press.

Carstensen, L. L., & Charles, S. T. (1994). The salience of emotion across the adult life span. *Psychology and Aging, 9,* 259–264.

Carstensen, L., Pasupathi, M., Mayr, U., & Nesselroade, J. R. (2000). Emotional experience in everyday life across the adult life span. *Journal of Personality and Social Psychology, 79,* 644–655.

Carver, C. S., Sutton, S. K., & Scheier, M. F. (2000). Action, emotion, and personality: Emerging conceptual integration. *Personality and Social Psychology Bulletin, 26,* 741–751.

Catanzaro, S. J., & Mearns, J. (1990). Measuring generalized expectancies for negative mood regulation: Initial scale development and implications. *Journal of Personality Assessment, 54,* 546–563.

Davies, M., Stankov, L., & Roberts, R. D. (1998). Emotional intelligence: In search of an elusive construct. *Journal of Personality and Social Psychology, 75,* 989–1015.

Diehl, M., Coyle, N., & Labouvie-Vief, G. (1996). Age and sex differences in strategies of coping and defense across the life span. *Psychology and Aging, 11,* 127–139.

Diener, E., Sandvik, E., & Larsen, R. J. (1985). Age and sex effects for emotional intensity. *Developmental Psychology, 21,* 542–546.

Dodge, K. A. (1989). Coordinating responses to aversive stimuli: Introduction to a special section on the development of emotion regulation. *Development Psychology, 25,* 339–342.

Duclos, S. E., & Laird, J. D. (2001). The deliberate control of emotional experience through control of expressions. *Cognition and Emotion, 15,* 27–56.

Eisenberg, N., Fabes, R. A., Guthrie, I. K., & Reiser, M. (2000). Dispositional emotionality and regulation: Their role in predicting quality of social functioning. *Journal of Personality and Social Psychology, 78,* 136–157.

Epstein, S., & Meier, P. (1989). Constructive thinking: A broad coping variable with specific components. *Journal of Personality and Social Psychology, 57,* 332–350.

Feldman, D. C. (1996). The nature, antecedents and consequences of underemployment. *Journal of Management, 22,* 385–407.

Forgas, J. P., & Vargas, P. T. (1999). Affect, goals, and the self-regulation of behavior. In R. S. Wyer (Ed.), *Perspectives on behavioral self-regulation.* Hillsdale, NJ: Erlbaum.

Fox, N. A. (1989). Psychophysiological correlates of emotional reactivity during the first year of life. *Developmental Psychology, 25,* 364–372.

Fox, S., & Spector, P. E. (2000). Relations of emotional intelligence, practical intelligence, general intelligence, and trait affectivity with interview outcomes: It's not just "G." *Journal of Organizational Behavior, 21,* 203–220.

Frijda, N. H. (1986). *The emotions.* Cambridge: Cambridge University Press.

Garnefski, N., Kraaij, V., & Spinhoven, P. (2001). Negative life events, cognitive emotion regulation, and emotional problems. *Personality and Individual Differences, 30,* 1311–1327.

Goleman, D. (1995). *Emotional intelligence.* New York: Bantam Books.

Gramzow, R. H., Sedikides, C., Panter, A. T., & Insko, C. A. (2000). Aspects of self-regulation and self-structure as predictors of perceived emotional distress. *Personality and Social Psychology Bulletin, 26,* 188–205.

Griner, L. A., & Smith, C. A. (2000). Contributions of motivational orientation to appraisal and emotion. *Personality and Social Psychology Bulletin, 26,* 727–740.

Gross, J. (1998a). Antecedent- and response-focused emotion regulation: Divergent consequences for experience, expression, and physiology. *Journal of Personality and Social Psychology, 74,* 224–237.

Gross, J. (1998b). The emerging field of emotion regulation: An integrative review. *Review of General Psychology, 2,* 271–299.

Gross, J. J. (1999). Emotion and emotion regulation. In L. A. Pervin & J. O. John (Eds.), *Handbook of personality: Theory and research* (2nd ed., pp. 525–552). New York: Guilford Press.

Gross, J. J., Carstensen, L. L., Pasupathi, M., Tsai, J., Skorpen, C. G., & Hsu, A.Y.C. (1997). Emotion and aging: Experience, expression, and control. *Psychology and Aging, 12,* 590–599.

Heckhausen, J. (2000). Evolutionary perspectives on human motivation. *American Behavioral Scientist, 43,* 1015–1029.

Heckhausen, J., & Schulz, R. (1999). The primacy of primary control is a human universal: A reply to Gould's (1999) critique of the life-span theory of control. *Psychological Review, 106,* 605–609.

Higgins, E. T. (2001). Promotion and prevention experiences: Relating emotions to nonemotional motivational states. In J. Forgas (Ed.), *Handbook of affect and social cognition.* Hillsdale, NJ: Erlbaum.

Judge, T. A., & Larsen, R. J. (2001). Dispositional affect and job satisfaction: A review and theoretical extension. *Organizational Behavior and Human Decision Processes, 86,* 67–98. [Special issue]

Kokkonen, M., & Pulkkinen, L. (1999). Emotion regulation strategies in relation to personality characteristics indicating low and high self-control of emotions. *Personality and Individual Differences, 27,* 913–932.

Labouvie-Vief, G., Hakim-Larson, J., DeVoe, M., & Schoeberlin, S. (1989). Emotions and self-regulation: A life span view. *Human Development, 32,* 279–299.

Larsen, R. J. (2000a). Toward a science of mood regulation. *Psychological Inquiry, 11,* 129–141.

Larsen, R. J. (2000b). Maintaining hedonic balance. *Psychological Inquiry, 11,* 218–225.

Lawton, M. P., Kleban, M. H., Rajagopal, D., & Dean, J. (1992). Dimensions of affective experience in three age groups. *Psychology and Aging, 7,* 171–184.

Lazarus, R. S. (1984). On the primacy of cognition. *American Psychologist, 39,* 124–129.

Lazarus, R. S. (1991). Cognition and motivation in emotion. *American Psychologist, 46,* 352–367.

Lazarus, R. S., & Folkman, S. (1984). *Stress, appraisal, and coping.* New York: Springer.

London, M. (1998). *Career barriers: How people experience, overcome, and avoid failure.* Hillsdale, NJ: Erlbaum.

Malatesta, C. Z., & Kalnok, C. (1984). Emotional experience in younger and older adults. *Journal of Gerontology, 39,* 301–308.

Martin, L. L., & Tesser, A. (1996). *Striving and feeling: Interactions among goals, affect, and self-regulation.* Hillsdale, NJ: Erlbaum.

Martinez-Pons, M. (1999–2000). Emotional intelligence as a self-regulatory process: A social-cognitive view. *Imagination, Cognition, and Personality, 19,* 331–350.

Mayer, J. D., & Salovey, P. (1995). Emotional intelligence and the construction and regulation of feelings. *Applied and Preventive Psychology, 4,* 197–208.

Mayer, J. D., & Salovey, P. (1997). What is emotional intelligence? In P. Salovey & D. Sluyter (Eds.) *Emotional development and emotional intelligence: Educational implications.* New York: Basic Books.

McCann, E. J., & Garcia, T. (1999). Maintaining motivation and regulating emotion: Measuring individual differences in academic volitional strategies. *Learning and Individual Differences, 11,* 259–279.

McConatha, J. T., & Huba, H. M. (1999). Primary, secondary, and emotional control across adulthood. *Current Psychology: Developmental, Learning, Personality, Social, 18,* 164–170.

Morris, J. A., & Feldman, D. C. (1997). Managing emotions in the workplace. *Journal of Managerial Issues, 9,* 257–274.

Morris, W. N. (1999). The mood system. In D. Kahneman & E. Diener (Eds.), *Well being: The foundations of hedonic psychology.* Thousand Oaks, CA: Sage.

Morris, W. N., & Reilly, N. P. (1987). Toward the self-regulation of mood: Theory and research. *Motivation and Emotion, 11,* 215–249.

O'Brien, T. B., & DeLongis, A. (1996). The interactional context of problem-, emotion-, and relationship-focused coping: The role of the Big Five personality factors. *Journal of Personality, 64,* 775–813.

Parkinson, B., & Totterdell, P. (1999). Classifying affect-regulation strategies. *Cognition and Emotion, 13,* 277–303.

Roger, D., & Hesshoever, W. (1987). The construction and preliminary validation of a scale for measuring emotional control. *Personality and Individual Differences, 8,* 527–534.

Roger, D., & Najarian, B. (1989). The construction and validation of a new scale for measuring emotion control. *Personality and Individual Differences, 10,* 845–853.

Salovey, P., Mayer, J. D., Goldman, S. L., Turvey, C., & Palfai, T. P. (1995). Emotional attention, clarity, and repair: Exploring emotional intelligence using the Trait Meta-Mood Scale. In J. Pennebaker (Ed.), *Emotion, disclosure, and health.* Washington, DC: American Psychological Association.

Scheier, M. F., Weintraub, J. K., & Carver, C. S. (1986). Coping with stress: Divergent strategies of optimists and pessimists. *Journal of Personality and Social Psychology, 51,* 1257–1264.

Smith, C. A., & Kirby, L. D. (2001). Affect and cognitive appraisal processes. In J. Forgas (Ed.), *Handbook of affect and social cognition.* Hillsdale, NJ: Erlbaum.

Surmann, A. T. (1999). Negative mood regulation expectancies, coping, and depressive symptoms among American nurses. *Journal of Social Psychology, 139,* 540–543.

Thayer, R. E. (1996). *The origin of everyday moods: Managing energy, tension, and stress.* New York: Oxford University Press.

Thompson, R. A. (1994). Emotion regulation: A theme in search of definition. *Monographs of the Society for Research in Child Development, 59,* 25–52.

Tobin, R. M., Graziano, W. G., Vanman, E. J., & Tassinary, L. G. (2000). Personality, emotional experience, and efforts to control emotions. *Journal of Personality and Social Psychology, 79,* 656–669.

Underwood, M. K. (1997). Top ten pressing questions about the development of emotion regulation. *Motivation and Emotion, 21,* 127–146.

Walden, T. A., & Smith, M. C. (1997). Emotion regulation. *Motivation and Emotion, 21,* 7–25.

Wanberg, C. R., Kanfer, R., & Rotundo, M. (1999). Unemployed individuals: Motives, job search competencies, and job search constraints as predictors of job seeking and reemployment. *Journal of Applied Psychology, 84,* 897–910.

Warr, P., & Downing, J. (2000). Learning strategies, learning anxiety, and knowledge acquisition. *British Journal of Psychology, 91,* 311–333.

CHAPTER 14

Affect and Work
Looking Back to the Future
Ruth Kanfer
Richard J. Klimoski

Affect (encompassing moods, emotions, and affect regulation) plays a key role in virtually all important life activities, including the development of language, schooling, social adjustment, marital relations, parenting, and successful aging. Yet over the past four decades, affect has been accorded a relatively minor role in the study of workplace behavior and adjustment. In the organizational domain, affect has tended to be relegated to junior status in one of two related ways: (1) as a dependent variable (such as job satisfaction) of dubious value as a causal determinant of action or (2) as a unidimensional input variable to cognitive-motivational theories of action. The chapters in this book attest to the growing consensus that affect represents a multidimensional construct of causal consequence in work-related thought and action. During the past fifteen years, organizational personnel and researchers have been carefully scrutinizing the individual, organizational, and transactional determinants of affective responses in the workplace and their relation to traditional measures of individual and organizational effectiveness. Their initial findings show that affective states, traits, moods, and emotions play a central role in employee perceptions of the workplace, beliefs about work and the organization,

We thank Bob Lord and Phillip Ackerman for their helpful comments and suggestions.

decisions made in the workplace, and behaviors displayed at work. Advances in the conceptualization and measurement of moods and emotions have spurred research into the dynamics underlying these processes and the potential implications of these processes for improving human resource management and organizational practices. In short, the elevation of affect in organizational psychology to the status enjoyed previously only by cognition and motivation heralds a new era in organizational psychology that holds great promise for closer alignment of organizational behavior theory and practice at multiple levels of analysis.

As the chapters in this book illustrate, the winds of change are beginning to blow across the entire field of organizational psychology. Questions about how to study work-related affect abound. For example, which emotions should we study, and how do they differ in their implications for workplace behaviors? Which of the many person and situation variables are most relevant in the study of work affect, and what is the relative role of these factors on the experience, expression, and regulation of different emotions? How do person-situation transactions influence unusual but important displays of motivation, courage, altruism, and contemptible behavior in the workplace? Which person-situation transactions have the greatest influence on long-term career success and employee development? What are the mechanisms underlying emotional contagion in the workplace? What are the costs and benefits of co-action on employee behavior, decision making, and organizational effectiveness?

At present, there is no grand theory to address such questions, nor do we believe that one is likely to develop in the near future. Rather, we view the study of work-related affect as comprising a loose confederation of approaches that share a core set of beliefs about the nature, influence, and importance of affect. We note three implicit assumptions that underlie most approaches: (1) that affect represents an unobservable yet potent psychological driver of cognition and action, (2) that it represents a dynamic state influenced by both intra-individual and extraindividual forces, and (3) that it plays a key role in employee behaviors and organizational outcomes. Some approaches emphasize the contributions of the individual to affective states, others emphasize the contributions of organizational practices, and yet others focus on the determinants and consequences of specific, frequent person-organization transactions. As such, we anticipate that new knowledge in the field will continue to build in a cumulative but dispersed manner.

The wide array of targeted approaches also makes it difficult to develop a clear picture of the broader domain. In this chapter, we provide a meta-framework to begin the process of coordinating diverse psychological and organizational approaches to work-related affect. Obviously, the framework is tentative and incomplete; for example, the model does not address temporal influences on person-situation dynamics. Rather, we offer the model as a heuristic for summarizing where we have been, what we have learned, and continuing gaps in our knowledge.

A Heuristic Meta-Framework

We begin by drawing from Plato's triarchic model that distinguishes traits in terms of their relation to cognition, conation (motivation), and affect. By extending this framework, we propose a model in which these components of the human mind form the interactional nexus for ongoing transactions between internal and external forces. Two features of our conceptualization of affect warrant note. First, we accord affect a central role (equal to cognition and conation) in its impact on action. Second, as shown in Figure 14.1, affect, cognition, and conation are portrayed as reciprocally related. That is, changes in any one term are posited to have potential influence on the other two terms in the nexus. Research may focus on the single or joint influence of these constructs on action.

Next, consistent with an interactionist view in the context of work, we distinguish two basic pressures on the nexus; intraindividual (person) forces and extraindividual (situational) forces. As portrayed in the figure, each force may be further be decomposed by level of analysis or content. External forces are depicted as overlapping life spaces, comprising work and nonwork life domains (such as family, social, and financial). Work-related forces may be decomposed further in terms of level of analysis. Internal forces include physiological, experiential, regulatory, and self systems, such as hormones, feelings, self-regulatory mechanisms, and self-esteem.

As depicted by the double-headed arrows in Figure 14.1, the heuristic framework proposes that person and situation forces are

Figure 14.1. A Heuristic Meta-Framework of Affect and Work.

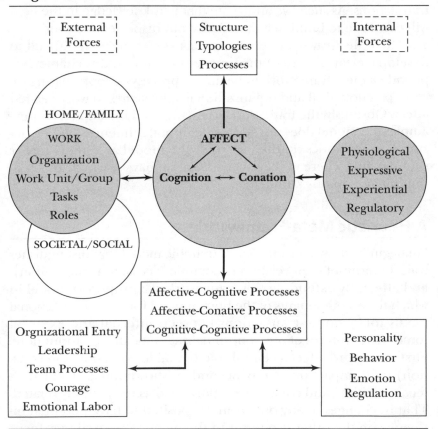

Note: Circles denote construct relations and levels; boxes denote research domains and related organizational topics.

reciprocally related to the nexus. These reciprocal relations yield three distinct pathways of affect influence. The first pathway runs from the nexus outward to the internal and external environment. Examples of research investigating these paths include studies on the effects of affective-cognitive and affective-conative interactions on decision making, task performance, and self-efficacy.

The second pathway focuses on the influence of person and situation forces on the nexus. Examples of research investigating these paths include work on how organizational socialization practices influence employee beliefs, feelings, and behavior (see Ashforth and Saks, Chapter Ten, this volume), investigations of how physiological processes affect feelings (see Lord and Harvey, Chapter Four, this volume), and studies on the role of self-regulatory variables on affect-related behaviors (see Pugh, Chapter Five, and Kanfer and Kantrowitz, Chapter Thirteen, both this volume).

The third affect influence pathway runs from person (or situation) onto the nexus as well as to the other domain. Cognitive appraisal theories, for example, suggest that extraindividual forces, such as a divorce, influence the nexus of thoughts, beliefs, and motive tendencies, as well as the individual's regulatory strategies for coping with appraised threats and challenges. However, as research reviewed by Lord and Harvey (this volume) suggests, divorce might also exert a direct, nonconscious influence on the individual's physiological state, with delayed effects on higher-order affective-cognitive-conative processes. Although most contemporary theories of emotion subscribe to the notion that cognitive appraisal is primary (and that changes in person features flow from such appraisals), it is often the case that individuals experience changes in mood state prior to consciously mediated appraisal processing. For example, individuals who experience job loss often report physiological symptoms, such as anxiety, prior to conscious appraisal of the event and implementation of coping strategies. Similarly, the September 11, 2001, attacks on World Trade Center and the Pentagon yielded many reports of changes in mood state prior to conscious appraisal of the event with respect to work beliefs and action tendencies. Our model allows for both processing possibilities, although clearly this is an area that warrants greater research attention.

The meta-framework provides a foundation on which to organize extant research literature. The boxes shown in Figure 14.1 provide a rough mapping of where psychological and organizational research on specific topics fits into the larger nomological network of construct relations. For example, basic research on the structure and measurement of affect, as discussed in Part One of this book, focuses on more complete specification of the affect construct. In contrast, research on affect in organizational entry, leadership, emotional labor, the work-family interface, and career adjustment typically emphasize the relationship between external forces and interactions within the nexus. Research on emotion regulation tends to examine the relationship between regulatory strategies and nexus interactions. Research on discrete emotions, such as anger or joy, may focus on either nexus (such as affective-cognitive processes associated with anger response tendencies) or the influence of such emotions on internal or external conditions (such as the effects of anger on emotion regulation strategies or the effects of anger on task performance, respectively). Obviously, not all research in the affect domain maps precisely onto the model, and cross-fertilization across research areas may shift the focus of a line of inquiry substantially over time.

Gaps in Our Knowledge

The heuristic framework provides an inductive overview of our current understanding about work-related affect. In this section, we use the framework as a guide for identifying current gaps in our knowledge based on both our experiences and the research literature. Specifically, we discuss five issues for future research: (1) moods and emotions, (2) affect goals and inductions, (3) person influences, and (4) affect-motivation relations, and (5) criterion issues.

Moods and Emotions: Variations on a Theme or Distinct Systems?

The majority of studies in organizational psychology focus on emotions rather than moods. Research on work-related emotions indicates that events of personal significance, such as an insult by a coworker, tend to spark an appraisal process that elicits felt emotion and a particular pattern of emotional responses. In contrast, although much is known about trait influences on moods and the consequences of mood states on behavior, few studies have examined the external and situational determinants of work-related moods.

Although moods and emotions may be distinguished along a number of dimensions, most investigators argue for the substantial overlap between these constructs. Accordingly, we make no distinction between these constructs in our meta-framework. Nonetheless, we believe that further consideration of the differences between emotions and moods may provide insight into a number of vexing issues in the organizational domain. In contrast to events that elicit emotions, moods tend to be diffuse, longer lasting, and of unspecified origins, although often associated with some theme, such as promotion, job layoff, and supervisory relations. As such, we propose two ideas: (1) that study of the mood–emotion distinction in the workplace may be better conceptualized in terms of the distinction between events and episodes and (2) that the event-episode distinction may be usefully applied to understanding the influence of organizational practices on different types of employee affect.

Our first suggestion, that we distinguish between events and episodes, draws from the affective events theory (AET) of Weiss and Cropanzano (1996), who note that an individual's affect may be characterized as episodic, that is, as a series of transactions organized around an issue or theme, such as team communications, supervisory relations, or layoffs. In contrast to event-based reactions, these emotion episodes occur over time and involve "subevents" that may produce distinct emotional responses.

We suggest that such episodes are importantly related to moods. For example, themed transactions related to job promotion are often associated with positive moods, whereas themed transactions related to job layoffs are typically associated with negative moods. Additional research is needed to investigate the relationships between common work-related themes, moods, emotion regulation strategies, and behavior. Lack of career progress, for example, may be associated with a sad mood state, a low level of emotion regulation, and withdrawal behaviors. In contrast, poor supervisory relations may be associated with an angry mood, high levels of ineffective emotion regulation, and hostile or aggressive behavior.

The event-episode distinction may also prove useful for coordinating the effects of organizational influences to different forms of employee affect in the workplace. In particular, organizational practices, such as leadership and socialization, can be described as thematic episodes containing a series of transactions that occur over time, each of which may fall below the activation threshold associated with event-emotion processing but may exert cumulative influence on the nexus over time. Examples of transactions that may contribute to work mood include the recounting of organizational stories, reliable patterns of team interaction following task feedback, and patterns of interpersonal leadership communications. Whereas events associated with emotions tend to be singular, brief, and generally unambiguous with respect to functional and motivational significance, organizational transactions that influence moods are proposed to be subtle, repetitive, and only obliquely related to the individual's sense of identity and well-being. Indeed, for many employees, these occurrences often go unrecognized as events and are regarded simply as an integral part of the workplace landscape. That is, the occurrence of a transaction within an episode is not perceived to have motivational significance and is not likely to trigger an appraisal, although the cumulative effect of affectively toned transactions may condition the individual's beliefs or action tendencies.

The conceptualization of organizational influences in terms of their event versus episodic character raises a host of interesting empirical questions. For example, what are the most salient parameters of organizational phenomena associated with employee moods and emotions (for example, diffuseness, temporal intensity)? What organizational conditions yield a dissociation of mood and emotion (for example, happy and angry, sad and proud)? Do individual differences in emotional sensitivities mediate episode-mood relations in the same manner as they appear to mediate event-emotion relations? From a pragmatic perspective, it is also important to consider whether the insidious and repetitive nature of particular organizational transactions produces persistent mood states that are less easily modified than emotion response tendencies. That is, how readily can different mood states be altered, and do mood states differ in their tenacity? Finally, what are the consequences of different types of organizational practices aimed at altering mood states (rather than emotions) on job behavior and satisfaction?

Goals, Induction Strategies, and Affect Paradoxes

At the broadest level, both organizations and individuals tend to agree that employee and organizational goals are typically well served by strategies that reduce an individual's negative affect and increase an individual's positive affect. Diverse topics in organizational psychology, such as organizational justice, job design, and job satisfaction, share this basic view. Nonetheless, there are many situations in which individual and organization goal progress may be advanced by enhancing negative affect or reducing positive affect. The literature is replete with anecdotal stories of how a negative emotion, such as anger, spurred constructive action and higher levels of performance (for example, the "I'll show you" syndrome), or how a positive emotion, such as pride, promoted complacency and subsequently lower levels of performance. Similarly, organizations frequently engage in practices designed to increase negative emotion (such as anxiety over a competitor's progress) for the purpose of eliciting further work effort or designed to dampen positive emotions (such as pride in task success) for the purpose of increasing conformity. The question of how these widely used, paradoxical affect induction strategies relate to broader affective states associated with employee well-being and work productivity is intriguing and of substantial importance to organizational personnel.

We propose that the first step in understanding this relation is to consider the conditions and purposes for which individuals and organizations use affect induction strategies. One possibility, consistent with theories of self-regulation, is that affect induction strategies in general represent effortful actions undertaken to support conative or cognitive processing for the accomplishment of a specific goal. That is, by inducing particular moods and emotions, individuals and organizations seek to take advantage of naturally occurring affective-conative and affective-cognitive interactions that occur in the nexus. Such regulatory strategies may be used to enhance the dominant emotion or mood or induce a different emotion or mood if the current affective state is deemed insufficient for meeting the cognitive and conative demands of the goal. Paradoxical induction strategies, in which individuals and organizations induce proximal negative emotions in order to produce distal outcomes associated with positive affect, represent an important tool in the arsenal of strategies for goal accomplishment. Trainees who do well on their first exam, for example, often engage in paradoxical handicapping strategies that increase negative affect following high levels of performance for the purpose of supporting continued task effort and protecting self-esteem.

Individual and organizational induction strategies are obviously useful, but they are not without risk. For example, the specifics of an emotional event may yield a different response pattern to the affect induction than intended. An individual who induces anxiety in order to facilitate study effort may become so anxious during study that he is unable to concentrate on the material. Individual differences in emotional makeup can also mediate the effectiveness of paradoxical organizational practices. The success of paradoxical induction strategies among military recruits in basic training, for example, appears to depend partly on the individual differences in emotional sensitivities and ego-strength and coping strategy tendencies. Finally, there may be important asymmetries in the consequences of using negative versus positive affect induction strategies, the relative effectiveness of individual versus organizationally initiated induction strategies, or the longer-term effects of such strategies on mood entrainment and job effectiveness. Individuals and organizations that implement paradoxical induction strategies at the wrong time or without regard for how such affect is likely to resolve may alter cognitive and conative processing in unintended and dysfunctional ways.

Person Influences: Expanding the Construct Network

To date, organizational research on person determinants and consequences of affect has focused on individual differences in physiological and personality traits, such as positive and negative affectivity. Although trait approaches to work affect have potentially important implications for personnel selection, classification, and human resource management, we think that investigation of other individual differences may prove fruitful as well. Historical variables, such as cultural history, may importantly affect employee appraisals of workplace events and emotion regulation strategies. Given the growing diversity of the American workplace, such differences in life experiences may help in the development of more tailored management practices to address entrained employee tendencies.

Other variables that warrant further investigation are age and gender (see Kanfer and Kantrowitz, Chapter Thirteen, this volume). Developmental research findings indicate that older adults tend to report less frequent negative emotions and more frequent use of secondary emotion regulation strategies than younger adults. Carstensen (1992) explains these findings in terms of developmental changes in motives for social interactions. Research by

Diehl, Coyle, and Labouvie-Vief (1996) found that both age and gender influenced self-reported emotion regulation strategy use. Specifically, younger adults reported more frequent use of aggressive coping strategies than did older adults, and women reported greater use of internalizing and self-punitive emotion regulation strategies than men did. These trans-situational findings are particularly important as the U.S. workplace is increasingly populated by women and older workers.

Affect and Conation: The New Frontier?

Our meta-framework suggests that affect exerts its effects on organizational and personal outcomes through its interactions with cognition and conation. Although many studies document the reciprocal influence of affect and cognition on a host of outcomes, surprisingly few organizational studies have examined the affect-conation interface—that is, the way in which affect influences employee motivation and goal striving and in which motives and organizational practices (designed to enhance motivation) influence employee mood and emotions.

Three lines of streams of research may be delineated in this area. The first line of inquiry pertains to the ways in which moods and emotions influence goal choice and patterns of goal striving (i.e., affect → conation processes). Research on the effects of mood on decision making provides an excellent foundation for future work on how basic mood states, such as sadness and joy, may influence deliberative processes in the choice of proximal and distal work goals. Additional research on the unique effects of specific emotions, such as anger, and self-emotions, such as shame and remorse, is also important for future investigation. With respect to the influence of moods and emotions, theory and research in the clinical and stress-coping literatures provide substantial evidence on the differential effectiveness of primary and secondary means of regulating emotions in the service of the attainment of broad life goals, such as subjective well-being, and narrow behavioral goals, such as anger management.

The second stream of research pertains to the mediational role of conation in affect-cognition relations (affect → conation → cognition processes). Carver and Scheier (1990), for example, note that affect influences motivational processes, such as task engagement and disengagement. Other research indicates that associated motivational processes, such as forming implementation intentions, affect the availability of goal-related cognitions (Goschke & Kuhl, 1993). The influence of affect on goal setting, goal striving, and goal abandonment represents affective-conative processes that directly affect cognitions.

The third line of research relates to how individual differences in motives and motivational practices may influence moods and emotions (conation → affect processes). Recent research by Brockner and Higgins (2001), for example, suggests that individual differences in regulatory focus (prevention versus promotion) influence the character of the affective response. Although motives and emotional traits tend to be related (for example, negative relation between achievement and negative affectivity), an individual's current concerns are likely to affect the initiation and direction of emotional responses.

These lines of inquiry could also be applied to understanding organizational influences on employee cognition, conation, and affect. For example, organizational practices may influence employee moods and emotions indirectly through conative processes. Organizational symbols, for example, may increase the salience of affiliative motives and increase the frequency of appraisals that produce positive emotional responses. And downsizing may increase the salience of prevention motives and stimulate more frequent negatively toned event appraisals. Additional research is needed to delineate the independent influence of these practices on motive strength and work affect.

Focus on the Criterion

The early chapters of this book review what is known about the nature of affect and affect-related processes. The later chapters show the state of affairs relative to the status of thinking, models, and data associated with affect-linked organizational phenomena or problematics. With regard to such phenomena, in our view, while much is known, much more is not well understood. We feel that the applied work being done must absorb and use the wisdom of recent discoveries in the field. At a minimum, this requires sensitivity to the often subtle and interactive effects of affect, cognition, and the context. While some might be motivated to search for more general, even grand theories, at least for the near future, we would advocate attempts at integrating the findings of basic research in the service of a more focused effort.

This implies that investigators start with a careful description of the criterion space of interest. Whether it be the modeling of persistence of a trainee in the face of failure, the quality of the dyadic relationship between a supervisor and a worker, the accuracy of decision making in work teams, or attempting to explain the level of commitment felt by workers toward the firm, affect will have a role. But the task before us is nothing less than to establish just how, when, where and why affect has its effects. To accomplish this task requires awareness of and expertise in the domain of interest. Moreover, while phrasing the task this way may make the point self-evident, we feel that it is important to be explicit in saying that this will call for narrower (that is, context-specific) rather than sweeping attempts at model building.

Three aspects of this suggestion are worth emphasizing. The first is that contemporary investigators must be willing to review and absorb in detail that which is already known about basic processes that are most surely implicated in most aspects of organizational life. To the point, how should our research goals, hypotheses, designs, methods, and measures be altered to take advantage of such available knowledge? In this regard, as a thought experiment, we invite readers to review one of the later chapters from the perspective of the findings reported in earlier ones and ask how, with the benefit of hindsight, we could redesign a published study on a topic to be more informative and useful. And if the findings of the basic research literature were to be accepted and adopted with some enthusiasm by the applied investigator, also consider how the very research questions themselves might be reformulated for maximum value to practice.

A second implication is that the investigator must be willing to examine and attempt to model what have been termed multilevel effects (Klein & Kozlowski, 2000). As we have already noted in several places in this chapter, the experience and regulation of affect is under the influence of several sets of forces. It is an embedded phenomenon. Forces (processes) will operate at the most basic level of physiology, but also at the level of interpersonal relations (as they unfold in the work unit and the family unit) and within the macrocontext of mass media messages and popular culture. Indeed, as we finish working on this book, the emotional impact of the terrorist attacks of September 11, 2001, along with America's military response, and the heinous and puzzling anthrax scare, serves as a backdrop to much of work life. Its salience is in flux as affected by events and mass media coverage. This societal context is certainly one that must be viewed as relevant by any investigator about to embark on research designed to understand or model the role of affect on an aspect of organizational life today, whether it is the temperament of the customer service representative, the productivity of a worker, attendance patterns at work, or the rate of violence in the workplace.

This multilevel perspective, however, can be adopted only with a key understanding of the criterion phenomenon of interest (DiNisi, 2000). The latter will serve as the basis for intuiting the nature and number of levels that must be brought into considerations of research design and measurement. A firm grasp of the criterion space also can inform the choice of mathematical tools used to model the interplay among levels in order to account for variance in dependent variables (Chen & Bliese, in press). Thus, the manifestation, regulation, and impact of affect are not only under the influence of forces operating at multiple levels but among these forces at multiple levels.

A third aspect of our position is that research on affect needs to include considerations of time and the temporal component of key explanatory processes. The admonition to do this has been offered by others (Tuckman, 1965; Likert, 1967; McGrath, 1988). This has been in recognition that many organizational phenomena—individual learning, group dynamics, or organizational change, for example—unfold over time.

In the context of this book, such advice presents special challenges. One challenge relates to the fact that the mechanisms and processes implicated in emotion and affect will operate (unfold) at differing rates but operate to a cumulative effect. Thus, automatic and physiological responses to stimuli, at outlined in several chapters in this book, get activated (processed) at millisecond speeds. But social and interpersonal processes take more time and may unfold over minutes (as in group meetings) or even weeks (as with a feud between two workers). Moreover, some processes may be linked to stimuli occurring at predictable intervals (such as receiving a paycheck on a weekly basis), while others are much more random (such as having to deal with three hostile customers in a row). In a related manner, forces may cancel out the effects of one another if they unfold in certain sequences (for example, it is easier to ruin a good mood than to remediate a foul one). Finally, we know that individuals are adaptable. Nominally positive or noxious stimuli have different effects with repetition over different periods of time. Fortunately, recent developments in theory and in methodology have been great (Goodman, Ancona, Lawrence, & Tushman, 2001). But it remains up to the investigator with an intimate awareness of the criterion space to make use of this new knowledge.

Conclusion

It is clear that work life and organizations are imbued with affect and that the study of work affect is gaining rapid momentum in organizational psychology. For most individuals, work occupies the largest waking segment of adult life. During young adulthood, work provides the primary context in which individuals continue to develop intellectual, social, and technical skills and career goals. In Western countries, successful transition into the workforce represents a key indicator of an individual's overall adjustment in society. During middle and later adulthood, work provides an important venue for social interaction and support and affirmation of one's identity, and it affords opportunities for the expression of achievement motives in the form of workplace accomplishments and career success. In short, the workplace provides a rich matrix for the study affect in relation to the cognitive and conative processes involved in subjective well-being, goal striving, and behavioral adjustment.

The study of affect related to work is also important to organizations. Technological, demographic, economic, and workplace design trends have led to a new conceptualization of human capital that emphasizes the employee's affective response tendencies and regulatory skills in the context of training, organizational socialization, teamwork, leadership, and organizational change. Talent in the expression and regulation of affect is explicitly sought for an ever widening range of jobs, from sales associate to chief executive officer. Retrospective accounts of spectacular organizational successes and failures frequently allude to the role of employee affect and the effectiveness of the leadership in the use of affect to enhance employee commitment and work motivation. In short, affective processes are recognized as a major influence on the dynamics of organizational effectiveness.

The question facing organizational researchers at this point is not whether affect is an important topic but how best to carve the study of work affect at its joints. Similar to motivation, affect and affect regulation may be conceptualized as an independent variable, a dependent variable, a mediating or moderator variable, or a set of processes. Affect may be investigated as a characteristic or outcome at the individual, work group, team, and organizational levels of analysis. The multidimensional structure of emotions further permits investigation of broad affective tendencies, as well as study of specific emotions related to the self or the environment.

We do not believe there is a single best approach; rather, the dominance of any particular approach will depend jointly on organizational needs and advances in supporting scientific disciplines. The current popularity of trait-based approaches, for example, draws from new psychological theories of emotion and dual organizational concerns about the effectiveness of extant models in personnel selection for jobs that involve substantial social interaction and demand emotional intelligence, and the high costs of ineffective regulation of negative emotions.

Recent changes in political and economic conditions suggest that future organizational concerns about the determinants and consequences of team effectiveness will continue to grow. In the postindustrial era, teams, rather than individuals, increasingly represent the basic unit of analysis in performance, prompting interest in how to optimize team performance through member composition, structure, and leadership. Psychological research on the mechanisms and processes underlying emotional contagion and transformational leadership represent two lines of research that bear directly on team effectiveness.

Although the current enthusiasm for the study of affect related to work runs high, we think it is also important to raise a cautionary note. As indicated in our meta-framework, affect operates in the context of cognition and conation. Researchers have long recognized the importance of these interrelations on the antecedents of affect but have tended to neglect the interrelationships among these elements with respect to the consequences of affect. That is, understanding the consequences of affect for individual and organizational outcomes requires explicit consideration of cognitive-resource and conative-goal factors at the appropriate level of analysis. Attempts to study the consequences of affect separately from these factors run the risk of building sophisticated but practically useless theories. Individual and organizational goal conflicts, for example, may yield a dramatically different pattern of affect-related behaviors than occurs when individual and organizational goals are in alignment. Team capabilities are likely to play an important role in determining the direction and persistence of emotional responses to events. In cohesive teams with substantial experience in resource mobilization, events that trigger fear may yield implementation of problem-focused coping strategies. In contrast, in newly formed or less cohesive teams, events that trigger fear may prompt more emotion-focused coping that builds team cohesion but fail to mobilize resources to reduce the perceived external threat.

It is an exciting time for research on affect and work. Advances in knowledge about affective processes have enhanced our capabilities and understanding of affect in the workplace, and shifting organizational priorities provide the motivation for applying this knowledge to the workplace in new ways. Our continued positive emotionality about the field, however, will depend critically on the extent to which research yields new knowledge and fosters the development of practical procedures that significantly enhance individual well-being and organizational productivity.

References

Brockner, J., & Higgins, E. T. (2001). Regulatory focus theory: Implications for the study of emotions at work. *Organizational Behavior and Human Decision Processes, 86,* 35–66.

Carstensen, L. L. (1992). Social and emotional patterns in adulthood: Support for socioemotional selectivity theory. *Psychology and Aging, 7,* 331–338.

Carver, C. S., & Scheer, M. F. (1990). Origins and functions of positive and negative affect. *Psychological Review, 97,* 91–35.

Chen, G., & Bliese, P. D. (in press). The role of different levels of leadership in predicting self and collective efficacy. *Journal of Applied Psychology.*

Diehl, M., Coyle, N., & Labouvie-Vief, G. (1996). Age and sex differences in strategies of coping and defense across the life span. *Psychology and Aging, 11,* 127–139.

DiNisi, A. (2000). Performance appraisal and performance management. In K. Klein & S.W.J. Koslowski (Eds.), *Multilevel theory, research and methods in organizations* (pp. 121–156). San Francisco: Jossey-Bass.

Goodman, P. S., Ancona, D. G., Lawrence, B. S., & Tushman, M. L. (2001). Special topic forum on time and organizational research. *Academy of Management Review, 26,* 507–511.

Goschke, T., & Kuhl, J. (1993). Representation of intentions: Persisting activation in memory. *Journal of Experimental Psychology: Learning, Memory, and Cognition, 19,* 1211–1226.

Klein, K. J., & Kozlowski, S.W.J. (Eds.). (2000). *Multilevel theory, research, and methods in organizations.* San Francisco: Jossey-Bass.

Likert, R. (1967). *The human organization: Its management and value.* New York: McGraw-Hill.

McGrath, J. E. (1988). *The social psychology of time.* Thousand Oaks, CA: Sage.

Tuckman, B. W. (1965). Developmental sequence in small groups. *Psychological Bulletin, 63,* 384–399.

Weiss, H. M., & Cropanzano, R. (1996). Affective events theory: A theoretical discussion of the structure, causes, and consequences of affective experiences at work. In L. L. Cummings & B. M. Staw (Eds.), *Research in organizational behavior* (Vol. 18, pp. 1–74). Stamford, CT: JAI Press.

Name Index

Subject Index